Acknowledgements

This book, our lives, and you the reader would not be here today if not for the countless millions of people around the world and throughout time that have been imprisoned, tortured, or killed in the act of resisting oppression and struggling for freedom—freedom from exploitation, oppression, and violence, and freedom to live as one chooses. We pay our humble respects to the nameless freedom fighters, revolutionaries, and liberationists that defend the Earth, animal, and human communities.

We also take this opportunity to thank our friends, families (human and nonhuman), colleagues, and supporters. This project would never have materialized if not for AK Press and its many dedicated collective members. Above all, we appreciate the support of Lorna, Charles, and Ramsey, and applaud the mission and vision of the press. Nor, of course, would this book have emerged without the cooperation, hard work, solidarity, and patience of its amazing array of authors, both those in and outside prison. We are grateful too for the many people that have aided us or this book in some way: Melissa Rodriguez, Daniel M., Jenny, Shelly, Stephanie with Boston ADL, Eric C. Blair, Ben, Yvone Pollock, Bron Taylor, Richard Kahn, Davey Garland, John Zerzan, Takis Fotopolous, Carl Boggs, Craig Mazer of IMPACT Press, Rosalie Little Thunder, Autumn Marie from Critical Resistance, and everyone from Break the Chains. Our many friends that have been there with us along the completion of this project include Jay, Jeremy, Jared, Brian, Jill, Eli Moore, Daria, Ben, Leslie, Jimmy, Kevin, Andrew and Heather, Cameron Naficy, Nathan Nobis, Jackie Orr, Don Mitchell, Micere Mugo, Winston Grady-Willis, Alison Mountz, Stephanie, Justin Goodman, Houston Animal Rights Team, Central New York Earth First!, the Center on Animal Liberation Affairs, Gary Yourofsky, Josh Harper, Kevin Jonas, Leana Stormont, Jason P., Erin Ryan Fitzgerald, Billy, Nick, Joel, Vicki, Jennifer, Greg, Andy, Amber, Loren, Justin, Brian, Amy, and Kevin from Syracuse Animal Rights Organization, Andy Stepanian, Matt and everyone from ADL Long Island, Nick, David, and Stephanie from Hugs for Puppies, elana levy, Nik Hensey, Jason Bayless, the Alternatives to Violence Program, Chris, Lisa, and Robert with the Program on the Analysis and Resolution of Conflicts (PARC) and the PARC crew from 2003–2004, Paulette and everyone from the Jericho Amnesty Movement, Anarchist Black Cross South Chicago, Mike Roselle, Chris Hannah from G7, Joel Kovel, Takis Fotopolous, Nik Taylor, DJ Rose, Charles Patterson, John Sorenson, Charles Patterson, Matthew Calarco, Karen Davis, Jim Mason, Paul Watson, Alison Watson, David Rovics, Scott Lyons, Peter McLaren, Doug Kellner, and Ward Churchill. Finally, with great love for ("Osama Bin") Gadget, who left this world the day we finished this book, you will be much missed dear friend.

Dedication

This book is dedicated to all who are willing to stand in the way of the destruction of the Earth and its sundry living inhabitants. This book also is dedicated to all political prisoners who fought/fight for a peaceful and loving world where ALL are respected.

Much of the profits of this book will go to political prisoners and prisoner of war defense committees, as well as to aboveground environmental organizations that support revolutionary environmentalism, such as Break the Chains, the Prisoners Of Conscience Committee, the Jericho Amnesty Movement, and the Earth Liberation Prisoners Support Network.

Contents

Foreword
Experimenting with Truth

Bron Taylor

It is with a distinct sense of déjà vu that in December 2005, I began writing this foreword, during yet another round-up of activists arrested for crimes the United States government labels "ecoterrorism."[1] The arrests occurred in five different states, and the allegations included a series of arson attacks on federal buildings associated with US agricultural and forest practices, and private companies involved in logging or lumber production, as well as the downing of a transmission tower in the Pacific Northwest. The actions were claimed by the Earth Liberation Front and, in one case, as a joint effort between the Earth Liberation Front and the Animal Liberation Front. Most of the activists arrested as suspects in these crimes face prison terms of up to twenty years if convicted, and one or more could even serve a life sentence.

On 23 December 2005, a day after finishing what I thought would be the final draft of this foreword, I learned that one of those arrested, William C. Rodgers, committed suicide while awaiting extradition from Arizona to Washington State to face accusations springing from a string of arson attacks, including on federal research facilities involved in the genetic modification of poplar trees, and the burning of several buildings at the Vail ski resort in Colorado, which was expanding into habitat considered by biologists to be critical to the survival of the endangered Canadian Lynx. The forty-year-old proprietor of a radical bookstore in Prescott, Arizona, was well known and beloved in his community and among radical environmentalists who knew him, as well as by his students from the days when he worked in outdoor environmental education for Lesley University's Audubon Expedition Institute and for Prescott College. The crimes he was suspected of, and his refusal to remain incarcerated, underscore the high stakes that are involved when activists turn to extra-legal tactics in their resistance to the destructive forces of an always expansionist and predatory market capitalism.

These arrests reminded me of the first time I had heard about such tactics being deployed, in the late 1980s, when five activists were arrested

1

for sabotage in several incidents in the Southwest. They were charged with attempting to down transmission towers coming from a nuclear power plant in Arizona, and for sabotage of ski lifts at a resort planning to expand and further desecrate lands considered sacred to many American Indians. The suspects were all eventually convicted and those most directly involved served several years in prison.

Probably like many who will read the book you now hold, I was drawn to such bold acts of resistance both out of raw curiosity (who *are* these people and what is motivating them?), and because of my own frustration and recognition that mainstream environmental strategies had been unable to halt or even significantly slow an intensifying environmental crisis. I wondered if direct action—both civil disobedience and sabotage—might provide more effective means of environmental struggle. I left my academic enclave in order to meet the activists promoting such tactics in an effort to determine whether there was promise or peril (or both) in the approaches with which they were experimenting. I thereby began a long journey, researching and writing about radical environmentalism and ecological resistance movements.[2]

When looking back at twenty-five years of environment-related resistance since the founding of Earth First!, I find more similarities than differences between the 1980s and now. Some factions and branches of the resistance, perhaps especially the most militant ones, have grown and expanded their fields of operation. There are more who express primitivist and/or anarchist ideologies. There appears to be less tension and more cooperation between animal and earth liberationists. Greater numbers of activists are both advocating and practicing sabotage and arson. More activists articulate a rationale for armed struggle—although they are still few in number, none seem to call for the deployment of such tactics immediately, and there are no examples of such violence as yet. Among Earth First! activists, there seems to be a decreasing interest in deep ecology and spiritually-focused approaches to ecological resistance in favor of more cultural and political approaches. At the same time, however, there has been more interest in spirituality within anarchist subcultures that, generally speaking, used to view religion as simply a way in which elites legitimate their power. Clearly, there is increasing fusion between radical environmentalism, and urban punk and anarchist subcultures. Yet most of the internal points of contention remain, including whether these movements are radical or revolutionary, and what these terms mean.

Igniting a Revolution represents an intensification of a political instinct that until the mid 1990s was largely just talk—the effort to cross class, ethnic, gender, and ideological divides and build new kinds of radical alliances, like those between earth and animal liberationists, Black liberationists, Native Americans, and anti-imperialists. This book is both a reflection of new multi-issue global alliance politics and a contribution to their potential formation. In *Igniting a Revolution*, Steven Best and Anthony J. Nocella, II have assembled fascinating and rarely heard voices that seek to intensify and unify the gathering resistance to the destructive forces of global market capitalism.

This volume will interest any reader who wishes to hear directly from some of the leading intellectuals, activists, and prisoners involved in these movements. The insights gained by listening directly to these voices—rather than by accepting the sometimes biased and often ill-informed interpretation of these movements by their adversaries, journalists, and many academics—can hardly be underestimated. Perhaps most important is to hear for oneself what motivates these activists; such attentiveness illustrates that many of them speak not only with anger about the injustices they perceive, but also with passion and love for the world they consider endangered. *Igniting a Revolution* thus provides little-known histories and perspectives from activists and political prisoners on the front lines of the resistance, those who are now beginning to talk with one another. With a little imagination, this book may provide the next best thing to joining radical activists in the trees, urban neighborhoods, prisons, or what Edward Abbey called "nightwork," that is, sabotage under the cover of darkness.

Yet before you read on, I would offer a few cautions.

First, I would urge that readers understand that these essays do not represent the whole spectrum of opinion in the environmental movement (whether mainstream or radical), nor do they, in most cases, explore the possible rebuttals or alternative approaches that other activists would offer. It is worth noting one critical reason for at least some of the disagreement among activists: it is exceedingly difficult to determine what the levers of social change are, or how to counter the power that inheres to corporations and the governments who generally serve their interests. Consequently, it is inevitable that among people who care about and seek to slow or halt global warming, species extinctions, or promote greater equity among human beings, there would be diverse approaches offered as the most effective means toward the desired ends. This particular book, by focusing on what the editors call "revolutionary environmentalism," provides a unique window into such visions and related political perspectives and practices.

Second, I would stress that revolutionary rhetoric often does not match the reality on the ground. It is one thing to argue that it is morally permissible or politically effective to deploy a given tactic, and another to undertake that action. It is yet another thing for readers who agree with the position to then put it into practice. Here I am thinking especially about the rationale for tactics involving property destruction, or tactics that seek to injure or kill adversaries. There have always been more people who are willing to argue for the permissibility or necessity of such violence than who are willing to put their ideas into practice.[3] Perhaps as the ecological crisis grows ever more severe, the most militant and martial rhetoric will converge with activist practices. To date, however, there are still relatively few activists who defend the use of violence and very few indeed who have elected to actually harm people in an effort to achieve their goals.[4]

Certainly, many who hear the term "revolutionary" will have a visceral, fearful reaction. But it is worth underscoring from the outset that for many, the term "revolutionary" is concerned primarily with making lasting, systemic change. The revolutionaries featured in this book seek to overturn contemporary social and ecological conditions that they judge to be anti-democratic and anti-ecological in favor of democratic, environmentally-sustainable ecosystems and communities. Many of them fervently believe their demands and visions cannot be realized within the constraints of current social arrangements, without abolishing these systems altogether.

Such qualifications made, there is no doubt that for many who identify with revolutionary environmentalism, there is both a willingness, if not insistence, that more militant tactics are necessary, including sabotage, and sometimes actions even more risky to activists and adversaries alike. So anyone drawn to such tactics should be clearheaded—for this is serious business. The authorities have steadily increased the penalties for such actions. The **PATRIOT** Act and other laws have further empowered government surveillance, increasing the likelihood and costs of apprehension. The case of Jeffrey Luers, from whom you can hear directly in this volume, is instructive. He was convicted for torching several sport utility vehicles in an action that resulted in no injuries, and sentenced to over 22 years in prison.

This draconian sentence reminded me of Saul Alinsky's *Rules for Radicals*, which asserts that arrests and jail can be very good for a revolutionary or social change movement by dramatizing the cause, making its leaders martyrs, and inspiring others to action. Alinsky added that jail can provide precious time to think carefully about and refine goals and strategies. But he also argued that if the incarceration is too long it will be counterproductive, removing the revolutionary from action.[5] To Alinsky's concerns I would add that long incarcerations can discourage followers while costing the movement time and resources as these are shifted into prisoner support.[6] Some activists and, no doubt, contributors to this volume, would view Alinsky's rules as quaint and obsolete, but it is certainly worth discussing if and when Alinsky's rules should be ignored or followed.

Third, while appreciating the many contributions of this groundbreaking volume, it is also important to recognize its limitations. Despite the many essays included in this anthology, few activists have the time or inclination to focus on movement history. Consequently, commonly received depictions of the alleged racism or other faults of earlier activists are sometimes based on thin evidence, or statements ripped out of context, which have become magnified through oral transmission. In my view, the depiction of some of the early founders of Earth First! as racist provides a good example.[7] Some criticisms of certain writings were made that ignored the context or qualifications that accompanied the offending statements. Often these criticisms were made by political rivals uninterested in fairness, but the criticisms were subsequently taken at face value, passed on orally and in later writings, becoming something of their own reality. Just as it would be wise to avoid taking criticisms of specific figures at face value, so is it ill advised to accept uncritically romantic depictions of individual activists or specific movement branches. A critical approach leads to appreciation of both virtues as well as limitations, failings, and sometimes, outright unreasonableness.[8]

Finally, I think ongoing, critical thinking about the reasons for the emergence and intensification of "radical" or "revolutionary" environmentalism is crucially important. Clearly, contemporary political institutions have been corrupted by corporate power and wealth. It is certainly understandable why some would question even civilization itself, given its obvious destructive power and inertia, and decide therefore that the only appropriate response is a comprehensive revolution. Some articles in this volume present forceful arguments for such approaches. If a revolutionary response is indeed justifiable or is the only reasonable response, then such strategies will stand up to critical scrutiny.

There are a number of questions that seem seldom raised by those most inclined to urge a revolutionary response, however. One might ask, for instance, how compelling is an ideology that requires a highly optimistic view of the very species that is responsible for so much destruction? That there are elites who are more responsible than others does not seem to overturn this question, for few people seem immune from desiring greater affluence or power when the opportunity is present. From this, a second question follows: Does an ideology, revolutionary or not, have the resources within it to bridle the abuse of power, even if wielded by the revolutionary agents themselves? It is understandable that those intent on halting destruction and living in the revolutionary (or at least, the resistant) moment, would not be focused on this latter question. But before we conclude any ideology is worth our energy, let alone our prospective liberty, it would be wise to have an answer to this question.

It is, essentially, the age old question central to social philosophy: How can we order our common lives to promote the commonwealth and protect the weak? While revolutionary environmentalists have arguably contributed to moral evolution by insisting that the commonwealth be understood to include all forms of life, it is less certain they have found a compelling answer to how we achieve and maintain it. This may, indeed, be an unobtainable task, but it is a worthy pursuit. It is, therefore, important to scrutinize every proffered solution, both means and ends, to see which sorts of political systems might actually be compatible with the flourishing of ecosystems in which they are situated.

Then again, it is only through "experiments with truth" (to borrow a phrase from Gandhi's autobiography) during concrete political struggles that we have a chance to discover or recover viable solutions.[9] Perhaps generations from now, revolutionary environmentalists will be lauded for making a decisive contribution to a sustainable future by having the courage to experiment boldly with paths to it. And perhaps some key elements of the solution will be found in the pages of this important and provocative collection.

In an anthology I complied entitled *Ecological Resistance Movements*, I spoke about how values are linked to and embedded in narratives. I urged readers to consider whether they found any of the stories in that volume inspiring, and if the forms of resistance described and analyzed there made sense, and were worth emulating. The same question seems equally pertinent here. The narratives and voices in this volume flow within the broader currents of progressive environmentalism and social justice movements. Which of them are compelling emotionally, and square with your own moral sentiments? Which make the most sense strategically? This volume, carefully considered within the light of social movement histories and the analysis of them, might well help us discern how we might more effectively stand up for life on earth.

Notes

1. "6 Arrested Years after Ecoterrorist Acts," *The New York Times*, December 9, 2005, A18.

2. For my own interpretive work about the movement, see "The Religion and Politics of Earth First!" *The Ecologist* 21, no. 6 [November/December] (1991): 258–66, and Taylor, Bron, ed. *Ecological Resistance Movements: The Global Emergence of Radical and Popular Environmentalism* (New York: State University of New York Press, 1995). The most synthetic introduction I have written to the radical movements is "Radical Environmentalism" and "Earth First! and the Earth Liberation Front," which appear in the *Encyclopedia of Religion and Nature* (Taylor, Bron, ed. London & NY: Continuum, 2005, v 2, 1326–35 and v 1, 518–24). These and other essays exploring these movements are available online at <http://www.religionandnature.com/bron>.

3. Anthony J. Nocella, II and Richard Kahn. "Serious Politics, Serious Consequences: Reinventing Direct Action's Educational Strategies." December 20, 2005. <http://www.animalliberationfront.com/Philosophy/Motivation2Education.htm>

4. I have written about the likelihood of violence springing from these movements in three articles: "Religion, Violence, and Radical Environmentalism: From Earth First! to the Unabomber to the Earth Liberation Front," *Terrorism and Political Violence* 10 no. 4 (1998): 10–42; "Threat Assessments and Radical Environmentalism," *Terrorism and Political Violence* 15 no. 4 (Winter 2004): 172–83; and "Revisiting Ecoterrorism." In *Religionen Im Konflikt*, edited by Vasilios N. Makrides and Jörg Rüpke. Münster, Germany: Aschendorff, 2004. This last article explains why animal liberationist subcultures are more likely to engage in intentional violence than are environmental liberationists. While this book suggests that the likelihood of intentional violence emerging from members of these groups may well be increasing, it is still worth asking—before we consider them to be some subset of terrorists (if they are): Where are the bodies? It is also important to note that in environmental conflicts, the overwhelming proportion of violence has been directed at activists, and this is particularly true in the global south. For a somewhat dated introduction that nevertheless demonstrates the trend, see Helvarg, David. *The War Against the Greens*. San Francisco: Sierra Club, 1992.

5. Alinsky, Saul. *Rules for Radicals: A Pragmatic Primer for Realistic Radicals.* New York: Vintage, 1971. See esp. "Time in Jail" (155–58) in which he explains both the positive and potentially negative aspects of incarceration. One positive aspect he mentions is the rare opportunity to reflect and refine one's strategic thinking. On the negative side, he comments, "the trouble with a long jail sentence is that (a) a revolutionary is removed from action for such a extended period of time that he loses touch, and (b) if you are gone long enough everybody forgets about you."

6. This is one reason that Edward Abbey crafted *The Monkeywrench Gang*'s "Code of the Eco-Warrior" to include, "if you get caught you're on your own" (NY: Avon, 1975).

7. A good specific example is the article by Miss Ann Thropy (a pseudonym for Christopher Manes), who wrote with regard to environmental decline, "the only real hope...is an enormous decline in human population." He added that AIDS has advantages over other cataclysms that might otherwise reduce population, especially because "it only affects humans" and therefore "has the potential to significantly reduce human population without harming other life forms" (see "Population and AIDS," *Earth First!* 7 no. 5 (1 May 1987): 32. Those who criticized this writer and the journal editors for publishing the article, charging that it was misanthropic or callous, never cited an important qualification made in the article, that "None of this is intended to disregard or discount the suffering of AIDS victims." The critics universally ignored the central contention of the article, that human overpopulation itself causes great suffering, both of humans and among the broader life community, and important context of the overall argument. One need not endorse the argument to note that a careful reading of the article reveals that some of the criticism of it was not based on a full and fair understanding of it.

8. For example, I am thinking of Judi Bari, one of the contending figures for power and influence in the movement from the middle of the 1980s until her death in 1997, at the age of 47. An important figure certainly to those who considered themselves involved in a revolutionary movement, she spoke early and eventually published an article about "Revolutionary Ecology" in *Capitalism, Nature, Socialism: A Journal of Socialist Ecology* 8 no. 2 (1997): 145–49. Those who knew her understood she was a complicated character—charismatic, funny, passionate—as well as one who was not obviously politically effective. Some activists concluded she had become emotionally troubled and ineffective. Still others fought fiercely against those who recalled her less effective or unsavory sides. In my view, it is better to neither exaggerate the virtues or vices of the individuals involved in concrete social struggles. Imperfect people can make significant contributions and sometimes they make missteps that have been devastating to their own causes. There are valuable lessons both ways.

9. For a way into the conundrums, readers could start with my analysis of green social philosophy, "Deep Ecology and Its Social Philosophy," in *Beneath the Surface: Critical Essays on Deep Ecology*, edited by Eric Katz, Andrew Light and David Rothenberg. Cambridge, Massachusetts: MIT Press, 2000 or with Andrew Bard Schmookler's *The Parable of the Tribes: The Problem of Power in Social Evolution.* Berkeley, California: University of California Press, 1984 and Andrew Dobson's *Green Political Thought: An Introduction.* London: Unwin Hyman, 1990.

Introduction

A Fire in the Belly of the Beast: The Emergence of Revolutionary Environmentalism

Steven Best and Anthony J. Nocella, II

Barely out of the starting gates, on the heels of the bloody and genocidal century that preceded it, the 21st century already is a time of war, violence, environmental disasters, and terrorism against human populations, animals, and the Earth as a whole. This omnicidal assault is waged by powerful and greedy forces, above all, by transnational corporations, national and international banks, and G8 alliances. Stretching their tentacles across the Earth, they hire nation states as their cops, juntas, hit men, dictators, and loan sharks to extract natural resources, enforce regimes of total exploitation, and snuff out all resistance. These menacing foes are part of a coherent *system* rooted in the global capitalist market currently in the final stages of the privatization and commodification of the natural and social worlds.

The net result of millennia of western culture, and roughly two hundred thousand years of the reign of *Homo sapiens* as a whole, is hideously visible in the current ecological crisis involving dynamics such as air and water pollution, acid rain, genetic crop pollution, chemical poisoning, species extinction, rainforest destruction, coral reef deterioration, disappearance of wetlands, desertification, and global warming.[1] This planetary crisis is caused by forces that include human overpopulation, hyperdevelopment, mass production, overconsumption, agribusiness, militarism, and a cancerous greed for power and profit that consumes, entraps, or kills everything in its path.

With the exception of a few sparkles of democracy, egalitarianism, and enlightenment, western cultural development is a dark stretch of hierarchy, domination, violence and destruction, all predicated on the pernicious ideologies and institutions of statism, classism, sexism, racism, speciesism, and anthropocentrism. Despite great works of philosophy, music, art, and architecture, regardless of brilliant advances in science and technology—much of which was built on the backs of the enslaved and exploited—the western world (which claims superiority over all other cultures) has created few social forms deserving the name "civilization." Rather, it spirals headlong toward barbarism, self-destruction, and oblivion. Indeed, the very concept of "civilization" is problematic as western cultures have defined it in antithesis to everything wild, non-domestic, animalic, primal, emotional, instinctual, and female, all forces to be subdued and conquered.

As global temperatures climb, icecaps and glaciers melt, sea-levels rise, and forests fall, the short-lived human empire has begun to devour itself and implode like a collapsing white dwarf star. The Earth itself—the bulk of which has been domesticated, colonized, commodified, bred and cross-bred, genetically engineered, and cloned—is refuting the myths and fallacies of Progress, Development, Science, Technology, the Free Market, and Neo-Liberalism, while demonstrating the inherent *contradiction* between capitalism and ecology.

This book is a rebel yell. It is a manifesto for a new social movement that we call "revolutionary environmentalism." It stands in solidarity with all struggles outside the western world and northern hemisphere, but it calls for a revolution within. As the Earth Liberation Front once stated in a communiqué, "Welcome to the struggle of all species to be free. We are the burning rage of a dying planet." Fed up with apathy, lies, and excuses; driven by passion and anger; moving through the night in black clothes and balaclavas; armed with the healing fire of resistance; the Earth Liberation Front is just one of many radical groups attacking exploiters and sabotaging nihilists who would trade in cultural and biological diversity for another mansion or yacht.[2] These guerilla warriors are joined by people of color protesting chemical poisoning of their communities, Chipko activists protecting forests in India, the Ogoni people fighting Shell Oil in Nigeria, and countless other indigenous peoples—from Central Africa and the Amazon Basin to the Canadian subarctic and the tropical forests of Asia—fighting pollution, mining, deforestation, biopiracy, oil and gas drilling, agribusiness, and other methods of human, animal, and Earth exploitation.

Global in its vision, *Igniting a Revolution* nonetheless arises from the belly of the beast, from the "core" states that control their "satellites," from the corporate command centers of the great imperialist powers, the u.s. above all.[3] This book is shaped by the era of "global terrorism;" the so-called "clash of civilizations;" struggles over dwindling natural resources; and the intensification of state repression against "eco-terrorism," liberation movements, and dissent of any kind. *Igniting a Revolution* was conceived amidst the smoke and rubble of 9/11; it was written during the blasts of 3/11 (Madrid, 2004) and 7/7 (London, 2005); assembled throughout the u.s. terrorist war against Iraq and the encroaching fascism of phenomena such as the u.s.a. PATRIOT Act and u.k. "rules of unacceptable behaviors;" and finalized under the spectral shadow of ecological disintegration, biological meltdown, and impending global chaos.

Increasingly, calls for moderation, compromise, and the slow march through institutions can be seen as treacherous and grotesquely inadequate. With the planet in the throes of dramatic climate change, ecological destabilization, and the sixth great extinction crisis in its history (this one having human not natural causes), "reasonableness" and "moderation" seem to be entirely unreasonable and immoderate, as "extreme" and "radical" actions appear simply as necessary and appropriate. After decades of environmental struggles in the west, we are nevertheless losing ground in the battle to preserve species, ecosystems, wilderness, and human communities. Politics as usual just won't cut it anymore.[4]

Origins of Western Environmentalism

"Environmentalism," a term developed in the modern western world, is an articulated philosophical and political concern human beings have with the destructive impact of their societies and lifeways on their surroundings and the natural world that sustains them. Most improbable in societies that respect and live in harmony with nature, environmentalism is a symptom of a disease. It is a manifestation of a dualistic outlook whereby human beings see themselves as separate from nature, view it as mere resources for their use, and seek to bend it to their will. Ecological lifeways in harmony with nature are primal, but environmentalism is a modern development.[5] Environmentalism is a necessary step toward healing the pathologies of a destructive and domineering society, but some forms of environmentalism, as we will show, only treat the symptoms of disease while others seek to eliminate its causes.

There are many histories of environmentalism appropriate to various national, geographical, or cultural settings, such as may be found in Australia, Asia, england, Finland, Germany, or the u.s. Our brief narrative here only touches on a few points relevant to traditions in north amerika and Europe during the 19th and 20th centuries, but verges toward a broader international (though mostly western) narrative.[6] Ideas, tactics, groups, and movements often flow from one nation to another, such that by the 1990s western "environmentalism"—which is simultaneously a general name and multiple tendencies—becomes an international movement that connects with indigenous struggles in the southern hemisphere and expands on a planetary scale.[7]

While one can always find antecedents to any "beginning," environmentalism emerged as a prominent new social concern in the u.k. and u.s. during the first half of the 19th century, largely in reaction to the social and environmental destruction wrought by capitalist industrialization processes. With the onset of the Industrial Revolution in London, the urban setting became a grim, overcrowded, polluted, smog-choked, disease-ridden prisonhouse of squalor and ugliness. In his poem, "Jerusalem" (1804), William Blake decried the city's "dark satanic mills," and in novels such as *Hard Times* (1854) Charles Dickens vividly portrayed the hellish lives of the urban poor. In protest against encroaching industrialization, groups of English weavers known as Luddites took up their sledgehammers in 1811 and attacked the machines that mass produced inferior products, eliminated their jobs, and destroyed their communities. The state crushed the burgeoning social movement, handing out death sentences for sabotage, and industrialization rolled right along under the banner of Progress, Democracy, and Freedom.[8]

As various radicals and social reformers organized against the destructive effects of industrialization on working classes in cities such as London and Manchester, a new sensibility emerged in the late 18th century, championed by Romantic poets, artists, and thinkers who were concerned with the impact of capitalism on the beloved countryside and forests of england. Within the belly of the industrial beast, William Blake, William Wordsworth, Samuel Taylor Coleridge, John Keats, and others observed with alarm how both outer and inner worlds were threatened by mechanistic science, the technological onslaught, and the ruthless commodification of nature and human relations. Following the lead of Jean-Jacques Rousseau who declared everything natural to be free and good (before corrupted by society), they praised nature as the antithesis to all that was rotten in modern life, and extolled the beauty and divinity of the wild.

In the early 19th century, Romanticism spread from england to amerika where it took on similar form in the guise of "Transcendentalism." Millennia after Native Americans established roots on the continent and lived with reverence for the Earth, transcendentalists such as Ralph Waldo Emerson, Henry David Thoreau, and John Muir embraced a similar pantheistic outlook. They rejected the prevailing Puritan ideology that saw nature as evil and repulsive—as something to be conquered not contemplated— and they spoke rapturously of the divine spirit manifest in all things. They extolled mountains, rivers, and forests as sacred and essential to authentic life, unlike the existence corrupted by the teeming crowds, breathless pace, and gross capitalist values of cities. They understood that the "temple destroyers, devotees of raging commercialism" (Muir), represented by railroad, lumber, mining, land, and farming interests, were rapidly colonizing the wild and exploiting the Earth. In their writings and speeches, Transcendentalists encouraged aesthetic and spiritual appreciation of nature, sparked public awareness about the widespread "war against wilderness" (Thoreau), and launched an amerikan tradition of environmental legislation and protection.

The evolution of "environmentalism" in the u.s. provides an instructive case study of the complexities and politics of the discourse and movement. According to a standard narrative, amerikan environmentalism emerged in the 19th century when privileged white males such as Emerson, Thoreau, Muir, and various conservationists became active in education and legislation efforts.[9] The story continues by relating how later figures, such as Aldo Leopold, carried the baton of a budding new movement. It emphasizes the importance of Rachel Carson's book, *Silent Spring* (1963), then brings the tale to a climax by describing the sea of white faces demonstrating in the streets on the first Earth Day in 1970.

Although we have certainly oversimplified, the basic outlines of this history have been told often, and it is important to note that the narrative leaves out two important facts. First, many of the founders and pioneers of amerikan environmentalism were classist, racist, and sexist, such that their spiritual attunement to nature did not free them from pernicious prejudices of the time.[10] Early environmentalists, prosperous white men, contrasted a "vigorous manliness" ethic in the pursuit of wilderness to the "effeminate weakness" of city life. Romantics, primitivists, and antimodernists, they celebrated the "savage virtues" that the man of leisure cultivates in the canyons and forests of wild amerika. Their emphasis on rugged individualism and solitary journeys into wilderness hardly encouraged social awareness or activism. During heady political times of slavery, civil war, and genocide against Native Americans, some naturalists, such as Muir, remained apolitical and even misanthropic. Thoreau, in contrast, participated in the Underground Railroad, protested against the Fugitive Slave Law, supported John Brown and his party, and encouraged tax resistance and civil disobedience in general. He thereby stands out as an early eco-radical, one with a holistic outlook that encompassed both wilderness and social justice issues, and who exerted a great influence on the politics of civil disobedience and direct action associated with radical environmentalism.

Amidst the struggles of oppressed groups and the Dickensian horrors of industrialization, the nineteenth century understanding of "environment" in the u.s. was that of a pristine wilderness, such as could be enjoyed exclusively by people of privilege and leisure. Unfortunately, this elitist and myopic definition discounted the *urban* environment that plagued working classes, and it set a regressive historical standard that has come under fire but still stands.

The nature/urban dualism was far less rigid in england, however, where many 19th century champions of wilderness protection and nature were also vigorous social reformers. William Blake deified wilderness but also repudiated slavery and championed racial and sexual equality. Octavia Hill (1838–1912) founded the National Trust, an influential nature preservation society, as she worked to improve housing and increase public spaces for the poor. Radical prophet, poet, pacifist, and labor activist Edward Carpenter (1844–1929) advocated vegetarianism, anti-vivisection, women's liberation, and gay sexuality, as he organized campaigns against air pollution and echoed Thoreau's call for the "simplification of life." Similarly, Henry Salt (1851–1939) was a socialist, pacifist, and champion of social reform in schools, prisons, and other institutions. He was also a naturalist, vegetarian, proponent of animal rights, and early animal liberationist. In 1891, he formed the Humanitarian League, which set out to ban hunting as a sport. This organization was a forerunner of the League against Cruel Sports (founded in 1924), as well as modern hunt-saboteur groups from which emerged the Animal Liberation Front (see below).[11]

Clearly, the understanding of "revolutionary environmentalism" will vary according to one's definition of "environment." If the definition focuses on "wilderness" apart from cities, communities, and health issues, then it will exclude the plight and struggles of women, people of color, workers, children, and other victims of oppression who work, live, play and attend school in toxic surroundings that sicken, deform, and kill. If, however, the definition of revolutionary environmentalism is broadened to include environmental justice (see below) and indigenous struggles against corporate exploitation and imperialism—which bring to the table key issues of race and class—then the contributions of Native Americans, Black liberationists, Latino/as, non-western peoples, and others can be duly recognized and integrated into a broader and more powerful resistance movement.

One must look to the 19th century roots of modern environmentalism to understand why, in the u.s. and elsewhere, the environmental movement is still comprised predominantly of middle or upper class white people. Tragically, narrow definitions of the "environment" and ideologies such as elitism, racism, sexism, and misanthropy persisted throughout the 20th century, often surfacing in movements such as deep ecology and Earth First! Such attitudes—while not endorsed by all deep ecologists or Earth First!ers and which by no means capture the complexity of their positions and politics—were not exactly welcome mats for women, workers, and people of color, who regardless were preoccupied with their own forms of oppression and survival needs.

A second and related problem with the standard historical narrative of amerikan environmentalism is that it leaves out the important roles played by oppressed and marginalized groups. Long before Rachel Carson, African-American abolitionists opposed the use of chemicals such as arsenic being used to grow crops. Women's chapters in the Sierra Club and Audubon societies played a significant role in furthering the aesthetic appreciation of nature. Women were not only wilderness advocates but also urban environmentalists. These activists included the "sewer socialists" of the late 19th century who militated for better sanitation conditions in cities; Alice Hamilton (1869–1970), a pioneer of occupational health and safety; and Jane Addams (1860–1935), whose activism on behalf of women, children, workers, and people of color was inseparable from her push for better housing, working, and sanitation conditions.[12] Anticipating by six decades the environmental justice movement that emerged in the 1980s (see below), Grace Fryer and other "Radium girls" sickened from radium poisoning sued the company responsible and raised awareness about the dangers of this deadly substance.

Modern radical groups have roots in forgotten social histories, such as we see in today's environmental justice movement. Similarly, well before the sabotage and monkeywrenching actions of the Animal and Earth Liberation Fronts, the Sea Shepherd Conservation Society, and Earth First!,

Native nations, rebellious slaves, abolitionists, Luddites, suffragettes, and others damaged machinery, destroyed property, and set buildings ablaze. Contemporary direct action and civil disobedience tactics, moreover, have immediate roots in the civil rights struggles of the 1950s and 1960s, and of course reach back to militants such as Gandhi, Thoreau, and Tolstoy. Thus, the modern environmental movement hardly emerged in a vacuum, nor did it evolve without deep imprints from intense struggles over class, race, and gender.

The Ferment of the 1960s

Rachel Carson's book, *Silent Spring* (1963), is often credited with sparking the modern environmental movement. It captured the attention of the nation with its vivid prose and dire warning of the systemic poisoning effects of newly invented pesticides, especially DDT. In an era that promoted "better living through chemicals," DDT and other deadly substances were spread liberally across the land, from the suburban lawns of New Jersey to the agricultural fields of California where migrant workers toiled, with firsthand knowledge of their deadly effects. Carson's book prompted President John F. Kennedy to order the President's Science Advisory Committee to examine her claims against pesticides. Despite ferocious opposition from the chemical industries, her research was vindicated and DDT was eventually banned—although the use of countless other deadly chemicals thereafter increased and continued to poison soil, crops, animals, rivers, and human communities and bodies.

Exclusive focus on Carson's great achievements tends to cloud the importance of other contemporaries. In the 1950s, for instance, Murray Bookchin wrote numerous articles and books on the poisoning of the environment and food supply by nuclear testing, pesticides, herbicides, and various additives and preservatives.[13] During the same period, he also merged anarchism and ecology in a new revolutionary framework he later called social ecology. Bookchin argued that all environmental problems are deep-rooted social problems and therefore demand far-reaching social solutions. Biologist Barry Commoner also protested against nuclear testing in the 1950s, warning of the dangers of radioactive fallout, and he helped bring about the 1963 nuclear test ban treaty. A national figure, Commoner wrote on a wide range of issues including pollution, the dangers of fossil fuels, and alternative technologies. His books, such as *The Closing Circle: Nature, Man, and Technology* (1971), provided clear understandings of the "laws of ecology" and how modern society recklessly violated them. Populist and progressive, Commoner provided another early attempt to connect environmentalism to left-wing politics and broad social agendas.

Yet it is clear that the modern environmental movement did not arise because of Rachel Carson, or a few other key individuals (including David Brower). It emerged and sustained itself in the larger *social context* of the 1960s, as shaped by the struggles of the "new social movements" (radical students, countercultural youth, Black liberation, feminism, Chicano/Mexican-American, peace, anti-nuclear, and gay/lesbian/bisexual/transsexual).[14] These movements, in turn, arose amidst the turmoil spawned by the civil rights struggles of the 1950s. During the 1960s, however, Blacks and a number of white radicals rejected environmentalism as a bourgeois concern, elitist and racist cause, reactionary primitivism, and even dangerous diversion from the hard-won focus on civil rights and the Vietnam War. The political mindset was dominated by humanist and anthropocentric concerns, and even "progressive" figures and groups were unprepared to embrace an emerging new ethic that challenged human species identity as Lord and Master of the wild. As they began to take shape in the 1960s, environmental concerns were—and mostly remain—"enlightened anthropocentric" worries that if people do not better protect "their" environment, human existence will be gravely threatened.

At the turn of the decade in 1970, however, the future of the environmental movement seemed bright. Riding the crest of 1960s turmoil and protests that were beginning to wane, environmentalism became a mass concern and new political movement. The first Earth Day on April 22, 1970 drew 20 million people to the streets, lectures, and teach-ins throughout the nation, making it the largest expression of public support for any cause in amerikan history. In this "decade of environmentalism," the u.s. Congress passed new laws such as the Clean Air Act, and in 1970 President Nixon created the Environmental Protection Agency. Some environmental organizations such as the Sierra Club (founded by John Muir in 1892) existed before the new movement, but grew in members, influence, and wealth like never before. The larger groups—known as the "Gang of Ten"—planted roots in Washington, DC, where they clamored for respectability and influence with politicians and polluters.

The movement's insider/growth-oriented recipe for success, however, quickly turned into a formula for disaster.[15] Many battles were won in treating the symptoms of a worsening ecological crisis, but the war against its causes was lost, or rather never fought in the first place. Potentially a radical force and check on capitalist profit, accumulation, and growth dynamics, the u.s. environmental movement was largely a white, male, middle-class affair, cut off from the populist forces and the street energy that helped spawn it. Co-opted and institutionalized, in bed with government and industry, mindful of the "taboo against social intervention in the production system" (Commoner), defense of Mother Earth became just another bland, reformist, compromised-based, single-interest lobbying effort.

Increasingly, the Gang of Ten resembled the corporations they criticized and, in fact, evolved into corporations and self-interested money-making machines. Within behemoths such as the Wilderness Society, the Environmental Defense Fund, and the Sierra Club, decision-making originated from professionals at the top who neither had, nor sought, citizen input from the grassroots level. The Gang of Ten hired accountants and

MBAs over activists, they spent more time on mass mailing campaigns than actual advocacy, and their riches were squandered largely on sustaining bloated budgets and six-figure salaries rather than protecting the environment. They brokered compromise deals to win votes for legislation that was watered-down, constantly revised to strengthen corporate interests, and poorly enforced. They not only did not fund grassroots groups, they even worked against them at times, forming alliances instead with corporate exploiters. Perversely, Gang of Ten organizations often legitimated and profited from greenwashing campaigns that presented corporate enemies of the environment as benevolent stewards and beacons of progress.[16]

Radical Backlash and the Grassroots Revolution

As Gang of Ten-type organizations emerging in the u.s. and Europe spread throughout the globe (the World Wildlife Fund, for instance, established bases in over one hundred countries), they created a bureaucratic organization paradigm that shaped the structure of Western environmentalism. Yet, while mainstream environmental machines churned away ineffectively, and the plundering of the Earth expanded in scope and pace, waves of new approaches that used militant tactics and sought radical change surged forward in the u.s., the u.k., and throughout the globe.

These emerging groups were motivated by profound dissatisfaction with mainstream environmentalism that was corporate, careerist, compromising, and—a key issue for many—divorced from the complex of social-environmental issues affecting women, the poor, workers, and people of color. Adopting more confrontational tactics and radical politics, the new orientations repudiated reformist models that sought merely to manage a growing environmental crisis through diluted legislation, illusory techno-fixes, and market-based "solutions" for market-based problems. Realizing the futility of working through the political and legal structures of corporate-controlled states, many groups adopted direct action tactics whereby they confronted oppressors on their own high-pressure terms through actions ranging from blockades to sabotage. Direct action is not just a tactic, but rather a process whereby activists develop decentralized and egalitarian politics based on cells, affinity groups, and consensus decision-making models. Within these democratic forms, direct activists use civil disobedience and/or sabotage tactics to empower themselves against corporate-state structures and facilitate social change impossible to achieve through pre-approved political channels.

Throughout the 1970s, the American Indian Movement (AIM) was absorbed in the struggle to defend itself from violent government attacks, fighting to preserve "Sovereignty, Land and Culture." In 1971, Greenpeace was born as a new kind of direct action group protesting nuclear testing and protecting whales, but it condemned sabotage and degenerated into a Gang of Ten bureaucracy. In 1972, drawing on a host of spiritual sources including Native wisdom, Norwegian philosopher Arne Naess formulated the biocentric "deep ecology" alternative to the anthropocentric "shallow ecology" of mainstream environmentalism, thereby promoting ecological and Earth-centered perspectives. The same year, Green Parties emerged in Australia, Canada, and New Zealand, spread to the u.k. in 1973, surfaced in Germany by the end of the decade, and migrated thereafter to the u.s. and throughout the world. Broad-based and alliance-oriented, the international Green movement is organized around "core values" that include ecology, democracy, peace, feminism, respect for diversity, and social justice. In 1974, French writer Françoise d'Eaubonne coined the term "ecofeminism" and the new framework was developed worldwide. As evident in groundbreaking analyses such as Carolyn Merchant's book, *The Death of Nature: Women, Ecology, and the Scientific Revolution* (1980), ecofeminists demonstrated strong links between the oppression of women and the domination of nature, such that ecology and feminism supported and required one another.

Evicted from Greenpeace in 1975 for the "violent" act of throwing a sealer's club out of harm's way, Canadian Paul Watson turned to confrontational and sabotage-oriented actions to defend sea animals from attack, eventually founding the Sea Shepherd Conservation Society. From the direct action culture of hunt saboteurs in england, the Animal Liberation Front (ALF) was born in 1976. Freeing animals from captivity, attacking with hammers and fire, the ALF became a transnational underground group that advocated nonviolence, as u.k. splinter groups such as the Animal Rights Militia and the Justice Department urged attacking exploiters themselves, not just their property.[17] Beginning in the mid-1970s, anti-nuclear and peace movements mushroomed in the u.s. and throughout Europe, especially in Germany, inspiring millions of people to embrace direct action and radical politics in the struggle for an ecological society. The u.s. Clamshell Alliance, for instance, formed in 1976 to stop the construction of nuclear reactors in the small town of Seabrook, New Hampshire. Despite thousands of members engaged in constant mass civil disobedience the Clamshell Alliance failed to prevent the completion of the Seabrook facility, but it was a key part of a larger movement that thwarted the development of nuclear power in the u.s. It was also an essential component of and contributor to an emerging "cultural revolution" that sought to change economic, political, and social structures in democratic and egalitarian directions, using direct action and anarchist-inspired tactics.[18]

Direct action strategies, grassroots movements, and radical politics continued to proliferate during the 1980s. The ALF migrated to the u.s. and throughout the world as Earth First! emerged in 1980 and changed the face of environmental struggle with militant civil disobedience and monkeywrenching actions. Earth First! spread from the u.s. to Australia in the early 1980s, and to the u.k. and Europe at large beginning in 1990. In the u.k., Earth First! landed amidst a political culture already radicalized in the 1980s by the Green Anarchist movement and magazine, which helped to promote Earth First! ideas and actions. Both Green Anarchism and Earth First! embraced "anarcho-primitivist" philosophies that repudiated "civilization" (defined as a complex of structures of domination such as technology, division of labor, and domestication that emerged 10,000 years ago with agricultural society) and advocated a return to hunting and gathering society. Primitivism was becoming more influential in the u.s. as well, developed in its most radical form by John Zerzan.

Beginning in 1986, Murray Bookchin launched fierce attacks on deep ecology, Earth First!, and primitivism. On the surface, Bookchin's blend of anarchism and ecology seemed compatible with other anarchist philosophies, but his emphasis was social not personal, rational not spiritual, and forward not backward looking. He thereby excoriated these approaches—not always accurately—as mystical, asocial, apolitical, irrational, and atavistic, wholly unsuited for his goal to build a revolutionary social movement that could abolish oppression and transcend a capitalist system rooted in "grow-or-die" imperatives.[19] Many activists understood the value of a social ecology orientation, but rejected Bookchin's forced option of *either* social ecology *or* deep ecology. These people included Earth First! member Judi Bari, who worked in theory and practice to synthesize social ecology, deep ecology, and ecofeminism in a "revolutionary ecology" approach that was immensely influential in the u.k. during the 1990s.[20]

During the late 1970s and early 1980s, the u.s. environmental movement broadened in scope and diversity with the proliferation of thousands of grass-roots environmental groups. These were organized by women, people of color, and community members to fight corporate pollution and exploitation. With no patrons, politicians, or corporate sponsors to answer to or offend, grassroots groups—such as spearheaded by Lois Gibbs to protest the 20,000 tons of chemical waste that sickened her community of Love Canal, New York—adopted a confrontational, no compromise approach and won battles the professionalized mainstream would or could not fight.[21]

A critical part of the grassroots revolution was the "environmental justice" movement that engaged environment, race, and social justice issues as one complex. Building on a long and sordid u.s. tradition of racism and discrimination, corporations and polluters targeted the poor, disenfranchised, and people of color to produce and discard their lethal substances. Far from the trimmed lawns and picket fences of privileged white neighborhoods, corporations ensconced themselves near people of color, where they built landfills and manufacturing plants, dumped hazardous and nuclear waste, operated incinerators, spewed deadly chemicals, and turned neighborhoods into toxic badlands. To protect their communities from *real* "eco-terrorism," Native Americans, Asian Americans, Blacks, and Hispanics organized and fought back, proving that marginalized did not mean powerless.[22]

An early expression of environmental justice was the Black revolutionary group, MOVE, founded in 1972 by John Africa and Donald Glassey. MOVE railed against industrial pollution, and related social and environmental problems to the exploitative dynamics of capitalism.[23] Cesar Chavez emerged as a pioneer in the environmental justice movement. In 1962, Chavez organized grape pickers into the National Farm Workers Association, later to become the United Farm Workers of America. Influenced by the non-violent tactics of Gandhi and Dr. Martin Luther King, Jr., Chavez fasted and marched to bring public attention to the plight of farm workers and he led national boycotts against grape growers in California. In the 1980s, Chavez called attention to "the plague of pesticides on our land and our food," such as was poisoning consumers and had a direct effect on farm workers in the form of high cancer rates and birth defects in their children. The u.s. environmental justice movement reached a high point in October 1991, when the first National People of Color Environmental Leadership Summit convened. This conference proved that "it was possible to build a multi-issue, multiracial environmental movement around *justice*. Environmental activism was shown to be alive and well in African American, Latino/a American, Asian American, and Native American communities."[24]

The 1990s in england was a key period when activists broke decisively with mainstream environmentalism. In a nation with traditional bonds to a countryside increasingly threatened by development, activists undertook major anti-roads campaigns to protect what precious little wilderness existed, and the number of direct actions rose dramatically.[25] Breaking from the constraints of u.k. Earth First! in order to employ ALF-style sabotage tactics, the Earth Liberation Front (ELF) formed in the early 1990s, and spread like a brushfire throughout Ireland, Germany, France, Eastern Europe, Australia, the u.s., and elsewhere. In defense of the Earth, the ELF burned down housing complexes under construction, torched SUVs and ski lodges, and ripped up biotech crops.

As ELF "elves" made their merry way across the u.s. and Europe, transnational corporations such as ExxonMobil, Shell Oil, ChevronTexaco, and Monsanto were advancing deep into the southern hemisphere and other areas ripe for "trade" and "development." Their predatory advances were supported by new legal treaties and institutions, such as the Free Trade Area of the Americas (FTAA) and the World Trade Organization (WTO), and bolstered by corrupt client states and brutal military forces. The onslaught of hydroelectric dams, commercial foresting, road building, mining, and agribusiness threatened lands, communities, and livelihoods. Indigenous peoples formed new "ecological resistance movements" (Taylor) and fought back in every possible way. The Zapatistas, for instance, announced their presence to the world just after midnight on January 1, 1994, the day that the North American Free Trade Agreement—a new imperialist weapon to undermine workers, the environment, and the rights and autonomy of indigenous populations—became operative in Mexico, the u.s., and Canada. The Zapatistas are a stellar example of the new revolutionary politics. Alliance-oriented, egalitarian, and global in outlook, they promote feminist values, consensus decision-making, ecological principles, a respect for all life, and the support and/or use of armed struggle.

As dramatically evident in the 1999 "Battle of Seattle," "anti-" or "alter-globalization" groups throughout the world recognized their common interests and fates, and formed unprecedented kinds of alliances.[26] The interests of workers, animals, and the environment alike were gravely threatened in a new world order where the WTO could override the laws of any nation state as "barriers to free trade." Global capitalism was the common enemy recognized by world groups and peoples. Bridging national boundaries, North-South divisions, different political causes, and borders between activists of privileged and non-privileged communities, alter-globalization movements prefigured the future of revolutionary environmentalism as a global, anti-capitalist/anti-imperialist alliance politics, diverse in class, race, and gender composition.

Conceptualizing Revolutionary Environmentalism

In the last three decades, there has been growing awareness that environmentalism cannot succeed without social justice and social justice cannot be realized without environmentalism.[27] To be sure, defending forests and protecting whales are crucial actions to take, for they protect evolutionary processes and ecological systems vital to the planet and all species and peoples within it. Yet at the same time, it is also critical to fight side-by-side with oppressed peoples in order to address all forms of environmental destruction and build a movement far greater in numbers and strength than possible with a single-issue focus. Such a holistic orientation can be seen in the international Green network, the u.s. environmental justice movement, Earth First! efforts (as initiated by Judi Bari) to join with timber workers, alter-globalization channels, Zapatista coalition building, and often in the communiqués and actions of ALF and ELF activists. Examples of broad alliance politics are visible also in recent efforts to build bridges among animal, Earth, and Black liberationists and anti-imperialists (as evident in this book). These various dynamics are part and parcel of the emergence of global revolutionary environmentalism.

There are key similarities between what has been called "radical environmentalism"—which includes social ecology, deep ecology, ecofeminism, Earth First!, and primitivism—and what we term "revolutionary environmentalism."[28] Among other things, both approaches reject mainstream environmentalism, attack core ideologies and/or institutions that have caused the ecological crisis, often adopt spiritual outlooks and see nature as sacred, reject the binary opposition separating humans from nature, and in many cases defend or adopt illegal tactics such as civil disobedience or monkeywrenching. However, a key distinguishing trait of revolutionary environmentalism is that it supports and/or employs illegal tactics ranging from property destruction for the purpose of economic sabotage to guerilla warfare and armed struggle, recognizing that violent methods of resistance are often appropriate against fascist regimes and right-wing dictatorships. Revolutionary environmentalism seeks to counter forces of oppression with equally potent forms of resistance, and uses militant tactics when they are justified, necessary, and effective. With the advance of the global capitalist juggernaut and increasing deterioration of the Earth's ecological systems, ever more people may realize that no viable future will arise without militant actions and large-scale social transformation, a process that requires abolishing global capitalism and imperialism, and would thereby embrace revolutionary environmentalism.[29]

As evident in the communiqués of the ALF and ELF, as well as in the views of Black liberationists, anarchists, and anti-imperialists, many activists are explicitly revolutionary in their rhetoric, analysis, vision, and political identities. Revolutionary environmentalists renounce reformist approaches that aim only to manage the symptoms of the global ecological crisis and never dare or think to probe its underlying dynamics and causes. Revolutionary environmentalists seek to end the destruction of nature and peoples, not merely to slow its pace, temper its effects, or plug holes in a dam set to burst. They don't act to "manage" the catastrophic consequences of the project to dominate nature; they work to abolish the very hierarchy whereby humans live as if they were separate from nature and pursue the deluded goal of mastery and control. The objectives thought necessary by revolutionary environmentalists cannot be realized within the present world system, and require a rupture with it.

Revolutionary environmentalists recognize the need for fundamental changes on many levels, such as with human psychologies (informed by anthropocentric worldviews, values, and identities), interpersonal relations (mediated by racism, sexism, speciesism, ageism, classism, homophobia, and elitism), social institutions (governed by authoritarian, plutocratic, and corrupt or pseudo-democratic forms), technologies (enforcing labor and exploitation imperatives and driven by fossil-fuels that cause pollution and global warming), and the prevailing economic system (an inherently destructive and unsustainable global capitalism driven by profit, production, and consumption imperatives). Revolutionary environmentalists see "separate" problems as related to the larger system of global capitalism and reject the reformist notion of "green capitalism" as a naïve oxymoron. They repudiate the logics of marketization, economic growth, and industrialization as inherently violent, exploitative, and destructive, and seek ecological, democratic, and egalitarian alternatives.

As the dynamics that brought about global warming, rainforest destruction, species extinction, and poisoning of communities are not reducible to any single factor or cause—be it agricultural society, the rise of states, anthropocentrism, speciesism, patriarchy, racism, colonialism, industrialism, technocracy, or capitalism—all radical groups and orientations that can effectively challenge the ideologies and institutions implicated in domination and ecological destruction have a relevant role to play in the global social-environmental struggle. While standpoints such as

deep ecology, social ecology, ecofeminism, animal liberation, Black liberation, and the ELF are all important, none can accomplish systemic social
transformation by itself. Working together, however, through a diversity of
critiques and tactics that mobilize different communities, a flank of militant groups and positions can drive a battering ram into the structures of
power and domination and open the door to a new future.

Thus, revolutionary environmentalism is not a *single group*, but rather
a *collective movement* rooted in specific tactics and goals (such as just discussed), and organized as multi-issue, multiracial alliances that can mount
effective opposition to capitalism and other modes of domination. We do
not have in mind here a super-movement that embraces all struggles, but
rather numerous alliance networks that may form larger collectives with
other groups in fluid and dynamic ways, and are as global in vision and
reach as is transnational capitalism.[30] Although there is diversity in unity,
there must also be unity in diversity. Solidarity can emerge in recognition
of the fact that all forms of oppression are directly or indirectly related to
the values, institutions, and *system* of global capitalism and related hierarchical structures. To be unified and effective, however, anti-capitalist and
anti-imperialist alliances require mutual sharing, respectful learning, and
psychological growth, such that, for instance, Black liberationists, ecofeminists, and animal liberationists can help one another overcome racism,
sexism, and speciesism.

New social movements and Greens have failed to realize their radical potential. They have abandoned their original demands for radical
social change and become integrated into capitalist structures that have
eliminated "existing socialist countries" as well as social democracies in a
global triumph of neoliberalism. A new revolutionary force must therefore
emerge, one that will build on the achievements of classical democratic,
libertarian socialist, and anarchist traditions; incorporate radical green,
feminist, and indigenous struggles; synthesize animal, Earth, and human
liberation politics and standpoints; and build a global social-ecological
revolution capable of abolishing transnational capitalism so that just and
ecological societies can be constructed in its place.

Using This Book

Similar to our last effort, *Terrorists or Freedom Fighters? Reflections
on the Liberation of Animals* (Lantern Books, 2004), we seek in this book
to present a rich diversity of radical voices and perspectives. Thus, we employ a pluralist, multipersectival, interdisciplinary, boundary-transgress-
ing, bridge-building approach, bringing together sundry people and positions that ordinarily never meet. *Igniting a Revolution* breaks down various
walls and borders, such as typically exist between academics and activists,
scholars and political prisoners (former and current), whites and people
of color, men and women, and human and animal rights advocates. This
volume features a wide array of critical perspectives on social and envi-

ronmental issues, ranging from social ecology, deep ecology, Earth First!, ecofeminism, and primitivism to Native Americans, Black liberationists, political prisoners, and animal/Earth liberation movements.

Igniting a Revolution was organized according to the principles of radical feminist and anarchist philosophy, in order to give voice to oppressed peoples rather than present yet another selection from the privileged few. In this weighty volume of over forty diverse contributions, we have made a special effort to reach out to and include those activists who still sit in prison for their political "crimes" against the corporate-state complex. Yet because our focus is on people struggling from within the belly of the beast, we do not include those battling corporate ecocide, neoliberalism, and biopiracy in India, Brazil, Ecuador, Africa, Chiapas, and elsewhere.[31]

An important task of this book—and of revolutionary environmentalism as well—is to decouple environmentalism from white, male, privileged positions; diversify it along class, gender, racial, ethnic, and other lines; and remove it from its single-issue pedestal. Still today, in the u.s. and other western nations, mainstream environmentalism fails to reach out to women, the poor, workers, migrants, and people of color whose immediate problems have more to do with toxic waste and chemical poisoning than a vanishing wilderness, although clearly these are interconnected issues.[32] Yet there are many promising signs in the last three decades and contemporary context whereby the struggles for Earth, animal, and human liberation are being *conceived of and fought for as one*. From a broad perspective, revolutionary environmentalism is a class, race, gender, and culture war that aims to abolish every system of domination, including that of human beings over nature.

This anthology is divided into seven sections that explore different aspects of the ever-deepening, global social-environmental crisis. Each section begins with a poem by a renowned activist-poet relevant to its general themes, as we close the book with a poem, and include an appendix of rarely collected ELF communiqués.

Section I provides historical, philosophical, and political overviews of revolutionary environmentalism, with a focus on deep ecology, social ecology, Earth First!, and the ELF.

Section II reflects on the pathologies of consumerism, the ideologies of mass media, and the politics of everyday life that call into question one's own complicity in the machines of destruction.

Section III dissects Christianity and orthodox religion from an ecological standpoint, and discusses the importance of spiritual connections among one another and to the Earth from numerous standpoints.

Section IV explores the "anarcho-primitivism" perspective which assails "civilization" as irredeemably rooted in domination, and thus calls for a return to primal ways of living.

Section V spotlights academics, political prisoners, Black liberationists, and animal liberationists who share personal experiences with state repression while offering hope for continued struggle.

Section VI explores the justifications for sabotage tactics as a much-needed weapon in defense of the Earth, as it also discusses their limitations and advances larger visions for social change.

Section VII examines the commonalities among various oppressed groups and radical struggles, and underscores the need for a broad social/environmental movement for revolutionary change.

Our Goals

Igniting a Revolution is written by and for Earth liberationists, animal liberationists, Black liberationists, Native Americans, ecofeminists, political prisoners, primitivists, saboteurs, grassroots activists, and militant academics. It reaches out to exploited workers, indigenous peoples, subsistence farmers, tribes pushed to the brink of extinction, guerilla armies, armed insurgents, disenfranchised youth, and to all others who struggle against the advancing juggernaut of global capitalism, neo-fascism, imperialism, militarism, and phony wars on terrorism that front for attacks on dissent and democracy. This book does not offer analysis or theory for its own sake, it is, rather, a political intervention to help spread resistance and change. It is not a haphazard collection of thoughts, but a strategic effort to unite radical struggles in the western world and beyond. It is not a history book, but a book to help make history.

This volume aims to promote thought, provoke anger, stir passion, emphasize commonalities, establish connections, advocate systemic thinking, and, ultimately, to galvanize militant action appropriate to the level of the destruction of the Earth and its sundry inhabitants and communities. While the voices in this book speak in different ways on social, political, and environmental issues, together they recognize the insanity, injustice, and unsustainability of the current world order, as they seek profound transformation on many different levels.

Windows of opportunity are closing. The actions that human beings now collectively take or fail to take will determine whether the future is hopeful or bleak. The revolution that this planet desperately needs at this crucial juncture will involve, among other things, a movement to abolish anthropocentrism, speciesism, racism, patriarchy, homophobia, and prejudices and hierarchies of all kinds. In a revolutionary process, people throughout the world will reconstitute social institutions in a form that promotes autonomy, self-determination of nations and peoples, decentralization and democratization of political life, non-market relations, guaranteed rights for humans and animals, an ethics of respect for nature and all life, and the harmonization of the social and natural worlds.

The Earth will survive—indeed, it will regenerate and flourish—without us, but we will not survive without a healthy Earth. Numerous hominid species such as *Homo Neanderthalensis* have perished because they could not adapt to changing conditions, and countless human civilizations have collapsed for ecological reasons. Clearly, there is no guarantee that *Homo sapiens* will exist in the near future, as the dystopian visions of films such as *Mad Max* or *Waterworld* may actually be realized. Nor is there is any promise that serious forms of revolutionary environmentalism can or will arise, given problems such as the factionalism and egoism that typically tears political groups apart and/or the fierce political repression always directed against resistance movements. Yet as social and ecological situations continue to deteriorate globally, the struggles for ecology and justice may grow ever more radical and intense.

Amidst so many doubts and uncertainties, there is nonetheless no question whatsoever that the quality of the future—if humanity and other imperiled species have one—depends on the strength of global resistance movements and the possibilities for revolutionary change.

May this collection of readings help blaze the trail forward and ignite this revolution. We invite you to read, reflect, resist, and revolt.

Notes

1. The claim that we currently are witnessing an advanced ecological "crisis," upon which the argument for revolutionary struggle rests, means that there is an emergency situation in the ecology of the Earth as a whole that needs urgent attention. If we do not address ecological problems immediately and with radical measures that target causes not symptoms, severe, world-altering consequences will play out over a long-term period. Signs of major stress of the world's eco-systems are everywhere, from denuded forests and depleted fisheries to vanishing wilderness and global climate change. As one indicator of massive disruption, the proportion of species human beings are driving to extinction "might easily reach 20 percent by 2022 and rise as high as 50 percent or more thereafter" (Wilson, Edward O. *The Future of Life*. New York: Knopf, 2002). Given the proliferating amount of solid, internationally assembled scientific data supporting the ecological crisis claim, it can no longer be dismissed as "alarmist;" the burden of proof, rather has shifted to those "skeptics," "realists," and "optimists" in radical denial of the growing catastrophe to prove why complacency is not blindness and insanity. For reliable data on the crisis, see the various reports, papers, and annual *Vital Signs* and *State of the World* publications by the Worldwatch Institute. On the impact of *Homo sapiens* over time, see "The Pleistocene-Holocene Event" <http://rewilding.org/thesixthgreatextinction.htm>. On the serious environmental effects of agribusiness and global meat and dairy production/consumption systems (which include deforestation, desertification, water pollution, species extinction, resource waste, and global warming), see Robbins, John. *The Food Revolution: How Your Diet Can Help Save Your Life and Our World*. Berkeley, CA: Conari Press, 2001. The environmental impact of militarism and war is another often overlooked, but critical factor, as militaries and warfare are major contributors to air pollution, ozone depletion, poisoned rivers, contaminated soil, use of land mass, consumption of energy and resources, release of toxic, radioactive, and chemical waste, and of course the threat of nuclear holocaust. See Bertell, Rosalie. *Planet Earth: The Newest Weapon of War*. Montréal: Black Rose Books, 2001.

2. Consider, for instance, how ExxonMobil has aggressively lobbied the Bush administration to block alternative energy approaches and maintain fossil fuels as the dominant energy source for the future; see "The Hydrogen Hypocrites." <http://www.globalpolicy.org/security/natres/oil/2003/0211hy.htm>

3. In solidarity with the language of resistance used by many Black liberationists and anti-imperialists, throughout this introduction we substitute "u.s.," "amerika," "england," and "u.k." for "US," "America," "England," and "UK." We graffiti the names only of these two main imperialist powers.

4. See Dowie, Mark. *Losing Ground: American Environmentalism at the Close of the Twentieth Century*. Cambridge, Massachusetts: MIT Press, 1995; and Speth, James Gustave. *Red Sky at Morning: America and the Crisis of the Global Environment*. New Haven, CT: Yale University Press, 2004.

5. Whereas some indulge in mythologizing and romanticizing past cultures, it is a well-known fact that massive environmental destruction is not caused by modern western societies alone, but rather was characteristic of numerous earlier societies that hunted animals to extinction and laid waste to their surroundings to the extent their technologies allowed. See Diamond, Jared. *Collapse: How Societies Choose to Fail or Succeed*. New York: Viking, 2004; Redman, Charles L. *Human Impact on Ancient Environments*. Tucson: University of Arizona Press, 1999; and Carter, Vernon and Tom Dale. *Topsoil and Civilization*. Norman, OK: University of Oklahoma Press, 1975.

6. Needless to say, in our limited space here, we cannot possibly discuss in detail key individuals, groups, and concepts important to the history of western environmentalism. We are tracing some of the streams that feed into the river of revolutionary environmentalism as we define it, and many other histories and perspectives are needed for a fuller picture. This focus means that we are more concerned with providing a broad sketch and conceptual framework rather than a critical assessment of every figure and development we mention.

7. On the topic of global environmentalism, see Guha, Ramachandra. *Environmentalism: A Global History*. Cartersville, GA: Longman, 1999. The differences between Northern and Southern forms of environmentalism is discussed by Ramachandra Guha, Juan Martinez-Alier, and Juan Martinez in *Varieties of Environmentalism: Essays North and South*. London: Earthscan Publications, 1997.

8. As they are so often misunderstood, it is important to emphasize that Luddites were not about mindless attacks on machinery or reactionary fears of "progress," but rather rejection of a mechanistic approach to life, care for craftsmanship, and concern over threats to core values such as freedom and dignity. For an illuminating account of Luddites past and present, see Sale, Kirkpatrick. *Rebels Against the Future: The Luddites and Their War on the Industrial Revolution*. Cambridge, MA: Perseus Publishing, 1995.

9. For an example of a standard, single-focus narrative on the history of u.s. environmentalism, see Nash, Roderick. *Wilderness and the American Mind*. New Haven: Yale University Press, 1967. To read an alternative, far broader account that links environmental and social history by including the fight for safe working and living conditions and the struggles of women, labor, and others, see Gottlieb, Robert. *Forcing the Spring: The Transformation of the American Environmental Movement*. Washington, DC: Island Press, 1993. Marcy Darnovsky provides an excellent social history of environmentalism in her essay, "Stories Less Told: Histories of US Environmentalism," *Socialist Review* Vol 22 No. 4 (October–December, 1992): 11–54. Darnovsky notes that "Too sharp a focus on wilderness blurs the environmental significance of everyday life...In limiting their scope as they do, the standard [environmental] histories contribute to still-widespread associations of the environment as a place separate from daily life and innocent of social relations" (28).

10. See Dowie, *Losing Ground*.

11. Salt's book, *Animal Rights: Considered in Relation to Social Progress* (1892), was pioneering both in its use of the term "rights" (in an english culture dominated by utilitarianism no less), and its holistic vision that presents human and animal rights as inseparable elements of moral progress. Salt also was a key influence on Gandhi, and thereby on subsequent history in two key ways: his book, *A Plea for Vegetarianism* (1886), prompted Gandhi to return to vegetarianism (this time to honor ethical reasons not religious tradition) and thereby formulate a wider ethic of life; in addition, Salt introduced Gandhi to the works of Thoreau, thus spreading the tradition of civil disobedience.

12. On the early role of women in the emerging environmental movement, see Fox, Stephen. *The American Conservation Movement: John Muir and His Legacy*. Madison: The University of Wisconsin, 1991.

13. See, for instance, Bookchin, Murray. *Our Synthetic Environment*. New York: Knopf, 1962 (published under the pseudonym of "Lewis Herber").

14. For a historical and critical analysis of new social movements, see Boggs, Carl. *Social Movements and Political Power: Emerging Forms of Radicalism in the West*. Philadelphia: Temple University Press, 1987.

15. For critiques of mainstream environmentalism, see Sale, Kirkpatrick. *The Green Revolution: The American Environmental Movement 1962–1992*. New York: Hill and Wang, 1993; and Dowie, *Losing Ground*. More recently, Michael Shellenberger and Ted Nordhaus proclaimed the "death of Environmentalism," arguing that it rests upon "unexamined assumptions, outdated concepts, and exhausted strategies." <http://www.grist.org/news/maindish/2005/01/13/doe-reprint/> Renouncing the mainstream's single-issue approach, they call for broadening environmentalism into a multi-issue social movement. Many grassroots activists, however, found their vision far too narrow. For multiracial critiques of their analysis, see Blain, Ludovic, "Ain't I an Environmentalist?" <http://www.grist.org/comments/soapbox/2005/05/31/blain-death/>; Aguilar, Oscar, "Why I Am Not an Environmentalist." <http://www.grist.org/comments/soapbox/2005/05/31/aguilar/index.html>; and Gelobter, Michel, et al, "The Soul of Environmentalism: Rediscovering Transformational Politics in the 21ˢᵗ Century." <http://www.rprogress.org/soul/soul.pdf>

16. For examples of greenwashing and "environmental" groups serving the cause of corporate propaganda, see Dowie, *Losing Ground*, 53–59; and Rampton, Sheldon and John Stauber, *Toxic Sludge is Good For You!* Monroe, Maine: Common Courage Press, 1999.

17. See Best, Steven and Anthony J. Nocella, II, eds. *Terrorists or Freedom Fighters? Reflections on the Liberation of Animals*. New York: Lantern Books, 2004.

18. See Epstein, Barbara. *Political Protest and Cultural Revolution: Non-Violent Direct Action of the 1970s and 1980s*. Berkeley, CA: University of California Press, 1991.

19. By far and away, the harshest critic of deep ecology, Earth First!, and primitivism—all reviled as being racist, misanthropic, mystical, irrational, and atavistic—is social ecologist Murray Bookchin (see, for example, Bookchin, Murray. *Re-Enchanting Humanity: A Defense of the Human Spirit Against Anti-Humanism, Misanthropy, Mysticism, and Primitivism*. London: Cassell, 1995). Although Bookchin makes a number of important points against these movements, he often takes statements out of context and fails to account for the diversity and competing divisions within groups, such as existed in Earth First! between the "wilders" (e.g., Dave Foreman and Christopher Manes) and the social-oriented "holies" (e.g., Judi Bari and Darryl Cherney). For critiques of Bookchin's one-dimensional readings of deep ecology and Earth First!, see Taylor, Bron. "Earth First! and Global Narratives of Popular Ecological Resistance." In *Ecological Resistance Movements: The Global Emergence of Radical and Popular Environmentalism*, edited by Bron Taylor. Albany: State University of New York Press, 1995. Also see Taylor's essay "The Religion and Politics of Earth First!," *The Ecologist* 21 66, (November–December, 1991).

20. Bari, Judi. "Revolutionary Ecology: Biocentrism and Deep Ecology." <http://www.judi-bari.org/revolutionary-ecology.html>

21. In her transformation from housewife to environmentalist, emblematic of the politicization of citizens at the grassroots level in the 1980s and 1990s, Gibbs organized her neighborhood against Hooker Chemical Company, created the Love Canal Homeowners Association, sparked President Carter's approval of a paid evacuation for the 900 families stranded in Love Canal, and was a force behind the creation of the Superfund—all without membership in the Gang of Ten. In 1981 she created the Center for Health, Environment & Justice <http://www.chej.org/>, and subsequently won numerous honors.

22. A good introduction to the environmental justice movement is Bullard, Robert D. ed., *Unequal Protection: Environmental Justice & Communities of Color*. San Francisco: Sierra Club Books, 1994. In an interview with *Earth First! Journal*, Bullard clarifies the environmental justice position by emphasizing that it does not favor human environments over wilderness and other species, but rather includes those issues in a broader framework. As he puts it, "environmental justice incorporates the idea that we are just as much concerned about wetlands, birds and wilderness areas, but we're also concerned with urban habitats, where people live in cities, about reservations, about things that are happening along the US-Mexican border, about children that are being poisoned by lead in housing and kids playing outside in contaminated playgrounds." <http://www.ejnet.org/ej/bullard.html> Also see Fisk, Daniel, ed. *The Struggle for Ecological Democracy: Environmental Justice Movements in the United States*. New York: Guilford Press, 1998, and Sachs, Aaron, "Eco-Justice: Linking Human Rights and the Environment," *Worldwatch Institute Paper* #127 (December 1995). A helpful online resource for environmental justice can be found at: <http://www.ejnet.org/ej/index.html>. For critiques of the environmental movement as dominated by white, privileged interests, and calls for a multiracial environmental movement, see Gelobter, Michel, et al. "The Soul of Environmentalism: Rediscovering Transformational Politics in the 21st Century;" Blain, Ludovic. "Ain't I an Environmentalist?;" Brown, Adrienne Maree. "Rainbow Warrior." <http://www.grist.org/comments/soapbox/2005/03/15/brown/>; Strikland, Eliza. "The New Face of Environmentalism." <http://www.truthout.org/issues_05/111005EB.shtml>; and Osayande, Ewuare. "Choking Back Black Liberation: Revisioning Environmentalism." <http://www.seac.org/threshold-backup/sept04.pdf>

23. According to John Africa, "MOVE's work is to stop industry from poisoning the air, the water, the soil, and to put an end to the enslavement of life—people, animals, any form of life" (cited at <http://religiousmovements.lib.virginia.edu/nrms/Move.html>). MOVE's subversive presence in Philadelphia ended dramatically when police dropped a bomb on their house, killing six adults and five children. While MOVE is widely recognized as a radical and innovative movement, many members of the feminist and lesbian, gay, bisexual, transgender, queer (LGBTQ) communities believe that MOVE founders adopted regressive views toward women and homosexuals based on a dogmatic, patriarchal, and homophobic interpretation of "natural law."

24. Bullard, Robert D. "Environmental Justice For All." In *Unequal Protection: Environmental Justice & Communities of Color*, edited by Robert D. Bullard, San Francisco: Sierra Club Books, 1997, 7.

25. On the history of environmentalism in england, see Wall, Derek. *Green History: Reader in Environmental Literature, Philosophy, and Politics*. London: Routledge, 2003. For recent histories of sabotage and direct action tactics, see Wall's earlier book, *Earth First and the Anti-Roads Movement: Radical Environmentalism and Comparative Social Movements*. London: Routledge, 1999; and also Seel, Benjamin, Matthew Paterson, and Brian Doherty eds., *Direct Action in British Environmentalism*. London: Routledge, 2000. For an excellent example of the broad sense of revolutionary environmentalism that we are articulating here—an uncompromising, anti-hierarchy, anti-capitalist, anti-imperialist social-ecological movement in solidarity with all oppressed world peoples and species—see the u.k. journal, *Do or Die: Voices from the Ecological Resistance*.

26. On the resistance movements against global capitalism, see Brecher, Jeremy, Tim Costello, and Brendan Smith. *Globalization From Below: The Power of Solidarity*. Cambridge, Massachusetts: South End Press, 2000; and Kahn, Richard and Douglas Kellner. "Resisting Globalization." In *The Blackwell Companion to Globalization*, edited by G. Ritzer, Malden MA: Blackwell Publishers, 2006.

27. For a thorough exploration of the social-environmental relationship from a radical anarchist perspective that builds on social ecology and offers concrete proposals for a revolutionary remaking of the world, see Fotopolous, Takis. *Towards An Inclusive Democracy: The Crisis of the Growth Economy and the Need for a New Liberatory Project*. London/New York: Cassell/Continuum, 1997. We also recommend essays in the journal *Democracy and Nature*, some of which are online at <http://www.democracynature.org/dn/>.

28. For significant works on "radical environmentalism," see Manes, Christopher. *Green Rage: Radical Environmentalism and the Unmaking of Civilization*. Boston: Little, Brown and Company, 1990; Scarce, Rik. *Eco-Warriors: Understanding the Radical Environmental Movement*. Chicago: The Noble Press, Inc., 1990; and Merchant, Carolyn. *Radical Ecology: The Search For a Livable World*. New York: Routledge, 1992. Bron Taylor provides a useful overview of "Radical Environmentalism" and "Earth First! and the Earth Liberation Front" in the *Encyclopedia of Religion and Nature*. London: Thoemmes, 2005, available online at <http://www.religionandnature.com/ern/sample.htm>. Another useful article, from an eco-socialist and revolutionary perspective, is Foster, John Bellamy, "Organizing Ecological Revolution," *Monthly Review* Volume 7 Number 5. <http://www.monthlyreview.org/1005jbf. htm>.

29. It is critical to point out that contributors to this volume use different terms to talk about similar or the same things; thus, in addition to "revolutionary environmentalism," one will also see references to "radical environmentalism," "radical ecology," or "revolutionary ecology." It is natural that different people discussing new ecological resistance movements will use different terminology, and we did not attempt to impose our own discourse of "revolutionary environmentalism" on any of the authors, although some do use the term "revolutionary environmentalism." While there is general consensus on the need for a militant resistance movement and revolutionary social transformation, we leave it to the reader to interpret and compare the different philosophical and political perspectives.

30. In 1996, for instance, the Zapatistas organized a global "encuentro" during which over 3,000 grassroots activists and intellectuals from 42 countries assembled to discuss strategies for a worldwide struggle against neoliberalism. In response to the Zapatista's call for an "intercontinental network of resistance, recognizing differences and acknowledging similarities," the People's Global Action Network was formed, a group explicitly committed to anti-capitalist, anti-imperialist, and ecological positions (see <http://www.nadir.org/nadir/initiativ/agp/en/index.htm>). For more examples of global politics and networks that report on news, actions, and campaigns from around the world, covering human rights, animal rights, and environmental struggles, see *One World* <http://www.oneworld.net/>, *Protest.Net* <http://www.protest.net/>, and *Indymedia* <http://www.indymedia.org/en/index.shtml>.

31. For some of the works chronicling the ecological and political battles around the globe, see Merchant, Carolyn, *Radical Ecology: The Search For a Livable World*; Peet, Richard and Michael Watts, eds. *Liberation Ecologies: Environment, Development, Social Movements*. London: Routledge, 1996; Taylor, ed., *Ecological Resistance Movements: The Global Emergence of Radical and Popular Environmentalism*; and Chapter 8 in Scarce, *Eco-Warriors: Understanding the Radical Environmental Movement*.

32. For an attempt to forge a grassroots alliance politics that links environmental justice with broad social concerns, developing an anti-racist, anti-imperialist, anti-authoritarian, feminist, queer and trans-liberationist movement against global capitalism, see the "Colours of Resistance" group at <http://colours.mahost.org/>. Also see the race-based critiques of Shellenberger and Nordhaus in footnote 15 above.

Part I

THE HISTORY AND NATURE OF REVOLUTIONARY ENVIRONMENTALISM

"Starting from the very reasonable, but unfortunately revolutionary concept that social practices which threaten the continuation of life on Earth must be changed, we need a theory of revolutionary ecology that will encompass social and biological issues, class struggle, and a recognition of the role of global corporate capitalism in the oppression of peoples and the destruction of nature." *Judi Bari*

"No real social change has ever been brought about without a revolution...revolution is but thought carried into action." *Emma Goldman*

"I throw a Molotov cocktail at the precinct, you know how we think...
FBI spyin on us throu the radio antennas
And them hidden cameras in the streetlight watchin society
With no respect for the people's right to privacy...
Bring the power back to the street, where the people live
We sick of workin for crumbs and fillin up the prisons
Dyin over money and relyin on religion for help
We do for self like ants in a colony
Organize the wealth into a socialist economy
A way of life based off the common need
And all my comrades is ready, we just spreadin the seed."
Dead Prez

"The planet is not dying. It is being killed. And the people killing it have names and addresses." *Utah Phillips*

Poems From Prison

Marilyn Buck

Velvet Fans

butterfly wings falter
poisoned or commodified.
trapped inside heavy-metal safes
fluttering across N A S D A Q screens

butterflies are gone
velvet fans stir the wind no more
flowers shrivel, unkissed
their lavish aspirations
    drop on despondent earth

American Gothic

Gaunt-eyed farmers
stand stripped
earth turned over
by hands
waving a piece of paper

Prayer

I pray that the poor
recover
breathe deeply sun-dappled
reclamation a repast
of sweet relief

i pray that the martyred and murdered
rise
in the light of infant-cradled
smiles rainbow chants
and morning hymns

i pray that the innocent
restore
ebony-boned crescendos
glory sounds drumming
upon the shores

i pray that the predators
perish
swallowed by their greed—stuffed
sump pumps gulping
in the wind

i pray that the globe-grabbing cannibals
consume
themselves roasted in black gold
wraiths irradiated
by wrung-earth remains

i pray that the demons
drown
beneath the pounding footprints
left by audacious dancers
in the dawn

let us pray that day and night
embrace
subversive lovers unafraid
of sweat-redemption
emancipation's creed

let us pray
let us pray
amen

After the Wave

let's take a walk
to remember the world
the earth that used to be
before syphilitic sirens soared

don't be afraid
it's only rubble now
rocks hunker behind torn-down trees
shriek their loss into the wind

don't be afraid of the wind
yes, a fire wave then
burned the breath
and flayed the cities' flanks

the wind weeps now
crowns death's sybarites
and cools scorched skeletons
memory's wind clatters

don't be afraid
yes, we will die
but not today, let's leave
dread's shoes in caves below

let's take a walk
if you do not come I will go alone
if I do not see the sky
I will die

Mapping

furies:
draw a map with wings
        flapping free
                butterflies

rebel against kingdom-maker's maps
    cross lines & intersections
    conjure rising waters
        move boulders
    confound the four directions
        of arrogant landgrabbers
strike down wall-builders
    with winged wrath
wipe their maps from the windscreens

fly down paths
    hidden in mapped dust
        willow trees will trip pursuers

Revolutionary Environmentalism
An Introduction

Mark Somma

In the contemporary political context, revolutionary environmentalism must be understood in relation to what it departs from, namely, "mainstream environmentalism." For committed environmentalists, revolutionary environmentalism represents the future of political struggle as mainstream environmentalism has proven itself to be inadequate to the task of responding to the crisis in the natural world and the corruption in politics.

In the view of the revolutionary environmentalist, mainstream environmentalism follows what Norwegian philosopher and activist Arne Naess criticized as "shallow ecology." For Naess, shallow ecology is a reform-oriented, technocratic outlook that seeks accommodation with the existing corporate economic and interest-group political system. It is mired in the burdens of organizational maintenance via donations and grants, and contracts are crucial to mainstream environmental leadership. Revolving door ambitions motivate decisions by mainstream environmental leaders as they move from corporate positions to government appointments to interest group leadership. In some ways, they become indistinguishable from their corporate adversaries who travel through much the same career pathways. Shallow ecology also is distinguished, Naess argues, by a human-centered or "anthropocentric" outlook that is alienated from nature and clings to a dysfunctional vision of mastery and control that lies at the root of the environmental crisis.

In direct contrast, revolutionary environmentalism, as I present it here, relies heavily on Naess' concept of "deep ecology." Deep ecology differs fundamentally from shallow ecology on two key points. Politically, it rejects bureaucratic models of change and seeks far more than reforms within a technocratic system of exploitation of nature; philosophically, it advances a "biocentric" worldview that aims to reintegrate human beings into nature through radically different forms of selfhood, values, and ethics.

This essay aims to clarify some key differences between mainstream and revolutionary environmentalism, between shallow and deep ecology. Clearly, different interpretations of revolutionary environmentalism exist, but most perspectives share some attachment to deep ecology. Deep ecology engages the fundamental problem of anthropocentrism and human alienation from nature. Yet, while the philosophical aspects of deep ecology are profound, the political aspects are themselves "shallow" and fail to develop an adequate theory and practice of forging new social institutions. I draw a distinction between radical actions and revolutionary change, and I argue that while tactics such as direct action and ecotage may be "radical," they are not revolutionary because they cannot, by themselves, bring about a qualitatively new social system. Such transformation requires a *new social movement* and *a positive vision of a new society*, the likes of which does not yet exist and remains to be invented.

The Logic of Revolution

A profound transformation awaits us in the immediate future as we grapple with the ravaging effects of human society against nature. The changes needed to heal the planet and the rift between human beings and nature far exceeds any reasonable interpretation of the word "reform." The change required is *revolutionary*—it is systemic and far-reaching in scope: it demands a different conceptual paradigm, new values and lifeways, and a dramatically different set of social institutions. Radical actions and organizing may help push society in the proper direction, but radical is a word best left to describe behavior and tactics. The Earth Liberation Front burns down logging company trucks to stop the destruction of a specific old-growth forest—that's radical direct action. But forming a new society that values old-growth trees and thus preempts their destruction from the start—that is revolutionary. The demand for change is radical; the overthrow and replacement of the existing social paradigms and institutions of society constitutes revolution. As yet, too little written work exists establishing a workable "deep ecology" politics and biocentric society. Radical tactics to defend nature and life only take us partway toward our goal of a society that respects nature and lives in harmony with life.

Radical tactics and revolutionary ideologies and politics evolve as environmental destruction accelerates and mainstream approaches fail to stop the destruction and adequately defend nature. Consequently, emergent radical groups splinter from their parent organizations. Thus, Earth First! arose from the Sierra Club and, in the early 1990s, a branch of Earth First! became the Earth Liberation Front. Likewise, in 1975, Paul Watson broke with Greenpeace when it condemned the use of sabotage tactics. He subsequently started the Sea Shepherd Conservation Society, a direct action group which he termed "the most aggressive, no-nonsense, and determined conservation organization in the world." Increasingly, environmentalists urge radical tactics to meet the mounting crisis in the natural world.

Much of the informational fuel for their insistence on radical tactics comes from the scientific community whose research into such diverse fields as herpetology, climatology, and Arctic ecology shows dramatic declines in species populations and habitats.

Revolutionary Semantics and Biocentrism

Successful insurgencies require a clear political message in order to communicate effectively with the populace. It's a requirement that revolutionary environmentalism doesn't yet meet, as it presents a muddled political message. It's primarily a message of "don't," as in, "don't do this and don't do that," but doesn't provide a viable framework for positive action to bring about social transformation. Several contemporary attempts to codify a revolutionary environmental message exist beginning with Arne Naess' famous essay on deep ecology (1989), the work of George Sessions (1987, 1993), Bill Devall (1980, 1988), and their collaboration (1985), in addition to Warwick Fox (1984, 1990) and poets like Gary Snyder (1969, 1990). Perhaps the most easily digestible version of deep ecology's political message is Bill McKibbens' *The End of Nature* (1989, 1999). The following summary abbreviates the deep ecology argument that many versions of revolutionary environmentalism assume.

Shallow ecology represents the cultural and political battles over pollution and resource scarcity. Culturally and philosophically, shallow ecology remains tied to anthropocentrism, the view that human existence and wants are the central fact of the universe. Such widely-held beliefs that wilderness is wasted unless developed, or the all-encompassing modern social experience of consumerism, tie directly to anthropocentric orientations. Politically, the battle joins mainstream environmental groups with the conventional tactics of campaign donations, legislation, litigation, and media-organized argumentation. Shallow ecology assumes that the ecological problems can be fixed without fundamental personal and social transformation, and thus that a series of minor reforms are sufficient.

Deep ecology begins by rejecting human-centered arguments about the relationship between society and the environment. All life ought to enjoy certain (undefined) rights and human society must recognize the interrelatedness and the intrinsic value of nature. Thus, deep ecology involves a break with the mechanistic ontology of nature, requires a system of ethics based on biocentrism (or "ecocentrism"), and an application of equality and justice extending to the natural world. The real difference between shallow and deep ecology is conflicting theories of natural reality. Each, for example, sees the forest as an entirely different phenomenon; for shallow ecology the forest becomes a collection of discrete resources measured by their respective values to an exploitative human society; for deep ecology, the forest has an intrinsic value distinct from human society's use for it. A central statement of deep ecology is the eight key platform principles developed by Bill Devall and George Sessions in their book, *Deep Ecology* (70).

The Platform Principles of the Deep Ecology Movement

1. The well-being and flourishing of human and nonhuman Life on Earth have value in themselves. These values are independent of the usefulness of the nonhuman world for human purposes.

2. Richness and diversity of life forms contribute to the realization of these values and are also values in themselves.

3. Humans have no right to reduce this richness and diversity except to satisfy vital human needs.

4. The flourishing of human life and cultures is compatible with a substantial decrease of the human population. The flourishing of nonhuman life requires such a decrease.

5. Present human interference with the nonhuman world is excessive, and the situation is rapidly worsening.

6. Policies must therefore be changed. These policies affect basic economic, technological, and ideological structures. The resulting state of affairs will be deeply different from the present.

7. The ideological change is mainly that of appreciating life quality rather than adhering to an increasingly higher standard of living. There will be a profound awareness of the difference between big and great.

8. Those who subscribe to the foregoing points have an obligation directly or indirectly to try to implement the necessary changes.

Devall and Sessions amplify the deep ecology thesis set forth by Aldo Leopold and Arne Naess. Their eight key principles further the daunting task of elucidating deep ecology and give us better, albeit nascent, guidelines for behavior. The strong emphasis on biocentricity, the recognition of a crisis in the natural world, and the call to action are standard signposts of deep ecology. The eight principles represent a working, but not definitive, platform for revolutionary environmentalism.

Deep ecology calls for the abolition of the consumer lifestyle that dominates modern society and individual aspirations, and the need for each individual to "self-realize," an expansion of the consciousness to identify with other living things. It calls for an immediate and determined effort to reduce human populations. Deep ecology argues that human society needs to accommodate its technological and material progress to the greater value of biodiversity (Naess 1988, 1989).[1] First-person accounts of participation in the Earth Liberation Front and other radical environmental organizations yield derivations, often abbreviated, of deep ecology principles. Rarely does mass recruitment occur. Individuals come to revolutionary environmentalism via word of mouth and moving from one group to a more radical one. The potent combination of changing beliefs and behaviors, such as the decision to switch to a vegetarian or vegan diet, encourages personal growth and steers individuals away from anthropocentric orientations and toward biocentricity. The changes in belief and behavior meet deep ecology's admonition to "self-realization."

The biocentric philosophy of deep ecology underlies such groups as Earth First!, the Sea Shepherd Conservation Society, and the Earth Liberation Front. Timber companies, ski resorts, transgenic bioengineered seed laboratories and warehouses, animal factory farms, animal testing laboratories, and so-called "trophy homes" (luxury homes built in previously undeveloped natural settings) receive the brunt of radicals' attacks. The political message, obviously derived from its deep ecology base, states that nature matters for its own sake, that non-human life has inalienable rights, and that biodiversity trumps consumerism.

The biocentrism of revolutionary environmentalism shares elements with the message of its mainstream environmental cousins, although the cousins quickly disavow sabotage tactics as a legitimate tool in the environmental debate. Direct action activists believe that a strong sympathy for direct action exists among rank and file mainstream environmentalists. As Paul Watson said about Sea Shepherd, "We're the ladies of the night, everyone wants to be with us, but no one wants to be seen with us." The political message of revolutionary environmentalism distinguishes itself in its acceptance of direct action. The radicals argue that mainstream environmentalism cannot succeed. Success requires fundamental change, and mainstream environmentalists remain tied to a belief in incremental or "reform" change. But little evidence supports any claim of mainstream environmental success. The most powerful argument against mainstream environmentalism comes, not from radical environmentalists, but from the world's scientists who carefully chronicle a steady series of deterioration in the natural world (Wilson).

Through the second half of the 20th century, mainstream environmental groups sought to influence political change via campaign donations, technical disputes over legislative language, and the fight over appointees to executive agencies. Mainstream environmental groups compromised with corporations and politicians accordingly. They measured themselves by conventional standards—the amount of political access, the size of their bank accounts and professional staffs, and their senior members' ability to move through the revolving door of political appointment and interest group leadership (Dowie). "Environmental" lawyers now work for natural resource companies and Earth Day became a chance for corporations to "green" their images by collaborating with environmental organizations to sponsor local events. Relative to the scope of the problem, existing reform fails. Like a vehicle not equipped with brakes, the momentum of economic growth seems to have an inertia that can only be stopped with a crash.

Despite their differences, mainstream and radical environmentalists argue that calamities loom large in our immediate future. The list of calamities easily divides into the anthropocentric and the biocentric, that is, those that affect human society and those that affect non-human life. Examples of anthropocentric or human-centered calamity include coastal cities swamped by storm surges and rising seas or exponential increases in skin cancer deaths. Biocentric or non-human-centered calamities, like extinctions, receive much greater attention among radical environmentalists and scientists than the general public (unless the animal or plant in question captures public favor like elephants or wolves or redwoods). An excellent example of biocentric calamity with little public attention is the frightening decline in frog populations and their sharply increasing mutation rates, likely due to increasing ultraviolet radiation and synthetic chemicals (Blaustein and Wake; on possible ties to coral reef diseases, see Carey). The passion of revolutionary environmentalists lies in their identification with biotic life and all of nature, and their belief that they fight for the innocent and the integrity of an evolving natural world under attack. One of the cardinal failures of mainstream environmentalists is their inability to discard their anthropocentric orientation.

Leaving behind their conventional mainstream counterparts, revolutionary environmentalists assess the state of the environment, the extent of biodiversity destruction, the power of corporate control over political and policy decisions, and make the choice to fight in a more militant and confrontational way. From Dave Foreman, founder of Earth First!, George Sessions, and Bill Devall come three claims that lead them to radical politics: (1) non-human life is intrinsically valuable (derived immediately from deep ecology); (2) an unprecedented biotic extinction process is underway; and (3) corporate economic power so thoroughly dominates national governments, particularly the powerful Western democracies, that normal political processes are unavailable to solve the ecological crisis.[2]

The Social Deficit of Deep Ecology

Hence arises revolutionary environmentalism and its attendant social prescriptions: spiritual awakening, ecological education, and fundamental political and economic change. Here, however, the political message of revolutionary environmentalism wanes. Despite its sophistication and comprehensiveness, the tight theoretical blueprint of capitalism and interest-group republic electoral politics remains unmatched by any rigorous theory of the transition to—and nature of—a future ecological society. Revolutionary environmentalism spins off bits and pieces of decentralized socialism, libertarian anarchy, even tribalism, but does not advance a coherent alternative to global capitalism. It remains primarily a philosophy of "don't" in the face of ecological destruction and environmental alteration. The powerful positive message of deep ecology needs integration into the practical social and economic life of ordinary citizens.

Revolutionary environmentalism's social and political philosophy needs to meld past practice with prescription, as did every successful revolution, whether political or spiritual. The message should emphasize the positive qualities of technology and demonstrate that science and agriculture need not be the enemy of nature. Organic farming benefits greatly from technology in natural pesticides and fertilizers. Solar power, geothermal power, and energy conservation are all dependent upon scientific research and technological advancement. Ours is not a failure of technology, but of society. But no guide to society comes forth to compete with the failing politics and exploitative economics of capitalism. Yet some noteworthy efforts to identify new forms of societal organizing exist. Recent work by Carter (1999) is useful as it nicely sums previous work in the activist and scholarly literature. Carter argues that social change requires decentralized, egalitarian, and cooperative autonomy. He uses "interrelatedness" to replace the individualism of contemporary societies. The decentralization and egalitarianism of the "co-op" represents the political schematic of "green" politics, such as it exists.

Wendell Berry's seminal work, *The Unsettling of America* (1977), condemns corporate agriculture's domination of rural America and its destructive effect on the physical environment and culture. Equally important, Berry presents solutions, some ancient and some futuristic, to our environmental crisis. Successful first steps exist in the practices proposed by a constructive environmentalism, including California's 1991 creation of ten eco-regions for the purpose of managing environmental protection and resource management (see Lipschutz).

Across the spectrum of environmental groups, some shared policy prescriptions emerge. The right to "stand" in court for nature and for a strong alteration of land-use are among the significant changes proposed by varying combinations of environmental actors. Massive expansion of "roadless wilderness," complete protection of the remaining "old-growth" forests, and a concerted effort to change our energy policy are also positions shared by most, if not all, environmentalists. Some European countries, notably Germany, adopt a "precautionary principle" that requires new practices to prove in advance of implementation, that their effects on the natural world will be benign, instead of waiting until environmental damage occurs and arguing about possible solutions. If some new technology or practice poses a potentially serious and irreversible environmental effect, then the precautionary principle states that the technology or practice should not be used.

The advancements in sophisticated decentralized energy technology and organic food production exemplify an environmentally friendlier society, and rescue revolutionary environmentalism from its dour scowl and hectoring admonitions. Policy recommendations should argue for tax changes in public policy to promote smaller family size, financial advantage to builders and consumers using sophisticated renewable energy systems, and incentives to adopt organic farming methods while discouraging the polluting, wasteful practices of current corporate agriculture. Of particular importance is the need to shift from a meat-based diet to a plant-based diet in order to conserve resources, revitalize the land, river, and forests, and end immoral forms of animal exploitation in factory farms and slaughterhouses (Robbins). Revolutionary environmentalism must argue its own merits, and not merely the sins of its foes.

Hope for the Future

Almost everyone draws a line of defense around what needs to be protected. Few of us willingly accept personal physical assault, or the theft of our property. For many people of the world, the loss of certain freedoms and liberties spark protest and violent rebellions. Nations go to war to protect their sovereignty, their boundaries, and their independence. Revolutionary environmentalists draw lines of defense around nature. For some, depletion of the last 5% of US old growth forest provokes counterattacks against the timber companies. For others, the extinction rates and the treatment of animals become sufficient grounds for militant mobilization. For Paul Watson and the Sea Shepherd Conservation Society, whales and other sea mammals deserve the same right to life that humans demand for themselves. As environmental damage accrues and people experience its effects in concrete ways, revolutionary environmentalists might gain more public support.

An epiphany struck the world's scientific community recently as the scope and breadth of human-induced ecological and environmental change came to light. Even as the majesty of nature reveals itself continuously, scientists noted the loss of species, the changes in habitat, and the saturation of ecologies with pollution. The materialism and drive to exploit nature that are inherent logics of capitalism only ensure the acceleration of ecological destruction. A similar epiphany may reach the mass society. The first great catastrophe that clearly derives from human-induced environmental damage and captures media attention may alter public perceptions of revolutionary environmentalists so that instead of being damned as "terrorists"—they will be praised as heroes. One of the common statements of revolutionary environmentalist leaders is that our grandchildren and great-grandchildren won't ask why we didn't more aggressively prosecute direct-action environmental activists, but why we didn't join them to help defend nature.

The extent of change required in human society to share the earth with its other inhabitants daunts nearly every observer. But revolutionary environmentalists remain undaunted. They insist that the needed changes can be accomplished. Their insistence arises from their sense of hope for a human society that respects the world of life that surrounds us. Despite the fact that they face violent attacks by corporate security or long-term prison sentences, they remain committed to a defense of nature. Their websites and written statements speak of the sanctity of all life, our moral responsibility to nature, and their vision for a human society in harmony with the natural world. Revolutionary environmentalists see a future of progress and peace that encompasses all life.

Bibliography

Berry, Wendell. *The Unsettling of America: Culture & Agriculture*. San Francisco: Sierra Club Books, 1977.

Blaustien, Andrew R. and D. B. Wake, "The Puzzle of the Declining Amphibian Populations," *Scientific American* 272 (1995): 52–57.

Bookchin, Murray, and David Foreman. *Defending the Earth*. Boston: South End Press, 1991.

Bryner, Gary C. *Gaia's Wager: Environmental Movements and the Challenge of Sustainability*. Maryland: Rowman & Littlefield, 2001.

Carey, Cynthia, "Infectious disease and world-wide decline of amphibian populations with comments on emerging diseases in coral reef organisms and humans,." *Environmental Health Perspectives* 108 Sup. 1 (2000): 143–50.

Carson, Rachel. *Silent Spring*. New York: Houghton Mifflin Company, 1962.

Carter, Alan. *A Radical Green Political Theory*. New York: Routledge, 1999.

Chew, Sing C. *World Ecological Degradation: Accumulation, Urbanization, and Deforestation 3000 B.C.–A.D. 2000*. Maryland: Rowman & Littlefield, 2001.

Devall, Bill, "The Deep Ecology Movement," *Natural Resources Journal* 20 (1980): 299–322.

___. *Simple in Means, Rich in Ends: Practicing Deep Ecology*. Salt Lake City, Utah: Gibbs-Smith, 1988.

Devall, Bill and George Session. *Deep Ecology: Living as if Nature Mattered*. Salt Lake City, Utah: 1985.

Dowie, Mark. *Losing Ground: American Environmentalism at the Close of the Twentieth Century*. Cambridge, MA: The MIT Press, 1995.

Foreman, David and Bill Haywood, eds. *Ecodefense: A Field Guide to Monkeywrenching*. Tucson, Arizona: Ned Ludd Books, 1985.

___. *Confessions of an Eco-Warrior*. New York: Harmony Books, 1990.

Fox, Warwick, "Deep Ecology: A New Philosophy of Our Time?" *The Ecologist* 14 (1984): 194–200.

___. *Toward a Transpersonal Ecology: Developing New Foundations for Environmentalism*. Boston: Shambala, 1990.

Lipschutz, Ronnie D. and Judith Mayer. "Not Seeing the Forests for the Trees: Rights, Rules, and the Renegotiation of Resource Management Regimes." In *The State and Social Power in Global Environmental Politics*, edited by Ronnie Lipschutz and Ken Conca. New York: Cornell University Press, 1996.

McKibben, Bill. *The End of Nature*. Toronto: Anchor Books, 1989 & 1999.

Naess, Arne. *Gandhi and Group Conflict*. Oslo: Universitetsforlaget, 1973.

___. "Self-Realization: An Ecological Approach to Being in the World." In *Thinking Like a Mountain: Toward a Council of All Beings*, edited by John Seed, et al. Philadelphia: New Society Press, 1988.

___. *Ecology, Community, and Lifestyle: Outline of an Ecosophy*. Cambridge: Cambridge University Press, 1989.

___. "The Deep Ecological Movement: Some Philosophical Aspects." In *Environmental Philosophy*, edited by Michael Zimmerman. New Jersey: Prentice Hall, 1993.

Ophuls, William and A. Stephen Boyan Jr. *Ecology and the Politics of Scarcity Revisited*. New York: W.W. Freeman, 1992.

Robbins, John. *The Food Revolution*. Berkeley, CA: Conari Press, 2001.

Sagoff, Mark. "'I am no Greenpeacer, but....' or Environmentalism, Risk Communication, and the Lower Middle Class." In *Business Ethics and the Environment: The Public Policy Debate*, edited by Michael Hoffman. Connecticut: Greenwood Publishing, 1990.

Sessions, George. "The Deep Ecology Movement: A Review." *Environmental Ethics* 11 (1987): 105–25

___. "Introduction to Deep Ecology. " In *Environmental Philosophy*, edited by Michael Zimmerman. New Jersey: Prentice Hall,1993.

Snyder, Gary. *Turtle Island*. New York: New Direction, 1969.

___. *The Practice of the Wild*. San Francisco: North Point, 1990.

Notes

1. The line of "deep ecology" reasoning predates Naess' finding roots in Buddhism, Taoism, Spinoza, and Thoreau among others. In fact, periods of "deep ecology" reasoning reoccur across time and place, often arising contemporarily with regional ecological declines (Chew 2001).

2. Foreman, 1990; Sessions, 1987; Devall, 1980; an insightful derivation of Foreman's version of "green" politics can be found in Sagoff (1990); similar critiques, outside deep ecology, include Bryner, 2001; and Ophuls and Boyan, 1992.

A Spark That Ignited a Flame
The Evolution of the Earth Liberation Front[1]

Noel Molland

In 2005, the FBI described the Earth Liberation Front (ELF) as America's greatest domestic terrorist threat, one responsible for over 1,200 "criminal incidents" and tens of millions of dollars in property damage. Yet ten years ago practically no one in America had even heard of the Earth Liberation Front. So how did this threat develop? What is its history? And what are the aims of the Earth Liberation Front?

Deep Ecology Roots

In 1972, the Norwegian activist philosopher, Arne Naess, devised the environmental philosophy known as Deep Ecology. At its core, Deep Ecology draws from an age-old recognition that humans are not the measure for all things on planet Earth. Deep Ecology recognizes that humans are merely one species on a planet teeming with different species and that all species, both plant and animal, have intrinsic value and are worthy of equal consideration.

In 1980, a small group of American environmentalists, taking Deep Ecology as their ideological guide, formed themselves into "Earth First!," a movement that literally puts the ecological "needs" of planet Earth over human interests, and thereby replaces anthropocentrism with biocentrism. Earth First! soon became synonymous with decentralized mass protests, civil disobedience, ecotage, and direct action. As a movement new and fresh in its philosophy and tactics, Earth First! proved very popular and spread rapidly around the globe, coming eventually to Britain in 1991.

British Earth First!

In 1991, British consciousness was alarmed with concerns about huge environmental issues such as Bovine Spongiform Encephalopathy (Mad Cow Disease), CFCs damaging the ozone layer, and global warming. More and more people were adopting a vegetarian diet and even in mainstream politics environmentalism was on the agenda, culminating with the

Green Party of England & Wales securing a landmark 15% of the popular vote during the 1989 European Parliament Elections.

However despite the popular concern about the environment, many people were finding the established paths of environmental concern highly frustrating. Groups like Greenpeace were centralized in their structure and focused on fundraising, such that they appeared more interested in one's money than one's help as an activist. Likewise the mainstream political system was a cul-de-sac for the young enthusiastic environmentalist. For example, despite the resounding European election success in 1989, the Green Party of England & Wales failed to win a single European Parliamentary seat.

People felt frustrated at the obstacles which constantly silenced the environmental voice within the British political system and this frustration was compounded with the lack of opportunity for people to be able to do anything active themselves for the established groups like Greenpeace, other than to help raise money so the "professional" campaigners could do their actions. Added to this was the fact that in 1991 a lot of environmentally minded people had become involved with protests against the Gulf War, which helped to introduce them to alternative politics. So when Earth First! arrived in Britain offering a legal, non-hierarchical, "You care about the environment? Then do something!" attitude, it found a willing and receptive audience.

British Earth First! didn't just want to stop the environmental damage from getting any worse—it tried to undo some of the damage that had already occurred. To quote from an early British EF! information sheet:

> Earth First! does not believe it is enough to preserve the last strongholds of nature. We must re-create the forests, heaths and marshes that once covered this land and reintroduce the lost species like the wolf, the bear and the boar. It is not enough to oppose new roads, industrial developments and urban expansion. We must set the land free!

EF! had a vision and it was one that many people wanted to be a part of and so it became Britain's fastest growing social movement at that time.

The Early Years

When Earth First! started in Britain its actions were generally small and on a local scale. For example, Mid-Somerset Earth First! organized a successful protest which stopped the destruction of a small local woodland in the Glastonbury area of Somerset.

However the founders of British Earth First! were always looking to try and make a national impact and within less than a year of its founding, British Earth First! started making national headlines as it organized Britain's first anti-road protest at Twyford Down in Hampshire. Twyford Down was exactly what British activists had been waiting for and it acted as a huge magnet for would-be eco-activists. Literally hundreds of people from across Britain made their way to Twyford Down to protest against the destruction of the natural habitat and oppose the building of this new road. The protests caught the imagination of protesters, media, and police alike.

Initially Twyford Down started off as a normal "go along at the weekend" style protest. People would turn up, shout and chant slogans, blow whistles, beat drums, and try to occupy something (maybe a bulldozer or a digger) until they are either arrested or just simply chucked off by the police. However the sheer number of people attending the protests at Twyford Down meant that very quickly the weekend protests became daily protests. Then some of the protesters decided to set up a permanent protest camp, called The Dongas, and the creation of the protest camp acted as an additional draw for young would-be activists.

The Donga camp not only offered people the opportunity to travel long distances to join in the protests, secure in the knowledge they had somewhere safe to stay, the camp also acted as a training ground where people could learn new skills and tactics. The tactics being used by British Earth First! at the time included everything from sit-downs and lock-ons to active machine sabotage.

Although the battle of Twyford Down was ultimately lost, it helped to really establish radical decentralized environmentalism in Britain, and demonstrated to the authorities that British EF! was a new force to be reckoned with.

The Earth Liberation Front Emerges

In 1992, whilst Twyford Down was raging, British Earth First! had its first national gathering, held in Brighton. At that gathering some people argued that as EF! was becoming so popular as a movement that everyone needed to make sure EF! maintained its popularity by not associating with overt law breaking. In effect, these people wanted to distance themselves from the illegal ecotage tactics that were starting to be linked to some British EF! actions.

Although there was not universal agreement for this proposal, it was ultimately accepted that British Earth First! would concentrate on mass demonstrations and civil disobedience. If people wished to carry out ecotage, then this would be done under a new name—that of the Earth Liberation Front (ELF).

The name Earth Liberation Front was chosen as a direct copying of the already established "Animal Liberation Front" (ALF) which emerged in England in 1976. The ALF was organized in small autonomous cells which carried out illegal non-violent direct action against animal exploiters. The founders of the ELF wanted radical environmentalists to work on the same basis and have a similar name, hoping that people would instantly understand how the ELF operated and what its goals were.

Similar to the ALF, the ELF guidelines make it clear that their actions are non-violent in nature, attacking the property of exploiters, but never the exploiters themselves, in order to eliminate or weaken their ability to cause harm to animals and the Earth. The three stated goals are:

• To inflict maximum economic damage on those profiting from the destruction and exploitation of the natural environment

• To reveal and educate the public about the atrocities committed against the earth and all species that populate it

• To take all necessary precautions against harming any animal—human and nonhuman.

Any direct action taken to halt ecological destruction whilst keeping to the preceding guidelines could, if claimed as such, be considered an ELF action.

The reason why the founders of the ELF were so keen to see such a movement established in Britain can be understood by looking at the events which were occurring in Britain at the time. The Earth Liberation Front (or Elves as they are known) argue that Earth First!-type activity can only ever go so far against the earth abusers. The early Elves argued that mass protest and civil disobedience is limited in its scope and sooner or later the legal system inevitably works in favor of the earth rapist and environment destroyer.

For example, in November 1993 anti-road activists were able to delay the M11 road building scheme by over a month as they squatted—in a tree house—in a 300-year-old sweet chestnut tree. But eventually and inevitably, the legal system worked against the activists and on the 7th December 1993, 200 police officers, 150 contractors, and dozens of Sheriff of London Officers arrived to evict the tree house activists. The police literally formed a ring around the tree and the individual activists were plucked off one at a time.

With the legal system so heavily weighed against the activists there was nothing that could be done—legally at least. Once the tree-sitters had been evicted, it took approximately three minutes for the grand old tree to be lost forever—a terrible act of environmental destruction by the Department of Transport.

In recognition that legal protestors are always limited by the law in their actions, the Elves argued that illegal action is needed to help the eco-resistance movement. The Elves hoped that illegal action would aid the earth liberation movement in exactly the same way similar action had helped the animal liberation movement. So rather than forming road blocks, ELF activists set fire to the roads. Rather than sitting in front of a bulldozer, ELF activists physically disabled the machine.

In effect, the Elves wanted to become an eco-ALF that will do whatever is necessary to save the planet and its inhabitants. Like the ALF, the Earth Liberation Front is opposed to using physical violence against their targets but do not regard economic sabotage as violent; rather, they see it as the most effective form of protest and resistance to the destruction of the earth.

Once the ELF was created as a concept, its activists very quickly went round establishing the ELF as a real movement. In the early days ELF actions tended to be small and more token than having a real impact. For example, during British Earth First!'s Mahogany Means Murder campaign of the early 1990s, Elves would mingle in with the EF! activists and whilst the EF! activists dropped their banners and blockaded the premises, the Elves would be busy gluing the locks of the buildings that the EF! activists were occupying.

Similarly, during the early 1990s the supermarket chain Sainsbury's applied for planning permission to build a store just outside Yeovil in Somerset. EF! responded to this by squatting an empty supermarket in the centre of Yeovil to draw attention to the fact there was a perfectly good building already built that could be used. EF! also started a nationwide campaign against Sainsbury's which involved protests up and down the country. The ELF, wishing to help out their EF! brothers and sisters, also joined in the campaign and started doing a number of small actions like going into the supermarkets, filling up a trolley full of frozen meat, and then leaving it to defrost in a warm part of the store. Besides these token actions, the ELF also launched an arson attack on a supermarket in southern England. Sainsbury's backed down and did not build their supermarket.

April Fool's Earth Night 1992

Another tool of the Earth Liberation Front during its early days was the use of "Earth Nights." British Elves learnt that in Australia eco-activists had "Earth Nights" where ecotage was carried out on a specific night. The ELF liked the sound of these Earth Nights and decided to bring them to Europe.

On the First of April 1992, an April Fool's Earth Night was declared. This was one of the first ever Earth Nights and the Elves wanted to use it to demonstrate their serious intent. On that night the Earth Liberation Front targeted Fisons, a peat company who they accused of destroying the peat bogs on Hatfield and Thorne Moors. The Elves attacked property belonging to Fisons and destroyed a number of pumps, trucks and other machinery. The estimated damage was between £50,000–75,000 ($85,000–130,000 US). Prior to the ELF action, legal campaigners—the mainstream group, Friends of the Earth—had spent two years asking gardeners to boycott peat products, but this was having only a limited effect and the ELF hoped this would give a new emphasis to the anti-peat campaign. A communiqué, published in *Green Anarchist* magazine at the time, outlined the Elves' demands:

"All our peat bogs must be preserved in their entirety, for the sake of the plants, animals and our national heritage. Cynically donating small amounts will do no good. The water table will drop, and the bog will dry out and die, unless it is preserved fully. FISONS MUST LEAVE ALL OF IT ALONE—NOW!"

This particular ELF action stands out in ELF history as it was one of the first ELF actions to occur independently of any British EF! campaign. It caused a considerable amount of damage and it used a press release.

ELF Press Releases

The effort to fully document the actions of the Earth Liberation Front in Britain and Europe is almost impossible because European Elves very rarely use press releases. Quite often an ELF-style activist will hit-and-run without leaving any clue as to who did the damage. From a security point of view this is very logical, as the less evidence an activist leaves the less chance there is of being caught. But from a chronicler's point of view this means that it is very hard to keep an accurate record of their actions. ELF-style activists, if they do claim an action, are also very good at using a name entirely different to the ELF in order to avoid conspiracy charges.

What is known about the ELF is that during the early years it made great strides to develop itself as a movement. British Elves contacted like-minded people across Europe, spreading the word of their new movement. Countries specifically targeted by these ELF missionaries included France, Spain, Germany, and Holland.

The ELF Becomes International

The Earth Liberation Front very quickly spread across Europe. To name just some of the early actions, the ELF in Holland targeted Amsterdam Airport, damaged cars, destroyed hunting platforms, and attacked oil exploration equipment. In a German forest near Frankfurt, Elves damaged dredgers being used to destroy the forest in preparation for urban expansion, whilst elsewhere in Germany activists targeted McDonald's restaurants, hunting platforms, and neo-Nazi political groups. There was even a report that a group calling itself "Radical Brigades for Ecological Defence" in Russia had damaged seven bulldozers in the Kaliningrad area.

In Britain the response of the police to the newly emerging ELF movement was to try to discredit the Earth Liberation Front by falsely claiming in the media that it was setting lethal traps for construction workers. In 1994, Dutch authorities claimed that ecotage actions in their country were carried out by British activists travelling across the North Sea. The British ELF, responding through activist publications, disputed the Dutch police's claims, saying that Dutch people were more than capable of undertaking their own actions. And later on that year the British activists' theory proved correct when the Dutch police arrested a Dutch man who was destined to become the world's first ever Earth Liberation Front prisoner, Paul S.

In court, Dutch eco-activist Paul S. was accused of carrying out an 18-month sabotage campaign against road construction sites in Holland. Because Paul failed to offer any political reason for his sabotage, other than he cared for the environment, the Dutch Government tried to have him declared insane. Happily this cynical ploy failed and Paul served a three-year jail sentence instead. The jailing of Paul S. did not deter the ELF, and instead many saw Paul's case as a reason to re-double their efforts.

Direct Actions Around The World

Across the world in 1993 and 1994, there was a flurry of radical environmental direct actions. In Scandinavia, eco-saboteurs started to attack road construction sites. A German group calling itself The Moles took up a railway line and dug tunnels under a road in an attempt to stop a nuclear convoy from travelling by either rail or road. The tunnels under the road were designed to allow normal vehicles to cross over the tunnels without any problem, but would collapse if they were driven over by a hundred ton nuclear convoy vehicle. New Zealand activists graffitied McDonald's restaurants with pro-forest slogans. In one incident, a New Zealand environmental campaigner was arrested and fined after he threw a brick through a McDonald's window in protest against its complicity with rainforest deforestation. And in Australia, two activists calling themselves the Pacific Popular Front set fire to a French Embassy in protest against French nuclear tests in the South Pacific.

The Police Strike Back

By 1995, radical environmentalism was starting to reach new heights in Britain. During a mass trespass at Whately Quarry in Somerset, England, people openly torched quarry construction machinery, and in April 1995 eco-saboteurs even raided the central London offices of the Department of Transport and damaged more than 100 computers.

The police response to the growing popularity of environmental direct action, and their attempt to curb the actions of the Animal Liberation Front (it was estimated, by the police, that five ALF actions happened every single night in Britain) was to carry out a series of raids against known animal rights and environmental activists. Throughout 1995 British police carried out a total of 55 raids across Britain, and even raided a man in Italy, as they investigated the activities of the ALF and ELF.

These police dragnets were largely regarded as a fishing expedition and information-gathering exercise, but they also laid the ground for a series of coordinated dawn raids on January 16, 1996, against six men charged with involvement in a five-year-long conspiracy to incite animal and earth liberation direct action. Subsequently, in 1997, after a long and complicated trial, three of those men were convicted of Conspiracy to Incite Persons Unknown to Commit Criminal Damage and each was sentenced to three years imprisonment.

Oppression Across Europe

At the same time of the police repression in Britain, similar repression was happening across Europe. In 1997 the Dutch police raided the offices of a radical environmental magazine, *Ravage*, after it published a press release by the Earth Liberation Front claiming responsibility for detonating a bomb inside an empty building owned by a German company linked to dumping toxic waste. In Finland, the Animal Liberation Front Supporters Group was actually forced to temporarily close down when the police used a couple of ALF arsons as the perfect excuse to harass known activists.

Despite all this repression, the actions continued and in an admittance of defeat the British Government announced that all new road construction plans were being put on hold because the Government could no longer afford the cost of policing the anti-roads protests and securing the sites from ecoteurs. For example, it is said that the security costs alone for the Newbury Bypass anti-road protests exceeded £20,000,000 (about $35,000,000 US), and the Government just couldn't keep on affording these high costs.

But as soon as the road wars ended, Genetically Modified crops reared their ugly heads in Britain, and GM crops became the new target for many eco-activists, leading to the destruction of any GM crop site which could be located. Some of these actions were done in the open, in full view of the media and police, while other strikes took place during the dead of night, and avoided the otherwise inevitable court proceedings.

Eco-Actions Continue

Despite all the police repression across Europe, eco-militants around Europe and Scandinavia continued in their work. In Finland, road construction machinery was targeted, and petrol stations and McDonald's restaurants all lost their windows at the hands of the ELF. In Italy, eco-saboteurs calling themselves "The Grey Wolves" ripped up high speed railway lines in the Northern Italian Alps. Activists in Spain cut the cables on machinery used to construct the controversial Itoiz dam, thereby delaying the project by a full 12 months. In Ireland, the Gaelic Earth Liberation Front tore up GM crop sites. A man in Sweden was accused of incitement to violence after he allegedly published details on how to sabotage road construction machinery. Whilst in Poland, eco-activists destroyed a ski lift construction which threatened a forested area. Across Europe, activists had unleashed a tide of Animal and Earth Liberation activity which no one could stop.

Ecotage in America

By the mid-1990s, the activities of the European Earth Liberation Front movement were reported increasingly in sympathetic American and Canadian publications. So it was inevitable that eventually the name of the Earth Liberation Front would make a transatlantic crossing and be used in

North America. But long before the name of the ELF was attributed to any North American action there had been a history of economic sabotage actions across the continent. For example, in 1989 the Earth First! "Arizona Five" targeted power lines providing power to a nuclear plant. Then in the early 1990s unnamed ecoteurs decommissioned the logging vehicles which were destroying wilderness areas. In one incident ecoteurs hot-wired some logging vehicles and used them to smash into each other before running over the loggers' hut. In another incident ecoteurs slipped past a sleeping security guard and poured "an abrasive foreign substance" into the logging machines' fuel tanks before disappearing into the night. The action was only discovered the next day as several machines wailed their final swan songs while their engines seized up. However all these latter actions were largely done anonymously.

The first time the title of "Earth Liberation" was used in North America was in 1995 when a Canadian group calling itself the Earth Liberation Army (ELA) started targeting trophy hunters. On the 19th of June 1995 the ELA firebombed the business of a Guide Outfitter in British Columbia. The ELA also went on to damage a hunting lodge and burned down a "Wildlife Museum" (a museum full of stuffed animals). The European Elves welcomed these actions and declared the ELA to be "transatlantic cousins." Later that same year, on October 8, eco-activists torched six railway cars at the Weyerhaeuser mill in Grand Prairie, Alberta. It was estimated that each car contained 400 bales of pulp.

But it wasn't until 1996 that the name "Earth Liberation Front" was first Used in North America. On Columbus Day, October 14, saboteurs glued the locks on a Chevron petrol station in Eugene, Oregon and spray painted "504 YEARS OF GENOCIDE" and "ELF" on its walls. Activists undertook identical action on the same day against a public relations office and McDonald's restaurant in Eugene. Two days later (on International Anti-McDonald's Day), at Grants Pass, Oregon, the ELF glued the locks and spray painted slogans in support of the British McLibel Two (two activists being sued for libel by McDonald's after they distributed a leaflet entitled "What's Wrong With McDonald's?"). On October 17, two more McDonald's restaurants had their locks glued and walls painted with slogans.

Oregon ecoteurs struck repeatedly thereafter. On July 17, 1997, for example, they disabled three logging machines, a feller buncher, a dozer, and an articulated loader in Mount Hood, Oregon. Less than a week later, the ELF destroyed heavy machinery including three dump trucks, two hydraulic excavators, and two front loaders at Cougar Hot Springs, Oregon. On October 27, 1996, the Earth Liberation Front made their mark in Detroit, Michigan, by setting fire to a truck and spray painting various slogans onto a US Forest Services Rangers Station.

The European Elves were delighted with the development of the ELF movement in America and openly applauded these actions through anonymous letters in a series of publications. However not everyone felt the same way and some British and American Earth First! activists, who disapproved of the ELF, actually started to criticize the European ELF and their supporters for publicizing the American actions.

However neither the ELF nor their supporters were deterred by the criticism and a couple of months later, on Christmas Day, 1996, a group calling itself the "Great Lakes Earth Liberation Front" raided Jack Brower Fur Farm, Bath, Michigan, and released 150 mink. Then on March 15, 1997, the "Great Lakes Earth Liberation Front" claimed credit for a raid on Eberts fur farm in Belhiem, Ontario, which led to the releasing of 240 mink. Two weeks later, on March 31, Eberts fur farm was hit for a second time and 1,500 additional mink were released. However on that occasion five people from Detroit were arrested and charged with theft, possession of burglary tools, and possession of stolen items.

ALF and ELF Unite

After the Great Lakes ELF actions a new phenomenon occurred in North America; a series of actions started to be carried out under the banners of both of ELF and ALF. During the early days, the European Elves had gone to great lengths, through a series of letters published anonymously in sympathetic publications, to argue the links between animal rights and ecological destruction. And although some ELF cells, like the Westcountry Wildlife Cell of the Earth Liberation Front (who were active in Britain during the early and mid-1990s), actively carried out actions with strong animal rights themes (such as targeting anglers, spiking trees on behalf of the woodland animals, and so on), no group had ever used both the ELF and ALF names together.

All that changed on March 14, 1997 when American activists spiked 47 trees in the Robinson Scott Clearcut area in Oregon. A press release by the "Animal Liberation Front Eco-Animal Defense Unit" claimed the action was a joint effort between the ALF and ELF, and warned of more collaborative actions to come. Five days later, the "Bay Area Cell of the Earth and Animal Liberation Front" claimed responsibility for firebombing an animal research laboratory at the University of California in Davis, California. On November 29, 1997, moreover, there was a joint ALF and ELF claim of responsibility for another Oregon action that released 500 wild horses and torched a Bureau of Land Management coral in Burns to protest BLM policies to round up wild horses and allow thousands to be sold for slaughter.

A Flurry of Activity in North America

The North American movement was growing and increasingly emboldened. On the day after the Cougar Hot Springs action in Oregon, anonymous eco-activists used a loader to rip up 115 meters of railway track used by Weyerhaeuser mill in Grand Prairie, Alberta. They also crashed the loader into an electricity pole taking out the main power line. Three months later, on October 27, 1997, an anonymous person fired a high powered rifle into the empty office of the plant manager of the Alberta Energy Company in Hythe, Alberta.

Then on December 29, activists in Grand Prairie used a chainsaw to take down 17 power lines which supplied power to oil wells. This action was followed up on the 1st of February 1998 with an arson attack on a skidder belonging to the Vidar Forestry Technology of Hythe based in Alberta.

Similarly, the action continued unabated in the US. On the 2nd of February 1998, construction machinery in North Brunswick, New Jersey, received extensive damage and had the words "Eco-Defense" and "Earth Liberation" spray painted over it. On the 21st of June 1998, the US Forest Service wildlife research centre near Olympia, Washington, was set on fire with a second fire at the animal damage control building. These fires were claimed jointly by the ALF and ELF.

Four days later, the Earth Liberation Front struck the Mexican Consulate in Boston, MA, leaving symbolic red hand prints and messages of solidarity with the Zapatistas and the Chiapas people. A week subsequent, on July 3, in a daring daylight raid, ALF and ELF activists released 310 animals from the United Vaccines experimental research fur farm in Madison, Wisconsin.

On the 31st of July and the 1st of August 1998, two separate explosions occurred at the well sites of the Alberta Energy Company in Beaverlodge. This was followed up, on August 24th, with a blast destroying the equipment shed at the Suncor Energy well in Hinton, Alberta. Four people were arrested for that action but the charges were later dropped.

Undeterred by the Canadian arrests, on September 20, 1998, the Earth Liberation Front in Davis, California, sabotaged seven "large yellow machines of death" by filling their tanks with sand, destroying wires, and slashing tires. The Canadian arrests also did not appear to deter Canadian activists either as there was a report that in October 1998 a bomb exploded at an unstaffed oil well in Hythe, Alberta, causing $10,000 damage.

Vail, Colorado and Beyond

Then, on the 18th of October 1998, "on behalf of the lynx," the Earth Liberation Front planted incendiary devices in five buildings and four ski lifts in Vail, Colorado. All the devices ignited reducing the ski lift to ashes causing $14,000,000 in damages. This was the most dramatic and costly ELF attack to date, and was a watershed event. The police and media response was instant and America became very aware that the Earth Liberation Front was now truly established within its borders.

But if the police thought their raids and questioning of known eco-activists, following the Vail fire, might deter the ELF they were very wrong. On Christmas Day 1998, the ELF torched the US Forest Industry's Corporate Headquarters in Medford, Oregon. The North American ELF was here to stay and the rest, as they say, is history...

Notes

1. This article is dedicated to the memory of the Italian eco-activists Soledad Maria Rosas and Edoardo Massari. In 1999 Soledad and Edoardo along with Silvano Pellissero were arrested, accused of a Grey Wolves action which saw the sabotaging of a high speed railway line construction site in the northern Italian Alps. Whilst awaiting trial, both Soledad and Eduardo died whilst in police custody. Silvano was sentenced in early February 2000 to six years and eight months imprisonment. May we never forget the names of those who have died fighting to save our Mother Earth.

To Cast a Giant Shadow
Revolutionary Ecology and Its Practical Implementation Through the Earth Liberation Front

Davey Garland

We are the Elfin,[1]
Those who carry the
Torch and flame,
To live or die
And no surrender,
We are the venom of our
Mother's fiery rain.

—From "Night of the Elfin," (written after the first Earth Night,
5 Nov 1992), in *Ecowars and Other Poems*, Davey Garland.

Carving Out a New Role

In order to discuss the nature of "revolutionary ecology," one must grasp how, where and by whom its ideas were used. As I will analyze it within the historical context of Britain during the 1990s, "revolutionary ecology" was formed from a hybrid of ideas taken from the social and deep ecology camps, and put into practice in the actions of Earth First! (EF!) groups and the Earth Liberation Front (ELF). The key concepts of deep ecology—such as the notion of living in harmony with nature, respect for all species, developing appropriate or non-dominating forms of technology, and the belief that everything has intrinsic value—stem from the writings of Norwegian philosopher, Arne Naess. The work of Naess, along with others such as American deep ecologists Bill Devall and George Sessions, helps to illustrate how modern society has alienated and isolated humans from nature. Deep ecology argues that to be reconnected with the natural worlds, we must enter into a new *self-realization* process rooted in identification with the non-human world. Earth First! was inspired by and grounded in this biocentric philosophy when it emerged upon the environmental campaign scene in 1980, as was the ELF later born out of Earth First! UK.

Social ecology, on the other hand, calls for a libertarian and decentralized model of social organization which rejects all forms of hierarchy including the human attempt to dominate nature. Founder Murray Bookchin insists that all environmental problems are social problems and cannot be solved apart from attacking hierarchical institutions such as patriarchy, class, racism, and the state. Above all, Bookchin argues, we must overcome capitalism in favor of decentralized and autonomous communities guided by the principles of ecology and anarchism. For Bookchin and his followers, deep ecology is a primitivistic, misanthropic, and spiritualist outlook that favors individualist over social methods of change. It is the social and political fabric of society, namely hierarchy and power systems, that has to be deconstructed and realigned if we are to go forward; such a complex project is hardly a matter of just abandoning an alienated mode of existence for some spiritual nirvana. Social ecologists reject much of the deep ecology message, arguing, for example, that society cannot dispose of its technological evolution, but rather should harmonize technology with ecology. Nor does society need to greatly reduce the large human population the planet now holds, so long as it develops sustainable forms of production and consumption.

However, activists including the late Judi Bari and organizations such as MOVE, a US black radical group, embraced deep ecology as they urged that social injustice and ecological destruction shared a common source. Derek Wall notes that:

> The beliefs of both Bari and MOVE suggest that a distinction can be made between social and asocial forms of deep ecology. While both reject anthropocentric approaches, asocial deep ecology ignores the fact that ecological destruction is the product of particular social practices and institutions, or at least is mediated through them. Equally, while neither Bari's approach nor that of MOVE rejects intrinsic worth of other species, both do also embrace human-justice issues (1999, 149–50).

Many ideas from both social and deep ecology philosophies were instrumental in forming the practical realization of resistance amongst the radical environmental movement in Britain during the early 1990s. I stress that activists drew from *each* of these outlooks, as neither would have fully stood up on its own, mainly due to the broadness and diversity of communities and people to which the movement wanted to appeal. Rather, each was modified to fit the specific situations that activists were experiencing during community actions.

Personally, I had been inspired by Bari, and later by MOVE, but never felt happy with the deep ecology label, as my own political history prevented me from adopting a strict biocentric approach. I saw it as unrealistic within a heavily populated and urbanized Britain, as I also felt uncomfortable with some elements of the movement, such as expressed in comments from Dave Foreman that often seemed racist and blatantly misanthropic. I was attracted to both Bari and Bookchin, though on occasion was confused as to where my true alliances lay. In retrospect, I was nearer to Bari in taking up a pragmatic community organizing approach, jumping from one issue to another, be it animal, land, labor, or human rights.

It was only in early 1994 after reading an article by US labor and environmental activist Orin Langelle (and eventually meeting him) that "revolutionary ecology" resolved my confusion. For activists like me who were campaigning on a number of diverse issues, revolutionary ecology bridged the social/deep ecology divide, taking the best from both philosophies: it held a socio-political theoretical base, as it also urged the importance of new relations with nature. Revolutionary ecology acknowledged the many institutional (and not merely personal or ideological) obstacles, such as including the power of the state, that we would have to overcome if we were to achieve our aims and rebuild our communities. As Orin Langelle sums up the holistic emphasis of this approach:

> Revolutionary ecology recognizes that all forms of life are equal and practices of domination (which run the gamut from homophobia to racism to speciesism etc) are part of a control pattern that leads to the exploitation of all forms, which includes our living, breathing planet: Gaia. An injury to one is an injury to all (1994).

This quote not only demonstrates a deep ecology attitude of embracing all life and respecting all those sections of the community (human and non-human) which are exploited or repressed; its political tone also touches a raw nerve in someone who would not necessarily fit into the traditional model of an environmentalist; i.e. white, middle-class, and university educated. There were many activists from ordinary working class or peripheral backgrounds who became aware of environmental issues through health or social campaigns within their community, workplace, or squat. Others became attuned to ecological issues by drawing upon their experiences within the animal liberation movement, whereby they fought against vivisection or employed guerilla tactics as hunt-saboteurs. The animal rights activists were not just more hardened and rough-edged than some who were entering the radical environmental movement for the first time. They were typically more versed in direct action, being more political and more flexible in their approach, and were certainly unwilling to follow a narrow and organized theory of protest, which at times Earth First! advocated.

Beyond Earth First! The Emergence of the ELFin

Many of these more seasoned direct action types were responsible for pulling Earth First! UK out from its political naivety in order to adopt a more confrontational style. This did not occur until the radical environmental movement was brought into the real world of having to stand by its words or lose face. The ability to appear tough was challenged, and slogans such as "No Compromise in Defense of Mother Earth!," became empty words when EF!UK failed to fully acknowledge, let alone support, one of Britain's most significant ecotage strikes involving the destruction of peat cutting machinery at Thorne Moore in Yorkshire. The Moore had been stripped by Fisons company for some years and had been the focus of major campaigns for many mainstream environmental groups, most notably Friends of the Earth. Immediately following the sabotage, there was panic within the EF! office in London, as activists rushed to distance themselves from the incident, as did many other ecological organizations.

Booth (1994) acknowledges this juncture in the movement's development, noticing how the two distinct wings decided to separate two different types of action in the aftermath of Thorne Moore:

> At Brighton roughly the same time (April 1992) EF! held a meeting which agreed the two groups shouldn't be critical of each other and that EF! would adopt a policy that monkeywrenching was "neither condemned nor condoned. Sabotage was to be claimed under the ELF (Earth Liberation Front) banner. This distancing formula was then used by the manipulative eco-bureaucrat tendency to marginalize the ELF, the opposite intention to that of the Brighton meeting (1994, 46).

This "respectable" (or ecocratic) wing of EF! very often refused to mention direct action or sabotage in their periodicals or statements. They preferred the non-violent direct action (NVDA) and Gandhian methods from anti-nuclear and peace movement circles that increasingly influenced the environmental movement away from the UK context towards problems that were occurring on the other side of the world.

The pacifist approach was very much an empty, if not short-lived, philosophy. It attracted attention, ruffled some feathers, and even stirred the blood to fight and protect one's environment, but it lacked body and depth and was culturally remote from the harsh life and times of Thatcher's Britain. Revolutionary ecology is and has been for me an instinctive feeling that has its roots foremost in the attachment to one's immediate community. Dissent and reaction were born once the community came under threat.

I also found it ironic that EF!UK was spouting the radical rhetoric of US activists such as David Foreman and Christopher Manes, whilst past social/ecologist/animal rights advocates from our own shores such as Edward Carpenter and Henry Salt were forgotten. We needed to search back into our own history of environmental resistance, so as to stamp our own identity upon radical environmentalism, and not just be an export destination for some elements of EF!US or to act as one of its satellites.

This led me to the conclusion that the radical environmental movement would best advance if it focused upon issues that were culturally close to people's hearts—such as the air and water pollution problems in their own community. This was the way to motivate citizens to look to problems in their own backyards, rather than to issues and struggles beyond their borders. For those activists who pursued a more radical agenda of action, however, it was to Europe (and ultimately our own British tradition) that we looked for inspiration, through such groups as the Autonomen in Germany, the anti-nuclear movement in France, and the Angry Brigade or Diggers in Britain, all of which had been ignored by many new activists who were captivated by the media road show of EF!US. Public resistance to the destruction of our planet would not be mobilized through the tokenistic rainforest defense campaigns that initially brought EF! into the limelight, but rather by focusing on the vast road building program that the government had initiated that threatened to flatten hundreds of miles of meadow and fields. One of the early anti-roads campaigners of the 1970s, John Tyme, summed up the anti-roads sentiments of many activists, especially those who, like me, lived in the countryside:

> None of our national enemies have so mutilated our cities, undermined the long term economic movement of people and goods, destroyed our industrial base, diminished our ability to plan our community life and reduced our capacity to feed ourselves (1978, 1).

This greater goal of building a new society inspired us to contact those sectors of the community that were alien to most environmentalists; namely the employees who worked in offending places of pollution, or construction sites. At a large Tropical Timber protest in Oxford, for example, over 400 activists who had blockaded a timber yard refused to move until the bosses had agreed that, if they sent home their staff, they would not dock them any pay. Environmental activists actually addressed the workers in their mess hall (Garland, 96).

The model of building communities of resistance did not just come from the European tradition, it also emerged from the efforts of the late US activist Judi Bari. As both an EF! and labor organizer for the Industrial Workers of the World (IWW), Bari saw that:

> There is no way that a few individuals, no matter how brave, can bring about the massive social change necessary to save the planet. So we began to organize with local people, planning our logging blockades around issues that had local community support. We also began to build alliances with progressive timber workers based on our common interests against the big corporations. As our successes grew, more women and more people with families and roots in the community began calling themselves Earth First!ers in our area (1994, 221).

The aim was to reinscribe the classical labor maxim: "Agitate, Educate, and Organize," putting it onto the agenda of ecological action. Revolutionary ecology provided a holistic model for this, covering civil rights to biodiversity. In order to mobilize the anti-roads and other campaigns to tired and frustrated communities, it was vital that the militant wing of EF! be able to hand down tactics and knowledge without creating a vanguardist or sanctimonious attitude. Regularly, activists found themselves discussing techniques and ideas for blockades or sabotage with local people from all backgrounds and professions. During the Twyford Down road protests, one activist pointed out how locals "took part in the EF! protest, either bodily or by bringing food. When asked where his children were, one local dressed in a Barbour and green Wellington boots, replied that they were off 'tampering with some machinery, not to worry'" (Wall, 1999, 137).

Turning Ink into Monkeywrenches

This cross-fertilization of information made the movement less hierarchical and more accountable. This was assisted at first by *Green Anarchist* magazine, which had predated EF!'s incursion into Britain by nearly ten years. *GA* would regularly print descriptions of all actions, blockading techniques, and the raids of ELF or ALF cells. *GA* would suffer later for this, when across the country police raided its readers and writers, with six standing trial for incitement to violence. But the *GA* collective, and those it sought to connect with in EF!, built a production and communication network that for the first few years of EF!, assisted in mobilizing groups of activists at a moment's notice. By the autumn of 1992, complementary papers/zines began to appear such as *Do or Die*, which sought to combine EF! and ELF activities that were not being reported by the official EF! paper, *Wild*. Around the same time, *Green Revolution* emerged demonstrating a strong internationalist and socialist flavor in its columns. By April 1994, ELF sympathizers were selling the *Terra-ist*—an unapologetic revolutionary ecology magazine—at demonstrations, and cops were arresting the street vendors.

These magazines were not alone in advocating such militant action; there were underground publications being produced like *Partizan*, inspired by the French Marquis Nazi resistance groups, which sought to list names and addresses of company directors as well to offer advice on how to attack their premises. The state reaction to this was paranoid, with thousands of pounds spent on security. Within all these publications, the ELF and others hardened their call to direct action through the International Earth Nights, which, though based upon original EF!US tactics, were now more coordinated and themed.

But all of these could not be mobilized without the resistance culture, rooted in the minimalist philosophy of accomplishing political goals with little or no resources. As Jasper acknowledges,

> Considerable attention to resources makes the interaction between most protest groups and their opponents less interesting, since the opponents usually have greater resources and so win in the long run. But what is often interesting is how those with few resources manage to attain certain goals despite their handicap—precisely through strategy and culture (1997, 297).

This culture of conjuring something out of nothing was not just akin to the political movements that inspired us, but also found in the images to which we aligned ourselves. In their communiqués, ELF activists took on various names, such as Tara and the Sea Elves, Gandalf, Faradawn, or Twinkle Toes the Tooth Fairy. This comedy would hold a darker side, inspiring people to take action at the Vail ski resort, in Colorado in October 1998 (Faust, 1998). The design and images of sabotage manuals regularly invoked these fairytale/Celtic icons as for instance the *Book of Bells* (a sabotage manual) was taken from the *Book of Kells*, the renowned Irish manuscript featuring ornate illuminations of the four Gospels. *GA* even printed t-shirts including, "I Believe in Faeries," which portrayed a fairy sitting on a dozer while trashing it (see below), and one with the word "Terra-ist" with the image of a bulls-eye and a list of past successful raids on the back.

The projection of resistance could not be dependent on myths alone; the activists had to tap into the TV and comic culture also. By using familiar images from most people's childhood we hoped to attract a wider audience, especially those from the younger generation. In some ways, this strategy was akin to the tactic of *detournement,* or image subversion, employed by the Situationist International in the 1950s and 1960s. As the Situationists attempted to intensify the class conflict through films and manifestos, the elves deployed artistic means to agitate in favor of the environment. Messages of resistance were intertwined through familiar characters, such as *Asterix* or the *Magic Roundabout*, and were utilized for their alternative and counterculture status. Following an example from the late 1970s–1980s when anti-nuclear activists fighting the proposed nuclear power station at Plogoff, northern Bretagne, incorporated the French comic hero Asterix into their protest culture, anti-roads protesters borrowed this character and transformed him into a champion of the movement through the comic book, *Asterix and the Road Monster*. This depicted fellow character, Obelex, with a huge ELF logo on his chest, swinging Romans above his head. Apart from the action, the comic book made a concerted effort to valorize worker solidarity, animal rights, feminism, and local communities against the corporate forces stacked up against them.

Asterix and the Road Monster—Road blockades, Roman Style!

Some of the graphics designed for Earth Night evoked this imagery further, using various contemporary resistance figures in circulation at this time. These included Tank Girl, dark Jesters, black cats, or even the logo from the 1960s cult TV series, *UFO*, with a pair of ears to give an elfin feel to it.

These kinds of icons successfully intensified the resistance, as they endowed the movement with a sense of carnival, the absurd, and humor. With no spokespersons or press office, the ELF was only seen through their masks and annoying antics. This type of Carnival and humorous resistance does not just create an exploration of social alternatives, it also builds an avenue for new desires and emotions that are not always associated with conventional protest and resistance (Szerkinsky, 97).

This Carnivalization of EF! and the ELF helped to instill a sense of dis/organization, or at least aided the creation of horizontal forms of decision making. For those who advocated a more militant and revolutionary stand, this dis/organization meshed with the anarchist lifestyle, and also worked with a variety of activists and their cells, thereby helping to construct affinity groups of trust and stability. The principle that each member contributes something vital and useful to the cause, and that all things can be utilized to create havoc or resistance, matches Jordan's observations about how groups best function, in terms of flat hierarchies:

> Flat hierarchies are an ethical statement. They are a belief that all who participate in a dis/organization have something (not necessarily the same thing) to contribute and that forms of co-ordination must strive to draw all the worth they can from everyone's contribution. In practice, this means ensuring open access to all co-ordinating meetings, as well as leaving space for spontaneous reinterpretation of actions. If a co-ordination network is truly flat, there is no privileged decision-making point; instead, at

any moment, a decision can be revisited by those involved. While this seems on the face of it to remove all notion of co-ordination from dis/organization, it ensures that the decisions taken do not strangle improvisation (2002, 69–70).

Anarchist notions of dis/organization were already present in Europe and held sway in many of the direct action groups there, especially in the anti-nuclear movement. They captured the imagination of fellow environmentalists who, unlike their British counterparts, were far more willing to employ confrontational tactics and more extreme forms of sabotage.

Going International

The spread of ecological direct action into other European countries was essential for the ELF, especially as this form of action and motivation was waning in Britain, being replaced by an almost benign *pixieing*, a new term for anonymous sabotage. Elves felt that mounting actions in Europe would revive flagging efforts in the UK and they sought to exploit networks and links which were at times very limited or weak. Thus, some Elves began to travel through Europe, setting up meetings and conducting interviews, thereby spreading the knowledge of the ELF and further publicizing the designated Earth Nights. The first country outside the UK to embrace the ELF was the Netherlands. In the autumn of 1993, Elves sat in the office of *NN* magazine, an anarchist bi-weekly, in the center of Amsterdam and told their story. The journalists were fascinated by the description of activities such as Twyford Down along with the different approaches the ELF wanted to take, especially with regard to social causes.

The Earth Night Poster that Launched the Dutch "Backlash"

This interview must have caught the imagination of Dutch activists, as a few weeks later on Halloween, an auspicious occasion for the Elves, Earth Night started with the destruction of a fuel tanker at Schipol airport in Amsterdam. Over a period of seven nights, various actions targeting vivisection labs, cars, and several diggers unfolded across the country. These actions in the Netherlands started a trend that for 18 months spread to other European countries and were reported in magazines in Finland, Germany, Poland, and the Czech Republic. These new networks produced many results such as the vandalizing of construction machinery or petrol stations. What was most important for the European movement was that the ELF encouraged debate about the need for a holistic model that sought the liberation of people, animals, and the earth. Consequently they called for solidarity with struggles in developing countries, including the Zapatista resistance to the Mexican government and the Nigerian Ogoni tribe's battle against the aggression of Shell Oil (Garland, 1998). Many of these actions set the tone for later actions, and certainly inspired new saboteurs to emerge in the US.

Embracing the Darkness: New Methods for a New Millennium

In such a brief overview, it is impossible to give a detailed analysis of the nature and meaning of "revolutionary ecology" as it emerged in Britain, apart from showing that for a few of us, myself in particular, a mixture of deep and social ecology was the fuel that stoked the fire of resistance against all forms of oppression. Infusing biocentric values with an anarchist politics, the ELF emerged because no other group was willing to go that extra mile, to take the increased risk, and to squarely declare open warfare against those who sought to destroy the earth and its inhabitants.

The ELF was a new resistance we craved for, and one that I personally still hope will take up the gauntlet where others' approaches have failed or compromised their values. Although not a social movement in the sense advocated by Bookchin and other social ecologists, the ELF's ecological and anarchistic message is revolutionary to the extent that no others have ever dared (apart from possibly MOVE) to utilize such radical tactics or to embrace so many in its ethics and its cause. Its cell-like structure and hit-and-run sabotage tactics inspire other social movements to radicalize their actions. Some of us see the ELF as a necessary tool for the period we are in, to deal with the forces stacked against us. The militancy and resolve of the ELF is akin to the tactics and spirit of Paul Watson's ORCA (Oceanic Research and Conservation Action) Force and Sea Shepherd Conservation Society, which sunk and destroyed parts of the Icelandic and Norwegian Whaling fleets. Though Watson's actions were condemned by many mainstream anti-whaling groups including Greenpeace, he correctly stands by his principle that there can be no compromise in the face of such devastation of the earth and when so much is at stake.

By combining aspects of social and deep ecology, we can produce a radical politics, ethics, identity, and a way of living that defends animals, biodiversity, and the environment, while also attacking a global capitalist system that is based upon greed and exploitation. The ELF demonstrated this holistic and inclusive approach in practice, openly stating in its Earth Night literature the need for all groups—from feminists and workers to animal liberationists and anti-nuclear activists—to join and work together. Unity meant, certainly for me, to combine deep and social ecology, as much as linking various groups into a common struggle. Within an elf's heart lies a vital feeling: an injury to one is an injury to all. The ELF has tried to bring substance to this line through its many activities. Revolutionary ecology, however, is not just about action, it is a philosophy characterized by humility towards nature, creativity, flexibility, and humor, while employing key tenets of anarchism to oppose corporate and state. In a world that is still intent upon destroying nature and itself, these traits, along with a determined endeavor to produce and mobilize a new resistance culture, are vital.

The tools of resistance are changing fast, with *hacktivism* and other technological methods becoming more frequent in undermining corporatism and government policy within the 21st century. The Elves are still here, though night time is a little longer for them these days, as cyberspace can provide that extra darkness and shadow time to carry out their activities, and allows them to be more efficient than they could ever be with just a "monkeywrench" and other standard implements in the saboteur's toolkit. The ELF is evolving with the times, and likely will employ and develop new methods such as cybertage, but it will always be *defining tactics from the field* (Langelle, 1994), fighting corporate ecocide by any means necessary (short of physical violence).

If I were to sum up the revolutionary ecologist, then it would be as the character in *Scaramouche*, the dual personality of actor and avenger. He/she may be the gentle fool, the clown, the writer, the hacker, the poet and painter with the world as their stage, but their blade is as deadly as their wit. Sabatini sums us up rightly, I believe:

> He was born with a gift of laughter and sense that the world was mad. And that was his patrimony.

Elves cross the Atlantic, Vail, CO 1998

Bibliography

Bari, Judi. *Timber Wars and Other Writings*. Monroe: Common Courage Press, 1994.

Booth, Steve. *Into the 1990s with the Green Anarchist*. Green Anarchist Publications, 1988.

Faust, Jan. "Earth Liberation Who?" ABC News. 1996. <http://www.environmentalnepal.com.np/articles_d.asp?id=186>

Garland, DJC. "Tactics, Organization and Conflict within the Radical Environmental Movement in Britain." Diss. Lancaster University, 1998.

Jasper, James M. *The Art of Moral Protest*. Chicago: The University of Chicago Press, 1997.

Jordan, Tim. *Activism!* London: Reakion Books, 2002.

Langelle, Orin, "Revolutionary Ecology," *Earth First! Journal* (1994).

Sabatini. *Scaramouche*. 1921. <www.bartleby.com/66/87/47787.html>

Szerzyniski, Bronislaw. "Performing Politics: The Dramactics of Environmental Protest." In *Culture and Economy After the Cultural Turn*, edited by Larry Ray & Andrew Sayer. London: Sage, 1999.

Tyme, J. *Motorways versus Democracy*. London: Macmillan, 1978.

Wall, Derek. *Earth First and the Anti-Roads Movement*. London: Routledge, 1999.

Notes

1. "Elfin" is a fraternity amongst members of the ELF.

Ontological Anarchism

The Philosophical Roots of Revolutionary Environmentalism

Michael Becker

History is on the side of the Earth Liberation Front. ELF communiqués demonstrate a fundamental critique of contemporary technology and global capitalism, and a radical reassessment of human relations with one another and the natural world. The philosophy and tactics of direct action environmentalism are timely and necessary. Like the sorcerer's apprentice, both technological society and indigenous communities are becoming ensnared by a blind technological imperative. The will to technical control has a long history in Western culture, specifically in its subject-centered (will-centered) metaphysics.[1] Western technological society denies the reality of anything other than human subjective striving. Only the ego, its desires and satisfactions, and its reflexive, self-awareness is meaningful. Starting from this subject-centered standpoint, the development of Western society has been marked by an expansive technological framework that transforms everything into interrelated, efficient systems designed for the exploitation of nature. That nothing of any worth is held to exist, save the human will and its conquests, is the epitome of Western *nihilism*.[2] The revolutionary nature of the ELF and similar direct action politics lies precisely in bringing to awareness technological nihilism by directly confronting the bloodletting of the Earth. To be blunt, nihilistic, Western technoculture and its unfolding in the development of the capitalist world-economy, is a predatory, and systematic assault on the Earth. In defense of life, revolutionary environmentalists employ direct action tactics to stop the extreme violence and destruction.

This essay examines the philosophical underpinnings of revolutionary environmentalism. "Revolution," in Theda Skocpol's definition, involves an overturning of dominant social and political groups along with the prevailing norms, ideas, and laws that justify their privileged position. In the current context, socioeconomic, political, and ecological crises cause an explosive upwelling of violent resistance from subordinate groups in society. Revolutionary struggle emerges through the articulation of ideas and tactics appropriate for turbulent political conditions and social transformation.[3] In the context of dire environmental threats, direct action environmentalists, by thought and deed, are clarifying a set of principles that challenge prevailing norms of technological manipulation, private property in animals and nature, and the idea of humans as masters and controllers of the natural world. In the face of the methodical assault on nature, ELF resistance stems from a deep sense of affinity with all life, one associated with biocentrism and deep ecology. Biocentric principles of identification with nonhuman plant and animal life in revolutionary environmentalism have been well documented.[4] Such identification springs from a fundamentally different ontology (a theory of the nature of "Being" or "reality"). ELF communiqués convey a sense of existence in which life—human and nonhuman—is constituted through a creative process, unifying all distinct entities in a constantly unfolding field. Such an understanding of the interrelatedness of life processes—and a recognition that biotic systems are currently being violated and dismantled by global capitalism—drives revolutionary action and provides a basis for reconstituting society in a manner that is appropriate to current ecological crises.

While the biocentric outlook is often associated with figures like Aldo Leopold and Arne Naess, here the focus is on the work of 20th century German philosopher Martin Heidegger, specifically his later writings concerning technology. I also address the similarities among Heidegger, the ELF, and traditional Native American spiritual teachings. Both Heidegger and Native American perspectives provide a useful interpretive context for illuminating the revolutionary significance of the philosophy and tactics of the ELF. Heidegger and Native American figures alike develop a dynamic and holistic ontology that focuses on the multiple ways in which human beings experience Being. For Heidegger, "Being" is not a noun, but a verb; it is not a static entity or concept, but rather a vibrant and creative process of which humans are a part. By contrast, the history of Western metaphysics, from Plato and Descartes to modern science and current times, has been characterized by definitions of "Being" in terms of a specific kind of "being"—disconnected, static things that take on meaning only in schemes of human manipulation. Given technological nihilism and ecological decline, static and mechanistic conceptions of the natural world have shown themselves to be dangerous illusions and are rapidly becoming outdated as new holistic ontologies and sciences emerge. Through their defiant eco-defense, revolutionary environmentalists are attacking and helping to supplant worn out and dysfunctional worldviews. Their political action is rooted in a spiritual reconnection with our natural surroundings and planetary companions. In fact, ELF philosophy and actions mark a historical turning toward the earliest sources of our consciousness of being at home within the world of nature. It is within this profoundly spiritual identification with the natural world, and in the action that it inspires, that the revolutionary character of the ELF is rooted.

Over time, Western metaphysics has constantly deepened the focus on human subjective agency. Consequently, it has sharpened the focus on gaining control over the natural and social worlds, as advancing technologies and sciences (such as genetic engineering and, most recently, nanotechnology) increase its manipulative powers to ever more dangerous levels. By contrast, the ontology underlying ELF actions is directed toward spiritual identification and non-interference with the natural world, and demands a wholly different approach to and use of technology and science. Being is a creative, dynamic, interconnected whole. Both the openness to the independent reality of "others," and the insistence that this openness can emerge in a variety of ways, leads into what I will term *ontological anarchism*. Taking "an-arche" in a literal sense meaning "absence of a ruling principle," ontological anarchism insists on a ready openness to the experience of Being. Rejecting the notion that there is a final, definitive account of "ultimate reality," ontological anarchism instead holds that the experience of Being may be "told" in many different forms—from science and ceremony to philosophy and poetry.

In addition, ontological anarchism states that any particular being must be accepted as a unique kind of life with its own interests. Think of Kant's categorical imperative applied to any entity: "Never treat a living thing as a mere means to one's end, but rather as an end in itself." Ontological anarchism thus provides a basis for surmounting Western nihilism in two key ways, each involving a radically different conception of freedom. First, it orients "freedom" toward an awareness of how each entity achieves its unique essence. Freedom is not the ability of the human will to range without limits; rather, it is the inherent movement from within each entity that defines its own, irreducible nature. Second, ontological anarchism believes that the creative process of Being "frees"—in that through this process all things come into being. That is, freedom and Being should be thought together; existence is precisely the "freeing" or emerging of entities into presence. Ontological anarchism means one cannot control or exploit either the unique character of particular entities (such as animals, plants, or ecosystems) any more than one can control or exploit the unique, dynamic process of Being itself.

If we apply both of these transgressive conceptions of freedom to social reality and everyday life, the most fundamental bases of Western nihilism and its current political/economic form—transnational capitalism—are radically undermined. Efficiency, the demand for maximum control, the conversion of nature into profit, the demeaning of experiences that fall outside the norm of calculation, and so on, give way to new values, novel types and applications of science and technology, and different conceptions of freedom that can inform a new ecological society. It is in just this sense that necessary, revolutionary historic change is on the side of the ELF. In my view this is precisely the meaning of "earth liberation."

I. Competing Paradigms of Technology

In many respects, the discourse in ELF and other direct action communiqués reflects a critical interpretation of technology similar to that offered in Martin Heidegger's later works—namely, that technology is a historical *and* ontological formation. That is, technology is characteristic of a late stage of western historical development marked by an almost complete withdrawal of an awareness of Being or "nature as a whole." Technology might be better grasped as the name of a historical epoch rooted in Western metaphysics and centering on synthesizing all entities—inanimate objects, animals, and people—into an enclosed, self-regulating (or cybernetic) system of control.[5] Heidegger's interpretation of technology turns on a crucial distinction between a "correct" definition and an "essential" understanding of technology. The commonly accepted, "correct" view is obvious: technology is a human activity oriented toward efficient means-ends relationships. This definition is anthropological. Technology is unique to humans—and instrumental—it improves the efficiency of cause-effect relationships. Typically, the correct definition also holds that technology is neutral, its proper construction and appropriate use depending entirely on human direction and with no logic or unique character of its own. Such a view is "correct" in that it can be used to refer to any particular tool at any specific time in history, but it serves to obscure the deeper issue of how and why modernity is singularly devoted to technological control.

An easy acceptance of the mundane definition of technology, Heidegger notes, "makes us utterly blind to the essence of technology" (see below).[6] Accepting that technology is merely neutral—"always already"—contextualizes responses to difficult technological issues. Profound technical problems and powers ranging from weapons of mass destruction and genetic engineering to reproductive technologies presumably must be resolved by establishing proper control over technology. The underlying conception of human beings as directors and masters of "natural resources," methods, and machines goes unexamined. But it is precisely such an assumption about human nature and purpose that lies at the core of our technical appropriation of the natural world. Seeing technology as a neutral tool "conditions every attempt to bring man into the right relationship with technology. Everything depends on our manipulation of technology. We will get technology...in hand. We will master it. The will to mastery becomes all the more urgent the more technology threatens to slip from human control."[7] That which is "conditioning" us—the "will to mastery" and the "urgency" of technical problems that impede or defy our attempts to control nature—is characteristic of our technological age. In fact it is precisely these historically-constituted factors that comprise the *essence* of technology.

For Heidegger, three phrases help orient us to the "essence of technology." They are "challenging forth" (*herausfordern*), "standing reserve" (*bestand*), and "enframing" (*gestell*). The first term refers to the essence of technology as it is disclosed within technological activity; the second explores the way objects appear or stand forth within the historical mode of technological appropriation; and the third represents the "destiny" of technology, the historical conjunction between Being as a whole, creative process, and a profoundly mistaken Western conception of Being which brings about destructive forms of technical development and social organization.

II. Reductionism and "Challenging Forth"

"Challenging forth" is Heidegger's term for the way in which entities are revealed through modern technological practice. The common element of such practice is a constant provocation, an insistence that nature continually yield more resources through increasingly efficient processes. Challenging forth describes the command character of technological activity, such that nature, in all aspects, is viewed as something that opens itself up as a grid, ready for unlimited appropriation. Technological praxis ceaselessly channels nature into increasingly complex, extractive, and manipulative systems. Challenging forth describes the difference between a windmill and a wind-powered electric generator. In the first instance, there is a direct relationship between the air flow and the movement of the windmill's sails. The wind's currents can be appreciated as such and are directly related to the need that is served. In the second instance, the currents are perceived only as a calculable resource generated through a turbine and stored within the electric grid. They are reduced to a unit within the electrical system available for use in innumerable, potentially infinite applications.[8] As a whole, technology can be grasped as a series of modes of challenging forth: mountains are viewed as mining districts, forests are mere timber resources, and rivers nothing but power sources to be harnessed for human use. The essential manifestation of the four basic elements—earth, air, fire, and water—is elided as they are all challenged within increasingly complex, resource and energy intensive, and ecologically destructive systems of appropriation.

Ultimately, the philosophy and science of cybernetics epitomizes the challenging forth character of modern technological life. In contrast to earlier modes of practice, challenging forth is typified by a constant demand for greater efficiency. Nature, in turn, is viewed exclusively in terms of manipulability. Human beings thus come to dominate nature, as nature appears to open itself up for the taking. For Heidegger, however, as we will see below, appropriate, less invasive technical means—those that are not rooted in assault and expropriation—are possible. But this possibility can only be realized by first grasping and moving beyond the ontological-historical conditions that continue to underlie modern technological domination.

ELF communiqués reveal a similar critical interpretation of technological practice. The command character of challenging forth is revealed in the activists' sense of the provocative nature of the business ventures they target in illegal direct actions. In a series of 2000 and 2001 communiqués from Long Island that concerned the torching of luxury homes threatening sensitive pine barren habitat and an important aquifer, activists spoke of the virtual assault mentality of the developers. The communiqué held that the "Earth is being murdered." The writers speak of the "rape of the Earth" by the Earth's "oppressors." The activists vowed to counter such destruction as long as the "Earth is butchered." ELF activists' identification with the Zapatista Army of National Liberation (EZLN) in Chiapas, Mexico is rooted in an attack on a corporate-state apparatus that wages "a war against the environment" as well as "a war against the people who live sustainably within it."[9]

In my view these pronouncements are not mere ideological hyperbole. A profound anger against and resolve to stop the inherently destructive, "command and control" technological orientation toward nature emanates from the communiqués. In public forums, activists cite statistics on the rapidly accelerating extinction crisis, but not with clinical detachment. Instead, they deploy these damning facts to bear witness to the violent appropriation of nature that they are passionately contesting.[10] Such concern is further demonstrated in videos produced by the press offices of the ELF and the Animal Liberation Front (ALF). In the current age, defined domestically by intense state repression of dissent coded as a "war against terrorism," ELF and ALF communiqués give voice to a real, if hidden "terrorism" *against* the *Earth* as it is bulldozed into oblivion, as forests splintered by the chainsaw crash to the ground, and ocean waters are befouled by oil spills and toxic wastes. One becomes aware of the terror experienced by billions of factory-farmed, genetically and chemically manipulated animals confined in cages, force-fed, and then butchered for their flesh, bodily products, and fluids. One must bear witness to the terror expressed in the eyes of a circus-caged elephant that rampages in fear and anger against its keepers.[11]

The testimony to the destruction of nature expressed in ELF communiqués and videos provides the critical counterpoint to the hidden everyday violence of technological appropriation. That activists recognize the assault as a systematic form of destruction is clear in their repeated reference to "genocide" against animal nations. Recognition of the inherently violent nature of technological assault on the Earth is a prerequisite to becoming aware of the essentially violent character of modern technological culture. In fact, bringing to consciousness the exploitative character of modern technical appropriation of the Earth, comprises, in large part, the truly revolutionary character of the ELF and similar groups. These are the only "environmental" groups that have fully grasped that the current integration of modern technics and corporate capital results in systematic violence against all nature, including animals and human beings. Further, the ELF is among the few groups to forcefully bring to the attention of millions of people such a basic and important insight regarding the techno-corporate matrix. Consistently, the ELF, ALF, and other revolutionary forces criticize single-issue environmental organizations for failing to understand the systemic and urgent nature of the omnicidal assault on the Earth by corporate technics. A statement from the ELF press office reads:

> The Earth Liberation Front does not commit merely symbolic acts to simply gain attention to any particular issues. It is not concerned merely with logging, genetic engineering, or even the environment for that matter. Its purpose is to liberate the earth. *The earth, and therefore all of us born to it, are under attack.* We are under attack by a system which values profit over life, which has, and will, kill anything to satisfy its never ending greed. We have seen a recent history rich in the destruction of peoples, cultures, and environments. We have seen the results of millions of years of evolution destroyed in the relative blink of an eye [emphasis added].[12]

It is only in the context of the increasingly intense and destructive technological assault on the Earth that one can grasp ELF arguments that revolutionary direct action is a form of *self-defense*, whereby activists—self-conscious extensions of nature—represent the Earth and strive to protect it from attack.[13] In a communiqué entitled "Weapons of Resistance," EZLN Subcomandante Marcos explained that the struggle is not for better food, housing, medical care, and dignified work for the Zapatistas themselves. For to gain these things at the expense of others who would remain in poverty is to lose the struggle; indeed, it is to become complicit in that against which the Zapatistas fight. "That is why we Zapatistas are fighters, because we want 'For everyone, everything, nothing for ourselves.'" The ELF extends the Zapatista principle to all of our relations on Earth. While each ELF action may have symbolic significance as an act in the name of liberation of the Earth from its oppressors, the actions are also efforts to stop a specific instance of violent assault by Western technical culture and corporate interests against a particular niche in the web of all life. We might say—again extending the phrase to *all* beings, human and non-human—that "none are free until all are free."

III. Nature as "Standing Reserve"

A second characteristic of the essence of technology is the "standing" or visible aspect of natural entities set up through challenging forth. Standing involves the way in which things commonly appear when they are positioned to be exploited by the technological praxis of challenging forth.[14] *Bestand* or "standing reserve" expresses the way in which entities within a technological framework appear to Western subjects as constantly on stand-by for their appropriation. Every thing appears to constantly avail itself to courses of action oriented toward maximum efficiency. Every thing seems tailored for human purposes and ready to be used. Every thing ostensibly is available for instantaneous manipulation. It is "the whole objective inventory in terms of which the world *appears* [emphasis added]."[15]

With the development of modern technology, we perceive the world differently. "The world now appears as an object open to the attacks of calculative thought.... Nature becomes a gigantic gasoline station, an energy source for modern technology and industry."[16] "The Earth itself can show itself only as the object of assault.... Nature appears everywhere...as the object of technology."[17] Today, some of the most forbidding and pristine places on the globe are being opened up for development. Why? Because these places, like all of nature, only appear to us as nothing but manipulable resources, open and ready for extraction. As such they tend to be used without consequence to the ecosystem from which they are taken, ultimately, harming human beings themselves.

The advent of standing reserve as an "inclusive rubric" actually undermines even the objective character of individual entities. Reduced to a level that excludes any meaning other than sheer usefulness, entities lose even their stance as independent objects. The standing reserve is the appearance of entities as "mere material...a function of objectification." Something as massive as an airliner, as long as it stands within the automatic functioning of the transportation system, "conceals itself as to what and how it is." In essence, it is "standing reserve...ordered to ensure the possibility of transportation."[18] Integrated within the transportation system the airliner is an ordered unit on standby, constantly ready for use. It appears within the totality of the ordered, cybernetic system as a standardized unit, not as a distinct object with unique properties. For Heidegger this pattern holds for all manner of entities integrated into technical systems and even for persons insofar as their production and consumption needs and habits are determined, calculable factors within the rubric of standing reserve. The crucial issue is whether—from transportation and energy to communications and food—it will be possible to relate to artifacts, other humans, animals, and the Earth in multiple ways—primarily in ways that allow each entity to take its own unique course according to its own nature—and not *only* in a coercive manner that converts all entities into units of technically efficient, functioning systems.

ELF communiqués are meant to alert us to the fact that we already stand at this dangerous threshold. A communiqué from 1999 explains the grounds for the liberation of beagle puppies from Marshall farms in upstate New York. Marshall is a breeder for Huntingdon Life Sciences (HLS), the main target of a radical animal rights group, Stop Huntingdon Animal Cruelty (SHAC). The thirty liberated puppies were among "hundreds of beagle puppies *waiting to be shipped* to vivisection labs [emphasis added]."[19] Within the essence of technologically-ordered cybernetic systems, these animals literally do not appear as dogs, as living beings or even as independent objects. Rather, they are mere resources, material, or commodities within a giant "scientific" research system ordered for corporate profits. That puppies are punched in the face, slammed against walls, or otherwise abused is obviously shocking and disgusting. That they are subject to the pointless cruelties of vivisection and product testing is simply monstrous and horrific. But the entrapment of the beagles in the first place occurs within a technological context in which nature, in whatever form, disappears and is able to show itself only as standing by or on reserve for manipulative use. These puppies are not living beings with needs and wants, but rather inert factors of production in the corporate research and commodification system.

Language in the communiqués that express the conversion of minerals, plants, and animals into mere materials and commodities parallels Heidegger's notion of the "ordering of the orderable." A tree-spiking action in Brown County and Monroe County Indiana state parks was "a warning to all those who want to turn the beings of the Earth into cash."[20] Similarly, a Wisconsin communiqué concerning genetic modification of white pine trees notes that forest "management" treats "wildlife as some numbers on a graph." The Forest Service coordinates with timber companies in "an insane desire to make money and control Life."[21] Direct action tactics, as briefly mentioned above are, on the one hand, self-defense against the assault on a planet that, except for its self-conscious manifestations, cannot defend itself. In addition, they are motivated by a reaction to the technical control of the corporate-state structure that characterizes the conversion of humankind itself into standing reserve as the only "natural" relationship humans have with the Earth.

IV. Enframing and the Forgetting of Being

The third and most complex term Heidegger uses to discuss the essence of technology is Enframing (*Gestell*). Heidegger refers to the essence of technology as a "way of revealing." By this phrase Heidegger has in mind an epoch as defined by a historically conditioned response of human beings to Being. In each epoch the response to Being is rooted in fundamental words (*Grundworte*) that the most important thinkers of that period have coined to orient human beings toward Being. The pre-Socratics conveyed a poetic experience of the mystery of Being: they grasped how the unity of Being concealed itself to allow the coming-to-presence of beings in their particularity. The elemental forces of nature (such as water, air, and fire) described by the Milesians are not literally meant to represent the "stuff" of the universe, but rather the ultimately unnameable process of unity diversifying into plurality and reuniting into oneness. Their poetic utterances name the oneness of Being which can never be perceived through the senses but only grasped intuitively.

Yet, since Plato, Western metaphysics has been marked by an increasing tendency to neglect or forget the question of Being. Instead, Western philosophers have consistently tried to represent Being in terms of a specific kind of being—be it the Platonic form of the Good, Aristotelian substance, Augustinian will of God, Leibnizian monad, or Cartesian *res cogitans*. The foundational works of Western metaphysics have consistently served to increasingly obscure rather than to illuminate Being. For Heidegger, this "errant" characteristic of Western metaphysics, the increasing turn away from Being, marks the inherent nihilism of the West. "Enframing" refers to the historical extension of technological nihilism, involving the embrace of technology across all manner of activities and throughout the globe. Corporate globalization is the vehicle for a pre-existing historical destiny: the world-wide extension of Enframing.

With the discovery of natural "laws" such as gravity and motion, the application of mathematical certainty to the investigation of physical processes and the development of automated machinery in farming and production, the essence of technology—Enframing—moved toward its extreme point. Being has become completely obscured in a metaphysics of subjective certainty and control corresponding with the technological-capitalist practice of total domination over nature and all life. Wonder at and evocation of Being through language, arts, and ceremony recedes into oblivion. In the forefront stands "Enframing," conditioning thought and practice to a cybernetic, nihilistic response to the question of Being.

As it stands at present, Heidegger believes, Enframing is our "destiny." Heidegger claims that Nietzsche's doctrine of the will to power (the foundational words of the epoch of Enframing) epitomizes the subject-centered, nihilistic extreme of Western metaphysics. In Heidegger's interpretation, will to power is a process of constant self-overcoming, in which the will is only alive, insofar as it constantly over-powers. The relentless insistence in our times that everything and everyone move more efficiently and effectively is a reflection of the ontological view that all of nature—and especially human action—is driven by a will to increased power.

We obviously do not expect to find a comprehensive ontology in the ELF and revolutionary communiqués. Implicit in the communiqués, however, is a clear awareness of the manner in which corporate, mass-consumer capitalism continually integrates nature into technical production systems. There is recognition both of an underlying structure of technological practice, and that such practice is rooted in Western history. In a single page introduction to one of its volumes, the ELF press office refers to the technological system or the systematic destruction of nature eleven times.[22] A communiqué regarding the firing of two USDA Animal Damage Control Buildings in Olympia, Washington identifies facilities "which make it a *daily routine* to kill and destroy wildlife [emphasis added]." It is precisely the increasing tendency toward the routinization of a technical orientation toward life that is Enframing. Activists write that "animals are being turned into machines for human consumption."[23] In fact, the description of natural entities as machines is becoming increasingly frequent.[24] But it is not merely the commodification of nature to which revolutionary environmentalists object; more fundamentally, it is the setting upon the world and the reduction of nature to useable bits of material. More importantly, eco-saboteurs recognize this process as an impersonal force rooted in current institutions and political ideology. "This world is dying. All that is beautiful about the world is being destroyed." Anger and rage is specifically directed "at this system."

It is against a predominant systemic pattern that presents itself as rightful and economically vital that ELF and ALF activists fight. Consider the infamous torching of a newly built ski lodge at Vail, Colorado in 1998. The action was aimed at preventing the destruction of sensitive Canadian Lynx habitat. The action was fueled in part by outrage at the fur industry "which cares only about fur quality and maximum 'production' and death."[25] The authors of the communiqué clearly identify a mentality and practice of maximizing productive systems as the general threat to human and nonhuman beings. There is a certain depersonalization of the issue in this language which is appropriate insofar as the technology of "genocide" against natural entities is buttressed by a will to control nature and make it "useful."[26] Rod Coronado, a Pascua Yaqui Indian and veteran of direct action environmentalism in the Sea Shepherd Conservation Society, the ALF, and other groups, recognizes the historical continuity between the decimation of his tribe and the systematic destruction of animals killed by the fur industry. The "invasion and conquest in the 'new world' [is] continually being directed toward indigenous animal people....threatening the very last nations of wild beings."[27] Similarly, in the communiqué on the Joe Romania car dealership fire, the authors refer to the "continuous assault on both the planet and ourselves."[28] In each of these instances the communiqués refer at least obliquely to the sense that the current level of ecological destruction derives from sources fundamental to Western history and a Western conception of "nature" as "resources" to be, at best, "managed."

Both Heidegger and revolutionary environmentalists share a deep foreboding about the extent of the crisis posed by our utter separation from Being. Heidegger writes of humans as the beings who, early on, hearkened to Being, but who emerge, in the end, as "the laboring animal who is left to the giddy whirl of its products so that it may tear itself to pieces and annihilate itself in empty nothingness."[29] It is not merely the physical devastation of thermonuclear war (or, in our day, global warming) that Heidegger has in mind here. It is the philosophical and spiritual poverty wrought by Enframing whereby humans are incapable of grasping the extent to which technical control has excluded a sense of interrelatedness with others as part of a unified, awe-inspiring, and fragile process of Being. Confident talk of values is part of "the armament mechanism of the plan," and that which is esteemed as progress is really an "anarchy of catastrophes" confirming "the extreme blindness to the oblivion of Being."[30] Direct action strikes similarly reflect "the rage of a dying planet." Activists are motivated by a commitment to divert us from a "path towards annihilation," recognizing that the ultimate effect of destroying biotic diversity is "suicide." It is morally impossible for ELF activists to "allow the rich to parade around in their armored existence, leaving a wasteland behind in their tire tracks."[31] Blindness to oblivion, annihilation, and the socio-ecological wasteland is the tragic condition of the current epoch of Enframing.

The essence of technology can only continue as long as its destructiveness is concealed. The revolutionary nature of the ELF lies in bringing the onto-historical conditions of technological culture and the capitalist exploitation of nature directly in to the foreground of social consciousness.

V. Openings for Change

Yet, for both Heidegger and revolutionary environmentalists, there exist possibilities for transformation despite the destructiveness of Enframing. In the midst of technological peril—indeed, precisely because the peril strikes at and thus awakens us to the bond between human and nonhuman life—there emerges a sense of solidarity of human with nonhuman beings. Looking at the well-heeled, bureaucratic discourse of "human resource management" and "personnel resources," the challenging forth of human beings into standing reserve is fairly evident. Factory-farmed cows, pigs, and chickens obviously have it far worse than people, but in both cases the purpose is to harness resources for maximum efficiency and profit. Ultimately human and nonhuman beings are similarly enframed within one giant "gasoline station." It is precisely the experience of this solidarity which must be constantly rearticulated—in arts, poetry, ceremony, music, and especially in socioeconomic and political action—in order to provide a historically and ontologically authentic break with the metaphysics of technical control and capitalist exploitation. Action will only be truly revolutionary if it revolves around engagement in solidarity with nature, where liberation is always seen both as human liberation from the confines of Enframing and simultaneously as liberation of animal nations and eco-regions from human technics. Anything less will always lapse back into the false and oppressive hierarchy of "man" over "nature" and "man" over "animals" with attendant effects of technological, disciplinary control over humans, nonhumans, and the Earth. Using a familiar title from the anarchist Crimethinc collective, revolutionary environmentalism is truly an instance of "fighting for our lives" where the pronoun refers to *all* life not just human life.

Heidegger describes the possibility of transformation through a return of Being as a re-figured humanism.[32] It is the possibility of suspending the will and attaining a lucid sense of the free play of Being within which all of life emerges and is sustained. A human being, like any entity, *is*—s/he stands forth as present. But "his distinctive feature lies in [the fact] that he, as the being who thinks, is open to Being....Man *is* essentially this relationship of responding to Being."[33] Human *being*, in essence, is the experience of awareness of Being. Such experience is the clearing of a space (symbolically represented, for example, in the building of an arbor for a ceremony or in the awesome silence created by the space within a cathedral or a grove of old-growth Redwoods), and the patient readiness for Being to be brought to language.[34]

Given the appropriate bearing and evocation through language, human beings can become aware of dwelling, along with all other existent beings, within Being—the open realm within which entities are "released" into presence (*Gelassenhait*—or "releasement"). What comes to the fore in suspension of willed manipulation is an embrace of other beings and the enduring process of evolution within which all beings emerge and develop. By reflecting on or experiencing oneself within the dimension of freedom that is the domain through which all beings pass, human beings can repair the willed manipulation inherent in calculative thinking and realize a patient equanimity toward Life.[35]

It is only in the context of this reawakened sense of the unity of life that revolutionary action gains an authentic basis. It is this engagement with "the Other" that shows that ELF actions are truly about defense of plant and animal life, and they demonstrate genuine liberation concerns that typically are trapped within Enframing. That is to say, ELF (and similar) actions, show themselves as part of a dynamic and necessary historical *evolution and transformation process*, not merely a gesture of opposition and negation, because of their profound solidarity with animals and the Earth. Such guidance and solidarity thus serves as a general basis for a post-Enframing, post-capitalist order, an ecological, not a capitalist society.

What will change is, first, the pre-eminence of Enframing as that which animates the epoch and, correspondingly, our relationship to technology. No longer will technical solutions be sought after in realms of activity where technique is not applicable. No longer will everyday activities be pervaded by the standardization and frenzied pace of technology. No longer will nature be looked upon as a homogenous field of resources to be extracted and exploited. No longer will resource-intensive and polluting technologies be utilized simply because they serve the blind interests of corporations over the needs of the Earth. No longer will human beings take from the Earth without thought of the far-reaching consequences of such actions on all present and future forms of life. Critics would wrongly denounce this position as atavistic, primitivist, or anti-science/technology. But as the turning toward the re-emergence of Being unfolds, both through revolutionary action rooted in solidarity with nature and through new, non-exploitative modes of acting in the world, technics will not disappear; instead, the limits of technology as a mode of revealing will begin to be discerned so that new forms and uses of technology can emerge. Questions about technology will center on whether a given technology can be developed and used so that plant and animal life can appear as it is and not be reduced to standing reserve. The question, for Heidegger, is not whether technology, in the sense of a set of tools, is done away with, but whether Enframing is surmounted.

It is in this sense of releasement that Heidegger writes, "Mortals dwell in that they save the earth....Saving does not only snatch something from a danger. To save really means to set something free into its own presencing."[36] I take this as the literal equivalent of the masked ALF activist reclaiming a puppy from a research lab so that it can become a dog rather than a unit of research, or an ELF activist who stops the destruction of an aquifer or forest so that it can remain an aquifer or forest rather than become a water or wood resource. It is just this new ethos which must guide a revolutionary reconstruction of society on grounds that preserve the openness to Being and the ability of each kind of being to become what it is in its essence.

VI. Ontological Anarchism and Native American Spirituality

For those who charge Heidegger with merely recycling, and not transcending, Western anthropocentrism, it is important to note that there are possibilities here for an emerging post-humanism—a new orientation to nature beyond egocentric forms of human agency and towards interrelation with other beings and Being itself. Heidegger's philosophy allows for multiple modes of engagement with others and nature as equals, all of them rooted in a relationship of solidarity, respect, and concern.[37] I call this kind of pluralistic, egalitarian, and ecological outlook *ontological anarchism*. It begins with the rejection of the illegitimate "rule" of metaphysical constructs that have served to justify unlimited technological appropriation of the world. In place of Enframing with its subjectivist metaphysical underpinnings, ontological anarchism proclaims a multiplicity of forms of experience in which a sense of revealing comes to the fore—such as in art, music, religion, and philosophy. One such experience, a pre-dominant theme of spiritual re-awakening in the ELF communiqués, is found in Native American philosophy and practice.

A reverence for the sacred power of nature pervades ELF writings and communiqués (as well as the texts of radical environmental organizations including Earth First!).[38] Spiritual identity with animal nations is a recurrent theme in ELF communiqués. A November 1997 communiqué concerns an arson event against the Bureau of Land Management (BLM) horse corral at Burns, Oregon, and an earlier ALF arson event at a Redmond, Oregon slaughterhouse and horsemeat processing plant. The focus of liberation was wild horses on BLM lands who had been classified as invasive and non-native, and were in the process of being rounded up and auctioned for slaughter. In defending the arson attack, activists speak of the "genocide against the horse nation." The Vail arson event occurred, in part, in defense of the "mink and fox nations." More generally activists speak of "wildlife nations" and abhor the destructive forces that hate and kill off the spirit of that which is wild.[39]

Spiritual identity with the Earth's creatures understood as "relations" of different "nations" is, of course, central to traditional Native American practice. In a sweat lodge ceremony even the rocks are acknowledged as the old ones who know everything because they have been here from the beginning. The closing prayer of the sweat lodge invokes "all my relations," meaning a prayer to all one's relatives with whom one is constantly connected. The prayer is an acknowledgement and reminder of that connection. Linda Hogan, a Chickasaw poet, powerfully evokes the living-remembering connection forged in the sweat lodge:

> The entire world is brought inside the enclosure...smoking cedar accompanies this arrival of everything....Young lithe willow branches remember their lives rooted in the ground, the sun their leaves took in... that minerals rose up in their trunks...and that planets turned above their brief, slender lives....Wind arrives from the four directions. It has moved through caves and breathed through our bodies. It is the same air elk have inhaled....Remembering is the purpose of the ceremony....It is the mending of a broken connection between us and the rest....the words "All my relations"...create a relationship with other people, with animals, with the land. To have health it is necessary to keep all these relations in mind.[40]

Obviously it is difficult for a person from a Western, rational-scientific-technological context to grasp the notion of a willow pole "remembering." The point is that the willow has an essence as a willow. As a natural being, it is also connected to other beings (such as the minerals flowing in its sap). Precisely the same is true for human beings, and ceremonies like a sweat lodge or a bear dance enable a spiritual identity with specific relations or with Being as a whole. In such ceremonies the reflexive association with oneself as ego is often surmounted by a more authentic prayerful voice. Such a voice in song or prayer can attain a simultaneity of self and "relation." Ego and other is surmounted by a spiritual connection of beings. The identity with horse nations in the communiqué stems from this kind of remembering/acknowledging spiritual relationship.

In fact, this is the very meaning of the "Earth *Liberation* Front." ELF activists seek to literally free plant and animal species as well as natural environments and people from a cultural-political-economic construct and system that would convert them from what they essentially are into commodities for exploitation and profit. "Welcome to the struggle of all species to be free."[41] At the same time, these efforts are oriented around a spiritual practice of identity with the species and environments being liberated. At the close of one communiqué is a petition for others to "stop the slaughter and save our Mother Earth." Again, identification of Earth as the first mother—the life generating and life sustaining force from which all creatures live—is central to Native American belief and practice. The act of saving as restoration lies both in deed and in spiritual recognition. This is a restorative surmounting which unites actor and the fullness of the life giving ground from which all our relations thrive.

In profound ways, traditional Native American spirituality exhibits parallels to Heideggerian ontology and can provide a more substantial basis for environmental direct action, specifically regarding the evocation of an unseen and unnameable, but all encompassing spiritual power. The article "Oglala Metaphysics" recounts an extraordinary dialogue between JR Walker—a Euro-American physician who lived among, and was accepted by, Oglala *wicasa wakan* (or "medicine men")—and a number of such Oglala figures, including Finger. Finger describes how there are eight separate elements—the sky, the Sun, the Earth, the rocks, the moon, the winged, the wind, and the beautiful white buffalo calf woman who brought the pipe and the first ceremonies to the Lakota people. Yet each of these elements are one—*Wakan Tanka*, the Great Spirit, or *Taku Skanskan* which is the living spirit in each thing, giving it its essence and causing it to behave in its own unique fashion. Walker asks whether the sun and *Taku Skanskan*, are the same. Finger responds that this is not so, that the sun is in the sky only half of the time. But Finger adds that it is the sky which symbolizes *skan* because *skan* "is a Spirit and all that mankind can see of him is the blue of the sky."[42]

What is fascinating here is the idea that a being which symbolically epitomizes the spirit cannot be delineated as a thing. The vault of the sky, a continuum within which everything unfolds, is taken to represent the unity of spirit which is unseen but through which every being takes its course. Similarly, for Heidegger, Being—the One—is never grasped directly in the same way as a particular being. Yet, in certain modes of experience and language one easily grasps the unity within which each particular kind of being develops. It is just that sense of the hidden interconnectedness of all life which animates the actions of ELF defenders of life. Insofar as the ideas and actions of revolutionary environmentalism help to elucidate an ethic based in spiritual, ontological unity, it advances a profound challenge to the culture of technological control.

VII. From the Provocation of Social Ecology to an Ethic of Sacredness

Environmentalists of whatever stripe who embrace spiritual principles akin to deep ecology have been criticized not only for overlooking socio-economic factors that perpetuate illegitimate forms of hierarchy in society, but also for embracing an apolitical mystical view or even a potentially theocratic belief system. The most persistent (often needlessly vitriolic) such critic of deep ecology is Murray Bookchin. Bookchin claims that "In failing to emphasize the unique characteristics of human societies and to give full due to the self-reflective role of human consciousness, deep ecologists essentially evade the *social* roots of the ecological crisis."[43] Worse, for Bookchin, "nature worship" ranges from innocuous and politically irrelevant New Age beliefs to the reintroduction of authoritarian religious potentates. Religion submerges the individual in an authoritarian collectivistic whole ruled over by "divine" masters. "The Paleolithic shaman, in reindeer skins and horns, is the predecessor of the Pharaoh, the Buddha, and, in more recent times, of Hitler, Stalin, and Mussolini."[44] Similarly, Daniel Deudney has pointed to the holistic emphasis of deep ecology as a potential threat to those very issues of separation (namely between church and state) that have been a mainstay of religious tolerance in the West.[45]

There is no question that Enframing emerges with the beginnings of capitalism and deepens along with the development of its corporate, mass-consumer form. The practical significance of studies of the interconnection between this mode of political/economic system and ecological destruction cannot be overemphasized. It is also unnecessary to point out that the institutional forms of the state and the corporation must be overturned, not least of all because they reflect the very hierarchy and oppression rooted in "man's" domination of "nature." Still, both Bookchin and Deudney recognize that a political practice that incorporates ceremonies reflecting ecological principles holds promise. At one point Bookchin himself, in speaking of Hopi horticultural ceremonies and other similar "preliterate" spiritual/natural practices, wrote eloquently about the "ecological ceremonial" and the profoundly important role it plays in integrating individual, society, and nature.[46] Similarly, Deudney imagines that, as a "civic religion," Earth religion could provide a basis for self discipline without an all-powerful state, while redirecting "topophilia" from nationalism to identification both with local geography and with the Earth as a living whole.[47]

Aside from these observations, for anyone who understands the anarchical structure and decision-making milieu out of which revolutionary environmental and animal liberation groups emerge, it is quite clear that the movement is not likely to evolve into a theocracy. The very point of ontological anarchism is that there is no single referent for the experience of solidarity with nature or animals or for the meditative grasp of Being. In the most common Native American ceremonial practice, the sweat lodge, this point is reflected by the sweat runner who clearly articulates his or her role as one who simply pours the water and directs the ceremony. Each participant has an opportunity to pray, sing, or speak in whatever form they wish. It is specifically and authentically pluralistic insofar as the ceremony is an avenue for direct communication between an individual person and the Spirit of Life. Any experience an individual has is recognized as unique and meaningful for that particular person. This is not the stuff of theocracy.

Instead what ELF communiqués reveal is something both much less and much more far-reaching: namely that spiritual biocentrism can serve as an important philosophical and spiritual component for seriously and directly contesting corporate, mass-consumer capitalism. Clearly, as it unfolds in, say, a Sun Dance ceremony, or manifests in spirit in ELF ecotage strikes, Native American sacred practice is no feel-good, religious flavor of the month. Moreover, in its decentralized form and its ontological anarchism such practice provides a basis for multiple forms of expression of human interrelation with all of our relations on the Earth. But unless and until an ethos rooted in biocentrism becomes a matter of course alongside consensus-based forms of governance, environmentalism will always be consigned to a series of half measures concerning humans and their need to "manage resources." In this context the inherently destructive practices of technological Enframing will never be decisively surmounted. Native American spiritual practice is fundamental to a revolutionary shift in thought and everyday behavior because, for the first time in the West, the most fundamentally destructive hierarchy, that of human dominion over nature and all nonhuman beings, is decisively challenged.

Heidegger's re-figured humanism, deep ecology, and Native American ceremonial practice are different in many respects, yet are fundamentally related in their ontological anarchism. As I have emphasized, this outlook is marked by a radical egalitarianism wherein the intrinsic worth and interdependence of all beings is acknowledged, honored, and celebrated. Moreover, it opens a way for the healing of an antagonistic relationship between human beings and the Earth. An ethos of care for one another in the human and human-nonhuman communities can be born from this. In Book VIII of his *Republic*, Plato spoke satirically of the folly of democracy where even "horses and asses have a way of marching along with all the rights and dignities of free men." Naturally, animals neither march (a strange activity reserved for certain groups of humans) nor participate in politics. Lacking a voice, the animals' and the Earth's well-being must be preserved and protected by ethical beings who strive to care for Others, particularly those Others whose voices have not been heard. Like Native Americans, ELF activists hear these voices speaking from the realm of the sacred. Such recognition of the sacredness of the Earth and her creatures is crucial to surmounting the nihilism of Western metaphysics and restoring dignity to human and nonhuman beings alike.

Notes

1. With good reason, much has been written of the decisive role of Descartes in the development of subject-centered, Western metaphysics. With the formulation *cogito ergo sum* ("I think, therefore I am"), certainty becomes the coin of the realm and only the *cogito* can be certain of its own intellectual activities, even of existence itself: hence, the radicalizing of subjectivity. Insufficient attention has been paid, in this regard, to the parallel notion of the will as the decisive seat of meaningful or purposive action. Specifically, I am thinking of St. Augustine's early description of the deficient will—the turning of the will away from God towards that out of which the will was created—nothing (Saint Augustine, *The City of God*, trans. Marcus Dodds (New York: The Modern Library), 385–88). The association of human willing and a turn of the will toward nothingness is fundamental to the subsequent deepening of will-oriented nihilism in the West. In the modern period, the interpretation of the will as decisive in effective human action is most apparent in Schopenhauer and Nietzsche. The

point is that both the point of reference for knowing and effective action is rooted exclusively in subjective agency.

2. Heidegger's various accounts of nihilism—the abandonment of being, forgetting about the questions of Being, the errancy in Western metaphysics—run well beyond the scope of this paper. Suffice it to say that, as in the Native American context, and in the context of deep ecology, the sense is that technological society serves to undermine and alienate experiences of the spirit, specifically a deep inner experience of the felt or lived relationship between one's self and earth. Technological society is nihilistic in that it cuts off access to any sense of the sacred.

3. Skocpol, Theda. *States and Social Revolutions*. New York: Cambridge University Press, 1979.

4. See, for example, the work of Bron Taylor, especially, "Ecology and Nature Religion" in the *Encyclopedia of Religion*, 2005. "Earth and Nature-Based Spirituality From Deep Ecology to Radical Environmentalism" (part I), *Religion* 31 2 (2001): 175–93. "Earth and Nature-Based Spirituality From Earth First! and Bioregionalism to Scientific Paganism and the New Age" (part II), *Religion* 31 3 (2001): 225–45.

5. Martin Heidegger, *The Question Concerning Technology*, trans.by William Lovitt (New York: Harper and Row Publishers, 1977), 4.

6. Ibid.

7. Ibid., 5.

8. This distinction is questionable. In his classic article, "The Historical Roots of our Ecological Crisis," Lynn White focuses precisely on the harnessing of wind and water power during the Middle Ages, approximately between A.D. 800 and 1000 (along with the vertical "knife" plow) as the origin of an entirely new, technically-oriented approach to nature. White remarks that from these beginnings "but with remarkable consistency of style, the West rapidly expanded its skills in the development of power machinery, labor saving devices, and automation" (White, Lynn, "The Historical Roots of Our Ecological Crisis," *Science* v l 155 (March 1967): 1203–07). Still, the point is that the technological direction of the West lies not merely in more machines but in a different way of thinking about nature and the human relationship with the natural world.

9. *Resistance*, unnumbered volume: 3. One of the leading figures in the direct action movement, Rod Coronado, whose Pasua Yaqui ancestors had engaged in a rebellion against Spanish conquistadores, speaks of the insight he had early on in his activism when trying to stop the slaughter of harbor seals in Canada. It suddenly dawned on him that the genocide against animal nations, including the seals, was part of the same process of the genocide of the Spanish against his people. (Rod Coronado. CSU Fresno, Fresno, CA. 14 Feb. 2003.)

10. Comments by Gary Yourofsky, Carl Rosebraugh, Kim Marks, Rod Coronado, Leslie Pickering, and Paul Watson at the "Revolutionary Environmentalism: A Dialogue Among Activists and Academics." Fresno, CA, 13–14 Feb. 2003.

11. See videos by PETA, the Animal Liberation Front, and the Earth Liberation Front—of particular interest in this regard is the ELF video *Igniting the Revolution*, ELF Press Office, 2002. Gary Yourofsky, a former PETA spokesperson and activist who liberated 542 mink from a farm in Canada, was first moved toward a militant animal rights position by his seeing the chained and caged animals "backstage" at the zoo. He sensed the deep fear and rage in the animals' eyes, and witnessed the neurotic behavior induced by their confinement.

12. lesliejames, *Resistance* unnumbered volume: 1.

13. Self, as we allude to below, must be considered in the context of the Indian word "mahatama"—the wider self which includes all that self relates to itself as itself. Ultimately, this self-relation must move beyond the relation of particular things to a relation to the whole, to nature or Being. The true, wider self, is a relation involving acknowledgement of the whole to which one is constantly related. See Naess, Arne. "Identification as a Source of Deep Ecological Attitudes." In *Deep Ecology*, edited by Michael Tobias. Santa Monica, CA: IMT Productions, 1985.

14. Heidegger, "The Question Concerning Technology," 17.

15. Martin Heidegger, *Poetry, Language, Thought*, trans. Albert Hofstadter (New York: Harper and Row, 1971), 111.

16. Martin Heidegger, *Discourse on Thinking*. trans. John M. Anderson and E. Hans Freund, intro. John M. Anderson (New York: Harper and Row, 1966), 50.

17. Heidegger, "The Word of Nietzsche: God is Dead," in *The Question Concerning Technology*, 100.

18. Heidegger, "The Question Concerning Technology," 17.

19. See *No Compromise* website.

20. *Resistance* unnumbered volume: 3.

21. Ibid., 4.

22. *Resistance* vol. 2 # 2: 1.

23. *Resistance* vol. 3: 15.

24. Even a cursory scan of the internet generates numerous references to animals and plants as machines. According to James Robl, president of Hematech LLC, "Cows are ideal factories." Hematech works in partnership with Kirin Brewing Co. to produce human immunoglobulins in cows. Paul Elias, AP Biotechnology writer notes that this has involved 672 attempts at cloning cows with six live births, two of which died within 48 hours. For us the significance lies in the manner in which cows have been reduced to research units in a systematic attempt to turn them from their essence as bovine creatures into manufacturing facilities (<http://www.heraldsun.com/healthneeds/34-256485.html>). In a similar vein, bio-engineered mice designed for myriad research projects are described as ideal "research tools."

25. *Resistance* vol. 3: 4.

26. One is reminded of Arendt's conception of the banality of evil inasmuch as those who turn animals into machines are enmeshed within an onto-historical horizon of meaningful action which cannot be "controlled," but rather is destined from within Enframing. After all, it is not just natural "resources" that are systematically channeled into corporate systems. Personnel, human resources, human genetic material, and labor power show the extent to which, within the essence of technology, human beings also become something to be ordered within the orderable. The actions of those directing the mechanization of animals are themselves determined within the movement of Enframing.

27. Rod Coronado interview in *Underground* Issue #17 (Winter/Spring, 2002): 17.

28. *Resistance* vol 2 # 1: 13.

29. Heidegger, *Overcoming Metaphysics*, 85

30. Martin Heidegger, *Identity and Difference*, trans. Joan Stambaugh (New York: Harper and Row, 1969), 71.

31. Each of these citations is from *Resistance* vol. 2 #1.

32. Heidegger's ontology tends towards a fundamental dualism between human beings with their special charge to "safeguard Being" and all other sentient and non-sentient beings. Ontological anarchism is meant to correct this privileging of human reason, even the specific language of a "new humanism." Humans and each of the non-human animals have their own unique ways of coming into being. In fact, the distortions of technological culture eviscerate both humans and animals (animals in a much more brutal fashion by literally turning them into machine products for consumption as I note below) by forming them into units fit for various systems. Heidegger's ontology, despite its privileging of human reason, is a step toward simply recognizing the various unique qualities of different kinds of animals including humans.

33. Heidegger, *Identity and Difference*, 31.

34. It is in this sense, in my view, that one can best understand Heidegger's famous statement that "Language is the House of Being."

35. At the same time, it is at this point that the divergence of Heidegger and the ELF is most stark. Radical direct action is quite at odds with what has been described as Heidegger's "super-passive optimism," as summarized in his statement to *Der Spiegel* magazine that "Only a God can save us," along with his fascist politics. Indeed, I would argue that it is a conception of intellectual life at an oracular and "stellar" remove from the prosaic world of politics that best accounts for Heidegger's grotesque, absurd, and unforgivable involvement with the Nazis.

36. Heidegger, *Poetry, Language, Thought*, 150.

37. Heidegger can rightly be criticized for a tendency to emphasize an alleged inner connection between Greek and German language as the sole path to a recovery of a sense of Being. On the other hand, in some instances Heidegger points to non-western traditions and language as actually better exemplifying the human belonging together with Being. See for example "A Dialogue on Language" which concerns Zen Buddhism. Martin Heidegger, *On the Way to Language*, trans. Peter Hertz (San Francisco: Harper Collins, 1971), 1–56.

38. Bron Taylor's work has been instrumental in documenting the diversity and pervasive influence of Native American religious themes in revolutionary environmentalism. See for example Bron Taylor, "Earth and Nature-Based Spirituality: From Deep Ecology to Radical Environmentalism," *Religion* 31 (2001), 175–203. Totem animals and other Native American religious symbols are encountered frequently, especially among Earth First activists. This has been effectively depicted by Taylor in his video presentation *Radical Environmentalism: Promise or Peril*, presented at the "Revolutionary Environmentalism" conference at CSU Fresno, 13 March.

39. Each of these references is from *Resistance #3*.

40. Hogan, Linda. "Sweat Lodge Ceremony." In *Native Heritage: Personal Accounts by American Indians 1790 to the Present*, edited by Arlene Hirschfelder. New York: McMillan, 1995.

41. *Resistance* Unnumbered Volume: 3.

42. "Oglala Metaphysics." In *Teachings From the American Earth: Indian Religion and Philosophy*, edited by Dennis Tedlock and Barbara Tedlock. New York: Liveright, 1975.

43. Bookchin, Murray, "Social Ecology Versus Deep Ecology," *Socialist Review* Vol. 88 no. 3 (1988): 19.

44. Ibid. Leaving aside the faulty analogy, it is rare for Bookchin to operate so sloppily in anthropological matters. In many tribal societies, the shaman's authority is linked directly to his success in healing. If he does not heal, he is not paid, and eventually is disrespected, treated contemptuously, and often shunned.

45. Deudney, Daniel. "In Search of Gaian Politics: Earth Religion's Challenge to Modern Western Civilization." In *Ecological Resistance Movements: the Global Emergence of Radical and Popular Environmentalism*, edited by Bron Taylor (Albany, New York: State University of New York Press, 1995), 299. In my view, the real battle concerning Western "values" at least in the short run will concern the right of property. It is on this legal and philosophical foundation that corporations continue to gain legal title to destructive appropriation of nature.

46. Murray Bookchin, *The Ecology of Freedom: The Emergence and Dissolution of Hierarchy*, (Oakland: AK Press, 2005), see the chapter entitled "The Outlook of Organic Society." Perhaps more noteworthy is the (only momentary) rapprochement between Bookchin and David Foreman who Bookchin, in other quarters, labels an "eco-brutalist." On Bookchin's qualified embrace of deep ecology see Bookchin, Murray and David Foreman, *Defending the Earth*, edited by Steve Chase (Boston: South End Press, 1991).

47. Deudney, "In Search of Gaian Politics," 299.

Shades of Green
Examining Cooperation Between Radical and Mainstream Environmentalists

Matthew Walton and Jessica Widay

"The end result of this kind of [radical] thinking—to which we are
painfully close in the United States—is an ideological stalemate in
which opposed camps are increasingly unable even to
communicate." *Martin Lewis*

Mutual criticism appears to be the status quo between "radical" and "mainstream" environmentalists.[1] Where we might expect cooperation between groups with similar goals of protecting the natural environment, philosophical and tactical differences have lead to a rhetoric of condemnation and disrespect. This antagonism has made cooperation in environmental campaigns difficult between the two camps. It is possible, however, to bridge these seemingly irreconcilable differences and allow for collaboration. Groups that move away from the mainstream by adopting a more radical philosophy—while continuing to use traditional tactics—open up new possibilities for cooperation across the environmentalist spectrum. In this essay, we will look at one group that utilizes such an approach, and analyze the characteristics that set it apart from mainstream environmental groups and allow for complementary action with radical organizations.

We begin by providing an overview of the development of rhetoric within the environmental movement, particularly between the radical and mainstream wings. Then we examine the case of the Headwaters Forest campaign in Northern California, where the Environmental Protection Information Center (EPIC), a group that would traditionally be considered mainstream, and Earth First! (EF!), a radical group, are demonstrating a new model of complementary action and positive rhetoric towards one another. We conclude by identifying factors that contribute to this cooperative spirit and demonstrate how EPIC represents a new category of progressive environmental organizations that are defined by a mixture of characteristics common to both mainstream and radical organizations.

New organizations of this type can engage the environmental movement in a way that changes both the level of cooperation and the nature of the rhetoric between the two opposing camps.

Rhetoric Within the Environmental Movement

In 1980, five men who had little in common beyond their mutual love for the outdoors, united in the shared sentiment that the environmental movement was not doing enough to protect the world's wilderness. The moderate stance of the mainstream movement was becoming increasingly ineffective, they argued. In its place, a new group was needed that would "say what needs to be said and do what needs to be done and take the strong actions" that wilderness protection requires (Dave Foreman, quoted in Manes, 70). Following in the tradition of Edward Abbey's *Monkeywrench Gang*, members of this new group, dubbed Earth First!, set out to undertake direct action that illustrated their motto: No compromise in defense of Mother Earth.[2]

The emergence of EF! ushered in an era of uneasy cooperation between the existing mainstream and emerging radical wings of the environmental movement. Moderate groups issued public support for Earth First!'s ambitious conservation goals, while denouncing its ecotage tactics.[3] Only a decade earlier, the Sierra Club had ousted its executive director, David Brower, for his radical leanings and no compromise stance. Similarly, when Greenpeace founder Paul Watson undertook dramatic actions against Atlantic seal hunters that garnered much media attention, he was removed from his leadership position in the organization.[4]

Earth First! developed at a time when mainstream environmental groups were becoming more professional in nature, with structured bureaucracies and highly-paid leadership. They had established relationships with policymakers and were experiencing success in their use of legislative and judicial strategies. The radical actions of new guerilla groups threatened to destroy moderates' hard-won credibility and authority within the Washington scene. The concern was that the negative publicity from ecotage and direct action would alienate potential supporters, jeopardize donations and funding, and harm the still somewhat fragile image of the environmental movement.

This fear that radical groups may undo the tenuous progress made by mainstream organizations has resulted in an uneasy, and often antagonistic, relationship. Mainstream environmentalists argue that radical actions hurt, rather than help, the cause, resulting in "self-defeating" behavior. As one mainstreamer asserts, "the quest for purity [i.e. no compromise] will in the end only undercut the prospects for change" (Lewis, 12). Thus, while established organizations applaud the *aims* of Earth First! and other groups that make use of direct action, they are quick to distance themselves from their *tactics*.

Similarly, radical environmental activist groups such as Earth First! have expressed mixed feelings toward more moderate groups. Initially, direct action groups set out not to replace the mainstream movement, but to complement it. As Dave Foreman noted at EF!'s inaugural rally, "the main reason for Earth First! is to create a broader spectrum within the environmental community" (*Earth First!* Vol 21 No 1 (Nov. 2000): 9). While moderate organizations undertook valuable actions that often met with success, EF!ers and other radicals felt that these actions alone were insufficient. The very first issue of the *EF! Journal*, which laid out the organization's mission, stated, "Lobbying, lawsuits, magazines, press releases, outings, and research papers are fine. But they are not enough" (Vol 1 No 1 (Nov. 1980): 1). The legal approaches of mainstream organizations, they argued, often result in compromised outcomes. Litigation may take years to resolve, during which time environmental destruction continues. Furthermore, the end result of a lawsuit may be a negotiated settlement that sacrifices some environmental resources in order to protect others. EF!'s no compromise stance decries such trade-offs, and demands that all available means of defending the earth be utilized. As Dave Foreman asserted, "Earth First! will use [traditional tactics], but we will also use demonstrations, confrontations, and more creative tactics" (Ibid., 1).

EF! explicitly stated that although they adopted more radical action in support of their no compromise position, they did not pass judgment on the mainstream groups for working largely within the system: "Earth First! will set forth the pure, hard-line, radical position of those who believe in the Earth first. We are not in competition with more moderate conservation groups nor do we wish to criticize them" (*Earth First!*, Vol. 1 No. 1 (Nov. 1980)). Moreover, EF! organizers envisioned a symbiotic relationship between the two wings of the movement. EF! founder Howie Wolke reflected, "When I helped found Earth First!, I thought that it would be the 'sacrificial lamb' of the environmental movement; we would make the Sierra Club look moderate by taking positions that most people would consider ridiculous" (quoted in Manes, 18).

This separate-but-complementary form of interaction has proved unsustainable, however. The very basis of radical environmental activism—no compromise—makes acquiescence to more pragmatic approaches impossible. While moderate groups broker deals with legislators and industry, radical groups view these actions as unacceptable. An example of mainstream compromise that was unacceptable to the radical movement can be seen in a bill sponsored by Morris K. Udall (D-AZ) in 1981 that dealt with radioactive waste. Anti-nuclear activists were appalled at the fact that the bill protected the nuclear industry from citizen complaints, but mainstream groups supported it, reasoning that Udall was "one of their best friends in Congress" (Sale, 57).

In short order, the rhetoric of partnership between mainstream and radical environmentalism has broken down into one of harsh criticism, mutual antagonism, and insults. In their more recent calls to activists, EF!

asks, "Are you tired of namby-pamby environmental groups? Are you tired of over-paid corporate environmentalists who suck up to bureaucrats and industry? Have you become disempowered by the reductionist approach of environmental professionals and scientists? If you answered yes to any of these questions, then Earth First! is for you" (*Earth First!* Vol 21 No 1 (Nov. 2000): 4). Radical activists regularly refer to mainstream organizations as "emasculated," "compromised," and "naive." EF! member Karen Coulter decries the mainstream as "hopelessly anthropocentric, interested in the benefits ('resources') nature provides to humans while not standing up for the intrinsic rights of other species and for ecological integrity" (Ibid., 79).

This antipathy does not characterize all radical/non-radical interaction, however. Occasionally we witness collaboration between groups such as Earth First! and other organizations that do not adopt such an "extreme" stance. Radical groups often synchronize their actions to support mainstream campaigns. It is not uncommon, for instance, for radical activists to participate in tree-sits in Pacific Northwest forests that more moderate groups are seeking to protect through legal injunctions (Scarce, 1990). One way to facilitate such cooperation among groups that embrace different organizational tactics is through harmonization of philosophy. Groups that cooperate with radical organizations are not the moderate organizations of the mainstream. Rather, they represent a different form of environmental activism that falls somewhere in between the moderate and the radical. Although these groups often rely largely on traditional tactics, they are willing to undertake more direct, confrontational (though still legal) actions than their mainstream counterparts. More importantly, they adopt a no compromise position, which aligns them more closely with radical organizations in terms of philosophy. Rather than criticize such progressive activist groups as "namby-pamby," Earth First! and others are turning to them as partners in the struggle for conservation.[5]

Headwater Forest: A Case for Collaboration

To illustrate the complementary action between radical and non-radical environmental groups, we turn to the case of the Environmental Protection Information Center, a group trying to protect Northern Californian wilderness. EPIC was formed in 1977, and uses "an integrated, science-based approach [to activism] that combines public education, citizen advocacy and strategic litigation" in its efforts to protect and restore local wildlife and habitats.[6] In the early 1990s, EPIC became involved in the fight to save Northern California's Headwater Forest.

By most standards EPIC would be considered a mainstream environmental activism organization. They hold rallies and demonstrations and their most effective tool is litigation that stops the destructive practices of extractive corporations, often halting them permanently and imposing significant fines. In contrast to a group like Earth First!, which is also active in Northwest California, EPIC does not engage in more radical direct action tactics such as sit-ins, tree-spiking, or chaining oneself to a bulldozer. Although it is likely that there is some overlap in membership between EPIC and EF!, EPIC publicly distances itself from its more radical cousin. However, in a news article in 2003, Cynthia Elkins of EPIC stated that although there was no coordination between her organization and the more radical activists, both groups "clearly watch each other's actions" (quoted in Driscoll). This is a far cry from the usual nasty rhetoric traded back and forth by mainstream and radical environmentalists. Moreover, as we will demonstrate, although the groups do not explicitly coordinate their actions, they are actively cooperating in the campaign to save the Headwaters Forest.

EPIC and EF! frequently disseminate news and updates about each other's actions to their respective communities. The EF! journal published an article praising the legal victory achieved by the partnership of EPIC and the Sierra Club over the Maxxam/Pacific Lumber companies in the Headwaters Forest case. In 1998, EPIC publicly denounced the killing of EF! activist David "Gypsy" Chain, who was protesting clear-cutting by Pacific Lumber. The organization used their connections to lead other environmental groups in the region in demanding an investigation into the incident.

The groups' support of one another has influenced their own respective strategies. While Earth First! continues to use direct action techniques, they have also become more amenable to traditional tactics, particularly as EPIC's legal strategies seem to be bearing fruit. In a rare compliment bestowed on the mainstream from the radical, EF!er Josh Brown acknowledged that many different groups have contributed to the campaign to save the Headwaters Forest, but "what has kept Headwaters standing is EPIC and the lawsuits they've filed" (quoted in Harrison, 1996).

One of the easiest ways that mainstream and radical groups can work together without actively coordinating their activities is through complementary action. EPIC and Earth First! were doing just this in the spring of 2003. While EPIC and the Sierra Club were fighting a lawsuit to stop Pacific Lumber from exploiting a loophole in a deal brokered in 1999, EF! was setting up direct action camps to ensure that no matter what the outcome of the legal case, loggers would not be able to continue their destructive practices (Kim). These direct actions by radical groups opened up a space for legal action to be taken by more mainstream organizations.[7]

This case demonstrates that, despite the usual nasty rhetoric, there is occasionally some degree of cooperation between radical and non-radical environmental groups. The question becomes: in what situations is this cooperation likely to occur and why does it happen?

The Newstream: Somewhere In Between

As we can see, the relationship among members of the environmental movement is anything but clear-cut. It is at times cooperative, at times combative. The nature of interaction is often determined by two key group characteristics: philosophy and tactics. Philosophy can range from a belief in "no compromise," which advocates stopping at nothing to defend wilderness areas, to that of pragmatism, which argues that strategic actions including deal-making are most effective. Tactics may include direct actions such as tree-spiking and human blockades, or they may center on more conventional strategies such as lobbying, demonstrations, and public education. The radical and mainstream movements are categorized according to these characteristics in the chart below.

	Radical	Mainstream
Tactics	Direct Action	Traditional Action
Philosophy	No Compromise	Pragmatic Strategy

Groups cannot always be easily characterized across a radical-moderate divide using these variables, however. In the case study above, Earth First! is a clear example of a radical environmental group. However, labeling EPIC is not as easy a task. While their methods are firmly within the realm of the traditional, EPIC has adopted a stance that is much closer to the no compromise position of EF! than the pragmatism of the mainstream. What we are seeing in the case of EPIC is a combination of factors that have created space for cooperative action between the mainstream and the radical. In embracing this type of approach, EPIC has evolved into a new breed of environmental organization, one that utilizes the traditional tactics of the mainstream while mimicking radical groups in refusing to make concessions in defense of the planet. We refer to this type of organization as a *Newstream Environmental Group*, and its position in the environmental movement is illustrated in the chart below.

	Radical	Newstream	Mainstream
Tactics	Direct Action	Traditional Action	Traditional Action
Philosophy	No Compromise	No Compromise	Pragmatic Strategy

Superficially, newstream environmental organizations appear to be a part of the mainstream. They utilize traditional activist tactics such as litigation, media coverage, and public demonstrations. Because they are often local in nature, newstream organization goals pertain to specific areas only, making their position appear more moderate than that of radicals that promote the protection of wilderness everywhere. However, they differ from traditional mainstream organizations in several important ways.

First, although their tactics are very similar to moderate groups, newstream organizations are willing to carry out more extreme actions. Undoubtedly, these actions still stop far short of the radical direct actions of groups like Earth First!, but they are nonetheless more directly confrontational than most mainstream organizations would be comfortable with, particularly in causing significant economic damage to corporations through lawsuits. In addition, the philosophy on which newstream activist organizations are based is that of no compromise rather than pragmatic bargaining. Their actions may be mild in comparison to those of EF!, but newstream groups are just as intent on refusing to compromise with politicians and corporations. This stance distances newstream groups from moderate organizations that view the struggle for environmental protection as a long war, in which specific battles must be strategically sacrificed. While some (including many radicals) perceive an inherent tension between the use of traditional legal strategies and a no compromise stance, newstream groups view them as compatible. Legal tactics are simply one strategy at their disposal. If lawsuits fail, the groups do not resign themselves to sacrificing that specific battle. Rather, the groups remain committed to utilizing alternative actions to secure environmental protection if legal options result in a less-than-ideal outcome. As one activist noted, "You've got to use every tool that you can... We didn't put much faith in the lawsuit at first... we were trying to stall until it got into Court" (Myra Finkelstein, quoted in Scarce, 3).

This shared philosophy has allowed newstream groups to succeed where mainstream groups have often failed in their ability to establish cooperative relationships with radical organizations. The radical environmental movement is founded upon the belief that the Earth deserves nothing short of total protection; in order to achieve this goal, humans should stop at nothing. By definition, this philosophy is non-negotiable, and because it is so central to radical environmentalism, there is little room for cooperation with groups that do not share the same view. Radical activists themselves have indicated that it is not the reformist actions of mainstream organizations that are problematic. Indeed, Dave Foreman has often noted that there is a clear "need for other groups less radical than Earth First! and other methods" (quoted in Manes, 19). Rather, it is the divergent philosophies, which radicals interpret as a lack of commitment on the part of moderates, which create a gulf between the two wings of the movement. Newstream groups can successfully bridge this gulf.

Forging the Newstream

Cooperation between radical and non-radical environmental activist groups is not easy or automatic, however. Collaboration is most likely when groups find themselves in close proximity. Newstream groups are most often local groups that focus on a specific environmental issue close to members' homes. The nearness of the threat encourages members to adopt a no compromise philosophy. Groups that may not necessarily be overly interested in increasing national or globally protected lands are naturally more concerned with saving the forest located down the road from their home. This hard-line stance endears newstream groups to radical organizations, who share their zeal for rejecting all concessions in their efforts to stop ecological degradation. We can see the tendency for such partnering of national radical groups with local newstream organizations illustrated in a case in British Columbia. In the late 1980s, a group of activists from the radical Friends of the Wolf cooperated with the local Western Canada Wilderness Committee (WCWC). Friends of the Wolf provided direct financial support to WCWC so that it could file a lawsuit to prohibit wolf hunts in the province (Scarce).

Membership overlap between newstream and radical organizations also facilitates group cooperation. Environmentalists that are members of both types of organizations can appreciate the strengths of each and can serve as advocates of inter-group cooperation. As individuals in radical groups like EF! begin to see the efficacy of certain traditional actions such as lawsuits, and members of mainstream groups begin to realize that traditional actions are not always sufficient to halt the degradation of the planet, activists will be increasingly comfortable moving between the two communities. Newstream adoption of a no compromise philosophy makes radical environmentalists more likely to form strategic alliances or to join their ranks.

Radicals are also more likely to align with newstream groups when the groups carry out direct actions. These actions are still located within the traditional realm, yet are more confrontational in nature. The refusal of newstream groups to enter into a cozy relationship with industry and legislators wins the support of radical organizations. Whereas mainstream groups are often afraid to criticize government bureaucrats, newstream groups actively expose their shortcomings and failed promises. This can lead to newstream groups being labeled as radical. While, according to our definitions, this characterization is not entirely accurate, the groups do not always oppose it. Rather than attempt to avoid all association with more "extreme" groups for fear of a tarnished reputation, newstream organizations persist in their struggle.

The development of newstream groups that we have identified here is primarily a result of mainstream organizations moving in the direction of radical groups in their philosophical basis. By definition, it would be impossible for radical environmental organizations to adopt the techniques of the mainstream. However, an important aspect of this phenomenon is the recognition by radical activists that these progressive groups are not only beneficial to the movement, but in many cases, a necessary complement to radical action. Activists on both sides are beginning to realize that the defense of mother Earth will require that every voice be heard.

The very nature of radical environmental organizations is such that sustained collaboration with more moderate groups is unlikely at best, impossible at worst. And we do not wish to make a call to radical activists to temper either their philosophy or their tactics. Yet, the EPIC example points the way to a middle path of environmental activism that could bridge the gap between these two extremes, creating the potential for cooperation that could be both effective and sustainable. The changing rhetoric between radical environmentalists and those who are more moderate in their actions reflects this evolution.

Confrontation and disagreement can be replaced by a language of respect and cooperation. This rhetoric remains the exception to the rule, however. Time will tell whether or not groups within the middle ground will continue to emerge and grow, fostering this rhetoric of support while still allowing for both radical and mainstream activism. If so, we can expect a more unified and effective environmental movement in the future.

Bibliography

Driscoll, John, "Moving into a new EPIC-Fresh realms of activism," *Eureka Times Standard*, 17 August 2003.

Earth First! The Radical Environmental Journal Volume 1 Number 1 (November 1980) & Volume 21 Number 1 (November 2000).

Harrison, Christa, "Junk Bonds and Redwood Forests," *Random Lengths*, Earth Day 1996.

Jonas, Kevin. "Bricks and Bullhorns." In *Terrorists or Freedom Fighters: Reflections on the Liberation of Animals*, edited by Steven Best and Anthony J. Nocella, II. New York: Lantern Books, 2004.

Kim, Katherine Cowy, "Hole in Headwaters Deal Threatens to Turn Triumph into Travesty," *Pacific News Service*, 29 October 2003.

Lewis, Martin W. *Green Delusions: An Environmentalist Critique of Radical Environmentalism*. Durham, NC: Duke University Press, 1992.

Manes, Christopher. *Green Rage: Radical Environmentalism and the Unmaking of Civilization*. Boston, MA: Little, Brown and Company, 1990.

Kirkpatrick, Sale. *The Green Revolution*. New York: Hill and Wang, 1993.

Scarce, Rik. *Eco-Warriors: Understanding the Radical Environmental Movement*. Chicago: The Noble Press, 1990.

Notes

1. We broadly define "mainstream environmental activists" as those who utilize traditional political tactics (such as lobbying and campaigns to raise public awareness) and take a pragmatic approach to solving environmental problems (negotiating land usage or limiting emissions, for example) within existing legal structures. "Radical activists," in contrast, are those that utilize non-traditional tactics (ranging from civil disobedience and tree-sits to sabotage and arson) and are not willing to make concessions in their defense of the Earth. Rik Scarce (1990) defines radical activists not only according to their tactics and approach,

but their aims (protection of biodiversity), organization (non-hierarchical and loosely-based), personal wealth (minimal), and prospects of success (limited). While we see the value in including such additional characteristics, we feel that tactics and philosophy are the most important defining features of radical versus mainstream activists, and that they provide the greatest explanatory power for the questions under investigation in this essay.

2. "Direct action" can be broadly defined as acts individuals or groups initiate against a political target, without maneuvering within the legal system, in order to prevent or stop an objectionable practice. This is as opposed to indirect actions, such as electing a representative to work on one's behalf. Direct action may be extra-legal, involving destruction of property or trespassing, but it also often takes legal forms such as demonstrations and boycotts. "No compromise" describes a way of thinking in which adherents (across the political spectrum) are absolutely unwilling to accept anything other than a complete achievement of their goals. They believe that there is no room for concessions or negotiations, thus rejecting pragmatic approaches in which immediate goals may be sacrificed in the name of future success.

3. Dave Foreman and many Earth First!ers have since given up ecotage tactics. However, they are still espoused by many within the organization. An article in the November/December 2003 issue of the *Earth First! Journal* specifically promotes direct action, both legal and illegal. In addition, ecotage is utilized by other radical environmental organizations, most notably the Earth Liberation Front.

4. In 1977, Watson intervened in the clubbing of a baby seal by taking a club from the sealer and throwing it in the water. The Board of Directors of Greenpeace considered this to be destruction of property and asked him to resign from the board; when he refused, he was voted off.

5. We do not believe that Earth First! is representative of the entire radical environmental movement. In fact, the organization would be considered much more moderate than a group like the Earth Liberation Front (ELF). The ELF relies almost exclusively on economic sabotage and guerilla actions to prevent the destruction of the Earth. However, EF!'s tactics are nonetheless firmly within the radical camp and for our purposes here, they provide a good example of a radical group that is engaging in positive action and rhetoric with a non-radical group.

6. See <http://www.wildcalifornia.org>.

7. This same approach has been very effective within the animal liberation movement, particularly in the case of the SHAC (Stop Huntingdon Animal Cruelty) campaign against the notorious animal testing corporation, Huntingdon Life Sciences. Without direct communication, the (legal) aboveground actions have been complemented by (illegal) underground actions of the ALF (Animal Liberation Front), strengthening the campaign and resulting in benefits for both groups. Jonas refers to this tactic as the "one-two punch." Companies targeted by aboveground groups respond quicker to public pressure when it is coupled with the threat of underground action, and the ALF enjoys more widespread publicity when an aboveground group like SHAC defends their actions (see Jonas, 2004).

Part II

SUSTAINABILITY AND THE POLITICS OF CONSUMPTION

"Let your life be a counter-friction to stop the machine. What I have to do is to see, at any rate, that I do not lend myself to the wrong which I condemn." *Henry David Thoreau*

"Live simply so that others may simply live." *Mohandas K. Gandhi*

"In a consumer society there are inevitably two kinds of slaves: the prisoners of addiction and the prisoners of envy." *Ivan Illich*

"I am going to fight capitalism even if it kills me. It is wrong that people like you should be comfortable and well fed while all around you people are starving." *Sylvia Pankhurst*

Lakota Woableze (Lakota Perception)

Rosalie Little Thunder

Nituwepi he? (Who are you?)

Oyate ki hunh samyeic'iyapi (Some people have gone too far),
Taku ki iyuha tawaic'ilapi (They think they "own" everything),
Taku yuha-pica sni hena ekeyas (Even those things not to be owned),
Hakablayela waokahnigapi (Their understanding is so superficial),
Wacintankapi ki slolyapi sni (They don't know self-discipline),
Kagisnisniyan wosotapi (They use up things carelessly),
Na hecena isam cinpi (And they want even more),
Hogan s'e wawiyakpa wastelakapi (Like fish, they like shiny things),
Na ipi slolkiyapi sni (And they don't know when they are full),
Maka ki tohantan (The Earth always was),
Na tohantan kte (And it will always be)
Niye ca niglasotapi kte (It is you who will cause yourself to perish)
Nituwepi he? (Who are you?)

Takoja Timmy

Takoja Tim, blessed with the eyes of the ancestors
Dropped his little bag at my feet
Human noises unnecessary
"I'm here," it all said.
Bagful of codes
Access

Looking at the mountains whizzing by
I wondered what was within him
"How much does this van weigh?"
2,000 plus pounds maybe
"What do you weigh?"

130 pounds
What?

Mango juice dripping down his chin
"Where does this come from?"
I don't know, far away
"How does it get here?"
Trucks and planes
"Not for us then"
Not?

"Why do people need new things all the time, like cars?
Look at all the cars to be fixed in the junk yards.
Would the Earth cave in if we took it all out?
Only make things when we need to."
Stop eating the Earth?
Stop?

"We want to be related to the buffalo cause they're smart
Little trees learn to be smart from old trees, right?
The rocks are really smart too
The wind must be too
Water
Us?"

Piles and piles of rocks of different shapes and colors
"For my mom, for my sisters, for my uncle
Some for my friends and still more
For the people I haven't met yet
Can't keep them," can't stop
Flow of goodness
Nothing is really
Ours

"Unci, it must be hard to try to be right all the time
Try to take all your stuff to the Spirit World
So easy to listen to old people
Can you hear them?"
Listen now
Shhh

Takoja Tim, he grew taller and wiser than me
He didn't pack up his bag and leave
He comes by now and then
Ancestors' knowing grin
Messenger generation
Spirit of the Earth
Help

What is a Morally Defensible Level of Consumption?

Robert Jensen

Most of the discussion of the Earth Liberation Front focuses on its tactics. Can property destruction be justified morally in the struggle to slow the human assault on the non-human world? If so, is it a good strategy? When ELF activists destroy, damage, or deface sport utility vehicles, the two key questions are: Is that ethical? Is it likely to be politically effective?

Others in this volume take up those questions. I want to ask a different ethical question, of ELF members and all of us. It is a question far more complex and difficult. It is a question about which there can be no posturing and glib moralizing. And it is, I believe, one of the central ethical questions of our time.

Whatever arguments one might want to have about the pace of global warming and toxic waste accumulation, about the rate at which humans are degrading the earth's capacity to sustain life, and about how long before our current way of living destroys the planet, one thing is beyond contention: If all the people of the world consumed at the level of the typical middle-class US citizen, the game would be over tomorrow. The earth cannot sustain six billion people—and billions more to follow—living as we live in this country.

Over the long term, a society such as the contemporary United States is not sustainable. By "sustainable," I mean a system that would not exhaust the finite resources of the planet necessary for the survival of human and non-human life, and would not generate pollution and contamination at levels that make the planet unlivable. In the short term, US society can continue only if people in other parts of the world are consuming far less.

More than a fifth of the world's people still live in abject poverty (under $1 a day), and about half live below the barely more generous standard of $2 a day; at least half the world cannot meet basic expenditures for food, clothing, shelter, health, and education. The sources of poverty, like the causes of most social/political phenomena, are complex. But at the heart of worldwide inequality today is the continued economic domination of the underdeveloped world by the developed world—with US trade, foreign and military policy square in the center of that system of domination. It is that system which allows us to consume as we do, and it is that system which helps keep the poor of the world poor. In some parts of that underdeveloped world that is changing. For example, as rapid economic growth continues in China, analysts describe a "great consumption rush," with Chinese consumers "increasingly spending on private vehicles, computers, mobile phones, property, insurance and securities" ("Consumer China 2004." *Euromonitor International*. 2004. <http://www.business-in-asia. com/china_consumer.html>). But the overall pattern of disparity does not change; someone must bear the cost of unsustainable affluence.

So, those of us serious about our ecological future and global justice have to face this question: What is a morally defensible level of consumption?

Many people avoid the question by arguing that the key to overcoming those threats and disparities is political change, not lifestyle changes by individuals. That's certainly true; large-scale economic and political changes to overcome the problems inherent in capitalism and nation-states are required. But that doesn't obscure the need for people to address the question at the personal level, for two reasons.

First, precisely because the ecological problems require large-scale, global solutions, people in the United States have to reduce their consumption. Why should anyone in the so-called developing world take serious any claims about the need for environmental regulation made by people in the industrial world? If we in the developed world show so little interest in curbing our own ravenously destructive habits, what standing do we have to preach to others? How can meaningful international solutions be reached when the industrial world shows so little interest in such change?

Second, it's clear that if we are serious about meaningful change, political movements and personal choices cannot be separated. Our willingness and ability to work on the big-picture politics flow in part from our personal connection to the question. On any issue, we are most effective in political organizing as our commitment and understanding deepen. On environmental questions, that deepening comes in part with honest self-assessment about our own life choices and willingness to act.

An analogy to the struggle for racial justice is helpful. In the 1950s in the United States it certainly was true that no serious progress on the problem of racism was possible without abolishing Jim Crow laws and providing meaningful guarantees of voting rights for non-white people. But did that mean that anti-racist white people should have ignored the ways in which they engaged in racist behavior, perhaps unconscious and subtle, in their personal lives until those political changes were in place? Would we have accepted from politically active white people the claim that until the Voting Rights and Civil Rights acts were passed, personal behavior didn't matter? Or that once those laws were passed, that's all that white people need worry about? Of course not. We would point out that a real commitment to racial justice means that white people have to engage in self-criticism and commit to changing their attitudes and behavior, along with the pursuit of political change at the societal level. In such arenas, no one suggests it is acceptable to ignore accountability for personal behavior while pursuing political goals.

So, we return to the question: What is a morally defensible level of consumption?

The answer can't be that, until there is justice and equity, we should all consume at the level of the poorest on the planet. The poorest in the world live in misery and starve, and no one can be expected to adopt a lifestyle that leads to impoverishment and eventual death. Neither is it feasible to ask people to live at a bare subsistence level, the minimum needed to survive. Even if people were willing to do it, we couldn't be effective politically living at such a level. Perhaps if we all knew that we would face such a life unless economic and political change happened immediately, it would be a powerful motivator. But that is not the world in which we live.

In a complex world, there can be no easy answer to this question. But that doesn't mean we have nothing to say about the search for answers. Instead, we can look to common ethical principles for guidance. One of those is the assertion that we should treat others as we would like to be treated, a claim that shows up consistently in human thought and in religious teachings:

> None of you truly believes until he wishes for his brother what he wishes for himself (Islam).

> Do unto others as you would have them do unto you (Christianity).

> Act only on that maxim that you can will a universal law (the secular philosophy of Kant).

That concept easily could be extended to questions involving resources: Consume at that level which could be generalized to all other people. That is, the morally appropriate level of consumption is one that, if all people in the world lived at that level, life on the planet would be sustainable indefinitely.

Obviously, the sustainable level of consumption depends on the size of the human population. The current population of six billion will rise in the near future, perhaps as high as ten billion by the year 2100, barring catastrophe. Also relevant is the future of technological developments that might make more efficient and less polluting use of resources. But for purposes of this discussion, absolute precision is not required on either issue. The question of a sustainable level of consumption cannot be answered with great clarity. Instead, the goal is to assess where we stand today, and understand the direction in which me must move, with some sense of the urgency of the task. We can assume the population will continue to grow in the short term, and that whatever advances in technology lie before us they won't solve all our problems.

So, what we can say with confidence is that all the people of the world cannot live at the level of Donald Trump. A world of over six billion Donald Trumps is not sustainable.

For those of us who aren't Donald Trump, that may at first seem reassuring; it's easy to focus on the most outrageous consumers as the problem. But it's equally true that the middle-class US lifestyle also is not generalizable to the whole world. Take the simple issue of automobiles. Klaus Toepfer, head of the UN Environment Program, has made the point that China's aim of quadrupling its economy by 2020 can only occur if developed nations radically change their consumption habits to free up scarce resources for the world's poor. If China had the same density of private cars as a developed country like Germany, Toepfer said, it would have to produce 650 million vehicles, which the world's supply of metal and oil would be unable to sustain.

So, if we were to apply a golden rule of consumption (consume at a level that, if applied throughout the world, would allow all people a decent life consistent with long-term sustainability), we have to get rid of some of our cars. Actually, lots of our cars, and not just the SUVs. Again, it's easy to point at the most wasteful of the vehicles on the road, but the real problem is the number of vehicles out there and the transportation system in which they exist. The owner of a fuel-efficient small car is every bit as implicated in this as the driver of the gas-hog.

So, should everyone who owns a car stop driving? That certainly would improve the health of the planet, but it's not feasible immediately in a culture designed around individual car travel. Many people live in circumstances that make it impossible to maintain family, work, and social commitments without a car.

That means that large-scale change is necessary, most obviously the development of mass transit and the redesign of cities to make them less auto-dependent. But that doesn't mean that as we work for those changes, there is nothing individuals can do. Here's a short list:

- Do not buy an auto if it is feasible to live without one
- If one has to use an auto, create a car cooperative with others to share a vehicle
- As a member of a family unit, maintain the least number of vehicles possible
- Buy the smallest and most fuel-efficient car possible
- Use a car only when necessary, substituting walking, biking, or public transportation whenever possible

To be clear: My argument is not that everyone is morally compelled to spend all their time pondering and taking action to lower one's consumption. We do not live under conditions of our own making, and if we want to participate in the culture in a way that allows us to be politically effective, then no one can claim a position of purity. The question we should ask is not, "Have you met THE standard set down by some arbitrary authority?" but instead "Are you willing to confront the problem and make good-faith attempts to move in the right direction?"

If anyone doubts that our direction must be toward far less consumption, visit the website <http://www.myfootprint.org/> and run through the quick survey. Using the concept of the "ecological footprint"—assessing how much of the world it takes to support one's lifestyle—the quiz graphically illustrates just how far most of us are from a just and sustainable level. (For more detail on the concept of the footprint, go to <http://www.rprogress.org/programs/sustainability/ef/>.)

The reality is that, even in progressive circles where people are generally aware of the severity of the problem, many people have not taken these questions seriously. As "sacrifices" go, that simple list of actions concerning cars is trivial, yet I know many people who think of themselves as politically progressive but have not considered any of them (perhaps beyond looking at the gas mileage figures when they buy a car).

Left/radical/progressive politics is always a process of destruction and creation. We are arguing that certain systems (capitalism, imperialism) have to be destroyed, while at the same time we struggle to articulate and, where possible, create the alternatives. In that process, each of us will have different contributions to make, depending on background, temperament, circumstance, and constantly changing contingencies. For some people actively engaged in political organizing, for example, these kinds of day-to-day choices may seem less important. But we all need to confront the choices. Humans have well-developed rationalization skills; we are gifted at finding ways of convincing ourselves of the irrefutable truth of what we want to believe. Those of us actively engaged with movements for social justice have a responsibility to resist that.

No matter how many times I emphasize that I am not arguing that there is a magic formula we can use to set an appropriate level of consumption, some will assert that is my goal. Often people tell me, "Oh, you just think everyone should live like you do." That is not my contention, if for no other reason that I have not yet reached a level of consumption that meets this golden-rule standard.

I think the motivation behind such a seemingly deliberate misreading often is fear. As members of an affluent culture, the vast majority of us have become used to living with the creature comforts of that affluence, at whatever level we exist, and we typically like it. In many cases, we have become lazy (I certainly can see that in my own life). And knowing that the affluence is based on the unsustainable exploitation of natural resources and the unjust exploitation of vulnerable people in other parts of the world (as well as less privileged classes at home) can be difficult to live with. One coping mechanism is to ignore it. For the political reasons already outlined, I think that is a bad choice.

But there also is a personal cost to ignoring these difficult issues. It is my experience that when I have wrestled with these kinds of questions (such as becoming vegetarian, for both moral and ecological reasons; or giving up a car for an extended period; or in general reducing my participation in the mall-based culture of consumption), I have benefited immensely, both from the process of coming to the decision and the ramifications of the decision. I like life as a vegetarian better than as a meat-eater. I am a happier and healthier person when I ride a bicycle to work. I feel liberated in not buying things that people all around me clamor to buy.

But those decisions don't get me off the hook. Although I don't eat meat, I still eat dairy products, and I struggle daily with that decision. The honorable example set by a friend who is vegan reminds me of the importance of taking it to the next level. During the period when I didn't own a car, I rented or borrowed a car to travel for political events, but I also sometimes used those vehicles for personal trips that were purely a matter of convenience; since buying a car I still sometimes do that. A friend who walks virtually everywhere reminds me of how I fall short in this area. Although I stay away from the mall, I still eat out (a wasteful way to eat, given the way in which food is prepared in contemporary restaurants) more than I need to. A friend who grows and cooks his own food reminds me of that failure of mine.

I could produce a long list of my own choices that create such conflict in me every day, and along with that a list of people I know who do better at me in the struggle to consume less. Their examples force me to face my own shortcomings. But I am grateful for them and what they freely offer— the gift of making me uncomfortable, for it is that sense of being uncomfortable with my choices that pushes me to struggle with these issues.

At some point, the entire culture is going to have to face these questions. For politically progressive people, it is crucial that we not shy away from those questions now. There need be no imposition of right answers, but there must be an honest conversation, with a willingness to engage in self-criticism and be accountable to others. Such conversations will often be difficult and sometimes quite painful—as are conversations about how well white people are living true to anti-racist principles, or how well men are living true to feminist principles. Their difficulty does not give us the right to ignore the issues.

After reading an article of mine about the American empire, a woman wrote to me recently and said that she could see the importance of the underlying question about our consumption. She asked me a simple question: If I want to be part of a movement for global justice, do I have to give up my house? By the tone and content of her email, I assumed she was a middle-class person with a comfortable house that was bigger than she needed, a house that wouldn't meet the golden-rule test. To be part of the movement against US imperialism and for global justice, do folks have to give up these houses?

In the short term, the answer is no. There is much political work to be done, and running out today to sell off the bigger-than-needed house likely isn't the answer. But one has to acknowledge that if there is to be global justice, we can't live in these big houses indefinitely.

Some might say: That's easy for you to say; you probably don't live in a house. That's true; I live in a one-bedroom apartment and don't have to worry about giving up my house. But if I am to be honest, I have to worry about giving up my apartment. If I am serious about striving to live at a level that could be applied to all the people of the world and be sustainable, my one-bedroom apartment—though admittedly rather dumpy—is a luxury. I have my own refrigerator, which sits there gobbling up electricity all day. I take a hot shower every morning. When the Texas heat becomes uncomfortable, I can switch on the air conditioning. Most of the people of the world do not have those things, and it's not at all clear we could live sustainably if everyone in the world had a separate apartment with those luxuries.

We all are implicated. We all have to struggle. It won't be easy for any of us. It can be hard even to imagine how we as a species are going to find our way out of this mess.

But it is not an all-or-nothing scenario. The only thing worse than struggling with it imperfectly is to abandon the struggle altogether. Then not only will we have failed in our moral obligation to the rest of life on the planet, but we will have failed ourselves.

Contesting the Economic Order and Media Construction of Reality

Lauren E. Eastwood

"The nature of consumption at this precarious moment needs to be
re-cognized—seen again and thought anew—in such a manner that
its inseparability from nature becomes every bit as explicit as its deep
entanglement with politics, the economy and culture" (Pred, 151).

2004—the year of "An American Revolution." So claims the recent ad
campaign of the Chevrolet automobile company. While the use of "progressive" rhetoric to market products is not new, it represents one of the
significant mechanisms whereby the general public is convinced not to
contest the social and environmental costs associated with the production
of goods in this current phase of capitalism. Indeed, there are strong mechanisms that undermine the ability to draw the link between consumption
and environmental degradation. Articulating some of these mechanisms
allows us to begin to think through the ways in which current dynamics of
global capitalism necessitates an indoctrinated and "mediated" public.

That consumption is political is not a new argument. The anti-sweat-
shop movement, for example, has made apparent many of the human
costs of the current mobility of capital that is known as "globalization."
The argument that I wish to make in this essay takes up a slightly different
point. Not only have the connections between the environment, politics,
and consumption been minimized, glossed over, or simply made invisible,
but activities and ideologies which have the potential to contest the current economic order are likewise significantly diffused by the media. In
order for the current economic order to be upheld, we must be complicit in
the process of capital accumulation. Our complicity is, in part, constructed
through the mass media—both through advertising and through the lack
of reporting on social movements which contest the negative repercussions of globalization and environmental destruction.

The Current Economic Order

The 1980s and 90s saw the emergence of what is now known as "globalization"—the setting in place of institutions and ideologies that sup-

114

port the mobility of capital across the constructed borders of nation states. During this period, economies were "adjusted" by multilateral organizations such as the World Bank, international trade policies, such as the General Agreement on Tariff and Trade, were negotiated, and domestic polices, such as US welfare and environmental policies, were "reformed" to reflect the tenets of neoliberal economics.

The primacy of capital mobility has not come without human, animal, and environmental costs. From the Exxon Valdez oil spill and the Bhopal chemical disaster, to habitat destruction and the everyday local cases of toxic emissions that have spurred the emergence of the environmental justice movement, we can find no shortage of examples of the tension between the exigencies of industry on the one hand, and social and environmental welfare on the other. This economic order is upheld, in spite of its severe environmental and social repercussions, by a fairly complacent public. Potential critiques of the current economic order are diffused—partly through advertising's reconfiguration of potentially progressive language, and partly through the non-reporting in the news of activities which, in fact, challenge the status quo. The result is the manufacture of a public that is ignorant of current and ongoing struggles to make social change, and that can feel—based on the ways in which advertising takes up a progressive rhetoric—as though it is being transgressive when it is merely engaging in the process of consuming products.

Advertising and the Hijacking of Language

A key current example of this use of progressive language in the selling of products can be found in Chevrolet's "An American Revolution" campaign. Unlike, for example, the Bolivian revolution of October 2003, during which disenfranchised peasants and indigenous peoples rose up against a government willing to sell off Bolivia's natural resources at the expense of the poor, the "American Revolution" of Chevrolet's advertising campaign was instigated by the ruling capitalist class, and not the marginalized masses. Whereas standard US news outlets largely ignored the Bolivian revolution, one need only have access to billboards, television commercials, and a range of other advertising venues to be well aware of this "American Revolution." The ads depict very little text, with the exception of the slogan and images of the re-designed Chevy vehicles.

Revolutionary this is not. Even from a technological standpoint, the automobile has seen minimal reform over the last century since its invention, much less radical or "revolutionary" change. Regardless, the appropriation of the rhetoric of "revolution" by Chevrolet to characterize what is primarily an aesthetic alteration to its products, is part and parcel of the current context of neoliberal capitalism. While examples of the incorporation of progressive language into the marketing of products abound, the Chevrolet advertising campaign represents one of the more recent and egregious capturing of the language of change for the purpose of maintaining the status quo.

Rendering the politically-charged language of "revolution" reactionary, is made possible by the coupling of the term "revolution" with a call to consume. Through advertising, consumers are increasingly expected to associate "reality" with fantasy. While advertising has always presented a fantastic image of products and people, the age of "reality TV" stands as one example of the effectiveness of the blurring of fantasy and reality. Despite the fact that, on some level, viewers are aware that "reality" shows are crafted and constructed with a cast that is carefully chosen, and methodical editing of scenes prior to access by the viewer, the guise of "reality" is preserved through deliberate production mechanisms. In fact, one could make the argument that these shows are no more "real" or "artificial" than any other television production, such as national or local news. Rather than creating a production that is self-consciously constructed (i.e. not "real"), what is being produced through media-forms such as reality TV and "fake news,"[1] is the very construction of the "real."

This marks an age in which consumers have largely stopped questioning the fantastic world of the media—creating a condition that French post-modern theorist Jean Baudrillard terms "hyperreal." With the hyperreal, the fantasy or the simulation has superseded reality, and the distinction between illusion and reality, truth and falsehood, is irrevocably blurred. As Baudrillard describes,

> [a]bstraction today is no longer that of the map, the double, the mirror or the concept. Simulation is no longer that of a territory, a referential being or a substance. It is the generation by models of a real without origin or reality: a hyperreal. The territory no longer precedes the map, nor survives it. Henceforth, it is the map that precedes the territory—precession of simulacra—it is the map that engenders the territory (166).

In the world of the hyperreal, advertisers can utilize the fabricated reality, and a morphing of a rhetoric of change with a call to consume, to help generate a willing consumer who is complicit in the machinations of capital fluidity.

Indeed, the application of the terminology of "revolution" in the context of its association with a call to continued mass consumption signals an upping of the political ante. As capitalism continues to produce its discontents, it must take on and re-configure the very political and moral vocabulary that (formerly) signified a possible critique of its excesses and injustices. The coalescence of labor, environmental, and social justice movements that are leveling a concerted critique of global capitalism—such as that evidenced in the protests against the 1999 meeting of the World Trade Organization (WTO) in Seattle—represents a new terrain that has to be taken on by those who benefit from the complicity of mass society in the maintenance of the status quo. However, organized resistance to the vestiges of capitalist production and consumption, such as the concerted campaigns against genetically modified agricultural products, indicates that, while the goods are being proffered through ever more sophisticated networks, markets, and media, some are quite literally not buying it.

Advertising: Reassuring the (Potentially) Concerned Consumer

For decades, businesses have been constructing an image of corporate responsibility and environmental awareness through costly public relations campaigns (Karliner, Stauber and Rampton, 1995, 2002). The "green" corporation or environmentally "friendly" product depicted through advertising has been rivaled recently by the construction of the corporation as "family" or "corporate citizen." These moves are clearly responses to some level of consumer understanding of the negative environmental and social consequences of mass production and consumption. In fact, research indicates that negative public sentiment about Chevron as a corporation was transformed by Chevron's "People Do" campaign. While the ads were largely misrepresentations of Chevron's environmental concern and activities, consumers were convinced by the images proffered in the campaign (Karliner, 172–74).

The pervasiveness of this type of advertising campaign speaks to the fact that capitalism requires that consumers *not* be concerned about the environmental degradation and social costs caused by corporations in the process of producing goods. The economic order is, in part, upheld by savvy advertising campaigns designed to assure the consumer that his or her participation in the systems of mass production and consumption are, indeed, not harmful to the environment, animals, and/or humans.

Wal-Mart's television commercials exemplify this dynamic. Rather than focusing on particular products or their prices, Wal-Mart advertises happy employees who meld a sense of family and self-worth into their understandings of work. This stands in stark contrast to the testimonials of Wal-Mart employees that have emerged in recent legal battles. It also contradicts the research that indicates that Wal-Mart's impact on communities is destructive to the very values and comforts being marketed in the commercials (Mander and Boston, 1996).

In commercials such as these, we see not only what the corporation wants the consumer to think about the product, but, additionally, a palatable image of the corporation being marketed to the consumer. Capitalism requires that people feel as though their consumption is not harmful to communities, the environment, or themselves. In facilitating the construction of this mythology, the power of advertising should not be downplayed. As Baudrillard argues,

> those who pooh-pooh the ability of advertising and of the mass media in general to condition people have failed to grasp the peculiar logic upon which the media's efficacy reposes. For this is not a logic of propositions and proofs, but a logic of fables and of the willingness to go along with them. We do not believe in

such fables, but we cleave to them nevertheless. Basically, the "demonstration" of a product convinces no one, but it does serve to rationalize its purchase, which in any case either precedes or overwhelms all rational motives (1993, 404).

Thus, the terminology of revolution is associated, as in the Chevrolet ads, with a "new look" rather than with systemic social and political change. History and politics become hyperreal in the distorted perception of the consumer. However, this confusion is not an isolated experience. If it were only advertising where re-configurations of the meanings of resistance were taking place, then the effectiveness could be minimal. Instead, the connection between buying new cars and engaging in "revolutionary" activity is constructed in the context of a society which relies on consumerism as a fundamental tenet, purports to uphold values of individual gain and private property above most other values, and vilifies acts of resistance to the established economic order.

The Treadmill of Production

"Get out and contribute to the economy. As my wife said, 'It has never been more patriotic to go shopping.'" *Alex Pemelas, Miami-Dade County Mayor, speaking at a news conference shortly after the September 11 attacks on the World Trade Center (Vardy).*

As was clearly demonstrated in official responses to the economic slump following the terrorist attacks on the World Trade Center of September 11, 2001, US culture is closely aligned with consumerism. Miami-Dade County Mayor Pemelas' sentiments, quoted above, were publicly reiterated in a concerted effort by heads of state such as Blair, Bush, and Chrétien (Vardy 2001). With the heightened emphasis on hyper-consumption, even the classic American Dream has been transformed over the past couple of decades. Whereas attaining the American Dream once meant having the capacity for a suburban life with the trappings of middle-class status, it has moved to the level of hyper-consumption in terms of its associations with compulsive buying, conspicuous consumption, and attaining excessive wealth. In reality, however, ever fewer people can attain anything approaching the consumer fantasies as the gap between rich and poor widens and the bottom drops out of the middle class, who work harder for less.

Allan Schnaiberg's analysis (1980) of the systemic nature of production and consumption is a useful analytic framework for drawing out the complexities that are glossed over in many analyses of consumption. Standard treatments of consumption tend to see it as related only to individual wants and desires. The primary assumption is that the rational individual engages in the market by making logical decisions within budgetary constraints. The consumption process, however, has little to do with the fiction of rational choice and far more to do with psychological manipulation, and systemic and structural issues which constrain consumer choice.

Capital accumulation relies not only on the production of goods, but also, as was mentioned above in reference to Wal-Mart's campaigns, on the production of the willing consumer. According to Schnaiberg, and contrary to common consumerist rhetoric, "needs" are constructed and produced through advertising. Schnaiberg and Gould's use of the term "treadmill of production" is particularly apt here (1994). In this term, Schnaiberg and Gould intend to encapsulate how the process of production and consumption—rather than being a function of the rational actions and choices—is instead deeply connected to larger social relations that extend beyond the individual actor. For example, in looking at how modern US society has taken up the three "R"s of "reduce, reuse, and recycle," it is apparent that the only one of the three that gets implemented in any meaningful way is "recycle." This is due to the fact that to "reduce" or "reuse" interrupts the process of production and consumption, whereas recycling maintains productive and consumptive activity. Understanding our society as being deeply wedded to the ideology of the treadmill of production, whereby the production process must not be interrupted, allows us to question the existence of the individual actor in the marketplace. We can begin to analyze such fictions as producer autonomy in addition to consumer choice. Planned obsolescence of products (for example, the emergence of new technology such as the DVD to replace the VCR), the collusion of government with industry (in terms of tax laws and weakening environmental legislation), and other structural decisions which have implications for "consumer choice" can be integrated back into the analysis once we move away from the mythology of the autonomous individual and recognize the ways in which consumption and production are fundamentally social construction processes.

A key example of this kind of analysis can be applied to the automobile. While the car is often presented as central to US identity, and our landscape and culture is clearly marked by its ubiquity, the history of how this dominance came to be is not part of the lore. We are presented with the guise of "consumer choice" through the staging of various models, colors, upholstery, and other largely aesthetic choices. However, questions are rarely asked regarding why we are not given a range of personal transportation choices, or why the choices we do have are not less harmful to the environment, communities, or personal safety. As with many of our social or environmental problems, the causes are chalked up to individual decisions ("too many people driving," "we love our cars," and so on), rather than to problems revealed by the structural analysis of profit and mass production imperatives of the automobile industry.

Most US citizens do not know that General Motors, Firestone Tire, Standard Oil, Phillips Petroleum, and Mack Truck colluded to buy up efficient and popular urban trolley systems in the 1930s and 1940s with the express purpose of rendering them inoperable, and replacing them with buses. That these facts are not common knowledge contributes to the effectiveness of the mythology that individual choice precipitates the serious problems we have with automobiles today. Problems ranging from traffic jams and pollution, urban and suburban sprawl, and habitat destruction, to foreign oil dependency, oil wars, and geopolitical conflicts. Additionally, the myth of consumer sovereignty is undermined by the fact that the automobile industry has lobbied, not only to expand the highway system (at the cost of urban communities nationwide, which are bisected by four to six-lane highways), but also to oppose regulations on automobile fuel efficiency. Indeed, in this context, the fact that the term "An American Revolution" is copyrighted by an automobile industry is significant. The choices that we actually have as consumers—such as what color or shape we want our current car to be—are trivial. We are not allowed the space to think about, and advocate for, alternative transportation choices—choices which might reflect our concerns about our communities and our environment.

(Non)Reporting of Potentially Disruptive Activities

The constructed sense of reality in which hyper-consumption is disconnected from its environmental and social implications is carefully created through mass media in general, and not only through advertising. What additionally serves to uphold this sense of reality is the lack of popular reporting on activities, movements, and individuals who contest the repercussions of the current economic order. Furthermore, when such individuals or movements *are* treated in the popular press, their actions and motivations tend to remain disconnected from the larger political issues. Rather than being portrayed as reacting to the negative repercussions of processes of production and consumption, movements which contest the current economic order are represented as isolated and misdirected, a tactic that renders these larger political projects nearly invisible. As Eduardo Galeano argued of the 1960s,

> [t]he human murder by poverty in Latin America is secret; every year, without making a sound, three Hiroshima bombs explode over communities that have become accustomed to suffering with clenched teeth. This systematic violence is not apparent but is real and constantly increasing; its holocausts are not made known in the sensational press but in Food and Agricultural Organization statistics (15).

This sense of reality has implications for media stereotypes of activists contesting the WTO, for example, and for the absence of reporting such activities as those that took place in Bolivia in October of 2003. The discursive terrain is such that particular actions—those which support the current economic order—are deemed logical, rational, and laudable, while those actions and ideologies which contest neoliberal economic imperatives are made invisible, distorted, or rendered illogical and irrational in their representation. The confluence of advertising and popular representations of radical actions that contest the economic order creates a situation in which the complexities of actions are glossed over or distorted. Real revolutions or revolutionary actions and ideologies become invisible or unclear, while artificial ones are plastered in our view. It is within this context that *Time Magazine* can not only name George W. Bush "2004 Person of the Year," but can furthermore dub him as an "American Revolutionary" (*TIME Magazine*, front cover, December 27, 2004).

Clearly, as Pred indicates in the quotation which begins this essay, corporations and media have orchestrated in the public mind a disconnect between hyper-consumption and environmental degradation. While we recognize, on some level, that our consumerist society has environmental repercussions, the official policy of the United States, in terms of environmental degradation, is to place it as secondary to the economy. Likewise, the amassing of capital in the current stage of the building of empire has been disconnected from its human, animal, and environmental effects. The fact remains that current extractive industries and our fossil fuel-based economy, which emphasizes capital gain as the primary value over other concerns (environmental, labor, or human and animal rights) has devastating impacts on the environment and on people who are either incorporated as resources into the amassing of capital or who are least able to afford to avoid environmental degradation. As with past eras of empire building, the current phase of hyper-consumption necessitates environmental degradation. The connections between the "American Revolution" in terms of our automobile-based culture, for example, global warming, ever-expanding fossil fuel exploration, and the regular spilling of oil, to name just a few environmental costs, need to be re-instated. Additionally, expanding "the environment" to take on indigenous cosmologies (Churchill; Deloria) necessitates that we re-cognize (in Pred's terms) the ways in which particular humans have been incorporated as resources into treadmill of production under the rubric of the primacy of capital.

Revolutionary Activities: A Potential Window into the Repercussions of Capital Accumulation

> "Our clean waters are clouded with silt and the wastes of the white man; Mother Earth is being ravaged and squandered. To the Navajo people it seems as if these Europeans hate everything in nature....To Navajos, land was something no one could possess, any more than he could possess the air. Land is sacred to the Navajos...because it is the mother of all living. To the whites, this is paganism as well as communistic, and it has to be eradicated." *Fred Johnson, founding member of the Coalition for Navajo Liberation, speaking to the US Civil Rights Commission in 1974 (Quoted in Grinde and Johansen, 130–31)*

Occasionally, we are allowed glimpses of opportunities to begin to make the connections between the treadmill of production and its human and environmental costs. The response of corporate media to such opportunities is not surprising given the media's collusion with capital accumulation in this current phase of globalization. Rather than making the connections between hyper-consumption, environmental degradation, and human and animal rights violations clear, the popular media engages in several tactics which serve to maintain the invisibility of the connections between the way our current economic order is structured and the environmental and human casualties of this order. One tactic is to represent those individuals who contest the economic order as "terrorist," "rebel," or, as Fred Johnson aptly observes above, "communist." This latter term has been used to discredit movements that resist the impoverishment of Latin America by foreign interests. As Galeano argues,

> Latin America is a region of open veins. Everything, from the discovery until our times, has always been transmuted into European—or later United States—Capital, and as such has accumulated in distant centers of power (12).

This systemic impoverishment of Latin America has not gone uncontested. However, those who argue for the poor, including those who have used Liberation Theology to do so, have been labeled "communist" (Bonpane 2000). This has served not only to discredit the motives of individuals who have been fighting systematic oppression, but has also served to justify the use of military force (supported by the United States) to remove democratically elected leaders from power and to suppress popular movements.

As with information regarding the history of the automobile in the United States, the facts of US involvement in Latin American politics have not been readily available to the general public. These facts are inconsistent with the self-image of most US citizens as members of a superpower which is organized around spreading democracy and its partner, capitalism, across the globe. However, as Galeano argues, "[t]he more freedom is extended to business, the more prisons have to be built for those who suffer from that business" (Galeano, 11). The lived reality of those who experience the negative repercussions of "free trade" stands in stark contrast to its rhetorical association with "democracy."

It is this lived reality that came into the (limited) public eye in Chiapas, Mexico, on January 1, 1994, when the Zapatista Army of National Liberation (EZLN) "declared war on the Mexican Army, and launched the first post-Communist, post-modern, anti-neoliberal uprising in the Americas" (Ross, 4). This is true revolutionary activity in that those involved in the Zapatista movement have consistently recognized the effects of the imperatives and machinations of the economic order on their communities. This activity's timing in Chiapas speaks to this dynamic, in that the movement was designed to mark official resistance to the North American Free Trade Agreement—which was to go into effect on 1 January, 1994. Prior to the revolutionary activities of 1994, the EZLN publicly demonstrated on October 12, 1992, "to mark 500 years of heroic resistance by the indigenous peoples of the continent against would-be European conquest" (Ross, 7). The communiqués from the EZLN have indicated a strong resistance to the current economic order, as well as a very sophisticated comprehension of how the basis of this economic order has relied on the labor and blood of indigenous and other marginalized peoples of Latin America for the past 500 years.

The response by the investment community to EZLN activities is telling. The following statement of the Chase Manhattan Bank's "Emerging Markets Group," points to the primacy of capital over human rights or environmental costs:

> While Chiapas, in our opinion, does not pose a fundamental threat to Mexican political stability, it is perceived to be so by many in the investment community. The government will need to eliminate the Zapatistas to demonstrate their effective control of the national territory and security policy (quoted in Silverstein and Cockburn, 1).

This knowledge of the repercussions of the workings of current global capital, which is intimately held by those involved in the Zapatista (and other revolutionary) movements in Latin America, is not part of typical US reality. Instead, we continue to engage in the "hyperreal," and consume both images and products which uphold and justify the current economic order.

While the Zapatista critique of global neoliberal capitalism has received some press space, the movement itself is relatively unknown to the majority of US citizens. This is not necessarily the case with the actions of another organization that can be seen as contesting the current economic order. Actions that are attributed to the Earth Liberation Front (ELF) have received far more popular media attention than the revolutionary activities of the Zapatistas. In part, this is due to the domestic (US) location of these activities. However, the nature of the activities also strikes a particular chord with "American" values. The torching of SUVs or suburban developments, for example, hits precisely at one of the values that Americans hold dear—private property. The destruction of private property associated with ELF activities has been duly reported in the mass media. What we are lacking, however, is a forum for discussing the complexity of the issues wrapped up in all of ELF's targets. For example, not only do all of the targets represent opulence and hyper-consumption (both of which appear to be supported by most US citizens), but they also represent fascinating examples of the collusion of government and industry that have actually resulted in a reduction of consumer autonomy. The lack of discussion of this latter dynamic upholds the continued guise of consumer choice, when in reality (from biotechnology to the suburbanization of the United States) a complex array of decisions—decisions which serve to diminish consumer choice—have been made by a few individuals in powerful corporations. As with the automobile, we are presented—through advertising and a general rhetoric of individual autonomy in the market—with the illusion of choice, individual power, and venues for democratic participation in society and politics. As Baudrillard suggests,

> advertising's careful omission of objective processes and the social history of objects is simply a way of making it easier, by means of the imagination as a social agency, to impose the *real* order of production and exploitation (406).

Without a structural analysis of the ways in which our choices and desires—the desire to lead more environmentally friendly lifestyles, for example—are greatly constrained by decisions that are made outside of the public realm, we are left only with the explanation that "terrorists" torched SUVs or suburban homes. While this very well may be a media-ready reality, without a discussion of the historical and political complexities of consumption and expansion of production in the United States, we are not able to have complex discussions about the reality we would like to create—a reality that might better reflect our concerns about environmental degradation, destruction of habitat and species, and the human costs of capital accumulation.

Conclusions: From "Hyperreality" Back to "Reality"

When we begin to investigate the current terrain on which the consumption of media-ready images of "revolution" is taking place, we find a two-fold dynamic. On the one hand, we have the rhetoric of "revolution" deployed to sell automobiles, and on the other, we have the vilification or lack of analysis of activities which might be considered to be "revolutionary," or, if not revolutionary, at the very least pose a critique of the current economic order.

It is important to draw conceptual connections between the invisible hands of the media and the popular representations of those who contest the current economic order as "rebel," "terrorist," or "leftist/communist." Rather than representing those who challenge the economic order for what they potentially demonstrate about the current repercussions of capital accumulation, the dominant media's lack of reporting on actual revolutionary activities (such as the Zapatista's construction of autonomous zones in Mexico) demonstrates a need on the part of the general population to *not* know the ways in which we all participate, through our own consumption habits, in the degradation of the environment and the concomitant violation of human rights.

What is at stake is our ability to make informed decisions about foreign and domestic policy (policy-making processes in which we are largely uninvolved), as well as our participation in the treadmill of production. While the argument has been posited that "the media provide what the people want," the complicity of the media with capital accumulation and dominant ideologies calls this logic into question. As long as the media fail to draw more complex connections between world and local events, and the negative repercussions of capital accumulation, they are complicit in producing uninformed and compliant citizens.

While I am guessing that this is precisely the goal—as they themselves are powerful corporations and members of the ruling elite—this is not a seamless "hyperreal" enterprise without inherent conflicts and contradictions. The existence of those who contest the current economic order, either found in organized resistance, such as the Zapatista movement, or in individualized acts of resistance, signifies that there is, indeed, a "reality" beyond the carefully crafted world of advertising, hyper-consumption, and a complacent public.

Bibliography

Baudrillard, Jean. "Advertising." In *Social Theory: Roots and Branches*, 2nd Edition, edited by Peter Kivisto. Los Angeles: Roxbury Publishing Company, 1993.

___. "Simulacra and Simulations." In *Selected Writings*, 2nd Edition, edited by Mark Poster. Stanford: Stanford University Press, 1988.

Bonpane, Blase. *Guerrillas of Peace: Liberation Theology and the Central American Revolution*. New York: toExcel Press, 2000.

Churchill, Ward. *Struggle for the Land: Native North American Resistance to Genocide, Ecocide, and Colonization*. San Francisco: City Lights Books, 2002.

Deloria, Vine, Jr. *God is Red: A Native View of Religion*. Colorado: Fulcrum Publishing, 2003.

Galeano, Eduardo. *Open Veins of Latin America: Five Centuries of the Pillage of a Continent*. New York: Monthly Review Press, 1973.

Grinde, Donald and Bruce Johansen. *Ecocide of Native America: Environmental Destruction of Indian Lands and Peoples*. Santa Fe: Clear Light Publishers, 1995.

Karliner, Joshua. *The Corporate Planet: Ecology and Politics in the Age of Globalization*. San Francisco: Sierra Club Books, 1997.

Mander, K., and A. Boston. "Wal-Mart: A Global Retailer." In *The Case Against the Global Economy*, edited by J. Mander and E. Goldsmith. San Francisco: Sierra Club Books, 1996.

Pred, Allan. "The Nature of Denaturalized Consumption and Everyday Life." In *Remaking Reality: Nature at the Millenium*, edited by Bruce Braun and Noel Castree. New York: Routledge Press, 1998.

Ross, John. *The War Against Oblivion: The Zapatista Chronicles 1994–2000*. Philadelphia: Common Courage Press, 2000.

Schnaiberg, Allan. *The Environment: From Surplus to Scarcity*. New York: Oxford University Press, 1980.

Schnaiberg, Allan and Kenneth Gould. *Environment and Society: The Enduring Conflict*. New York: St. Martin's Press, 1994.

Silverstein, Ken and Alexander Cockburn. "Major US Bank Urges Zapatista Wipe-Out: 'A litmus test for Mexico's stability,'" *Counterpunch* Vol 2, No 3, (February 1, 1995).

Stauber, John and Sheldon Rampton. *Toxic Sludge is Good For You: Lies, Damn Lies, and the Public Relations Industry*. Maine: Common Courage Press, 1995.

___. *Trust Us, We're Experts: How Industry Manipulates Science and Gambles with Your Future*. US: Penguin Putnam Press, 2002.

Vardy, Jill. "Shopping is Patriotic, Leaders Say." *National Post*, Canada. 28 Sept. 2001.

Notes

1. "Fake news" employs pre-packaged news stories that look like "news," but in fact are corporate propaganda fictions produced by a PR firm. These stories are sent to local and national outlets who typically run the entire package without commentary on its pseudo-status. For examples and analysis of fake news, see Stauber and Rampton (1995, 2002) and the Center for Media and Democracy <http://www.prwatch.org/nofakenews>.

The Revolution in Everyday Life[1]

Adam Weissman

Revolutionary environmentalism? Overthrowing capitalism? Smashing the state? These phrases may inspire true believers, but to just about anyone else, they sound silly, sinister, or even insane. Most people in the United States see industrial capitalist civilization as a basic fact of life, the very mechanism of their survival. If revolutionary environmentalists ever hope to radically alter human society, we must do more than simply resist ecological destruction—we must demonstrate new and better ways to survive and thrive, as we actively begin to create a new and better world.

Ecological sabotage is a poetic expression of love for a living Earth, and resistance to the threat to its survival posed by a decadent, small-minded culture blinded by the empty promises of commodity and wealth-acquisition. Through this ecological propaganda of the deed, direct actionists expose the irrelevance of the petty laws that humans have created to enforce their illusory notions of ownership and property. Eco-saboteurs declare their independence from a ravenous, insatiable industrial civilization that will leave no stone unturned, no mineral deposit unmined, no oil reserve untapped, no rainforest unlogged where there is a dollar to be made; they swear an oath of loyalty to the countless lives that hinge on its destruction.

Attacking the machines, disobeying a culture that tells us to be apathetic in the face of atrocity, embracing the darkness, and striking in silence—these are romantic notions—but by the same token represent an incomplete model of resistance. This civilization has ensnared every aspect of our lives—its commodities and concepts shape our understanding of our world to the point where we come to believe that we cannot survive without them. Yet for all the hypocritical talk of "freedom" spouted by warmongering windbags, we are so weighted down with invisible chains that we don't know what it is to truly be free.

From our earliest years, we are indoctrinated by well-trained parents, television, toys, and foods marketed as toys. We spend 12 years in basic schooling where we learn obedience, conformity, and fear of authority. We learn that the system is larger than all of us and that we do not own our own lives. We learn that apathetic boredom is "maturity," and "good be-havior" must be accepted as the fundamental reality of everyday life. We learn of a limited range of options in how we live our lives. We may choose families or the single life, we may pursue a myriad of careers, we may decide to be suburbanites or city dwellers, but fundamentally, we are all workers and consumers and are led to believe that this cycle—generating capital through labor and expending it to acquire commodities—is a fun-damental and unavoidable reality of survival. As real as the need for food and warmth.

If the very civilization that is making earth unlivable is necessary for our survival, how can we ever stop the destruction? As important as it is that we act in defiance of unjust, hypocritical laws as we strike out against the worst abuses of the planet, it is equally critical that we resist this cul-ture's ownership of our daily lives and prove that our survival need not hinge on the destruction of the Earth.

Rather than investing all of our hopes in a future revolution, what if we could *immediately* demonstrate practical approaches to satisfying our fundamental needs outside of the framework of the worker-consumer lifestyle that has been presented to us as our only option in life? With ap-proaches that embody values in contrast to everything wrong with this society—ecological sustainability over consumptive excess, egalitarianism over hierarchy, cooperative community over competitive self-centeredness, justice over exploitation—we can create a new culture that can grow and inspire multitudes to limit their dependence on and identification with industrial capitalist society as we seek to build another, better world. Revo-lutionary environmentalism and social change, then, is reconceived so that in addition to large-scale institutional change in the future, we can begin a revolution in everyday life right now as we create new practices and in-stitutions for living our values. This essay offers numerous examples of an ongoing revolution in everyday life and a new world in the making.

Waste Recovery

Known as dumpster diving,[2] curb crawling,[3] trash trolling,[4] urban scavenging,[5] or just plain old garbage picking,[6] practitioners of the art of recovering useable resources from the waste of a hyperconsumptive so-ciety are able to dramatically curtail or altogether eliminate their need to purchase commodities.[7] Whether finding couches on the curbside; re-covering fresh, clean food from the dumpster of retailers; building librar-ies from discarded books; supplying kitchens with reclaimed appliances, plates, and silverware; creating wardrobes out of discarded clothing; or re-covering everything from replacement computer parts to entire systems,[8] foragers find that they rarely have to use money to acquire the items they need.[9] In the process, they reduce waste, limit their personal environmen-tal impact, curtail their economic complicity with the socially and ecologi-cally destructive multinational corporations responsible for the creation of most consumer goods, relieve the pressure to work two or three jobs to make ends meet, and avoid funding corrupt, militaristic governments by limiting their contribution to sales and income taxes.[10] In rural areas, gleaners harvest fruits and vegetables spilled and left behind by inefficient industrial farming practices.[11]

Urban scavenging is a key component in renewing community around the principle of mutual aid.[12] Many urban foragers recover goods in groups. Some use recovered food for communal meals,[13] sometimes in communal living spaces. Scavengers frequently point each other to reliable sites to recover useable goods.

For many, urban scavenging is rooted in "freeganism," an ethic of economic non-participation in the conventional consumer economy. The term is a response and light jab at the concept of veganism, a lifestyle based on refusing to purchase and use products made from animals, their secretions, and products tested on animals.[14] Freegans, by contrast, focus on eliminating—to the best of their ability—ALL consumer purchases from their lives, recognizing that industrial, capitalist mass-production is responsible for injustice, exploitation, and environmental destruction even in the case of products that don't come to the retail shelf by way of the slaughterhouse or animal testing lab.[15]

Freegans recognize that products that are "socially responsible" in some ways, are often exploitative in others.[16] Bananas,[17] coffee,[18] and chocolate[19] are vegan in the sense that they aren't made from animals or their secretions, but they are hardly "cruelty-free" or even "animal friendly." The standard corporate model for producing these commodities involves clearcutting wildlife-rich rainforests to create plantations, heavy spraying with toxic insecticides, and severe exploitation of peasant farm workers. Discarding the myth that we cannot survive without buying, freegans embrace a myriad of alternative survival strategies.

Food Not Bombs

Food Not Bombs (FNB) is a global grassroots movement founded to challenge the waste of massive military spending in a world where hundreds of millions are starving.[20] Over 200 FNB chapters on six continents recover food that would otherwise go to waste—either foraged or donated by retailers who would discard it. With these foods, they prepare hot, wholesome, vegetarian meals to share on streets and in parks. Rather than "serving the poor," FNB shares food with ANYONE who wants to eat, shucking the paternalistic notion of charity for the unfortunate, and instead promoting the idea that we can share and help one another as equals without a profit incentive. While our society, for the most part, accepts that giving to the destitute and desperate is admirable, challenging the assumption that we should expect payment from those who can afford to pay for what we give them is subversive.[21]

Wild Foraging

Humans began as a species of plant foragers—in anthropological terms, we have only recently adopting hunting and agriculture as means to provide food. Seeking to recapture this ancient and sustainable means of sustenance, some are rediscovering traditional wild foods and medicinal herbs. In the New York City area, naturalist Steve Brill leads tours in local parks introducing urbanites and suburbanites to edible and medicinal wild plants and mushrooms. Books like Brill's *The Wild Vegetarian Cookbook*, videos like Brill's *Foraging with the "Wildman*," and zines like *Wildroots' Feral Forager: A Guide to Living off of Nature's Bounty* are helping to widely disseminate this information, germinating a new culture of wild foraging, even in heavily urbanized areas.[22]

Rewilding

While some practice wild foraging in the contexts of fairly urbanized lives, others go further, adopting a primal, wilderness-based existence—living in birch bark lodges, building stone tools, cooking on an open fire, living in an interdependent community, and healing with traditional medicine and wild herbs. Many rewilders are anarcho-primitivists, believing that civilization and "progress" have been disasters for the earth and its human and nonhuman inhabitants, and that the most egalitarian and ecologically sustainable human lifestyle can be found in primitive cultures. Anarcho-primitivists seek to recapture this way of life, and view rewilders as pioneers of a return to ancient ways of living.[23] Sadly, many rewilders have embraced the killing of animals for food and clothing through hunting and trapping.[24]

Freecycle, Freemarkets, and Free Stores

Freecycle is a network of regional email lists where waste-conscious people post items they wish to give away, and individuals seeking to acquire items without purchasing them post the items they are looking for. Giver and receiver make contact over email and arrange to meet to transfer the item with no expectation of reciprocity beyond gratitude. Freecycle.org's "Freemeets" resemble flea markets where all available items are offered free of charge. People donate items they wish to share and acquire items they can use.

This is also the concept behind Really, Really Freemarkets. People happily share books, magazines, clothing, records, food, and artwork. Freemarkets complement free goods with services, performance, and activities—massage, dance, comedy, music, tarot readings—anything that can be shared freely.[25]

Projects such as Freecycle and Freemarkets foster community, prevent useable goods from becoming waste, provide a practical venue for an ethic of sharing, and break down the idea that the distribution and acquisition of goods must be accompanied by the exchange of money. A smaller but more permanent version of this concept is the free store, where people can donate or freely take a plethora of useful goods any day of the year. By attaching cooperative values to a permanent community institution, freestores allow this ethic to become a part of everyday life. Sharing becomes second nature, while looking to fulfill needs in the competitive capitalist marketplaces ceases to be a necessity.[26]

Squatters and Guerilla Gardeners

Squatters and "guerilla gardeners" are challenging the idea that the property deed of an absentee owner should prevent urban communities from making use of empty, abandoned buildings and lots. Squatters take debilitated buildings and convert them into living spaces and vital community centers. Guerilla gardeners find abandoned, often garbage-filled lots, and rehabilitate them into beautiful green spaces, oases in deserts of asphalt and concrete where city dwellers can witness the miracle of growing plants, cultivate the food they eat, breathe fresh oxygen, and develop an appreciation for the nonhuman world.[27]

Alternative Media and Infoshops

When major corporations own the mass media, and corporate advertisers routinely influence and distort even "news" coverage, mainstream newspapers, magazines, television, and radio simply can't be trusted.[28] In response to this compromised information stream, a global independent media movement has flourished with the commitment to bring people credible information without corporate bias. Alternative media makers present news and opinions in a myriad of formats—websites, pirate radio stations, free newspapers and magazines, books on topics too dangerous for corporate publishers, "zines" (small print run, often highly personal, magazines, commonly reflecting a punk visual and cultural esthetic), satellite and public access television, podcasting and streaming audio and video content, subversive videos and DVDs, independent documentary films, and public speaking and presentations.

Independent Media Centers (IMCs) have sprung up in cities around the globe, providing venues and resources for the creation and dissemination of news and information without the distorting filter of corporate ideology. These centers are managed collectively through consensus decision-making that eschews hierarchy.[29]

Infoshops are other community-building institutions committed to creating space in communities for expression and dialogue about radical ideas. Infoshops integrate elements of libraries, bookstores, cafes, and community centers. While some infoshops are based in squatted buildings, others operate out of rented storefronts to maximize exposure to the general public. The shelves of infoshops are filled with magazines and books by radical philosophers, exposés of injustices hidden by the corporate media, and practical guides to activism and anti-capitalist living. While most infoshops do sell books, many also have lending libraries that encourage people to both donate and borrow books. Infoshops are full of free publications including pamphlets, newspapers, zines, and magazines. Alternative press publications that expose corporate hegemony and preach sedition rarely find their way into chain bookstores, so infoshops provide a critical venue for these voices to share information and ideas with people in a vast array of communities. Conversely, infoshops provide information to local communities from a vast array of sources that they wouldn't otherwise be exposed to. In addition to publications, infoshops also provide space for poetry readings, music events, art exhibits, lectures, workshops, discussions with authors, slide presentations, and films.

Infoshops are run not only for communities, but by them. They are staffed not by paid employees, but by local volunteers. Decisions are made not by an owner or manager but by the volunteers themselves, who participate in nonhierarchical collectives generally based on consensus decision-making policies. Most infoshops actually encourage people to "hang out," and many have tables and cafés for this reason. Infoshops offer meeting space to activist groups, provide bulletin boards for notices on community events, and serve as points of convergence in moments of crisis, like after a violent police attack and mass arrest at a peaceful demonstration.

Holistic Medicine

Holistic healthcare providers are upending the traditional medical model by shifting the focus from expensive, often dangerous, patented pharmaceuticals designed to treat diseases as isolated phenomena to a focus on prevention, overall health, and an understanding of the relationship between energy and health. Alternative therapies rely more on diet, exercise, stress management procedures like acupuncture and spine adjustment, herbs and vitamin supplementation, than they do on patented pharmaceuticals, and often achieve far better results. They offer the promise of healthcare without dependence on monopolistic, animal-testing,[30] and polluting[31] megacorporations like Glaxo and Merck.

Defending Our Communities

These few examples only scratch the surface. Throughout the US and around the world, people are engaging in projects and practices that prove that we can live—and live better—without contributing to ecological destruction, financing corporate atrocities, or depending on corporate-controlled governments for our survival. Strategies like health care cost-sharing, medic collectives that provide free care to protesters and striking workers, community-based disaster relief,[32] and collectively-run community centers explore the promise of cooperative, nonhierarchical, self-managed institutions as a more humane and sustainable approach to providing for people's needs than the free market.

Efforts to build a more just and sustainable culture are a complement to direct resistance to the destruction of ecosystems, and large-scale institutional change.[33] Some campaigns combine both approaches. Principles of ecological sustainability, egalitarianism, autonomy from state or corporate power, cooperative mutual aid, and consensus decision-making can be embodied in the collectives we build to take direct against the destruction of biotic and urban communities—from tree villages in ancient forests[34] to community gardens.

It should come as little surprise that the capitalist system, based on an ideology that views fierce competition as a natural imperative, has attempted to crush these new approaches to living rather than co-exist or cede ground to them. Time and again, corporations, state institutions serving their interests, and corporate front groups have undermined such projects. Retail stores deliberately damage merchandise as they discard it to prevent scavenging. Sharing food is criminalized, and Food Not Bombs activists are surveilled by the FBI and arrested on felonies.[35] Squatters[36] are evicted and the buildings torched.[37] Community gardens are bulldozed.[38] Respected alternative physicians are smeared as "quacks."[39] Police forcibly remove ecodefenders from tree villages.[40] Critical mass bike rides[41] face mass arrests.[42]

Just as we resist the destruction of biotic communities, we must also defend the communities, institutions, and practices of the new culture that we are building. The struggle to preserve and protect our spaces and way of life powerfully dramatizes the conflict between the real needs of people trying to live decent, ethical, sustainable lives, and a government more interested in defending the economic interests of landlords, car manufacturers, pharmaceutical companies, and wasteful retailers. People facing similar threats can come together to defend our communities. In New York City, the More Gardens Coalition,[43] an alliance of community gardeners and supporters, built a citywide campaign of resistance to the destruction of gardens, exposing the officials and private interests behind the destruction of the gardens, winning broad public sympathy. Along with education and protest, garden defenders chained their bodies to stationary objects in gardens to blockade these cherished spaces from bulldozers.[44] While the activists were eventually removed, these passionate defense efforts heightened public outcry against the destruction of these cherished spaces, to the point where the city was forced to agree to leave 138 gardens unmolested.

Many of these projects stretch beyond our conventional understanding of environmentalism. A *radical* approach must address our relationship to our world not simply in abstract terms, but must relate to the values and institutions that guide our everyday lives. Challenging the hierarchy, materialism, commodification, and competitiveness that are intrinsic to industrial capitalist society is absolutely necessary if we hope to stem ecological destruction.

Rethinking Revolution

If the very civilization that is making earth unlivable is also necessary for our survival, how can we ever stop the destruction? After all, aren't we, as taxpayers, workers, and consumers part of the problem? In the United States, tax dollars provide corporate welfare for cattle-grazing and logging on public lands, and fund hideously cruel experiments on animals, military atrocities, and the mass incarceration of people of color, which benefits private prison management corporations, prison supply and construction contractors.

With very few exceptions, our paid work almost guarantees some level of complicity. In many cases, it is those who enjoy the lowest levels of economic privilege who carry out the most savage tasks—spraying pesticides, slaughtering animals, ravaging forests with chainsaws and bulldozers, stripping the seas of life with longlines and driftnets, and bombing cities. Yet, without the secretary, accountant, checkout clerk, franchise owner and graphic designer, the businesses responsible for these exploitative practices could not exist.

As consumers, even our most seemingly benign purchases contribute to ecological destruction and social injustice. We rarely consider the enormously complex series of steps that bring a product to market. So long as people view their survival as dependent on compliant participation in our industrial capitalist civilization, they will view it and its ravages as necessary evils. To truly liberate the future and cast off the yoke of domination we must complement direct resistance to ecocide with efforts to limit our support for the economy that is responsible for the destruction in the first place—building new lives and new cultures based on kinship and community rather than domination and destruction.

If we are to build a revolutionary movement with the power to truly challenge the status quo, we must demonstrate that the principles we uphold offer not only planetary survival, but a better everyday life. For most working people, the threat of not being able to pay rent is much more immediate than loss of biodiversity or global climate change. Considering this, it is not particularly surprising that beyond groups fighting environmental racism in low-income neighborhoods of color, the US environmental movement remains mostly white and middle class.[45]

People need a clean environment and require wilderness more than they realize, but they also need food, shelter, health, community, security, intellectual stimulation, and joy in their lives. When we build a movement that demonstrates the capacity to offer all of these things, while challenging the greed, misery, and destruction of megacorporations, their puppet government, and the entire capitalist-industrialist model, then we can begin to build broad support and engagement in ecological resistance struggles, and finally have a real chance to liberate this world.

Notes

1. Thanks to Rebecca Lerner, Eileen Patrick, Hal Weiss, Homefries, Madeline Nelson, Steven Best, Anthony Nocella, Peter Muller, Aresh Javadi, Christine Karatnytsky, Jonathan Goldberg, Eric Laursen, Chuck Munsen, Thadaeus, Spencer Sunshine, and especially Hillary Rettig for their insights and support in the writing of this article.

2. <http://www.allthingsfrugal.com/dumpster.htm>

3. <http://ths.gardenweb.com/forums/load/treasure/msg0912375430751.html>

4. <http://www.portlandphoenix.com/features/this_just_in/documents/02831864.asp>

5. <http://www.everything2.com/index.pl?node_id=1140523>

6. <http://www.colum.edu/echo/back/spring05/features1.html>

7. <http://houstonpress.com/issues/2004-11-25/news/feature.html>

8. See for example <http://www.rocklincoln.com/dumpsterdiving.htm>, <http://tristateobserver.com/modules.php?op=modload&name=News&file=article&sid=3330>, <http://www.paladin-press.com/authormo_1202.aspx>, <http://www.cat.org.au/skippy/>, <http://w3.tvi.edu/~cgulick/dda.htm>, and <http://www.streettech.com/archives_DIY/dumpsterTech.html>.

9. <http://www.geocities.com/CapitolHill/Lobby/3609/lib_whyfreegan.html>

10. <http://www.redefiningprogress.org/media/clips/030527_sac.html> and <http://www.geocities.com/CapitolHill/Lobby/3609/lib_whyfreegan.html>

11. <http://frugalliving.about.com/od/savewhenshoppingforfood/a/blgleaning.htm>

12. See for example, <http://www.zmag.org/content/showarticle.cfm?SectionID=5&ItemID=1389>.

13. <http://www.girlrobot.com/blog/jim_casebolt_et_al.html>

14. For an explanation of the freegan critique of veganism, see <http://crimethinc.com/library/english/veganism.html>, <http://freegan.info/?page=Liberating>, and <http://freegan.info/?page=WhyFreegan>.

15. The website< http://freegan.info> offers an online directory of favorite scavenging sites in different areas and similar guides are distributed in print form. The creators of Freegan.info run tours where groups are introduced to reliable trash-picking sites. Directory creators and tour organizers hope that their readers and tour participants will then be inspired to seek out other promising locations on their own, which can be added to the future tours and directories.

16. <http://freegan.info/?page=DestructiveProducts>

17. <http://www.rainforestrelief.org/What_to_Avoid_and_Alternatives/Bananas.html>

18. <http://www.rainforestrelief.org/documents/Do_I_Dare.pdf>

19. <http://freegan.info/?page=chocolate>

20. See <http://foodnotbombs.net/firstindex.html,and http://freegan.info/?page=WorldHunger>

21. <http://foodnotbombs.net/>

22. For more information on foraging, check out <http://www.wildmanstevebrill.com>.

23. Anarcho-primitivist thinking is not uncommon among those practicing the more urbanized forms of anti-capitalist living described in this article, many of whom see their lifestyles as attempts to embody elements of primitive lifestyles and values in the context of our present civilization, with hope of eventually pulling all of our society in their direction.

24. For a critique of the "man the hunter" myth, see Jim Mason's book, *The Unnatural Order*. (New York: Lantern Books, 2005).

25. <http://www.indybay.org/news/2004/06/1683917.php>

26. For more information on these alternatives to commodity markets and consumerism, see <http://freecycle.org/, http://freegan.info/?page=Freemarkets>, and <http://freegan.info/?page=freestores>.

27. To learn more about squatting, see <http://freegan.info/?page=Squatlinks. Additional information on guerilla gardening can be found at http://moregardens.org/>.

28. <http://www.fair.org/index.php?page=101>

29. <http://indymedia.org>

30. <http://www.corpwatch.org/article.php?id=12462>

31. <http://www.sdearthtimes.com/et0203/et0203s18.html>

32. Established in the immediate aftermath of the Hurricane Katrine disaster, Algiers, New Orleans' volunteer-managed Common Ground Wellness Center has provided services to poor communities that had previously received little or no assistance from the government or bureaucratic relief agencies. Common Ground is run by a volunteer staff of locals and supporters from around the country, "medics, doctors, cooks, communications technicians, and community organizers" <http://www.indybay.org/news/2005/09/1767321.php>. Projects include "community garbage pick-up program; mobile kitchens to provide free hot meals to a first aid clinic; and a mobile first aid station; and bicycles for volunteers and residents to transport aid around the area; and a free school for children."

33. For an in-depth strategic analysis of how resistance and alternative institution building can complement each other, see Dominick, Brian. "An Introduction to Dual Power Strategy." <http://sandiego.indymedia.org/en/2002/09/2403.shtml>.

34. To prevent logging of the less than five percent of original old growth forests left in North America <http://www.ran.org/ran_campaigns/old_growth/>, communities of resistance have been forged in the tops of ancient trees in the temperate rainforests of the Pacific Northwest. Tree villages are series of inhabited, rudimentary treehouses on circular platforms, interconnected by networks of rope traverses, constructed largely of salvaged materials. Inhabitants of tree villages like Oregon's Red Cloud Thunder pose an immediate impediment to logging operations. None of the trees connected by the village can be felled without putting everyone living in the tree village's life at risk. Loggers, unwilling to risk murder charges, are thus forced to leave these trees standing. <http://www.efn.org/~redcloud/direct.html>

35. <http://www.practicalanarchy.org/fnb_crass2.html>

36. <http://squat.net/archiv/nopermission.html>

37. Eviction of CHARAS <http://www.geocities.com/zorikh/charas.html> and Casa del Sol <http://www.ainfos.ca/05/jan/ainfos00040.html>.

38. <http://www.terrain.org/essays/13/light.htm>

39. <http://www.quackpotwatch.org>

40. <http://www.eco-action.org/dod/no5/region_north.htm>

41. Autonomously organized and lacking leaders or central planners, critical masses are collective rides where hundreds, sometimes thousands, take to the streets at once using human-powered transportation. In a reversal of the norm, drivers of muscle cars and behemoth SUVs are forced to adapt to the pace of skaters and bicyclists. Critical masses suggest the promise of a car-free society, one where pedestrians don't risk their lives every time they cross the street, where getting from one place to another doesn't mean generating smog or complicity in imperialist oil wars. From critical masses, cyclists gain a sense of solidarity and validation—and even safety, for those who are terrified to bike or skate on streets filled with road-raging motorists.

42. <http://www.democracynow.org/article.pl?sid=04/08/30/1453256>

43. <http://www.moregardens.org/?q=node/4>

44. <http://userpage.fu-berlin.de/~garten/Buch/Stoneenglisch.htm>

45. The Coalition Against Environmental Racism defines environmental racism as "the exclusion of people of color in the decision-making process and the disproportionate impact of environmental hazards, including pollution, resource depletion, and waste disposal, on the health and wealth of people of color." <http://gladstone.uoregon.edu/~caer/>

Part III

RELIGION AND SPIRITUALITY

"Honor the Earth, our Mother.
Honor the Elders.
Honor all with whom we share the Earth:
Four-legged, two-legged, winged ones,
Swimmers, crawlers, plant and rock people.
Walk in balance and beauty." *Native American Elder*

"But if you have no relationship with the living things on this earth, you may lose whatever relationship you have with humanity." *Krishnamurti*

"Kindness and compassion toward all living things
is a mark of a civilized society. Racism, economic deprival, dog fighting
and cock fighting, bullfighting and rodeos
are cut from the same fabric: violence." *Cesar Chavez*

I don't want to live where they are killing me

Kalamu ya Salaam

1.

it's crazy. most of us
kind of assume that where we are born
is home, where our first kiss was, learning to walk, literally,
throwing our first stone at someone in anger,
sitting at the table a mouth full of mother's meatloaf
or was it strawberry pie, or even monkey bread—
those twisted strings of dough that were a wonderful
combination of chewy cake and sweet stuffing—
catching the bus home from school with friends,
the first drink, wasn't it when uncle teddy
served you beer at thanksgiving, you were five?
like that, we think of that location in the mythic sense

the high drama that came later, the desperately sought
trysts, sneaking to liaison with someone you know you
ought to avoid, or the first time you got together
with someone whom you wanted the whole world
to know you were committed to being with for life,
or so you thought, how wonderful the world looked
as you lay dreaming on your back your head
secure in a special someone's lap, or how short
the walk after the dance from the club to the parking lot,
what you wouldn't have given for a reprise of that heaven
the way a lover looks when their whole face smiles
just because you came around the corner with
a yellow tulip in your hand and a pack of almond m&m's
secreted behind your back as you whispered
smokey's ooh baby baby into an eagerly waiting ear

actually those were the preludes—the real high drama
came some years later, the first time calling someone,
anyone, to come and get you out of jail, which you were in
for doing something stupid, something really, really
stupid, and then there was the accident when you banged
up someone's new car, but those were just the breaks, not
the actual high drama of sitting sullen in some counselor's
waiting room, your head thrown back to the wall
avoiding the eyes of your better half who was now
the loyal opposition and whose eyes were the same eyes
only smaller in the head of the child to whom you
could not some how find the right words to make sense
of this mess that was formerly your marriage

where these scenes take place, the parlor in which
a cousin's camera has caught you crying, the foggy mirror
where you examined yourself, one flight up in a total
stranger's house and sheepishly you wonder what were you
doing in this blue tiled bathroom so very early in the morning
when you were supposed to be somewhere else—life is what
some people call this, and where you live your life, shouldn't
that be the place you call home?

2.

the water. my god the water. the angry water
rain roaring sideways with the force of a freight train,
smashing your resolve to ride it out, or inching
down an interstate at two miles an hour so call evacuating
from the water. the dirty, angry water, running
if you were lucky enough to have wheels and a wallet
with plastic in it. the water. you will dream of
wet mountains falling on you and wake up gasping
for air as though you were drowning, oh the water
deeper than any pool you've ever swam in,
water more terrible than anything you can think
of, another middle passage, except this time
they don't even provide ships

I used to wonder how my ancestors survived
the Atlantic, Katrina has answered that question,
I wonder no more—there is a faith that is beyond
faith, a belief when there is nothing left to believe in,
no, not god, well, yes, god, for some, for many, it was
jesus, a few humduallahed, or whatever, but it was also
whatever that visited this terror upon us, and so
to keep believing in whatever, now takes something

the mind can not imagine, the realization that in order
to live you had to survive and in order to survive
you had to do whatever needed to be done, few
of us really, really know what we will do
when we've got nothing but have to find something
to keep us going, how you manage your sanity
in the water, corpses floating by, gas flames
bubbling up from some leaking underground line,
and you sitting on a roof and you just pissed
on yourself because, well, because there was
no where to go and do your business, five days
of filth, no water but flood water, no food but
hot sun, no sanitation but being careful where
you stepped, where you slept, where you turned
your back and eliminated, being careful to survive

twelve days later and you still don't know where
all your family is, if you've got faith, you're about
to use it all—is this what our ancestors saw?

3.

it is over a month later and you still can't walk
on the land that used to be your backyard,
they treat you like a tourist, you can only
be driven down your street in a big bus,
you can only look out the window at what twisted,
funk encrusted little remains of all you ever owned
and some kid with a gun won't let you go
to get big mama's bible

this shit is fucked up, that's what it is,
fucked up and foul, the smell of a million
toilets overflowing, of food that been rotting
for days inside a refrigerator that became
an oven because the electricity was off and
the sun was beaming down ninety degrees or more

and the worse part is that none of what you
already went through is the worst part, the worst
is yet to come as government peoples with
boxes and things they stick into the ground
tell you that even if the water hadn't drowned
you, something called toxicity has made it
impossible for you to stay here, they are
telling you it is impossible for you to stay
in the house that been in your family

for over fifty years even though it's still standing
it's impossible to live here, and what shall
we call this? what shall we tell the children
when they ask: when are we going home?

4.

I don't want to live anywhere where they have
tried to kill us even if it was once a place
I called home—but still and all, my bones
don't cotton to Boston, I can't breath
that thinness they call air in Colorado,
a Minnesota snow angel don't mean shit
to me, and still and all, even with all of that,
all the many complaints that taint my
appreciation of charity, help and shelter,
even though I know there is no turning back
to drier times, still, as still as a fan when
the man done cut the 'lectric off, still,
regardless of how much I hate the taste
of bland food, still, I may never go back,
not to live, maybe for a used to be
visit, like how every now and then you
go by a graveyard... I am not bitter, I am
just trying to answer the question:
what is life without a home?
what is life, without
a home? and how long does it take
to grow a new one?

Jains, the ALF, and the ELF: Antagonists or Allies?

Charlotte Laws

"Do not injure, abuse, oppress, enslave, insult, torment, torture, or kill any living being."[1] Do these words sound extremist or incendiary? Could they be scrawled in red paint on a vivisection laboratory wall by a member of the Animal Liberation Front (ALF) or screamed through a bull horn at a PETA protest outside a fur salon? They could, but in fact, they come directly from ancient Jain scripture.

"To pollute, to disturb, to hurt and to destroy the...earth, water, air, animal life, vegetation...is a sinful act....To cut a forest...is considered a very serious offense."[2] Do these comments come from Julia Butterfly Hill, an angry sailor on the Sea Shepherd, or an SUV-destroying member of the Earth Liberation Front (ELF)? They could, but again, they are venerable Jain teachings.

Jainism is one of the world's oldest religions, originating as early as 950 BCE; it was revised and expanded in 550 BCE by Lord Mahavir, a prince from Bihar, India. This relatively obscure religion with a modest number of followers could have waned in the first few centuries; instead it spread throughout South Asia and can be found in most parts of the world today. Its increase in popularity over time is often attributed to the disproportionate number of prominent and affluent figures, such as kings, who converted to the faith or adopted its principles. The first emperor of India became a Jain towards the end of his life,[3] and Gandhi was deeply influenced by Jain thought.[4]

Although ancient, Jain philosophy is directly relevant to the social and ecological crises of modern day as they pertain to the human alienation from nature, the technological imperatives of control, and a modern society organized around the dynamic of endless growth and expansion. Its fundamental tenet of nonviolence towards all nonhumans corresponds seamlessly with the contemporary animal rights agenda, a connection that most Western or capitalistic ideologies lack.

Jainism promotes a non-speciesist and pacifist philosophy, arguing against ecological imbalance, pollution, and inflicting violence upon any living being.[5] In a sense, it provides for a convergence of animal rights/ liberation philosophy and environmentalism, which are often at odds because animal rights emphasizes individual sentient beings, while environmentalism seeks to protect entire species and ecosystems. Environmentalists may hold that individual members of a species can be sacrificed in order to benefit the whole, whereas animal advocates find this notion abhorrent. By advancing an ethic that encompasses both living beings and the earth, Jains dissolve such tensions, and honor both animal rights and environmental worldviews.

Jain philosophy can do more than assuage the animal rights vs. environmental conflict; it can aid the movements themselves in their battle against the anthropocentric worldview. Jains can be embraced as ideological and political allies of the ALF and ELF contingent who fight with spray paint and homemade fire-bombs. Jains may refrain from "violent" behavior themselves, but they do not disparage resistance strategies involving ecotage and animal rescue.

Although nonviolent and nonjudgmental, Jain philosophy has much in common with direct action philosophy. Both have a strong ethical nature, recognizing the innate value of living beings and the natural world. Both emphasize a holistic and non-materialistic philosophy that positions them outside the social mainstream. Both the ascetic Jains and the action-oriented ALF and ELF, moreover, make great personal sacrifices to adhere to what they believe to be right, evincing a commitment similar in strength to the abolitionists, suffragettes, and adversaries of the Nazi regime. Although Jain philosophy has quietistic implications, its similarities with animal and earth liberation—such as its rejection of speciesism, its all-encompassing nature ethic and holistic outlook, and its condemnation of causing injury to life—outweigh the differences, such that animal liberationists and revolutionary environmentalists can consider them their allies.

Fighting the Cultural Authorities

Although the word "radical" is commonly taken to mean extreme, deviant, disruptive, or fanatical, this is not an accurate definition of the term. Stemming from the Latin "radix," it means to get to the root of something or to dig below the surface of a situation. Authoritarian forces, usually those who seek to maintain the status quo, utilize words such as "radical" or "terrorist" in order to marginalize and discredit those perceived as their adversaries.

A term can be tweaked over time to have a less-than-noble connotation in order to stigmatize or condemn a person, organization, or tactic. The Animal and Earth Liberation Fronts have never caused the death of a human, yet they are labeled "terrorists," "radicals," and "extremists" by the FBI, mass media, and industries that exploit animals and the environment for profit.

"Witch" was the disreputable buzz word of the Spanish Inquisition. As evidenced by the procedures outlined in *The Hammer of the Witches*, church authorities demanded an outward display of remorse from the accused heretics and a public renouncement of their so-called wrongdoing. Absent this, they feared these "witches" would be martyrs, converting the remainder of the community to an unconventional way of thinking, subverting the mores, morals, and religious precepts of the time.

It was much the same in the US during the 1950s when Joseph McCarthy, chairman of the Senate Government Operations Committee, embarked upon a "patriotic" enterprise to weed out suspected "communists." He pressured those whom he deemed unamerican to confess, repent and name names. His overzealous campaign led to mandatory loyalty oaths for teachers, actors, clergy, union members, and others as well as to character assassination, intimidation, blacklisting, and a vicious tone of intolerance throughout the nation.[6] Anyone with an ideologically divergent view was likely to be perceived as a threat and a target. This is clearly a situation the ALF and ELF are familiar with today, as the weapons of persecution shift from "communism" to "terrorism," from a "Red Scare" to a new "Green Scare."

To allow alternate visions to exist, such as those promoted by the ALF or ELF, is a threat to consumerism, corporate control, and the guilt-free lifestyle of indulging in meat, fur, SUVs, and other exploitative commodities. ALF and ELF philosophies challenge the necessity of vivisection, drilling for oil in Alaska, factory farming, rainforest decimation, urban sprawl, and wanton corporate expansion. The "cultural authorities" may hold that capitalism should not be sacrificed or even tamed for the sake of preserving the environment. They often refuse to give up convenience or the "might makes right tradition" that has—from their perspective—led to American hegemony and accomplishment.

Because Jains do not aim to alter the behavior of others or sneak into labs at midnight to rescue distressed animals, they are not perceived as threats to the status quo. Their philosophy is one of setting an example, rather than attempting to dictate or control the behavior of others. Most Jains hold to moral relativism and to the notion that there are many legitimate perspectives to a situation rather than one truth. Jainism celebrates fluidity and flexibility, conveying an element of uncertainty about what qualifies as "right and wrong." It is for this reason that they would not criticize the illegal or "violent" tactics used by the ALF and the ELF.

As opposed to more malleable Jain precepts, the ALF and ELF belief systems tend to coincide with some form of moral absolutism, regardless of whether the framework is consequentialist, like that of Peter Singer, or deontological, like that of Tom Regan.[7] Most ALF and ELF members hold that violent acts against nonhumans and/or the environment are immoral and that direct action is necessary to combat these conspicuous wrongs. To be lenient on their ideological opponents—as Jains might be inclined to do—would be shameful and antithetical to their mission.

While the ALF and the ELF would no doubt appreciate the Jain emphasis on nonviolence, they would view it as politically naive and self-defeating in the context of a corporate-controlled state. They would describe Jain nonintervention as ineffective, ultimately leading to a society of greater violence through toleration of it. They would argue that the powerful will continue to manipulate, mistreat, and murder the powerless for profit until society is propelled in the compassionate and ethical direction by those with an active commitment to change. This means advocacy and combat, rather than the passive Jain tactic of "setting an example."

In spite of the divergent approaches to morality and action by a Jain and a member of the ALF or ELF, both step outside the conventional, anthropocentric paradigm to prioritize the interests and needs of animals and the environment. Unlike most of their contemporaries, they have an expanded moral vision, holding that nonhuman living beings have interests and inherent value, apart from their usefulness to people. Jains, the ALF, and the ELF are admirably radical in this way.

They are in good company. The abolitionists, who fought to end slavery in the US between the 1830s and the Civil War, were derided by Southerners and called dangerous fanatics by Northerners. Analogous to the animal and environmental movements, the anti-slavery campaign encompassed a slew of clashing personalities who embarked upon varied tactics. Some wrote articles or freed their own slaves, while others used violence to institute change. Harriet Tubman, along with others who defied anti-slavery laws, took between 40,000 and 100,000 slaves to safety through the Underground Railroad,[8] and Nat Turner led a violent slave revolt that led to the deaths of at least 51 people.[9] Just as financial interests today take precedence over the lives of animals and the integrity of the environment, in the 1800s "Black people in the US were told that their slavery was an 'economic necessity' to be continued for the good of the country."[10]

In the nineteenth and early twentieth centuries, the suffrage movement proceeded down a similar path. From it sprang a multiplicity of voices and maneuvers by different groups and individuals, all aimed at securing rights for women. Those outside the movement—and even many within—were critical of the unconventional tactics of Alice Paul and other members of the Congressional Union of Women Suffrage (CUWS) who engaged in civil disobedience, chaining themselves to the White House fence. When they were jailed, they embarked upon hunger strikes and were force-fed by the legal authorities. Their controversial tactics were successful in the end and arguably gained women the right to vote in 1920. Drawing on the philosophical resources influenced by Jainism, the ALF and the ELF expand these modern resistance traditions to extend rights to all living beings and protect the earth from injury, violence, and exploitation.

Practical and Impractical Connections

Ahimsa—which originates from Sanskrit and means "without violence"[10]—is the central tenet of the Jain religion. Nonviolence towards all living beings is the single, predominant cultural value embedded within all aspects of Jain life. In fact, Jainism prohibits intentional physical injury to humans, animals, plants, and microorganisms—especially for those who wish to lead the purest existence, such as the monks and teachers—as well as negative thoughts and harsh speech. The Saman Suttam—the only text approved by all Jain sects and translated as "The Essence of Jainism"— commands that one "not use harsh words or speak what is harmful to other living beings; even if it is true, because it is sinful."[11] Absence of ill will towards every creature is essential; it is considered violent for a Jain to do otherwise within Jainism's very broad definition of "violence."

Animal and environmental activists have an altogether different definition of what qualifies as "violence." They often resort to name-calling, threats, and harassment tactics, not to mention damaging personal property. But they feel that such actions are justified, even required, in order to counter the real violence which they see as the abuse and murder of nonhumans or the despoilment of the environment. Their retaliation is what one might call a form of "extensional self-defense"[12]—the act of protecting the innocent and powerless from attack.

Scottish political economist, Adam Smith, wrote *The Wealth of Nations* in 1776 where he criticized the "vile maxim"—the idea that those in control selfishly take all for themselves, and leave nothing for other people. The phrase the "violent maxim" could be used to describe how the human species violently takes all for themselves—through overuse and abuse—leaving virtually nothing for other species. This plunder and killing is usually done for economic advantage and is usually informed by a "might is right" philosophy.

Is damaging personal property always, or ever, a "violent" act? Perhaps surprisingly, there is no easy answer. For example, if one breaks the windows of a car with a hammer, is this considered violent? What if it is your automobile? Does intention matter? What if you break someone else's window to rescue a puppy from the debilitating heat? What if you rescue your own dog from your own car? Is the cost of replacing the personal property relevant? Is it violent to tear to shreds a piece of paper belonging to someone else? Do you have to be angry with this person for it to be considered violent? Is it violent to experiment on an animal? To raze a rainforest to the ground?

It seems "violence" is dependent upon subjective interpretation, context, and other contingent factors, such that there may be no single, absolute, or objective definition. One could argue, of course, that some definitions of terms such as "violence" and "terrorism" make more sense than others, insofar as they are rich, nuanced, impartial, and sensitive to context.

However they are defined, "violent acts" can involve pragmatic difficulties. For example, Jain activities are highly limited. The laity are asked to avoid killing living beings, and thus should not ingest animal products or root vegetables or enter into objectionable professions, such as farming. Jains tend to live in cities so as to protect the land and avoid digging in the earth because small beings can be injured or killed in the process. Jains often buy farm animals in order to save their lives.

Those who wish to follow scripture in an orthodox way must adhere to even more stringent rules. They wear white robes or go naked and are prohibited from driving a car or running so as not to trample on insects or tiny life forms. Walking requires carrying a small broom; they must sweep the path prior to setting their foot on the dirt. They abstain from sex so as to spare the lives of millions of sperm cells, and avoid baths so as not to harm minute forms of water-borne life. These ascetics will use mouth cloths in order to protect small beings in the air, as well as refrain from clapping, fanning themselves, or setting fires.[13]

The monks or ascetics are forbidden to prepare food, thus are dependent upon the laity for basic survival. Consequently, they must rely upon the "less moral" people to feed them, house them, and generally take care of them. Their extreme pacifism and asceticism makes their lives quixotic. Thus we encounter a utopian dilemma. A world full of obedient Jains would result in suicide by starvation—an act, by the way, endorsed by Jainism as a spiritual ideal—or virtual immobility and the inability to perpetuate the species due to the prohibition against intercourse. Who would remain to pass on the beauty of *ahimsa*?

ALF and ELF members would no doubt call the Jain method laudable, but dub it internally inconsistent and impractical when strictly followed. They might add that Jains, animal rights advocates, and environmentalists must survive in order to enlighten the world about the innate value of all living beings and to reduce—or eliminate—cruel behavior and callous indifference towards other beings.

The revolutionaries called the ALF and ELF may also face the impractical consequences of their ideals.[14] Their behavior arguably advances their goals when practiced on a limited basis by a few cells of activists here and there because a property "attack," for example, may heighten public awareness and end exploitive conduct by a particular corporation or individual. Due to this type of "encouragement," fur farms have been shut down, repeatedly vandalized buildings have become uninsurable, and vivisectors have become intimidated and sought other lines of work.

Periodic and unpredictable ALF and ELF actions play a symbolic role in alerting the masses to the fact that war has been waged against an uncompassionate, financially insatiable system that dismisses the interests of nonhumans and ignores the needs of the earth. These acts of sabotage, harassment, and animal liberation (or "property theft") can also serve to keep their opponents on their toes, to motivate and inspire others in the movement, and to directly free animals in dire distress.

An increase of sporadic and random attacks into a wide-scale project, however, is problematic for the ALF and the ELF. First there is a *philosophical* problem involving a possible slippery slope. Everyone—even a conscientious animal rights advocate or environmentalist—probably participates in objectionable behavior at some point, at least from someone's perspective. For example, some animal activists shun the practice of dining with carnivores, or tenting houses for termite work, since rodents can be killed in the process. Others may engage in these activities. Some environmentalists may criticize those who drive cars or who fasten the occasional plastic diaper to their newborn, since the item will dwell in a landfill for years. Some condemn those who have children in the first place. Could a person be targeted for driving a car, buying diapers, having children, or choosing the wrong dinner companion? It is unlikely, but possible, especially if direct action advocates become over-zealous or their tactics become less focused. The criteria for selecting a target could become lax or imprecise, especially when one considers the fact that ALF and ELF cells are decentralized and self-determined. Apart from a few rules that ALF or ELF activists must follow—such as abstaining from physical violence against opponents—those acting in the name of animal or earth liberation might assume they have *carte blanche* powers to attack whoever they want. As no commander sets an agenda, targets could be chosen based on convenience or the particular passions of one member rather than on which business or person commits the most heinous "moral crimes."

This invokes a second concern: there is a *practical* problem involved with a steep escalation of direct action. There are millions of activities, industries, businesses, and individuals impeding the goals of the ALF and the ELF, but they cannot all be coerced into change. If one fast food restaurant is continually attacked by the ALF or ELF, why ignore the others? If a researcher is routinely harassed for torturing animals, why are butchers and slaughterhouse workers—who may contribute to greater suffering and death—often left alone?

It is for reasons such as these that one might urge the ALF and the ELF to direct their energy towards only the most flagrant offenders and routinely publicize the rationale behind selecting one business, organization, or individual over others. An action or series of actions can be more effective when part of a larger campaign. Documentation, witnesses, and video footage are invaluable public relations tools.

The ALF and the ELF might be well-advised to focus their efforts on activities that are most easily embraced by the public—such as rescuing distressed puppies from research labs—rather than actions more readily perceived as "violent" or "offensive," such as vandalizing a corporate executive's car or smoke-bombing his private home. Animal rescues are more frequently applauded than "crimes" involving property damage. Moreover, animal abusers can easily be seen as "victims" if the ALF and the ELF choose the wrong targets or do not properly convey their message within what is widely acknowledged as a hostile media environment.

The nature of any war arguably includes an element of chaos and passion, but the more the ALF and the ELF—and their "press agents"—show the logic and necessity behind their actions, the more they will gain public support and the sooner they will win. A practical decision must be made each time the ALF and the ELF don their fatigues.

Sacrificing Freedom

In addition to the link between Jains and ALF/ELF members regarding the practical or impractical consequences of their actions, there are likewise connections on freedom-related issues. Those who adhere to Jain, animal or environmental philosophies sacrifice personal freedom in order to conduct themselves in accordance with their rigorous beliefs. In the case of ALF and ELF members, they face a possible loss of external freedom if they are imprisoned or punished for circumventing the law.

Apart from metaphysical distinctions—such as in the determinism vs. free-will debate[15]—one can discuss a real world freedom, which could be sorted into two categories. The first could be called "active," "positive," or "internal"[16] and the other called "passive," "negative," or "external."[17] Limiting freedom in the first sense is self-imposed; it involves restricting or altering behavior in order to act in accordance with one's beliefs, such as when one adheres to a vegan lifestyle or rescues spiders from one's home. In the second sense, limiting freedom means there is an outside constraint or some form of coercion. In other words, a person is unable to act in a chosen way due to external forces, such as when legal authorities thwart an animal rescue operation by tossing an activist in jail. It is natural for everyone to experience both types of freedom loss; however, the restrictions for Jains, and committed animal activists and environmentalists can be arduous, even burdensome at times.

Jain founder, Lord Mahavir, knew what arduous meant: he was a master of self-restraint. At age 30, he left his affluent home bare foot, relinquished his worldly possessions, went without food for extensive periods, and spent much of his time in a devout meditational state. In fact, it is said that he spent twelve years in deep silence. He also restricted his activities substantially to avoid harming or annoying other living beings including animals, birds, and plants.

A similar story of self-denial is told about the founder of the Buddhist religion, Siddhartha Gautama. In search of truth, the story says that he "slept on brambles, ate one grain of rice or one bean each day, and neglected and tortured his body until his spine could be poking through his stomach and his ribs stuck out like camel hooves."[18] Martin Luther, an Augustinian monk who lived in the sixteenth century, serves as another example of intense self-discipline. During his Catholic years, he fasted, wore uncomfortable clothes on purpose, and regularly chained himself to his bed to remind him of his sins.

The most observant Jains are self-proclaimed ascetics, although they endure harsh conditions for "purity" or "*Ahimsa*-related" reasons rather than to punish themselves. Most committed members of the animal rights/liberation and environmentalist movements might not describe themselves in this way; however, strong parallels exist. An ascetic is someone who practices "severe self-discipline," [19] often for "religious or spiritual reasons."[20] Animal and environmental philosophies require extreme curtailment of personal behavior and have been likened to religions by some. In their arguably tendentious book, *The Animal Rights Crusade*, authors James Jaspers and Dorothy Nelkin criticize the animal rights movement as a moral crusade and label the ALF as "fundamentalists."[21] "In the strident style of Old Testament prophets," they say, "scolding and condemning their society, [animal rights] organizers point to evils that surround them."[22]

Although a fashion model may deprive herself of food in order to retain her job, or a business owner may toil for hours in order to increase his income, the most committed animal and environmental activists—like Jains—live onerous and unselfish lives of daily personal sacrifice for the sake of what they deem a greater good.

For ALF and ELF members to adopt a philosophically consistent lifestyle in this speciesist and anthropocentric world is challenging, and typically begins with a commitment to veganism. They must, for example, exhibit patience, energy, self-control, and self-deprivation. An animal activist could spend hours searching for non-leather belts, plastic shoes, vegan food, cruelty-free household products and cosmetics not tested on animals. The plastic shoes may be uncomfortable, even painful to wear. The activist may want to avoid charitable organizations and stock holdings with objectionable ties that could otherwise be the most profitable choice. He or she may refuse cars with leather seats, or avoid movies and plays that extol the virtues of hunting or fishing. It might be necessary to decline invitations to the horse races, zoo, circus, community barbecue, or Thanksgiving meal. He or she may have to avoid certain science classes or even—like the Jains—entire professions. The principled activist may also feel compelled to rescue dogs from the pound or to buy lobsters from the grocery store in order to set them free. He or she may endure teasing and vitriol from unsympathetic family members. In short, while a commitment to animal rights and environmentalism can be liberating to the soul, in practical matters it can make everyday life more complicated. It requires sacrifice and arguably an element of withdrawal from the world, which could be described as quasi-asceticism.

The ALF and ELF extend themselves further than the Jains by risking the second type of freedom which involves external constraints imposed by others. They may rescue animals from factory farms or vivisection labs, spike trees, sabotage logging or construction equipment, set fires, release mink from fur farms, obstruct hunters from their prey, protect seals from the spiked clubs of sealers, deface buildings with bold red letters, or conduct a myriad of other illegal acts. In each case, they risk loss of freedom, injury, or worse. Some activists have died in the line of duty, and many sit in prison right now. It is selfless to give up inward freedom and to put outward freedom at risk. However, radical activists know it is a minor sacrifice in comparison with the suffering animals endure and the plight of the earth. Nonhuman species cannot escape their circumstance. They are at the mercy of human society which almost always opts to disregard their pain, treat their lives as disposable, and neglect the health of the earth as a whole.

Forging a Political Coalition

According to Noam Chomsky, revolutions are not two-sided as people are traditionally taught, but three-sided.[23] In addition to the agendas promulgated by the two warring powers, the common folk have their own goals, which are often contrary to those of the commanders, armies, states, and even "revolutionaries." For example, during the US Civil War, the populace may have hoped for personal safety, survival of their homes and plantations, and a government headed by a villager rather than an aristocrat or member of the social elite.

Despite his seemingly expansive view, Chomsky fails—like most thinkers—to recognize that there are an infinite number of perspectives on any subject. More importantly, as a "humanist," he is oblivious to the fact that other species have interests, that they too have "sides" that need representing and protecting in almost any situation, including combat.

Nonhuman species are excluded from the discourse each time a politician, news reporter, or military leader talks about the human casualties and property damage from a war or human-created disaster, but fails to mention the animal fatalities and ramifications for the environment. Defined as commodities and property objects, nonhuman species have no standing in court, and their needs are rarely given consideration when legislators develop policy. Therefore, the ALF and ELF, in conjunction with other animal/environmental supporters, must represent nonhuman interests—regardless of whether the battlefield is in the courtroom, at city hall, or on the street.

The ALF and the ELF serve as soldiers, even though many within their own general advocacy movements may never support their controversial tactics. Animal welfare and rescue groups act as nurses, patching up the daily wounds. Like-minded academics provide strategies and maps for the forces, while sympathetic writers emerge as wartime correspondents. Those involved in human rights movements make suitable "allies" due to their experience with similar struggles, and Jains—and others with pacifistic ideologies—can play an integral role in the political arena. They can negotiate a temporary withdrawal on one front in exchange for substantial ground on another, such as when a campaign against a business is temporarily abandoned in return for removing a few objectionable products from the shelves. Even-tempered Jains are arguably better suited for entering into these mediations and reasoning with their ideological opponents than hard-core activists who expect immediate victory.

In India, Jains are over-represented in the fields of politics and finance because the requirements for compassionate living prohibit them from entering professions that contribute directly to the death, injury, or mistreatment of animals and plants. These religious prohibitions have turned out to be advantageous, propelling them into white-collar positions of power and prestige, resulting in improvements for the nonhumans in their communities.

The pliable and relative nature of Jain philosophy—which allows for compromise, composure, and openness to other views—makes Jains attractive political prospects in India, America, and around the world. It is widely acknowledged that flexibility, negotiating talents, and the ability to "set an example" are useful, even essential, when serving as a council member, commissioner, assemblyman, congresswoman, or community leader. In addition, a Jain can authentically represent all beings—the humans, animals and the environment—in his or her district, thus allowing the ALF and the ELF jointly to support a candidate for office.

Advancing progressive societal change can be an arduous and frustrating process that requires patience and "baby steps." The sluggish system is loathsome to most animal and environmental activists who are passionate about their cause and concerned about the dire consequences for nonhumans when gradual, rather than rapid, shifts occur. Many animal rights supporters and environmentalists stand firm, opposed to bargaining with the "enemy." This inflexibility may be commendable, but it may not be politically savvy or constructive in the long run; at least without more moderate allies, such as Jains, coming to their defense. The composed Jains are more practical in this way. They are well-equipped for combating the formidable and time-consuming political, legal, and procedural hurdles that require patience and finesse.

According to the Jain Center of Southern California, countless numbers of people throughout the world are becoming enlightened to the Jain lifestyle and religion. Currently, there are eight to ten million followers in India and 20,000 practicing Jain families in America.[24] There are no doubt thousands more who adhere to the principle of nonviolence, but do not associate themselves with the religion.

As people throughout the world become aware of Jainism, there are likely to be new animal and environmental recruits who share a devotion to ahimsa and a willingness to step forward in leadership roles. They may describe themselves as Jewish Jains, Christian Jains, Muslim Jains, Agnostic Jains, Atheist Jains, or just plain Jains. They may refuse labels altogether, but become accomplished diplomats and negotiators for the cause.

Plunging into politics and community leadership—on the local, state, and national level—is integral to the success of animal rights/liberation and environmentalism. Endorsing career politicians who are not true supporters of the movement can no longer remain the prevailing strategy;

those within the movement must run for office themselves, acknowledging—either personally or publicly—that all beings are their constituents, deserving of consideration. Jains and pacifists may not be willing to join the ALF and the ELF on the front lines, but they are well-equipped to pass them a political shield.

Notes

1. See Pravin K. Shah, *Jainism: Religion of Compassion and Ecology*, 1st ed. (North America: Jaina Education Committee, June 2001), 23.

2. See Sargarmai Jain, *An Introduction to Jaina Sadhana* (India: University of Madras, 1995), 82–83.

3. See <http://hinduwebsite.com>.

4. See George Woodcock, *Mohandas Gandhi* (New York: The Viking Press, 1971), 60.

5. See Sargarmal Jain and Sri Jinendra Varni, *Saman Suttam* (India: Sarva Seva Sangh Prakashan, 1993), 55. See also Pravin K. Shah, 25.

6. See *The New Encyclopedia Britannica*. 15th Edition, Volume 7, 610–11.

7. For discussions about consequentialist (utilitarian) and deontological (rule and duty-oriented) ethics, see Williams, Bernard. "Contemporary Philosophy: A Second Look." In *The Blackwell Companion to Philosophy*, edited by Nicholas Bunnin and E.P. Tsui-James (Oxford: Blackwell Publishers Ltd., 1996), 32–34. To read the philosophies of Regan and Singer, see Tom Regan and Peter Singer, *Animal Rights and Human Obligations*, 2nd ed. (New Jersey: Prentice-Hall Inc., 1989), 73–86 and 105–14.

8. See *The New Encyclopedia Britannica*, vol. 12, 126.

9. Ibid, 66.

10. See Marjorie Spiegel, *The Dreaded Comparison* (USA: New Society Publishers, 1988), 17.

11. See *Concise Oxford English Dictionary*, 11th ed. (Oxford: Oxford University Press, 2004), 27.

12. See Sargarmal Jain and Sri Jinendra Varni, *Saman Suttam* (India: Sarva Seva Sangh Prakashan, 1993), 149.

13. The term "extension self-defense" was coined by Steven Best to argue that humans can serve as legitimate proxy agents for animals in order to secure their right to self-defense which animals themselves are powerless to exercise in many cases.

14. See Lawrence A. Babb, *Absent Lord: Ascetics and Kings in Jain Ritual Culture* (Berkeley: University of California Press, 1996), 56.

15. The refusal by ALF and ELF to compromise on animal and environmental issues could itself be called impractical, especially within the political sphere where negotiation is essential for progress.

16. See Ted Honderich, *How Free Are You? The Determinism Problem* (Oxford: Oxford University Press, 1993).

17. See Baruch Spinoza for different senses of freedom, *Ethics and Selected Letters* (Indianapolis: Hackett Publishing Company, 1982), 57.

18. See Max Lerner ed., *Essential Works of John Stuart Mill* (New York: Bantam Books, 1961), 255–360. See also David Archard, "Political and Social Philosophy." In *The Blackwell Companion to Philosophy*, edited by Nicholas Bunnin and E.P. Tsui-James (Oxford: Blackwell Publishers, Ltd., 1996), 258.

19. See Earl Schipper, *Religions of the World* (Grand Rapids: Baker Book House, 1982), 61.

20. See *Concise Oxford English Dictionary,* 11th ed. (Oxford: Oxford University Press, 2004), 75. See also *The American Heritage Dictionary of the English Language* (New York: Dell Publishing Company, 1970), 41.

20. See *Shorter Oxford English Dictionary,* 5th ed. (Oxford: Oxford University press, 2002), 127.

21. See James M Jasper and Dorothy Nelkin, *The Animal Rights Crusade: The Growth of a Moral Protest* (New York: The Free Press, 1992), 9.

22. See James M Jasper and Dorothy Nelkin, *The Animal Rights Crusade: The Growth of a Moral Protest* (New York: The Free Press, 1992), 8.

23. See Noam Chomsky, "Opposing Privilege and Power." In *Dialogues* by Jerry Brown (Berkeley: Berkeley Hills Books, 1998), 214.

24. See Shah, 7.

In the Beginning
God Created the Earth and "Ecoterrorism"[1]

L. A. Kemmerer

Most of us do not view "ecoterrorism" as a standard Sunday activity for mainstream Christians. In fact, the ignoble (and misleading) title "ecoterrorism" strongly suggests something less than exemplary behavior. Yet surprising as it may seem, many of the activities of "ecoterrorists" are firmly supported by Christian scripture.[2] Moreover, scriptural support comes from the heart of the Christian tradition: the first two chapters of Genesis, Prophets, the injunction to love, and the life of Jesus.

Two fundamental teachings are critical to an eco-sensitive spirituality: a sense of interconnections—including an appreciation for the majesty and fragility of creation—and a call to action on behalf of creation (Gulick, 185-87). Christian scripture offers both. Due to length constraints, this essay explores only a few key Biblical passages and concepts. It supports what many would consider a radical, theologically-based eco-justice movement. Though this interpretation is by no means fundamentalist or mainstream, it stems from a reasoned, literal exploration of scripture, one that has been supported by both theologians and scholars.

Genesis and Creation: Interconnections, Majesty, and Fragility

"In the beginning when God created the heavens and the earth, the earth was a formless void and darkness covered the face of the deep, while a wind from God swept over the face of the waters" (Genesis 1:1). Genesis Chapter One and Two provide the Christian account of creation (a Hebrew/Jewish text also accepted by Islam). Creation preceded the Fall of humanity, which occurs in Genesis Chapter Three. The Fall radically alters the perfect, God-given universe in which the first people are placed. Only in Genesis Chapters One and Two do we see the world as God hoped it would be. How do these chapters reveal God's intent for this spinning globe?

Much of importance is revealed in Genesis 1:1–25. In the six days of creation the deity creates all that we know of the universe: light, the sky, the great bodies of water and land, vegetation, heavenly bodies, and living creatures, including birds, fish, and land-animals. The Creator repeatedly observes that what has been created is "good," and when creation is complete God notes that what has been done is "very good" (Genesis 1:25). Scripture demonstrates that God cares about the natural world and all living things "because they are 'good' in themselves" before people are formed (Wybrow, 264).

Genesis One is clear as to how God viewed the natural world even before people were created—it is God's, and it is good. Genesis One reveals the importance of the natural world to God. Theologians, cognizant of this, have included nature in their vision, "interpreting it as God's good creation, a revealing pathway to the knowledge of God, and a partner in human salvation" (Johnson, 6). How can we not wonder at the majesty of creation that the deity proclaims to be "good" long before human beings are placed on the earth? How can we fail to see our interconnections with beings created together on the sixth day—our partners in salvation? Indeed, it is not surprising that Christianity, "for roughly fifteen centuries... held the natural world in some form of close relationship with humanity and God in their doctrinal and moral reflection" (Johnson, 17).

In his controversial essay, "The Historic Roots of Our Ecologic Crisis (1967), Lynn White noted: "What people do about their ecology depends on what they think about themselves in relation to things around them" (1205). Genesis One has stirred much controversy concerning the rightful place of humankind because, among other things, we are made "in the image of God" and given "dominion." White accused Christianity of being "the most anthropocentric religion the world has seen" (1205). Does Christianity place humans above and apart from the rest of creation such that all else is merely a support system for our purposes? Genesis states:

> Then God said, "Let us make humankind in our image, according to our likeness; and let them have dominion over the fish of the sea and over the birds of the air, and over the cattle, and over all the wild animals of the earth, and over every creeping thing that creeps upon the earth. So God created humankind in his image, in the image of God he created them; male and female he created them (1:26).

What does it mean to be made "in the image of God?" "No expression in Genesis 1 has been debated more forcefully by biblical scholars and theologians alike than the 'image of God,' in the attempt to discover what qualities the image of God bestows" on human beings (Hiebert, 137).

Being made "in the image of God" suggests that we have God-like responsibilities. In the Biblical world, in Egypt and Mesopotamia, kings were regarded as "the image or likeness of the deity" in both "function and position." The king was viewed as "the representative of the deity, with a divine mandate to rule" (Hiebert, 138). In this light, to be made in the "image of God" grants humans "a unique function...as God's representative in creation" (Hiebert, 138). If we have a special place in creation, it "is to be understood primarily in terms of special responsibility" (Kinsley, 172).

What is our special role amid creation? The natural world is God's, and it is good. "[I]maging god, we must love the world and take care of it" (DeWitt, 2000, 306). Perhaps, to "image God is to image God's love and law... to be endowed with dignified responsibility to reflect God's goodness, righteousness, and holiness...to reflect the wisdom, love, and justice of God" (DeWitt, 2003, 354). Biblical creation reveals that we are part of creation, "with special responsibilities," and that "we find God in and through" creation (Cobb, 506–07).

"Dominion" is perhaps the most misunderstood and misrepresented concept in the Hebrew Bible (Hutterman, 282). Dominion is offered to humans over "every living thing that moves upon the earth," which excludes vegetation, land, seas, and the earth itself. Human dominion is decidedly restricted (Hutterman, 283). To better comprehend the limited nature of human dominion, we return to scripture. Immediately after the passage offering "dominion," it is written:

> God said, "See, I have given you every plant yielding seed that is upon the face of all the earth, and every tree with seed in its fruit; you shall have them for food. And to every beast of the earth, and to every bird of the air, and to everything that creeps on the earth, everything that has the breath of life, I have given every green plant for food. And it was so." God saw everything that he had made, and indeed it was very good. And there was evening and there was morning, the sixth day.

Creation is complete only after the deity explains what we are to eat; only then does God pronounces creation to be "very good" (1:31)—then God rests. Humans are to have "dominion," but an "herb-eating dominion is hardly a license for tyranny" (Linzey, 1995, 126). The diet provided by the Creator indicates a divine preference for a world without bloodshed, without the fear and suffering entailed in predators and prey, without deadly exploitation. We are given dominion, but are not instructed by God "to kill animals or touch plants in their basic existence" (Hutterman, 283). Biblical creation is exceptional in the extent to which "[p]eace is the norm of the cosmos from the beginning" (Wink, 188). While the Bible admits violence (such as flesh-eating) in Genesis Chapter Nine, this does not detract from God's original intent. (Indeed, the ensuing Biblical violence, and God's dismay over what had come to pass, speaks to flesh-eating as a degenerate practice that the deity struggles to accept for the sake of a fallen creation.)

Many Christians point to the order of creation to justify a human-centered outlook: we are the final act of creation, which occurred in a particular order, for a particular reason. By this common way of thinking, creation is assumed to unfold such that the last act of creation is the most important, the most precious, and the most entitled. Is there a Christian hierarchy that places humanity above and apart from the rest of creation?

Scripture does not support the assertion that people are created last *because they are the apex of creation*. In fact, this point of view is made ridiculous by the existence of two creation accounts in the first two chapters of Genesis. The second account reports:

> In the day that the Lord God made the earth and the heavens…a stream would rise from the earth, and water the whole face of the ground—then the Lord God formed man from the dust of the ground, and breathed into his nostrils the breath of life; and the man became a living being. And the Lord God planted a garden in Eden, in the east; and there he put the man whom he had formed. Out of the ground the LORD God made to grow every tree that is pleasant to the sight and good for food…
>
> Then the Lord God said, "It is not good that the man should be alone; I will make him a helper as his partner." So out of the ground the Lord God formed every animal of the field and every bird of the air…but for man there was not found a helper as his partner. So the LORD God…took one of his ribs…[and made] a woman and brought her to the man (Gen. 2:4-9, 18–22).

The order of creation here looks very different from that of Genesis One: basic earthly elements, man, vegetation, more complex inanimate matter, animals, and finally woman. If we are to assume that the order of creation establishes a hierarchy, how will this hierarchy be understood in two such diverse accounts of creation? While the two accounts of creation are often understood to play very different roles, it is difficult to defend hierarchical interpretations that hold for only one creation story. If we are to find a hierarchy of being in creation, how are we to make sense of a creation account in which vegetation and all other animals are created between man and woman? The order of creation is best viewed as irrelevant to status and privilege. Just because God created humans first or last does not override the more important implications of creation: all that exists is good and it is God's.

Genesis Chapter Two provides other key passages. For example, God "took the man and put him in the garden of Eden to till and keep it," telling the man that he might eat of every tree but one (2:15–16). (As in Genesis Chapter One, there is no mention of animals being given to human beings for food.) Here we find the most explicit account of what human beings—or at least men—are to *do*. The Hebrew word often translated as "till" in Genesis Two (*'abad*), is translated as "serve" in other portions of the Bible, such as Joshua 24:15: "Choose this day whom you will serve, whether the gods your ancestors served… or the Gods of the Amorites" (DeWitt, "Behemoth," 204). The first man is a gardener, intended to "serve" and keep the garden, as "slave to master" (Hiebert, 140). The "Biblical expectation that human beings will 'serve the garden' means that" we are to tend creation "as an act of service" (DeWitt, "Three," 354). Service holds a place of prestige in many religions, and is understood to be foundational to Christianity. With regard to the natural world—creation—human "service should reflect God's love for the world" (DeWitt, 354).

The word "keep" also appears in Numbers 6:24: "The Lord bless you and keep you" (DeWitt, 353). "Keep" implies a vitality, a nurturing of "life-sustaining and life-fulfilling relationships.... [This] is an extremely rich word with a deeply penetrating meaning that evokes a loving, caring, sustaining keeping" (DeWitt, 353). We are to "keep" God's fragile bounty. As God keeps us so should we "keep" God's earth (DeWitt, 303).

"Dominion," viewed in its biblical context, a context of service wherein we are charged to serve and keep creation in all its splendor and vitality, requires submission and diligence, and reveals our rightful role with respect to Creator and creation. Genesis Chapter Two reveals man "as the servant, not the master, of the land. It emphasizes human dependence on, rather than dominion over, the earth" (Hiebert, 140). People, all other animals, and vegetation are connected—made from the same arable soil—emphasizing that we are "not distinguished from other forms of life but identified with them" (Hiebert, 139). The human being and animals alike are called "living beings" (Hiebert, 139). Though Genesis only mentions that God has put the breath of life into human beings, we later find that all animate creatures have the breath of life (Genesis 2:7). This suggests that the deity "does not grant the first human being a soul or spiritual character different from the animals, since this breath is the physical breath of all animate life" (cf. Gen. 7:22). Animals are created from the same soil, given the same breath of life, and intended as helpers and companions in the task of keeping the garden.

> It is not good that the man should be alone; I will make him a helper as his partner....God formed every animal of the field and every bird of the air...but for the man there was not found a helper as his partner. So the Lord God...made...woman and brought her to the man (Genesis 2:18–22).

While no "partner" was found, partnership was God's intent when creating other animals, and the role of "helper" intended for other species—helping to serve and keep creation—is never revoked.

Eco-Justice: The Christian Call to Action

Christian love is understood to originate in the munificence of divine love and to connect each of us with the Almighty (Allen, vol 12, 214). 1 John 4:8 and 1 John 4:16 state simply, "God is love." In this passage love is "not merely an attribute of God but defines his nature, though in a practical rather than philosophic sense....God's nature is not exhausted by the quality of love, but love governs all its aspects and expressions" (Buttrick 12: 280). Christians are called to copy this example. Almost all Christians agree that love is "the paramount scripture...essential to the Christian way of life" (Allen 12: 214). The love of Jesus—God as love—demands a life of *radical* compassion. Christian sensitivity to suffering measures our fidelity to a compassionate Creator. Any theology that "desensitizes us to suffering" of any kind "cannot properly be a theology centered on the divine vindication of innocent suffering" (Linzey, 1997, 132). An understanding of

Christian love, or of God's love, that limits care and affection "is spiritually impoverished" (Linzey, 1997, 131).

It ought to be an embarrassment that Christians so often and so loudly vocalize their central tenet of love while congregations and ministers alike demonstrate and teach that love turned toward other living beings, or the natural world, is misplaced. Indeed, some of the most adamant voices raised against respect for the earth are to be found in pulpits and the Christian press. Jesus demonstrates compassion; love in action. Christian love is expected to aim for that generous love demonstrated by God. For practicing Christians, love is understood to be limitless. All religions, and "especially Christianity, teach that one can expand one's capacity to love, and ought consciously to do so" (Halley, unpublished manuscript).

"In the story of the Good Samaritan and elsewhere, Christ expanded the idea of 'love your neighbor' outwards from the small circle of 'Jews' to a much larger circle of people including Samaritans.... St. Paul continued the process (Gal 3:28), extending the circle to include all gentiles.... Perhaps there is no limit" (Halley, unpublished). Romans 8 and Colossians 1, demonstrate that Jesus died to redeem *all* of creation. We are still in much need of stretching our heart-strings to include all that God has called "good."

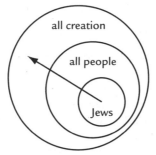

Jesus modeled a life of all-embracing love that entailed the ultimate sacrifice: "In the light of Jesus, Christian loving can only properly be defined in terms of that kind of loving which costs us something" (Linzey, 1997, 102). The beatitudes teach that "those who are persecuted for righteousness' sake" are blessed, and "theirs is the kingdom of heaven" (Mat 5:10). Christians are warned that "all who want to live a godly life in Christ Jesus will be persecuted" (2 Tim. 3:12, also see John 15:18–25 and Rom. 8:35–36). Scripture demands *sacrificial* love.

Christianity is rooted in "compassionate service to others" and affirms personal "responsibility to 'care for creation'" (French, 488). How should Christian love be manifest toward nature in contemporary times? God's love for all of creation confers intrinsic value to all of God's creatures and creations. It is this fundamental measure of worth which serves as the foundation of justice. Christians are called by God to love what God loves, to value what God values, and to join with God in the process of redemption—to restore the right relationships of a good creation in a fallen world.

Justice understood in this light is not simply "rendering to each their due," but is more profoundly understood as "rendering to each their dignity as a creation of God." Christians are called by God to restore dignity by remedying the injustices that violate the dignity of God's creation (Martin-Schramm, 440).

The love of Jesus and his renunciation of oppression must now include contemporary oppression brought to nature by humans. His distaste for conventional hierarchies must now include a rejection of the idea that humans are above, or apart, from nature. "His healing stories can be extended to the deteriorating ecosystems of our planet; his practice of eating with outcasts is pertinent to the extinction of species and loss of habitats due to human over-development and consumption" (McFague, 35).

If the earth is indeed creation, a sacrament of the glory of God with its own intrinsic value, then, for those of the Christian persuasion, ongoing destruction of Earth bears the marks of deep sinfulness. Through greed, self-interest, ignorance, and injustice, human beings are bringing violent disfigurement and death to this living, evolving planet that God created as "very good" (Gen 1:31). Ecocide, biocide, genocide—these new terms attempt to name the killing of ecosystems and species that are meant to radiate the glory of God but, instead, end up broken or extinct. "One of the 'books' [in creation] that teaches about the ultimate Giver of life is being ruined: as matter for religious concern, this has the character of moral imperative" (Johnson, 15).

Daily violence toward creation, intensified and aggrandized by modern industries such as factory farming, technology such as automobiles, and household products such as Styrofoam and pesticides would seem immeasurably worse than any violence a handful of people might have brought to the earth in Noah's time, violence which did not threaten the ozone layer or entire species. Yet even the violence of Noah's day was appalling in the eye of the deity—so shocking and objectionable that the Almighty determined to make an end of all that had been created rather than maintain a world of such violence.

The life of Jesus and his moral imperative to act on behalf of the downtrodden are "easily extended to nature: nature is the 'new poor;' nature deserves justice"—all of creation is worthy of our attention and spiritual energy (McFague, 30). For those who are human-centered in their vision, the "inclusion of nature as the 'new poor' may seem sentimental or even ludicrous... but it does not seem so from either a theocentric or a cosmocentric point of view. If the Redeemer is the Creator, then surely God cares also for the other 99 percent of creation, not just for the 1 percent (actually, less than 1 percent) that humans constitute" (McFague, 35). The justice and care that Christians believe their human neighbors, especially oppressed neighbors, deserve "should be extended to the natural world. What this will mean in practice is complex, varied, and costly," as is love and care for needy human neighbors.

The "*principle* that Jesus' ministry is focused on God's oppressed creatures must, in our day, include the deteriorating planet" (McFague, 35). The function of the church is as "guardian of creation" (Daneel, 535). Christianity has "an important role to play in the pursuit of sustainable community" (Hallman, 467). "Jesus does not propose armed revolution. But he does lay the foundations for social revolution" (Wink, 183). The life of Jesus calls us to extend moral consideration—justice and compassion—"from the human neighbor to 'otherkind' and the earth itself.... Solidarity with victims... and action on behalf of justice widen out to embrace life systems and other species" (Johnson, 15). Our conflict with nature is damaging, and is waged against the helpless and the innocent, causing extinctions, soil erosion, deforestation, and climate change. Our way of life brings "carnage and many casualties, as in any war... highlighting the need for the moral equivalent of planetary peacemaking" (French, 487).

Religion is rooted in faith; faith is expressed in action. The religious life includes "both reflection and action, contemplation and practice" (Mische, 591). Christians are to reflect personal faith, their understanding of our divinely ordained role to serve and keep God's creation, in daily life. Christianity calls for an all-embracing love, and action on behalf of the needy and the defenseless. Jesus spoke against greed and oppression; he commanded us to help those in need—*whoever* "those" might be. Jesus "abhors both passivity and violence"—but not all forms of violence (Wink, 189). Jesus did not call for tranquility but for activism that "seeks out conflict, elicits conflict, exacerbates conflict" in order to move "against perceived injustice proactively with the same alacrity as the most hawkish militarist" (Wink, 192). It is not surprising, then, that Jesus was stirred to overturn the tables of those who profited at the expense of devotees and the sacred.

Jesus entered the temple and drove out all who were selling and buying in the temple, and he overturned the tables of the money changers and seats of those who sold doves. He said to them, "It is written, 'My house shall be called a house of prayer;' but you are making it a den of robbers." (Mat. 21:12).

According to scripture, in the temple he found people selling cattle, sheep, and doves, and the money changers seated at their tables. Making a whip of cords, he drove all of them out of the temple, both the sheep and the cattle. He also poured out the coins of the money changers and overturned their tables. He told those who were selling doves, "Take these things out of here! Stop making my Father's house a marketplace!" (John 2:14–16).

It is critical to note that "turning over tables" is not violence against life. Many "eco-terrorist actions" fit this long biblical tradition of radical Christian activism. Is this not sensible given our present transgressions against the earth—against what is rightly God's? Does not our current way of life defile that which we were charged to serve and keep?

"*Anger* bristles through the prophets, and why not? The Biblically astute Thomas [Aquinas, *Summa Theologiae*] said that anger looks to the
good of justice, so that those who do not have it in the face of injustice love
justice too little. Thomas loved John Chrysostom's dictum: 'Whoever is not
angry when there is cause for anger, sins!'" (Maguire 419). Christians have
cause to be angry with individuals who profit at the expense of the earth,
at the expense of all of us, at the expense of our rightful relations with God
and creation. Faced with the realities of today, more radical actions are
not only appropriate, but necessary; "[s]imple, sensible approaches won't
do it" (Maguire, 419).

Given our wayward civilization, how are Christians to confess "creation's integrity in word and deed" (DeWitt, 2000, 305)? Some work with
the government to change and create policies that limit the damage we
cause to the natural order, and to promote policies that are earth-sustain-
ing (French, 488). Others simply "turn to the earth, respecting it and caring for it in local, ordinary, mundane ways" (McFague, 33). Still others
"seeking God's will on earth," are called to direct action: for "wild creatures
this may mean a benign beholding by human onlookers. For threatened
creatures and kinds it will involve rescue work, considered incomplete until the rescued are liberated from human keeping into self-sustaining habitats" (DeWitt, 2000, 304). Yet other strong Christians are called to "turn
over the tables," to use physical force against property—"violence" that
harms no life—in defense of God's beautiful and fragile Earth. Does not
the value of God's creation, and the Christian duty to the Creator, surpass
human property rights?

Many activists do not consider violence against property to be a form
of violence. Many members of the ALF and ELF consider only threats
against life to be violence. Based on the dictionary definition, this seems
disingenuous. In *Empty Cages*, Tom Regan writes:

> The American Heritage College Dictionary defines violence as
> physical force exerted for the purpose of violating, damaging, or
> abusing, it does not say that the damage must involve a sentient
> being. We do not need to hurt someone in order to use violence
> against something. If the ALF uses an incendiary device to level
> a building, they engage in some serious violence. To speak of the
> "violent destruction of property" is not a contradiction in terms.
> Why persist in denying the obvious (188–89)?

While Jesus spoke repeatedly of a new moral order, an order of equality and love, and acted with righteous violence against property toward
those who set up shop in the temple, the prophets frequently behaved in
bizarre ways with intent to gain the attention of humans—in the hope of
calling people away from doom, back to God. It is difficult to turn people away from their customary daily lives; it is yet more difficult to bring
about a deep spiritual change that alters behavior. "Conversion of socially
entrenched valuations is an area needing attention if this earth is not to
die....The effort to supplant the dominant consciousness with an alterna-

tive social consciousness seeks a revolution in affect. The target is 'the heart' (Isa. 51:7; Jer. 4:4; 4:14; 31:35; Amos 6:6)" (Maguire, 418). This is the role of prophecy.

"Prophecy is essentially eccentric, coming from the Greek, outside the center. The center is where the addicts of comfort and safety dwell. Prophecy leaves them and pushes to the edges where new horizons can be seen. Resistance to the dominant consciousness anchored in ill-gotten privilege is the essence of prophetic eccentricity" (Maguire, 420). The prophets stood for truth; they stood against those with power (Wink, 188). They were persecuted for stepping outside the center, for threatening the established order. Christians, too, must expect persecution when we move outside the center to align with God rather than humanity. Christians are to "rejoice and be glad" when persecuted, for it is written that when persecuted, "your reward is great in heaven, for in the same way they persecuted the prophets who were before you" (Mat. 5:11).

Radical actions on behalf of God, sometimes motivated by righteous anger, are fundamental to scripture and to religious history. Again, consider the prophets. Isaiah wandered "naked and barefoot" for three years (20:204). Micah also abandoned clothing along with other conventional ways of behaving: "Therefore I must howl and wail and go naked" (1:8). "Nakedness was taboo in Judaism" (Wink, 179). Nudity became recognized as one of the indicators of prophecy so that when Saul stripped, people asked: "Is Saul also among the prophets?' (1 Sam. 19:24). "Jeremiah harnessed himself to a yoke and was seen, understandably enough, as a 'madman' (27:3; 29:26). Ezekiel cut off his hair with a sword and scattered it to the winds (5:1–2). Jesus was so intemperate he was seen as 'a prophet like one of the old prophets' (Mark 6:15). He was a scandal because, as Walter Brueggeman says, he violated 'propriety, reason, and good public order'" (Maguire, 420–21). And shouldn't we all for the cause of God? Should we not use even the most radical actions, short of harming life, to gain attention and bring a conversion of heart on behalf of this creation that we were charged to serve and tend and instead savage, exploit, and terrorize (Maguire, 419)? "The prophets intuited that only outrage speaks to outrage.... Only shock gets through" (Maguire, 420). With prophecy as a model, and a radical change from our present course of doom as the goal, biblical "shock therapy," is a legitimate Christian approach to serving and tending the earth.

Like prophets of old, those in today's eco-justice movement warn of disasters that will befall the earth if we do not change our ways—if we do not have a change of heart that carries with it a change in the way we live. "Radical" contemporary environmental activists (and animal rights activists) employ methods that parallel those of the prophets. The animal rights group, People for the Ethical Treatment of Animals, does an annual naked march on Fur Free Friday, the day after Thanksgiving, in order to protest loudly against buying and wearing fur on the busiest shopping day of the year. They stage mock clubbings of women in which fur coats are torn from the "victims" and they are left lying naked—in blood-red paint—on a busy sidewalk. Protestors against the World Trade Organization in Seattle, Washington (November of 1999), put on *extra* "garments" to make an eco-statement on behalf of endangered turtles. "Two hundred and forty people dressed as turtles marched together with a twenty foot inflatable sea turtle float" (Sea). For those who witnessed the event, whether in person or on TV, such a lively herd of turtles was impossible to ignore; their eco-message was carried to the masses via outlandish, turtle-clad activists. Many of these protestors were arrested for their efforts; persecution is to be expected for those who act on behalf of God's good creation.

Biblically, such modern persecution is light-weight. Jesus provides a paradigm "for a way of life that ends on the cross" because the powerful have a vested interest in oppression. The Animal Liberation Front and the Earth Liberation Front are just two liberation groups that use "shock therapy," or destruction of property on behalf of the planet and its many enslaved and endangered creatures, are not likely to be awarded medals by law enforcement—or by local churches. In the first decade of the twenty-first century they are more likely to be labeled "eco-terrorists" or "animal rights terrorists," and to serve time in jail—fighting for justice against the powers that be remains costly 2000 years after the death of Jesus. Never mind that such radicals, who destroy only property, who sacrifice their time to protect and defend oppressed creation, and who risk their freedom for God's good creation, are employing shock-techniques recognizable as those of the prophets, and are walking closer to the footprints of Jesus than most of the rest of us ever will.

And God Declared Defense of the Earth to Be Good

Spiritual eco-justice requires a sense of interconnections, a deep and abiding respect for nature, "reinforced by a spiritual power to act on its behalf" (Gulick, 194). Christianity offers both.

Genesis Chapter One and Two provide the only accounts of what God intended for creation—the only account of planet Earth before it was sullied by the fall. These chapters reveal the value of all that has been created—all of which is already good in God's sight before human beings are created. All creatures are interconnected through the Creator, through the breath of life. A close reading of scripture does not support the view that dominion allows us to harm the earth or other animals for our benefit. For example, there is no Biblical support for the common Christian claim that animals were created as food for people. On the contrary, we are made in God's image, to serve and care for creation.

Preeminent teachings of love, and the life of social activism modeled by Jesus, indicate that Christians are called to act on behalf of creation because it is God's, because it is good, and because we have been charged to keep and serve creation. Toward this end, Christians have at their disposal outrageous acts pioneered by the prophets, and violence against property—a violence that risks no life—modeled by Jesus. Indeed, ideally Christians will find themselves on a little-trodden path laid out by one no less than Jesus, a spirituality of self-sacrificing service that reaches out to protect and defend the whole of God's wondrous creation.

Bibliography

Allen, Clifton J. *Broadman Bible Commentary*, 12 vols. Nashville: Broadman Press, 1971.

Buttrick, George Arthur, ed. and trans. *The Interpreter's Bible*, 12 vols. New York: Abingdon, 1956.

Cobb, John B Jr. "Christianity, Economics, and Ecology." In *Christianity and Ecology: Seeking the Well-Being of Earth and Humans*, edited by Dieter T. Hessel and Rosemary Radford Ruether. Cambridge: Harvard University Press. 2000, 497–511.

Coffin, Sloane. "The Politics of Compassion: The Heart is a Little to the Left." In *Harvard Divinity Bulletin*. 28, 2/3 (1999): 11–12.

Daneel, Marthinus L. "Earthkeeping Churches at the African Grass Roots." In *Christianity and Ecology: Seeking the Well-Being of Earth and Humans*, edited by Dieter T. Hessel and Rosemary Radford Ruether. Cambridge: Harvard University Press, 2000, 531–52.

DeWitt, Calvin. "Behemoth and Batrachians in the Eye of God." In *Christianity and Ecology: Seeking the Well-Being of Earth and Humans*, edited by Dieter T. Hessel and Rosemary Radford Ruether. Cambridge: Harvard University Press, 2000.

___."The Three Big Questions." In *Worldviews, Religion, and the Environment: A Global Anthology*, edited by Richard C. Foltz. Belmont: Wadsworth, 2003.

French, William C. "Ecological Security and Policies of Restraint." In *Christianity and Ecology: Seeking the Well-Being of Earth and Humans*, edited by Dieter T. Hessel and Rosemary Radford Ruether. Cambridge: Harvard University Press, 2000.

Gulick, Walter B. "The Bible and Ecological Spirituality." *Theology Today* 48.2 (July 1991): 182–194.

Halley, John. Unpublished communications to author. May 1999 and Sept 2004.

Hallman, David G. "Climate Change: Ethics, Justice, and Sustainable Community." In *Christianity and Ecology: Seeking the Well-Being of Earth and Humans*, edited by Dieter T. Hessel and Rosemary Radford Ruether. Cambridge: Harvard University Press. 2000.

Hiebert, Theodore. "The Human Vocation: Origins and Transformations in Christian Traditions." In *Christianity and Ecology: Seeking the Well-Being of Earth and Humans*, edited by Dieter T. Hessel and Rosemary Radford Ruether. Cambridge: Harvard University Press, 2000.

Hutterman, Aloys. "Genesis 1—The Most Misunderstood Part of the Bible." In *Worldviews, Religion, and the Environment: A Global Anthology*, edited by Richard C. Foltz. Belmont: Wadsworth, 2003.

Johnson, Elizabeth A. "Losing and Finding Creation in the Christian Tradition." In *Christianity and Ecology: Seeking the Well-Being of Earth and Humans*, edited by Dieter T. Hessel and Rosemary Radford Ruether. Cambridge: Harvard University Press, 2000.

Kinsley, David. *Ecology and Religion: Ecological Spirituality in the Cross Cultural Perspective*. Englewood Cliffs: Prentice Hall, 1995.

Linzey, Andrew. *Animal Theology*. Chicago: University of Illinois Press, 1995.

___.and Dan Cohn-Sherbok. *After Noah: Animals and the Liberation of Theology*. London: Mowbray, 1997.

Maguire, Daniel C. "Population, Consumption, Ecology: The Triple Problematic." In *Christianity and Ecology: Seeking the Well-Being of Earth and Humans*, edited by Dieter T. Hessel and Rosemary Radford Ruether. Cambridge: Harvard University Press, 2000.

Martin-Schramm, James B. "Incentives, Consumption Patterns, and Population Policies: A Christian Ethical Perspective." In *Christianity and Ecology: Seeking the Well-Being of Earth and Humans*, edited by Dieter T. Hessel and Rosemary Radford Ruether. Cambridge: Harvard University Press, 2000.

McFague, Sallie. "An Ecological Christology: Does Christianity Have It?" In *Christianity and Ecology: Seeking the Well-Being of Earth and Humans,* eds. Dieter T. Hessel and Rosemary Radford Ruether. Cambridge: Harvard Univerity Press, 2000.

Mische, Patricia M. "The Integrity of Creation: Challenges and Opportunities for Praxis." In *Christianity and Ecology: Seeking the Well-Being of Earth and Humans,* eds. Dieter T. Hessel and Rosemary Radford Ruether. Cambridge: Harvard University Press, 2000.

Peterson, Anna. "In and of the World?: Christian Theological Anthropology and Environmental Ethics." In *Worldviews, Religion, and the Environment: A Global Anthology,* edited by Richard C. Foltz. Belmont: Wadsworth, 2003.

Regan, Tom. *Empty Cages: Facing the Challenge of Animal Rights*. New York: Rowman & Littlefield, 2004.

Sea Turtle Restoration Project. "Press Release." 12/02/99. <http://www.seaturtles.org/press_release2.cfm?pressID=40>

White, Lynn Jr., "The Historical Roots of Our Ecologic Crisis," *Science* 155, (1967): 1203–07.

Wink, Walter. *Engaging the Powers: Discernment and Resistance in a World of Domination.* Minneapolis: Fortress, 1992.

Wybrow, Richard Cameron. "The Bible, Baconism, and Mastery over Nature: The Old Testament and Its Modern Misreading." Diss, McMaster University, 1990. In *Ecology and Religion: Ecological Spirituality in the Cross Cultural Perspective,* edited by David Kinsley. Englewood Cliffs: Prentice Hall, 1995.

Notes

1. Special thanks for feedback on this essay to colleagues (and friends) Rev. Kim Woeste, Dr. Walter Gulick, and Dr. John Halley.

2. Biblical quotes are from the *New Revised Standard Version.*

Gwarth-E-Lass: Stick Standing Strong

Wanbli Watakpe and Paula Ostrovsky

For our daughter Victoria Lakota
and all the coming generations of indigenous children.

You turned to face me and asked, with that smirk and crazy look
in your eyes, how many flesh offerings I was going to give. I said
seven. You turned away, and then, just as abruptly, turned back
again, looked at me, and said "s-e-v-e-n-n-n" in your *iktomi* voice.
"S-e-v-e-n," I said back defiantly, more embarrassed than anything else and shot back to you: "How many you giving, Leonard??" You stopped a minute then grew tall, stood very straight,
looked me squarely in the eyes and said fifty. "Fifty?" I said. "Ok,"
I muttered to myself. You must have noticed this but said nothing. We gave 50 pieces of flesh together, about 30 of us warriors.
This is what we will do again, give flesh together, my brother.

They have you in a box. Thirty years of withstanding their
torture, for defending your land and your People. Leonard Peltier,
you are the mighty one, Stick-Standing-Strong; I remember when
the Native Tribes in the north gave you that name, I was there.
Our enemies won't hurt you any more where you're going, but
before you depart there is a ceremony we must finish so they will
know your name. The Northwest American Indian Movement is
back, your warrior brothers are charging again and we ain't leaving without you. We've come to take you home, Leonard...

Our lives and struggles are always connected to the land. Our creation
stories take place in our land, we are from it, we ARE it. When concerned environmentalists try to protect other species from extinction they
often do not see indigenous people also as endangered. When they do not
see our fight for the land the same as they see theirs, they allow their sub-
conscious ethnocentric beliefs that perceive our plight as solely political to
skew their views, confuse their minds, and harden their hearts. It is not we
who have to adjust our beliefs and language to fit in a wider environmental
agenda. It is the environmentalists who must learn to see our plight as the
original issue to address, from which all concerns for Mother Earth under
the present global reality stem. Yet what the Western world labels as "environmental" and our social plight—our indigenous fight for the land—are

one and the same thing. We ask the readers to stretch their minds and for once adjust to an indigenous framework.

Rectifying the Language

Our enemy does not totally grasp our inter-being with the land the Creator gave us to care for, but they understand this much: without our land we cease to be, we become shadows and start to die. Hence the reason for all of the enemy's policies of removal, relocation, and displacement, of plundering our Mother Earth, especially our sacred sites, those places that connect us with our *Tunkasila* (Grandfather) more than any other place on this Earth. Consequently, we move further and further away from our original instructions, to the point that we don't know them anymore.

All we have left to connect us with those original instructions, the land, and who we are is our ceremonies. Our indigenous movement only prospers when guided by our ceremonies; the moment it is corrupted or betrayed by the western Ego game of recognition and worldly accumulation of objects and comfort, it ceases to thrive. In the Lakota way we must strive to be *ikce wicasa*, an ordinary person who has learned humility before the Creator, ready to meet Him with no shame. Our indigenous movement has been derailed by those so-called leaders that succumbed to the western temptations, but now it is again back in the hands of the warriors, the foot soldiers, the "footnotes in western history." Our inspiration and strength comes from our warrior brother Leonard Peltier, who has withstood three decades of the torture of a wrongful imprisonment and continues to resist with dignity.

As warriors in a sacred path we will use what the enemy can never have, the knowledge that as much as he tries to twist our truth with his science, *we belong here*. As much as he tries to defile our land with asphalt, concrete, and poisons, *the land is ours*. As much as he tries to appropriate our culture and our ceremonies, they will always be our own unique way to reach The Creator. As much as he tries to crush and imprison our spirits, they rise above his prisons and his lies.

In this way, the enemy may have the body of our warrior Leonard Peltier—who stood tall to defend our people and our land—locked up in a cage, but his spirit soars and makes us take flight unafraid. Each day they keep him imprisoned his spirit grows stronger; each day they have to invent a new lie to justify his incarceration, they grow weaker. It might not be obvious in the human frame of time and space, but we have already won.

Leonard's life unfolds as an ancient sacred ceremony. He is like a sun dancer in the last round when the piercing takes place. This is how we should know his story, exorcising the tale we keep hearing over and over from the mouths and pens of the colonial executioners, the oppressor's words carefully assembled to uphold their myth.

The mere utterance of the oppressor's language traumatizes our history. Those alien words—idiosyncratic encumbrances, words that are awkward for an indigenous tongue, carrying their jungle-of-junk culture—diffuse, affix, and re-invent to obfuscate meaning and fit circumstances. As Confucius said, we need to rectify the language, because our invaders are not going to do it. They call us "Indians," our land "America," their invasion "discovery," our genocide "conquest," our massacres "battles," the battles they lose "murders," our sacred places the "devil's places," and on and on, ad infinitum. They need to perpetuate their lies to be able to continue living, walking on our ancestors' bones, raping our Mother Earth, as if it was their hard-earned right. We must begin to use our own words to wake up from this nightmare and begin our healing.

The (Second) Siege of Wounded Knee

A lonely hamlet called the Wounded Knee ville was occupied and seized in the early morning hours on February 27, 1973 under the pretense of going to an "Indian pow-wow." The forces that assembled there were from the superpower's elite law enforcement community: the FBI and US Marshals with additional help from the Department of War (now Department of the Interior) and the Bureau of Indian Affairs (BIA). The superpower government provided training for all of the BIA officers and also the Special Operations Group which trained its elite rangers at the School of the Americas in Fort Benning, Georgia. The "Tribal Council" also had their own police and the Chairman had deputized a local militia called the GOONs or GOON Squad.

The puppet tribal government and its pawns soon understood that they were in danger of being exposed before a worldwide audience. They rushed to devise a way to cut off exposure through their media. The first thing was to organize a local support group and next look for a viable scapegoat. That was not hard to find—in fact the scapegoat was too willing, and held up at the historic Wounded Knee, "America's" most visible mass grave.

This most unlikely group of warriors was not only not hiding but taking up arms and challenging the superpower, calling them out. We had no army, no money, no education and no support, two hundred warriors at most, but we held up the most powerful forces in the world for the next 71 days. We resisted the culture that spawned the Crusades against the Islamic world, dropped the Atomic Bomb on innocent Japanese civilians, and now pretended to stand as guardian against tyranny worldwide.

Over the next three years, with the support of the superpower's federal law enforcement agencies providing intelligence, arms and money, the puppet government was successful in putting down a potential revolt on the Pine Ridge reservation. This alliance between tribal governments and US interests still pollutes all tribal life and keeps a thumb on the pulse of the Indigenous community.

Leonard Peltier was in Pine Ridge at the request of the Oglala People. His mission was to protect them from Dick Wilson (the US government's puppet dictator at the time), the FBI, and the GOONs, and to assist with security in Dennis Banks' trial being held in Custer, South Dakota. The FBI was not in the Pine Ridge Indian Reservation to enforce the law, but rather to support the Tribal Council system, its rogue dictator and murderer Dick Wilson, and any actions taken against Oglala Sioux Civil Rights Organization and AIM. In return, Dick Wilson gave away a quarter of the Pine Ridge Reservation to the State of South Dakota, and established the white town in Martin and Bennet County on prime ranching land.

The "crime scene" in which they have framed Peltier was actually a *battleground*. On June 26, 1975, armed US government combatants illegally entered non-US territory, and attacked a group of armed civilians defending their land and families. Leonard Peltier was among those resisting the aggression. Two FBI agents who attacked the AIM camp, allegedly to serve a warrant they did not have, prompted the firefight that led to the assassination of Joseph Bedell Stuntz, a young warrior who was developing into a formidable leader, and ultimately their own deaths as well. The BIA and Tribal GOON squad were also present along with several hundred law enforcement types in military garb, and supported by helicopters and armored vehicles. They fired all day against, perhaps, two dozen people, half of whom were unarmed females and children. It was a miracle this attack did not conclude with their massacre.

The Trial

The FBI is responsible for protecting and investigating capital crime on reservations. This mission is in stark contrast with their causing and engaging in a firefight to allegedly serve a warrant they did not have, for a minor robbery case, on a person who was not there. After the melee and killings they gratuitously caused, the FBI framed and charged Peltier for the deaths of two agents. Peltier fled to Canada, but was extradited and forced to serve trial in the US in 1977.

Peltier's extradition from Canada and trial in the US was another travesty that mocked even the US' own laws and judicial system. In order to obtain his extradition from Canada, US attorneys, together with the US prosecutor in Canada, conspired with the FBI to coerce Myrtle Poor Bear, a woman with a history of mental health issues, to sign affidavits implicating Leonard Peltier in the shooting of the FBI agents. Peltier was charged with the "murder" of the two agents and given two consecutive life sentences.

During Peltier's trial, key evidence that exonerated him was withheld, witnesses were held and intimidated by the FBI, the FBI had "exparte" communications (meaning that they met outside the courtroom to go over what needed to happen to convict Peltier) with a judge trying the case. Peltier's defense team was infiltrated, and the prosecution was receiving first-hand information concerning the defense. We have reason to believe infiltration was still occurring as recently as June, 2005.

As it has often done historically with indigenous issues, the US government acknowledges its misconduct but washes its hands of the case. The United States Court of Appeals for the Eighth Circuit ruled in 1986 that the prosecution had indeed withheld evidence which would have been favorable to Leonard Peltier and would have allowed him to cross-examine witnesses more effectively. But it still upheld Leonard's conviction. Even the Tenth Circuit Court stated: "Much of the government behavior at the Pine Ridge Reservation and in prosecuting Mr. Peltier is to be condemned. The government withheld documents. It intimidated witnesses. These facts are undisputed....But [this] is a question we have no authority to review." Even US Attorney, Lynn Crooks, has admitted the government does not know who shot the agents, but continues his work to ensure Leonard never again walks this earth a free man.

They say there is nothing they can do to change Leonard's fate, but they can certainly torture him, and move him at will. This western government operates with man-made laws and violates them at will because its men wrote them. This is a convenient exercise but also has a tactical purpose since it is used to distract people from the real intentions, which are not honorable, and do not include us. We do not operate by those intentions or laws. There is no man who can make a law to keep the salmon from swimming upstream, but they can certainly destroy the river. We operate by the spiritual laws, the law of the ceremony.

The Injustice Continues

The government still refuses to release over 140,000 pages of documents related to the case, many of which are being destroyed. The FBI is afraid of the truth. The Minneapolis FBI office has most of these documents. This is the same office that withheld documents on 9/11 and Timothy McVeigh.

This FBI "policy" of targeting Leonard Peltier has never ended. The agency has intervened at every juncture in which Leonard could have some hope of freedom, including presidential clemency and parole, by launching systematic and officially sanctioned campaigns of misinformation and disinformation.

A memorandum, recently obtained by Peltier's legal team through the Freedom of Information Act, describes an FBI meeting in 1993 regarding the agency's intervention against Peltier's clemency bid and contains instructions to "get the story out publicly through *Reader's Digest, Life, Detective Magazine,* or other publications which have worked closely with the FBI over the years." It also instructs that if Pulitzer Prize winner journalists Mike Royko and Jack Anderson wrote a "fictionalized" story or column FBI Headquarters should respond displaying Clarke's (FBI Director at the time) name to show their "level of concern with bad information."

Other memoranda describe the FBI pressuring Robert Redford, Senator Daniel Inouye, and Judge Heaney to change their stance of public support for Leonard Peltier. On July 15, 1994, the FBI Agents Association and the Society of Former Agents of the FBI ran an ad in the *Washington Post* and hundreds of agents marched opposing clemency for Peltier.

. More recently, in 2003, the FBI paid Kamook Nichols (a woman closely associated with the AIM leadership and an acquaintance of Peltier) to testify in the Arlo Looking Cloud trial regarding the murder of Anna Mae Aquash. In this trial she stated, out of context, and without being asked, that Leonard had confessed to her that he had killed the agents. She also implicated Leonard in the murder of his dear friend Anna Mae. She contends she participated in this legal charade to help bring justice for "her friend" Anna Mae, even though Anna Mae was having an affair with her husband (Dennis Banks) and she had stated to me [Russ Redner] in 1994 that she "was glad the bitch was dead."

Soon after the Looking Cloud trial, in a ceremony attended by many FBI agents, Kamook Nichols married Robert Ecoffey, former head of the GOON squad who was later promoted to US Marshal. It is obvious that the transcripts stemming from this trial will be used against Leonard in his next parole hearing, when we will see another FBI campaign of mis/disinformation using a much more FBI-friendly media, expertly manipulated and prepped by the Bush administration.

How much money and time has the FBI dedicated to ensure Leonard Peltier dies in prison? What other prisoner of the US gets this special treatment from the government? While the top agency charged to guard national security pours so much of its resources into making sure a man who is already in prison does not get justice, that same agency lets key evidence that would have prevented the 9/11 attacks slide. The FBI's obsession with Leonard Peltier borders on psychotic and prevents it from doing the job with which it has been entrusted, making the agency dangerous and obsolete.

Wars of Aggression and the New Resistance

With the objective of showing all those who are fighting for the land to what extremes the government of the United States will go to crush our efforts, we seek to expose the vendetta against our beloved warrior. At this point, Leonard's life is endangered. He is sixty years old, in poor health, and at the whim of his captors who have already attempted to break him and murder him. Now they render him to some of their worse prisons, taking away what little they have allowed him; they've restricted ceremonies, limited contact with his loved ones, and taken his painting and right to fresh air. The FBI-led society, forever enforcing their laws upon indigenous generation after generation, has not relented on his case. Even their Presidents—some cowards, some racists, others automatons, and most puppets, but tyrants all of them—dance to the tune of the FBI.

George W. Bush, the latest Emperor, is well anchored inside the western box of democracy and the disingenuous idea that Nations can only attain a just government and freedom based upon the Americanists' imperialist and intrusive perspective. Bush has it correct when he states, "This is war," and among his few more eloquent quips' "War is a dangerous place." I am still trying to figure where that place ends, but for us, the indigenous peoples of these lands, it has been reality for too long. War is exactly what was occurring on the battlefield in the Oglala, Pine Ridge Theater from 1973 to 1976. Even though the US war and policies of destruction against the indigenous people have never stopped, that era and its "Reign of Terror" represents one of the most violent periods in contemporary times and coincides with the COINTELPRO operations led by the FBI against all groups they considered anti-American. Today we have to contend with a resurrection of those operations in the intelligence activities endorsed by the Patriot Act.

Those that supported the government's intrusion and use of military/paramilitary clandestine operations also condoned the liquidation of Tribal sovereignty. Among those was the puppet government, the Tribal council, backed by the US. This was (is) really a deliberate obstruction of true democracy, of our original forms of government. Why? The answers are varied but the bottom line is the land and resources, it is always the land and resources. The second consideration is a hard line on any potential sacred Resistance by Indigenous People. "War on Terror" echoes a familiar refrain, just like "nits make lice" or "the only good Indian is a dead one" (unless, of course, that Indian is your school mascot).

The war that the invaders, now calling themselves "Americans," waged against our people, who today are called "Indians," lasted nearly two centuries in its active phase. The scene of the event that unleashed the Reign of Terror is set in the historic place where once the same US Army massacred a mostly unarmed group of refugees from a band of the Lakota Nation who were merely seeking safety at the Red Cloud Agency. They were surrounded and held at gunpoint on Wounded Knee Creek in 1890, eventually suffering a terrible fate. They were gunned down by the 7th Cavalry—the same Cavalry that had been wiped out only a few short years before at the Little Big Horn Creek in the Cheyenne Nation, now called Montana. Every square inch of "America" is a battleground.

The vengeful and dirty campaign against Leonard Peltier is what those who stand up for indigenous peoples and their land can expect in return from a government that professes to be the leading example of freedom, justice, and democracy. Only a true philosophical unity among those in the global struggle can contend with the government's monstrous capacity to inflict harm to those that question its actions and intent. I believe an indigenous framework could provide such an encompassing purpose. To get behind such an idea, and perhaps take leadership from the indigenous peoples, will take great courage and introspection from the progressive groups all over the world who, in spite of their commitment to their causes, still benefit from our stolen land.

Until all the social justice and liberation movements recognize and deal with the origin of "the beast" that threatens their causes, all their efforts will remain superficial and little real change will occur. Acknowledging and addressing that this country was created through the theft of indigenous lands, destruction of natural resources central to indigenous life, and genocide of the indigenous peoples will catalyze a much needed change in consciousness in all the righteous people who struggle for justice against this global empire.

We can then start by cleaning house from the proverbial "belly of the beast." It is time to stop sidestepping this elephant in the living room that seems to escape the consciousness of most activists today. It is not possible to genuinely support the animal and plant peoples, the Palestinian people, the Iraqi people, or the indigenous people in Chiapas in their struggles against removal, genocide and land theft, while ignoring the same plight of the indigenous peoples of this land, especially when this oversight is carried out by people who still benefit and live off our stolen land. Our wounds are deep, and the torment that created them is unforgettable. We know we cannot go back in time, but what can be done today is to put an end to the assault on indigenous people and indigenous land that has been taking place without reprieve since the beginning of this country.

We implore all people of conscience to unite with us in demanding: "Enough is enough, America! Ya Basta!" You must all assume your responsibility by making sure this country honors its treaties, stops taking and destroying Indigenous lands and their resources, respects Indigenous sovereignty and culture here and abroad, rectifies the language of history, and frees the warriors, their People and lands. And, as historical beings yourselves, be determined to affect our futures together.

The Animal Question
Uncovering the Roots of Our Domination of Nature and Each Other[1]

Jim Mason

Some think human society seems to be steadily going insane. Ridiculous hatreds and wars rage around the world. We foul our global nest, wipe out the planet's life, and make life more and more miserable for ourselves.

I don't think we are going insane; I think we have just not learned to look deeply enough into the causes of our current social and environmental problems. I believe, with a growing number of others, that these problems began several millennia ago when our ancestors took up farming, broke the ancient bonds with the living world, and put human beings above all other life.

Because of this, we have no sense of kinship with other life on this planet, hence no good sense of belonging here. We are arrogant. The living world is a thing beneath us—to be either used up or kept at bay. We are pathologically alienated from nature.

A World Alive and Ensouled

Our distant ancestors—those tribal "forager" societies before agriculture began about 10,000 BC—lived not merely close to, but *in* and *with* nature. I call them "primal" people, since theirs is the oldest and most universal human lifeway. For them, food and materials came not by working the soil, not by controlling the lives and growth of plants and animals, but by incredibly detailed knowledge about them. They lived with daily reminders of their interconnections with the living beings around them and with constant awareness of how taking from the world might affect their lives. All of this evolved into the various tribal religions seen around the world. What they all have in common is a deep emotional attachment to, and respect for, the living world.

Alienated from the natural world, our modern minds are too maimed to fully grasp how thoroughly the primal mind was fed by its environment—particularly by the moving, living beings in it. The early human mind literally took its shape and substance—its basic images and ideas—from the plants and animals around it. It came to know which plants out of hundreds made the best foods, medicines, and materials. It came to know the life cycles and day-to-day habits of dozens of kinds of animals intimately enough to be able to predict when and where a hunt might be most successful. It came to know how all of the above might be affected by weather, seasons, and the other forces in nature. Primal people knew the land, their foraging territory, probably better than any modern ecologist could. They had, after all, generations of wisdom and experience living in it and, most of all, a feeling for it that no books or journals can ever convey.

Animals intrigued early human beings with their size, speed, strength, and behavior. They were believed to have powers humans did not. For primal humans—especially those with the flowering mind, consciousness, and culture of modern *Homo sapiens* about 45,000 years ago—the animals in their foraging lands were the most impressive, the most fascinating living beings in the world. Measured in terms of the amount of human wonder they caused, animals were the most wonderful things out there. The primal relationship with the animals/powers of the living world was not a hierarchy but more of a *partnership* in which human beings had interactions and a strong sense of interdependence with them.

Other things in nature impressed us, too, like dark forests, violent storms, and rivers swollen by flood waters. Yet animals impressed us in ways that the rest of nature could not. Why animals? Why do animals figure so centrally to the process of mind formation? Why isn't the child moved by stuffed plants and figures of trees and rocks? Animals, like us, move freely; and they are more obviously like people than are trees, rivers, and other things in nature. Animals have eyes, ears, hair, and other organs like us; and they sleep, eat, defecate, copulate, give birth, play, fight, die, and carry on many of the same activities that we do. Animals are active, noisy, colorful characters, all of which make them most informative. In contrast, the rest of nature is background—relatively amorphous, still inscrutable, and not much help to the budding brain.

Somewhat similar to us yet somewhat different, animals forced comparisons, categories, and conclusions. Of all the things in nature, animals stood out most. They were rich food for the developing mind. Animals provoked abstract and metaphysical thinking, and thereby drove and shaped human intelligence.

From Souls to Slaves

As movers of the mind, thought, and feeling, animals are very strong stuff to human beings. No wonder our ancestors believed they had souls and powers. After centuries of manipulative animal husbandry, however, men gained conscious control over animals and their life processes. In reducing them to physical submission, people reduced animals *psychically* as well. Castrated, yoked, harnessed, hobbled, penned, and shackled, domestic animals were thoroughly subdued. They had none of that wild, mysterious power of their ancestors when they were stalked by hunter-foragers. Domestic animals were disempowered by confinement, selective breeding, and familiarity with humans. They gradually came to be seen more with contempt than awe.

In subjugating domestic animals, farmers reduced animals and nature, in general, because crop-conscious farmers saw wild species as pests, and natural elements as threats. But it was animal husbandry in particular that nudged people from seeing animals as spiritual powers to viewing them as commodities and tools. It drastically upset the ancient human-animal relationship, changing it from partnership to master-and-slave, from being kin with the natural world to being lord over it.

As farming and the agrarian worldview took hold some ten thousand years ago, human beings saw themselves, for the first time, as distinct from the rest of nature. This dualistic worldview spread with farming from Mesopotamia to the rest of the ancient world. It was already well developed by the time written history begins circa 3,000 BC, and it grew to greater size and strength in Greece, Rome, and the other great empires of the ancient world. It is the foundation of Judaism and Christianity, which have taught that human beings have "dominion" over animals and nature, and it thereby forms the ideological backbone of Western culture. I call this outlook *dominionism*—the view that human beings have a God-given power or right to use and control the living world for their exclusive benefit. Throughout the changing vagaries of over two millennia of Western culture, the one constant has been adherence to the dominionist worldview and it is at the root of the crises in our social and natural worlds today.

Misothery, Misogyny, and Racism: The Reduction of Animals, Women, and People of Color

Dominionism positions us as superior to, and distinct from, the living world. From that illusory position, we can only despise and deny the animal and natural wherever we see it in the world or in ourselves. To dissect this attitude of contempt for nature wherever we find it, whether in forests, animals, or our own bodies, I have coined the word *misothery*. It literally means hatred and contempt for animals and, by extension, the natural world as a whole, especially its animal-like aspects. One writer, for example has described nature as "red in tooth and claw," that is, as violent and bloodthirsty like predatory animals. We use the expression, "it's a dog-eat-dog world" in display of our condescension toward animals (as we ironically justify brutal social competition as some kind of natural law). The mainstream media still refer to ultra-violent criminals as "animals," "beasts," and "brutes," as it features shows entitled "When Animals

Attack" that position humans as victims of nature, rather than aggressors against it.

The trouble is, we have deep neuroses and anxieties about our own animality, as we try in endless ways to repress the fact that *we are animals*. We are anxious about our bodies and their cycles and functions, for instance, because they remind us of our closeness to animals. Projected outwards against nature, misothery bounces back against us. We project our fear and hatred of nature not only onto other animals, but also onto ourselves and onto any other people whose physical differences places them, we think, below us—nearer to animals and nature than to us. The result is that we are repressed, inhibited, psychologically crippled, and at war with ourselves and the world around us.

On the dominionist ladder or hierarchy of being, women of one's own group are a step down. They have been regarded as "near the animal state," according to Sir Keith Thomas in his survey of European attitudes in *Man and the Natural World*. Other writers have explained how the subjugation of women under patriarchy began with the animal-domesticating, animal-herding tribes of the ancient Middle East. These first male supremacists rewrote creation stories and other myths, destroyed goddess cults, introduced misogyny into poetry and myths, and ultimately reduced the status of women.

Down another step or two on the hierarchy are people whom we call *Others* because they do not look like us, or speak another language, or are somehow different. How far down the hierarchy they are depends on their usefulness and their distance from nature. Male Others may outrank the women of one's group if they are "civilized"—that is, if they have a similar *agri-culture* with dominionism, patriarchy, royalty, wealth, monumental art, urban centers, and so on.

On the rungs below Others stand animals, first those useful to men, then, farther down, all the rest. At the very bottom of the ladder is raw, chaotic nature itself, composed of invisible organisms and an unclassifiable mass of life that feeds, grows, dies, and stinks in dark, mysterious places. This is muck, swamp, steamy jungle, and all backwaters and wildernesses far from the pruned orchards and weeded crop rows of agrarian civilization; this is nature least useful, nature most mysterious, and therefore nature most hostile and sinister.

This mentality of hierarchy and misothery draws on the animal breeder's obsessions with bloodlines and breeding purity, as it did in Nazi Germany and the segregated South, as it still does today among neo-Nazis and white supremacists. The rhetoric of all these racists speaks of the breeder's obsessions, and the extremity of their actions betrays the depth of their fear and hatred of "lower" nature. The Nazis ranted against Jews, gypsies, Poles, and other "mongrel races," and then methodically tried to exterminate them. Southern segregationists preached against "race mixing" and used lynchings, mob violence, and terrorist campaigns to keep people of color "in their place." This is why, despite all the efforts of science and civil rights campaigns, the racial hatred still lies, like a great aquifer, just beneath the surface of consciousness in our culture. On occasion, it wells upward and becomes a very conscious, very political cause.

The Animal Question

Biologically speaking, human beings have been too successful at the expense of other species. For one thing, our numbers have swollen quite recently. The global human population first reached a billion about 1830; it swelled to 2.5 billion only 40 years ago. Our numbers are 6.5 billion today and they increase by about 90 million every year.

The average human being today uses dozens of times more energy and materials than ever before. We have become very materialistic animals. We boast of our affluence barely realizing that, ultimately, all of our wealth consists of stuff taken from the environment.

Consequently, human voracity has set off a snowballing destruction in the world's food chains. Since we began steadily intensifying human food production through agriculture 10,000 years ago, we have just as steadily wiped out species after species. Biologists fear that the impact of human existence is setting off mass extinctions that could eradicate a fourth of the world's remaining species in the next 50 years.

The scale of war and massacre has increased with the scale of both technology and society. In sheer numbers, the 20th century has been the bloodiest in history. In that century alone, nearly 36 million were killed in the various wars. An incredible 120 million more were killed by the various genocidal programs carried out by governments. Human devastation—this huge, this constant spiral of destruction—must have some basic causes, which most people avoid looking for too deeply. Those few who do undertake such searching believe that our nature-alienated, dominionist worldview itself is the basic cause of self-inflicted violence on a huge scale. A well-known critic was Sigmund Freud, who wrote that, "Men have gained control over the forces of nature to such an extent that with their help they would have no difficulty in exterminating one another to the last man. They know this, and hence comes a large part of the current unrest, their unhappiness, and their mood of anxiety."

As for the human impact on the planet, many are concerned but few are looking for basic causes. We see a torrent of writings calling for "radical" (and words to that effect) changes in our worldview and our relations with the living world. Dominionism is under attack—at least in a few small, obscure circles of intellectuals. In their argot, we must address the "Nature Question." The rhetoric is strong, but they and the movers and shakers of conservation and environmentalism, with rare exceptions, stop dead in their tracks when they approach the Animal Question—the whole sticky mess of human views toward, relations with, and uses of animals, and how these need to be radically changed.

This part of the Nature Question (are animals not part of nature?) is oddly off limits. Should an environmentalist step on it accidentally, he or she usually jumps back to safety in the remoteness of discussions about trees or the abstractions of biodiversity and species. The Animal Question is regarded as illegitimate, silly, and peripheral—as are those who address it. One's bigness and seriousness as a thinker on the Nature Question is measured, in part, by how well one steers clear of the Animal Question.

Yet, on the contrary, the Animal Question lies at the very heart of the Nature Question. Animals have always been the soul, spirit, and embodiment of the living world. To exclude discussion of relations with animals from the discussion of our relations with nature is to miss the most crucial point. Emotionally, culturally, psychically, symbolically—just about any way you want to measure it—animals are the most vital beings in the living world. They are fundamental to our worldview; they are central to our sense of existence in this world. If we continue to regard them with misothery on the mind, we will continue to see the world and ourselves as savage and violent, females and different *Others* as inferior, our sexuality and biology as shameful, and war as inevitable. We are fooling ourselves if we think we can deal with the big picture, the mangled mess of our relations with nature, without a soul-searching examination of our dealings with animals. For if we try to steer around the Animal Question, then of course we leave it in place, forever to trouble our relations with nature. We can't undo dominionism without a good overhaul of our views of and relations toward animals.

When we come to institutions such as the experimental laboratory, factory farm, and the slaughterhouse, the calls for a "radical" or "fundamental" overhaul of relations with the living world suddenly go silent. Indeed, no reasonable person challenges these bastions of dominionism. Those who do so are pegged as the "lunatic fringe," which is a handy way of disposing of them and their troublesome ideas. The overwhelming perception is that these uses of animals are well justified in that they confer great benefits to the human species. That perception is, of course, both the source and the lasting strength of dominionism.

If we want a truly *fundamental* overhaul of our dominionist worldview, then we are going to have to deal with the most difficult issues, which are meat-eating and animal experimentation. Many, of course, will refuse to step onto these sacred grounds. They will simply fall back on familiar dominionist axioms and stand their ground. To be charitable, we must excuse them, for many, if not most, people are simply not inclined toward soul-searching and changing their habits. Age, subculture, and other circumstances tend to instill a certain inflexibility in many people, and it is probably best not to bother them. But for those hardy souls who genuinely want to help reconstruct our worldview, our sense of ourselves, and our human spirit, nothing can be off limits for re-examination and soul-searching.

Non-Patriarchal Manhood

One good place to start undoing the dominionist worldview is with ideas about sex and gender. Patriarchy is not good for human society, but men are reluctant to tackle their role in it. Men today needn't feel responsible for the attitudes of people who lived 5,000 years ago. Men do have a huge responsibility, however, to participate in the processes of restoring female principles, status, and power to society and of building an egalitarian sexual ethic. These are difficult tasks, of course, and no group that has long enjoyed supremacy and privilege of any kind has ever relinquished them gladly.

These and other chores offer plenty of opportunities for men to find and build on their humanity, as opposed to carrying on boyish displays of macho manhood. In the past, men showed bravery in the hunt or in battle; they showed "strength" in taking pain and dishing it out without feeling. Instead of macho displays, the modern man can show genuine human bravery and strength. He can be brave enough to tackle the thorny strands of tradition that warp human society and threaten the living world. Men can have the strength to accept an equal role in the house, at work, in bed, and in society as a whole.

Men, the predominant makers and users of pornography, can have the bravery and strength to dismantle this industry that degrades women, the human body, sexuality, and nature. Men, whose traditional masculine culture values stoicism, detachment, and control of others, can use their strength to uproot those values and to build a culture that values empathy, altruism, and kinship with all Others—regardless of sex, race, or species.

Return to the Primal Worldview—Through Science

We are coming full circle around to the kind of awareness held by primal human society. The sciences of biology and ecology help us to see the awesome web of life in the world and the human place in it. We see the cycles of birth, life, death, and rebirth that keep all of nature alive and evolving. We can see the whole living world as a kind of First Being made up of many lesser beings, of which we are one. Instead of viewing this living world as a divine miracle, we understand it through biology and evolutionary science and we are just as awed. We feel for animals whom we see as kindred beings; they give us a sense of belonging, of membership in the Great Family of life in this world. Our ancestors gained this worldview through real experience; we are gaining it, ironically, through science.

This emerging global view conflicts with many of the main beliefs of the West's agrarian religion, which sees this world as a temporary testing ground for humankind, as a lowly way station full of soulless beings whose despicable existence offers temptations to sin and evil. It will be interesting to see if religion's various branches can accommodate the emerging understanding of humans as beings kindred with others in the living world. If they cannot, they will become increasingly irrelevant. If they are unable to join the rest of us in coming to terms with nature and finding kinship among the life around us, they will cease to provide spiritual guidance and comfort, and they will fall away as religions have done before.

Western religion needs to come to terms with its ancestor religions—the "idolaters," "pagans," goddesses, worshippers, and the other belief systems that the monotheists so ruthlessly tried to stamp out. Many traces of these are alive and well today in the developing world despite centuries of mostly Christian and Islamic missionary campaigns. Judaism, to its credit, never sought to impose its theology and its God on other peoples and cultures. If Christianity and Islam can get beyond their current phase of rigid fundamentalism and their obsessions with the "revealed word of God" on the printed page, they could help mend the spiritual fabric of humanity torn by genocidal war, racism, and the social and economic inequalities that drive terrorism and make us all fear for the future. Ironically, it is the fundamentalists of both sides who, although they share the same worldview, are tearing most at that fabric.

When they recognize that human spirituality began with awe of life on earth and that humanity has always found comfort in a sense of kinship with the living world, perhaps they will see the need for, and the wisdom in, coming full circle to the primal worldview.

My own view is that the primal worldview, updated by a scientific understanding of the living world, offers the best hope for a human spirituality. Life on earth is the miracle, the sacred. The dynamic living world is the creator, the First Being, the sustainer, and the final resting place for all living beings—humans included. We humans evolved with other living beings; their lives informed our lives. They provided models for our existence; they shaped our minds and culture. With dominionism out of the way, we could better apply our sciences to understand our world and our place in it. Then we could enjoy a deep sense of kinship with the other animals and of belonging in our living world.

Then, once again, we could feel for this world. We could feel included in the awesome family of living beings. We could feel our continuum with the living world. We could, once again, feel a genuine sense of the sacred in the world.

Notes

1. For a far more detailed discussion of the ideas in this essay, see my book, *An Unnatural Order: The Roots of Our Destruction of Nature* (Lantern Books, New York, 2005).

Part IV

PRIMITIVISM AND THE CRITIQUE OF CIVILIZATION

"Wilderness transformed into city streets, subways, giant buildings, and factories resulted in the complete substitution of the real world for the artificial world of the urban man....Surrounded by an artificial universe, when the warning signals are not the shape of the sky, the cry of the animals, the changing of seasons, but the simple flashing of the traffic light and the wail of the ambulance and police car, urban people have no idea what the natural universe is like." *Vine Deloria*

"We come upon a contention which is so astonishing that we must dwell upon it. This contention holds that what we call our civilization is largely responsible for our misery, and that we should be much happier if we gave it up and returned to primitive conditions." *Sigmund Freud*

"To combat cultural genocide, one needs a critique of civilization itself." *Gary Snyder*

Death Has Already Arrived

Levana Saxon

Blue Jay hops down the tree, seed in beak same routine for
40 million years.
She knows something that
we are pretending to not know.
She knows this will all be over soon.
The wave of extinction is catching up to her a dark hungry Death
approaching, unsure of when it will arrive there is nothing to be
done except continue to collect seeds.
Unless of course you are a human.
Then there is much to do.

Death was thrown out of his delicate dance with Life by us.
We stopped the music,
we stepped on his date's toes.
Pretending he doesn't exist, he grows
bigger, trying to get our attention
but we are too caught up in our self-absorption to notice him.
And now
he's got a serious addiction.

We avoid Death,
try to box him up and bury him like he never existed as soon as he
appears.
We pretend we aren't causing the fastest annihilation of life in
65 million years.
We are smart enough to get to the moon, peer into the universe,
peek into our molecular structures, build skyscrapers and blow
them up, but we can't figure out how to get out of this predicament.

We can't figure out how to stop some highly programmed and
uncreative humans from destroying it all.
I guess 'cause,
we are programmed ourselves, and not nearly as creative as we
could be.

While we play the capitalist games of the aristocracy, doing our part to uphold patriarchy and white supremacy Death creeps closer straight laughing at us, because he knows that we could stop this whole mess overnight.

Living galaxies can awaken the star birthing capacity of dormant galaxies by orbiting with them.
Molecules cling together in intimate embrace and become life.
Tissues clutch to bones that protect organs all desperately holding each other so that body can live.
If atoms decided to have a system of measurements to figure out who was more worthy of benefits than other atoms, this whole matter thing would have never happened.
Imagine if the Sun got tired of the Earth dancing around him and bounced.

We are relationships vibrating on every level and when we reject relationships we embody disintegration and collapse.

There is nothing more natural than adoration.
There is nothing more primal than curiosity.
We are born beholding beauty in every body we meet, human, turtle, grass blade.
Then something happens
like a star we burn out.

The Universe didn't create us to just sit here and scrap.
She wanted friends she could relate with, she could play with and create with.
But we are just sitting up in here,
in her
and ignoring our whole reason for being.
Too busy shopping and doing our hair
spirits and bodies under siege by chemical warfare walking on poisoned earth, suffocating under concrete our minds under attack by TV, billboards, bulletins, schools, hearts-beat overwhelmed can't take any more we resort to zombification, thinking it's easier, but under this spell we let this nation become Death's delivery man

Death has already arrived
taking up hundreds of thousands of us
now ancestors singing from the other side to the seeds in our DNA
to germinate, urging us to get together and sprout some dormant potential to create.
Like the burned out galaxy that orbits ours, we can be re-ignited with some kind of intimate embrace that is our birthright and our responsibility.

Not so mysterious what we can do you see, Like any co-dependency, Death needs an intervention.

Death will stop short when his supply
of global capitalism and colonialism runs dry and is replaced with networks of local autonomous co-ops loosely organized When racism is replaced with justice and fear with liberation a culture of rape replaced with love and reform with revolution When the prisons are replaced with gardens and schools replaced with learning oil replaced with wind and solar, Death will stop his yearning When agribusiness fields are split up into 40 acre sections and with mules are given out in reparations When the indigenous nations of every land get recognition and 500 years of affirmative action for white people ends When borders become passageways and all the fences fall over Death will sit with Life and renegotiate our future.

The Lies of Progress

Robert Thaxton (aka Rob Los Ricos)

Progress is a lie used to justify the domination of the world by Europeans and their post-colonial bastard offspring. Global warming, chemical warfare, women and children sold into slavery: it's all the price of progress. Genocide isn't a concern of progress, progress is only concerned with economics.

Let's imagine a people living peacefully along the shores of a lake, as their ancestors have done for centuries. Families share garden plots and homes. People hunt and fish. The people, as a whole, are healthy. No one goes hungry, and their culture of dancing, festivals, folk medicine, and sharing encourages everyone to integrate into the community.

This is unacceptable. These people are not generating profits for corporations or banks, or paying taxes to a government. These people and their land need to be developed. Let's have a look at these people after a couple of generations of progress.

First of all, disease killed off a great many of them when they first encountered *Haoles* (Hawaiian for "death breathers"). With liquor and firearms, the developers corrupted a few of the people to help seize lands once held in common by the community. The majority of the people refused to go along with this plan, so the military was brought in to subjugate them. With military occupation achieved, progress picked up steam.

A dam was built upstream from the lake, to provide electricity for future development. Water is also diverted from the lake for use by the town that has grown around the military base. A paper and lumber mill once employed some of the people, but when the forest was gone, the mills closed.

The lake is full of mercury and dioxin—by-products of industrial processes. People still eat the fish, which gives them cancer. The land is all owned by former military leaders, who raise cattle on it. Jobs are hard to come by and most people work servicing the military: doing laundry, cooking food, prostituting themselves. The soldiers, in return give the people unwanted children, venereal diseases, liquor, and drugs.

This is progress on a micro level, and this progress has been repeated over and over again—in the Americas, Africa, Asia, even in Europe.

On a larger scale, the lie of progress is even easier to see. Look at Argentina. Once, it had an economy built around beef production. After the Great Depression, Argentinians were determined to progress into a first world nation, like Canada or Australia. It took them 50 years, but they made it.

Unfortunately for them, this wasn't acceptable to global corporate and financial interests. You see, first world nations require a great deal of the world's natural resources to maintain their affluent lifestyles. There just isn't enough! No, there is only enough for a few first world countries. I don't know—how about eight?! So the IMF and World Bank stepped into Argentina, and destroyed its economy. Just ten years ago, Argentina was a prosperous country. Now its economy is all but imaginary, the currency unstable, unemployment is greater than 50 percent, and the economy is centered around debt-servicing, just like any other third world country. This is progress: the disempowerment of local people in order to increase the power of global corporations and financial institutions.

A tiny minority of people are waging an unrelenting war against the Earth and its inhabitants. Knowing very well that they can never rule the entire planet, they've decided to destroy what they don't need and hoard what they do.

They use methods which proved effective in the era of European colonialism—dividing populations so that they constantly make war on one another, poisoning the water supply, forcing people into concentrated population centers to better control them, rewarding "leaders" who will do the dirty work for a piece of the action, eliminating "troublemakers," etc.

The most hideous aspect of this death culture is that the powerful have convinced the weak to desire their obliteration. Actually, the powerful get the weak to destroy themselves and do it as a sacramental duty.

Some of the weak can see the destruction they are visiting upon their world. They do what they can to limit the destruction they cause. They utterly fail to realize that the lesser of two evils is still evil. These "kinder-gentler" destroyers are so afraid of looking at the consequences of their actions that they fight whole-heartedly to defend the rights of the powerful to destroy our world, and denounce any efforts to oppose the machinations of the death-culture.

Because, you see, not everyone is blind to the workings of the killers of the Earth. Not only that, but there are still millions of people who are not connected to the apparatus of the death-culture. These two types of people not only try to minimize their impact on the living planet, but they fight to stop the death machines. The powerful and the weak alike hate the primitivists.

The powerful must destroy them in order to maintain their privileged status. The weak must destroy them so that they don't have to face their own cowardice. Also, they—being weak—are totally dependent on the death-culture—without it, they would suffer and perish immediately, rather than slowly.

The powerful and the weak make war on the uncooperative, the wild and the free. They are as effective as they are heartless. The powerful use fear to force the weak to kill the rebellious and the free. The weak are motivated by fear—fear of offending their masters, fear of losing their illusionary status, fear of being killed themselves.

If fear is the only motivation the weak understand, perhaps it's time for the uncooperative to make the weak fear that which they have embraced.

Perhaps its time for the brave and free to make the powerful awake in their bunkers.

Perhaps it is time to go on the offensive, and make the powerful and weak alike pay for their crimes against nature.

Perhaps it's time for a two-sided war.

Attack the System

Craig "Critter" Marshall

Being that I'm on the opposite side of the strands of razor wire from most contributors to this book, I may be in a better position to say something important about the corporations that profit from the destruction and exploitation of nature or, in the capitalist ledger, "natural resources." The mainstream environmental movements claim that the ELF's tactics are too extreme. In contrast, I feel that ELF actions are not "extreme" *enough.*

My co-defendant, Jeff Leurs, is serving 22 years and 8 months for burning a few SUVs. If his lawyer hadn't died in the middle of our trial, forcing the prosecution into offering me a much improved plea deal of 5 ½ years, I'd also be serving an absurdly long sentence for an action with minimal results. Most people do not get caught for their sabotage actions, which only proves how effective planning and dedication can be. If people are risking many years of their lives, however, shouldn't they undertake actions that are far more effective than torching a couple of trucks? I'm fairly sure that if my co-conspirator and I had burnt down the entire factory that produced the SUVs we wouldn't have been facing much more than the 22 plus years meted out to Jeff. Though such an action would have been a great improvement over what we accomplished, I believe even that would not have gone far enough, for another factory would be built and the destruction of the earth would continue with little interruption.

What we need to attack is the totality of the death machine that is industrial society, AKA: civilization. As the earth and its creatures are being assaulted 24 hours a day on an enormous scale, how can we hope to stop this destruction by doing utterly ineffective actions such as burning a few trucks? Those who attack the logging industry are making bigger, longer-lasting dents in the machines' armor, but these too are still just dents. We need to cut off the head of the monster.

No matter how many animals are rescued, no matter how many trees are saved, if the current technological state progresses or even carries on at the rate it is currently destroying planetary ecosystems, life on this planet is doomed. Civilization as we know it depends on the domination and exploitation of every type of "resource" (whether living beings or their habitat), and cannot exist without such exploitation. Before the rise of agricultural society, humans were once mostly nomadic, only settling into permanent villages as plants and animals were domesticated. The exploitation of these life forms allowed the populations of early civilization to increase, which in turn called for the "need" to further exploit plant and animal populations.

Flash 10,000 years into the future, to today. There are very few places on earth where humans have not tried (and for the most part succeeded) to form dominating relationships over the life-forms that dwell there. The vast majority of the so-called civilized world has been scarred and/or covered with concrete. The current rate of species extinction rivals that of the time of the dinosaurs 65 million years ago, and while saving a grove of trees or the hostages at a factory farm is a noble cause, it is still applying a band-aid to a gaping chest wound.

If we could save every animal in the world from suffering in factory farms and laboratories, what good, in the long run, would it do if there were no wild places left to free them? Conversely, what would be the point of protecting the last wild spaces if the animals were all domesticated, their wild spirits broken? The struggles to save life and land are inseparable. Every aspect of civilization conspires against all that is wild. It is the totality of human domination, not just one element, that dooms life.

Our struggles cannot ever hope to be effective as long as we each only focus on one aspect of the *dis-ease* of civilization. We must attack the totality of industrial society every single day. We must be relentless in our struggles, for civilization continually advances its death march. We must challenge the assumptions that are integral to the everyday existence of industrial society. The majority of people fighting for the liberation of one life-form unknowingly or unthinkingly support the oppression of many others every day. No? Well then it's safe to assume you don't use electricity? I do realize there are necessary evils if we want to be effective in our struggles, such as the use of petro-fuels for ecotage actions that can bankrupt corporations. But we must be aware of the negative impact our actions and tools have on ecosystems, both local and distant.

Of course I am not condemning anyone who goes out and torches a sawmill; if that's what you want to do, by all means burn the fucker to the ground. At the very least you will be make this political hostage smile. But just be aware that you are not stopping the earth's destruction—at best you are only slowing it down.

We need to relearn how to coexist with nature, to live in ecosystems rather than on "top of them." As has been said, "We have seen the enemy and it is us." It is hypocritical to attack one aspect of industrial society's nature-destroying machinery at night only to lend support to another aspect by making purchases in the morning. We cannot carry on with our lives in the manner taught to us by those who condone civilization (and its inherent destructiveness), and ever expect to end any form of domination.

Civilization, from its inception, has been rooted in domination; it depends on it for continued survival.

We need to get back to a sustainable culture—one where we live in harmony with nature—but this will never happen as long as industrial wastes, from packaging to poisons, are being pumped out by corporations whose only concern is profits. People have been led to believe that comfort and security come from working at least half of their waking hours, so they can buy things that will save them time and energy. Am I the only one who sees the utter absurdity of this? Fortunately not, but more of those who see it need to realize that even if they stop participating in this work-consume-die culture, the others who are still taking part are helping to poison all of us.

While burning down a sawmill may slow the ecocide being perpetrated by industry, I think a much more effective tactic is to take out the consumer goods before the point of production by destroying the power-plants and laboratories that enable such a cancerous society to exist. Every moment that is not being spent on destroying industrial society is tantamount to condoning its destruction of us and every other life form. We are being poisoned by toxins that are being pumped out 24 hours a day, yet the average person spends less than 24 seconds a week doing anything about it. Hopefully this doesn't make you pat yourself on the back if you do more—hopefully, it makes you realize that those of us who are doing something need to attack even harder.

Each of us must face the totality and decide whether we want to continue to strike at the fingers of the beast that has all life in a chokehold, or if we need to strike at the head. Don't get me wrong, biting off one of these fingers is never a bad thing, but unless it is part of a larger strategy it is not going to put an end to the human domination of animals and nature.

We will never succeed in convincing corporate interests to stop the exploitation of animals and the earth, it is against their "nature." We want to defend life at all costs, they want to protect an exploitative way of life no matter what the cost. Their job is to make as much money as possible regardless of the suffering. Our job is to put the bastards out of business.

Against Civilization, For Reconnection to Life!

Terra Greenbrier

Civilization saturates us to the core. On physical, mental, emotional and spiritual levels, we are born manufactured in Civilization's image. It has torn each of us from our wild selves and the wild world that we rely on for survival. It flows in our blood, projecting itself onto the world around us and representing itself as "reality." To perpetuate itself, it demands that we must separate, isolate, categorize, label, package and inevitably devour our own inner wildness, and the unmolested places around us that we have come to call "wilderness."

Existing as an interlocking complex of physical, social, emotional, spiritual, and psychological systems, Civilization is not defined merely by physical places or specific eras of history. The word itself refers to the phenomenon of the "City," which first appeared at different times in different places around the world. But the "civilizing process" looks similar in all these places. The transition from nomadic, foraging lifestyles, to sedentary, horticultural society, with its complex economic and property systems as well as various types of social hierarchies, define this process. This process has tended to result in the rise of the City—a glaring example of ecological imbalance and social alienation. Both in pre-industrial contexts, as with the Aztecs of Mesoamerica, and in industrial contexts, such as our own, it's clear that such scenarios have been, and continue to be, recipes for disaster.

A Deepening Disconnection...

An underlying logic of domination and control fuels Civilization. The physical institutions that reflect and enforce this logic include school, work, media, science, medicine, religious institutions, the nation-state and its military, political systems, and economies. Concepts like Progress, patriarchy, domestication, reason, morality, and politics constitute a social foundation for the Machine. These systems and values that surround us separate us from directly experiencing the diversity and inter-relatedness of the living world. Living within the circle of life, as an integral part of a whole organism, forms a basis for our relationships with other humans. Without this primal relatedness, the roles and assumptions that predefine us in Civilization control our own self-image, and consequently our understanding of the humans around us.

In Civilization, we surround ourselves with symbolic culture: predetermined measurements of time, representations of the world through language, number, science, history, myth—culture itself. We wear synthetic clothing, live in wasteful and isolating shelters, eat toxic food made in factories, spend our time in artificial and sterile environments doing monotonous and tedious things to keep the machine of Progress and Capital running, in exchange for money or diplomas. We take drugs to keep our caged wild selves from hurting ourselves or lashing out at those around us. We numb our pain and depression with alcohol, or distract ourselves from it with superficial pursuits like pop culture, junk food, shopping, or religion. Surely the point has been made crystalline that Civilization must collapse or be made to collapse, by many a rambling street person and anti-civ writer.

But what hasn't seemed so clear, is how we might go about destroying Civilization in our own lives; how one might free oneself from our physical dependence on it, and the mental, social, emotional, and spiritual psychoses that come from this dependence. Like an addiction, Civilization convinces us we need it to live.

The thousand year-old legacy of hoarding, warring, and ecological imbalance that has brought us here to the edge of catastrophe, reflects what's been a steadily deepening disconnection with the physical world around us. It's this disconnection and desensitization that has allowed us in modern, industrial society to justify living far beyond the limits of the planet's life-support systems, and to objectify and exploit our non-human neighbors, as well as each other. In many Civilized cultures, animal exploitation, racism, and sexism are just some of the more familiar manifestations of this objectifying impulse. In our collective denial, we imagine ourselves as super-humans, trusting in the brave new world of high technology to finally allow us to supersede our messy human-ness.

A Cancerous Trajectory...

Within leftist and liberal political circles, this cancerous trajectory is so often accepted as unchangeable reality. We are encouraged to grasp at crumbs of inclusion thrown to us by the systems that maintain this ongoing fantasy of human superiority and technological utopia. Mass Society and its movements boil down our passions and convictions into one monolithic voice, with a goal of palatability at the forefront. Our desires for sanity and balance are constantly co-opted by the "Spectacle"—the all-encompassing world of mass media and its conformist and consumerist values that tell us who we are and why we are alive. To dare to live outside of it becomes either a matter of societal privilege, or just sheer luck.

In taking this critical analysis to the next step of confrontation, we continuously seek practical courses of action from which to express our opposition. Reform-oriented campaigns are crafted to appeal to society's "moral conscience," while playing right into the hands of the political systems that guard the royal towers. Even the courageous and righteous direct actions of the Earth Liberation Front (ELF), while aimed at institutions profiting off ecocide, can only go so far toward toppling their foundations: the logic of Civilization and all its institutions. While Ted Kaczynski may have spoken eloquently of some of the fundamental causes of the destruction of earth, his actions too were limited in their effectiveness. In terms of an anti-civilization praxis, they can hardly be considered a threat. This is not to discount their worth. They serve a necessary purpose: propaganda by the deed. But symbolically exposing the perpetrators of ecocide is only one facet of our opposition to the Megamachine. We are also creating examples of possibilities of life outside of, and in opposition to, the institutions that control us.

An all-too common mistake comes with the creation of "alternatives" to destructive lifestyles that still rely on mass society, industrialism, the nation state. These efforts usually simply reproduce the logic of civilized thinking, existing in a comfortable social niche. They are easily "recuperated" back into the Spectacle, and offered up for consumption in the marketplace. The failure to challenge the most basic assumptions of society keeps us constantly dissatisfied and miserable, with just enough distractions to allow us to avoid this uncomfortable realization.

Nation-state organization and industrial technology have enabled the domination of the individual by "the majority," and suppressed the self-regulating, anarchic nature of life. They work counter to any physical patterns we could observe in wild nature. Even if masses of people all simultaneously removed themselves from industrial society by self-organizing "alternative" lifestyles, it should be clear that the corporate/state powers wouldn't allow it to happen without a fight. Their very existence depends on our dependence on them. "Democracy" itself is an institution that follows the logic of civilization perfectly. It serves to alienate us from our own power over our lives, controlling our personal and collective desires and values, channeling it into the marketplace of ideas and products.

Catalyzing situations...

From this perspective, and seen as a matter of community and self-defense, one might welcome the dissolution of the physical infrastructure of civilization—industrialism—before it renders life on earth, and human freedom itself, dysfunctional. This is not a call to "bring on industrial collapse," but rather a sobering acceptance of the inevitability of such a collapse (or series of collapses), and a call to gather with others in decentralized, bioregionally-based communities in order to survive it (those of us who actually want to anyway). In creating a multiplicity of examples of life without the super-system that only takes and gives nothing back, we can pass on information and experiences with different methods of ecological culture, while also defending our communities from those who would take control.

What took thousands of years to come to this point could take even longer to unravel. But we can get the process started by creating, or merely participating in, catalyzing situations. Through these situations we might urge people to question the ecological wisdom of a human-centered, control-oriented culture. Global warming, power failures, computer glitches, and damage incurred by nature's whims in the form of hurricanes and floods, can all provide fertile ground for further, and more lasting, destabilization of the industrial infrastructure. This infrastructure is very tangible, and thus physically vulnerable. With enough people acting directly and simultaneously, around the world, interconnected systems of domination COULD, theoretically, crash. Without this megamachinery clouding our vision of how to live in balance, people might just begin to sober up out of our collective hallucinations. The potential for living outside the institutions that control us may just seem to make a lot more sense, and propel us to start living with a realistic, biocentric view of ourselves on planet earth.

Many radicals and anarchists see no point in even embarking on such a project, considering what appears to be the average mindset in industrial culture. "People don't want to destroy civilization," claim the already defeated. But consider this: (1) just because it seems at this point in time that most modern humans don't want to destroy civilization, it doesn't mean that will always be the case; and (2) if one deeply believes that civilization must end in order for humans to be truly liberated and live in harmony within nature, why should we deny our convictions by working toward a "more realistic," less suffocating (for western societies) world, thus prolonging the painful effects of civilization on the entire planet?

And besides, what is more unrealistic than believing that there is sufficient time (before the collapse of our planet's life-support systems, or the complete technocratic control of physical reality, whichever comes first) to build a broad-based, multi-ethnic/racial/sexual/generational social movement? One that is so cohesive and powerful that it can resist the highly technocratic mechanisms of state repression long enough to allow millions to re-organize into decentralized, anarcho-communist, worker controlled, ecologically harmonious, classless, international networks of syndicates that can maintain a global non-capitalist trade system that doesn't contribute to the degradation of the earth, or require that people work soul-killing, monotonous jobs to maintain it, and preserves peoples' individual freedoms, as well as returning stolen lands to native people, and administering reparations to Africans and others for slavery and other atrocities... It's a nice fantasy...

Scattering Seeds...

In the time we have left before the wild chaos of nature takes back control from the hands of (a small, elite network of) the human species, we might embark on the project of asking ourselves what seeds we can scatter here that will one day sprout from the compost of our decadent society.

Visions of a post-civilized world have become more and more vivid to many of us who are attempting to live in ecological balance, free of our mental cages of domestication. "Rewilding" is not a political strategy aimed at organizing masses or exercising "freedom of speech." It's an impulse toward personal and communal liberation that looks at the past for inspiration and wisdom, and toward the future to adapt and prepare for new and drastic changes in our daily lives. It also looks at the situation as it currently stands, and accepts both the impoverishment we have inherited, and the possibilities that we have to work with. Breaking free from our domestication helps us survive both physically and psychologically amidst waste and boredom. It allows us to confront the subtle, psychic logic of Civilization within ourselves, and reclaim our Self from the false self that we were taught to create and project to the world.

As opposed to hyper-competitive systems like capitalism, sharing and cooperation make life easier. This is a very old idea, of course—perhaps even instinctual to our species. If seen within this context, modern decentralized DIY networks could not only render civilization useless, but they could be used to subvert it—much in the same way the Black Panthers or the American Indian Movement included morning breakfast programs for children and community-based cultural education in their strategy, or like the German autonomous squatting communities in the 1980s. Food, housing, education, health, trade, communication, music, and art can all be seen in terms of a postindustrial reality. It's not up to us to figure out how, and if, these things will function in the future for anyone other than ourselves and our immediate communities, but we can begin the task of that exploration now, and share it with the world around us.

Beyond "Society"...

A large part of that exploratory process can include a deep questioning of the very existence of some elements of modern life that often go unquestioned, such as systems of food production, education, and technology; mass society; and "culture" itself. Rather than merely looking to adapt these elements into our lives in a more participatory or ecological way, we can incorporate into our cultural conversations an active self-questioning of the very origins and functioning of these activities in our daily lives. Even without taking drastic measures like abandoning agriculture and modern medicine, we can take our process of unlearning and deconstructing our socialization—our domestication—beyond where most radicals have typically gone before. Picking up where others have left off, we can move from veganism and organic agriculture to urban/suburban edible landscaping and wild food foraging; from Waldorf and Montessori schools to "unschooling," cooperative homeschooling projects rooted in self-directed, ecologically-based learning; from community theater and recycled object art to invisible theater and surrealism.

Learning and practicing earth-based lifeways can help us gain a more direct understanding of life without civilization's constructs, inspired by the wisdom of those who live them. Having been domesticated already, we can never return to a purely "wild" existence. Instead, "going feral" is a way of escaping the dense layers of our domestication. By peeling back our alienation from nature's cycles and stories just a few layers, we enter the realms of permaculture, edible landscaping, wild food foraging, earthen building, and even subsistence hunting. These experiences can help us resolve the basic crisis in our psyches, or what Chellis Glendenning refers to as "the original trauma," in her important book *My Name is Chellis and I'm in Recovery from Western Civilization.*

On a personal level, an ethic of "truth-speaking" and "radical honesty" can transform our highly mediated interpersonal relationships into directly lived, interactive, and participatory exchanges. These transformations can allow for a deeper and more powerful level of healing and collaboration. Without the tedium of social relationships simply filling time between work and school, our connections can set off wildfires, personally and socially.

The task that lies before us is both old and new. We are everything that has come before us, and at the same time, like nothing that has ever come before. Within a process of constant self-questioning, we can only become more open to the infinity of possible futures.

What is Liberation?

John Zerzan

As the "Movement" of the 60s collapsed, some refused to accept defeat and decided to remain active "by other means," namely, tactics of violence. The Weather Underground began a campaign of bombs aimed at corporate and security offices in 1970. There was a string of bombings that petered out by about 1975 in which no target involved injury or death. The Black Liberation Army also took to the field, followed in 1973 by the Symbionese Liberation Army; neither had qualms about inflicting casualties on the enemy. There were several other less well-known groups, too, that didn't want to quit even though the bottom had clearly dropped out of the global wave of 60s militancy.

My personal take on this post-60s turn to violence is that it was the politics of desperation. Without in any way discounting the very high level of personal courage involved, there really seemed to be no one in those days who felt that "picking up the gun" (or planting the bomb) was going to reverse the end of that era of contestation. I had been a participant in San Francisco and Berkeley radicalism, and to me the relatively sudden end of those days of upsurge and optimism was unmistakable. It was as if one day it was plainly all over. Nobody knew what to do about it; very few showed up for projects; the absence of energy was palpable. Things went on to some degree, but the beating heart of it all was missing.

This is my own memory, still vivid. Maybe others experienced it differently. In any case, the feeling of defeat or closure is what marked for me the sad pointlessness of the early- to mid-70s tactic of violence. And that feeling has carried over, many years later, so that my first reaction to militant tactics today was that it is again the politics of desperation.

But I can see that such a carry-over reaction, in terms of ELF and ALF acts in particular, is not appropriate, because there are major differences between the activities of groups like these and what went down 30 years ago.

The politics of the earlier illegalists was straight-up backward, for one thing. It could hardly have been more authoritarian, as in *Marxist-Leninist* (the Weather Underground, for example). In fact, hierarchy was the model across the board, as remarkable as it may seem today; this fact seems to be routinely omitted from films and memoirs on the subject. Yeah, just one thing missing: the embarrassing core philosophy of these outfits.

ELF and ALF worldviews, if I may speak of them together in this context, could hardly be more dissimilar from that of the earlier hierarchical, vanguardist militants. Instead of aiming at seizing state power (the goal of the left in general, though leftists occasionally deny this), these liberationists want to dissolve political power. They are motivated toward autonomy and a multiplicity of approaches, rather than toward collectivizing structures and universalized solutions. They are anti-statist, and also apply their anti-authoritarianism internally in their anti-hierarchical relations with one another. Instead of accepting the false and deadly promises of Progress and the global Megamachine, the earth-based, life-based ELF and ALF attack corporate components of the systematic destruction of nature, its habitats and species.

Occasionally the left employs passing rhetoric in favor of the natural world, but more often doesn't even bother—which is a modicum of "truth in advertising." It isn't possible to affirm the globalized social world, with its foundation of domination of nature and mass production/consumption for all, while remaining in any real sense in favor of reconnecting with the earth. The stale humanism of the left prevents it from abandoning the ideology of dominating nature. In contrast, the ALF/ELF have abandoned humanism in favor of some form of biocentrism, and a vastly fuller concept of liberation.

ELF and ALF communiqués provide truly inspiring alternative visions to the senile, putrefying mantras of the left. These joyous and determined messages, backed up by arsons, sabotage, strikes against animal torturers, and the like, spell out the nature of the accelerating, deepening, totalizing crisis and show us how much of "civilization" must go.

As I see it, these passionate, searing critiques are echoed by another part of the emerging contemporary resistance, which goes by names such as green anarchy, anti-civilization, anarcho-primitivism. As part of this latter current, I salute my ELF and ALF comrades who are on the cutting edge of the fight to stop the all-devouring beast of technology and civilization. The humanist left is an enormous failure that must be superseded. There is a growing realization worldwide of the deep roots of a culture that becomes unhealthier and more grotesque by the day. There is but one global civilization now, revealing its deadly essence as its basic institutions bring forth their sterile fruit. Specialization and domestication drive the mechanism of control ever further and deeper, bringing new levels of desolation, standardization, exploitation, and extermination.

Are we willing to break with the dominant approaches, with those—like the left—that accept civilization, mass society, the techno-culture and the destination of death? Do we not need a paradigm shift that will make us unafraid to defend the earth and challenge our own domestication?

Indigenous struggles against empires and globalization have, of course, been going on for centuries. I think that is also a part of the new resistance, revealing how people who are not part of industrial modernity, and who have lived on the earth without destroying it, are defending *their* world against all odds. It is paradoxical in a way that what is new discovers what is old and true, and sees its enduring value.

All the rhetoric of the prevailing world rings false, including the worn-out rhetoric of pseudo-opposition to the dominant order. Visions, actions, and analyses are urgently required that break completely with the institutions and assumptions of civilization—a worldview that dates back only 10,000 disastrous years. Indigenous, earth-based, non-industrial solutions, for example, can help us imagine modes of human life that existed in communion with the natural world, instead of the domesticating, conquest-style approaches of civilization.

Part V

REPRESSION AND RESISTANCE

"I don't care if I fall as long as someone else picks up my gun and keeps on shooting." *Che Guevara's dying words*

"Revolution builds in stages; it isn't cool or romantic; it's bold and vicious; it's stalking and being stalked—the opposition rising above our level of violence to repress us, and our forces learning how to counter this repression and again pulling ourselves above their level of violence." *George L. Jackson*

"Jails and prisons are designed to break human beings, to convert the population into specimens in a zoo—obedient to our keepers, but dangerous to each other." *Angela Davis*

"If they aren't able to destroy the desire for freedom, they won't break you." *Bobby Sands*

In the spirit of Paul Robeson and the words of Chairman Fred Hampton...
This here is a tale from the real. No play on Broadway, showcase Sunday or
Hollywood scene. Now...

The Troubles I've Seen

Fred Hampton Jr.

You've mace me & attacked me. Transferred me from prison to prison.
Oh! tape record this also, for I want the world to listen.
I've been forced to drink toxic water in order to survive.
While you bring in Black bodies by the boatload & call it
war on crime.

I know Brothers who were sentenced to 2 but ended up serving 10.
I'm aware of countless numbers of cats in these camps who went
to bed but never got up again.
Have you ever seen them enter with pride? Headstrong and sane.
And then leave out broken thinking a number is their name?
You ever seen a genius go crazy? A mastermind dismantled?
How about a Man being shot up with more shit than a horse can
handle.

I've seen Grandfathers placed in cells with their own offspring.
And I've seen Men of principle resort to do the strangest of things.
I've seen a Brother bleed & bleed to damn near no blood was left.
I heard him say hell *must* be better. I heard him pray for quick
death.

I've seen Black Men classified as C-numbers held over a quarter of
a century.

And I've seen White Men with triple murders leave the penitentiary.
Ever had to choose from what you need & what is necessary?
Ever been exploited by a prison commissary?
Heard of Women turning tricks for sanitary tissue?
You ever been searched in a manner that truly dissed you?
Imagine four grown Men forced in the same room.
What if the pigs that beat you served you your food?
I've had property pissed on and given bogus charges.
I can't count the cats in comas, let alone beat unconscious.
I've been awakened at three in the morning & told it's time to ride.

God knows how many murders you've classified as suicide.
I've lost count of the times I heard them say guilty.
How many babies who haven't lived, but yet got the death penalty.
Did you know that Mumia was moved & placed in seg.?
And given trumped up charges for refusing to cut his dreads.
Like magicians you drop drugs from thin air.
Murdered George in Quentin and claimed he was strapped in his chair.
How many "problem prisoners" were popped with ice picks?
From corn to shanks you still farmers planting shit.
You keep me isolated and caged 24 a day.
I've seen the effect of those who you claim to rehabilitate.
Now I know what you mean when you use the term "correct."
For, I've experienced yo' bad, brutal ass, Uncut, in the raw &
Undressed!

—Dedicated to the memories of Albert "Nuh" Washington, Field Marshall George Jackson, Young Man-Child Jonathon Jackson, Min. K.T., Don T. Taylor, Merle Africa, Attica 32, Ajamu Nassar, Mandigo, David Walker, Amb. Mark Sheppard, Calvin DeAngelo Moore, Santana, Willie Enoch, Mike Williams, Larry Roberson, Shaka Sankofa, and all casualties endured behind enemy lines.

From Protest To Resistance

Jeffrey "Free" Luers

In the late Summer of 1997, Southern California was rocked by storms. The meteorologists blamed El Niño and the nightly news featured "Storm Watch." In my 18 years I had never witnessed any storms like these, not in California.

My friend Aspen and I sat on the beach through the storm pounding away on our drums, voices rising high into the night. We reached out to the fury of the storms, into the crashing waves. The raw power of it all filled us with life.

Not more than 20 miles north we saw lightning fill the sky. The cities of Long Beach and Seal Beach were under a tornado watch. The day before a water spout had touched down just off shore. Anyone with a lick of sense was staying inside and riding out the storm.

Not us, we were doing magik. This is what Aspen lived for. I met her canvassing for the Sierra Club. She was assigned the task of teaching me how to convince people to give up their money. Thankfully, she taught me so much more.

It was Aspen who first taught me how to feel the rhythm of Mother Earth and how to reach beyond everything I've ever known. Aspen was a totally free soul. When she taught me things it was more like sharing ancient knowledge. She did not teach me my spirituality, she simply showed me how to find it.

Most nights after work we would go out for chai tea and talk for hours. We were an odd pair. She with an earthy look, dread locks and peaceful presence. I, on the other hand, wore spikes and chains and sported a bright orange mohawk. We were from two different worlds, stuck in the middle of America's second largest city and all we ever talked about was nature and social justice.

One night while sharing a joint she told me about the time she spent in the Redwoods. She told me about a group called Earth First! She shared stories about stopping logging and the joys of camaraderie, and in a hushed voice she told me stories of monkeywrenching.

My eyes lit up. This is what I wanted, someone I could get active with. I'd been involved in protests in LA, but it was largely symbolic. I'd been introduced to the Animal Liberation Front (ALF) and I'd done a few minor actions. But frankly, I was still too scared to go out and do stuff on my own. I needed to do more. I needed to leave my comfort zone. My life in LA was stifling. It was time for me to cut my ties and move on.

A few months later, Aspen and I parted ways with smiles. I was on my way to Eugene, Oregon. Something deep inside me told me I would find my destiny there. I knew very little about the city other than what the University was like. I had a few friends I could stay with until I had a place of my own. But it was something more that called to me. My heart told me Eugene was where everything was going to kick off.

I arrived in January 1998. One month after my 19th birthday. By February, I had plugged into the local activist community and was living out in Fall Creek—an old-growth Douglas Fir Forest, preparing to defend it. I spent nearly two months living out there alone, going to town only when necessary. I camped under a single tarp, my only source of water was the creek. I learned the deer trails, observed the habits of the squirrels, birds and owls. I listened to the frogs and crickets, and I watched salamanders mate. By day, I would get soaked in the rains and by night I'd dry out by a fire. I sang to the forest, the animals, and the sky. I lost myself in the rhythm of life around me.

As I climbed the big trees, setting lines in preparation for the tree sit, I was overwhelmed with the sense that these trees were sentient beings. Soon I was climbing just to sit and sway in the branches of the upper canopy. I had come home.

In the hustle and bustle of modern life we rarely have time to stop or slow down. We move through life so quickly from school to work in our quest for meaning. Striving to make ends meet, to get the next "must have." Before we know it, life has passed us by and in the end few can say what it was to truly live.

Some people say "science killed magik." I don't think it is knowledge that killed magik, it is how we applied it. When I talk to people about communicating with animals and trees or about the power of the Earth, most laugh. We have been indoctrinated to believe that we are not of the Earth, that somehow we are separate from all other life on this planet. We have been taught to believe that the Earth and her creatures exist solely for people to use and exploit. Nothing could be further from the truth.

Mother Earth is a giant living organism. Much as our bodies are made up of cells and organs that together give us life, so, too, is the Earth. The Earth is the giver of life whether by miracle or happenstance. It is only the combined symbiotic existence of the Earth's creatures and geophysical features that allow life to flourish on this planet.

All life is interconnected, making a web in which the survival of any one species rests on the survival of many others. As oxygen breathing mammals, our existence depends on the forests, plankton, and alga that produce the air we breathe. These entities are dependent upon the complex webs of life that ensure their survival. When any one of these diverse ecosystems become adversely affected, a chain reaction starts culminating in a global environmental crisis if left unchecked.

Living in the forest, I learned more about life than I ever had in school. I sat alone for hours with my back against an old growth tree. The forest around me was more than 600 years old, evolution at its perfection. To be able to sit and take everything in, to experience all the forest had to offer, through every one of my senses—this is the reason we are alive. The meaning of life is simple: enjoy it.

The forest was so harmonious it was hard to believe that it was in danger. Who in their right mind would destroy an entire ecosystem in order to make phone books and ass wipe?

I had a lot of time to ponder these questions, as well as question my own beliefs. The last package of supplies I had received had zines written by Rod Coronado, as well as some *Earth First! Journal*s. I was inspired by Rod's words, and for the first time I was exposed to the Earth Liberation Front. I read the history of the ELF's evolution and commentaries about how the ELF and ALF should work more together.

My road to militancy had begun in LA and this had just reconfirmed my belief. However, I had made a decision to try every other method first. After all I'd be a hypocrite to resort to the sword before diplomacy had failed.

One day in April, the Forest Service started building roads into the forest. They cut down trees and buried streams, leaving torn earth in their wake. There was a sense of urgency now. The "sit" had to go up.

In town we rushed together supplies. In two days the campaign would officially begin. That night I sat behind the log mill that had bought the "right" to destroy public land. I'd sat in this spot on many nights. Months ago I had tested the security systems and discovered only motion sensitive lights—nothing had changed. I knew all of this could end right now with one match.

As I sat there thinking about my options, an owl appeared. It swooped over my head and circled me three times, as if to tell me something. As quickly as it had appeared, it was gone. I was profoundly affected by this encounter. I remembered my oath to myself. My path had already been set in motion, I had to see it through!

The months passed. I left my tree sit for the ground, believing I could be more effective there. I'd watched from the treetops as ancient trees were felled to make way for the road. I vowed never again would I sit by and watch what I could stop.

Under the light of billions of stars and the solemn gaze of the moon, the pickax came crashing down penetrating gravel and dirt. This must have been the third time in as many days I'd helped dig up this culvert. Each time the road was shut down, building stopped and they had to fix it. Each night, masked defenders would dig it up again. The neatly piled log deck would become a convoluted disarray spread across the road. Road blocks were doused with gasoline to serve as burning barriers. This forest would not be allowed to fall.

Each morning the battlefield was set. Road workers and Freddies (Forest Service Law Enforcement Officers, also LEOs) were met with new blockades and 20–30 masked and camouflaged individuals. The confrontations could be fierce lasting days or weeks, but the most heated lasted only hours. Ultimately, the roads were built, but we reclaimed them, and in the end, we controlled more than ten miles of roads. The signs were very clear. "Beware of Caltrops," another warned "If trees fall, blood spills."

At any given time there were more than two dozen road blocks. Walls were built with second growth felled in road construction, as well as walls made out of dug up culverts. Pitfalls the size of Freddie Broncos were dug in the road and covered with tarps and dirt. Tunnels, tripods, bipods, mono-poles, and other platforms were used as lock downs

We maintained a myriad of trails through the forest. I could get anywhere faster on foot than a vehicle on an unobstructed road. We had 24-hour security using radios and drums to communicate. And each night under the cover of darkness, the fairie folk would take to the road ripping and tearing until Wild Earth was free again.

As our control over the forest grew, so did the heavy handed tactics of the LEOs. Many people, some as young as 15, were assaulted. One young man was hit in the head with the flat of a machete, another was buried up to his waist by a bulldozer, while the Freddies looked on laughing.

In raids designed to intimidate, as much as reclaim control of the road, the Freddies would descend en masse upon our camps. Our water jugs were punctured with knives, our food dumped out and stepped on, and our kitchen ware was stolen or tossed into the woods. Our camp sites were dismantled, thrown into the road—possessions and all—then set ablaze. Arson is not a tactic practiced solely by dissidents.

During one raid and road closure, a comrade and I were holding a road block platform. The LEOs had parked a bulldozer next to the platform so four officers could climb up to remove us. The platform would not go without a fight. As the LEOs gained the platform, I cut the support lines and we began to shake the platform in order to make it fall taking us all with it.

With frightened expressions the officers leaped back to the safety of the bulldozer leaving us on our still standing, if leaning platform. Unsure of what to do next, one officer snatched a stout branch off our platform that we had been using as a support for the tarp. Using it as a makeshift club, he began to try and knock our food and water off the platform.

Thinking quickly (or not thinking at all), I jumped in front of the supplies to protect them with my body. I thought surely he would not hit me. Officer Friendly raised his club and began to strike me in the thighs and waist.

"We see you hurting him and we are videotaping," tree sitters shouted from above.

This officer had just crossed a line that ought never be crossed. I caught the next swing mid-stroke disarming the thug in uniform. Much to the surprise of the LEOs.

"How would you like it if I hit you?" I screamed, as I raised the club. "You wouldn't like it very much, would you?"

The tough guy officer on the far end of the dozer provoked "Go ahead. It will be the last time you hit a cop."

What he didn't know is that it would not have the first. I moved toward the new threat.

"It'll be the last time you draw breath, pig!"

"Everyone back off, he's serious," the head honcho down on the ground instructed.

The Freddies retreated and made no other attempt to remove us. We held the platform through the day and long into the night. Around midnight, still being watched by LEOs, we agreed that with a lack of supplies and a badly leaning structure, we could not hold the blockade for any length of time. Grudgingly, we decided to abandon the structure.

Despite the short lived victory, that platform was the only roadblock at Fall Creek to ever repel an eviction attempt.

Less than a month later we had reclaimed the roads. My partner and I were holding the gate at the only entrance to the series of roads that comprised the timber sale. Sometime around 3 AM she took watch while I slept.

I awoke to her screams of pain, and cries for help. It was still dark out. I jumped out of my sleeping bag to see two armed men in full camouflage. One man was trying to wrestle her to the ground, the other was near the gate and me.

A primal instinct to protect my loved ones roused in me. I charged her assailant taking him down and landing on top. As I raised my fist, I was suddenly aware I was looking down on Officer Friendly. In the same instant, he screamed for help and before I could react, I was hit from behind by bad guy number two.

As the officers fumbled with compliance holds, I calmly said "I'm not resisting," and went limp.

Fuck, I thought. How am I gonna get out of this one?

Fortunately, my partner's screams had brought backup with a video camera. They were able to videotape the officers being out of uniform, as well as the fact that it was only 5 AM and the sun had not risen.

At the jail, I was placed in maximum custody. No phone call. No charges. No nothing. Locked in my cell I stewed on the possibilities until around 10 PM when I gave up on getting out that day.

I had no idea that the entire jail was on lock down due to a large rowdy crowd protesting my arrest. Sometime around 2 AM an officer opened my door.

"You Free?"

"No, I'm in jail."

"Roll up, you're getting out."

What? I grabbed my stuff and went down to see the release officer who had denied my release ten hours ago. She asked the same questions again. Did I have an address? No. Did I have a phone number? No. If let out, would I check in? Hey, she didn't ask that before.

By 3 AM they were literally kicking me out of jail. Outside I was met by approximately 100 sleeping protesters. They had refused to leave until my release. Even though I wasn't in jail, I ended up spending the night anyway.

Weeks later, I was indicted on 17 Federal charges. One felony assault with a deadly weapon on an officer, and 16 misdemeanors. The Judge threw out the assault on grounds of self-defense and the lack of a weapon. And I plead out to the other charges agreeing to 30 days in jail on an unrelated resisting arrest.

I served my time in a Federal Correction Institution and was released in January 1999. I spent the rest of that winter alone in a tree sit thinking about what direction my life was going to take.

That Spring, I dedicated my life to full scale resistance. I had realized no amount of protest or begging for redress would stop the onslaught against life and freedom that the state endorses. I had been lied to too many times by Government Officials. I had been beaten and witnessed my friends beaten by a brutish police force too often. While those responsible for the injustices continued with business as usual. I could tolerate no more. It was time to walk a different path.

By the time I was arrested in June 2000, I had engaged in street battles with cops during riots; sabotage and armed forest defense. When it came to dealing with the State and greedy corporations, the word "please" was no longer in my vocabulary.

In Spring of 2000, I found myself returning to Eugene. I'd spent the last couple of months hopping trains and hitchhiking. Upon my return, I found myself thrust into the role of security for Eugene's Seven Week Revolt (which, ironically, was nine weeks long). There would be workshops, squatting, forest defense, and it would all end with a Reclaim the Streets, Reclaim the City demonstration on June 18th.

On June 18, 1999, the city was rocked by organized rioting as part of a worldwide day of resistance to the G8. The police sustained several injuries and were forced to retreat on multiple occasions. Damage was in the tens of thousands of dollars. Banks and police were the hardest hit, incurring the biggest losses. The city was covered in political graffiti. Eugene was suddenly center stage in the United States anti-capitalist movement.

This year's event was billed as a historic reenactment of last year's festivities. Of course, the problem with advertising a revolution is the police state prepares for one.

For nine weeks Eugene was a hot bed of police and anarchist activity. Folks were gathering en masse at parks, streets, cafes, and bars, while the police and SWAT Team patrolled the city—four officers to a car.

The city was tense. I really believed something big could kick off. The energy and repression were boiling to a head. I would not have been surprised if the opening shots of the second American Revolution had been fired. Impromptu marches were starting all over the city, and no corporate chain store was safe, as groups of people would simply walk in and walk out with food and beer. The police substation in the Whiteaker neighborhood had been attacked not once, but twice, and cops routinely were forced back into their cars when they tried to stop or arrest somebody.

I, too, was planning something to go along with the seven week revolt. During my time traveling I'd spend many a night shooting out windows of big car dealerships with my slingshot. It was a perfect way to rack up some good damage amounts, shattering those giant showroom windows and taking out the windows on those pricey SUVs. Very quickly I learned security for these places was often minimal. I'd never encountered anything more than lights and cameras.

I began to put together an idea of how to go about torching a dealership. It would be so easy to rig up a few devices and place them under some SUVs. I wanted to send a strong message to the car and oil industry, as well as to the public that not only is the extensive use of fossil fuels in this country contributing dangerously to global warming, it is also directly responsible for the hostile and imperialistic foreign policy of the US Government. These acts of injustice would be resisted.

The Seven Week Revolt put me back on my home turf and provided my opportunity. The city was ripe for action, and I wanted to help fuel the fire. I wasn't planning on a major action, just something big enough to raise the issue and inspire other actions.

I believed a clandestine attack on an SUV dealership—one of the symbolic hearts of industrial greed and power—during the gathering would inspire and encourage others to resist.

I targeted Romania Chevrolet because Chevy is a subsidiary of General Motors. Romania was the second largest dealership in Eugene. The truck and SUV dealership was selling a commercial fleet of vehicles (as opposed to those marketed to the public). The dealership was also located near the college campus providing an easy opportunity to get in and out.

The "where" and the "why" were easy issues to solve. However, I still needed to figure out how.

One day during a discussion with my friend and trusted ally, Craig "Critter" Marshall, he spoke of wanting to take his own actions further. Critter and I had worked together extensively on numerous tree sit campaigns. The level of trust between us allowed for very open and blunt conversations. After a few exploratory questions and the requisite security precaution of plausible deniability, we figured out we were on the same page. I shared my theory on car dealerships.

Excitedly, we set about our plan. For close to a month, we observed our target. Romania had private security, something I had yet to encounter at a car lot. Still, there are ways around security guards. We just had to learn the routine.

The dealership was also near homes which meant we needed to learn if anyone worked late or had any regular night activities that would have to be accounted for. The other concern was regular police patrols, as the neighborhood was part of the University District.

Finally, because of the many bars and restaurants nearby we needed to learn any regular pedestrian traffic, particularly when these establishments closed.

Once we had gathered the necessary information about our target and the surrounding area, we set about deciding our goals. We passed the idea around that we could take out the whole dealership. I could have easily rigged multiple devices to ignite at the same time and we could have punctured all the gas tanks on the vehicles to further feed the conflagration. Other ideas involved leaving graffiti behind or other messages.

Ultimately, for the sake of simplicity, and because this would be our first time working together in such a manner, we decided to use one device each and place them under two separate vehicles. It would not be a big fire, but to get the point across, it wouldn't have to be. Come the early hours of Friday, June 16th, we would strike. By the morning of June 18th our communiqué would be public knowledge. If all went well, the black block would rally and last year's uprising would look like a picnic.

All did not go well. On the night of June 14th, I was arrested while doing Cop Watch. Three local activists had been stopped by four police officers for the heinous crime of riding a bike at night with no headlamp. During the stop, I videotaped the police giving a warning to a couple riding by for the same infraction. I notified the police that any action now would qualify as select enforcement, and that I would be more than happy to provide all sides with copies of the tape.

During the course of the stop, the crowd had grown to about 20–25 people. The officers, too, had multiplied to eight including SWAT members. The Commanding Officer ordered no citations be given and that the police leave before things escalated. But, the pigs had come to pick a fight, and they weren't leaving without one.

As I stood on the sidewalk filming, the officers dispersed. One walked directly toward me. I focused the camera on him as he came closer—ten feet, five feet, he walked right at me. His shoulder lowered as he walked into me. He threw his arm around my throat as he dragged me behind the police car.

If I'm honest, I would have to say that most times I would have fought back, as much out of instinct as pride. This time, I simply held the camera and captured my own beating. It's kind of funny now if you can picture my head slammed into the road, and I'm laying face down with camera held out in front of me and pointed back.

The police got what they wanted. My beating triggered a response: the crowd charged, batons were raised and the smell of pepper spray filled the air. Mine would not be the only arrest that night.

The next morning I was released from jail. In a little more than twelve hours, I was supposed to slip through the darkness with a gallon of gas and a lighter. First things first, though. I went and had breakfast, then I went and took a nap. At 4 PM I met up with Critter at a gathering in the park. Against my better judgment, I assured him we were still on.

For the better part of the last year I had worked frequently by myself on actions, except on a few occasions when I would join with others for a specific action or event. I preferred working by myself because it brought out the best in me. I alone was responsible for planning and carrying out the action. I was free to listen to my instinct and change plans as needed without affecting any others. In this way I was able to incorporate a lot more ritual and magik in my actions, which was important to me.

Working alone I was also fully aware of my own abilities and limitations. I paid more attention to the details because I didn't have anyone to double-check me. By myself, I felt more careful and focused.

For whatever reasons, I was always nervous when working with others. It never reflected in my performance, but on this night it reflected in my judgment.

In times past, I saw to it that all incriminating evidence was properly disposed of prior to any action. On the evening of June 15th, I failed to take that necessary precaution, thinking it was detail that could be taken care of after the fact. I felt compelled to stick to our schedule, and we were already falling behind and so to both Critter's and my detriment, loose ends were left untied.

As I rigged the devices, and triple checked that no fingerprints or hairs would be left on anything going to the scene, I had a very bad feeling. I'd felt it all day. Something was wrong. Every instinct I had screamed at me to walk away. Maybe Critter felt it too. But we had made a commitment to each other, and our sense of honor made us keep it. Had we communicated our feelings perhaps things would have been different.

Unbeknownst to us, not more than 200 feet away, sat an undercover detective spying on us. (During the course of my trials, three different reasons were given for the surveillance. The most frightening being someone told the detectives to keep an eye on me, but no detective could recall who gave the order or who else attended the meeting.)

It was time we loaded the car I had borrowed earlier in the day. I had told the owner that I intended to go camping out at Fall Creek. I can still vividly remember the look she gave me when I picked up the car. It was like she could see right through me. I could tell she didn't want me to take it. She would later tell me her instincts said something was wrong. Still she gave me the car because she trusted me. I betrayed her trust that night and got her involved in something she had absolutely nothing to do with. I will always regret that. I will forever be sorry and ashamed for my betrayal, and the fact that the consequences of my actions touched the lives of innocent people.

As we pulled out of the driveway, the detective signaled to his partners, "The subjects are in motion."

At the first red light another of the three detectives called in a positive ID: "Jeff Luers is the passenger."

None of their communications came in on my scanner. All was quiet. We drove on, completely oblivious to the fact that we were being tailed by three vehicles. Yet, deep down that bad feeling persisted.

We turned onto a side street. The vehicle behind us did as well. Warning bells rang in my head. Another turn and it was gone. We kept repeating this game of cat and mouse until we were satisfied that we were not being followed by a specific car. We rationalized that it was only coincidence that there was always a vehicle behind us. After all, it was a busy night, school had just let out for the summer and traffic was everywhere. We forget the age old axiom, "Just because you're paranoid, doesn't mean they're not after you."

One last drive by the target, no cars behind us. Let's go! We parked about a block away. Critter grabbed the pack with the devices. From here we knew our parts. Together we walked through a dark parking lot across the street from Romania. We crossed the street to a bike path that would lead us back around to Romania. If we had paused for a few moments, the detective now following us on foot would have run right into us.

My heart was pounding. A few hundred feet left to go. Suddenly, I was in the headlights of a big black SUV. It drove by slowly like it was getting ready to pull into a home. Shit! I did not want to be seen. I had my hood up and my head down. I might have looked suspicious, but I knew I wasn't recognizable.

After a quick talk we decided to go on with it. We'd come too far now, with no time for second-guessing, it was now or never.

We reached the hedge that separated the properties. This was our cover and our entrance point. Quickly we ducked behind the hedge. We made our way crawling between the building and the row of new trucks.

In our planning, we had decided on the middle two trucks of the back row. We had observed that security never walked back here and there was another row of trucks buffering us from his path. While this row was closer to the building of a non-target, if the guard decided to change his route and patrol this lot before the other lot, we would be safely out of harm's way when the devices ignited. We wanted to ensure the safety of people as much as possible.

The downside to this is that we could not place the devices under the engines where they would have caused the most damage. Instead we had to place them under the gas tanks and hope the fire would be intense enough to do the trick.

Critter reached his truck first, as I crawled on to mine. He handed me a device as I prepared the fuses. The final assembly complete, I placed my device under the left rear tire and below the gas tank. With the flick of a lighter my fate was set in motion.

We ran through the back of the lot until we reached the street. We walked as calmly as anyone could in the situation until we reached the shadows near the car. From there we sprinted.

Once inside the car we felt safe. Critter turned the key and off we drove. We had only pulled out a few feet when the headlight of a big black SUV pulled in behind us. My heart skipped a beat. It was the same one that had passed us earlier. The thought that it was a cop didn't even cross my mind. We both figured it was a concerned citizen, as it continued to follow us.

About 15 minutes later my scanner was a buzz of activity. A fire had been reported at Romania Chevrolet. The car erupted with laughter as we cackled. At that moment the SUV behind us didn't matter, we had done it. No matter what happened now we had put the ball into motion.

After a while the SUV faded. We pulled off the highway and pulled into an Albertsons to grab some beer; head up to Fall Creek and establish our alibi. Then we saw the flashing lights coming off the highway. Not far behind was a big black SUV.

I turned to Critter and our eyes met. I didn't have to say it he already knew. "We're going to jail, bro. Got a smoke?"

Casually, we both rolled our cigarettes as we sat on the hood of the car waiting for our "traffic ticket." Then they took Critter and put him in a police car. I was left to observe the illegal search of our car.

Here is where I made a fatal error. When asked if I had been anywhere near Franklin Blvd. (the street Romania is located on), I said, "No."

"What would you say if I told you I had three officers ID you there?"

"I'd like to speak to my attorney."

"You are under arrest for Criminal Mischief."

"Can I finish my smoke?"

"No!"

I took two more drags before allowing myself to be cuffed. It was my last act of defiance as a free man.

Two trials and one year later I was convicted of three counts of Arson in the First Degree, two counts of Attempted Arson, four counts of Manufacture and Possession of a Destructive Device, and two counts of Criminal Mischief. The only two charges I actually beat were Conspiracy to Commit Arson with "Persons Unknown." I was sentenced to 22 years and 8 months.

The Prosecutor tried for a year to get me to plea bargain in exchange for my cooperation. The first offer was to testify against Critter. Then after they gave him a five-year deal, they wanted me to debrief about the ELF, my cell, and other cells I knew about. I steadfastly refused to deal and claimed no affiliation to any group. Each refusal was met with a re-indictment on new charges.

My attorney tried again and again to get me the same deal Critter received. Each time the prosecutor accused me of being an ELF leader and uncooperative. After each failed attempt, my attorney would ask me why they thought I was a leader. I never answered him.

The truth is I could think of a dozen reasons why they might think that. But, ultimately, I think the real reason they labeled me an ELF leader isn't because of any role I played in Fall Creek or the community. They needed to catch a "leader" after years of catching no one. They needed to set an example.

Their idea backfired. Thousands of people have been inspired to fight back because of this injustice.

Was a fire that destroyed one SUV worth 22 years of my life? Of course, I wish things were different.

I wish that the world was not run by powerful military, government, and big money men. I wish that people had more rights than corporations. I regret that people have to fight for their freedom and to protect Mother Earth.

Most of all, I regret that I am an American citizen, that my privilege and lifestyle has been the root cause of oppression and suffering for so many. I am saddened that most of my fellow citizens are, at best, unaware of the death and injury dealt to the indigenous people and citizens of other nations in order to serve American interests; oblivious to the destruction and pillaging of the earth to secure American opulence. And I am ashamed and disgusted because, at worst, my fellow citizens are aware and are indifferent.

So, we must continue to struggle, to educate and make aware, to challenge and fight back. Always we must seek the balance between building a better future and destroying an old civilization corrupted by values and morals that lead us to our death. We cannot waver in the face of repression. We must find strength in our fear, for if we fail to act, if we fail to win, our government and the corporations that finance them will take our last semblance of freedom in the process of destroying our world.

Now more than ever we need a unified front. Our voices must be heard and our actions must be felt. Our only silence should be our footfalls in the dark of night.

Mojo Workin'

Ashanti Omowali Alston

They think they can wipe you out!

"'This so-called war against terrorism has degenerated into another one of the phony, politicized no-win wars we've been through since Korea,' a senior government expert burst out in an interview with a *Spotlight* correspondent. 'The American public should realize that we do have the scientific and technical means, the psychological and operational know-how, to wipe out terrorism in a year—if the bureaucrats give us the go-ahead and the resources. And the next time it hears that terrorists have created an international crisis, the public should get up and demand that the administration do so.'"

What an honor. Yeah, truly an honor to write an article for those who represent homegrown revolutionary terrorists, as far as the Government tags you. Well, you're my kind of people. They called us the same names, and we were, and still are, Freedom Fighters. So, right on! Andy Stepanian, you brought me into this. We met at that panel discussion in upstate, upscale Vassar College in 2000, and I wondered, "Who is this young white boy who just got finished doing some prison time for this Animal Rights...no, Liberation???" And you came out not afraid but more determined than ever to do ya thing and spread the word that despite these fascist muthafuckas attempts to snatch y'all who believe in Animal Liberation out of your waters, the waters said *Welcome* and you who still wanna jump in...Come on!

I had two things, then and there, that drew me to think more seriously about speciesism and this crazy movement of young white folks who have raised the issue of human AND nonhuman life as a unity against those forces we called White Kapitalist Amerika or Babylon. One was Andy's story itself, a story of dedication to a belief in justice and against oppression. And the second thing was the issue itself, which I had never really thought about in such a way against the background of my own people's struggle. Something about it was new, yet ancient. It was about vision that expanded one's understanding of the kind of world we wanted to create out of this Madness. It was a call to the simplicity of Indigenous Folks' world-

224

view. Yet, it was also the direct outgrowth of the insanity of this over-technologically developed capitalist system's drive to manufacture all forms of life as it deemed profitable.

Nonhuman life with rights. Hmmm. McDonald's as the enemy. We can kick Colonel Sanders' ass? Oh, yeah! Black children know McDonald's before they know their ABCs, and will never know the revolutionary organizations and political prisoners who are fighting to keep the Dream alive and moving towards our liberation from this Madness. We have recognized for a long time that our communities are saturated with fast-food joints and well as liquor stores. We have also recognized for a long time that the pollution, lead-poisoning, garbage dumps, asthma, etc., etc., are all a part of the genocidal shit we face. We, too, are working hard to recover, actually, the unity and dignity of Life even when it finds us "dead" in the middle of its most urbanized major cities. Our movements have common ground even when it doesn't seem that way to our constituencies.

But I bet you there are others who DO recognize it: the government, the state, the FBI, these racist muthafuckas who know the potential power of alliance and got plenty experience in counter-intelligence operations to throw wrenches into our alliance efforts. But I'm like Steven Best, who knows that our movements have the smarts and the daring to throw the monkeywrench back into THEIR machinery, and we can do it like the Zapatistas say in "Walking while Asking," hey, we can get better as we go. Therefore, as we learn and grow we say again, *Babylon, you coming down. Down. Down. Down!!!!* Vision up. Alliance-building up. Babylon, what? Downdowndown!

That quote at the top of this essay I got that from a far-right wing rag in 1978. I was, at the time, in the Federal Prison of Marion, Illinois. This particular prison had taken the place of Alcatraz as the prison that held folks whom other prisons deemed too much. I was sent there as a political prisoner—Black Panther Party-Black Liberation Army—from the federal prison of Lewisburg, Pennsylvania, where prisoner resistance to new fascist measures had caused a "spontaneous fire" to erupt in the industry's warehouse. Don't ask me. I was on my fourth year, I believe. Prison time for me was one of reflection and escape. But for now, let's just talk about reflection.

Imagine. People wanna be free, and if that somehow frustrates the plans of racists, government, and big business then you can expect trouble. Our Black Liberation phase had just rose out of the Civil Rights movement and it would not have come out of that particular movement if the peaceful, visionary liberal civil rights movement had not met constant repression from the State institutions and The State-in-the-heads of other reactionary folks, white folks, who just would not understand. Anyhow, you know that if your desire to be free fucks with The Plan you are gonna be subject to some things that's gonna make life miserable for you, maybe take it a step beyond and make life, your life, stop. Just like that. Maybe find three bodies in the bottom of a lake. Fellow revolutionaries just disappeared. (i.e. The State: We are going to "disappear" them niggers and nigger-lovers. Nothing personal. Just wanna communicate a message to others that we aint having it. Not here.) But folks wanna be free. Blame it on the Free "anarchist" Gene. Can't help it.

Then came the Black Power or Liberation phase with a new force of youth, new ideas, new energy and a really different kind of courage. Believe me, it took courage to do a sit-down strike or a pray-in in the face of powerful fire-department water hoses getting ready to wash your behind, painfully, down the next two blocks, as a communication device saying, "Get your ass back in your place!" It took courage because these were the same folks, my folks, who had been terrorized for generations and it did, yes it did, instill tremendous fear within us and in our communities of White Power as we understood it. But dignity demanded that we face it, that terrifying force, as a first step, so to speak, towards our freedom. Yeah, I didn't understand that then, but later, in prison, I did. What courage!

It needs to be said that though our struggle took off to new heights, it was those very liberal government administrations who dug even more viciously into our movement. John F. Kennedy being the prime one. J. Edgar Hoover of the FBI, autonomous nut that he was, had in common with Super Liberal, John F. Kennedy the one objective that only matters to them: SAVE THE EMPIRE. They don't play games. Profits and power means a lot of folks gotta suffer. That's capitalism, baby. Nothing personal. The historical records are clear. Y'all know them. Even preparing for this writing, I was reading Steve Best's website (which I am sure f-ed up our computer here, ha!) and the clarity which he has about the State, about government/big business collusion, about the new advanced levels of fascist/surveillance society...YOU KNOW. You know what to expect. But know as well, that we did too, on some level. It was just being young, inexperienced in that "knowing," a "knowing" still hampered by a naiveté which caught us off-guard even as our dialogues and newspapers reported: FASCISM.

The 60s through the 70s were the greatest revolutionary period in this country. The visions were so dynamic, alive, creative. ALL POWER TO THE PEOPLE! The Black Panther Party (BPP) brought it all together, sort of like a bridge. Black power for Black people, Brown power for Brown people, Asian Power, Red Power, Power to the workers, Women Power, power to all the oppressed groups. Yeah. The Revolutionary People's Constitutional Convention was like the Zapatista Encuentro Against Neo-Liberalism and For Humanity. The government/big corporate powers HAD to stop that shit! The BPP, American Indian Movement, the Chicano liberation, and Puerto Rican Independence movements had to really dig in for some fierce battles. Some of our forces had to go "underground" for real. IMAGINE: People just wanna be free!

IMAGINE: Black power is taking off. Folks are thinking Community Control of the institutions that are vital to the health and welfare of our people and secure the best futures for our children. After 400 years of Hell, pure Hell. Terrorized. Suffering from internalized oppression. Can't even look Mister White Kapitalist Man in the face. Look down, look down, nigger! And then here we come. The *African* generation that declared *Ya Basta!* It ends here! When we walked down them streets we walked proud, fearless. Our heads held high as a mutha...PIG! THE PIG POWER STRUC-TURE. PIG POLITICIAN. PIG LANDLORD. PIG. (Yeah, I know. The language today may not sit well with you, my Animal and Earth Liberation allies, but just understand its power then and the new power of your language influence today. It's all good, as it goes. And I got a story to share related to this before I sign off. Ha!)

We, as the BPP, gave a defiant frame to identify our enemies, which also determined who were our friends. Never before had a broad, multi-sector generation of victims within the brain of the Empire taken to such defiance, rebellion, and movement. But this Pig Power Structure came after us with a vengeance! You wanna know why many of us went Underground? Think of why some of you have, or why so many of you have come to support you own Underground. Though there are class and race differences, believe me, what we have in common is the justice and simplicity of our visions for the worlds we wanted. The Weather Underground were our ALLIES, and I am proud of them and the risks they took against their privileged backgrounds. Awesome, daring. Hell, we all made mistakes, but we gave it our best shots...or bombs (strategically placed propaganda-bombs, ha!). But let us not forget: we acted to keep Dreams alive and to keep at least one step ahead of the Death-Dealers, the Destroyers, the Dominators. They, on their part, recovered rather quickly after an initial surprise, and went to the Drawing Board. *Hmmm. We've been here before. These kids have built a movement. Must be communists behind it. Whatever. NEUTRALIZE THEM, BY...ANY...MEANS...NECESSARY!!!* And so, like they have done with so many revolutionary movements around the world that have challenged Amerikkkan domination, they set out, with efficiency, methodically, to SAVE THE EMPIRE. That meant they were coming after the Underground and in such a way that all the aboveground, legal, social and captive nations folks would get the message. Its over! And sometimes it surely felt like it was.

Animal Liberation and Earth Liberation folks: know that there are over 150, maybe 200 Political Prisoners now within the brain of the Empire. Some of them have been imprisoned for over 30 years. You need to know who they are and how they got there. You have your predecessor visionaries there. You have those of us who took up guns, bombs, hammers, as well as the weapons of paper and pen, and bodies as wrenches thrown into various oppression machineries. I hope that you learn who they are and work for their liberation as vigorously as you do AL and EL Political Prisoners. But I also want you to know who they are because their circumstances are what the Empire wants you to know can be yours if you continue. Obviously you are not going to stop. Why should you. **The Empire has got to come down—down, down, down!**

The existence of Political Prisoners is also the living stories connecting us through generations. To know what has happened before you, before most of you were even born, is but a step away from where you live (literally). Locked away in them prisons are the voices, the memories, and the still living defiant desires of our Dreams. Here are the victims of RICO, and other business-as-usual repressive tactics: Know *them* as Knowing Yourself and Know Your Enemies, and as Sun Tzu says, in one hundred battles you will never know defeat. They are there. Reach out to them and the readings from Ward Churchill and others on COINTELPRO and the latest updates on Patriot Acts will all help you.

Being invited to speak at several Animal-Earth liberation conferences has also taught me a lot. Like about the connection between human AND nonhuman oppression and the LOUD, SCREAMING similarities between the treatment and maintenance of our oppressions. As I watched the videos and listened to Andy and young folk after young folk "break it down," my understanding was broadened in welcoming yet some discomforting ways, because I, too, have to realize my own conceptions, ideas, and behaviors towards other worlds that are still mired in oppression. But, I am here, present, open. Sooooo compartmentalized this advanced technological capitalist, patriarchal society (thanks bell hooks) is, and sooooo compartmentalized it make us. US as individuals. And then I realize that folks of color like Rod Coronado, Rob Los Ricos, Puck, and Warcry not only bring color to this critical movement but the challenges that such a movement needs to grow through. So, Puck raises the issue of *critical* anti-racist struggle within the Earth/Animal liberation movements, and Rod frames it as arising out of "sacred Indigenous resistance" and sees himself as a guerilla fighter who realizes that community work with both elders and youth is as important as the guerilla strike against the fur industry or Huntingdon Life Sciences. For me, as I have said in any of the conferences I've been invited to, I give the wisdom of my experience to new liberation movements which now have so much in common with Black Panther, Students for a Democratic Society, Republic of New Afrika, Nation of Islam, MOVE, the Weather Underground, etc.

This is it in short: While the government and big business interests are directing fire towards your ass, you have to continue to be smart and resourceful. But if I can tell you what's most important to me, then it that you also learn to know yourself as products of this Madness and how, if you are uncritical about it, the very oppressive behaviors that fuel government and big business will poison your own good intentions. But it will be *YOU*. COINTELPRO didn't destroy the BPP. It merely capped on our own weaknesses that we couldn't or didn't have the understandings and tools to transform at the time. Racism, sexism, classism, homophobia, impatience. Dogmatism, arrogance, scientism. Need I go on? New needs are: Accountability, responsibility, sensitivity, creativity, resilience...COMMUNITY. SPIRITUALITY, even if it has to come in secular forms, you better have ways to draw extraordinary strength in those times when the shit really gets rough and you most feel all alone.

Bridging is also a form of remembering. Many nationalisms are reminders of days of living close to the land, even for those of us who have never actually set foot on our folks' lost pre-industrialized lands. For urban Black folks we have those stories of that nation called Down South, stories which continue to get fertilized by more memories of folks recently here from the Caribbean islands, from Rastas, to just earth folks from Barbados and Haiti. Reminders that it wasn't always The Land of Concrete, Steel, Machinery, Computers, McDonald's, and State. We, like many folks from all ethnic groups here, have idyllic stories of pre-conquest Amerikkka, and the desire to get the wisdom, and share in the experience that present-day Indigenous folks keep alive. It has been these things that my experience with you have brought back to me. I remember, strangely. Yeah, something ancient, yet so new. MOVE, ain't that the message of MOVE?

The BPP revolutionized black nationalism by making it expand its tight boundaries. Boundaries necessary at one time, but which had to be broken through as our understanding expanded of how more of the interlocking systems of oppression operated. Our nationalism was enriched with internationalism, anti-sexism, anti-kapitalism because we heard under the Silence the LOUD, SCREAMING voices of other victims, some of whom were under our own boots. There were similarities between the treatment and maintenance of our oppressions. Hard truths, but necessary to face. We learned to speak new languages and helped to popularize those new languages into the mainstream. Today, as I be hanging with Animal Liberation folks (and know that my comrades make fun of me) I know that my presence and AIM's presence and MOVE's presence and Puck's presence and Rod Coronado's presence also means that there is an awesome potential for the kind of alliances that can set a new stage to this revolutionary spirit within the Brain. IMAGINE: Massive headaches within the Brain of the Empire caused by the ongoing work of our various movements BRIDGING with each other, working out our differences, respecting our autonomy, rethinking power, community, boundaries, ethics, solidarity, identity, etc. All the things that our enemies CAN'T do cuz the muthafuckas are terminally stuck. Right on.

I was reading Rob Los Ricos' *The Revolutionary Imperative of Going Native*, where he says,

> There are plenty of...subversive cultures we, as insurrectionary green anarchists, can look back upon to help us envision alternatives to the shitstem we're currently mired in. Sadly, we cannot return to the past. We can only learn from its examples. The pertinent question to be answered at this point is: are such cultures of resistance achievable in the 21st century? Franz Fanon's monumental book, *The Wretched of the Earth* suggests that it's not only possible, but necessary in order to rid the world of residual colonialization and imperialism.

Now I can get with Rob's insurrectionary green anarchists. He sounds like a 21ˢᵗ century insurgent Green Panther in Zapatista *pasa montaña* challenging us here within the Brain, the position Che Guevara envied. It challenges us to envision and to work to bring visions to fruition. *A world where many worlds fit*. Lord knows that we need that kind of guidance here. And inherent in that guidance is the internal challenge coming from the words of my sista Puck from her article, "Facing Off the Radical Environmental Lynch Mob: On Healing and Decolonizing:"

> The process of colonization is painful and dehumanizes both the oppressors and the oppressed. We all have so much healing to do. The dominant Western culture is killing the planet. We need to love the land, build real ties with and learn from people whose ways of life are more in tune with the Earth and are less oppressive to people.
>
> How will we be able to do this if we're stuck in an insular scene, congratulating ourselves and pretending that nothing is wrong? We need to find ways to support each other, care for each other, rip off our blinders and talk frankly about the problems we face.

Sounds like Assata Shakur's wisdom to me. The key to revolution in Babylon is us, in power through the people who care enough to jump on in the water.

Last thing is my little story, sort of related to fears of jumping in any new situation you got a desire to know more about.

Coming back from a conference with that damn Andy again, ha! We're driving back, me in the back seat just relaxing. It's a long drive. So, we gotta stop and get gas. We pull in. Across from us in the station is one of them trucks used to haul animals. What! Andy and fellow passengers, out of animal/earth-loving curiosity, get out of the car to check it out. OK, some farm animals are in it. Not many. Maybe five or six. Some grown, some babies. They ask the drivers, *Where ya going? Oh, to the slaughterhouse to get rid of them*. Now, I'm still in the back seat and I already see colored lights flashing from the heads of my companions. Back they come to the car. Huddle. Talk. What should we do? WE? I'm like, oh shit—ME too? Yep. *This is how we do it*. So, after a minute, no more, WE agreed to ask the drivers if would they sell any of the animals to us and if so, for how much? Drivers (father and son) say yes, and at such and such a price. OK, wait a minute. Back to the car. Huddle. How much money we got. Not much, but we got enough to buy the pig. *THE PIG!* Oh, my lord, what would my comrades think of this? Of me...*SAVING A PIG!* Ha! They go to the Father, negotiate and next thing I know, they coming back to our car with a baby pig in their arms. Shit. But I'm loving it. I like their spirit, their spunk, their DO-IT-NESS. Into the car safely comes our new friend and off we go. New York City, here we come. Now, this wasn't even an underground action. This was just a simple humane transaction. Just like other stuff I learned that day about Animal Liberation like their ethical concerns about freeing animals and making sure there are home-places already established to take them. Hell, I didn't know that. Sounds like the earlier abolitionist movement and the Underground Railroad to me. And folks wanna know why this movement continues to grow? And why the government is out to destroy them? Same as with the Panthers, it wasn't our guns that scared them. It was our visions and ideas, and the good, wholesome, loving, and daring ***doings*** that were catching on and had the potential to spread like wildfire. Ashanti, you've been through yet another learning experience and again reaffirmed your faith in the saying:

YOUTH MAKES THE REVOLUTION.

And they think they can wipe you out!

WE NEED TO FREE ***ALL*** OUR POLITICAL PRISONERS!,
THE SHAC 7
THE MOVE 9
LEONARD PELTIER
ROB LOS RICOS
PANTHERS & BLA SOLDIERS
WEATHER SOLDIERS
NEW AFRIKAN POWS
MUMIA
THE COYOTE
LIFE
LIFE
LIFE

ALL POWER THRU THE PEOPLE!

GOOD MORNING REVOLUTION,

AS ALWAYS, WE ACCEPT YOUR INVITATION TO JOIN YOUR NEW DAY!

Facing the Agents of Omnicide
Hope in a Dark Time

Josh Harper

I have been asked to write this article about the repression and brutality I have experienced as an activist. My goal is not to play the outraged protestor, naively shocked when State and Industry respond to a threat. These entities will not even react within the confines of their own laws when their power is compromised, and I see as inevitable some of the consequences my community has faced for being sincere in their desire to change the world. So, instead of a woe-is-me tale of jail cells and grand juries, I hope to present my experiences alongside an explanation of how I have endured and my hopes for the future. To give readers the full story, let's go back to October 26th, 1986.

I was eleven years old that day. My father was driving me to school in his rusted-out Ford truck. It was early, and cold, and I was busy dreading another day of compulsory education when a story on the radio caught my attention. The University of Oregon had been broken into by a group of masked "terrorists." They ransacked and vandalized the place, "stole" animals, and spray painted the words "Animal Liberation Front" on the walls. The authorities were looking for them, and the announcer assured his audience that these scofflaws would be brought to justice. Quotes from school officials and law enforcement followed. The motivation of the criminals was hardly discussed, but I gathered that they were opposed to animal research.

That night I turned on the television news and watched stock footage of the ALF flickering across the screen. I stared at the people in masks and thought of the good guys and bad guys from the pages of comic books. I knew that these so-called "terrorists" didn't fit the mold of evil-doers. They had acted selflessly on someone else's behalf despite the possible consequences to their own well-being. Seeing them juxtaposed against armed FBI agents, angry faculty members, and the mad doctors from the vivisection labs made everything clear to me. I wasn't an animal liberationist, I was just a kid, but I knew right from wrong, and I knew I was on the side of the ALF. To me, they were real-life superheroes, and in a sick reversal of the timeless pulp fiction cliché, they were being hunted by the bad guys.

Five years had passed when George Bush Sr. started his pet war in Iraq. Protests sprang up across the state and I followed the corporate news stories about the anti-war anarchists being handily defeated by the long arm of the law. One day at school, a kid I knew handed me a newspaper called *The Student Insurgent*. I took it home and read an analysis of the war I had not previously been exposed to. My first encounter with alternative media brought tears to my eyes and anger to my heart. I would never trust my television again. One page had several pictures of victims of the US bombings alongside an announcement for a rally against the war that very night. Soon I found myself down at the Federal Building for my first protest, and my first confrontation with law enforcement.

The demonstration that night was sickeningly peaceful, at least on the protestors' part. Considering the number of people being killed so that US Oil companies could see greater profits, pacifism seemed a comfortable form of non-resistance. We were all chanting slogans and waving banners when a group of people near the doors began a sit-in. Everything suddenly went into a frenzy. I heard screams well up in front of me, and "Clear the area!" barked over and over again into a megaphone. People began fleeing, and in every direction I ran I encountered a cop. Police seemed to be raining from the sky and coming up from the cracks in the sidewalk. As I neared a set of stairs one hit me sharply in the ribs with a billy club. I crumpled and fell down the stairs but didn't dare remain there; the officer was still coming at me. My legs were carrying me away as fast as they could when I had my first introduction to tear gas. Someone grabbed my arm and implored me to come with them.

My mystery friend took me and a group of other young activists to Skinners Butte, a nearby hill covered with trees. We all began speaking of what we had seen, who had gotten arrested, and what should be done next. One group of people argued passionately for a campaign of non-violent resistance. A young anarchist interrupted them and opined that this war was being fought for profit, and as such, we had to insure that money was being lost by corporations and the government every day the war continued. I went back and forth for days as to what course of action I should take. In the end, I decided to go out and break windows of banks and other institutions profiting from the war.

Eventually (and allegedly), that war came to an end, but my knowledge of other injustices was growing. My sister, who I love more than anyone in the world, was sexually assaulted by one of her teachers. The lawyers, judges, and jurors in her case treated her as inferior not just because she was a young woman, but also because she was born disabled. They let her attacker got off with a slap on the wrist. I visited her right after the case ended, and her despair was palpable. Every moment I spent in her presence was a reminder of my own deeply sexist attitudes, the same attitudes which had allowed the man who molested her to go free. Face-to-face with my own prejudices, I began confronting all my assumptions about the hierarchies that surrounded me. Eventually this process led me to a rejection of anthropocentrism.

My newfound ethics prompted me to go vegan and join the newly formed Liberation Collective in Portland. Soon we started traveling to demonstrations, making food for tree-sitters, and distributing copies of *Earth First! Journal, No Compromise, Live Wild or Die,* and other eco-revolutionary literature. These publications reacquainted me with the Animal Liberation Front. I felt the same admiration for them as I had when I was eleven years old, and I soon found myself organizing ALF support events. The activist community in Oregon was taking notice of me for being dedicated, outspoken, and relentless. Unbeknownst to me, I was also getting some other attention…

One day I was sitting on my front porch, when two men came up the stairs. I assumed they were missionaries or salesmen. As I tried to think of a way to escape their sales pitch, one of them suddenly pulled out a badge and said they were investigating a noise complaint. Instinct told me he was lying. As I stood and attempted to leave, one of the men confirmed my gut reaction and told me that they were FBI agents. He pulled out a list of license plate numbers and told me my house had been under surveillance. He was in the middle of asking who had been visiting me when I closed the door.

Soon afterwards my friend Joshua Kielas and I began work on *Breaking Free Video Magazine,* a periodical VHS series documenting direct action and protest for earth and animal liberation. We had solicited footage of actions from around the world and attempted to track down rare tapes of underground actions. Our mail began arriving open, and one day the studio we were producing from appeared to have been entered while we were gone. I started noticing people following me to and from Joshua's house. One day we went to a demonstration at the University of Oregon, outside the same labs the ALF had destroyed around ten years prior. A vivisector targeted during that raid, Richard Morocco, struck me in the chest during the protest. When I complained to the police they told me that nothing would be done about it. They did tell me, however, that they were keeping an eye on me.

During this time period I was practicing voluntary arrest frequently, and as such was regularly in conflict with law enforcement. Police attacks on activists were becoming regular. I had been arrested at a demonstration in Anaheim, California, and even though I was the one who had been repeatedly struck, I was charged with multiple counts of assault and battery. A surveillance tape showed me being passive while the police repeatedly shoved and hit me, but a conservative jury declared that I had made unwanted contact with the officer's hands and arms with my chest and stomach. I was subsequently sentenced to forty five days in the Orange County jail.

While I was in jail, I received two beatings at the hands of prison guards. At one point I was handcuffed and hit in the back of the head repeatedly for refusing to wear leather boots. Another time I was pushed down a flight of escalators by a guard. When I hit the bottom he joined a colleague in kicking and stomping on me. Neither of these incidents was as bad as the horrible violence directed against the jail's primarily African and Chicano population each and every day.

When I began my sentence, I declared that I was on hunger strike, thinking that passive resistance could reach the conscience of the judge, and soften the hearts of the police. My opinion soon changed when I realized that judges have no conscience and police have no hearts. While serving my time, I began discussing politics with inmates who rightly saw Gandhi's "Token of Suffering" as a tactic which did little to threaten the State and its corporate masters. As my body began to take damage from the prolonged refusal of food, my thoughts turned to the animal abusers, clear cutters, dam builders, developers, and their ilk sitting comfortably in their warm homes, enjoying dinner. Why should I suffer while they enjoy the fruits of their plunder? I was released after thirty six days without eating. I decided then that I was going to focus my energy on methods of battle that were more meaningful.

After recuperating, I joined up with some friends to sabotage a whale hunt off the Olympic Peninsula, Washington state. Local supporters confided that their friends at the Sheriffs office had been spying on us. We later found out that a Joint Terrorism Task Force had been formed near the small town of Sequim, where our group made its base of operations. After three months of freezing cold water, rough waves, and bad food, the hunters went into action. We were ready. Jake Conroy and I were arrested for interrupting the hunt with smoke canisters, fire extinguishers, and flares. Our deeds on the water that day saved a young whale's life and taught me the true value of direct action. Initially accused of attempted murder, our charges were lowered to Felony Assault in the First Degree. We plead guilty to gross misdemeanor reckless endangerment charges, and returned to the ocean during the next hunting season to save another whale.

At this time, the heat surrounding the ELF was increasing literally and figuratively. The Earth Liberation Front, sister group to the ALF, was burning down businesses, vehicles, and developments that were further harming the planet. The shadowy organization had grown rapidly, largely due to the frustration many people were feeling with formerly radical groups such as Earth First! As the lefties and pacifists gained greater hold on aboveground resistance, the ELF offered an alternative for those determined to have an impact beyond banner hangs and giant turtle costumes. Their fires were rekindling the forgotten flames of rebellion that had been smothered by an increasingly timid environmental movement, and the FBI was taking notice. Special Agents began appearing everywhere trying to track down the elusive "elves." The Justice Department announced that the ELF had become their number one priority, and simultaneously sealed my status as their biggest fan. I wasn't startled when Marshals came looking for me hoping to gain my testimony on the Front's activities. I was just bewildered at how they went about it.

One day during my second season of the whale campaign I was crewing on my friend Brett's small boat, Stingray. We had patrolled the area all day with a device meant to scare gray whales from the hunt zone. The Coast Guard radioed us and claimed the device violated the Marine Mammal Protection Act, and that they were going to cite us. It soon became clear that was not their real intention. Coast Guard Cutters encircled our boat, and then a small fleet of Zodiacs skipped across the ocean towards us. The men on board were clearly not with the Guard. They had on shiny black jackets with the words, "Federal Agent" emblazoned across the back. One of them came aboard and served me with a subpoena to the Portland Federal Grand Jury.

Still, I got off easy that day. My friend Erin Abbot was run down by a Zodiac while she attempted to keep the whalers from their prey. One of her shoulder blades was split in half, many of her ribs were broken, and she was nearly killed by the spinning blades of the boats engine which passed only inches from her head. Rather than rescuing her, the Guard members who ran her down allowed her to remain in the water for five minutes before calling for a Medivac Helicopter. The courts never gave Erin justice, but all of us on the water that day will remember her courage for the rest of our lives.

When we returned to land that night, I placed a call to the ELF Press Officer, Craig Rosebraugh. Craig and I had known each other for years, and during that time he had been subpoenaed to grand juries repeatedly. He explained that Grand Juries are fact finding expeditions carried out by federal prosecutors. Once subpoenaed, a witness has no protection from self-incrimination, no right to an attorney in the grand jury room, no right to hear evidence presented against them, and no right to remain silent. Grand juries can jail US citizens for up to eighteen months without actually convicting them of a crime.

Craig agreed to handle any media interest in my subpoena and to help me find a place to stay in Portland. I left the whale campaign and headed south to meet up with other activists and determine how I would handle the grand jury. At one point, I was staying with some friends near San Francisco who lived with two pit bulls. As the dogs tore around the living room wrestling with each other, I thought of how lucky they were to be in a loving home rather than a vivisection lab, a puppy mill, or a blood sports arena. I felt a tug on my heart and walked outside. I can't fully explain what compelled me to do it, but I burned the subpoena and spit on the ashes.

The next day, I wrote an open letter to the Animal and Earth Liberation movement explaining that I would never provide information about our struggle to the US Attorneys office, and that I refused to even show up for the hearing. On the morning of my scheduled appearance, Craig read my statement to the hundred or so supporters who showed up outside the Federal Building in Portland. The newspapers declared me an "anarchist fugitive." I thought that was funny, since I was not hiding and was living at the exact address the FBI had last monitored. Months passed without incident and I thought that perhaps the feds had decided I was not worth their time.

A young vegan I had met during this time period invited me to speak at his high school. After my speech I left the building to get breakfast. Suddenly cars swooped in from all sides. I was surrounded by Federal Marshals, FBI, and local police, and arrested on a warrant for felony criminal contempt. After my bail hearing, supporters gathered several thousand dollars and made bond within minutes. I was released and placed on pretrial supervision. The judge presiding over the case issued a demand that I stop advocating, encouraging, or showing support for illegal actions in any manner. My lawyer countered that this was a violation of my first amendment rights, and asked; "Would Mr. Harper be allowed to wear a t-shirt exclaiming 'Hooray for Jaywalking'?" The judge replied that I would be in violation of his order if I publicly approved of jaywalking, and that I would be jailed.

This grand jury ended uneventfully. Stuart Sugarman, my genius council on the case, struck a deal where I would enter the grand jury room in exchange for the felony being dropped. I did enter the grand jury room, but like former President Ronald Reagan, I just couldn't remember anything once I got there. The jury was asking where I was on certain dates, who I knew, and what knowledge I had of ELF crimes. My answers kept coming back, "I don't recall," prompting a hilarious fist pounding episode by US Attorney Stephen Piefer. "Stop playing games with me, Mr. Harper," he screamed, "I will walk out of this room and pursue any sentence I can against you!" He insisted he had evidence that I had liberated rabbits from a farm in Philomath, Oregon, and participated in mink releases elsewhere in the Northwest. I just smiled politely and continued with my memory lapse. A few minutes later I left the federal building without incident. That Grand Jury dissolved soon afterwards, but it wasn't long before another subpoena arrived.

In 2001, I made a campaign video for Stop Huntingdon Animal Cruelty (SHAC), entitled "This Means War." The short film contained footage I had received from anonymous ALF members documenting a raid on Huntingdon Life Sciences (HLS). Sure enough, after the premier in New Jersey I was delivered another subpoena. Prosecutors asked me to turn over the video on September 12th, 2001, one day after real terrorists flew planes into the World Trade Center and the Pentagon. I showed up at the court house but refused to hand over the videotape and was released.

Since that time I have encountered more surveillance, harassment, and physical aggression than I can list here. The short version is as follows. After being run off the road by corporate goons and beaten by cops in Arkansas, I was arrested alongside several other protestors for the crime of walking in the street without a permit. I was then dragged off the police bus and served with a civil RICO (Racketeering Influenced and Corrupt Organization) lawsuit claiming more than ten million in damages that HLS investors expected me and other activists to repay. RICO was originally designed to protect small businesses from the mafia. Now it was being used to protect multi-billion dollar investment firms from kids with placards. Eventually the case was dropped after we defeated its main financer, Stephens Incorporated, by pressuring them to end their investment in Huntingdon.

After that debacle, I released *The Mandate*, a video which documented more of the protests and direct action against HLS and their associates. During my speaking tour promoting the short film, I was followed constantly by the FBI. When I returned home, I began organizing against local HLS collaborators and soon my home was raided by the Seattle Joint Terrorism Task Force. They claimed that items such as pictures of my sister at age three, childhood martial arts trophies, and old magazines were valuable evidence against me and packed them up alongside several boxes of my roommate's possessions. The FBI simultaneously raided the SHAC USA offices: the soldiers in the War on Terror did not find any WMDs, but did manage to confiscate copies of the sitcom, "Bosom Buddies," along with some dream diaries, computers, and random junk.

In the months following the raid, I found out that people, including one of my roommates, were offered money to spy on me. After moving to a new apartment, I began to suspect that my home was being entered while I was away, and one day had the suspicion confirmed when I found files rifled through, closet doors opened, and vegan outreach materials thrown around. I began noticing people following me around town and started hearing rumors of my name being mentioned to witnesses in grand juries. Then, one morning around 6 AM, there was a knock on my door. It was the FBI with a warrant for my arrest. Six others were arrested across the country that morning, all of us charged with conspiracy to violate the 1992 Animal Enterprise Protection Act. Four of us are charged with "Conspiracy to use an Interstate Tele-communications Facility for the Purpose of Harassment." Three of those arrested were also charged with additional counts and are facing more than 23 years in prison.

It is clear that in the age of the USA PATRIOT Act privacy is a thing of the past. Since the arrests I have learned that a long-time friend, Lisa Distefano, was actually an informant. Her mission was to spy on me and deliver details of my life to the FBI. The full depth of her betrayal will remain unknown until she testifies against me at trial. There were also warrants to install key sniffing programs on our computers and wiretaps in our homes. I have seen thousands of pages of phone calls, emails, and instant messenger conversations between me and my co-defendants, alongside transcripts of our writings and speaking engagements. Video surveillance was also taken of many of the defendants. This "evidence" is worthless; there clearly was no conspiracy, yet the "SHAC7" trial continues because the powerful men who have lost money due to the Huntingdon campaign also pull the strings of the so called justice system.

Compared to what other people in the effort for Earth and Animal Liberation have endured, I am lucky. In England, people have been killed for campaigning for animal rights. In South America, Africa, Asia, and elsewhere environmentalists have been "disappeared." Female comrades in the movement have complained of being sexually assaulted by security guards and police officers during protests, and a friend of mine from Europe was permanently disabled when a cop knocked her off a platform during a civil disobedience action. Looking to other movements, especially those comprised of fewer white people, rape, assassination, and the framing of innocent activists is commonplace. I fear that, as time goes by, we will be facing the same, and yet I continue on this path. I know full well that more prison time lays in my future, and that worse brutality is inevitable; still I will not hesitate to act on the convictions that the ALF first sparked in me at age eleven. Here is why.

At one time, in the area that is now San Francisco, early explorers reported seeing flocks of birds so great in number they would block out the sun for hours. French traders in Newfoundland wrote of migrating harp seals that covered the horizon as far as anyone could see, and ran for ten days and nights without stopping. Going further back in time, the area that is now Iraq was once so covered with trees and wildlife that the mothers and fathers of Earth's first terrible empire could never have imagined it would become a desert. Perhaps it was the spread of that early civilization that eventually led to the loss of the harp seals, of the sky shattering migrations of birds, and all the other wonders that disappear forever each and every day that we continue the war against wilderness.

The Human Empire is nearly complete. The last of wild areas that once covered the whole earth are falling to our advancing cities. The other animals on this planet have been taken from their homes and made our captives, stripped of their original form and domesticated for our use. With our increasingly dangerous technology, nature stands almost no chance of righting the wrongs we have inflicted against the free beings of this world, and on the world itself. Perhaps I am naïve, but despite all this horror I still see some promise for the future.

Tonight, a teenage girl and her friends might pick up hammers for the first time, and smash the windows of a nearby McDonald's. An officer from a mainstream environmental group may realize that they will never save those wetlands near his home with paperwork alone, so he decides to step into the night with a gas can in his hands. An old woman in Oregon may walk a path in the forest she has loved since she was a child, and pull spikes from her pockets to place in the trees she climbed long ago. Though these people are thousands of miles apart, they share something with the millions of others who will also step up to fight the twin scourge of animal slavery and eco-destruction—a spirit of indomitable resistance, a fearless desire to save what they love and free the voiceless billions from

their suffering. That teenage girl, that middle-aged career environmentalist, and that old woman all know what might await them as a consequence
of their actions, but their hope for a better tomorrow overrides their instinct for self-preservation. They will act anyway. We must follow them on
that path.

The government can jail some of us, but they can not stop the phenomenon of compassion. It reached me as a boy on my way to school, and
with each new action it has the chance of inspiring others to take sides.
So long as I know that new warriors join the fight, and that old veterans
refuse to bow, I will have hope that our small uprising will save the world.
Stay safe, keep fighting as long as you have a breath left in your body, and
victory may yet be ours.

From the Prisonhouse to the Slaughterhouse
Reflections on Lives in Captivity

Anthony Rayson

Capitalism can only provide the "freedom" of the charnel pit and the "democracy" of the mass grave. Driven by slavery of all sorts—prison, chattel, contract, wage, sexual—the global "market" is vicious and fights over the meat. Not just humans, but also animals are exploited in ghastly, Mengelesque-form. Trapped in factory-farmed concentration camps, enduring the gruesome nightmare of mechanized murder, genetically altered pigs, cattle, sheep, chickens, hens, and turkeys are transformed from living beings into commodities for the machines of planetary profit. Industrialized animals are crammed into tiny cages, raped for breeding purposes, and their offspring are forcibly fattened, confined, drugged, and rushed to slaughter, all for the cravings of carnivorous consumers.

Of course, it doesn't stop with the torture and murder of non-human animals who suffer and die in an endless variety of barbarities. Human animals, too, are subjected to the horrors of forced imprisonment, slavery, starvation, and all manner of unnecessary suffering, experimentation, and commodification.

We know that for capitalism to survive, it must endlessly expand, as its whole *modus operandi* is driven by the quest for the profits of elites, not the needs of the world. Mountains of non-biodegradable garbage, plastics, metal, and radioactive material continue to accumulate, as global capitalism devours and depletes dwindling natural resources. All the while, wars, or talk of more wars, are looming in the battle of the "fittest" for territory and scarce resources. It's a planetary ecological and social tsunami in the making.

It takes a response of equal intensity and clarity, bubbled from the underground up. For life itself, an orgiastic panorama of options, is based on "mutual aid," not the "survival of the fittest" like we've been deceptively led to believe. Evolution couldn't happen without cooperation. But, extinction is a distinct possibility, as a lying, dying, murdering system goes through its disgusting death throes.

We're all gravely threatened by the otherworldly murderous intent and "star wars" capabilities of the US system of neo-con warlord wannabes. Large corporations set their agendas in their mahogany boardrooms for their sycophantic media and other means they use to instill compliance and acceptance. Academia, even "radical" studies and the "academic Left," are centers for the detachment from and intellectualization of genocidal policy. The rulers of the global capitalist empire develop the "research" that enables maximal profit and control. NAFTA and the World Bank are there to "solve" the problems of third world "poverty" they generated in the first place. Hitler, no wonder you were so damned jealous. Your dream of a "Master Race" has been realized. Zeig Halliburton!

All aspects of coercive social life, such as the schools, the military, and mass culture constantly reinforce the "goodness" of their bullshit cause—the Washington-run, global terrorist campaign of pillage, theft, extermination, and lies. Those left alive should wear a McDonald's beanie and bleat when prompted. We get the "privilege" to dig our own graves, while we live a regulated life in service to our oppressors' addiction to wealth accumulation.

Of course, the authorities call their terrorist bombs, jails, guns, planes, and markets "counter-terrorism." We're supposed to be so proud when dead bodies of US GI's trickle back to the states (under orders not to be photographed), as the severely injured fade into the shadows of suffering. Talk about "animal abuse!" And just think of the "cradle of civilization," modern day Iraq. Bombed, poisoned, invaded, occupied, and degraded—they endure constant bloodshed and suffering, yet live on. No doubt, all the animals there are suffering terribly too, unless under the care of normal people. The whole system of for-profit torture must end. It's a modern day, worldwide Gulag and system of slavery.

Hugo L. A. Pinell, a political prisoner for 41 years, is a former comrade-in-arms of the legendary George Jackson. Here's what he has to say about how this system devastates our society:

> Our oppression and dehumanization and our living conditions worldwide, are worse than ever because we are dealing with the most vicious, malicious and inhumane forces in history. They control just about every aspect of our physical and social lives, and that is a reality we can't deny or ignore. But as agonizingly painful as this reality is, the biggest damage these monster criminals have inflicted upon our humanity is the one done to our mental faculties, through a systematic and dogmatic process, generation to generation."[1]

From this psychological imprisonment, flows all the degradations we must live through.

The Art of Mind Control

Subjugation can't function in a society of thinking, feeling people who haven't had their humanity lobotomized. Education, knowledge, truth, and the brave people who make them their life have been made "illegal" in a way. In the nineteenth century, it was against US law to educate slaves. Their native culture was beaten out of them and servility, Christianity, and hopelessness was forcefully inculcated.

The same goes today in a much more sophisticated, all-encompassing manner. From the minute a child is born, s/he is deluged with never-ending television and social suffocation. Normal human activity is filtered through a blizzard of corporate ideology and consumerism, leading to the intellectual torpor and vapidity that passes for social life. Even families aren't really families, as the parents are slaving away in the rat race, the latch-key kids are taught nonsense and obedience in schools. Their "free" time is gobbled up by the idiot box, movies, fast food, and computer games that trumpet the fascist cry of "Long Live Death!"

So, we live in a society rooted in the need to zombify its citizens, to mass manufacture armies of uneducated masses oblivious to their own best interests, unable to think critically and resist. I read a story about a gung-ho moron in a government death squad who reveled in the "opportunity" to massacre people in Fallujah. Like many soldiers, he was a deadbeat and lost soul. His passion was Tupac Shakur. But Tupac railed against the US slave state, not for it! Yet that was lost on him. He was killing men, women, and children in Iraq and being told he was a "hero."

The German Nazis specialized in the "Big Lie" and advanced the "science" of propaganda. With the end of World War II, the US made it a top priority to snatch up Nazi manipulators and put them at the head of the nascent CIA and other oppressive systems. The US competed with Russia, who had the same idea—a nationwide, deceptive system of capitalism, military aggression towards others, and intense repression at home. Russia had Stalin, Italy had Mussolini, and the US had John Foster Dulles.

All aspects of our lives are targeted, with the goal of mindless acquiescence to the wilting of our own being and the Time Machine-like response to the sirens that blare when the system wants us to do something—be it to cheerlead for mass murder, work obediently in factories, participate in their genocide, or become their jailers and kidnappers. Exploiting people in this manner is just a reflection of the treatment the Global Gulag accords the ecology of the Earth. Species extinction, resource depletion, global warming, chemical and radiation poisoning, decimation of the rainforests, and other signs of ecological collapse are causes and effects of the oppression placed upon people. It's the crux of our whole problem.

Drugs play a huge role in this too, because many drugs have a strong effect on our thinking and behavior. Heroin was brought in from the Marseilles Mafia in the wake of the massive bloodletting of WWII. Air America was the world's largest airline during the Vietnam genocide and they routinely smuggled massive amounts of heroin into the States, sometimes inside the bodies of dead GIs. I remember seeing pictures of junkies sprawled on stairwells, victims of a particularly pure dose. CIA agents inundated the inner cities with crack cocaine to destroy the environment of the Black community.

Strange Fruit of the Prison Industry

In the racist system of the US, it takes 500 times as much powdered cocaine (the drug of whites) as crack (the drug of blacks) to get the same mandatory sentence. Crack is a highly addictive and debilitating drug that ruins communities. Moreover, its hyper-illegal status makes it easy for police to round-up blacks and further devastate their community. Crack is the epitome of racist drug law. With few legal forms of commerce available, dealing drugs becomes a major part of the economic life in the 'hood. Even though most of the drugs are sold to white people, it is black people who are imprisoned and murdered because of them. Black women too are thrown into prisons, leaving their young children without mothers, in a slave-like acceleration in the punishment industry. An environment without love or hope is a doomed environment. Add the fact that poor black communities also suffer the lion's share of industrial waste dumps and inferior everything, and you have a systematically degraded environment that breeds despair and violence.

Prisons began as factories and police forces were created to capture slaves and suppress workers. This is still their function today. Cops of all kinds still basically take their orders from the corporations who pull the strings in Washington. "Gangs," "anarchists," and "terrorists" are all buzzwords that people almost automatically accede to in order not to involve themselves with whoever the government is targeting.

Prisons aren't about "crime control," they're about for-profit repression. In fact, they are a huge, government-run, criminal enterprise, wildly profitable, and completely paid for by ripped-off taxpayers. Think about prison environments for a moment. People screaming day and night. Rape and the spread of serious diseases—such as AIDS, hepatitis, venereal diseases, and everything else—is epidemic, as if deliberately cultured in a Petri dish. Violence, longing, bitterness, hopelessness, and self-loathing are coupled with the schooling in criminality. Useful programs within this madhouse environment have been gutted. There's no real rehabilitation, no social re-entry programs. People are left to live or die in this minimalist warehouse nightmare. Then, after consuming the prime of many lives, people are spit out of their dungeon and shoved into the glare of day without any clothes, housing, job prospects, or money. And a vast array of laws and stipulations nearly guarantee that parolees will soon return for some parole violation or new "crime."

There is an endless poisoning of community environments. First the system snatches up young, dynamic men and women, then forces them through a hellish prison world, then dumps them back into the community like human refuse. This insane system leaves people shell-shocked, embittered, and farther from being a positive asset to the community than when it seized them. In Amerika, the state tortures and tries to kill the spirit of people, whereas in client states like El Salvador, the US-trained authorities were allowed to go all the way—to torture, kill, and dump the mutilated bodies for the vultures to pick over—just like the US perfected in the Phoenix Program in Vietnam. Given that a community cannot live without a positive spirit and hope of genuine humanity, what miserable kind of world is this prison system really breeding?

Many of the most articulate and courageous thinkers and doers are locked down and kept from the public. Once prisoners raise their voice, they can expect severe repression—beatings, transfers to control units and supermax torture chambers, forced drugging, shackling, and other techniques unique to the US. A huge percentage of the young men from the most oppressed communities—Blacks, Latinos, and Native American men (and increasingly women)—have been ensnared in round-ups. Not just in large cities, but also in reservations, rural communities, along the US–Mexican border, suburbs, and elsewhere, people are continuously fed into the maw of Mammon to fatten the for-profit punishment industry.

So, really, the vibrancy of these communities, even though separated sexually, exists in the prisons of America today. Everything is concentrated from the violence and cruelty, to the love and insight. Meanwhile, the community state-inmates came from is left without direction; it is fearful and subjected to low-level occupation, surveillance, economic hardship, constant brainwash, desperation, and ignorance. Grassroots groups struggle to do useful community support work, for the young lions and lionesses, and the wise elders that they so vitally need, are locked away. The captives' families have a difficult, daily struggle just to keep on keeping on.

Those of us who have battled through a lifetime of lies and have regained our ability to think, have overcome our fear. We are thus capable of contributing our unique talents and interests to concentrate on addressing the crucial issue of prison reform. This is where the Kevin (Rashid) Johnsons and the Jeffrey Leurs are. To rebuild our communities and develop serious resistance requires that we collaborate closely with these brave and brilliant prisoners.

Another debilitating lie the government constantly tries to hammer into people is that prisoners are dangerous threats to the populace, when in fact they are culled from their own families and communities. Mostly, they comprise poor people of color convicted of non-violent, often victimless "crimes." Yet, every night on the news, the headline story is about the latest gruesome murder. But, of course, the media never bestows the same attention to the innumerable victims of the government killing machines, the industrial accidents, or the hell of prison life, where behind the razor wire people die like flies. Incarceration itself is a crime against humanity. No other animal treats itself or other species with such cruel contempt.

The prison industry is anti-life, constructed only to oppress, instill fear, and keep a monstrous regime in power.

Pedagogy of the Oppressed

To successfully overcome this horrible reality will require a reversal of the brainwashing process. We must break out of our atomized existence and learn to be thinking, feeling people again. All the struggles in the world are interconnected and these connections must be made in political alliances. Solidarity, a basic anarchist tenet, is extremely important for revolutionary change.

As government is increasingly targeting activists and organizers, such as Ward Churchill and the Anarchist Black Cross, more and more of these people will become prisoners. For the truth they speak is powerful and dangerous, like water to a wicked witch. Go to the prisons for the real truth about this society and know that the garbage you see and hear from governmental mouthpieces are lies.

Prisoners have experience with deprivation, lack of resources, repression, and so forth. They have adapted to their situation in ways that show resourcefulness we need to learn from. How do you cook food on a heater? How do you barter coffee, stamps, food, and various services to get what you need? More generally, how do you adapt to such a restrictive situation and still keep your sanity? Prisoners can teach the rest of us these type of vital skills.

One thing that really frustrates me is the obliviousness of outside people to the powerful education of which prisoners are capable. I focus much of my attention helping to get the word in and out of the gulags. Prisoners are immensely grateful when given empowering information. They start study groups and read zines until the cops confiscate them and then they write their own material. People on the outside seem to care only about how "professional" a zine looks and not the ideas it contains. Who is really in prison here, mentally? Without the humanity, freedom, and counsel from conscious prisoners, I myself would be in a constant state of dread and despair.

The labs where monkeys, cats, dogs, mice, rats, and all kinds of animals are forced to endure gruesome experiments which will destroy their sanity and life, is, was, and always has been, duplicated by people on human prisoners. Nazi vivisector, Joseph Mengele, learned his methods from US mentors and colleagues who came to Germany to teach him their techniques. At the close of WWII, the US grabbed the best and the brightest German "scientists" to learn the latest techniques in everything from developing hydrogen bombs to enforcing sensory deprivation in prisons and madhouses. Many of these evil police tactics we're seeing more of today—violent restraint techniques, high-frequency concussive blasts fired into crowds, tasers, mass pens of "pre-emptive" arrestees, and so on—are developed after experimentation on prisoners. Who better to learn from than the initial victims themselves?

The modern techniques of sadism, brainwashing, control, atomization, and obfuscation form an ever-expanding and all-encompassing field of "research." The shock-and-awe ghastliness of the US government knows no bounds, and the tens of millions of human beings vaporized in Hiroshima and Nagasaki, butchered throughout Central America, or killed and left for the starving dogs in Fallujah all bear grim testament to this sordid fact. The US is fascistic, or if you prefer, "democratic," which only means militarized corporatism. Sham elections don't affect that status one iota.

Like everybody else, I feel the pressure and bear witness to the carnage and suffering experienced throughout our world, because of this extreme aggressor nation. Personally, I gravitated to dealing almost exclusively with the prisons, because it became more and more clear to me that this was "ground zero" on the assault on Americans by the system. It's the "black hole" of society, constitutionally sanctioned slavery, where anything goes in the dungeons of the state. Court cases brought forth by prisoners have been dismissed by no less than by the US Supreme Court, citing a clause in the Thirteenth Amendment that sanctifies slavery for prisoners.

So, when the system makes anti-capitalist and anti-state activities "illegal," it has an unlimited source (or potential source) of slaves to exploit, without any moral accountability or economic responsibility. All expenses to feed and house prisoners are paid for by the governmental extortion racket known as taxes. Just as technological advances bring forth faster cars, so too does state repression evolve and streamline itself. And the folks with the brightest minds, who are the most giving to their communities, are often singled out for the most physical and psychological torment.

Black folks face the extreme, but all of us are likewise being menaced and targeted, as this system devours everything in its path. We need to look to the most oppressed in this nation (Blacks, natives, women, undesirables of every stripe) and assimilate the analyses of their experiences, so we can thoroughly build a conscious counterforce of life, love, liberation, and a giving humanity.

Dirty Old Prison Town

Stalags are everywhere nowadays and affect everybody. They kidnap their young bounty, usually in urban areas, as opportunities for round-ups for a million-and-one "violations" of their pro-slavery laws abound. Rural areas have been besieged by corporate farms, and the government has most people where they want them—atomized, television-watching, worker bees. Prisons come, and the glowing promises turn into community nightmares.

A brother we were able to help parole (a real rarity) in Alabama was telling me about a struggle in his community to prevent the erection of a prison. He said that at first the prison builders claimed they were constructing a strip mall! The politicians, gutless wonders as ever, never fail to crow for the greased wheel deal of a prison as a means of "economic development" in rural communities. The whoring-out of these hyenas gets shriller and hoarser, so naturally, we must all acquiesce, as our conservative press tries to disdainfully explain to us the wonders of "progress." So slap your "bring them home" ribbons on the back of your SUV and don't think anything of it. Condoleezza Rice, George W. Bush, Donald Rumsfeld, and Paul Wolfowitz will "take care of things." Kissinger is always there for advice.

A prison is the kiss of death to a community. They bully the whole country (and less convincingly, the world) with an unhealthy, deliberately ruinous, wasteful, oblivious, and punishing mindset. They also pollute pitilessly and "legally" cut local deals so they can maraud over all areas, economically and culturally. I'm talking about all the industries, factories, prisons, animal farms, military centers—all of it. Our hard work is exploited for profits, then taxes, so that industry and government can ruin our communities, force us into being their jailors and soldiers, and wreak devastation on our brothers and sisters all across the globe. Democracy in bloodthirsty action!

Recently, the state of Illinois was going to grace a poor black farming community in Kankakee County, with a women's prison. This was in Hopkins Park. They thought that they could use this to balm over centuries of slavery and institutional racism by bestowing a beautiful prison in their face. Well, guess what? The citizens responded with militant direct action! Living in Pembroke Township, they formed a group called Pembroke Advocates for Truth (PAT). Their newsletter, *Insight*, was the joyous rarity in activism—funny as hell and dead on. They didn't cater to the idea that they should welcome a prison. They saw it, rightfully so, as monstrous, as another example of the oppressive nature of this settler, cracker Empire!

Despite the fact that these folks vehemently rejected this project, poor though they continue to be, it was started anyway. Initially, it was planned to happen directly across from an organic farm. Due to agitation, it became known that this piece of land—the first piece actually sold to a state government for a prison by any state in decades (all other land had been "gratefully" ceded by municipalities)—was actually a sweetheart land deal between the crooked Governor, George Ryan and billionaire Kankakee developer, Tony Perry.

A prison always has its glaring lights on 24-hours a day.

Most have ominous towers occupied by shotgun-toting guards. The dumping of sewage, along with excessive pollution caused by this dreadful economic system of mass incarceration, means that communities are flooded with problems, not "solutions." Your "prison town" environment has been degraded in the most depressing of ways. Your area will henceforth be known for human suffering and misery for the "cause" of profits instead of whatever vibrancy it once possessed or the human potential that is forever squelched by this demented society. Natural habitats of animals are also forever being menaced by this unrelenting paving of farmland and the introduction of diesel and gas-spewing vehicles into previously peaceful, pastoral productive farmland. Everything, alive or dead—even inorganic—has a price on it and is subject to the devastation the system clumsily and wantonly causes.

Total Liberation

These are serious times and we are greatly in need of lucid, well-written narratives and analyses, crafted to be empowering and to offer instruction and guidance. We can rise above our fears, develop effective working habits, and operate with a driven determination. Humans must learn to usefully apply their energies to the greater good of their community, something that animals do instinctively. People would act spontaneously too, if allowed to be themselves as individuals who are naturally interested in mutually supportive, non-coercive community. But being programmed to function as obedient robots and soylent green-fed consumers is the opposite of genuine freedom and real life.

The marvelous brainpower human animals possess gives us the possibility to transcend this repressive and predatory social environment. But the baser instincts of power and greed which drive the small few who orchestrate this worldwide death march are holding our minds and bodies hostage, just like the animals they exploit. We must cross the fear line and develop our human capacities. Work your brain and decide where your greatest talents and interests lie, and weave your gifts into the social struggle. Mutual aid will see us all through, but it only works if you seriously apply yourself.

It's all part of the struggle for liberation—be it for humans, animals, or the Earth herself. People wrenched from poor neighborhoods are a vital part of the slaughterhouse environment this system requires to keep creaking along. Take away a third of the young black men in poor communities—in some areas the percentage kidnapped is well over 50%!—and then warehouse them in dreary prisons, and the social environment has been effectively decimated. Family members have no brothers, sons, or husbands to deal with the occupation and forced immiseration of their "expendable" communities of people. Increasingly, it's the women, mostly mothers of young children, who are wrenched from the embrace of their families and forced to languish in a cage.

Those who have gained useful knowledge must become the serious educators for others. Free education must be a fundamental part of all activist activity. The knowledge is accessible, through websites, zines, distros, tapes, etc. We should seize the media and adapt what is useful to the situation at hand, as we continually, "raise some fucking issues" as Lorenzo Komboa Ervin eloquently puts it.

I call it "agitation-education." Our fellow humans are all being treated like minks on a farm, in one form or another. To liberate them means to be supportive of them and help them rekindle their sense of self. A person who overcomes his or her fear of the state, is an animal finally freed and capable of anything.

Notes

1. This quote is taken from a foreword Hugo L. A. Pinell wrote for a new publication I currently am editing, entitled *George Jackson Lives!*

Taking Back Our Land: Who's Going To Stop Us?

The Native Youth Movement Warriors Society

Kanahus Pellkey

The Native Youth Movement (NYM) is a Native Peoples' Liberation Movement, fighting for our People, our Land, and our way of Life. The Native Youth Movement is a Warriors Society: the Young Warriors serve as the Physical protectors, and the OGs (Original Guerillas) act as the Advisor Warriors, giving direction through lessons, age old teachings, previous battles, and from the Spirits and our Ancestors who have passed on this responsibility of defending our Indian way. The Native Youth Movement is becoming a Grand Council of young and veteran, battle-tested Warriors.

Here in the Secwepemc Nation, the Secwepemc Native Youth Movement and the grassroots Secwepemc—comprised of Elders, youth, and traditional land-users—have been fighting to protect our mountains from a massive expansion by Sun Peaks Resort Corporation. This alpine area has been the lifeline of survival for countless generations of Secwepemc and is now being severely threatened by ski resort development. The 2010 Winter Olympics is planned to take place in our backyard and the province and corporations intent to build 200 ski resorts, which would destroy our mountains here in so-called British Columbia. The destruction here is non-stop, a fact that verifies the urgency to defend the lands now. If we wait any longer these mountains will be raped of everything needed to carry on our traditional way of life.

Formed in 1990 in Winnipeg, Manitoba, inspired by the Mohawk Armed Uprising at Oka, Québèc, Canada, and seeking an alternative to high Native Gang rates, NYM is a continuation of 500 years of Native Resistance to Colonization. NYM is a Unity point for Young Warriors from many organizations, Nations, and Societies throughout Turtle Island. We receive our direction from our true Elders, those who left our instructions in the rocks, the stars, songs, War stories, and way of life that we must insure continues forever. NYM is a part of the Prophecy of the Eagle and the Condor, when all of our Nations will once again unite and Take Back our

Land, and the Youth will once again be the majority of our populations. That time is now. This Unity and true power scares our enemy so much they will not stop until they feel we are no longer a threat to their evil and devilish crackah ways.

NYM uses Education, Agitation, and Direct Action to achieve our goal—Freedom! We will not be stopped until Freedom is achieved.

The NYM Outlook

NATURAL LAW: "The Creator give us a Law. The Creator give us a Way of Life, and he created Indigenous People. We have a Right to live as the Creator wants us to be, to live on this land, our country."—Bobby C. Billie, Traditional Seminole Nation

TAKE BACK THE LAND: This is Indian Land. We must re-claim what's rightfully ours, for the Future of our Red People. We won't stop until we Win! "When one falls a thousand will take his place"—Fred Hampton Sr.

PROTECT AND RESPECT OUR WOMEN AND CHILDREN: No child molesters, no rapist, no women beaters. Those who abuse our Life Givers and Future Leaders have no part in a Warriorz Society and will not be permitted to join NYM. We fight for Red Life, not Spiritual death.

SELF-DEFENSE: We have been attacked for 500 years. All actions against those on our Land, are purely Defensive. We must Defend Mother Earth from Destruction from the evil Invaders. We will Defend ourselves BY ANY MEANS NECESSARY.

NEVER COLLABORATE WITH THE ENEMY: Don't talk to Police. We have the capabilities to handle our own business, no matter the circumstances. Snitches get Stitches. Fuck The Police!

NO HEARSAY LYNCHINGS: Only take Face-to-Face communication as Truth, everything else is questionable and should not be believed or acted upon before Face-to-Face communication is established, and messages/rumors/gossip is confirmed. Internal breakdown and false egotistical pride got many people killed and locked down and can easily lead to the dismantling of the Movement and Organization. Don't believe the Hype.

Break Free From the Shackles of the Indian Reserves

Indigenous Peoples throughout the World are in a battle right now to protect their homelands and People. Some are fighting with guns, some are fighting with law, some are putting their lives on the front line, some are prisoners of war, and some are grassroots people asserting their rights by occupying their traditional lands again. No matter where Indigenous Peoples in this World are, they are all fighting against the same forces of encroachment, assimilation, greed, lies, money, racism, contamination, and destruction. We, as Indigenous Peoples, experience the effects of these forces on our everyday lives, but still only a handful of our people will stand and fight.

Here, in so-called Canada, in the Secwepemc Nation and on the Nes-konlith Indian Reserve, I see how being born into the confines of the Indi-an Reserve colonial system has taken the warrior spirit and conformed the views and values of our people. We were not meant to be confined to small tracts of land—we have vast homelands for a reason. Every Indigenous person needs to realize that if we remain content and happy, trapped on these little Indian reserves, they will have conquered us and we will lose all that our Creator has left for us. Remember that it was just a short time ago that our ancestors lived free out on the land, and that they would see the Indian reserves as an atrocity to our way of life and existence. Our Nations were enormous and powerful—full of pride and dignity. This is what we must fight for—this is what we must rebuild. We can't sit back and expect our Peoples and Nations to exist forever, especially with all the powerful political and economic forces against us, trying to assimilate us, colonize us, kill us, and make us forget that we exist as distinct Peoples.

There are many Native youth that do not receive any type of direc-tion, teaching, or values from their communities and families, leaving them a stranger to their own culture, Land, and Peoples. With no vision or hope for the future, many Aboriginal youth are themselves trapped within cities or on the rez, where the effects of post-colonial stress syndrome are prevalent: drugs, alcohol, domestic violence, suicide, disease, gangs, birth defects, pollution, sterilization, self-exploitation, and other outside influ-ences which devastate our Peoples. This is not the way our people were meant to live, conforming to a colonial system made to oppress and as-similate us. This man-made system has taken control of our Peoples and our Freedom, which has led us through the "Indian Dark Ages" to where we stand today. I choose to consciously resist the "white-man's system" in its entirety: its corruption, greed, destruction, lies, racism, assimilation, colonization, and evil.

The Secwepemc Nation is a sovereign Nation. We have never ceded, surrendered, or released our Nation to any foreign government. We have never signed a Treaty with any one. The Secwepemc have occupied this area since time immemorial and our culture, traditions, and identity flow from this land. It is inarguable that the Secwepemc have an ancient right to this land. Nevertheless, governments, corporations, and individuals continue to trample on the rights of our people, and destroy everything in their path.

Here in the Secwepemc Nation, grassroots Secwepemc, comprised of Elders, youth, and traditional land-users, have been fighting to protect our mountains from a massive expansion by Sun Peaks Resort Corporation. This alpine area has been the lifeline of survival for countless generations of Secwepemc, and is now being severely threatened by ski resort devel-opment. The destruction here is non-stop which verifies the urgency to defend the lands now. If we wait any longer these mountains will be raped of everything needed to carry on our traditional way of life.

This alpine area that is being threatened has always been our mountains we call *Skwelkwek'welt* and we hold an ancient responsibility to this land. Upon upholding my responsibility to take care of the land, I became actively involved in the Native Youth Movement. I have seen the British Columbia and Canadian governments and Sun Peaks Resort Corporations collaborate to drive my people off the mountain. They destroyed eight of our homes and bulldozed and desecrated two sweatlodges. RCMP and white settlers officers assaulted young women, and arrested over 75 Elders, youth, and traditional land-users.

Our right to the land is given to us by the Creator and is an ancient and inherent right. The word used in law and politics to explain this ancient right to traditional lands is "Aboriginal Title." It has been through the hard work and dedication of our ancestors that the legal framework to protect our rights is set out for us. Our ancestors thought about us, just as we must take into consideration the future generations.

We are born into a world of colonized thinkers, born into a time we did not choose. Born Secwepemc today, I show the symbol of assimilation and shed the light of our unwritten history. If I do not stand and fight against this war of genocide, history's words will speak "the Secwepemc are extinct." The task falls to my generation today to stand up and fight for all generations to come.

The great importance of our existence, the very essence of our identity, relies on the land and the ability to preserve and protect our land base within our Nations. Thousands upon thousands of unborn Indigenous Peoples depend on us here today. If we forget about them, will we join white-man's ways and leave them with scarred mountains, massacred forests, toxic waters, and extinct medicines, foods and animals? Will we leave them with no language, no culture, no traditions, no pride, and no identity? Or will we fight to protect those unborn and leave a legacy to remember?

Our struggle to protect our land and way of life is the lifeline to a vision. A vision where our Peoples will exist forever unscathed from the influences of the white-man's destruction; where our Peoples will be Free to exist as true to our identity as were our ancestors; where we will hold the ancestral power and pride of being Indigenous Peoples, and have control over our own lives and lands to finally receive true Justice and Freedom.

The truth of the matter is that the governments of Canada and British Columbia have forced their control over our people and land, and they will not stop. During this past year, many have sacrificed their own personal liberties for the freedom of their people and land, and are now caught in a battle with the court system. Innocent Secwepemc are being arrested, charged, and imprisoned for exercising their Title and Rights to the land. Yet, this relentless struggle must carry on.

Hope for the Future

Canada and British Columbia are never going to say, "This is Indian land." We have to say this ourselves and we have to truly believe this. It is from the grassroots people, the Elders, women, men, youth, and children that we will see change. It is from the fulfillment of protecting and reconnecting with our land, reviving our language, culture, traditions, and honoring and holding pride in our identity that we will win this battle. This is not just a battle over land, this is a battle within ourselves to recover our ancient warrior spirit that lies inside us all.

Through asserting our right to live on our land, we are challenging the whole government system and their control. By collectively asserting Aboriginal Title and control over our own lands, we will rebuild our Nations strong and powerful again. This is why the governments of Canada and British Columbia have waged wars of genocide against us: they want us to surrender to them.

If we, as Indigenous Peoples, want to see change, we must take action in order to make that change. We cannot remain true Indians by living on the rez. We must empower ourselves and leave these man-made reservation concentration camp borders. Go back to the land and the mountains to live and be free. This is where the fight is, where there is clean water and survival.

Native Youth Movement Women Warriorz Upholding Our Responsibilities

As the women, the child bearers, and the life-givers of our Nations, we need to realize that it has only been a short time since contact and colonization, since hospitals, western medicines, painkillers, and "doctors." We need to let go of the dependency upon their system and stop fearing what we already know is the right way to give birth. We don't need the Canadian, American, or any foreign occupying force to tell us—the Indigenous women of the Land—that we need to register our babies, that we need to go for regular check-ups in their hospitals, that we need an ultrasound or painkiller.

What we need is to let our own People know that we will rise with a new spirit of warrior women who will reclaim our rightful place in our societies and give birth to a new generation free from oppression and invisible to their system and control. We can have our babies free, we can let our babies live free. Our Nations depend on us—the future depends on us.

As women warriors it is up to us to ensure our traditions and customs are followed and upheld. We must strive to reclaim our rightful place in our societies and re-learn and revive our language, songs, dances, and ceremonies, as well as wear our traditional clothing, and make our tools and baskets. As women warriors we must conduct ourselves as traditional Indian women to hold onto our ways and let our Nations rise again.

As women warriors we must always acknowledge that the impressionable young women and girls are looking at us for examples of how to conduct themselves as women. We, as women, cannot let abuse in our communities continue. Our women warriors councils have an obligation to the children. When we have women and children that are disrespected in our communities, through abuse or rape, it is up to us to ensure our traditional laws are enforced, no matter how savage or "uncivilized" the rest may think it is. From the Caribbean to Secwepemc Territory, the penalty for sexual abuse is death. I speak about this because of the abuse that plagues our communities and takes a grip on the lives of our young women. It will not be tolerated any more because any abuse or disrespect on women is a disrespect to our Mother, the Earth.

We can no longer tolerate any type of disrespect by men, such as treating women like "bitches" and following the pitiful ways women are exploited in music videos and movies. To all you men out there that keep a woman around as a maid, cook, and sex toy, you better look at yourself because you are not a warrior, and certainly do not hold any respect or honor in the eyes of a traditional woman warrior.

We, as women warriors, need to stand strong and powerful again; we need to organize ourselves and work together in order to protect our Land, Water, and Peoples. We are the ones who will lead the way, we are the ones who will give birth to the future warriors and teach them what is needed to uphold our instructions from the Creator. We must always be alert and patrol our communities and territory, and watch for enemies. The day when Indian women and men will need to stand side by side to fight our enemy and demand the respect we deserve has come—it is NOW!

Cancel the 2010 Winter Olympics! Boycott Sun Peaks Ski Resort! Boycott BC Tourism! Boycott BC Beef! Free Leonard Peltier! Free Eddie Hatcher! No Tourism in Taino Territory—the Caribbean Islands! Arm Yourself and Fight for Life!

Speak the Truth, Go to Jail

Rik Scarce

It's the little things that bring back my 159 days in jail. A mention on the television news of a "grand jury." Talk of how "fair" our judicial system is and how "soft" our prisons have become. Even images of motorcycle gang members. And, of all things, the underside of our utility ladder at home. This is the story of my journey to jail for simply studying the radical environmental movement.

I spent more than five months in jail after refusing to answer some of the questions that were propounded to me by prosecutors running a federal grand jury. My recalcitrance was based on the First Amendment's free speech/free press clause and my belief that scholars, as much as journalists, are the public's fact-finders. We, too, are members of the press, and our essential role in a democracy needs to be protected, I felt. District and appeals courts disagreed. I was found in contempt of court and thus sentenced to do hard, boring time in the Spokane County (Washington) Jail until either a judge or I broke down. In my case, the judge blinked, deciding that my "coercive" treatment—permissible under the law—had magically transformed into "punishment," which was not permitted for contemptors, and so I was released. Never mind that, up until the judge finally realized I would not budge, I had eaten, slept, bathed, and *endured* under precisely the same circumstances as persons convicted of everything from violating court orders to manslaughter (they segregated the murderers, rapists, and child molesters elsewhere in the jailhouse).

Early on, my best friend inside was a huge, gimp-legged member of the Banditos motorcycle gang, and I think of him whenever I see bikers on the road. His wife's name was tattooed on his left forearm: Patee. On his right bicep was the Bandito's motto: If You Can't Be Well Loved, Be Well Hated. As for the utility ladder, my wife and stepson purchased it while I was "away." Ironically, the date of manufacture stamped under the top step of the ladder is "May 1993," the month I was locked away. Every time I use the ladder, I see that date. So much comes flooding in.

The Beginning

It all began in another May, one year and three days before I was incarcerated. Late on the afternoon of May 11, 1992, the Friday of finals week at Washington State University (WSU), where I was a Ph.D. student studying social movements and environmental sociology, I found two phone messages in my departmental mailbox. The same name and number—an extension on campus—was written on each one. I dialed the number and a voice said, "University Police." The police? When I was connected to the name on the message, I was asked to come over to the station, which was just across the street from my building. "I'd really rather not talk about this over the phone," the sergeant said.

When I arrived at the station, the sergeant introduced himself and an FBI agent who was with him. It was only then that I knew why I had been summoned. The prior summer, the Animal Liberation Front had broken into a laboratory on the Washington State campus. Some mice and mink were stolen, several coyotes were set free, and computers and other equipment were damaged. Because the lab was operated using federal funds, the FBI was called in to investigate. Over the intervening months, details of the case began to trickle out through the media, including the identity of the chief suspect, Rod Coronado. Rod was house-sitting for my family when the raid occurred.

I met Rod in the winter of 1989–90, while I was feverishly working on my first book, *Eco-Warriors: Understanding the Radical Environmental Movement*.[1] His story was very public, and it was one of the most fascinating in a movement that features everything from tree sitting to tree spiking. Rod first gained notoriety when, as an "agent" for the Sea Shepherd Conservation Society, he and an accomplice sunk two ships—half of the Icelandic whaling fleet—in less than an hour in 1986. The Sea Shepherds are akin to Greenpeace, but instead of buzzing rubber rafts around whaling ships to keep them from harpooning cetaceans, they ram their own vessels into those that they accuse of "outlaw" hunting.

Rod proved a difficult man to track down. Or perhaps he was checking me out. With a name like "Rik," I might have been an Icelandic secret agent for all he knew! Eventually, however, we made contact. He told me of his exploits as a Sea Shepherd and also as an animal rights activist. I found him likeable, gentle, and fierce. Rod held his beliefs as dearly as any radical environmentalist whom I interviewed, and that is saying quite a lot.

After I was accepted into the sociology Ph.D. program at Washington State, we remained in contact. At one point, I thought we had a deal for him to house-sit for my family in the summer of 1991, while we visited family on the East Coast, and I conducted dissertation research—I planned a more scholarly, theoretically-informed examination of the radical environmental movement that I had become so familiar with while writing my book. But for several weeks I heard nothing, and I was making other arrangements for someone to feed our cat—our only real concern while we were away—when Rod called and asked if he could still watch the place. He was eager to spend some quiet time in a far-away place writing and thinking, he said. Pullman, Washington, is far away enough to be considered near the edge of the earth, and we were pleased that our cat would have a full-time playmate.

On our return from the east coast, Rod picked us up at the airport. It was late. My wife, stepson, and I were still on east coast time and were exhausted from a long day of traveling. The next day was my stepson's birthday, and I woke up early, feeling the excitement that any parent does on a child's special day. When I opened the newspaper, I was stunned. There had been a raid on an animal experimentation station on my campus a couple of days before. It would change my life forever.

The Subpoena

Rod left town that morning. A few months later, he was mentioned in the local paper as a "person of interest" in the FBI's investigation of the raid. And a few months after that, I received the phone call from the campus police. That afternoon the sergeant and the FBI agent questioned me for about an hour about Rod and the raid. I invoked my First Amendment rights as a member of the press and refused to answer most of their questions. After the sergeant had me autograph a copy of my book, the FBI agent served me with a grand jury subpoena. I was to appear in less than a month.

I felt myself go flush. For months I had wondered if the government was going to show an interest in my relationship with Rod. His presence in my home while he was housesitting was very public; we lived in a duplex in the middle of a residential neighborhood, and Rod did not act secretive. But he had first been named a person of interest, and later an out-and-out suspect, in the raid. What might that portend for those who had had contact with Rod? In my book I included material from interviews with numerous persons responsible for serious criminal activity, and for my dissertation I was continuing to gather information from environmental activists who used a range of tactics to pursue the changes they desired. How might my dissertation research be affected? Would the government attempt to compel me to reveal details of my research that were obtained under promises of confidentiality?

Worst of all, though, was the possibility that I might go to jail. While working on my book, I had contacted a civil liberties attorney to inquire about any "shield law" protections that I might have under California's statutes, where I lived at the time. He spoke with colleagues, and the outlook, they agreed, was grim. In all likelihood, should a prosecutor come looking for information that I, an independent scholar, had obtained through promises of confidentiality, California's law would not protect me from jail if I refused to cooperate. I published my book and took my chances. Suddenly, the abstract threat of jail time, one that I had pondered and inquired about, was a very real danger.

I suppose what made it so bad—I lost ten pounds in the two weeks after the subpoena was foisted upon me, and I rarely slept more than a couple of hours a night—was that, from the start, I knew I had no choice. There was no way in hell I was going to cooperate with the grand jury if they came after my research data. More than anything else, what motivated my decision was my strong sense of justice. I was raised by a liberal-Democrat divorced mother in North Carolina in the midst of the civil rights movement, and I think my family's sympathy for equality and fairness under the law shaped me far more profoundly that I ever knew until I faced my own constitutional struggle. My upbringing gave me a spine that grows stiff when basic rights are threatened by any source, especially the government that is charged with protecting those rights. But this rights-spine of mine would have remained unknown to me had not the federal government crossed my path.

After my subpoena was served, it was almost two weeks before I located an attorney who would take my case and who I felt had enough experience with grand juries—Jeffry K. Finer of Spokane. One of the first things Jeffry did was secure a letter from the United States Attorney stating that I was not a suspect in the raid, and through the course of my ordeal this fact was stated in court as well. The government felt that I had information that might aid it in its investigation, and that is all it wanted.

But what else does a member of the press, whether journalist or scholar, ever really have? What we *do* is inform. Information is the obverse of our sole currency. On the reverse is trust: the trust of readers that believe we are honestly reporting information or data, and the trust of those who provide us with information that we will abide by our spoken and unspoken agreements with them—including assurances of confidentiality. As information gatherers and transmitters, we will be bankrupt—morally and professionally—if we do not treat our information, and the trusts of readers and informants, as so valuable that we would, in the worst case, defend it with our liberty.

Until the day I was hauled away, I never got over my fear of jail. During the months following receipt of my subpoena, my life was almost constantly miserable because of that anxiety. I never did sleep very well, I was irritable, my studies suffered, and so did my teaching. My stepson, whom I love dearly, came to live with us in the midst of it all. He was my joy and my despair. How could I be a father to him if I were locked away? How could I make him understand?

Despite the fact that I was not an object of the government's investigation, I felt I was a wanted man. Although not being pursued as a criminal, my liberty was at stake under the federal civil contempt of court statute.[2] So, too, was my interpersonal standing with those whom I depended upon for research data—members of the environmental activist community.

And my career within the profession of sociology would surely be affected by how I behaved as my case progressed.

On the first point, a civil contempt citation would come or not. That decision was entirely in the hands of the prosecutors and, ultimately, a judge. But I knew I would not budge should push come to shove. Second, I figured that environmentalists would appreciate my stance, but that some might nevertheless be anxious about participating in my research for fear that the government would pressure me for information any time it investigated crimes in which radical environmentalists were suspects.

As for professional concerns, to some extent they were resolved by the American Sociological Association's (ASA) especially courageous ethics statement on confidentiality. It read, "Confidential information provided by research participants must be treated as such by sociologists, even when this information enjoys no legal protection or privilege and legal force is applied."[3] Whether I had a stiff rights-spine or not, the ASA's expectation was that sociologists would treat confidential information as confidential *no matter what*. Few, however, had ever been placed in a position to take the ASA's edicts seriously.

The Nub: Confidentiality

The issue of confidentiality, and of my professional obligation to safeguard it, first arose as a result of what happened the day after Bill Clinton was elected president for his first term, November 4, 1992. That morning, I made my initial appearance before the grand jury investigating the WSU break-in. After answering a few preliminary questions, I asserted my Fifth Amendment right against self-incrimination in response to two additional queries. This was a torturous step for me. "Pleading the Fifth" was what gangsters did to avoid telling the truth about their illegal activities. When Jeffry, my attorney, first told me that I would likely have to do the same, I asked if doing so wouldn't amount to perjury, since I had done nothing wrong. No, he said. It's all part of the game; you have no idea what is on the prosecutor's mind. In my circumstances, immunity from prosecution was probably only going to come as a result of asserting my Fifth Amendment rights in front of the grand jury, and immunity—even for an innocent person—is necessary as protection against rogue prosecutors.

After making the first move in this game, I was immediately taken before a federal district court judge who signed a faxed Department of Justice form that immunized me from prosecution but that also compelled me to answer the prosecutor's questions. In other words, my Fifth Amendment rights had been stripped from me, as had my First Amendment right to withhold speech. "And this is America?" I thought to myself. "Whatever happened to constitutional 'protections?'"

Jeffry then requested a hearing on whether a "scholar's privilege" exempting me from grand jury testimony existed, and it took place in February 1993. At the hearing, I refused to say whether I had ever interviewed anyone involved in the WSU raid—a policy that I still adhere to. My concerns stop well short of that issue, for I do not believe that the government has the right to compel researchers to answer any questions at all about their research—otherwise, the First Amendment is only hollow words. Although the judge allowed Jeffry to assert a variety of legal arguments in support of my claim to a scholar's privilege, he nevertheless ruled that even a newspaper reporter in my position would have to testify.

I again found myself in front of the grand jury in March 1993. Over two days I was grilled for 7½ hours, and on 32 occasions I refused to answer the prosecutor's questions, saying,

> Your question calls for information that I have only by virtue of a confidential disclosure given to me in the course of my research activities. I cannot answer the question without actually breaching a confidential communication. Consequently, I decline to answer the question under my ethical obligations as a member of the American Sociological Association and pursuant to any privilege that may extend to journalists, researchers, and writers under the First Amendment.[4]

The grand jury met a month later, and I was summoned to answer the 32 questions (they actually only amounted to about ten questions, some of which were asked several different ways). I declined to answer the questions, again invoking the privilege, and I refused to answer three new questions for the same reason.

Immediately afterward, the prosecutor sought a contempt of court citation from the judge. Jeffry had anticipated this development, and at my contempt hearing we were joined by an attorney from the American Civil Liberties Union. As I wrote in *Journal of Contemporary Ethnography*, they argued "that the Supreme Court precedent, the First Amendment, and the common law," in this case a Washington State Supreme Court decision, "protect scholars from compelled testimony, or at the very least call for a balancing test between the government's interest in investigating crimes and the public's interest in an unfettered press. Those arguments were summarily dismissed by the court, which then found me in contempt."[5] I was booked and set free on my own recognizance pending my appeal to the Ninth US Circuit Court of Appeals.

When the appeals court ruled 3-0 against me in early May, the way was clear for my incarceration. The judge showed no interest in hearing my reasons for my stance when I appeared before him early on May 14. Instead, he ordered the US Marshals to take me away. I would not walk freely again until October.

Paying a lasting Price

Jail ended up not being the nightmare I feared. As I relate in my book, *Contempt of Court: One Scholar's Struggle for Free Speech from Behind Bars,*[6] I was welcomed as a hero by my fellow inmates. They saw me as someone who wouldn't "rat out" others, who refused the sweet temptation to be a snitch. Many inmates couldn't understand my position, however. When they heard that all I had to do was call the judge with a promise to cooperate with the grand jury and I would be set free, they thought I must be nuts. But I was inside for principle and I was inside for many other people, not just me.

So life inside wasn't so bad. It was boring and, of course, constraining. For more than five months I could not kiss my wife or hug my stepson. I was routinely strip-searched, and I ate terrible food. I also picked up attitudes and ways of speaking that were abhorrent to me outside, but inside they seemed normal. To my surprise, I made friends inside and met men whom I admired. Life in jail was winnowed to its essence, and I experienced a kind of democracy that surprised me. In our abstract state, all of us inside were even in social status. Oh, there were some who intimidated and others who cowered, but physical harm came only to those who invited it and no one need be intimidated by others.

My jailing was not the worst part of my ordeal, the part with lasting effects. Rather, it was that fearsome year that I spent fighting against going to jail that scarred me. Even today, a dozen years after my release, I have nightmares about being hunted down. Fearsome creatures—or sometimes regular old FBI agents—pursue me endlessly in my dreams; I always wake up before they get me, and it always takes a long time to go back to sleep. I did no wrong to justify such torture as I endured and continue to endure, other than conduct research on the radical environmental movement. That obtaining information and writing about it should effectively be a crime—which my case demonstrates it is—is itself a frightful specter, a nightmare that haunts our society.

Ironically, around the time I was imprisoned, when reporters asked FBI and Bureau of Alcohol, Tobacco, and Firearms agents how they could find out more about the ALF, they were told, "Read Scarce's book." Reporters may still be told the same thing. I wonder, though, how society is supposed to have access to the truth about social movements when those who write about activists in those movements are hunted down, brought before grand juries in their star chambers, and compelled to cooperate with the authorities on pain of imprisonment. And I wonder what kind of a society we have become when society's own fact-finders become official pariahs, consigned to the jails that are our culture's human wastebins, simply for attempting to comprehend those who oppose society's forces of domination. When those who would expose the truth are oppressed, we all pay a terrible price.

Notes

1. Scarce, Rik. *Eco-Warriors: Understanding the Radical Environmental Movement.* Chicago: The Noble Press, 1990.

2. *United States Code,* Title 28, §1826.

3. American Sociological Association, *Code of Ethics* (Washington, DC: American Sociological Association, 1984), 3.

4. In *Re Grand Jury Investigation and Testimony of James Richard Scarce,* Panel 92-1S (E.D. Washington), 1993, 36. After saying this complete statement a few times, the prosecutor and I agreed on a shorthand method of invoking the privilege.

5. Rik Scarce. "(No) Trial (But) Tribulations: When Courts and Ethnography Conflict." In *Journal of Contemporary Ethnography* 23(2) (1994): 123–49, 131. Interested readers may also wish to read my article, "Scholarly Ethics and Courtroom Antics" in *The American Sociologist* 26(1), (1995): 87–112.

6. Scarce, Rik. *Contempt of Court: One Scholar's Struggle for Free Speech from Behind Bars.* Walnut Creek, CA: AltaMira Press, 2005.

Armageddon Now!!

Sara Olson

> "I love people who harness themselves, an ox to a heavy cart, who pull
> like water buffalo, with massive patience, who strain in the mud and
> muck to move things forward, who do what has to be done, again and
> again." *Marge Piercy, "To be of Use"*

For such an overwhelmingly Christian nation, the United States is
chockfull of remarkably unforgiving people. Redemption! What a concept! Since we're all going down at Armageddon, why bother? In fact, the
quicker we hasten destruction, the better. That seems to be the path Somebody chose for everyone. That Somebody isn't named Jesus, Yahweh, God,
or one of various other surnames in a patriarchal pantheon. It's Somebody
with many different names acting under the holy aegis of the greed of corporate capitalism in cahoots with US imperialism.

For decades, Americans have believed that the rest of the world is just
plain jealous of what we have and, of course, of our "democratic" form of
government. So when anything untoward occurs elsewhere which hints
that people in "the rest of the world" might have a bone to pick with United
States foreign policy and its results—such as, perhaps, the overthrow of a
sovereign government, the takeover of its economy, or the brutal exploitation of its people—it's because the damned whiners aren't grateful for all
we've done for them by bringing Freedom and Democracy.

Since 9/11, an ugly culture of fear and repression has come to pass
in the United States. Ubiquitous color-coded warnings serve to remind us
how dangerous our world became on that day. One may ask, "Why did
9/11 happen? Why is the US so hated throughout the world?" Despite the
erstwhile investigation of the famous 9/11 Commission, or perhaps with its
collusion, the government covered up the answers. American media never
broached the idea that 9/11 was "blowback" for decades of American imperialism, and support of dictators and corrupt governments throughout
the world.

September 11 gave Americans a new sense of vulnerability, but provoked little thought or critical reflection. Genuine shock evolved into short-
lived searching ("What exactly is Islam?"), which segued into unimagina-

tive and shallow jingoism. Shortly after 9/11, someone launched a mini or follow-up terror: the Anthrax Terror. Anthrax was suddenly in the mail, a deadly, inhalable powder that could get anyone, anywhere, anytime. The omnipresent and democratic threat of Anthrax was no metaphor. It was especially Democratic too, since it targeted the then-minority leader in the US Senate, Tom Daschle, while eschewing Republicans. September 11 instilled a fear of The Other—well, of Arabs and Muslims—and a general paranoia. This made us ready to get religion, and George "Born Again" Dubya was the Preacher. His sermon: "The guv'mint can arrest anyone, anywhere, anytime to help keep Americans 'out of harm's way.'" Bush, Ashcroft, the FBI were to be our saviors, the Patriot Act our holy doctrine, our sacraments solemnized in the Church of the New Police State. We had only to sacrifice our Liberty, for Security.

With the advent of Bush II's takeover of Washington DC, we've seen the invasion and occupation of Afghanistan and Iraq (causing the deaths of over 100,000 innocent civilians), the Patriot Act, FBI surveillance and harassment of activists, and federal court-sanctioned secret mass arrests and deportations of Muslims based on racial/ethnic profiling. Across-the-board tax cuts for the ruling class are obscenely coupled with massive spending cuts in social welfare program for the poor and middle classes. With the gap between the rich and poor growing, along with the accompanying anger and resentment, *New York Times* columnist Paul Krugman describes a future in which wealthy Americans will live in walled communities guarded by a specialized urban police force. The US will look like a European medieval society, the majority of the population existing outside the elitist walls in a grim sci-fi environment, scrambling and grubbing for crumbs.

Within the harsh conditions of class domination, imprisonment is a crucial method of social control. The systems of federal, state, and corporate imprisonment—the Prison/Industrial Complex—are growth industries in the United States. While there has been much attention worldwide given to a huge American incarceration rate that has become a human rights travesty, criticism has brought no reduction in numbers. Incarceration is aimed at certain groups—Blacks, Latinos, and the poor. Thirteen percent of the Black male population is in prison, a fact that reflects the legacy of slavery. The US is the only western democracy that executes its citizens, many of them innocent of any crime. Those convicted of capital crimes are preponderantly black; 48% compared to a 40% overall rate for whites according to an October 2005 *New York Times* front page article. Women's imprisonment rates have doubled in recent years affecting, once again, Black, Latino, and poor women and their children. Sexual assault and rape of male and female prisoners are rampant. And there are many political prisoners and POWs, (people captured while fighting racist regimes and colonial domination) in US prisons—mostly people of color. However, the US does not recognize any prisoner as a "political" prisoner. All prisoners are simply lawbreakers.

A key tool of social control and profit in this country, American imprisonment and the use of torture techniques is also a US export business. Criminal justice policies that aim to increase prison populations, such as three strikes, mandatory minimum, and truth-in-sentencing laws are replicated in Canada, Mexico, Great Britain, and in some European countries. America's secretive, grossly dehumanizing, maxi-max isolation prisons are in Turkey, on US military-run facilities in Afghanistan, Iraq, and Guantanamo, Cuba, and in myriad "disappearance" penal units around the globe. People are "extraordinarily rendered," picked up randomly, then disappeared. These captive, victims of policies legalized by Alberto Gonzalez before he became US Attorney General, are starved, beaten, threatened with dogs and snakes, given electric shock, mocked, humiliated, and sexually assaulted. Demonized as "enemy combatants," they are stripped of all rights. Revelations of the country's torture policies and violations of international law at Abu Ghraib and Guantanamo Bay were broadcast to an initially shocked citizenry. They soon ran up against a wall of public apathy, a public ignorant of the fact that torture is common in US prisons, and that many techniques—later exported to Abu Ghraib and Guantanamo—were first perfected at home.

Fear keeps the American population silent about prisons and "criminals" in this country. While campaigning in the late 1980s and early 1990s, politicians told voters that criminals and weapons were proliferating on American streets, and throughout neighborhoods and cities. Democrats and Republicans alike pounded on the topic. They prompted national and local television to lead their nightly news with story upon story about CRIMINALS (a focus which, incidentally, attracted more terrified viewers and thus advertising revenues) until Americans were sufficiently afraid and clamored for more jails and prison.

The script worked. Politicians were able to save the people from "criminals" and to go on the take from corporations and special interests, doing their bidding for the right price. In the same process, prosecutors assumed the mantle of White Knight, building lucrative political careers while using the criminal justice apparatus to put away the "bad guys." In the war on drugs, the bad guys are around every corner. With guilt the first assumption, innocence is always illusory.

In nature, many of the large predators are diminishing in numbers. They disappear due to habitat destruction, eradication of vital links in their survival chain, or overhunting. There is an ascendant breed of predators at loose on Earth, the men and women who run and work for US multinational corporations. They use economic aid, bribery, threats, military coercion, and outright genocide to get what they want and need. They unleash their corporate agents, informed by policies steeped in greed and use of force, to destroy human life everyday through the production of poverty, disease, starvation, economic sanctions, military incursion, and war. The ultimate victim is the planet itself. Environmental devastation, wrought by capitalism and its state war machines, mirrors the reality of social destruction. If people of goodwill don't step up now in large numbers, it will be a nightmarish future we're passing on to our daughters and our sons.

The Earth needs an Operation Rescue. People must cease living as though the human species is the biggest asteroid to ever hit the planet. To do so, we'll have to empower ourselves to change the way we live our lives. Such a course may increase state repression but, given current trends, that likely will escalate whether or not people move forward in a decisive manner.

I was arrested in 1999 for my 1975 involvement in activities related to the Symbionese Liberation Army. I am currently incarcerated in California in one of the two largest women's prisons in the American Gulag, located across the road from each other. Central California Women's Facility and Valley State Prison for Women lock up seven to eight thousand women in approximately five square miles of militarized space. The sole goal of California's prison system is punishment. After release from a California prison, parole status lasts for three years. Contrary to propaganda, California parole offers no programs for rehabilitation or reintegration into society. In fact, felons are, by law, disallowed access to public housing, food stamps, and almost all jobs that offer a living wage. In many states, ex-felons are disenfranchised for life. Parole in California is a three-year holding period for prison re-entry. When the inmate population dips within the prisons, local law enforcement conducts parole sweeps to elevate inmate quotas to their maintenance levels for maximum public funding.

Although incarcerated, I still do what I've done before. I try to reach out through writing and talking with people within the prison and with the few allowed to visit me. That is what, it seems to me, any activist must do: educate and organize as creatively as possible under any circumstances one might face. I live under a high level of personal control, but I don't think there can be any doubt that control of every aspect of everyone's lives is the goal of US repressive agencies: CIA, DIA, NSA, DEA, FBI, and Homeland Security, our newly revamped COINTELPRO.

Since every person and every deed affects everyone and everything else, my politics have intersected with many other struggles for democracy and equality while dragging my family, friends, and people I didn't even know along with me. After I was arrested, people whose lives I may have brushed up against over twenty-five years before had their worlds turned upside down in the ensuing investigation. The government has bottomless pits of taxpayer dough to blow on investigations and prosecutions, and there's not a chance it won't do so. People must consider this when they decide to take a stand or to organize for change. However, as my fellow prisoners' many stories have taught me, anyone can be caught up anyway, and innocence, very often, means nothing.

Prison awaits many who opt to step outside the boundary of silence. Criminalizing dissent through new policies, such as the Patriot Act and its Orwellian concept of "domestic terrorism," is really just persecution-as-usual in the US. This tactic has been used throughout US history against workers, anti-war, anti-racist, and pro-woman struggles, and it is now being applied against those fighting for animal and earth liberation. The numbers of imprisoned in the US currently totals 2.3 million. There are approximately 6.9 million altogether in prisons, jails, and on parole/probation. These figures will increase if people don't act to stop non-corrective human warehousing. The fact that some are imprisoned and kept there for their political beliefs and actions alone, in a "democracy" with a Bill of Rights, must begin to be widely acknowledged.

So, what are you doing for the rest of your life? How many necessities, both natural and social—clean water and good schools, breathable air and Social Security, non-genetically modified food and affordable housing, rainforests and healthcare, and so on—have to vanish before people act? At a time when we desperately need collective action and solidarity against corporate predation, we can't afford separation and the illusion of individualism. Above all, in our work and struggles, we must never lose touch with each other. It's either solidarity and resistance, or...Armageddon...and it's now.

Part VI

DIRECT ACTION AND BEYOND

"If voting changed anything, they'd make it illegal." *Emma Goldman*

"It is not the oppressed who determine the means of resistance, but the oppressor." *Nelson Mandela*

"I don't even call it violence when it's in self defense; I call it intelligence." *Malcolm X*

Medusa Trilogy

Jesús Sepúlveda

In 2001, I went to the Museum of Modern Art in New York, and I saw an art installation called "Medusa." NY was a final destination, before coming back to Oregon, after a trip to Chile, where I was arrested at the airport and robbed in the streets. The installation was a sculpture representing Mother Earth with rails and freeways crossing all over her body. The image of a sick planet has nothing to do with a healthy and green Gaia. There, suspended in a room by wires, Gaia had become a grey Medusa: the planet under siege. But the representation created by the artist was only that: a representation of what was going on in the streets of NY and everywhere else.

Escrivania
Chile Odyssey 2001

Neither arrest nor robbery upon my return

It was three below zero when we crossed the Brooklyn Bridge

Welcome to New York City: The capital of the World in the New Millennium

We crossed four continents in a year

Not only does the mirror move
but also what is on the other side of the mirror

We walked arm-in-arm
without identity, without a wallet

there are surveillance towers, smart buildings, 20 million cameras
spy satellites, infrareds, barbed wire

Not only do the lens and the eye that spies move
but also the past and the landscape I write

A new millennium for a new world in the new citadel
as if the canals of Amsterdam
flowed into the Maipo River in the Andean foothills

Here there was neither an arrest nor a robbery
—just bureaucracy

Four peasant women sell ski masks
four Zapatistas eat homemade bread

What do you wish to see when you look through the window?
a tree. a sky. an enchanted house. silence.

Yesterday it didn't rain but it snowed
The day before yesterday it was hot
nena, ya me quiero mojar
or
vamos a la playa
oh oh oh oh oh

Cities that repent
Subterranean trains pass through the heart of the Medusa
She maintains her silence: spy planes, infrareds, command posts

One two three...hello....hello...are you there

Hunters use telescopic sights
masks. computers

The spotted animal crosses the plain
They talk about reality. They believe
they are justified in their observations.

We walk arm-in-arm
smiling

Each gesture is a stain that spreads
like an oasis in the desert

The oasis expands and breathes
taking form

The panther breathes and
exudes something I can't explain

To see in darkness
is not the same as seeing in darkness

Displacement is not equal to being in motion

To return home and to leave again
as if the knots of the trunk of the tree in my parents' house
no longer existed

as if the annual rings that remained
were the faces of those who have nearly disappeared

The hunters calculate the impact
and fail

They look from side to side
crazy hats at a costume party

They rest on their elbows
striking the keys

We walk, smiling

No hand leaves
a wallet in a trash can
No case ever closes

Here there was neither arrest nor robbery

The hour of gibberish is in every moment

Welcome to the Capital of the World

To see in darkness is to avoid mirages
The heart of the Medusa beats patiently

Not only do the mind and coincidental reality move
but also the weather and the time that remains

The eye of the hunter is false
It sees into nothing like nothing looks into the mirror
Machine-like

Its color is fictitious
Waxen eyelids

I offer my arm and we walk

Welcome again

The night breathes like a crouching panther
Its pupils open the morning
and close the evening until dawn

At midday we all go to the oasis to breathe

Den Bosch 2000—Oregon 2001
Translation by Paul Dresman

Pax Americana

What was Grandfather Bush doing digging up Geronimo's skull
from the graveyard
and later financing the regimen of the Third Reich?

What was Daddy Bush doing bankrolling the Contras
and supporting Baghdad in its fratricide against Iran?

What was Boy Bush doing when the Mossad agents filmed the aerial
spectacle
and two planes were swallowed by the columns of the czar and
Caesar, world center of business?

What were they doing when the black hawks dropped their bombs
on the
slums of Panama?

What were they doing when uranium was scattered
in the lungs of the survivors of the desert storm?

What were they doing when Panzer tanks invaded Poland?

What were they doing when they advertised war and 33 million
voices
echoed through the streets of the planet?

What became of all that?

Infamy lying the end of democracy overwhelming
misfortune

Or were they just shitting their pants
while Reagan drooled and babbled?

Four thousand fighters arrived to hold back the brand of the
apocalypse
against wind and betrayal

The sand storm blinded the false hawks who only wanted to go back
home
disappearing little by little till none were left

Violent hail strikes the blue helmets of homeland henchmen in the
line of fire

And from the depths the prayer of the sorceress
the witches and the wizard create a circle of protection
heard by the trees and the moss and lilies and the sun reappearing
and magnolias and hyacinths

Like a house of cards teetering on a wobbly table
the cluster bombs fall on a dead mother and her dead child

sowing death
and lying

Pax americana written as a screenplay that directs the kidnapping
and the atrocious crash into the columns of the dead

Pax americana that enclosed thousands in its concentration camps
in Guantanamo
or on its reservations in Montana, Idaho, California, New Mexico,
Arizona
or in its ghettos in Cincinnati, Atlanta, Detroit, Washington DC, New
York, Miami,
Los Angeles

Pax americana is a swastika that the masked ones set on fire

Pax americana is a ferocious freight train held back by white and
green and redblack workers' overalls around the world

Beelzebub's pitchfork has three heads: Aznar, Blaire, and Bush
and the Azores are the redoubt where they forge death
and lose eternal peace

What were they doing bombing Cambodia the Moneda Palace
Granada
invading the Bay of Pigs Texas Santo Domingo?

Sinking the Maine and sending white anthrax powder through the
mail?

What were they doing and why?

Like cold-blooded reptiles they carry out rites in sequoia forests
Like birds of prey they suck on skull and bones in holy fields

The cross of the Ku Klux Klan sets out on a crusade

Have you ever heard so many voices crying out?

People marched all over the world to seal the lid of the coffin

Poets chant a mantra for the torture chamber to disappear
Poets meditate on the verdure of this planet
Ora pro nobis in this uncertain time

Pax americana is a time bomb
that the conquistadors trigger when they march on Babylon
and burn themselves up

Dreams of incandescent light over a nightmare of black gold

The tanks of Zion sowed the desert with bodies of the dead
and a suicide hand challenges them

The directors of defense policy type up their own extinction
There are thirty mafiosi sipping coffee in the Pentagon
Their video game is lethal and legal
like a cobra that approaches from behind

Pax americana bites its own tail
and Clinton, Nixon or Polk gaze in the mirror
while licking their bloody cigars

The mothers and the widows
of the disappeared in South America
those dead of radiation poisoning in Hiroshima and Nagasaki
the forgotten of Armenia
the condemned at Wounded Knee

The shackled ancestors with dark skin
the Palestinians rounded up for a barrel of oil
that the rich uncle bought on sale
Misery exported to Taiwan, Indonesia, Brazil,
Haiti, Jamaica, Liberia

Amalgam of eyes
to drill holes with their gaze

Pax americana and the kingdom of abomination
Pax americana is a punctured eye
Pax americana is a broken lily and a broken mirror that shatters the
world
Pax americana is one son less and one dead grandfather
Pax americana is a hissing serpent in the shape of a dollar sign
Pax americana is a general caught by the leg and a banker
a financier
a bureaucrat
or a mormon pastor at every door
Pax americana is McDonald's plastic and bulldozer steel
Pax americana is a strange dream
that foresees the end of the ecosystem and leaves a desert in its path
Pax americana is a videotape with one, two, three thousand explosions
and millions of nameless dead
Pax americana is a skull and permanent war
Pax americana and the kingdom of abomination

Then what will they do when they devour everything and reach the
head?

The center of La Medusa will open an eternal grave-pit
that the rays of the gods will reach into
so that the children of their own territory
may destroy the war machine
with their hearts in their hands
and the intense sound of peace

February–September 2003
Translation by Kate Donahue & Amanda Powell
Editing: Janine & Jesús Sepúlveda

Utopia

Visualize being despoiled
being left with nothing
naked under springtime

Visualize laughing
abandoning your work the domus the nothingness
and resting facing springtime

Visualize forgetting
unlearning all your training
waddling like a duck in the middle of the garden

Visualize there being no race rage remedy religion
nor state
that the crystals which separate you from art shatter and slowly blur
away

Pay close attention to what I am saying

Visualize losing the fear the code the anorexia
and weapons boredom bulimia come to an end
and embrace your partner
and gather food from the trees
and harvest the crops
which keep you healthy through the winter

Visualize being free
without numbers or borders or archives
that you are relieved of the weight and your eyes bloom
and you abandon your job the domus the nothingness
and unlearn your name
and rest calmly in the midst of the garden

Radical Environmentalism: Is There Any Other Kind?

John Wade

Life on this planet is being destroyed at an amazing rate because of an entrenched political and economic system which encourages exploitative and wasteful behavior. The means to change an entrenched system cannot be found within that system, and so no amount of political lobbying or private benevolence will be able to halt this system's destruction. Humans have an advanced intellect and thus have a great capacity to use technology to bend the natural world to their will. Unfortunately, this species has failed to use its intellect to re-establish any sort of equilibrium with the rest of the Earth. In fact, some powerful groups and nations have so far used this intellect mostly for purposes of war, exploitation, and violence. Humans have destroyed much of the Earth's accessible open spaces, and poisoned the air, water, and soil. On the rare occasions that politicians talk about saving the environment it is in terms of what is "practical" or "cost-effective." In other words, "environmentalism in moderation." What is an acceptable arsenic-to-water ratio? How much cancer is too much cancer?

These are the compromises capitalism forces you to make by turning every question into one of monetary gain or loss. Arsenic is not a *choice*. Arsenic is *poison*. The problem is too huge to lay out in a short essay such as this. The Earth's temperature is rising. Natural resources are being consumed at an unsustainable rate. Open space and species are rapidly disappearing. The air we breathe and water we drink is contaminated. The human population is out of control. According to Lester Brown's book, *Plan B: Rescuing a Planet Under Stress and a Civilization in Trouble* (2003), the human population has more than doubled in just the past half-century: "The growth during those 50 years exceeded that during the four million years since we emerged as a distinct species." We are now well past the point where anything but a radical change in the way we live can save the Earth and ourselves from destruction. The only convincing argument against direct action could concern not its justification, but its effectiveness.

The two major arguments against the utility of direct action are that it scares away possible mainstream sympathizers to the environmental movement, and that its impact is negligible. Provided that direct action is nonviolent (the term "violent" is not appropriate to describe the destruction of property), it can be just as inspiring as it can be negatively polarizing. It is pretty clear that a short-term estimation of consequences would not look favorably on any isolated "extremist" action. Did the $250,000 in damages I personally inflicted on the corporate power structure have any significant effect on suburban sprawl, Ford Motor Company sales, or the fast-food industry? Probably not. However, the Earth Liberation Front is huge and it doesn't make sense to regard my actions as independent of the radical movement or mainstream environmental movement. The important thing to remember is that the difference between the Earth Liberation Front and the Sierra Club is not so much the *ends* but the *means*. Instead of limiting themselves to certain tools because of a wrong-headed public perception about what direct action is, environmentalists should value effective approaches from any direction.

The Federal Bureau of Investigation believes the Earth Liberation Front to be the fastest growing "domestic terrorist" group in the country. ELF acts of "vandalism" are not isolated incidents, but part of a thoughtful, coordinated campaign. Activists are striking back against exploitative corporations across the United States and the world. In Turkey, Mexico, China, and all over, hundreds of millions of dollars of property damage have been inflicted and a powerful message of resistance has been heard.

If sabotage works in today's environmental movement, it should come as no surprise that radical action is also historically an effective and not unusual method within other social movements. Another example of a social movement which was widely viewed as extreme at the time, is the movement to end slavery in the United States. There could be no such thing as an abolitionist without radicalism. According to Howard Zinn's book, *A People's History of the United States*, James Hammond, a slave owner and supporter of slavery, agrees: "But if your course was wholly different [i.e., if there were no violent reactions to slavery]—If you distilled nectar from your lips and discoursed sweetest music...do you imagine you could prevail on us to give up a thousand millions of dollars in the value of our slaves, and a thousand millions of dollars more in the depreciation of our land?"

History is filled with examples of social movements which would not have been successful without radical action. Any movement which seeks to transform any system in a profound way must, by its very definition, be radical. According to the *Merriam-Webster Dictionary* a "radical" is "a person who favors rapid and sweeping changes in laws and methods of government." This means that Thomas Jefferson, Mark Twain, and Jesus Christ were all radicals. They worked towards independence from England, the abolition of slavery, and a new interpretation of an old religion. While almost universally respected today, all these figures, and the movements they were a part of, were controversial (to say the least) during their time.

Having explored my views concerning the *solution*, let's take a quick look at the root of the *problem*. The economic order in the United States is such that most of the wealth is held by a small group of people. Like other countries, the economic order in the US is also the political order, as those with the money control the government. Without going into an analysis of the overall weakness of capitalism as an economic system, I will quickly underscore its two main flaws: capitalism devours natural resources, and it virtually guarantees the consolidation of political and economic power.

Our use of natural resources is limited only by our ability to extract them from the earth. The capitalist system of supply-and-demand regulates short-term use of resources, but provides no incentive for long-term conservation or sustainability. Rejecting a short-term profit maximization approach for a long-term focus would bring life back into equilibrium. A long-term perspective is both self-serving (it allows humans to continue living with at least a modicum of convenience in the future) and altruistic (it is good for the entire planet). If humans continue to use fossil fuels at the current rate, for example, very soon radical changes will be forced upon them through the myriad consequences of global warming and soil, air, and water pollution.

In addition, capitalism guarantees the consolidation of political and economic power. When I say that I am frustrated with the government, I really mean that I am frustrated with the corporate power structure and the political institutions as a part of that structure. The government does not even attempt to look after the people's interest, as evidenced by President Bush's recent tax cuts for the rich, his attacks on Social Security, and response to the victims of Katrina. To understand the consolidation of political and economic power, one must ask, "What is the primary concern of politicians?" The answer is "To be re-elected." So then how does a politician get re-elected? Through orchestrating a public perception of benevolence and, of course, through tons of money. So, now the question becomes, "Who has the money?" I think the answer to that is pretty obvious. Unfortunately, a serious lifestyle change would be bad for every major corporation in the United States. Is the use of fossil fuels good or bad for Exxon-Mobil? Is sprawl good for construction companies and developers? Is the lack of pollution controls good or bad for many corporations' short-term profit?

I do not think I have overestimated the urgency of the environmental cause. I maintain that something radical needs to be done while there is something left to save. We cannot continue to dig for oil in sensitive areas and build large tracts of unplanned suburban housing, and expect that future generations won't suffer the consequences. We also should not continue to pretend that negotiating with powerful groups—whose only concern is short-term monetary profit—has gotten us somewhere. Acts of vandalism against specific targets is an effective way to take away the profit motive that drives the exploitation of the environment. The radical environmental movement values life over property and carries this priority to its logical conclusion. Our vision is a world where human beings recognize that everything, including their own species, is a part of the environment.

What Goes Up Must Come Down

Derrick Jensen

As a long-time grassroots environmental activist, and as a creature living in the thrashing endgame of civilization, I am intimately acquainted with the landscape of loss, and have grown accustomed to carrying the daily weight of despair. I have walked clearcuts that wrap around mountains, drop into valleys, then climb ridges to fragment watershed after watershed. I've sat silent near empty streams that, two generations ago, were "lashed into whiteness" by uncountable salmon coming home to spawn and die.

A few years ago I began to feel pretty apocalyptic. But I hesitated to use that word, partly because of those drawings I've seen of crazy penitents carrying "The End is Near!" signs, and also because of the power of the word itself. Apocalypse. I didn't want to use the term lightly.

But then a friend and fellow activist said, "What will it take for you to finally call it an apocalypse? The death of the salmon? Global warming? The ozone hole? The reduction of krill populations off Antarctica by ninety percent? The turning of the sea off San Diego into a dead zone? The collapse of earthworm populations in the Midwest? The cutting of remnants of this continent's native forests? The extirpation of two hundred species per day? Four hundred? Six hundred? Give me a specific threshold, Derrick, a specific point at which you will finally use that word."

Do you believe that our culture will undergo a voluntary transformation to a sane and sustainable way of living?

I didn't think you would. I don't either, and neither does anyone I talk to. For the last couple of years I've taken to asking people this question, at talks and rallies, in libraries, on buses, in airplanes, at the grocery store, the hardware store. Everywhere. The answers range from emphatic "no"s to laughter. No one answers in the affirmative. One fellow at a talk did raise his hand, and when everyone looked at him, he dropped his hand, then said, sheepishly, "Oh, voluntary? Of course not." My next question: How would this understanding—that our culture will not voluntarily stop destroying the natural world, eliminating indigenous cultures, exploiting the poor, and killing those who resist—shift our strategy or tactics? The answer? Nobody knows, because we never talk about it.

This essay is about that shift in strategy and tactics.

I just got home from talking to a new friend, another long-time activist. She told me of a campaign she participated in a few years ago to try to stop the government and transnational timber corporations from spraying Agent Orange, a potent defoliant and cancer-causing agent, in the forests of Oregon. Whenever activists learned that a hillside was going to be sprayed, they assembled there, hoping their presence would stop the poisoning. But each time, like clockwork, the helicopters appeared, and each time, like clockwork, the helicopters dumped their loads of Agent Orange onto the hillside, onto the protesting activists. The campaign did not succeed.

"But," she said to me, "I'll tell you what did work. A bunch of Vietnam vets lived back in those hills, and they sent messages to the Bureau of Land Management, and to Weyerhaeuser, Boise Cascade, and the other timber companies, saying, 'We know the names of your helicopter pilots, and we know their addresses.'"

I waited for her to finish.

"You know what happened next?" she asked.

"I think I do," I responded.

"Exactly," she said. "The spraying stopped."

Closely allied to all of this is the second point, which might also be another way of saying the same thing. The same action can often seem immoral from one perspective and moral from another. What's more, the same action can often be moral from one perspective and immoral from another. From the perspective, for example, of salmon or other creatures, including humans, whose lives depend on free-flowing rivers, dams are murderous and immoral. From this perspective, to remove dams would be extremely moral. Those who make money from the generation of hydroelectricity, or who irrigate from reservoirs, or who live downriver and who very well might be killed if the dams were suddenly to burst, would probably take a dim view of the morality of someone intentionally blowing up the Grand Coulee or Glen Canyon dams. Of course the most moral thing to have done—defining morality in this case to be roughly similar to serving life—would have been to not build these or any other large dams in the first place. But they're built, and they continue to be built the world over, to the consistent short-term fiscal benefit of huge corporations—really the primary consideration of any political decision—and over the determined yet usually unsuccessful resistance of the poor.

The second most moral thing to do—continuing to define morality the same way—would be to let the water out slowly, and then breach the dams more or less gently, taking the survival needs (as opposed to the more abstract requirements of our economic system) of all humans and nonhumans into account as we let rivers once again run free. But the dams are there; they're killing the rivers. In the Northwest, salmon and sturgeon are fast disappearing from the region, and in the Southwest, the Colorado River no longer even reaches the ocean. The current political, economic, and social systems have shown themselves to not only be consistently unresponsive, but irredeemably detrimental to human and nonhuman needs. Faced with a choice between healthy functioning natural communities on one hand, and profits on the other hand, those in power of course always choose the latter option. What, then, becomes the most moral thing to do? Do we stand by and watch the last of the salmon die? Do we write letters and file lawsuits that we know in our hearts will ultimately not make much difference, or do we take out the dams ourselves?

Here are more questions: what would the rivers themselves want? Would it cause them additional pain to have the dams blown, or would they perceive that as their release from a cement cage?

I'm aiming at a far bigger and more profound target than the nearly twelve million cubic yards of cement that went into the Grand Coulee Dam. I want to examine the morality and feasibility of intentionally taking down not just dams but all of civilization. I aim to examine this as unflinchingly and honestly as I can, even, or especially, at the risk of examining topics normally considered off-limits to discourse.

I am not the first to make the case—as I have in my other work—that the industrial economy, indeed, civilization (which underpins and gives inevitable rise to it), is incompatible with human and nonhuman freedoms, and in fact with human and nonhuman life.[1] If you accept that the industrial economy—and beneath it, civilization—is destroying the planet and creating unprecedented human suffering among the poor (and if you don't accept this, go ahead and put this book down, back away slowly, turn on the television, and take some more soma: the drug should kick in soon enough, your agitation will disappear, you'll forget everything I've said, and then everything will be perfect again, just like the voices from the television tell you over and over), then it becomes clear that the best thing that can happen, from the perspective of essentially all nonhumans as well as the vast majority of humans, is for the industrial economy (and civilization) to go away, or in the shorter run for it to be slowed as much as humanly possible during the time we await its final collapse.

But here's the problem: this slowing of the industrial economy will inconvenience many of those who benefit from it, including nearly everyone in the United States. Many of those who will be inconvenienced identify so much more with their role as participants in the industrial economy than they do with being human, that they may very well consider this inconvenience to be a threat to their very lives. I'll discuss this more later, but for now the salient point is that those people will not allow themselves to be inconvenienced without a fight. What, then, becomes the right thing to do? Here's another way to ask this: Is it possible to talk about fundamental social change without asking ourselves questions we too often refuse to ask? Such as, "What if those in power are murderous? What if they're not willing to listen to reason at all? Should we continue to approach them nonviolently? When is violence an appropriate means to stop injustice?"

With the world dying—or rather being killed—we no longer have the luxury to ignore these questions. They are questions that won't go away.

For years now I've been talking about blowing up dams to help salmon, but suddenly today I realized I've been all wrong.

This understanding came as I read a description of attempts by ancient Egyptians to dam the Nile, and the Nile's resistance to these attempts. It was all a pretty straightforward process. The Egyptians would erect a dam, and the river would shrug it off, probably with as little effort as a horse quivering the skin of its shoulder to get rid of a fly.

By now, however, the concrete straitjackets have become massive enough that rivers have a harder time sloughing them off, the equivalent, to extend the above simile, to encasing a horse in concrete, leaving holes at head and tail to allow food and water to pass. The rivers need our help. (I first wrote "They may need our help," but even without me asking a couple of rivers strongly requested I remove the qualifier.) They can't do it themselves, at least in the short or medium run.

I've always wanted to blow up dams in order to save salmon, sturgeon, and other creatures whose lives depend on wild and living rivers. But that's not right. We need to blow up dams for the rivers themselves, so they can be again the rivers they once were, forever, the rivers they still want to be, the rivers they themselves are struggling and fighting to once again become.

Liberating rivers, blowing up dams. The difference may seem semantic to you—like "liberating" versus "invading" Iraq, like "creating temporary meadows" versus clearcutting—but it doesn't to me, for a number of reasons.

Rhetoric aside, both invading Iraq and clearcutting are motivated by the culture's obsession to control and exploit. The primary reason is to gain, maintain, and use resources—oil in the first case (as well as to provide a staging area for further invasions), trees in the second. Further, both invading and clearcutting damage landscapes, damage our habitat. They also enchain the natural world.

The primary motivation for liberating a river, on the other hand, isn't selfish, except as it benefits oneself to live in an intact, functioning natural community (duh!), and as doing good feels good.

This all leads to probably the most important question so far: with whom or what do you primarily identify? A way to get at that question is to ask: whom or what do your actions primarily benefit? Whom or what do you primarily serve?

Who or what primarily benefits from the invasion of Iraq? Let me put this more directly: who/what benefits from US access to Iraqi oil fields?

The US industrial economy, of course. If you care more about and identify more closely with the US industrial economy than you care about or identify with people killed by US bombs or bullets (or by the "blunt force trauma" of smackyface: the CIA's preferred term for beating captives, often to death)—people under whose land the oil resides—then you may support the US invasion of Iraq.

Similarly, if you identify more strongly with "forest products" corporations such as Weyerhaeuser or MAXXAM—or more broadly with the industrial economy—than you do with forests, you may support clearcutting.

Just today I saw an article in the local newspaper saying that local shrimp trawlers are complaining (accurately enough) about regulations California is (finally) putting in place to curtail the (extraordinary) damage done by trawling. Shrimp trawls are designed to maximize contact with the sea floor. They scrape away everything in their path, the undersea equivalent of clearcutting, picking up every living thing as they go. In some places eighty percent of the catch is "bycatch," that is, creatures the trawlers can't sell, and who are merely thrown overboard dead or dying.

Local trawlers say the regulations will force them out of business. Politicians say they'll hurt the local economy. This amounts to an explicit acknowledgment on both their parts that shrimping, and more broadly the local economy (and more broadly still the entire industrial economy) is predicated on harming and eventually destroying the landbase.

If you identify more closely with the local economy than the local landbase, it may make sense to you to support an economy that damages this landbase, your own habitat.

If, on the other hand, you identify more strongly with your landbase than with the economy, it may make sense to you to protect your landbase, your habitat. And since the industrial economy is poisoning us all, the same would be true for those who identify more closely with their own bodies and their own survival (and the survival of those they purport to love) than they do the industrial economy.

Who benefits from the removal of dams?

If you identify more closely with the Klamath River and its salmon, steelhead, lamprey, and other residents than you do with the agri-corporations which primarily benefit from taking the river's water, it may make sense to you to help the river return to running free, to liberate it from its concrete cage, or rather, to help it liberate itself. The same would be true for the Columbia, Colorado, Mississippi, Missouri, Sacramento, Nile, and all other rivers who would be better off without dams.

With what/whom do you most closely identify? Where is your primary allegiance? Where does your sense of skin extend, and what does it encompass? Does it include ExxonMobil, Monsanto, Microsoft? Do you give them fealty? Do you give them time, money? Do you serve them? Does it include the US government? Do you pledge it allegiance? Do you serve it? Does it include the land where you live? Do you act in its best interests?

I still haven't really gotten to the difference between liberating rivers and blowing up dams. It's one of focus, and intent. I've written elsewhere that if I were once again a child, faced only with the options of a child (i.e., no running away), but having the understanding I do now of the intractability of my father's violence, I would have killed him. But the point would not have been to kill him. The point would have been to liberate me and my family from the rapes and beatings, to stop the horrors.

Similarly, I don't have a thing for explosives. If I took out a dam, it wouldn't be so I could get off on the big kaboom. I'm not even sure it would be to help the salmon (although yesterday I saw seven baby Coho in the stream behind my home, and fell in love with them all over again). It would be to help the river, which in turn would help the salmon. It would be to stop the horrors.

I think it would be virtually impossible for even the most dogmatic pacifist to make a moral argument against immediately taking down every cell phone tower in the world. Cell phones are, of course, annoying as hell. That might be a good enough reason to take down the towers, but there are even better reasons. There is, of course, the very real possibility that tower transmissions cause cancers and other problems to humans and nonhumans alike. Even ignoring this, however, there's the fact that towers—cell phone, radio, and television—act as mass killing machines for migratory songbirds: five to 50 million per year.[2] These birds die so the jerk at the table next to you can yammer at full volume (of course) about his latest financial conquest.

To the direct killing of birds we can add as a cost of cell phones, the effect of speeded-up business communications, both because of the decreased quality of individual lives in a culture addicted to speed ("People who work for me should have phones in their bathrooms," said the CEO of one American corporation[3]) and on the natural world as a whole (the activities of the economic system are killing the planet: the higher the GNP, the more quickly the living are converted to the dead).

The question becomes, how do you take out a cell phone tower? I need to say up front that I'm a total novice at this sort of thing. I am, to slip into the language of the mean streets, a goody two-shoes. My whole life I've rarely done anything illegal, not out of an equation on my part of morality and obedience (or subservience) to laws—at least I hope not—but instead, partly because many illegal activities, such as using illegal drugs repulse or scare me, while others, such as insider trading, simply do not hold my interest. Even with those that do hold my interest—e.g., taking out dams, hacking, destroying (or otherwise liberating) corporate property—I'm not only almost completely ignorant of how to do it, but fairly nervous about getting caught. Don't get me wrong: I've raised a little hell in my time. Sometimes I go crazy and turn right on red without coming to a complete stop, and I routinely drive four or sometimes even nine miles over the speed limit. A few anarchist friends were trying to set up a talk where I'd share the stage with a couple of former Black Panthers. One of them did time for robbing a bank, the other for hijacking a plane. I thought a moment, then confessed, "I once shoplifted dog food from Wal-Mart." High fives were exchanged around the table.

I have to add that were I more attracted to illegal activities I would probably curtail them because of what I write. It's possible—though doubtful—that I've drawn at least a little attention from the powers-that-be, and the last thing I want to do is give them an excuse to pop me for something non-political (and frankly I'm not too keen on getting popped for something political either). If they want to come after me because of what I write, I'll take them on, and if someday I have the courage to quit writing and take out dams (note the plural: I don't agree with the Ploughshares tactic of turning yourself in if you destroy property belonging to the occupiers), they can try to catch me. But in the meantime, I'm not going to give them any cheap opportunities.

All of which is to say, I'm a coward. I'm going to write about how I would take down a cell phone tower here in town, but I'm not going to do it. If I were going to do it, I wouldn't be so stupid as to write about it, or even talk about it with anyone I didn't know and trust literally with my life. And all of that is to say that you FBI agents reading this essay (and the ones tracking my strokes on the keyboard) can go ahead and lose your erections. This isn't a confession. And even if your CIA buddies decide to play smackyface with me there isn't much I can confess (unless you count the survey stakes I've removed, but I've already written about that, and besides, removing survey stakes is a fundamental human duty).

Recon is always the first step in any military action, so I drive my mom's car to the cell phone tower behind Safeway. I take her car not out of some fiendishly clever plot to make it so if anything happens she'll get sent up the river instead of me, but because my car has been sitting on blocks in her driveway for more than a year now (I never knew, by the way, that moss would grow along the weatherstripping around the rear window).

There are two towers I know of in Crescent City. There's the one behind Safeway, and another off in the woods a few blocks north. The one closest to the grocery store is in the open, which would obviously make taking it down more problematic. The tower is enclosed in a chain-link fence topped by barbed wire. The two sides of this fence farthest from Safeway face thick woods, which might provide a solution to the problem of it being in the open. I'm certain the fence could be cut easily and quickly.

The problem is that I wouldn't know what to do next. There are a couple of sheds inside, and I'd imagine that some gasoline and matches could render the whole thing inoperable. That may be great for (temporarily) stopping the guy at the restaurant from bothering his neighbors, and would slow the destructive march of the economic system, if only ever so slightly, but it wouldn't do a damn thing for the birds. Unfortunately, the tower itself is probably three feet in diameter, hollow with a two-inch shell of some sort of metal.

I sit in my car and look at it. I'm nervous, as though even thinking about how I would do this is enough to draw cops to me. (The same is true now as I write this.) Of course if I were going to bring this down I would never have driven here for this reconnaissance. At least not during the middle of the afternoon. I would have parked far away and walked. And there's no way I would have done it in this town, either. Crescent City is too small, and I'm too well known. For crying out loud, at the (excellent) Thai restaurant two blocks south of this tower they know me well enough to always bring me a huge glass of water without me asking, and like me well enough to pack my salad rolls full to bursting (of course after they read this essay my future salad rolls may be limp and wrinkly). I'm almost surprised no one has stopped by while I'm sitting in this car, just to say hi and pass the time of day. I don't know what to do. I'm a writer. I have no more idea how to take down this tower than I would know how to write a computer virus, or than I would know how to perform brain or heart surgery. Worse, I'm spatially and mechanically inept—probably a couple of standard deviations from the norm—with a heavy dose of absent-mindedness thrown in for good measure (and it seems that absent-mindedness would be a tremendous curse to anyone contemplating anything deemed illegal by those in power).

An example of the spatial ineptitude: whenever I pack for a road trip, my mom always takes a look at my suitcase, sighs, and repacks everything in about half the space.

An unfortunate experience in eighth-grade woodshop class highlights the mechanical problems. For our final project, we got to build whatever we wanted. I chose a birdhouse. I was excited. From close observation I knew the birds in our area (though I no longer live in a region with meadowlarks, even recorded versions of their songs still make me smile), and from reading I knew their habits and preferences. In some cases I knew their Latin names. I cut each piece of wood as meticulously as I could, nailed them together as tight as they would go (admittedly there were a fair number of gaps where my cuts hadn't quite been straight), then put putty in the nail holes. I stained it all (an irregular) dark brown. On the final day of class we each brought our projects to the front, one at a time. The other pieces looked pretty good, and I got increasingly nervous as my turn approached. For good reason. When I held up my birdhouse, the entire class burst into laughter. One of them—I still remember your name, David Flagg, and you're still not on my short list of people to invite over to dinner—pointed at the lumps of still-white putty and shouted, "It looks like the birds have already been on it." Even the teacher laughed so hard he had to remove his shop glasses and wipe his eyes.

The infamous shower curtain episode makes clear my absent-mindedness. My shower curtain was hanging too far into the tub. It floated when I showered, and I often stepped on or even tripped over it. After only about a year of this, I decided to fix it and cut off the bottom of the shower curtain. Only later did I remember that the bar (which I had purchased and installed) was springloaded, and it was a simple matter to just raise it a few inches.

The point is that when it comes time for us to start taking out dams, I'm not sure I'm the one you want holding the explosives.

That said, here's what I'm thinking as I look at the cell phone tower. Basic principles. There are, I'd think, maybe six major ways to take down anything that's standing. You can dismantle it. You can cut it down. You can pull it down. You can blow it up. You can undermine it until it collapses. You can remove its supports and let it fall down on its own. This is all as true for civilization as it is for cell phone towers.

In the (smaller) case before us, I think we can dismiss out of hand dismantling and digging. So far as the former, the tower is constructed of two or three huge pieces, and so is obviously not a candidate for dismantling. And the big parking lot (as well as presumably deep footings, would certainly eliminate digging.

Pulling it down can be dismissed just as easily, unless you've got some big earth moving equipment and a hefty cable to attach fairly high up on the tower. I don't think my mom's car has the horsepower to move it (and I know mine sure as hell doesn't). I keep picturing that scene from *The Gods Must Be Crazy* where they attach one end of a cable to a tree and the other to a jeep, and end up winching their vehicle into the air. Oh, hello, officer. What am I doing up here? That's a very good question. My cell phone reception has been really crappy lately, and I thought I'd get better reception if I got closer to the antenna. And say, would you mind helping me down?

Cutting would probably work, so long as we're clear that we're not talking about hacksaws. This tower is big. A grinder wouldn't work either in this case. There are lots of cell phone and other towers out in the mountains, and so long as you had lookouts, grinders might work out there, but that much noise here in town seems contraindicated. Oh, hello, officer. What am I doing here? That's a very good question... But an acetylene torch might do the trick, although once again here in town there's a good chance it would draw some attention. And so far as me doing it, I have used acetylene torches, but you don't even want to hear about my experiences in metal shop class (and yes, David, I still remember you from there, too).

Explosives would have the advantage of it not mattering whether anyone notices, because timers are easy enough to make that even I could use them, so by the time the tower comes down I could easily be in another state (not quite so dramatic as it sounds here since I live about twenty minutes from the border). Additionally, in this case explosives would be safe. Although I've been saying this tower is "behind Safeway," it's way behind Safeway, in an old abandoned parking lot. The problem, once again, is that I know nothing about explosives. I was certainly a nerd in high school, college, and beyond, but evidently the wrong kind of nerd for the task at hand. While the science geeks were busy seeing what bizarre combinations of chemicals would blow things up, and dropping M-80s down toilets in (usually unsuccessful) attempts to get school cancelled (though being geeks I was never quite sure why they wanted to cancel school), me and my friends were reading books, and playing Dungeons and Dragons (and a hell of a lot of good that does me now: if only a +3 Dwarven War Hammer could bring down civilization, I'd be in great shape).

Ah, the pity of a misspent youth.

This all makes me wish I would have joined the Navy Seals, and learned how to blow things up. (I probably would have learned how to kill people too: strange, isn't it, how when the system's soldiers are taught to kill, that's banal—the final night at boot camp, drill instructors sometimes christen their students' new lives by saying, "You are now trained killers"[4]—but when someone who opposes the system even mentions the k-word, it's met with shock, horror, the fetishization of potential future victims, and the full power of the state, this latter manifesting as those who've been trained to kill in support of the centralization of power.) Or better, it makes me wish I had a friend who was a Navy Seal, and who shared my politics.

This leads us to removing the tower's supports and letting it fall on its own. That may be the easiest, and something even I could handle. The other tower, in the woods to the north, has about twenty guy wires. Everything I've read suggests these wires are even more deadly to birds than are the towers themselves. Some places you can pick up dead birds by the handful beneath the wires. Their necks are broken, skulls cracked, wings torn, beaks mangled. But I also know what happens when high tension wires are severed: those opposed to their own decapitation ought to be far away. Which leads us back to explosives.

But there's good news in all of this. I see giant bolts surrounding the base of the tower behind Safeway. I'd imagine they're secured very tightly, but for one of the few times in my life my physics degree might come in handy. Of course you don't really need a physics degree to understand that if you want to unscrew a tight bolt all you need is a long lever arm on your wrench. Just as Archimedes said, "Give me a long enough lever and a place to stand and I can move the world," I'll go on record as saying that if you give me a long enough lever arm I can unscrew any bolt in the world—oh, okay, maybe just a lot of bolts that are pretty damn tight. So a huge pipefitter's wrench with a long metal pipe over the end to extend your lever arm might be enough to get you the torque you'd need to loosen the base (failing that, you could always cut the bolts instead of the tower itself: remember, always attack the weakest point). Then walk away and wait for the next windstorm to do the trick.

All this talk of taking down towers makes me wish I was a farmer, not only because the farmers I've known have generally been crackerjack mechanics—I was a farmer (commercial beekeeper) in my twenties, and learned, to my dismay, that most farmers spend far more time with machines than animals—but also because back in the 1970s a group of farmers called the Bolt Weevils were pioneers in the art and science of taking down towers. They specialized in towers for high-tension electrical wires.

It all started (and I'm indebted to Mary Losure of Minnesota Public Radio for this account:[5] I'm not sure why, but accounts of the Bolt Weevils are fairly hard to come by) when the United Power Association and the Cooperative [sic] Power Association decided to put a 400 mile transmission line across Minnesota farmland between coal-fired generating stations in North Dakota and the industry and homes of the Twin Cities. As always, the poor would be screwed so the rich could benefit. First, as with water, most of this electricity would not be used to benefit human beings, but industry. Second, the utility corporations chose to put the powerlines across lands belonging to politically powerless family farmers rather than across huge corporate farms with political clout.

One of the farmers, Virgil Fuchs, became aware of the plan, and went door to door informing his neighbors. He was just in time: representatives from the utility corporations were right behind him trying to get farmers to sign easements. After Virgil's warning, not one farmer signed.

What follows is a story we've heard too many times, of local resistance overwhelmed by distant power, of politicians and bureaucrats who go out of their way to feign community interest while going just as far out of their way to stab these communities in the back. In essence, it's the story of civilization: of human beings and communities harmed, so cities and all they represent may grow.

Local townships passed resolutions disallowing the powerlines, and county boards refused permits for construction. The response by the corporations was to ignore local concerns and turn to the state for help. The farmers also turned to the state for help, speaking to their purported representatives. The response by the state government's Environmental Quality Council was predictable: public hearings were held, people voiced their opinions, and after discovering that opinions ran overwhelmingly against the powerlines, the state doctored the transcripts of the meetings (dropping out unfavorable testimony), then went ahead and granted the permits. One county sued, but the case was dismissed.

Government representatives promised they would at least let farmers know when construction would begin, but they lied. Suddenly one day surveyors showed up in Virgil Fuchs' fields.

Here is why, in many ways, I respect at least some family farmers more than most environmentalists: Fuchs fought back. He drove his tractor over the surveyors' equipment, and rammed their pickup truck.

It must be said, however, that Fuchs was, in some ways, risking less by doing this than had he done the same actions as an environmentalist. He was sentenced to community service, and eventually even the record of his arrest and conviction was expunged. You and I both know that any environmentalist who did this to equipment belonging to any extractive corporation would probably get charged with attempted murder, and receive at least 50 years in prison: remember that environmental activist Jeffrey Luers is serving more than 22 years for torching three SUVs in the middle of the night when no one was around, and three environmentalists face up to 80 years for allegedly torching an unoccupied logging truck. Similarly, when gun-wielding farmers in the Klamath Valley stood off sheriffs and sabotaged public dams to force water to be diverted away from salmon and toward their (publicly-subsidized) potato farms, sheriffs joined the fun and no one was arrested, let alone indicted, let alone prosecuted, let alone sent to prison, let alone shot. And they got the water. If you or I re-sabotage those dams to keep water for salmon (water for fish: what a quaint notion!), and we pull guns on sheriffs as we're doing so, we, too, wouldn't go to prison. But we would go to the cemetery.

Farmers began gathering, at Fuchs' farm, and at others across several counties. They fought the surveyors wherever and however they could. They'd suddenly, for example, gain permission from the county to dig a ditch across a road for this reason or that. One farmer stood next to the surveyors running his chainsaw so the workers couldn't communicate.

Local sheriffs did the right thing, or at least didn't do the wrong thing. One said,

> As sheriff of this county, I became involved when the landowners and other concerned citizens objected to trespasses of their property [by the power companies]. In the meantime the power companies expect my department to use unlimited force, if necessary, to accomplish their survey and ultimately the routing of the powerline. In my opinion this is a situation that began with the Environmental Quality Council, at the request of the power companies, and that's where the problem should be remanded for resolution. I will not point a gun at either the farmer or a surveyor. To point a gun is to be prepared to shoot, and this situation certainly does not justify either. It does justify a review of the conditions that bring about such citizen resistance.

Where is this sheriff when environmentalists need him? If only sheriffs would always defend local humans against distant corporations, or at the very least, not enforce the ends of these corporations through violence.

The governor also refused to intervene. That's where things stood when a new governor took office that winter. Things looked good for the farmers: the new governor considered himself a populist. As one farmer said, "He thought of himself as representative of the people, with a capital P, not of the bureaucracy or the bigwigs or the business people, and so he had, I think, a great hope and belief that he could get people together and solve the problems."

But when politicians present themselves as representatives of regular people it's time to start packing (either your luggage so you can flee, or a pistol, so you can, well, you know...you choose which).

The governor took to slipping off in secret to visit farmers at their homes. He told them he sympathized, and said, "You really got stuck in this case."

Philip Martin, head of United Power Association, sympathized too. He'd grown up on a farm, and he even knew and loved Virgil's mother— "She reminded me somewhat of my own mother," he said—but as from the beginning of civilization the demands of this deathly economic system trumped all human cares, feelings, and needs. Demand for electricity was growing by ten percent per year, construction of the lines had already begun, and the clock was ticking on interest of a $900 million federal loan. The logic was, "I may love my mother, but if the economic system—and more broadly civilization—demands it (or hell, even hints at it) I'll screw her over and leave her for dead."

Martin was clear on the source and solution of the problem: "We built all the way across North Dakota and we had one person protesting it. That was solved when the law enforcement—he did some damage—and the law enforcement there initiated the action to put him in prison, or jail. And pretty soon he said, 'I'll be a good boy, I won't do anything more,' and they let him out, and we built a transmission line. We didn't have any problem in North Dakota."

But, he continued, in Minnesota, "The law enforcement refused to enforce their own laws. We would go out and try to survey, and they would simply pull up all our stakes, they would destroy everything we had out there [Kinda makes you proud to be an American, don't it?]. And there was never anything done. President Norberg, who was president of the cooperative, and I were out there to many meetings. I drove a car with an escort in front of it and back of it with guns going off, sticking out the windows."

The farmers said the transmission lines would come in over their dead bodies.

They filed more lawsuits, which went to the Minnesota Supreme Court. The Supreme Court decided against them. This journey through the courts radicalized many of the farmers, who to that point had believed in the system. One farmer stated: "I had the feeling that it was all decided. The courts weren't acting as courts at all, they were just a front. And it was just a terrible, terrible shock to me. I thought, gee, this can't be."

That November, construction started in western Minnesota. When farmers protested, the corporations filed $500,000 lawsuits against them.

The farmers found allies, from former Vietnam War protesters to Quakers to musicians.

The corporations, of course, already had allies in the court system, and now the governor, and through him, police with guns. For all of his rhetoric, when push came to shove, the governor, as representative of the state's economic system, shoved the powerlines down the farmers' throats. He said, "You know, this is a nation of laws. And there's a lot of things that I don't like, you know, and I'm sure there's many things that you don't like, but there's a process that we can work, it's a process that's open. It's a process that people in November go and they make that mark on that ballot." Let me translate: "It does not matter whether this or any other particular law or action is good for humans or the landbase. It does not matter whether you like what happens to your landbase, to your children, or to you. It does not matter whether I like it. It does not matter if the laws were designed by and for the rich, and the same is true for the courts and law enforcement. It does not matter if we lie to you and put you through processes of sham public participation. Your participation in processes that affect your life, the lives of your children, and your landbase begins and ends with a checkmark on a ballot in a meaningless election. The only thing that matters is the growth of the economic system. If you don't like it, we will send in people with guns to put down resistance."

Farmers broke up construction sites and corporate representatives said construction would not continue without police protection. The governor sent in state troopers, with up to ten cars and twenty cops protecting individual dump trucks.

The state legislature considered a moratorium on construction until further health studies could be performed. It was already known that electrical lines can lower conception rates and milk production in dairy cows. And the state's own guidelines warned farmers against refueling their vehicles under the transmission lines, and warned school bus drivers against picking up or discharging children under them.

Across the state, people overwhelmingly favored the farmers over the utility corporations. But, as a corporate attorney argued, "The critical question for you as legislators is, is this a government of law, or of men?"

Think for a moment about that question, and think about its implications.

The legislators thought about it long enough to kill the moratorium.

By now the cops (who, too, may have sympathized, but who, too, were too enthralled with the machinery of civilization to follow their human hearts) were behind the powerline a hundred percent. They told farmers they couldn't assemble, couldn't drive county roads, couldn't stop on township roads, couldn't speak. When a farmer asked why cops were stopping farmers on county roads, the officer responded, "We will do whatever we can to get that powerline through." The farmer made the point that the officer did not say, "We are there to protect you," nor even "We are there to protect the workers."

In August, someone loosened the bolts on one of the 150-foot steel transmission towers. Soon after, it fell, and soon after that so did three more. People cut guard poles in half, they cut bolts three-quarters of the way through, then replaced them, waiting for someone to step on and break them.

The governor called out the FBI. A helicopter soon guarded the powerline, presaging the sort of surveillance that is now familiar to the poor in many parts of the country. There were more than seventy arrests in one county alone. But home-cooked justice prevailed this time, as even the two people convicted of felonies were sentenced only to community service. In some cases, everyone refused to testify against the farmers.

A reporter asked one farmer whether he agreed with those who were bringing down towers.

The farmer responded, "I wish a few more would come down, and I think they will, as time goes on. They shouldn't have done this to us in the first place. We've did everything we could lawfully. We went to Minneapolis, got lawyers, went through the courts. But either the judges are paid off, or they just don't realize what's going on here. I think there's a lot of different laws and ways you can look at it. There's moral laws, too. I don't know, I don't figure it's wrong what we're doing out here. Sure, people think you gotta stay with the law, but what is the law? Who makes it? We should have more of a say with what goes on in this state too, you know. They can't just run over us like a bunch of dogs."

Although the farmers ultimately lost—the powerlines have been operating for two decades now—over the next two years they knocked down ten more towers, and shot out thousands of insulators.

Dissatisfied even with victory, the power corporations wanted to make sure no one would ever again challenge their hegemony. In the words of Philip Martin, "We got the federal government to pass the law" that it's a federal crime to take down a tower transmitting electricity across state lines.

I'm sitting again by the cell phone towers, and this time I'm thinking, I could do this. There are, as with so many activities we may find intimidating, several categories of barriers to action. There's the intellectual: I must convince myself it's necessary. There's the emotional: I must feel it's necessary. There's the moral: I must know it's right. There's the consequential: I must be willing and prepared to deal with the effects of my actions. Related to this, there's the fearful: I must be willing to cross barriers of fear, both tangible, real, present-day fears; and conditioned fears that feel just as real and present but are not. (e.g., If I wanted to go waterskiing, which I don't, I would have to face not only whatever fears I might have of speeding behind a boat, but my visceral repulsion to waterskiing based on beatings associated with it when I was a child: there is no longer any danger of my father hitting anyone if I were to go waterskiing, but it still feels like there is. How many of our other fears have been inculcated into us by our families or the culture at large?) There's the technical: I must figure out how best to proceed. There are undoubtedly others I can't think of.

For someone to act—and this is a generic process, applying as much to asking someone out, as to weeding a garden, as to writing a book, as to removing cell phone towers, as to dismantling the entire infrastructure that supports this deathly system of slavery—each of these barriers to action must be overcome, or sometimes simply bypassed in moments of great embodiedness, identification, and feeling. (For example, if someone were attempting to strangle me (with bare hands, as opposed to the toxification of my total environment) my movement through these various barriers to action would, of necessity, be visceral and immediate (no pondering, just reaching for the pen to stab into his eye).)

Sure, I don't know how to take down a cell phone tower. But that's not why I don't act. One purpose of this essay is to help me, and perhaps others, to examine and if appropriate, move past these other barriers to then leave us only with the technical question of how-to, because so often how-to is actually the easiest question, the smallest barrier.

I could take out a cell phone tower. So could you. We're not stupid (I'm presuming no members of the current Administration have made it this far in the essay). And while our first few attempts may not be pretty— you'll notice I don't show you the first stories I ever wrote (at the time, my mother said they were good, yet now we both laugh when she says, "They were terrible, but I could never tell you that") and even now I don't show you my first drafts—but we would learn, just as we learn to do any technical task. I'm certain that if I made as many birdhouses as I write pages, not even David Flagg could laugh at them.

Practice makes perfect. This is as true of taking down cell phone towers as of writing. And fortunately, there are a lot of cell phone towers (I bet you never thought you'd see me append fortunately to a statement like that!). According to some estimates there are 138,000 cell phone towers in the US (more than 48,000 of which are over two hundred feet tall)[6] plus radio and television towers. And the number of American cell phone users went up another 23 million between 2000 and 2001, leading to 20,000 new towers.[7]

That's a lot of practice. If we just put our hearts and minds and hands to it, it probably won't take very long before we get pretty good at it, so that taking down towers becomes something natural, like breathing, like taking long deep breaths of cool fresh air. Soon enough, we'll wonder what took us so long to get started.

Notes

1. See, for example, Jensen, Derrick. *The Culture of Make Believe*. White River Junction: White River Junction, 2004; and *Endgame: The Collapse of Civilization and the Rebirth of Community*, New York: Seven Stories Press, 2006.

2. Malakoff, David. "Faulty Towers." *Audubon* <http://magazine.audubon.org/features0109/faulty_towers.html>

3. Schor, Juliet B. *The Overworked American: The Unexpected Decline of Leisure* (Basic Books, New York, 1991), 19.

4. Wilkinson, Bob. "Trained Killers." *Anderson Valley Advertiser*, 30 April 2003, 3.

5. Losure, Mary. "Powerline Blues." *Minnesota Public Radio News*. <http://news.mpr.org/features/200212/08_losurem_powerline/>

6. Sadovi, Carlos. "Cell Phone Technology Killing Songbirds, Too." *Chicago Sun-Times*, 30 Nov. 1999. <http://www.rense.com/politics5/songbirds.htm>

7. Wikle, Thomas A. "Cellular Tower Proliferation in the United States." *The American Geographical Society*. <http://www.amergeog.org/news.htm> See also <http://www.towerkill.com/>.

People Ain't Feeling This Bullshit

Leslie James Pickering

I was brought up to succeed. To get mine any way I can. Whatever it takes to get what you've got coming. And if you can't do it honest, do it dirty. If you ain't watching out for yours then you won't get it. Any money is good money, as long as it's yours. That's how they make us.

I actually remember a thought I had early in my childhood about how lucky I was to have been born white, male, and American. Not how fucked the world was, but how lucky I was, because the world was mine. I delivered newspapers seven days a week and memorized every word out of my teachers' mouths. I wanted to be an astronaut, until I realized that I could aim higher.

In America, the ends justify the means, and I am an American, home-grown. If I have to slaughter Iraqi civilians to get myself through college, then sign me up. If I have to flip burgers in a clown suit at McDonald's to make my American Dream come true, I count my blessings. Made in the USA.

But somewhere along the way I stopped giving a fuck. It wasn't that I stopped believing that the means could be justified. It was that I lost interest in the ends.

I see the high class. I see the prestige and the people groveling at your feet, the bling and the white picket fences, it's bullshit. My life's worth more than that. I want a fucking world worth living in, and I'm gonna get it or die trying.

In this "free country," the moment your ends aren't monetary, your means become questionable. You can destroy people, families, communities, and the entire quality of life on Earth for the almighty dollar and somehow be beyond question. But destroy even a few thousand dollars worth of property, for any other ends than money, and you'll quickly be reminded just how below the law this system regards its citizens.

We are above the law. The law is supposed to serve us, not imprison us or pave the way for our oppression. Fuck the law, it wasn't written for us. It's in place to keep us from getting free. Freedom is never gonna be on the ballot. Liberation ain't coming from holding a sign or writing a petition. The laws don't protect the people, they protect the system. So you want to know how to truly challenge the system? It's simple, break its laws, and get away with it.

You want to change the world? You want to save the Earth? You want to break free? Then get the fuck off your knees. You don't break free by begging.

They say we resort to breaking the law. There ain't no "resort" about it. I've resorted to begging, pleading, petitioning, and protesting for petty policy changes. I've resorted to walking their walk and talking their talk in front of their media and their courts. But I never had to "resort" to breaking the law, it was always a pleasure.

Breaking the law never compromised my morals. How could it when we're made to aspire to the world's worst criminals—the officials, the authorities, the rich and powerful who break the law on a daily basis? My problem ain't that these people are breaking the law, it's that they don't give a fuck about anything but money, and that I've been raised to be the same.

My problem is that I've been lied to. I've voluntarily ran myself through their courts too many times because I believed the lie that you can get free by begging and placing yourself in the mercy of this sick system. Even civil disobedience is a fucking bullshit lie, a filtration device to sort out dissidents and place them in the hands of the courts. It never got me anything but a criminal record and a few more knocks over the head. So fuck voluntary arrests and fuck any form of begging, we'll take our freedom whatever way we can get it.

We are made to mirror this system. To be machines driven by greed, fueled on the American Dream, bloodthirsty. Vicious and unrelenting, whatever it takes. Fuck the Earth, fuck the people, fuck the air we breathe and the water we drink, fuck our friends and family. Fuck anything and anyone that gets between you and all the money you can get your hands on.

So be it, only let freedom be our ends instead of money. You want to make a nation of heartless killers, but it's turning on you. You want to raise us on violence and yet expect us to make tax-deductible donations for our freedom? Fuck that. You reap what you sow.

We are America's chickens coming home to roost, the seeds of its own destruction. Middle class, upper class, lower class, working class, woman, man, white, black, brown, red, yellow…we've all been lied to and victimized by this system, yet we stand as the most significant force for revolution.

Guerillas have caused tens of millions of dollars in damages to the seemingly indestructible power structure. Riots have reduced cities to ruins. The powerful have been assassinated, computer viruses have wreaked havoc on institutions, and people have found new ways of living, loving, communicating, fighting, working, as revolutions speckle human history. So let's bring it on already.

There is no time or place better than right here, and right now. There is nobody more capable or more justified than you and I. The only thing stopping us is the belief in their bullshit lie that we can get free by begging for petty policy changes. There is no excuse for our passivity and we are the only ones to blame if we fail to even try.

We have a choice we make every day of our lives. We can fight each other or we can fight this system. We can struggle to get ahead of everyone else or we can struggle to get free. We can do the same bullshit that everyone is doing; go to school, go to work, go to the bank, go to the store, go to the retirement home, and go to the grave. Or we can fuck this system up and get free. We can live and die for this system or we can live and die for freedom and revolution.

We need a revolution. We need a revolutionary movement, passionate and powerful. Nothing's going to get any better while this reigns supreme. We need a complete reevaluation of our priorities and values as a people, and we need a revolutionary movement struggling with those as our objectives. We don't need a utopian dream, we need a fucking people's army, some hope and something to believe in, something to live and die for. We need to fucking change our world, and that starts with the overthrow of this system.

In his book on the Haitian revolution of 1791–1803, *The Black Jacobins*, C.L.R. James put it this way:

> The Slaves destroyed tirelessly. Like the peasants in the Jacquerie or the Luddite wreckers, they were seeking their salvation in the most obvious way, the destruction of what they knew was the cause of their sufferings; and if they destroyed much it was because they had suffered much. They knew that as long as these plantations stood their lot would be to labor on them until they dropped. The only thing was to destroy them. From their masters they had known rape, torture, degradation, and, at the slightest provocation, death. They returned in kind.[1]

There ain't nothing nice about it. Revolution is born of oppression. You're wrong if you think we wanted it like this, but you're just as wrong if you think we ain't gonna fight back like we mean it. The oppressed write the rules in our own struggles to break free, no one else. So you want the theory spelled out, here it is—the people aren't relating to the struggle.

We've all got plenty of our own problems. I've got the bills backed way up again and my brother's getting suicidal, so I ain't really thinking much about some trees off in some lumber mill somewhere. That's just how it is. People really have to find themselves in a unique position to care an awful lot about the abstractions that a lot of American middle-class movements are built around. Everyone I know is oppressed, but not everyone can identify with it.

I hated school, a lot of us did. I hated how adults were always telling me how to live my life and I hated the constant disrespect that I got as a youth growing up in America. I wanted to quit, but I didn't want to stay poor. I wanted liberation, but I couldn't quite identify with it.

Then I came across the Earth Liberation Front, and I liked that. There was something about how urgent and raw their struggle was that drew me in. I wasn't a tree hugger, I didn't really relate to that at all, but I was lost, like so many of us, looking for something, and this was as close as I've ever seen.

To tell the truth it was the criminality of that struggle that attracted me the most. I wasn't at all interested in holding signs and writing letters. I had already gone through too much to feel empowered by that kind of thing. But seeing buildings burn down is another story. If someone had written a letter to the superintendent I probably wouldn't even have cared; if someone held a protest at the Board of Education I'd probably forget about it pretty quick, but if the bus rolled up to a pile of ashes in the morning I could relate to that. That would change my life.

When the struggle doesn't relate directly to your oppression you're gonna have a hard time relating to the struggle. People that do find ways to relate to abstract struggles are usually satisfied with a minimal level of participation. That's when a struggle's doing more to shed your guilt than to break you free. And since we need to build a revolutionary movement, not another pastime, we're clearly doing something wrong.

So here's the strategy—relate the struggle to the people.

The primary responsibility of the struggle isn't to be saintly and righteous, it's to win. Not all that many people I come across are all that interested in *ahimsa*, they're just looking to break free. We're doing dirt everyday just to get by, so that kind of utopia is way too far out there for most the people I come across to relate to. We shouldn't be expecting oppressed people to relate to an abstract struggle, we should be working to relate the struggle to the people.

We need to identify with our own oppression. Stop running around the world searching for the lowest of the low when this shit's keeping you and your people down every day. Once you identify with your oppression you can start to find your community. These are the people who are bleeding like you're bleeding. You probably see them all the time, those other rats in the race. When you know your true community you can start to organize it. This is gonna look different in every circumstance. There's no map to follow because we haven't gotten there yet, and everybody's going somewhere different.

Over the last year and a half I've been developing a model of revolutionary community organizing through Arissa in Buffalo.[2] When something ain't working you try something else or give up, and we ain't about to give up. Our entire first year was devoted to a community needs assessment survey. Instead of going into a community organizing effort acting as if we already know what is wrong and what should be done about it, we took a survey to find what the rest of the community thought and used the results of that survey as the foundation for our local efforts in Buffalo.

As a result we've been developing several programs addressing needs like food, housing, incarceration, and corruption in local politics. We've got an ongoing revolutionary education program where we give multimedia presentations on historical revolutionary struggles on a regular basis.

I've found myself working in ways I never imagined, like organizing public forums with county legislators so people from the community could come and tell them what they think about the county budget crisis that's shutting down countless crucial services, arts and cultural programs, and causing thousands of layoffs in our county.

Whatever it takes. And it's going to take a revolutionary movement to create revolutionary change, so that's what we're working to build. For once I'm starting to see all kinds of people from the community—from youth too young to be in school to county legislators—saying that the system has failed us, and coming together to do something about it. And when the shit inevitably hits the fan around here everybody will know who's down, and nobody can say we didn't try to talk it out first.

You got a better theory and strategy? Then implement it. For real, I can hardly wait. Let's see some new shit start to happen. But fuck a theory and strategy with no action. We got too many of those. The struggle needs people, and the people need some inspiration, something to believe in, to live and die for. We're tired of this bullshit. No one is about to join another movement that ain't moving. We've gotta prove to the people that we are fighting to win, that revolution is possible, that together we can turn this motherfucker upside down and finally break free. Enough is enough.

Notes

1. C.L.R. James, *The Black Jacobins* (New York: Vintage Books, 1963), 88.

2. The primary goal of Arissa is to create a social and political revolution in the United States. We believe that none of the single issue problems—whether in the human or environmental categories—can be resolved until a political structure is put in place to allow for an atmosphere of change. Arissa will have reached its initial goal when that revolution occurs. Realizing that the citizens of the United States are nowhere near prepared for a revolution, we believe that public education is a priority. In order to build a revolutionary movement, we must first build a revolutionary consciousness. We believe there are sound reasons for fundamental political and social change in this country, and it is crucial to assist in allowing the people to understand this as well. See <http://www.arissa.org>.

Direct Action and the Heroic Ideal
An Ecofeminist Critique

Marti Kheel

I am seated at a plenary session at a national animal rights conference. A well-known animal rights activist and self-described "eco-warrior" is speaking to a large audience, his voice bellowing with anger. He declares that violence is a normal and acceptable response to the desecration of sacred places or art. Why, then, is it not a commonplace reaction to rainforest destruction? If activists truly valued these "cathedrals of nature," he continues, they would not simply picket, lobby, or dance around in silly costumes; they would rise up and rip those loggers limb from limb. The audience cheers and claps with enthusiasm, and gives him a standing ovation when he is done.

A few years later, I'm seated at an animal rights conference, listening to a panel on direct action. The facilitator introduces himself by giving his personal background: he was imprisoned for several years for overturning a car during an animal rights protest. He initiates the discussion by asking, How many people think that direct action is justified? People begin to raise their hands until it seems that all are raised—except mine. He has not specified what *type* of action he would like us to consider. Without that information, I cannot respond.

Direct action as a means of opposing injustice is a time-honored tradition, increasingly embraced by many members of the animal rights and environmental movements.[1] Direct action activists have made significant contributions. In addition to saving the lives of countless animals and curtailing environmental devastation, they have placed key issues in the forefront of discussions about animal liberation and environmental ethics. Many nature advocates now recognize that it is not enough to reform an inherently corrupt system; we must challenge the entire notion of nonhuman animals as property. Direct action activists have also advanced the discussion of what constitutes terrorism. Is it terrorism when someone rescues an animal who is being subjected to pain and suffering and ultimately death? When someone throws a brick in a window of a fur store? Or is terrorism, rather, the state of siege that is inflicted upon billions of animals everyday throughout the world? These types of discussions have advanced the animal liberation movement in significant ways.

Some forms of direct action can be valuable tools for social change. The ALF theft of videotapes from the Head Injury Clinic at the Neurological Institute in Pennsylvania, for example, documented extreme cruelty to primates and was instrumental in closing the laboratory.[2] But when direct action is endorsed uncritically in any and all forms, or embraced as a universal norm, it can do more harm than good. There is a marked distinction between liberating an animal from a laboratory, in which no risk to others exists, and burning down a building where someone could be injured.

When most animal rights advocates think of direct actions, they conjure up images of dramatic night-time raids, property destruction, and acts involving great personal risk. Freeing animals, bombing buildings, destroying research, seizing evidence of animal abuse, and targeting the homes of individuals involved in animal exploitation, all come to mind as examples. The uncritical endorsement of *heroic*[3] acts by some militant animal and environmental advocates, however, may inadvertently replicate the violent worldview that the protesters seek to supplant. Moreover, the focus on heroic actions also tends to eclipse the more frequent everyday acts of courage that form the fabric of social change. In this paper, I examine both the ethos that underlies heroic direct action, and the importance of ordinary acts of courage that can bring about social change.

It is understandable that people would resort to extreme actions in the face of the pervasive suffering of animals that persists and even grows, despite numerous campaigns against it. We live in a patriarchal and capitalist society which sanctions animal abuse as the norm. Billions of animals suffer and die every day for human profit, pleasure, and use. Nonhuman animals emerge into this world only to be prodded, choked, caged, pierced, bludgeoned, raped, gassed, branded, and otherwise assaulted. Their flesh and body products appear in our cosmetics, clothes, cars, and food. The mentality that underlies these forms of abuse conceives of animals as the "other," as mere objects with no independent identity, existing only to serve the needs of others.

The worldview that underlies animal abuse in Western culture derives from a similar mentality to the one which underlies the abuse of women. Women, like nonhuman animals, are viewed as Beasts or Bodies. The Beast is a symbol for all that is deemed not human, and thus evil, irrational, and wild. Civilization is achieved by driving out or killing the Beast.[4] On an inward level, this involves obliterating all vestiges of our own animality.[5] Outwardly, the triumph over the Beast has been enacted through the conquest of wilderness, with its concomitant claim to the lives of millions of animals driven from their homes.

The triumph over the demonic beast has been a recurring theme throughout patriarchal mythologies.[6] Typically, the slain Beast is a former divinity from the earlier matriarchal world. The serpents, dragons, and horned gods, who were at one time worshipped as divine, are transformed in patriarchal mythology into devils and monsters that must be slain. Thus Apollo slays Gaia's python; Perseus kills the three-headed Medusa (the triple goddess), who is described as having snakes writhing from her head; Hercules defeats the terrible multi-headed Hydra; and the pharaohs of later Egypt slay the dragon Apophys.[7] In the Middle Ages, there were countless renditions of St. George's prowess in killing the dragon to rescue the damsel in distress.

Today, the heroic battle against the Beast is reenacted as ritual drama in such masculine ventures as sport-hunting, bullfights, and rodeos. A similar mentality can be seen in the ritual degradation of women in pornography and rape. Just as "wild" animals are tied and bound in rodeos, women are tied and bound in pornographic magazines, or depicted in acts of submission.

The second image underlying the abuse of women and nonhuman animals appears less heroic, but is equally violent in its own way. It is the representation of women and nonhuman animals as mindless matter, objects that exist to serve the needs of superior, rational "Man." In this conception, animals are depicted as having different, unequal natures, rather than as wild or evil creatures that must be conquered and subdued. They are not so much irrational as nonrational beings. Along with women, they are viewed as mere "matter" (a word that, significantly, derives from the same root word as "mother"). In this conception, the bodies of women and animals are valued for their reproductive capacity and their flesh. Their bodies are also said to excite the appetites of men.

At times, women and nonhuman animals have also been idealized as pure and innocent, providing a nurturing influence that functions to moderate male aggression. Once again, their value lies only in their utility to others. They are considered damsels in distress, helpless victims who must be rescued from the evil "Beast." In this conception, protection becomes the mirror image of predation.[8] The predatory ethic that fuels the masculine conquest of the Beast is transformed into the ethic of heroic protection. Again, women and nonhuman animals are seen as devoid of independent identity, passive objects which reinforce the autonomous masculine self.

Patriarchal society presents us with intolerable choices. Everyday there is something more that we could be doing to alleviate the pervasive suffering that surrounds us. If we do nothing, we often feel complicit in this suffering. Engaging in some form of direct action can help assuage our feelings of helplessness, providing us with a sense of empowerment. Heroic forms of direct action in particular may seem to fulfill this search for empowerment, but they can also reflect an assertion of dominance and control.

Significantly, a number of individuals who engage in direct action view themselves as "eco-warriors" and relish their warrior role. Dave Foreman, one of the founders of Earth First! openly declares that "Earth First! is a warrior society."[9] The Earth First! logo of a raised fist, accompanied by the words "In Defense of Mother Earth," aptly exemplifies the warrior's mission: to "rescue the helpless female—in this case Mother Earth."[10] Paul Watson, director of the Sea Shepherd Conservation Society, similarly exemplifies the warrior model, drawing inspiration from two ancient Asian military strategists, and litters his writing with military metaphors: "war," "battle," "enemy," "weapons," and "defeat."[11] As captain of the Sea Shepherd, he rams fishing boats and fires shotguns in his battle to protect marine animals. He praises newsworthy actions that "hint of romance and piracy," claiming that "there is nothing wrong with being a terrorist as long as you win."[12] Militarism is more than a metaphor for Watson, who states that "Right now we're in the early stages of World War III. We are the navy to Earth First!'s army. It's the war to save the planet. This kind of action will be getting stronger....Eventually there will be open war."[13]

Martyrdom is a trait often praised by eco-warriors. In Watson's words, "The Earth warrior, like all warriors, must be prepared for death."[14] Always ready to embrace danger for a noble cause, the eco-warrior often denounces other forms of activism as cowardice. Behind these tirades lurks the specter of the sissy, with its link to the devalued female world. Watson scorns Greenpeace, the organization he helped to found, as "the Avon Ladies of the environmental movement."[15]

Animal liberation philosophers also typically employ the model of the heroic warrior, citing the "force of reason" in their "defense" of "animal rights."[16] Reason is viewed as the weapon of choice for compelling adherence to universal norms, such as "interests" and "rights." Proponents of direct action, by contrast, purport to move beyond the power of words, preferring physical force to achieve the goal of animal liberation. But as feminists have pointed out, both the logical power of "reason" and the physical power of force often fail to change people's hearts. What is needed, in addition, is the development of compassion for the nonhuman world, and an understanding of why such care is so singularly absent in our current culture.

A nineteenth-century organization of English children's kindness clubs, the Bands of Mercy, a wing of the Royal Society for the Prevention of Cruelty to Animals (RSPCA), understood the importance of reaching people's hearts, rather than only their minds. The Bands of Mercy provided the inspiration for the modern day organization of the same name, which later developed into the ALF. Founded in the 1870s by the anti-slavery activist, Catherine Smithies, as a branch of the RSPCA, the clubs required band members to sign a sworn statement promising that they would be "kind to all harmless living creatures, and try to protect them from cruel usage."[17] Members were also required to get thirty people to sign the oath in order to form a "band." These clubs were modeled after the widespread and internationally popular children's temperance clubs, the Bands of Hope; in addition to promoting kindness to animals, they required children to take vows of abstinence from alcohol.[18]

The kindness clubs and temperance organizations that sprang up in the latter part of the nineteenth-century were part of a larger movement, predominantly led by women, which sought to stem men's violence. These movements reflected the post-Darwinian belief in men's "animal nature," and the concomitant hope that women's benevolent influence would serve as a civilizing force. Promoting kindness and compassion, mostly in young boys, was viewed as a central purpose of many nineteenth-century women's organizations.

The twentieth-century organization, the Band of Mercy, which emerged in England, initially retained vestiges of its nineteenth-century namesake, the Bands of Mercy, endorsing the model of "active compassion."[19] Founded in 1972 by members of the Hunt Saboteur Association (HSA), the organization initially condoned property destruction, but only if it was used to stop animal abuse.[20] When Band members engaged in raids to damage vehicles used in the hunt, they claimed that they "would always leave a message to the hunters explaining the motives of their actions and the logic of animal liberation, while stating that they had nothing personal against any one individual."[21]

Over the next four years, the Band of Mercy extended its activities to arson and the first animal rescues. In 1976, the members decided to change the organization's name, claiming that it no longer seemed appropriate. The name of the new organization, the Animal Liberation Front, appears to have been designed to inspire fear, rather than compassion. As Noel Molland explains, the group wanted a new name that "would haunt the animal abusers. A name whose very mention could symbolize a whole ideology of a revolutionary movement."[22] The organization, however, still retained its commitment to nonviolence towards humans, and destruction only of property used for animal abuse.

By 1984, many direct action proponents had come to endorse violence as a necessary tactic for achieving success. The underlying rationale was that, given the resistance to legitimate forms of social change and the worsening conditions of animals, the ends justify the means. Patriarchal society, however, employs a similar logic in support of animal abuse. Animal experimenters cite the worthy benefits that will ensue when they "sacrifice" animals at the altar of science; nonhuman animals are merely tools in their single-minded search for "cures" or products. "Home demos," which target the homes of individuals engaged in animal abuse, show a similar singularity of focus: there is little concern that innocent people, including children, may be traumatized by their actions.[23] Yet every action occurs within a particular context and generates multiple reactions.

Feminist philosophers have underscored the need for contextual thinking as well as feelings of care.[24] In contrast to modern ethical theorists who base their arguments on abstract principles and universal rules, feminists point to the importance of understanding the context within which ethical decisions are made.[25] The two approaches find a parallel in the field of health. Allopathic medicine views the body as a battlefield in which the invading enemy—disease—needs to be countered with an arsenal of weapons, including radiation, surgery, and drugs. The physicians are the heroes who rescue the ailing body, overcoming the enemy combatants. Holistic healing, by contrast, seeks to understand the causes of disease, fortifying health so the body can regain strength to repel unwelcome intruders. Holistic healing focuses on preventing illness, rather than simply suppressing symptoms and declaring the battle "won."[26] In a similar vein, holistic ethics seek to understand the underlying roots of moral problems, with a view to removing them, and preventing their reoccurrence.

Direct action proponents might do well to consider trading in their military metaphors for the model of holistic health. Rather than viewing individual actions as surgical interventions designed to force enemy combatants into submission, they can be viewed as educational opportunities. The open rescues that liberate animals, while filming their liberation, exemplify the kind of direct action that helps individual beings, while also promoting empathy and an understanding of the larger context of animal oppression. Karen Davis illustrates this point in her description of the video of a liberation of several hens by the Australian Action Animal Rescue Team. As she states,

> We see the hens' suffering faces up close. We watch and hear a hen scream as she is lifted out of the molasses-like manure in which she is trapped in the pits beneath the cages. The video captures not only the terrible suffering of the hens being rescued, but the gentleness and firmness of the rescue team (as expressed, for example, by their hands), who, as an integral part of their videotaped operations, contact the police, get arrested, and explain their mission with the intention of putting battery-hen farming visibly on trial before the public and in the courtroom.[27]

At times, open rescuers do not reveal the particular operation that they target, preferring to put pressure on the industry as a whole. These open rescues contrast with the heroic mind-set of the masked warriors who focus on property destruction or the defeat of a single animal operation, neglecting to lay the base for the type of understanding that can prevent future abuse of nonhuman animals.

While the feminist ethic of care eschews abstract principles and universal rules in favor of a contextual approach to ethical conduct, it can draw on guidelines in evaluating particular situations and actions. Kim Stallwood proposes a useful set of criteria for assessing direct actions, based on the "core values of compassion, truth, nonviolence or *ahimsa*, and 'interbeing.'" In his words, he endorses direct action that:

• is motivated by a sense of compassion for all beings (human and nonhuman alike);

• tells the truth about animal cruelty and all resulting harms it causes to people and the environment;

• is accomplished with adherence to nonviolent principles to all beings (human and nonhuman alike) and property;

• is undertaken only after all consequences of the direct action and its impact on all people and animals are carefully considered by the protagonists, who are wiling to honestly and openly accept the consequences.[28]

Just as holistic health seeks to determine the causes of disease with a view to restoring health and preventing its recurrence, so too holistic ethics strive to determine the cause of moral problems, and the way to prevent them. Exploring the relation between masculine self-identity and violence toward nature may help to shed light on what is needed to transform our society's relation to the natural world.

It is well known that a large majority of members of the animal liberation movement are women.[29] It is also no secret that women are disproportionately represented in the more mundane work entailed in running an organization. A similar breakdown can be found in shelter and other rescue work, with far more women than men involved in the day-to-day care for nonhuman animals. Feminist activist pattrice jones speculates that despite men's greater visibility in direct actions, the gender representation there is probably comparable to that of the rest of the movement.[30] Although the secrecy surrounding direct actions makes it difficult to determine gender ratio, there is reason to believe that more men than women are drawn to the heroic model of activism.[31] jones concedes that "the combination of macho posturing by ALF spokesmen, the unstructured nature of the ALF cell system, and the essential lawlessness of the ALF" makes it possible for "disaffected and potentially violent young men...to use the ALF as an excuse to vent anger in inappropriate ways." She contends, however, that this liability can be remedied by media coverage which puts a "feminine face on the ALF." Although changing the "face of the ALF" may help to discourage violent forms of activism, foregrounding education and "active compassion" would, perhaps, change the ALF in more fundamental ways.

Examples of direct actions which combine active compassion and education can be found around the globe, including the Chipko tree-hugging movement in India, Julia Butterfly Hill's year-long tree sitting campaign in the US, and the Greenham Common missile protest in England. In the Chipko movement in the early 1970s, mountain villagers embraced trees in order to prevent environmentally devastating clear-cutting. Although the movement was originally organized and controlled by men, women organizers were catapulted into the spotlight when they spontaneously organized to persuade loggers to leave the forest.[32]

In a similar spirit, beginning in 1997, Julia Butterfly Hill, camped out for two years on the top of a California Coast Redwood tree in protest of the logging practices of Pacific Lumber Company.[33] Both forms of action illustrate the figurative and literal embracing of what the protesters hoped to protect in contrast to angry confrontations with a perceived enemy, which often alienate the public.[34]

The Women's Peace Camp in Greenham Common illustrates a similar compassionate form of activism.[35] In this instance, women embraced not what they wanted to protect, but the missiles they opposed. The Women's

Greenham Peace Camp began in England as a protest against the siting of the US Cruise Missiles at the Greenham Common. Throughout its nineteen years of existence, organizers engaged in multiple forms of imaginative, mostly nonviolent, playful direct actions. In 1982, for example, 30,000 women joined hands around the base in an "Embrace the Base" event. In other actions, women tied yarn around themselves and the war machinery, confusing the police officers who didn't know how to go about unknitting a web of women.

In all of these examples, protesters garnered widespread sympathy for their goals through creative actions that embodied their hopes and their dreams, rather than engaging in violent confrontations. Heroic direct actions, with their confrontational style, by contrast, tend to eclipse the everyday acts of courage that we can perform on behalf of nonhuman animals. Some of these more prosaic actions present themselves to us on a daily basis and are often lost or overlooked. My niece recently missed one of these opportunities. Sarah, raised as an orthodox Jew, was a natural-born animal rights activist from a very young age. A vegetarian from birth, she grew up viewing meat with a combination of horror and disgust. She teased her meat-eating friends by mimicking the animal they were consuming—flapping her arms when they ate a chicken and swishing them like a fish when they consumed a fish. She embarrassed her mother in public by hiding under the table whenever meat was served.

She was not deterred by authority figures from voicing her strong views about meat. On one occasion, when dining at a Rabbi's house, she challenged the Rabbi for condoning meat eating. "Meat eating is murder!" she instructed him. The Rabbi responded by explaining that that is not possible, since it would make most humans murderers. "Well, you are!" she responded, much to her mother's embarrassment.

As she grew up, her demonstrative acts of protest began to wane, but I had no reason to doubt that her zeal for the animal cause had abated. It therefore came as a shock when I learned that she was engaged to be married and planned to serve meat to her guests on her wedding day. Giving in to the pressure to conform, Sarah had missed a major opportunity to engage in a direct action. Had she chosen to serve vegetarian food, she could have expressed her care and compassion for nonhuman animals and potentially influenced a large number of people. While serving vegetarian food at a wedding might not jump to mind as an example of direct action, this type of challenge to the tyranny of convention exemplifies the everyday acts of resistance that form the fabric of social transformation.

Direct action on behalf of nonhuman animals can further be enriched through critical discussion of the heroic ideal. Is courage only an act of physical bravery? Must it always entail danger? Can courage, for some, be found in defying the tyranny of convention? How might "direct action" be redefined so that it incorporates everyday acts of courage? A feminist ethic of care and "compassionate activism" can provide an important contribution to answering these questions and to the development of new forms of

direct action that can help create a world of peace and nonviolence for all
living beings.

Bibliography

Adams, Carol. "Challenge of Animal Rights." The Animal Rights 2003
National Conference, sponsored by the Farm Animal Reform Movement, Los Angeles, California. 2003.

Bari, Judi, "The Secret History of Tree Spiking," *Earth First! Journal* Part
1 and 2 (1994): 264–328.

Best, Steven. "It's War! The Escalating Battle Between Activists and the
Corporate-State Complex." In *Terrorists or Freedom Fighters: Reflections on the Liberation of Animals*, edited by Steven Best and Anthony J. Nocella, II. New York: Lantern Books, 2004.

Boholm, Åsa, "Comparative Studies of Risk Perception: A Review of 20
Years of Research," *Journal of Risk Research* 1 (1998): 135–63.

Brown, Wendy. *Manhood and Politics: A Feminist Reading in Political
Theory.* Totawa, NJ: Rowman and Litttlefied, 1988.

Cole, Eve Browning and Susan C. McQuin, eds. *Explorations in Feminist
Ethics: Theory and Practice.* Bloomington: Indiana University Press,
1992.

Curtin, Deanne. "Toward an Ecological Ethic of Care." In *Ecological Feminist Philosophies,* edited by Karen J. Warren. Bloomington: Indiana
University Press, 1966.

Davis, Karen. "Open Rescues: Putting a Face on the Rescuers and on the
Rescued." In *Terrorists or Freedom Fighters: Reflections on the Libera-
tion of Animals*, edited by Steven Best and Anthony J. Nocella, II.
New York: Lantern Books, 2004.

Donovan, Josephine and Carol J. Adams, eds. *Beyond Animal Rights: A
Feminist Caring Ethic for the Treatment of Animals*. New York: Continuum, 1996.

French, Marilyn. *Beyond Power: On Women, Men, and Morals*. New York:
Summit Books, 1985.

Galvin, Shelley L. and Harold A. Herzog, Jr. "Attitudes and Dispositional
Optimism of Animal Rights Demonstrators." *Society and Animals* 6
(1988): 1.

Gilligan, Carol. *In a Different Voice: Psychological Theory and Women's
Development*. Cambridge, Massachusetts: Harvard University Press,
1993.

Green, Martin. *The Adventurous Male: Chapters in the History of the White
Male Mind*. University Park, Pennsylvania: Pennsylvania State University Press, 1993.

Guha, Ramachandra. *The Unquiet Woods: Ecological Change and Peasant Resistance in the Himalaya*. Expanded Edition. Berkeley: University of California Press, 2000.

Hoagland, Sarah. *Lesbian Ethics: Toward New Value*. Palo Alto, California: Institute of Lesbian Studies, 1989.

Jain, Shobita. "Standing Up for Trees: Women's Role in the Chipko Movement." *Unasylva* 36.4 (1984).

jones, pattrice. "Mothers with Monkeywrenches: Feminist Imperatives and the ALF." In *Terrorists or Freedom Fighters: Reflections on the Liberation of Animals*, edited by Steven Best and Anthony J. Nocella, II. New York: Lantern Books, 2004.

Kheel, Marti. "From Healing Herbs to Deadly Drugs: Western Medicine's War Against the Natural World." In *Healing the Wounds: The Promise of Ecofeminism*, edited by Judith Plant. Philadelphia: New Society Publisher, 1989.

Kheel, Marti. "From Heroic to Holistic Ethics: The Ecofeminist Challenge." In Greta Gaard, *Women, Animals, Nature*. Philadelphia: Temple University Press, 1993.

Larrabee, Mary Jeanne, ed. *An Ethic of Care: Feminist Interdisciplinary Perspectives*. New York: Routledge, 1993.

Massachusetts Society for the Prevention of Cruelty to Animals. "Our Dumb Animals" 20:3. Boston, Massachusetts, 1987.

Midgley, Mary. *Beast and Man: The Roots of Human Nature*. New York: Routledge, 1995.

Molland, Noel, "Thirty Years of Direct Action," *No Compromise* 18 (Summer 2002).

Plous, Scott, "Signs of Change Within the Animal Rights Movement: Results From Follow-Up Survey of Activists," *Journal of Comparative Psychology* 112 1 (1998): 48–54.

Plumwood, Val, "Integrating Ethical Frameworks for Animals, Humans, and Nature: A Critical Feminist Eco-Socialist Analysis," *Ethics and the Environment* 5.2 (2000): 285–322.

Pothier, Dick. "Animal-Rights Group Says it Vandalized Penn Laboratory." *Philadelphia Inquirer*. 30 May 1984.

Regan, Tom. *The Case for Animal Rights*. Berkeley and Los Angeles: University of California Press, 1983.

Robbins, Jim. "The Environmental Guerillas." *Boston Globe*. 27 March 1988.

Roseneil, Sasha. *Disarming Patriarchy: Feminism and Political Action at Greenham Common*. Buckingham: Open University Press, 1995.

Scarce, Rik. *Eco-Warriors: Understanding the Radical Environmental Movement*. Chicago: Noble Press, 1990.

Peter Singer. *Animal Liberation*. 2nd edition. New York: New York Review of Books, 1990.

Sjöö, Monica and Barbara Moor. *The Great Cosmic Mother: Rediscovering the Religion of the Earth*. San Francisco: Harper and Row, 1987.

Stallwood, Kim. "A Personal Overview of Direct Action in the United Kingdom and the United States." In *Terrorists or Freedom Fighters: Reflections on the Liberation of Animals,* edited by Steven Best and Anthony J. Nocella, II. New York: Lantern Books, 2004.

Watson, Paul. *Earthforce!: An Earth Warrior's Guide to Strategy.* Los Angeles, California: Chaco Press, 1993.

Watson, Paul. Presentation at the Animal Rights 2002 National Conference. Sponsored by the Farm Animal Reform Movement, McLean, Virginia, 2002.

Notes

1. The term "direct action" generally refers to both legal and illegal actions of an immediate nature designed to exert pressure toward social change. On one end of the spectrum, some conceive of direct action as tree spiking, liberating animals, arson, and other acts of eco-sabotage. On the other end are organizations, such as Friends of Animals, which consider veganism a form of direct action. My intention in this article is to challenge the preeminence of the heroic ideal in discussions of direct action, and to explore its masculinist underpinnings.

2. The tapes that were stolen were the actual footage taken by the experimenters themselves. For the full story see, Dick Pothier, "Animal-Rights Group Says it Vandalized Penn Laboratory," *Philadelphia Inquirer,* 30 May 1984.

3. Heroism in the Western world is traditionally associated with the notion of courage, sacrifice, and risk, all typical of conceptions of direct actions within the animal rights and environmental movements. The classic hero is also most commonly a male warrior who vanquishes foes and surmounts obstacles in an attempt to overcome "evil." The word "hero" derives from ancient Greek "*hieros*" and originally referred to the notion of a demi-god. The idea of glory, and immortalization through legend, is closely aligned with the classic notions of heroism.

4. I am indebted to Mary Midgley for my understanding and use of the term Beast. Midgley, Mary. *Beast and Man: The Roots of Human Nature.* New York: Routledge, 1995.

5. For an in-depth analysis of how masculine self-identity and Western civilization are founded upon the attempt to transcend animal and female nature, see Brown, Wendy. *Manhood and Politics: A Feminist Reading in Political Theory.* Totawa, N.J.: Rowman and Litttlefied, 1988, and French, Marilyn. *Beyond Power: On Women, Men, and Morals.* New York: Summit Books, 1985.

6. Portions of my discussion of the heroic Beast are drawn from Marti Kheel, "From Heroic to Holistic Ethics: The Ecofeminist Challenge." In *Women, Animals, Nature,* edited by Greta Gaard. Philadelphia: Temple University Press, 1993.

7. Monica Sjöö and Barbara Moor, *The Great Cosmic Mother: Rediscovering the Religion of the Earth* (San Francisco: Harper and Row, 1987), 250–51.

8. On the common worldview underlying predation and protection, See Hoagland, Sarah. *Lesbian Ethics: Toward New Value.* Palo Alto, California: Institute of Lesbian Studies, 1989.

9. Quoted in Jim Robbins, "The Environmental Guerillas," *Boston Globe Magazine,* 27 March 1988. Cited in Seager, Joni. *Earth Follies: Coming to Feminist Terms with the Global Environmental Crisis* (New York: Routledge, 1993), 227.

10. Joni Seager, 227.

11. Paul Watson. *Earthforce!: An Earth Warrior's Guide to Strategy*. Los Angeles, California: Chaco Press, 1993.

12. Paul Watson, Presentation at the Animal Rights 2002 National Conference, sponsored by Farm Animal Reform Movement, McLean, Virginia, June 28–July 3, 2002.

13. Quoted in Best, Steven. "It's War! The Escalating Battle Between Activists and the Corporate-State Complex." In *Terrorists or Freedom Fighters: Reflections on the Liberation of Animals*, ed. Steven Best and Anthony J. Nocella, II. New York: Lantern Books, 2004.

14. Paul Watson, 51.

15. Scarce, Rik. *Eco-Warriors: Understanding the Radical Environmental Movement* (Chicago: Noble Press, 1990), 102.

16. See Regan, Tom. *The Case for Animal Rights*. Berkeley and Los Angeles: University of California Press, 1983, and Singer, Peter. *Animal Liberation*, 2nd Edition. New York Review of Books, 1990. For critiques of the emphasis on reason in animal ethics, see the essays in *Beyond Animal Rights*, edited by Donovan and Adams. New York: Continuum, 1996.

17. *Our Dumb Animals* Volume 20 No.3 (1987).

18. The twentieth-century Band of Mercy maintained that some militant members of its nineteenth-century predecessor also sabotaged rifles, but conceded that no evidence exists to substantiate this claim. They appear to have drawn inspiration from a play performed by the earlier organization, in which a maid sabotaged the gun of a hunter, which subsequently burst in his face. See Molland, Noel, "Thirty Years of Direct Action," *No Compromise* 18 (Summer, 2002).

19. Ibid.

20. For an overview of the history of direct action, see Stallwood, Kim. "A Personal Overview of Direct Action in the United Kingdom and the United States." In *Terrorists or Freedom Fighters*.

21. Noel Molland, "Thirty Years of Direct Action."

22. Ibid.

23. Carol Adams gave a first-hand report, describing how traumatic it was for her children to have their own home picketed by anti-abortion activists. Panel presentation at The Animal Rights 2003 National Conference, sponsored by the Farm Animal Reform Movement, Los Angeles, 2–5 August 2003.

24. On the subject of a feminist ethic of care, see Gilligan, Carol. *In a Different Voice: Psychological Theory and Women's Development*. Cambridge, Massachusetts: Harvard University Press, 1993; Larrabee, Mary Jeanne, ed. *An Ethic of Care: Feminist Interdisciplinary Perspectives*. New York: Routledge, 1993; Cole, Eve Browning and Susan Coultrap McQuin, eds. *Explorations in Feminist Ethics: Theory and Practice*. Bloomington: Indiana University Press, 1992. For a discussion of an ethic of care in relation to nonhuman animals, see the essays in Donovan, Josephine and Carol J. Adams, eds. *Beyond Animal Rights*.

25. For discussions of contextual thinking in relation to nonhuman animals, see Plumwood, Val, *Ethics and the Environment* 5.2 (2000): 285–322, and Curtin, Deanne. "Toward an Ecological Ethic of Care." In *Ecological Feminist Philosophies*, edited by Karen J. Warren. Bloomington: Indiana University Press, 1966.

26. For a feminist critique of Western medicine's war against the natural world, see Kheel, Marti. "From Healing Herbs to Deadly Drugs: Western Medicine's War Against the Natural World." In *Healing the Wounds: The Promise of Ecofeminism*, edited by Judith Plant. Philadelphia: New Society Publisher, 1989.

27. Davis, Karen. "Open Rescues: Putting a Face on the Rescuers and on the Rescued." In *Terrorists or Freedom Fighters*.

28. Kim Stallwood. "A Personal Overview of Direct Action in the United Kingdom and the United States." In *Terrorists or Freedom Fighters*.

29. Researchers estimate that women constitute over seventy-five percent of the animal advocacy movement. See Galvin, Shelley L. and Harold A. Herzog, Jr., "Attitudes and Dispositional Optimism of Animal Rights Demonstrators," *Society and Animals* 6: 1 (1988), and Plous, Scott, "Signs of Change Within the Animal Rights Movement: Results From Follow-Up Survey of Activists," *Journal of Comparative Psychology* 112 1 (1998): 48–54.

30. jones, pattrice. "Mothers with Monkeywrenches: Feminist Imperatives and the ALF."In *Terrorists or Freedom Fighters*.

31. Men's disproportionate representation in risk-taking activities, especially those that involve physical threats to life, health, and the environment, is well documented in a number of studies. See, for example, Boholm, Åsa, "Comparative Studies of Risk Perception: A Review of 20 years of research," *Journal of Risk Research* 1 (1998): 135–63. For an in-depth analysis of the allure of adventure for men, see Green, Martin. *The Adventurous Male: Chapters in the History of the White Male Mind*. University Park, Pennsylvania: Pennsylvania State University Press, 1993.

32. Women's role in the Chikpo movement came to the fore in 1974, when the male organizers in the village of Reni were lured away to clear the way for the loggers. In addition to convincing the timber workers to leave the forest, the women also destroyed and guarded a bridge, preventing them from returning. For a detailed history of the Chipko movement see Guha, Ramachandra. *The Unquiet Woods: Ecological Change & Peasant Resistance in the Himalaya*. Berkeley: University Press, UC Press, 2000. For an analysis of the gender dynamics of the movement see Jain, Shobita, "Standing Up for Trees: Women's Role in the Chipko Movement," *Unasylva* 36.4 (1984).

33. For a chronicle of her tree sitting campaign, see Butterfly Hill, Julia. *The Legacy of Luna: The Story of a Tree, a Woman, and the Struggle to Save the Redwoods*. San Francisco: Harper Collins, 2000.

34. The above tree-hugging/sitting actions contrast with the tree spiking campaign of the early Earth First! movement. According to this tactic, spikes are placed in trees in order to deter logging. While tree huggers/sitters pose only a risk to themselves, tree spiking endangers others. Moreover, the threat is to the timber workers, rather than to the corporate decision-makers. Although Earth First!ers denied responsibility, at least one timber worker was badly injured by a tree spiking incident. Tree spiking was later renounced by the Northern California and Southern Oregon chapters of Earth First! EF! activist, Judi Bari, argued "If we are serious about putting Earth first, we need to choose tactics because they work, not because they seem macho or romantic." (Bari, Judi, "The Secret History of Tree Spiking," *Earth First! Journal* Parts 1 and 2 (1994): 264–328.

35. For a detailed history of the Greenham Women's Peace Camp, see Roseneil, Sasha. *Disarming Patriarchy: Feminism and Political Action at Greenham*. Buckingham: Open University Press, 1995.

Stomping with the elephants
Feminist principles for radical solidarity

pattrice jones

> "Pull or stab or cut or burn,
> She will ever yet return."
> *Robert Graves, "Marigolds"*

1. Evening

It's nighttime in Zululand and the men who have been working in the Thula Thula Exclusive Private Game Reserve are ready to retire, having captured and corralled several antelopes for a breeding program. The frantic antelopes mill about restlessly, not knowing what to do. Out of the twilight comes a herd of elephants. They encircle the enclosure, inspecting the situation. The people keep their distance, apprehensive of the elephants. The matriarch of the herd steps forward and uses her trunk to unlatch the bolts and open the gate. The antelopes escape into the enveloping darkness. The elephants disappear back into the night.

Witnesses use the word "rescue" to describe what they saw that night.[1] Whatever their previous beliefs about animals, they could not help but recognize the deliberate and purposeful nature of the actions of the elephant called "Nana" by local conservationists. Trusting their own eyes, they learned something that most people—including most animal and environmental activists—fail to appreciate: people aren't the only ones acting to undo the damage that people have done.

Putting ourselves in the place of the antelopes that night, we can learn something too: the outlook is very scary but help is at hand.

2. Emergency

I live at a sanctuary for chickens. The roosters are very loud. All day long, they check in with each other by crowing, which evolved as a way to maintain contact in the dense Asian forests where the wild jungle fowl still thrive.

Roosters raise a ruckus whenever they spot a predator or other threat to the flock. All the chickens within earshot respond immediately, taking cover until the danger has passed. In the event of a continuing hazard, the hens and other roosters add their voices to those of the roosters who raised the original alarm. The meaning of the ensuing cacophony is clear to anyone with ears to hear: This is an emergency.

If only human beings were so sensible! Every day, including today, we go about consuming and spending as if we had no knowledge of impending ecological disaster. Some people lash out at the "roosters" who issue warnings about global warming and other emergent crises. Most people ignore them. Even those who do heed the warnings do so without a sense of urgency proportionate to the dangers that face us. There's a breach between what we think and what we feel, a gap between what we know to be true and what we actually do.

As any earthquake survivor can tell you, disjunctions can be hazardous to your health. And, indeed, every day brings more evidence of the dangers of disconnection. In the wake of the Tsunami of 2004, Sri Lankan wildlife officials were stunned to discover that all of the animals at the Yala National Park had survived. Park workers and tourists perished as floodwaters surged through the refuge but the animals evidently sensed the danger in advance and retreated in time.[2] Accustomed to scanning the newspaper or the television rather than the skies, modern men and women do need a weatherman to know which way the wind blows. Like the park rangers of Sri Lanka, even people who are relatively more attuned to the natural world have lost their animal ability to sense and respond appropriately to impending natural disasters.

How else to explain our dumb numbness in the face of the facts? Nine of the ten hottest years on record have occurred since 1990. Thirteen percent of the planet's plant species are in danger of extinction.[3] One out of every ten bird species is likely to be extinct within the century.[4] Our own lives are in peril too. The World Resources Institute predicts that at least 3.5 billion people—that's more than half of us—will experience water shortages by 2025.[5] And, of course, we all are vulnerable to the escalating effects of climate change. For all species, the primary cause of extinction is habitat destruction. In these days of disappearing islands and catastrophic cataclysms, can there be any doubt that we have endangered ourselves?

Much of the damage cannot be undone. In the mountains of Mexico, the wild grasses that are the living ancestors of all maize have been forever polluted by genes from genetically engineered corn. The individual frogs and fish born with missing limbs or extra sex organs will never be the animals they would have been if their mothers had swum in water untainted by antibiotics and pesticides.[6] Shattered rocks and punctured atmospheres cannot be put together again.

How long will it be until we do whatever *can* be done to stop the violence and repair the damage? To what contortions of body and behavior will the progeny of today's sex-crossed fish and five-legged frogs descend in the interim? How does it feel to fly home after a season at the winter place to find that all of the food and housing has been chopped down or washed away? What, exactly, is a bird or a butterfly to do when she finds herself famished and homeless after a long migration? When will well-fed people, safe in *their* houses, *feel* the wing-flapping, heart-pounding, fur-raising sensation that says: "This is an emergency?"

Emergencies mandate immediate and effective direct action. Both critics and proponents of radical environmental activism ought to ponder the implications of that obligation. Those who would condemn radical direct action on behalf of earth and animals might first consider the fine line between complicity and underactivity. If they want their work to be fruitful, those who purport to be radical environmental activists must think carefully about efficacy in order to avoid wasting scarce resources on symbolic activities that might be emotionally satisfying but hardly meet the criteria for direct action.[7]

Particular care must be taken when contemplating actions that may lead to incarceration. Since we are in a state of emergency, we cannot afford to pay the price of years of relative inactivity for the dubious benefits of symbolic acts. All of which is to say that we must think strategically. In order to do so accurately, we must understand not only our own limitations but also the root causes of the problems we hope to solve.

3. Faultlines

How do you break a wild animal? The key can be found in the word itself: You sever connections.

To break or domesticate an animal you must first physically isolate the individual from the natural world. Then, you must cut all natural bonds to other animals by controlling sexual relations, interrupting the relationship between mother and child, and rupturing the structure of the extended family. You must alienate the animal from herself, so that she no longer expects her own will to control her own body. Finally, you must break the spirit, by humiliating and violating the animal in every possible way, including physical and sexual assault.

It's no accident that these are the same tactics used by abusive husbands to control their wives, or that analogous methods are used to bring wild plants under "cultivation." After all, "husbandry" refers to the breeding of plants and "livestock," while "grooms" are both breakers of horses and takers of brides.

We tend to think about sexism, speciesism, and environmental exploitation as separate, if sometimes intersecting or interlocking, problems. In truth, they are just different symptoms of the same injury.

While we don't have a word for this violation, we know it when we see it. It's the fault line running underneath all of the social and environmental disruptions that plague us and the planet. You can read all about it in Genesis or the platform of the Republican Party: Men have the right and the duty to subdue the earth, the animals, their own families, and the men of other faiths. You can see this ethos in action everywhere from the detention camps at Guantanamo Bay to the dead zone in the Chesapeake Bay.

At the heart of the problem is alienation, separation, dissociation. To imagine that you "own" a piece of land, you must first alienate yourself from it, psychologically tearing yourself out of the seamless fabric of your ecosystem in order to lay claim to part of it. In order to demarcate "your" land, you must create artificial boundaries, perhaps even erecting physical fences to separate it from the rest of the world. In creating and enforcing those borders you will probably hurt or scare animals and other people. To do so, you must dissociate yourself from your natural empathy for fellow beings.

To feel comfortable breaking the body or mind of another human or non-human animal, you must first wrench yourself out of the web of relationships that define ecosystems. Doing so necessarily culminates in disruptions to those systems.

To fail to perceive the detrimental ecological impact of your actions, particularly when your own health or life is threatened by the pollution or disruption you have created, you must divorce yourself from the evidence of your senses. Healthy animals notice dirty water or smoky air. Only a profoundly disoriented animal fails to respond to a perceptible change in climate.

Estrangement is both cause and consequence of the problem. We are cut off from the earth, other animals, each other, and ourselves. Those disconnections, in turn, allow us to do terrible things to the earth, other animals, each other, and ourselves. These actions increase the estrangement, and the cycle of violation and separation continues.

What started the cycle? Did it begin with the first "wife" or the first "livestock?" Was terror or hubris the motivation for that first enslavement? Did the story of "God the father"—alone in the sky, sacred and separate from his profane creations—predate and motivate the original denigration of the earth, or did men make up the story after the fact to rationalize what they had done?[8]

We may never be able to answer those questions about the origins of our disconnection but we can and must recognize and repair the ruptures that we have created within ourselves and in the world. We must learn to see, and act within our awareness of, the similar ways that women, plants, animals, and the planet are exploited and abused. We must recognize and cultivate our relationships with each other, with other animals, and with the ecosystems in which we are enmeshed. And we must make sure that our own hearts, minds, and hands are always connected. We must work to ensure our own basic integrity, so that what we think and feel and do are always consistent.

If breakage is the problem, then integrity is the answer. That means that we must embrace integrity as both end and means. That may mean using force to stop the violence.

4. Violence

Did the elephants who freed the antelopes commit violence? Some critics of radical environmental activism would say yes, since they tampered with locks and probably caused some property damage. But the very word "property" ought to give you a clue as to why such actions, whether undertaken by elephants or adolescents, ought not to be considered violent under any definition of the term.

Those who decry or defend "violence" in defense of the earth and animals often fail to first answer the question: What is violence? To adequately answer that question, one must attend to both concepts and context.

Words tend to reflect what most people mean when they say something. When most people say "violence," they are talking about some sort of *violation* by means of actual or threatened physical *force*. Both aspects—force and violation—must be present for an act to be considered violent. Passing a basketball involves physical force but is not violence. Forging a signature may cause emotional or economic injury but is not violence. Thus, in law as well as in popular imagination, there is a distinction between violence and justifiable use of force, as well as a distinction between violent and non-violent crime.

Most people consider intention when thinking about violence. Physical injuries caused accidentally are generally not considered the result of violence, unless the person who caused them could or should have known that they might occur. Similarly, acts that would be considered violently aggressive in some circumstances are considered to be justifiable use of force when undertaken in self-defense, unless the force used was excessive in relation to the threat.

The exceptions to the commonsense definition of violence, and the qualifications of those exceptions, highlight the importance of context, which is another factor that knee-jerk opponents and proponents of "violence" tend to neglect. Here, feminist ethics offer an avenue through what might seem like a jungle of ambiguity.

Like most women, many feminist ethicists tend to suspect invariable moral rules that leave no room for considerations of context. Thus, feminist viewpoints on nonviolence tend to be more nuanced and practical than abstract condemnations or defenses of "violence."

If we understand *violence* to be *injurious and unjustified use of force*, then we can never discern whether or not an act is violent apart from its context. We don't have to waste time arguing about abstractions because, as a matter of practical fact, violence always occurs within a material context. Furthermore, we can stop arguing about whether violence is ever okay. Justifiable use of force isn't violence. Instead of trying to justify "violence," we can turn attention instead to the rather more pressing problem of figuring out how much force is justified in defense of earth, plants, animals, and ourselves.

Where is the line between force and violence? We must attend carefully to that question. Violence is at the heart of the problems we seek to solve. Using violence to address those problems is like using genetic engineering of plants to solve the problem of pesticides. Adding fuel to the fire is not likely to put out the flames. At the same time, physical force often is required to defend ancient redwoods and baby seals from the chainsaws and clubs that menace them. In the long run, physical force may become more and more necessary to counteract the very great power of those who profit from the continued exploitation of people, plants, animals, and the earth herself.

In the context of the escalating environmental emergency, force may be necessary, but violence is never okay. Force is necessary when material problems require a physical solution that will not otherwise be forthcoming. Violence, as I have defined it, is intrinsically wrong and is particularly wrong-headed as a solution to problems that are founded in violence.

Where is the line between force and violence? That question can only be answered with reference to the details of the context in which it arises. An act that would be violent in one setting may be a justifiable use of force in another setting. Pushing a child so hard that she flies several feet in the air before hitting the ground is a justifiable, and perhaps even heroic, use of force when a little girl is standing in the path of an onrushing truck. But it would be severe child abuse if done by an angry parent at the head of a flight of stairs.

In contemplating the use of force in any given situation, we must ask first whether the action really is likely to result in a desired outcome. Next, we must ask whether the same outcome might be achieved as quickly and certainly (or, perhaps, even more quickly or certainly) by some other means. We also must ask whether the force contemplated is proportionate to the harm we are seeking to correct or prevent. Most people think that it would be okay to bash a man over the head, using potentially deadly force, if he were in the act of raping a child, but not if he were in the act of cheating a senior citizen out of $20.

Returning to the question that opened this section, is property damage violence? The question can only be answered by asking other questions. We must ask: What objects will be damaged? For what purpose? Using what kind of force? Will any living being be injured in any way? If the only potential "injury" is to "property rights," then I would argue that the act is not violent. Property rights are suspect within the worldview that holds that neither land nor animals are objects to be owned. In many instances, property rights are themselves violence or, at minimum, the result of past violence. The creation of "property" generally involves a process wherein land or animals are forcibly enclosed or wherein people or animals are alienated from the products of their labor. These are inherently violent processes, since they involve actual or threatened use of force to cause injury. Moreover, continuing violence is often needed to maintain property. From electrified fences around lakes to armed guards at grocery stores, the violence implicit in property is hidden in plain view every day.

Because violation of life is perhaps the most important cause of the problems that plague our planet, environmental activists and their apologists must take particular care to avoid a rhetoric of violence. Instead of reveling in militaristic terms that implicitly glorify violence, we must distinguish between legitimate use of force, and violence, which is always illegitimate. We can and should valorize those who dare to use justifiable force, putting their own bodies on the line in the process. We must not glorify those who use the plight of mother earth as an excuse for reckless aggression or selfish violence. By building strong relationships with each other, and with others who are working for earth and animal liberation, we will more easily see the difference between force and violence and better able to have the courage to use force when necessary, and the forbearance to always avoid violence.

5. Flower Power

All life depends on photosynthesis. People and all other animals depend on the bodies of plants for food, fuel, and shelter. People and all other animals also require the oxygen that is a by-product of the almost magical process by which plants convert light into food. Without plants, we could not live.

Without photosynthesis and its complement, photorespiration, plants could not live.

Photosynthesis requires light, water, and carbon dioxide in proper proportions.[9] Plants can die or are damaged by too much or too little light, water, or carbon dioxide. Despite the fact that our lives depend on it, humans have tampered with each of these essential elements of photosynthesis. Around the world, people have distorted and destroyed plant habitats by pumping, flooding, depleting, and tainting water; by cutting, burning, uprooting, and transplanting shade trees; and by poisoning the air that the plants need to breathe. At the same time, our collective folly has interfered with the global atmosphere. We have torn the protective mantle of the ozone layer, exposing the plants that sustain us to increased levels of the kind of ultraviolet light that can interfere with photosynthesis.[10]

Meanwhile, human activities such as burning fossil fuels have radically increased the amount of carbon dioxide in the atmosphere. The resulting climate changes will surely alter growing conditions such as temperature as well as availability of water. We don't know what impact the ever-increasing amount of carbon dioxide in the air that we share will have on plant photosynthesis and photorespiration, or in turn, what impact that will have on the availability of oxygen for the animals of the world.[11]

Like the spark of life itself, the energic exchange at the heart of photosynthesis cannot be faked or even fully explained. Scientists know, or believe that they know, quite a bit about *what* happens, but much remains unknown in the realms of *why* and *how*. Commonsense dictates that life-or-death mysteries be approached with hesitation and respect, yet some scientists are confronting the carbon dioxide conundrum not with more caution, but with ever greater recklessness. Even though we don't really know how or why plants balance photosynthesis (in which they consume carbon dioxide and release oxygen) and photorespiration (in which they consume oxygen and release carbon dioxide), some scientists intend to tamper with plants' genes to reduce photorespiration.[12]

Thanks to the promiscuity of pollen, both food crops and wild plants already have been contaminated by the genes of plants engineered to resist pesticides and it's possible that the genes of plants engineered to produce pharmaceutical or industrial chemicals also have gone astray.[13] Imagine what could happen if genes engineered to interfere with the mechanics of photosynthesis were to cross into wild plant populations.

The idea of using genetic engineering to tamper with the process upon which virtually all plant and animal life depends is an extreme case of the everyday hubris that leads humans to assume that they know best. Given the length of the list of things that seemed like a good idea at the time but turned out to be disastrous, this is a remarkably foolish assumption.

Since human animals are responsible for the ecological emergency in which we find ourselves, we do have an especial obligation to stop the violence, undo whatever damage can be undone, and ease the suffering of those who have been harmed. However, we must do so humbly, remembering that other species have a vested interest in our efforts, and rejecting the preposterous idea that we alone know what needs to be done.

So much destruction has devolved from our failure to attend to and act in concert with other species. We neither look nor listen carefully enough to perceive the patterns and rhythms of the actions of other species as they maintain balances with each other and their environments.

Our so-called "scientific" method requires us to deliberately narrow our range of perception, accepting as valid information only decontextualized "data" falling within the preset parameters circumscribed by our own experimental methodology. Most often, this means that we simply do not perceive anything that we did not previously conceive. Any stray sensations or ideas that penetrate this powerful perceptual filter are laughed off as illusory, brushed off as irrelevant, or (if all else fails) warped into a form that fits our fixed ideas. The extent to which ostensibly objective scientists have twisted their perceptions to fit their preconceptions would be comical if it weren't so tragic.[14]

Our ideas about plants are rigid and dismissive. We demonstrate contempt by both belittling plants and tinkering with their genetic integrity, as if they were our playthings rather than the source of all that we need to survive.[15] Such an attitude is only possible in the context of radical dissociation. We are so estranged from the rest of the world that we don't recognize our place in it. We think of ourselves as the owners and bosses of those without whom we could not survive. Anyone less alienated from the natural world might be mystified by our unjustified ideas about human singularity.

Plants and other animals appear better able than we to perceive and respond to each other's needs in a mutually gratifying manner. Countless animal pollinators and seed distributors help to propagate the plants that feed them without, apparently, feeling the need to claim credit for the process or to assert ownership of the resulting seedlings. For their part, plants have managed to feed themselves and the rest of us despite all manner of impediments imposed by people.

Plants are not passive, however inert they may seem to the human eye. Probing, probing, probing into the ground, roots seek out resources, break through barriers, and share information with other plants. Reaching, reaching, reaching toward the light, limbs and vines position leaves so that they can do what we all need them to do: transubstantiate light into food. While we do not—and may never—know anything about plant intentionality, we do know that plants are, indeed, actively responding to pesticides, genetic modification, and other assaults on their bodies.

What do plants know? What do they feel? Do they have projects? Are their efforts to counteract the harms done by humans intentional? Does it matter? What can we learn from them either way?

Some fundamentalist Christians laughingly dismiss the idea that people make choices or in any way control their own fates. To them, it seems self-evident that God—and only God—makes choices. Whatever they might *seem* to be doing, everyone else is just dumbly acting out God's will.

Most people take a similar view concerning the self-determination of plants and non-human animals. To them it seems self-evident that people—and only people—make choices. Whatever else they might *seem* to be doing, everyone else is just dumbly acting out laws of nature.

Our constructions of such concepts as consciousness and purpose have a built-in bias favoring animals, in general, and human animals, in particular. We have a hard time even imagining how awareness or intention might be realized in beings very different from ourselves. That's okay. We don't need to know or even be able to imagine everything. As long as we recognize that there are limits to our knowledge and imagination, and that things may be true even though we cannot perceive or prove them, then we can avoid the folly of unfounded assumptions loosely rooted in ignorance.

Are plants that participate in happy mutualisms with insects, fungi, or other plants *cooperating* with other beings? Are the "superweeds" that have evolved in response to pesticides trying to tell us something? In the end, what we think we know about such questions is irrelevant. We can and should learn from what plants are *doing*, taking guidance from the measures they have taken to preserve themselves and their ecosystems. Even if we don't know what the trees are "thinking," we can still follow their lead.

6. Terrorists

When US Secretary of Defense Donald Rumsfeld tried to hold a press conference in New Delhi in 2003, the press corps were greeted by scores of jeering Macaques monkeys, who shouted at them from the window ledges of surrounding buildings, literally making a mockery of the event.[16] In New Delhi, monkeys regularly break into the offices of the Defense Ministry, rifling through file cabinets and otherwise interfering with business as usual.

As with the witnesses to the antelope rescue, witnesses to these events know what they are seeing. "Monkeys are very furious," said Ujagar Singh, spokesman for the Patiala district in India, where pink-faced Rhesus monkeys have uprooted lawns and trashed houses.[17]

If the frequency of news reports are any guide, direct action by animals is on the rise. Elephants, apes, and monkeys in various regions of Africa and Asia are refusing to cede to the ideas that people have about who belongs where and who owns what. From baboons in South Africa, who break into houses not only to take food but also to pull clothes out of closets and urinate on them, to elephants in Indonesia, who have returned again and again to destroy the cash crops on a particular plantation, non-human animals in many places are actively contesting the privileges claimed by human beings.[18] Meanwhile, attacks by sharks, leopards, and even elephants are on the rise worldwide.[19]

Wildlife officials, and other experts in the affected regions, are unanimous in their assessment of the cause of the apparent increase in human-animal conflicts: habitat loss due to pollution or other human intrusions. Reading reports of animal responses to human activities, it seems to me that they can be divided into three categories: (1) incursions and attacks for the purpose of obtaining food or other necessities; (2) destruction, defacement and/or occupation of structures and locations claimed by people; and (3) expressions of discontent. The first category is relatively self-evident and includes some, but not all, of the attacks on the bodies of people. The third category includes acts against people or property that appear to have no material purpose other than the expression of anger or frustration. While we must be careful in relegating acts to this category, since there may be material ends that we are not able to discern, we must also remember that people are not the only animals who have feelings. Monkeys who engage in seemingly senseless acts of property destruction may well, like some human eco-activists, have mixed motives that include both emotional and rational aims.

Acts falling into the second category of animal reactions to human activities often are equivalent to the work undertaken by radical environmental activists. Indian elephants who repeatedly demolish cash crop plantations remind me of Indian farmers who demolish fields of genetically modified crops. Both are using the most direct method to remove noxious human introductions from the environment.

Animals have taken even more assertive measures to protect their habitats from human exploitation. I think, for example, of a region in Sierra Leone, which had been controlled by animals during a recent war but into which people now wish to relocate; the elephants have fought back, chasing people away and killing those who do not flee. Similarly, elephants killed 130 people in two years in the Indian state of Assam.

When animals use deadly force to protect their homes, should their acts be considered "violent?" Recalling the number of extinctions due to habitat loss, not to mention the number of individual animals who have starved or otherwise perished when their homes have been invaded or polluted by people, the concept of justifiable force in self-defense comes to mind. Many animals also confront hunters who deliberately seek to kill them, sometimes for food but sometimes for fur or trinkets. Hunters have found ever more insidious and violent ways to kill elephants, including jackfruit bombs, poisoned salt licks and water holes, electrified foot paths, and nets made out of nails.[20] Should we really be surprised when some elephants elect to fight back?

People almost always kill animals by some means when they fence off, cultivate, or build on land. When the new construction or cultivation is not, strictly speaking, necessary, ought not those killings be considered aggressive violence?

When, as is so often the case, poverty forces people into places formerly controlled by animals, then tragedy is sure to follow. One way or another, somebody who doesn't deserve to die is going to end up dead. People in the aggregate already have more than we need but because resources are not shared equitably, starving people often end up competing with starving animals on the outskirts of so-called civilization. This is why the struggle for earth and animals will never be won in the absence of social justice and *vice versa*.

When animals resist human expansionism, they often face harsh reprisals. In India and elsewhere, villagers have poisoned and speared elephants in retaliation for crop raids.[21] Despite government protections, baboons have been shot in South Africa, and monkeys have been killed *en masse* and dumped in sacks in India. Because killing monkeys is illegal in India, the Punjab state has instituted a monkey jail. As of 2004, more than a dozen monkeys were imprisoned for life in a 15 by 15 cell, some for "crimes" no more serious than destruction of property.

Like human rebels, animals who refuse to respect property rights or other concepts invented by people are increasingly called "terrorists" or accused of creating "terror" whether or not they have engaged in acts that might be considered violent. In the Punjabi struggle between the people and the monkeys, one local newspaper referred to a captured animal as a "terrorist monkey." Similarly, local news media report that elephants in the states of Assam and Tripura invade human settlements not only to find food but also "to create terror."

When people rise up against their oppressors, solidarity movements spring up around the world. When people are imprisoned for acts of resistance, whether these be in defense of earth, animal, or human rights, like-minded activists extend comfort and support to them. In India, Maneka Gandhi has stood up for the imprisoned monkeys, but otherwise, overt extensions of solidarity to animal rebels have not been forthcoming from animal advocates or other environmental activists.

Dare we step forward to say that rebel elephants are as deserving of solidarity as Zapatistas or Irish Catholics? Dare we assert that monkeys locked up by people are political prisoners and that their indefinite detention is just as unjustified as the permanent imprisonment of suspected "terrorists" now contemplated by the US government? Shouldn't we support all defenders of the earth, regardless of their species?

Officials have implored citizens not to feed the monkeys who occupy government buildings in New Delhi, but people come weekly, bearing bananas, anyway. Such common-sense expressions of material and moral support are heartening and ought to be emulated wherever animals are under fire for transgressing human rules.

One need not live near elephants or monkeys to find opportunities to express solidarity. In the US state of Virginia, for example, turkey vultures—who serve a vital ecological function in addition to being intrinsically valuable as individuals—have been literally under fire for their failure to respect suburban notions of cleanliness. With the aid of the federal government, local officials have shot these allegedly protected birds and hung them by their feet from the trees (purportedly to scare off others of their species) solely in order to spare humans the trouble of washing bird dropping from their cars and barbecue equipment.[22] In the state of Louisiana, bees bit back when children threw rocks at their hive. 40,000 bees—who also serve a vital ecological function in addition to being intrinsically valuable as individuals—were killed and another 80,000 captured in retaliation for the stings suffered by the aggressive children.[23]

We can and should support non-human rebels, whether they are fighting for their own lives or for the ecosystems that they share with other beings. As with the plants, we must also seek to learn what we can from the patterns of their actions. Escalation of attacks, property destruction, or other rebellious acts in a particular region may signal that the animals in the area, like those who sense the onrush of the Tsunami, may be more aware than we of impending ecological disaster. They also may know better than we what needs to be done to arrest or mitigate the detrimental effects of ongoing human activities.

7. Morning

"In the course of history, there comes a time when humanity is called to shift to a new level of consciousness...That time is now."
Wangari Maathai[24]

None of us evolved in isolation, whether as individuals or as a species. Evolution always occurs in context and relationship with others. For example, humans and dogs co-evolved. Like plants and pollinators, or ants and aphids, the progenitors of dogs and humans got together for mutual benefit. For all we know, our species might not have survived were it not for the additional reproductive success we gained through the association of proto-humans and proto-dogs. At night they helped to keep us safe and warm. But then, in what must be among the most brazen betrayals in natural history, humans turned around and made slaves out of their trusted friends.[25]

The good news is that evolution is ongoing. We can choose another path. We can recognize our kinship with other beings. We can recognize without being terrified by our dependence on them, and act accordingly.

If we really want to wage a war on "terror," then we need to learn to be less afraid. We don't need to enclose or control those upon whom our lives depend.

If we can recover our kinship with our non-human relatives, then we won't have to hide behind barricades, because we won't be alone anymore.

Can we do it? Yes. Will we do it? I don't know. I do know that we are not alone in the struggle to save the earth. The sooner we see that and act accordingly, the sooner we can begin to end our own awful estrangement and help to heal those we have hurt.

The current situation is more dangerous and perverse than any nightmare. Yet most people, including many who consider themselves to be environmentalists, slumber fitfully within the uneasy dream of human singularity. For the sake of the rhinos and the redwoods, and the canaries and the cornflowers too, I hope we wake up soon.

Notes

1. "Elephant unlatches gate to save South African antelopes." AFP. 8 April 2003; "Elephants on a rescue mission," South African Press Association, 9 April 2003.

2. Nelson, Sue, "Did Animals Have Quake Warning?" BBC, 31 December 2004.

3. Scheer, Roddy, "Researchers Predict Massive Avian Decline," E Magazine (December 2004).

4. Threatened Plants of the World by UNEP World Conservation Monitoring Centre (2001). See <http:// www.wcmc.org.uk /species/plants/overview.htm> for more information.

5. See the World Resources Institute online <http://www.wri.org> for more information.

6. For examples of the latest traumas endured by animals due to human impact on their habitats, see Coghlan, Andy, "Pollution Triggers Bizarre Behavior in Animals," New Scientist 01 (September 2004).

7. Only tactics that have an immediate impact on some element of the target problem qualify as direct action. Indirect action seeks change via more circuitous routes, such as seeking to change citizens' minds in the hope that they will, in turn, change their voting behavior, and that this will, in turn, lead to changed government policies. Rent strikes, boycotts, blockades, and demonstrations that substantially interfere with business as usual are direct action. Petition drives, letters to editors, community education, and demonstrations that are limited to symbolic expressions of opinion are indirect action. Flamboyant transgressions may be radical civil disobedience without being direct action. Sabotage that substantially interferes with ecologically destructive activities may be considered direct action. Sabotage that expresses the emotions of the activist but does not significantly prevent, hinder, mitigate, stop, or heal the effects of harmful activities must be considered indirect action. Whether such sabotage may be considered successful indirect action depends upon whether they really do have the intended indirect impact (such as changing people's minds or inspiring them to change their behaviors). For more on the critical distinction between direct and symbolic actions, see my articles "Marching in Circles" in *Freezerbox* at <http://www.freezerbox.com/archive/article.asp?id=264> and "Let's Put on a Show!" in *Press Action* at <http://www.pressaction.com/news/weblog/full_article/jones03142004>. Successful social change strategies generally require a coordinated combination of direct and indirect action tactics. For more on that in the context of animal liberation, see my chapter "Mothers with Monkeywrenches." In *Terrorists or Freedom Fighters? Reflections on the Liberation of Animals*, edited by Steven Best and Anthony J. Nocella, II. New York: Lantern Books, 2004.

8. The foundational texts of all of the patriarchal "faiths"—which many ecofeminists, like me, believe to be misogynist and speciesist political propaganda dressed up as spirituality—explicitly mandate the exploitation of women, earth, and animals. Like the violence that they promote, these ideologies are part of the problem and thus cannot be part of the solution. That is the reason why so many radical feminists, eco-activists, and animal liberationists embrace either atheism or earth-based spirituality.

9. Different plants have evolved to grow under a broad range of circumstances, including extremes ranging from deserts to rainforests. However, each plant requires a certain balance of water and light in order to thrive. Desert plants can drown if given too much water, while shade-loving plants can die from too much direct sunlight. Similarly, plants vary in their reactions to levels of carbon dioxide.

10. See the Australian Academy of Science primer on ozone depletion at <http://www.science.org.au/nova/004/004key.htm> for more information.

11. See the International Council for Local Environmental Initiatives briefing on climate change at <http://www.iclei.org/SB1.htm> for more information on the impact of increased levels of carbon dioxide in the atmosphere. See the chapter on photosynthesis in *Plants* by Irene Ridge (Oxford University Press, 2002) for a detailed discussion of the interaction of photosynthesis, photorespiration, and atmospheric carbon dioxide.

12. See *The Mystery of Photorespiration* at <http://amos.indiana.edu/library/scripts/photorespiration.html> for a brief and easy to understand example of one of the mysteries associated with photosynthesis.

13. Pearce, Fred, "Crops 'Widely Contaminated' By Genetically Modified DNA," *New Scientist* (23 February, 2004).

14. One thinks, for example, of "Drapetomia," which was the term coined in 1851 by Dr. Samuel Cartwright for the "disease" that led slaves to run away. See Randall, Vernallia R. *An Early History—African American Mental Health.* <http://academic.udayton.edu/health/01status/mental01.htm> for more examples of tragically silly "scientific" ideas about race.

15. Male attitudes toward women are remarkably similar to human attitudes toward plants. In both instances, the denigrated being has life-giving capabilities not possessed by the allegedly superior being, who depends upon the subordinated being for the continuation of life. In both instances, invasive scientific tinkering with the bodies of the denigrated beings stands in the stead of healthy respect for their reproductive capabilities. While feminist scholars and activists have focused increasing attention on the linkages between exploitation of women and exploitation of animals, we've not yet broken ground for the digging that needs to be done to get to the root of the earth-plant-animal-women conjunction.

16. Wang Andrew, "Monkeys Terrorize India Workers,Tourists," AP, 2 November 2003.

17. Barker, Kim, "Pesky, Protected Monkeys Doing Hard Time in Jail," *Chicago Tribune*, 16 September 2004.

18. See "Baboons on Rampage in South African Town," *AFP,* 16 June 2004, and "Indonesian worker escapes rampaging elephants," *New Straits Times*, 26 December, 2001.

19. See "Dead Zone May Boost Shark Attacks," BBC, 4 August 2004, Lengrade, Jayashree, "Wild Leopards on Human Killing Spree in Bombay," Reuters, 5 June 2004, and "Sierra Leone Villagers Flee Deadly Elephants," Reuters, 29 July 2004.

20. Ittaman, Shali, "Hunters Find Ingenious Ways to Kill Elephants," *Hindustan Times*, 1 May 2003.

21. See Hussain, Wasbir, "Angry Villages in India's Northeast Kill Five Elephants for Raiding Crops," AP, 11 October 2002.

22. "Virginia City Trying to Scare Away Vultures," AP, 3 December 2001.

23. "Kids Plus Rocks Equals 120,000 Angry Bees," Reuters, 16 August 2004.

24. Wangari Maathai recently won the Nobel Peace Prize for planting trees. She is the first African woman and the first environmentalist to win the prize, and she did it by founding and maintaining—despite vehement and at time violent opposition—an uncompromising program of direct action. For detailed information about Wangari Maathai's work, see her book, *The Green Belt Movement: Sharing the Approach and the Experience*. New York: Lantern Books, 2004. Two wide-ranging and very interesting interviews with Maathai may be accessed online at <http://www.satyamag.com/jul04/maathai.html> and <http://www.motherjones.com/news/ qa/2005/01/wangari_maathai.html> courtesy of *Satya* and *Mother Jones* magazines.

25. As Raul Valadez Azúa recently wrote in the official publication the *Asociación Mexicana de Médicos Veterinarios Especialistas en Pequeñas Especies*, "an important process of familiarity and posterior coevolution between *Canis lupus* and *Homo erectus*" lasted for about 40,000 years until *Homo sapiens* came along and "took advantage of familiarity" to capture puppies and begin the process we euphemistically call "domestication."

Part VII

SOCIAL MOVEMENTS AND ALLIANCE POLITICS

"There will never be a new world order until women are a part of it."
Alice Paul

"Hope and resiliency. These are your greatest strengths. We can work together. Sisters and brothers, all of one human family. Your generation and mine." *Leonard Peltier*

"They came down on us because we had a grassroots, real people's revolution, complete with the programs, complete with the unity, complete with the working coalitions, where we crossed racial lines."
Bobby Seale

"The aim is to listen and learn about the struggles, the resistance and rebel movements, support them and bind them together to build a national anti-capitalist, leftist program." *Subcomandante Marcos*

Ancestors & Angels

Drew Dellinger

I write words to catch up to the ancestors.
An angel told me the only way
to walk through fire
without getting burned
is to become fire.

Some days angels whisper
in my ear as I walk
down the street and I fall in love
with every person I meet,
and I think, maybe this
could be a bliss
like when Dante met
Beatrice.

Other days all I see
is my collusion
with illusion.
Ghosts of projection
masquerading
as the radiant angel
of love.

You know I feel like
the ancestors
brought us together.
I feel like the ancestors
brought us here and they
expect great things.

They
expect us to say what
we think and
live how

we feel and follow the hard paths
that bring us near joy.
They expect us
to nurture
all the children.

I write poems to welcome angels
and conjure ancestors.
I pray to the angels of politics
and love.

I pray for justice sake
not to be relieved of my frustrations,
at the same time burning sage
and asking ancestors for patience.

I march with the people
to the border
between nations
where
everything stops
except
the greed of corporations.

Thoughts like comets
calculating the complexity
of the complicity.

There is so much noise in the oceans
the whales can't hear each other.
We're making them crazy,
driving dolphins insane.
What kind of ancestors
are we?

Thoughts like comets
leaving craters
in the landscape of my consciousness.

I pray to ancestors and angels:

Meet me in the garden.
Meet me where spirit walks softly
in the cool of the evening.
Meet me in the garden
under the wings of the bird
of many colors.
Meet me
in the garden
of your longing.

Every breath
is a pilgrimage.

Every
breath
is a pilgrimage
to you.

I pray
to be
a conduit.

An angel told me:

the only way
to walk through fire—

become fire.

Armed Struggle, Guerilla Warfare, and the Social Movement Influences on "Direct Action"

Ann Hansen

My name is Ann Hansen. I am a 51-year-old Canadian woman who is currently on parole until the prison system has personally viewed my dead body. I was sentenced to "life" for conspiracy to rob an armored car guard, the British Columbia Hydro and Litton bombings, firebombing a Red Hot Video porn store, unlawful possession of explosives and weapons, auto theft, and possession of stolen property. I was arrested on January 20th, 1983 along with four others and charged with these "offences" for actions we carried out as members of an urban guerilla group called Direct Action.

As the name would indicate, our urban guerilla group identified ideologically with anarchism, and as such, we were struggling to help create a society in which power would rest as much as possible in the hands of the people. We were one of the first guerilla groups in North America to develop a critique not only of capitalism, but also socialism. Unlike most urban guerilla groups and social movements during the seventies and eighties, we did not blindly accept the concept that technology, progress, development, science, and material wealth are good in and of themselves. We also did not share the socialist view of the state as a revolutionary vehicle for the people. In our analysis the state is a repressive apparatus that concentrates power and decision-making in the hands of a small number of people who will inevitably become corrupted whether they be peasants, working class, middle class, or ruling class.

In retrospect, if I were to label the political analysis of our guerilla group, Direct Action, it would share more in common with green anarchism than any other ideology. Our politics evolved from our involvement with traditional native people who showed us how western thinking—in the form of patriarchy, capitalism, and even socialism—tended to objectify life on this planet. The traditional native peoples taught us how the objectification of life inherent in the philosophies of capitalism and socialism

340

reduced all life to mere material value, thus reinforcing one of the worst aspects of human nature: greed. Practically speaking this means all life is exploited, reducing the environment to a "natural resource" to be "developed" for profit. Animals, birds, fish, and insects become "products," "livestock," "pets," "game," and "pests." Women become sex objects to be exploited to sell "products," while humans in general become "consumers" and "producers." According to this way of thinking, the most important criterion in determining human value is a person's productivity within the economic system, and so "the unemployed" and "welfare cases" are considered a burden.

Our politics were also deeply rooted in the feminist, environmental, and anarchist movements of the 1970s. Many radicals' politics had evolved from these movements during the 1970s, however we decided to introduce a more militant practice by starting an urban guerilla group modelled after the western European guerilla groups such as the Red Army Faction (RAF) and the Red Brigades, as well as American guerilla groups such as the Black Liberation Army (BLA) and the Symbionese Liberation Army (SLA). These groups had, in turn, been modelled after the various anti-imperialist armed liberation movements active throughout most of the colonized world. In other words, our political ideology was patterned after the social movements of the Native peoples, the feminists, the environmentalists, and the anarchists, while our political practice drew inspiration from the various urban guerilla groups active globally. This created an interesting mix of armed struggle without the nationalism, vanguards, Marxism, or materialism so prevalent in the vast majority of active urban guerilla movements during the sixties and seventies.

Within the social context of North America, we didn't think that militant actions were *more* important than legal protest, but considering the virtual vacuum in terms of militancy, we decided this was the area in which we would have the most impact. We were not under any illusions that Direct Action on its own would spark a massive revolutionary movement, but we hoped that our actions in concert with the protests of the radical movement would contribute to building a stronger revolutionary movement. Even though the size and development of the revolutionary forces in Canada were miniscule at best, we did not think that controversial militant actions would inhibit them. On the contrary, history has shown that militant actions can be a catalyst for growth in the early phases of a revolutionary movement's development. We could talk and write about militancy until the proverbial cows came home, and it would still just be talk, so after much soul searching, we decided to *be* militants.

Considering once again how tiny the pockets of individual revolutionaries were in Canada during this period, we decided if we wanted to avoid being put under surveillance and then arrested by the police, it would be necessary to develop an underground clandestine organization in order to acquire the funds and identification needed to plan and carry out actions. In other words, the kind of large scale, high-tech actions we were planning would necessitate an illegal, underground lifestyle, otherwise the police would have no problem identifying who we were, and putting an end to our activities. We spent several years developing our analysis, and honing the skills we would need to live clandestinely and carry out high-tech actions.

In our analysis of capitalism, value is only placed on property and money. Unless human, animal, or environmental life could be transformed into some kind of monetary value it was considered useless. In the face of terrorist attacks targeting humans, despite the tears and fears displayed by corporate and political leaders in the media, the only time they really seem to respond is when such attacks threaten the loss of revenue, shares, investments, and wealth.

Time and again, we witnessed corporations pulling out of regions where their investments were in jeopardy. Time and again, we witnessed governments that were unable to protect corporate interests in their region topple. Time and again, we saw corporations make decisions based on share prices. And time and again, we saw politicians sing to whatever corporate piper was playing the tune. Based on these observations, we decided to direct our campaign against property.

This decision was based more on efficacy than on ethics. If a person wants to immobilize a car, they wouldn't damage the rear view mirror or the upholstery, they would ruin the engine; the most expensive and most difficult part of the car to repair. Using this analogy, if Canada's principal role within the global economy is a supplier of natural resources, then targeting those industries would be the best way to destabilize the Canadian economy. This is the strategy we decided to pursue.

Although this was our basic strategy, tactically there was a complex set of criteria that also had to be taken into account. For example, in order to gain public sympathy, it would be more effective to target an issue around which a popular struggle had already mobilized so people would understand why we had carried out the action. We could enhance the effectiveness of a popular movement by acting in concert with it, rather than in isolation and potentially hindering its development.

This leads to the next important criterion: timing. Timing would be critical because if we acted prematurely around a certain issue, the popular movement would see us as usurping their struggle rather than enhancing it. Therefore it was important that we acted only after the popular movement had exhausted all the legal avenues at their disposal, and could see that resorting to militant actions was the only avenue left. In some cases, this also meant waiting until a campaign of civil disobedience had also proven ineffective. In general it is important to use illegal, militant actions only as a last resort after all possible peaceful and legal measures have been exhausted, because the repercussions for everyone in the popular movement are always severe. If the popular movement does not see clearly that there is no other option left than militancy, then they may resent and blame the militants for the inevitable repression from the state.

In May 1982, Direct Action began its campaign by bombing four transformers at the Dunsmuir hydro substation. This substation was part of a British Columbia (BC) government mega-project called the Cheekeye-Dunsmuir Transmission Line. This was a one billion dollar project to build a hydro line from the BC mainland, under the Georgia Strait to Vancouver Island in order to allow for the expansion of the privately owned pulp and paper industry on the island. BC Hydro planned to fund the construction of this line by borrowing taxpayers' money in the form of pension plan funds. It would also involve cutting a huge swath of land along the beautiful coastline and spraying it with defoliants.

Ever since the inception of this plan, a number of different groups in the province had mobilized against it, including citizens living along the route of the line, native groups, unions, the teachers' federation, as well as people living on Vancouver Island who were opposed to the expansion of the pulp and paper industry. They were organized under the umbrella group, the Cheekeye-Dunsmuir Alliance, who spearheaded a campaign of letter writing, petitions, demonstrations, eventually culminating in civil disobedience actions during the summer of 1981. Citizens had taken to pulling up surveyor's stakes along the transmission route, and were blocking bulldozers from clearing the land. This was a popular struggle but unfortunately, by the spring of 1982, BC Hydro had begun installing hydro towers and transformers in substations along the route. They were in the final phases of construction with no end in sight.

Direct Action decided to blow up the transformers, only after the movement had failed to stop its construction, but before it was electrified. Our goals were to cause as much damage to the transformers as possible without injuring anyone or causing extreme discomfort to the people whose sympathies we were trying to win. An electrical blackout would have alienated the general public from our cause. After the smoke cleared, Direct Action destroyed the four transformers and an oil pumping station causing more than four million dollars in damage.

During the early 1980s, the anti-nuclear movement had been building a national campaign against Canada's role in the development of the cruise missile. This new weapon in the American nuclear arsenal was in the final phases of manufacture, and was about to be tested on Canadian soil. Nationally, a broad-based group, Operation Dismantle had been organizing public awareness campaigns and demonstrations, and in Toronto, the Cruise Missile Conversion Project (CMCP) and the Alliance for Non-Violent Action (ANVA) had been leafleting the workers at the Litton Systems plant where the guidance system for the cruise was being manufactured. They organized blockades of the plant and tried to convince the workers to pressure management to convert the plant to the production of peaceful technology. They also organized demonstrations and civil disobedience actions.

A Gallup Poll at the time indicated that 52% of Canadians were opposed to Canada's role in the manufacture and testing of the cruise missile.

Even within the reigning Liberal Party, a survey in April 1983 found that of 146 Liberal MPs, six opposed the cruise tests and another 115 refused to state their position. Their silence spoke volumes. Despite public opposition, the Canadian government signed agreements to test the cruise, and gave Litton Systems $48 million in grants and interest-free loans under "the corporate welfare" program from the Defense Industries Production Department, known as DIP.

By the fall of 1982, Direct Action decided to sabotage the Litton plant in an attempt to deter any further investment by the American mother plant, and to cause significant financial damage to the plant itself. It appeared as though the popular campaign to stop the manufacture of the guidance system, and the testing of the cruise on Canadian soil had failed.

On October 14th, 1982, Direct Action caused $4 million in damage to the Litton plant when a van filled with explosives detonated during the night. Unfortunately, when the bomb squad arrived *en masse*, the electronic frequency from their radio transmissions set off the electronic timing device, causing the bomb to explode twelve minutes prematurely. Despite numerous precautions to avoid injuries—such as driving the van across a flood lit lawn, parking against the most visible building to the security guards, leaving an unarmed stick of dynamite with a warning note and instructions, and phoning in a bomb threat with instructions—seven people were injured in the bombing. Direct Action issued an apology for the injuries and took responsibility in that we should never have put a bomb in a location that relied on authority figures clearing buildings and blocking roads to secure the safety of the public. Although this was a very serious error, mistakes are inevitable and we can't let our fear of making them paralyze the movement. Remaining passive in the face of today's global human and environmental destruction will create deeper scars than those resulting from the mistakes we will inevitably make by taking action.

After returning to BC in the fall of 1982, we encountered women who had been organizing to pressure the government to close down a franchise of violent pornography outlets, known as Red Hot Video, that within a year had expanded from one store to thirteen. This franchise distributed videos that had been pirated across the border from the United States. There was evidence to support the accusation that many of these videos were not dramatizations but, in fact, were real depictions of women in the sex trade who had been kidnapped and filmed being raped, and subjected to forced enemas. The women in these videos were seen clearly objecting to painful, violent acts, leaving no doubt in the viewer's mind that there was nothing consensual about it.

The women's movement in BC had tried every legal means at their disposal to force the government to act. They had invited the police to public screenings of the most violent videos available to demonstrate that their distribution violated the Motion Pictures Act and various hate crime laws. In response, the Attorney-General's office explained that the Motion Pictures Act did not refer to the magnetic storing of film, and that "gender" was not classified as an identifiable group under the hate crime laws. Understandably the women's community interpreted these explanations as the government's excuse to do nothing, and continued organizing demonstrations, petitions, and letter-writing campaigns directed at their members of parliament.

The government and justice system's unwillingness to respond led some women to approach the women of Direct Action to participate with them in a series of arsons aimed at burning down some of the Red Hot Videos. On the night of November 22nd, 1982, three separate groups of three women, each calling themselves the Wimmin's Fire Brigade, simultaneously fire-bombed three Red Hot Video outlets. One store was successfully burnt to the ground, another was partially burned, and a third attempt was aborted because a police car drove by just as they were about to throw some Molotov cocktails.

A few months after the Wimmin's Fire Brigade action, the five members of Direct Action were arrested. On the same day, in a raid whose timing was oddly coincidental, the RCMP charged the Victoria Red Hot Video store with three counts of distributing obscene material. Many activists believed the timing of these raids signified that the police felt compelled to lay charges or risk appearing less effective in dealing with violent pornography than the Wimmin's Fire Brigade.

In the aftermath of Direct Action and the Wimmin's Fire Brigade's 1982 campaigns, a number of popular myths were dispelled surrounding militant direct action. There is a commonly held view promoted by the mass media and perpetrated by the pacifist factions of the radical movement, that militant direct action has the effect of alienating the public from getting involved in issues, and marginalizes those involved from the mainstream. Consequently this myth supports the widely held belief that militant direct action is ineffective in "winning" a campaign, and will only serve to stimulate state repression that will inevitably result in the withering away of the popular movement.

The bombing of the Dunsmuir substation did very little to stop the completion of the Cheekeye-Dunsmuir transmission line. The line was electrified two months behind schedule, but in reality this is par for the course in terms of any type of mega-project construction. The most obvious contribution the bombing made to the movement against resource mega-projects was in heightening the media coverage and stimulating the debate around militant direct action. Considering the Cheekeye-Dunsmuir project was in its final stages of completion, and the popular movement was waning, the repression in the wake of the bombing had little impact on the Cheekeye-Dunsmuir Alliance.

However, the impact of the Litton bombing was much clearer. Even though this bombing was as controversial as they come due to the injury of innocent civilians, the numbers of people in attendance at demonstrations and protests in the weeks immediately following the bombing dramatically increased. Two weeks after the bombing, in Ottawa on October 30th, 1982, fifteen thousand people showed up at the largest anti-nuclear demonstration in Canadian history. And a month after the bombing, over seven hundred people showed up for a demonstration and civil disobedience action at Litton, despite heavy police propaganda regarding the repression the activists should anticipate.

Attendance in the mainstream anti-nuclear group, Operation Dismantle tripled in the year following the bombing. Most notably, the president of Litton Systems, Canada, Ronald Keating, stated in a *Globe and Mail* article that they had lost the contract to build the guidance system for an advanced version of the cruise missile due to the "protesters and the bombing." It is important to stress that the failure of Litton Systems, Canada to win this contract was not due to the bombing alone, but rather to the combination of the massive protests in concert with the militant direct action.

By far the most successful action was the Red Hot Video firebombing by the Wimmin's Fire Brigade. Within a year of the fire-bombings, the franchise had been whittled down from thirteen stores to only one. Success could also be measured in terms of popular support. In the days following the fire-bombings, radio phone-in shows devoted to the fire-bombings were inundated with supportive calls. Letters in the editorial sections of the newspapers also weighed in heavily in support of the action. Even the BC Federation of Women issued a statement articulating support for the motives of the action. The most obvious sign of public support was the large number of women who would show up at demonstrations, wearing red plastic fire hats and claiming to be members of the WFB. After the police raid on the Victoria store on January 20th, 1983, the Red Hot Video stores that hadn't already closed down, or changed their names or moved out of the province, were crippled in legal fees due to the ongoing series of raids by the RCMP.

The success of the Wimmin's Fire Brigade is indicative of the kind of militant direct action that is most effective in the North American political climate characterized by a relatively tiny revolutionary movement amidst a sea of privileged people who, by and large, identify as free and supportive of western "democracy." The Wimmin's Fire Brigade was successful because it acted around an issue that the vast majority of people supported, and used tactics with which ordinary people could identify.

I would suggest that this is the kind of tactical militant direct action that would be best used in today's climate as well, since little has changed since the early 1980s in terms of North American mass consciousness and the objective conditions of relative wealth and freedom. A militant direct action campaign initiated around issues with which the popular movement can already identify is more likely to be supported. This means the grassroots movement has to do its homework, educate the public, and use all the legal means at its disposal before launching into a militant direct action campaign.

Militant direct action using low-tech forms such as arson and property destruction, with which the average person can identify, is also far more likely to be supported than high-tech actions such as those necessitating explosives, robberies, and false identification. It is hard to attract militants to carry out actions if they have to live clandestinely in miniscule groups completely isolated from the movement, while trying to survive in a vast sea of hostile people. On a psychological level, it is a very unhealthy lifestyle leading to mistakes; on a political level, underground militants will feel isolated and find it difficult to communicate with their supporters, making it difficult to make enlightened decisions about future actions.

In the new millennium of the western world, successful groups using militant direct action share some common principles, tactics, and structures that also characterized the Wimmin's Fire Brigade. Some examples of these groups are the Earth Liberation Front (ELF), the Animal Liberation Front (ALF), the Ontario Coalition Against Poverty (OCAP), and the Black Bloc. Rather than attracting individuals to a clandestine underground organization that shares a strict ideology, these groups attract individuals who share a few common principles around which they can organize to carry out actions. As a result, they do not have to acquire false identification, live underground for the rest of their lives, or adhere to a rigid ideology. This puts less pressure on the individuals, allows them to carry on their normal lifestyle after the action, and remain in communication with the rest of the political community.

This is possible because these groups do not use high-tech actions but rather employ arson, property damage, and various monkeywrenching tactics. However, without a strict code of silence to which everyone abides around every aspect of the action, militants will soon end up in prison. Ever since 9/11 the consequences for getting busted for any type of political action can never be underestimated. The stakes may be high for those individuals who decide to engage in militant actions, but without a militant front as part of our revolutionary movement, the stakes for the survival of an inhabitable planet are even higher.

They Took Ulrike Meinhof's Brain
A Comparative Study of the Causes of and Justifications for Militant Direct Action

Maxwell Schnurer

"Every slave waits only for the moment the overseer lets his whip fall—in order to strangle him with his chains, if he still has strength enough and pride within himself. The power of the powerless receives its clear expression in spontaneous action, but that really is an individual thing."
Bommi Baumann, West German Urban Guerilla.

In 1976, Ulrike Meinhof—terrorist leader of the West German Marxist group, the Red Army Faction—was hung in a Munich prison.[1] There was significant public furor over Meinhof's death, in part because all four leaders of the Red Army Faction died suspiciously and many believed they were assassinated by the West German government. After she died, the West German government cut open her skull and removed her brain to study the alleged biological causes of her "deviant" behavior. For thirty years scientists secretly held Ulrike Meinhof's brain, and subjected it to a barrage of tests. Bernhard Bogerts, director of the psychiatric clinic at the University of Magdeburg, was one of the scientists who had the opportunity to examine Meinhof's brain. Bogerts believed that an earlier brain surgery for a tumor caused the aggression during the years she was in the Red Army Faction (Moulson).

Looking for a *biological* justification to view dissent as a form of social pathology or abnormality, scientists wanted to study the brain chemistry of an armed militant. Today, an entire class of intellectuals has emerged to interpret and explain what they think terrorists really want, and why they take extreme measures to get it. Meinhof's mad scientists are a part of this industry, along with military and academic theorists whose popular explanations of terrorist motivations often come down to "they hate us." Such misrepresentations of terrorism become an intellectual straightjacket that precludes us from understanding—in their true *communicative and sociological* depth and complexity—the use of armed struggle, terrorism, and ecotage as forms of political protest (Shapiro).[2] However hard they try, the reductive fetishists and biological determinists peering into Meinhof's

348

brain will never find the causes of her actions, or those of any armed militant, unless they leave the laboratory and confront the *socio-political conditions* that breed radicals and revolutionaries, as well as their own written accounts of their motivations.

Militants attack social institutions not because of faulty brain chemistry or damaged DNA, but rather for specific political reasons. Thus, rather than study the brains of dead terrorists, it seems far more fruitful to explore why militants *themselves* say they take up arms as a method of precipitating social change.[3] Leaving aside laboratories and the smell of formaldehyde, this essay turns instead to the memoirs, biographies, and communiqués of militant activists like the Red Army Faction, in order to illuminate their motivations for engaging in militant direct action.[4]

When we examine the varied justifications for radical direct action, we see, above all, young people coming to grips with privilege, expressing their outrage over social injustice, and presenting a political philosophy girded by the notion that privileged westerners should experience arsons and bombings in order to know what it is like to be a colonized subject of the third world. These readings offer a fruitful place to examine Earth Liberation Front (ELF) actions and the reactions they elicit. Similar to the Weather Underground's goal to bring the Vietnam War home to the US by bombing federal buildings, the Earth Liberation Front has unleashed property destruction and arson attacks against a number of economically and symbolically important targets such as timber industries, housing developments, and SUV dealers in order to bring the *ecological* war home by attacking corporate exploiters.

While making this comparison, it is crucial to understand a profound contemporary social turn, whereby the most dynamic and important political battles in many countries today have shifted from agitating for social justice within nations, to liberating animals and defending the *natural world*. Quite unlike the 1960s–1980s era, the main forms of "terrorism" confronting advanced industrial societies today stem from groups such as the Animal Liberation Front (ALF) and the ELF.[5] Yet in order to fully comprehend this political gestalt shift and begin to understand a group like the ELF, it is quite useful to undertake a comparative study that first examines the actions of—and state response to—the militants of the 1960s and 1970s, and then apply this knowledge to understanding contemporary militant groups such as the Earth Liberation Front.

This essay will thus compare "terrorist" groups then and now, and examine their justifications for sabotage, armed struggle, and "violent" action. The goal of the paper is not merely historical in nature. By comparing militant groups of past decades with the ELF, one can not only better understand contemporary radical politics, one can also help people become critically aware of the use and abuse of terrorist discourse today and formulate a rational assessment of the sharp conflicts between corporations and governments, on one side, and radical eco-militants on the other. Once one grasps how the politicized label of "terrorism" decontextualizes and delegitimates militant activism, one can better understand the motivations and goals of the ELF and other forms of militant direct action. It is crucial that people educate themselves about government reprisals to past militant groups so that they can properly interpret media reporting on "terrorism" in the tradition of "organic intellectuals," as defined by the Italian Marxist, Antonio Gramsci.[6]

A Million Revolutionaries: The Militant Left

"Our first outstanding accomplishment was piercing the myth of government invincibility." *David Gilbert, anti-imperialist political prisoner*

Looking at the militant leftist groups of the latter half of the twentieth-century, we find an astounding diversity of committed revolutionaries. In Italy, the Red Brigades and the autonomia movements came close to overthrowing the government during the late seventies, logging more than 700 bombings in a single six-month period. Most famously, in 1978, they kidnapped and killed Aldo Moro, the leading political opposition candidate. The Angry Brigades in the UK bombed industrial and military locations. In Canada, the group Direct Action bombed a missile manufacturing plant and set off firebombs in pornography shops. In America, the Weather Underground and the George Jackson Brigade bombed multiple targets, and the Black Liberation Army expropriated money through bank robberies, and retaliated against racist police officers. Across the globe, young people were becoming terrorists and shooting their way to notoriety.

All of the main terrorist groups mentioned are leftist politically, with several along the socialist/communist spectrum and several espouse anarchist philosophies. However, in many ways, the political ideology is less important than the willingness to use armed violence. In his introduction to *Armed Struggle in Italy 1976–1978*, Jean Weir argues that the sundry revolutionary groups operating then in Italy have a common orientation despite their diverse political differences. According to Weir, these groups

> have come together on the basis of affinity, [which] is based on simple means that are available to anyone and contains a strong element of creativity and joy in the knowledge that it is simple and effective to attack what is oppressing us directly, and that there is no need for endless documents of ideological justification for doing so (Weir, 5).

The real distinguishing factor among various left groups is the willingness to use violence as a means to achieve their ends. Activists used shooting, bombing, arson, and assassination to realize their goals. It is important to distinguish between groups who were armed for self-defense and sometimes were involved in shootouts with police (such as the Black Panther Party for Self Defense and the American Indian Movement) from groups who used violence offensively to attack institutions, and individuals such as white South African David Pratt who attempted to kill the founder of Apartheid, or the Weather Underground Organization placing bombs in the Pentagon.

In the case of the militant left, the study of armed groups has often been oversimplified. The astounding variety of groups has been reduced into a few famous revolutionaries as activists are forgotten. Despite hundreds of different bombings and arsons, the scope of their actions and diversity of tactics has been reduced to a few memorable campaigns.[7] Daniel Burton Rose explains that armed opposition to the United States government, for instance, has been rounded down to the Black Panthers (later the Black Liberation Army) and the Weather Underground when, "In reality there was a groundswell of armed protest against the US government from 65 into the early 70s." Such historical simplifications have the unfortunate effect of obscuring the full spectrum and intense nature of resistance, and therefore make current groups such as the ELF seem more like aberrations and anomalies rather than a continuation of a militant political tradition.[8]

What Made Meinhof a Threat?

"Words are senseless, outrage is no weapons; the Guerilla takes action."
Ulrike Meinhof

Emerging in 1969, the Red Army Faction was an underground revolutionary group that robbed banks, assassinated industry/government leaders, and bombed US Army bases. It was a close-knit cell of underground revolutionaries including Attorney Holgier Meins, Thorwald Proll, Horst Sohnlein, and Gudrun Ensslin. Fueled by Marxist fervor, they were most often identified with their leader, Andreas Baader, a tough action-oriented guerilla. Arguing that western nations would only understand what it was like in Vietnam when the daily bombings and terror of Vietnam was experienced by everyday West Germans, the Red Army Faction set about to show them what life was like during a colonialist war. Coupling a fierce anti-imperialist war ideology with Marxist criticism of the culture of production, Baader founded the Red Army Faction whose hallmark would be action against capital and the state.

In jail for burning the most prominent department store in Berlin, and under suspicion for a number of bombing attacks, Baader's actions had been undercut by his relatively quick capture and imprisonment. That would change with the help of Ulrike Meinhof. As an occasional reporter for a prominent television network, Meinhof and two other women smuggled pistols into the prison under the pretenses of a television interview and broke Andreas Baader out of jail. The Red Army Faction went on to terrorize the West German nation with several years of militant violent actions. More importantly they inspired further generations of militant direct action with their approach and willingness to use violence. In May 1972, the Red Army Faction bombed the American army base in Frankfurt, killing Lt. Col. Paul Bloomquist and injuring 13 soldiers (Vague, 44). Like the North American Black Panthers, the idea of young armed revolutionaries was immensely appealing to an increasingly media saturated

West German society. The Red Army Faction became a powerful symbol to youth around the globe.

Ulrike Meinhof was first known as a prominent West German Socialist intellectual and later as a member of the Red Army Faction. In a world dominated by the Cold War, Meinhof was a successful, bright, and well-regarded social critic. She edited a left-wing magazine, gave lectures, lived in society, was married to a prominent leader, and was considered to be one of the key voices of the West German intellectual left. Meinhof encountered the Red Army Faction when Andreas Baader and Gundrun Enslun spent two weeks at her house while fugitives from arson charges. When Baader and Enslun were captured, Meinhof's private support became more public by breaking Baader out of prison and joining the group underground.

Meinhof and the Red Army Faction presented a revolutionary movement of the left whose opposition to capital and the state would not be contained in the traditional methods of protest. Their tactics ensured them global notoriety, and radicals across the globe were paying attention.[9] Ron Eyerman and Andrew Jamison argue that social movements "develop worldviews that restructure cognition, that re-cognize reality itself" (165). The Red Army Faction was repositioning all of the rules about political protest and responsibility. The police response was intense, as evident in the development of a centralized database on terrorist subjects (Vague, 37–38). Police set roadblocks, arrested activists, and did all they could to catch the Red Army Faction.

Why was there so much pressure to catch them? Perhaps the rapid arrest of the activists would restore public confidence to a sagging German government. The sudden appeal of terrorism to the youth of the country must have been outrageous to the German leaders. Perhaps they later cut out Ulrike Meinhof's brain because they thought that the chemical makeup might help them understand her actions and the actions of the young people who followed in her footsteps. If this is the case then, the justification is disingenuous. Governments know why people become terrorists. Poor and oppressed people reach a point of crisis and the only rational response is to use all the tools available, which often includes armed struggle for the most desperate. But Meinhof was different. She didn't join because she was oppressed, quite the opposite, for she came from a wealthy and privileged background.

So what then did drive Meinhof to wage war against the state? In large part, the justifications she offers in her communiqués hinge on coming to grips with her middle-class position in society. Meinhof argues that: "Reality can only be perceived in a materialism related to struggle—class struggle and war" (Vague, 63). For the Red Army faction, recognizing inequality meant waging war to support the liberation struggles in the third world. If you were aware of the problems, then you were compelled to act—regardless of whether you lived in Hanoi or Stuttgart. The Red Army Faction were not the only activists who operated under this philosophy, for across the globe, activists were dealing with their privilege by engaging in armed struggle.

Coming to Grips with Privilege

"If you live in guilt you are never free." *David Pratt*

The mechanistic assumption of the capitalist system is that the citizens of a state should defend the society that accords them their privileges.[10] An upper-middle class person will have been rewarded with the financial benefits of their station and should never turn against the government. One of the reasons that Meinhof intrigued the state so much was that she defected from the system of benefits that her class position provided her.

What Meinhof and the rest of the Red Army Faction intended to do was to bring the experience of urban guerilla warfare (the kind that was going on in Vietnam, Algeria, and the Congo) to West Germany. As stated, their logic was that western citizens had access to the roots of the war machines that were operating in the third world, and yet were free from the brutality of life in a war zone. At the same time, because of their birth in a particular nation, Europeans could strike against the industrial and political decision-makers who caused these wars. Because West Germany was one of the most powerful, successful industrial nations in the world, activists were quick to see the colonial relationships with third world nations in terms of a global struggle. For privileged Germans, the role of action was a necessity in terms of their own authentic protest. If Africans were fighting for liberation against European soldiers and risking their lives, shouldn't European youth fight the war on the streets of Europe?

The Red Army Faction were not the only activists to view armed struggle as a response to privilege. Perhaps the clearest example comes from South Africa, where David Pratt, a white South African farmer, attempted to kill the architect of apartheid, Dr. Hendrick Verwoerd. Pratt's action was a direct response to the Sharpeville massacre where dozens of black South Africans were killed when the police opened fire on unarmed protesters challenging the passbook laws. The justification Pratt gave was that he had shot at the system of apartheid, and not at Verwoerd himself.

More interesting, Pratt described his time after the assassination attempt as "a hundred times happier than the past five years....If you know you must do something and you don't do it you are not free" (cited in Richards, 53). For Pratt, living in an unjust society necessitated action precisely because of his privilege. In a South Africa where he could travel freely and the black residents needed passbooks to move and were killed when protesting against such injustice, Pratt was moved to act. In part because he was able to gain access to Verwoerd, Pratt argued that he had a responsibility to act.

Other white activists have viewed their actions as earnest attempts to own up to privilege. David Gilbert, a white militant who was a part of the Weather Underground and a co-defendant of Black Nationalist Kuwasi Balagoon in the Brinks expropriation trial, argues that the privilege of white society made the commitment to revolution essential. According to Gilbert, he and his comrades might face police repression, but black and Latino activists were being killed by police. For Gilbert this meant using Weather Underground bombings to focus attention on the causes of oppressed people of color.

Similarly, when explaining why she was a part of revolutionary armed struggle in the United States, political prisoner and former underground guerilla warrior, Laura Whitehorn, outlines a justification that ties direct action to privilege. She writes:

> It seemed to me that those of us in the belly of the beast—citizens of the…[m]ilitary and political machinery inside the US…could play a significant role in shortening the war by increasing the material and political costs. That's why…I later took part in armed actions against targets like the NYC Patrolmen's Benevolent Association, the Israeli aircraft industries and the US War College and the Capitol Building (cited in *Enemies of the State*, 10).[11]

Bill Ayers, former Weather Underground member, was one of the organizers who helped to spearhead the creation of the organization at the 1969 Students for a Democratic Society (SDS) meeting. In the SDS organization a handful of radical student leaders created an underground American guerilla army from a youth protest organization. Ayers argues that the members of the Weather Underground "felt personally and specifically the full weight" of Vietnam (141).

With all this pressure, many activists felt as though they had to act. The militant actions included bombings and arsons, but were generally targeted at the public in an attempt to persuade them to act against war or imperialism. The application of militant pressure for focused political goals became a hallmark of the action of the era. Unlike the perception of indiscriminate violence wrought by the leftist bombers, the reality is that there was almost always a clear political goal and rationale associating each bomb with a target. Underlying the actions was a sense that activists wanted to shock a complacent public into outrage.

Shattering Paradigms Like Glass

> "People are tired of meetings, the classics, pointless marches, theoretical discussions that split hairs in four; endless distinctions, the monotony and poverty of certain political analyses. They prefer to make love, smoke, listen to music, go for walks, sleep, laugh, play, kill policemen, lame journalists, kill judges, blow up barracks." *Alfredo M. Bonanno*

These radical activists shared a belief that the government, corporate, and media systems were immune to traditional methods of change. Their view centers on the inability of these traditional tools to remedy what are perceived of as grave injustices. In the case of the Red Army Faction, their initial communiqué outlines their position that the growth of the urban guerilla is a direct reaction to the failure of parliamentary democracy

(Vague, 28). In their mind, the plodding path of traditional politics would never make the changes to stop the wars of colonialism that ravaged the third world. As a result, the armed action of Europeans was necessary to change the tenor of politics.

Similarly, the Angry Brigades of the UK defined the tepid political system as an unacceptable political outlet. Tom Vague reports on a filmed conversation about violence between members Chris Allen and Ian Purdie: "We're not just going to sit around and produce petitions against what you're doing. The bombings are not going to be the be-all and end-all of the situation. They're an announcement of a certain situation where we're no longer going to accept the confines of legality set by the state" (cited in Vague, 30). For the Angry Brigades and the Red Army Faction, traditional political agencies would never make the changes necessary for progressive social change, and thus violent responses were necessary.

Similarly, the Black Liberation Army (BLA) used armed struggle to communicate a shifting in position of racial hierarchy in the United States, a tactic to bring about cultural change within the black population. "The BLA has undertaken armed struggle as a means by which the social psychosis of fear, awe, and love of everything white people define as being of value, is purged from our people's minds" (Coordinating Committee, 10). For the BLA, the action of violence was a necessary move to dethrone the subservient position of a colonized, enslaved people.

Ann Hansen's book, *Direct Action*, tells the story of the radical Canadian guerilla group Direct Action. With the bombings of a weapon manufacturing plant, a power plant, and the arson of several pornography stores, the group was a radical voice of militant action in North America. One of its primary goals was to change the nature of the debates among radicals in order to "inject a more militant political philosophy and action into the movement for social change" (Hansen, 54).

These activists used militant direct action to redefine the political landscape. The actions of Hansen and the BLA suggest that attacks against institutions of the state can communicate ideas to the larger public, amplify protest messages, or redefine the political meaning of events. The bombings and arsons of these militants were specifically targeted, not only to bring about concrete political change, but also to challenge the paradigms of thought in society, be it the place of black people in a racist society, or the notion that a government can do no wrong.

From Trees to SUVs: the Changing Rhetoric of the ELF in the Era of Terror

> "Around here, we've elevated the word 'arson' to 'terrorism.'"
> *Bob Rivinius, director of the California Building Industry Association*

It might seem incongruous to move from groups like the Weather Underground and the Red Army Faction to the Earth Liberation Front. The ELF has never harmed anyone and has never taken up arms to fight the state. Despite the obvious differences, the wide net of post-September 11th terrorist discourse has portrayed the ELF in the light of both leftist terrorists like the RAF, and Al Qaeda. It is vital to disentangle the ELF from terrorist labeling and explore the justifications provided by Earth Liberation Front activists for their actions. ELF defenses of sabotage tactics are similar to those used by earlier urban guerillas, with the key difference that they are acting in defense of the earth rather than human beings.

Shrouded in the rhetoric of security, significant political changes are happening in the United States and the UK based on the fear of terrorism. Internment of immigrants, extra-legal detention of suspects at foreign military bases, authorization of the use of torture by CIA operatives, the dramatic increase in police and law enforcement power via the PATRIOT Act and Bush-approved warrantless wiretaps, and the swelling military/anti-terrorism budgets on both state and federal levels all emerged couched in the rhetoric of Homeland Security and terrorist threats.

It shouldn't be surprising to find that direct action activists such as the ALF and ELF became re-presented to the public as anti-business terrorists. New pieces of legislation presented as tools against terrorists like Al Qaeda have been used against ALF and ELF activists who have never harmed a living being. The insertion of terrorist labeling into environmental policy-making underscores a dramatic change in the nature of radical politics: animal liberation and defense of the earth is increasingly central to the broader struggle for rights and justice, something that is recognized by both radicals and police. While the nature of the subject (animals and the earth) that guerillas fight for may have changed, the response by government remains the same—intense direct repression.[12]

Like the Red Army Faction and the Weather Underground, many in the Earth Liberation Front justify their action in terms of coming to grips with their privilege, and tactically, most ELF actions are targeted at political goals. Unlike the Red Army Faction, the ELF doesn't carry weapons or engage in shoot-outs with the police. Their actions are generally driven by a sense of oncoming ecological destruction and motivated by the realization of the privilege that anthropocentrism offers humans. Tre Arrow, an accused ELF member, who is imprisoned in Canada, explains the roots of his actions in his love for the earth. "As long as these injustices continue towards me, the planet, our non-humyn animal friends and our brothers and sisters here and abroad then there is still work to do." For activists like Arrow, the imperative of action comes from the ongoing destruction which puts at risk the planet, animals, and humans.

This imperative comes from the experience of privilege. Witnessing massive environmental destruction and breakdown of the world's eco-systems necessitates action. Like Meinhof and members of the Weather Underground, the unearned benefits of anthropocentrism given to humans translates into disquiet for ELF members, and this becomes a justification for direct action to remedy the situation. Like the Black Liberation Army who hoped to elicit a philosophical change in the perspective of black audiences, the ELF hope that their actions will resonate with the larger public.

Similarly, the communiqués of the ELF highlight that, like the George Jackson Brigade, the targets of the ELF's wrath are politically appropriate. In 2001, Earth Liberation Front activists burned a warehouse filled with genetically modified cotton seed in Visalia, California. Their communiqué explained their actions:

> Engineering a suicide sequence into the plant world is the most dangerous new technology since nuclear power and needs to be stopped. We chose this warehouse because it contained massive quantities of transgenic cotton seed in storage. But now, this seed will no longer exist to contaminate the environment, enrich a sick corporation, or contribute to its warped research programs.

For ELF activists, these seeds represented an ecological catastrophe, one that they compare to nuclear power. The target is the warehouse because it does damage to the corporate infrastructure and because it directly removes an agent of harm from the environment. Also evident in this communiqué is the same kind of disdain for reformist politics that we see in many other militants like the Angry Brigades. The "sick corporation" is an agency that we can assume will never put ecology first. Thus the actions of the ELF are the only way to respond to corporate malfeasance in a world where the oversight institutions that should prevent this kind of research, are complicit with it.

While the tactics of the ELF fall outside the system of traditional politics, the justifications for arsons and ecological sabotage are precise and cover a global ecological scope. Activists like Arrow and former ALF prisoner, Rod Coronado are not single-issue environmental fanatics, but humans who view their actions within the context of other social justice causes. Coronado, for example, explains how his politics on fur trade are tied to his identity as an indigenous North American, saying: "the fur trade today is the modern incarnation of those very same people who murdered and destroyed my people and my homelands."

In other cases, the ELF has acted directly to support ongoing political campaigns or causes. Consider the example of the attempted arson of a Nike facility in Minnesota in 2001. The communiqué includes this justification: "This visit was in solidarity with all people of all nations to fight globalization, and to support the growing anti-global sentiment. This is also a call for direct action against globalization in solidarity with all of the anti-FTAA actions scheduled in Canada later this month." Not only does the ELF use arson to link their struggle for the earth to global human rights struggles and the campaign against Nike, they also connect Nike to the Free Trade Agreement of the Americas—a multinational treaty which undercuts environmental politics and opens new channels for corporate policies, and dollars to cross borders. This kind of strategic political action suggests a mature political awareness—one which shows the relations between the structures of capitalist economies to everyday suffering in the third world, thereby advancing a radical, holistic, anti-capitalist position much like the militants of the sixties and seventies. In some instances, like the arson of the Bloomington, Indiana Republican Party headquarters, the ELF specifically targeted developers interested in expanding interstate I-69. "The fire was set as a reminder to politicians such as John Hostettler that we are watching and that we will not sit idly by as they push for plans like I-69." ELF activists use arson to fight development, connecting the political Republican machine to the environmental catastrophe of highways in an astute presentation of ecological politics. Echoing the Weather Underground or the Red Army Faction, the targets and tactics of the ELF are precisely selected to maximize the political message of dissent and create new political ideology.

ELF activists justify their actions in the context of an ecological crisis that demands action, be it genetically modified food, or the destruction of a luxury resort. Just as a sense of privilege drove earlier militants, the ELF seems driven by a sense of ecological privilege. As humans become aware of the damages done to the earth, and of the failure of traditional remedies, many ELF activists see their actions as necessary responses to a system of destruction. The communiqué from the arson of a luxury home on Long Island, New York included this line: "It's time for the people of Long Island to put their foot down and no longer passively tolerate our island's rape." Here the activists call for a public who are engaged in ecological politics to forcibly stop the damage. The communiqué also explains who they view as the cause of these problems, "greedy corporate and personal interests." According to the ELF, "The rape of Earth puts everyone's life at risk" and thus action is justified. The ecological privilege is presented as a Jeremiad, a rhetorical claim of doom unless action is taken.

Although the militant activists of the sixties and seventies presented the difficulties of privilege as one of their chief justifications for action, there seems to be a real difference in the sense of the ELF activists' privilege. Many of them are also young white people, but their justifications don't seem to be tied to their identity as much as their portrayal of their enemies. Unlike the Red Army Faction or the Weather Underground, there is no reason to "bring the war home" because ELF members live near the destruction. Instead, the goal seems to center around the decision-makers who caused the act. In all of the ELF communiqués examined in this work, each of them outlines a specific person or industry that inspired the action. It is the looming danger presented by these enemies of ecology that provide the sense of urgency for many ELF communiqués. This is a kind of privilege—a sense that the current moment provides a space for ecological action that will not be available in the future. Action is necessary because inaction gives the space for enemies to further their attacks on the earth. In the case of the arson at Vail, Colorado, the impetus for action came from the impending development that threatened lynx habitat. Tactically, this notion of privilege parallels the justifications of access—because the

ELF have access to the implementation of an ecological destruction, they must act.

While justifying these actions, the Earth Liberation Front does not phrase their political claims in terms of general opposition to society. Rather their claims are couched in the frame of environmental necessity. For example, there is no ELF parallel to the *days of rage*, a Weather Underground organized action which involved several hundred militant youth fighting with police through the gold coast of Chicago. The ELF actions are generally covert acts of sabotage, not intended to attack consumers, and the public at large; instead, ELF actions traditionally pressure industries such as logging corporations and research laboratories.

Despite this lack of a public face, the symbolic meaning of the ELF is massive. As a tactical innovation, direct action against decision-makers represents a sea-change in North American activism. As a decentralized movement with nothing but ideology to sustain its members, the ELF presented a real departure from the kinds of politics of other movements. Without an entry barrier, many in North America found the label, tactics, and philosophy of the Earth Liberation Front appealing. As the actions of the ELF grew, so did the notoriety, and their tactics spread across the United States. The ELF focuses on increasing the costs to corporations by destroying equipment or facilities. These actions are buoyed by a philosophy which explains that loss of profits is the only message that corporations will acknowledge. Based on this philosophy, the ELF had never undertaken an attack on public consumers because they simply were not their target.

In 2003 and 2004 this changed, as popular consumer Sport Utility Vehicles (SUVs) became the target of actions in New Jersey, Oregon, Michigan, Pennsylvania, and, most notably, California. These actions struck at the heart of modern American consumer identity—the automobile. On August 22, 2004, ELF activists in Southern California attacked four of the largest auto dealerships during the night. More than 100 SUVs were painted and burned. Estimates put the damages between two and five million dollars. Usually, militant direct action on behalf of the earth occurs in protest of concrete political causes—like the ELF activists who destroyed the genetically modified seeds. But in the case of the activism of the Earth Liberation Front and their targeting of luxury SUVs, the operating rules seem to have changed. Instead of attacking the manufacturing facility, these activists struck against trucks awaiting sale in dealers' lots.

This kind of tactical move—to bring public criticism to the day-to-day experiences of people—is a controversial activist tactic. Sweatshop and animal rights campaigns have centered much of their advocacy on connecting the responsibility associated with the choices of shopping at the Gap or buying the processed remains of a dead animal to the consequences felt in the sweatshop or the slaughterhouse. The Earth Liberation Front SUV attacks seem to operate in a similar way. The paint and fires show the relationship between consumer choices and violence. They force some recognition between shopping for an SUV and the ecological impacts of the machines. In a society of privilege, the response of citizens who are reminded of the consequences of their shopping, is often retaliation and expressions of outrage. In an era when consumption is one of the chief mechanisms of identity formation, challenging it is extremely threatening. Looking at the responses of the public and authority figures can help us to understand how these kinds of actions elicit so much anger in the society.[13]

In the case of the ELF, the discourse of terrorism obscures the causes and impacts of direct action against consumerism. Attacks which are intended to communicate outrage with a system wholly out of sync with natural limits are represented as attacks on "our way of life"—mimicking the anti-terrorism rhetoric of government leaders. In the case of the SUV attacks, consumer outrage was a dominant theme to media coverage. *The New York Times* concluded their report on the attacks with a story of the California Hummer Owners group who came to show their support several days after the arson. Steve Reisman, the founder of the group said: "It's one thing to pass out leaflets and to put stickers on cars saying they pollute, but it's another to start setting fire to them" (Madigan, 20). Reisman and thirty other proud Hummer drivers gathered to rally support for the recently attacked dealership.

Reisman's quote helps us to understand the SUV arsons in the context of a larger national debate about the harms of SUVs and the responsibility of their drivers. Reisman knows that his vehicle is widely opposed. But because it is a perceived right of his life, he views the gigantic automobile with something more than consumerist lust, but rather a kind of religious sense of persecution. When the drivers gather to celebrate their automobiles they create a very strong public argument to defend the use of the automobile and challenge the very legitimacy of the debate about SUVs. In the end of *The New York Times* story, the punch line wasn't that SUVs were attacked, but that Hummer owners were celebrating their vehicles in response to the attack.

Consider the response of the law enforcement community to the ELF SUV attacks—a relatively small crime in the context of the crime in Los Angeles. First they arrested Josh Connolle, a 25-year-old solar panel installer. They held him for four days of interrogation, using intense psychological techniques to get him to confess. They took everything that could relate to the crime, including his computer, from his house, and trashed the coop that he shares with fourteen other people. Connolle contends that he was not picked up because he was a legitimate suspect, but because he was a global warming activist opposed to SUVs. Then someone emailed the *Los Angeles Times* explaining that they had the wrong suspect—and giving details of the action to prove authenticity. It turns out that the emails were sent by now-convicted Cal Tech student Billy Cottrell who felt bad that someone innocent was in jail. After a massive FBI scan on the Cal

Tech email system, Cottrell was picked up and matched with the surveillance tapes.[14]

Examining the Response

> "[T]hey do not understand that our revolutionary aim is to go towards another kind of attack on the State, that of convincing people that it is necessary to do something, even small, right from today, not start organizing for a final battle with the state itself." *Alfredo Bonanno*

In the current neo-McCarthyesque culture of the US, animal rights and environmental activists are demonized as terrorists. When it comes to the study of radical environmentalism, the debate over what causes people to torch resort hotels or graffiti Hummer SUVs is occurring in public dialogues and *it is essential that people be aware of the representations emerging around the discourse of terrorism and their political implications*. While the tactics may differ from terrorist groups like Al Qaeda, groups like the ELF receive similar attention from law enforcement. With the ALF and ELF topping the FBI most wanted domestic terrorist list, a juxtaposition of the responses to ELF and terrorist action seems in order.[15]

These kinds of reactions by law enforcement agencies are a highly under-theorized part of the contested meaning of radical protest. The public reaction to ELF actions creates public meaning by helping to articulate the protest as a threat to public order. When governments associate the Earth Liberation Front with terrorists like Al Qaeda, the ELF is thereby reduced to the paradigm of evil. Just as the responses to the militant direct action of the leftist terrorists of the 1970s and 1980s demonstrated the amount of fear governments have of militant ideas, the repression that emerged among the hunt for these SUV-painting activists was significant precisely because it was *so intense* and such a broad witch hunt. Clearly the police and FBI are trying to send a message to those who might sympathize with, defend, or participate in sabotage against corporations—they will face harsh persecution and penalties. Identifying such actions, as they intend to, as "terrorism"—the most extreme type of vilification today—diverts attention from the violent war on people, animals, and the planet. Such labeling helps to avoid any discussion of systematic violence in our society, deflecting attention from the causes, and toward the activists.[16]

ELF activists have noticed this kind of attention. In the communiqué released after an attack on SUVs in Erie, Pennsylvania, a clear criticism of the priorities of law enforcement emerges:

> We have absolutely no faith in the legal system of the state when it comes to protecting life, as it has repeatedly shown itself to care far more for the protection of commerce and profits than for its people and the natural environment. Clearly, the state itself causes and profits from many of the various atrocities against life that we must struggle against. To place faith in that same state as though it will act in the interests of justice and life is utter foolishness and a grave mistake.

For ELF activists, the focus of law enforcement energies to catch eco-activists is symptomatic of the bias of police and federal agents such that, as figures of the corporate-state complex, they protect the profits and property of exploiters. From the perspective of the ELF, however, the agents of law enforcement ignore corporations who break labor laws and environmental regulations, instead focusing their energies on catching eco-terrorists. Part of the activism of the ELF is to focus public scrutiny onto industries they deem dangerous.

This is a methodological transformation in the Earth Liberation Front whose actions against automobiles represent a vigorous public argument connecting automobile use to environmental harms. In an attempt to pressure the public, the symbolic burning of SUVs presents an attack on some sacred American space; an aggressive move not only toward the industries which are killing the planet, but the shoppers who sustain them. In a radical turn, the ELF are now bringing the environmental war home to consumers.

The Organic Intellectual and the Struggle over the Representation of the ELF

"Militancy has made a comeback." Jeremy Varon

We can never really know what drove Ulrike Meinhof to become an armed guerilla. Nor can we ultimately know what causes ELF activists to set off incendiary bombs at housing complexes in California, or the ski lodge at Vail, Colorado, or to turn their cans of spray paint to luxury automobile dealers. But the fact that the actions of Meinhof and the ELF are attacked with such vehement pathology in the popular media suggests that these actions strike deep into the political identity of the modern public. In the case of Meinhof, the actions of the Red Army Faction become swept away under the socio-scientific judgment of mental illness. In the case of the ELF, the articulation of pathology is quite similar. After the arson in Vail, Colorado, which burned a luxury resort down, Rocky Smith, spokesperson for Colorado Wild, attacked the ELF actions. "I just reject that thinking. I think it's sick," he said. "You saw it on September 11, 2001, on a grand scale. It's pathological"(Hughes).

The radical direct action groups of the sixties and the seventies had their political message re-articulated by the state using pathology and terrorism as tropes to dismiss dissent. When groups like the Weather Underground and the Red Army Faction turned their actions to attempting to persuade the public with direct action—attempting to *bring the war home*—the governments responded. First labeling the actions as terrorist and then portraying the activists themselves as sick, the German state did its best to protect the European citizenry from the critique of the Red Army Faction. The United States government used surveillance and political dismissal to prevent the ideas of the Weather Underground from "infecting" the public consciousness.

In the last few years, the Earth Liberation Front has evolved its version of "bringing the war home." The attacks on SUVs represent a paradigmatic change to bring pressure on the consumption and ecological impact of automobiles. As the ELF brought increased public attention and pressure on automobile culture, the government brought out a variety of justifications to fight the ideas presented by the SUV attacks. It is here where the contested meaning of direct action becomes visible that we can understand how public opinion turns. Understanding how narratives of pathology and the label of terrorism act to deny argumentative legitimacy to activism helps readers to better understand the Earth Liberation Front and all militant direct action.

This kind of reading will be increasingly necessary as the terrorist labeling of ELF militants grows stronger. Antonio Gramsci argues that community based, organic intellectuals can play a vital interpretive role, helping communities to critically read government propaganda. Gramsci suggests that these organic intellectuals can operate as "permanent persuaders" re-articulating dominant news stories to be comprehensible and motivating to people in their communities. This essay can help to provide the foundation for organic intellectuals to intervene in popular dialogue about terrorism and direct action for the earth, helping to better understand and combat terrorist representations.

Acknowledgements

The author would like to thank Steven Best, Elena Cattaneo, and Anthony J. Nocella, II for their assistance in the formation of this essay.

Bibliography

Ayers, Bill. *Fugitive Days*. New York: Penguin Books, 2003.

Armed Struggle in Italy 1976–1978: A Chronology. London: Elephant Editions, 1990.

Arrow, Tre. "Tre Arrow." <http://www.earthliberationfront.com>

Balagoon, Kuwasi. *A Soldier's Story: Writings by a Revolutionary New Afrikan Anarchist*. Montréal: Kersplebdeb Publishing, 2003.

BBC News World Edition. "Meinhof Brain Study Yields Clues." 12 November, 2002. <http://news.bbc.co.uk/2/hi/europe/2455647.stm.>

Baumann, Bommi. *How It All Began: The Personal Account of a West German Urban Guerrilla*. Trans. Ellenbogen, Helene and Parker, Wayne. Vancouver: Arsenal Pulp Press, 1975.

Best, Steven and Nocella, II, Anthony J. "Defining Terrorism." In *Terrorists or Freedom Fighters? Reflections on the Liberation of Animals*, edited by Best and Nocella. New York: Lantern Books, 2004.

Bite Back. "News from the frontlines." <http://www.directaction.info/news_jan04_03.htm>

Bonanno, Alfredo M. *Apart from the Obvious Exceptions: A Few Considerations by a Frequenter of the Courts*. London: Elephant Editions, 2003.

___. *Armed Joy*. Trans. Jean Weir. Baltimore: Firestarter Press, 2003.

Burton, Michael. "Rugged Individualists of the Road Unite! (Chicago)." In *Critical Mass: Bicycling's Defiant Celebration*, edited by Chris Carlsson. Oakland, CA: AK Press, 2002.

Carlsson, Chris. "Cycling Under the Radar: Assertive Desertion." In *Critical Mass: Bicycling's Defiant Celebration*. Oakland, CA: AK Press, 2002.

Coronado, Rod. "Rod Coronado: A Voice for Liberation an nterview with Mirha-Soleil." *Underground: The Magazine of the North American Animal Liberation Front Supporters Group 17* <http://www.kersplebedeb.com/mystuff/video/msr/coronado.html>

Earth Liberation Front Communiqué. "The Earth Liberation Front takes credit for torching the Delta & Pine Land Co. Research cotton gin in Visalia, California on February 20." *Infoshop.* <http://www.infoshop.org/news6/elf_cotton.html>

Earth Liberation Front Press Office. "US, Earth Liberation Front Claims Responsibility For Attempted Arson At Nike Outlet Store In Albertville, MN" *A-Infos.* <http://www.ainfos.ca/01/apr/ainfos00242.html>

___. "The ELF sets ablaze the GOP headquarters." *Infoshop.* September 19, 2000. <http://www.infoshop.org/news5/elf_vs_gop.html>

___. "ELF Burns another home on Long Island" *Infoshop.* December 21, 2000. <http://infoshop.org/news5/elf_christmas.html>

Enemies of the State: An Interview with Anti-Imperialist Political Prisoners David Gilbert, Laura Whitehorn and Marilyn Buck. Montréal: Arm the Spirit, 2002.

Eyerman, Ron and Jamison, Andrew. *Music and Social Movements: Mobilizing Traditions in the Twentieth Century*. Cambridge: Cambridge University Press, 1998.

___. *Social Movements: A Cognitive Approach*. University Park, Pennsylvania: Pennsylvania State University Press, 1991.

George Jackson Brigade. *Creating a Movement with Teeth: Communiqué's of the George Jackson Brigade*. Montréal: Arm the Spirit, 2003.

Gilbert, David. *No Surrender: Writings from An Anti-Imperialist Political Prisoner*. Montréal: Arm the Spirit Press. 2004.

Gramsci, Antonio. *Selections from the Prison Notebooks*. Trans. Hoare, Quintin and Smith, Geoffrey Nowell. New York: International Publishers, 1971.

Hansen, Ann. *Direct Action*. Oakland, CA: AK Press, 2002.

___. "Epilogue to Direct Action" *Anarchy* 53 (Spring/Summer 2002): 57–61.

Hughes, Joe. "Agents Raid Activist's Home in Arson Probe." *San Diego Union Tribune*. 29 August 2003, B1.

Hughes, Jim, "Eco-Terrorists Top FBI's List Attacks Intensify Since Fires 5 years Ago at Vail," *Denver Post*. October 18, 2003: B1.

Madigan, Nick. "Cries of Activism and Terrorism in S.U.V. Torching." *The New York Times*, 31 August 2003: 20.

Meinhof, Ulrike. "Communique." In *Hatred of Capitalism*, edited by Chris Kraus and Lotringer, Sylvere. New York: Semiotext(e), 2001.

Moulson, Geir. "German professor acknowledges he examined terrorist's preserved brain." Associated Press. 12 November 2002.

Muntaquim, Jalil. *On the Black Liberation Army*. Montréal: Arm the Spirit. 1997.

Murr, Andrew. "The physicist and the torched SUVs." *Newsweek*. (Nov 1, 2004): 30.

Richards, Vernon, ed. *Violence and Anarchism: a Polemic*. London: Freedom Press, 1993.

Rose, Daniel Burton. "Introduction." In *George Jackson Brigades: Creating a Movement with Teeth: Communiqués of the George Jackson Brigade*. Montréal: Arm the Spirit, 2003.

Shapiro, Michael J, "Representational Violence," *Peace Review*, (December 1988): 559.

This is Baader-Meinhoff. <http://www.baader-meinhof.com>

Vague. Tom. *Anarchy in the UK: The Angry Brigade*. Oakland, CA: AK Press, 1997.

___. *Televisionaries: the Red Army Faction Story 1963–1993*. Oakland, CA: AK Press, 1994.

Varon, Jeremy. *Bringing the War Home: The Weather Underground, The Red Army Faction and Revolutionary Violence in the Sixties and Seventies*. Berkeley: University of California Press, 2004.

Weir, Jean. *Armed Struggle in Italy 1976–1978*. Elephant Editions, 1990.

Whitehorn, Laura. cited in *Enemies of the State*.

Notes

1. The use of the term terrorist is a certain acknowledgement of the obvious—that all of the people studied used violence in order to terrorize people in an effort to bring about political change. This term says nothing about the complexity of each situation and action. Other terms that are used interchangeably with terrorist are "militant direct action" and "revolutionary." Some distinction can be made between the concepts, but almost all action attempts to threaten some public, and can be articulated as terrorist in nature. Rather than focus on the definition of a term, this work focuses on the specific actions, individuals, and groups who undertake action in an effort to better understand them.

2. Shapiro (1988) helps us to understand how the representation of a label can reduce a number of identities into a single idea—enabling a kind of mental shorthand that enables violence. In the case of terrorism, the threat construction and threat inflation go hand in

hand with a representation of terrorism that is ever present and constantly putting "us" at risk. Drawing on the work of Judith Butler, Shapiro helps to sketch out how bodies become translated into objects for violence.

3. Some might object, and say that biographies and memoirs can be biased, or even false. Many of the facts presented in biographies, however, are verifiable. Throughout the work I have used several sources on these activists in order to triangulate information, and where unsure, I have not used the data. Even though we can discuss the factual validity of memoirs and communiqués, there can be no debate that they provide significant rhetorical meaning for audiences. Documentation of revolutionary direct actions are disseminated through pamphlets, books published by radical presses, and through word of mouth. The stories of Red Army Faction actions resonated with members of Direct Action in Canada. The George Jackson Brigade named their group after the radical African American prison organizer. Even if the data is not verifiable, its impact for other activists, and on popular culture, can not be disputed, and thus should be studied.

4. If we base our methodology of inquiry on a pathological view of these participants' actions, we will never understand them. If we begin by looking for the sickness, the trauma, or the injustice which triggered her actions, then we will find ourselves in a field of study which examines the personal histories of radical activists looking for damage to explain their "aberrant" behavior. Instead, we should explore what the motivations for joining these groups.

5. One of the reasons for this paradigm change is the advancement of the ecology movement. Many environmental activists view a deep connection between the forces of social decay—governments that wage war or imprison activists of color—and the environmental crisis. In the case of the Earth Liberation Front, many of the actions focus on transversal political issues that cross borders—connecting SUV driving to the oil war in Iraq or linking genetically modified crops to starvation in the third world. The injustices that drove groups like the Weather Underground still exist, but the articulation of protest happens via environmental concepts.

6. Italian Communist, Antonio Gramsci, suggested that organic intellectuals—civic leaders and community members—could articulate ideas and help to translate government messages. Gramsci imagined a class of activist "permanent persuaders" (11) who could help to challenge the ideas that sustained an unjust society.

7. Jeremy Varon describes the scene in America after the massacre at Kent State in his book *Bringing the War Home*: "According to government figures, there were 281 attacks on ROTC buildings alone and a staggering 7,200 arrests on American campuses from June 1969–June 1970. In a special issue on "Guerilla Warfare in the United States," Scanlan's magazine documented close to 500 acts of arson or bombings (attempted or successful) of government, corporate, police, military, and university targets in the first six months of 1970" (178).

8. In order to answer these questions it is necessary to examine a history of radical, left wing, militant activists who have used armed struggle to achieve their goals. Of course government officials (whose job it is to prevent this kind of action) have a vested interest in preventing a full understanding of the scope and impact of these social movements. In an understanding act of complicity most academic researchers have shied away from such research. The increasing corporatization of the university system has only accelerated the pariah-like compartmentalization of the study of revolutionary movements in the university system. As public relations become more important than understanding phenomenon, work on the strain of social movements that are radical has all but disappeared. Therefore it is important to understand that even undertaking the project to further research these subjects is a radical departure from two primary axes of power in our society.

9. In almost every radical group that I studied, some reference to the Red Army Faction came up. Among the North American militants like Direct Action, the Weather Underground and the George Jackson Brigade, there is clear acknowledgement of the Red Army Faction's role as tactical progenitors for other militant groups. Their presence was celebrated, and in many cases solidarity actions occurred, such as the George Jackson Brigade's attack on a German car dealership which was initiated in support of imprisoned members of the Red Army Faction.

10. Antonio Gramsci (1971) most successfully articulated the concept of how the daily participation of individuals in a society will encourage them to continue to defend the status quo. Gramsci's conception of hegemony, which included the use of intellectuals to perpetuate the power of the state heavily informs this essay. Hegemony is the power of the state to retain control. Hegemony has two parts—one is the power of force (army police) and the other is the power of gifts, given to individuals to invest them in the value of the society.

11. Note that Whitehorn also justifies her actions in terms of an ongoing war and as a tactic intended to bring about additional costs to those in power (much like the justifications for ALF and ELF actions).

12. Increasingly, the contested nature of the modern political state will center on ecological changes. Natural disasters such as Hurricane Katrina are being articulated as military threats that require military solutions. Problems such as global warming seem to require the presence of the Army Corps of Engineers building walls of sand to stop floodwaters.

13. Michael Burton offers a vigorous discussion of car culture in his chapter in *Critical Mass: Bicycling's Defiant Celebration*. Burton argues that many participants in the monthly bicycle ride through traffic get involved because they see the terrible trap of automobile transportation (28). Carlsson describes the challenge that critical mass presents to people driving cars in another chapter in the same book.

> When someone becomes a daily bicyclist s/he makes and empathic break with one of the basic assumptions and "truths" of the dominant society: that you must have a car to get around. The actual experience of urban cycling refreshes the cyclist mentally and physically. That experience in turn inoculates the bicyclist against the disdain heaped on cyclists by "normal" people, often while they're driving. In addition, it begins to undermine all sorts of received truths, packaged and delivered by entertainment conglomerates with a vested interest in maintaining our dependence on steadily consuming their products in pursuit of an elusive happiness, or at least a satisfaction that we can't seem to get (78–79).

14. As Billy Cottrell accepted responsibility for being part of the attacks, the narrative of deviance emerged. Similarly to Meinhof, Cottrell has been diagnosed with a developmental disorder, Asperger's Syndrome, and labeled mentally unfit. "His lawyers hope to explain the apparent contradiction by showing that Cottrell has Asperger's Syndrome, a mild form of autism marked by an impaired ability to comprehend social situations. 'The question is: how can somebody so smart be so dumb?' says his attorney Marvin Rudnick. 'And Asperger's answers that question'" (Murr). Like Meinhof, the actions become explained as caused by their brain defects. In this we begin to see an example of how science operates not as a neutral operation, but as a part of a system which uses the explanatory tools of science to label and dismiss critics. In the world of behavioral science there is no justification for radical action for the earth because it is all pathological. The goal of scientists is to discover the illness behind each action—an interpretive turn that provides a medical justification for state intervention and control.

15. Part of the problem in the total failure to grasp the motivations of militants who turn to tactics of violence is the facile acceptance of the label of "terrorism." It is a virtual mantra drummed into public consciousness by the droning voices of corporate media, corporations who profit from exploiting the living world, and law enforcement agencies such as the Federal Bureau of Investigation (FBI), driven by their corporate masters and simplistic Good vs. Evil mythology, toward an obsessive pursuit of eco-activists in the ALF, ELF, Stop Huntingdon Animal Cruelty (SHAC), and other militant direct action groups. As Best and Nocella argue, terrorism is a political and semantically corrupt concept used against dissenting groups "to malign their cause and demonize them" (365).

16. One component of heavy responses to militant direct action is the attempt on the parts of governments to respond to respond to the *method* of terrorism as protest. The use of an extra-governmental path to bring pressure on a government official creates a non-negotiable request from a citizen. In the usual relationship between government official and citizen, the citizen has almost no power and the official can choose to listen or not listen to the complaints. But militant direct action, particularly pointed actions, make demands that can not be put off or denied. At stake is the very nature of complacent citizenry and a government in control.

The American Indian Movement in the 21st Century

Tony LoGrande and Robert Roche

America of the late 1960s was a place of political unrest and of racial turbulence. The war in Vietnam was daily becoming a point of contention, dividing Americans into "hawks" and "doves," and driving a wedge between the establishment and America's youth. The poor of the inner cities, particularly those of African descent, were beginning to find their voice and to protest against the deplorable conditions under which they were forced to live: the dreadful housing, the lack of meaningful employment, and the limited opportunities for quality education. These protests—against the war, against poverty and discrimination—were physical and visible, often militant, and occasionally violent. It was this atmosphere of social upheaval that gave birth to the American Indian Movement (AIM).

During the Summer of 1968, 200 or so socially aware members of the Native American community came together to discuss various issues bearing upon Native Americans in general, and those residing in Minnesota particularly. Among those issues were police brutality, slum housing, the 80% unemployment rate, and the flagrantly racist anti-Indian practices of the Minneapolis public school system. The community also challenged the equally racist and discriminatory policies of the Hennepin County welfare system toward Native Americans, and the questionable policies of the federal government in regard to Native Americans.

This meeting marked the nativity of the American Indian Movement. In addition to the issues mentioned above, the Movement was created to address the need to protect treaty rights, preserve traditional Native Culture and language, maintain traditional Native Spirituality, and fight for Indian Sovereignty. "Sovereignty, Land and Culture" was the rallying cry of the American Indian Movement back in its early days. And during the 60s and 70s, when activist protest and upheaval were the norm in this country (indeed, throughout the world) the activities in which the fledgling Movement took part were often militant if not straightforwardly violent—and had to be in order to get the world's attention.

In 1968, for example, the Minneapolis AIM Patrol organized to address police brutality, sometimes came into violent contact with the Minneapolis Police Force. Many in the public viewed AIM's 1969 occupation of Alcatraz Island (claiming it as Indian land), as a belligerent and intrusive act. AIM critics also disdained the takeover of an abandoned naval air station near Minneapolis in 1970—an act meant to focus attention on Indian education. Similarly, many were stunned when AIM forces occupied the offices of the Bureau of Indian Affairs (BIA) in Washington, DC to protest their dishonest and exploitative policies. Were these actions effective? For the most part, yes. They did draw attention to the plight of the Native American in the mid-20th century. Were they extreme? For the time, no, they were not.

AIM was involved in a number of activist incidents in the years following the Minneapolis and Alcatraz events, particularly in the early 1970s. In March 1970, to protest against BIA anti-Indian employment policies, activists commandeered the Bureau of Indian Affairs Office in Denver, Colorado. On July 7th of that year, AIM-led Native Americans were raided by Chicago Police and the FBI in their "Chicago American Indian Village," a tent city which had been pitched behind Wrigley Field to protest the lack of services provided to them by the city of Chicago. On Thanksgiving Day, 1970, the American Indian Movement seized the Mayflower II in Plymouth, Massachusetts. Members of AIM, including Russell Means and Dennis Banks, proclaimed Thanksgiving a national day of mourning to commemorate the theft of Indian lands by white colonists. These and many other incidents marked the turbulent early years of AIM.

But times change, as do social norms and expectations. Actions that were once thought to be justified, even appropriate, to advance a cause are now considered reckless acts of terrorism. Violence and militancy in the name of a movement, no matter how well-intentioned or noble, is no longer tolerated. Thus, as the contemporary world has changed, so has the American Indian Movement. "Sovereignty, Land and Culture" is still the rallying cry, the focal point of the Movement's efforts, but its methods have changed to adapt to the norms and expectations of the world around it. The byword today is no longer militant protest, but rather active and vigorous education. By reaching out with honest, truthful information and an affirmative and confident attitude, the American Indian Movement is daily accomplishing its goals. Even the occasional peaceful protest, such as the opening-day rally against Chief Wahoo at Jacobs Field in Cleveland, Ohio is actually an exercise in education.

Despite the fact that eight million Native People in the Americas were slaughtered by European "explorers" during the 23 years after *we discovered Christopher Columbus* in 1492; despite the fact that the Federal Government of the United States has been committing cultural genocide against our people in the years since; despite the fact that the same government has systematically deprived us of our treaty rights, our sacred ceremonies, rituals, and religion; and despite the fact that attempts have been made to trivialize us and dehumanize us through mockery, massacre and mayhem, we have retained our dignity, honesty, and courage. We have maintained our values throughout the horrors of sterilization, relocation, boarding schools, religious persecution, and assimilation, and the prejudice and discrimination that continue today. Through changing attitudes and the joint effort of our autonomous chapters, we, the American Indian Movement, must educate the Native Community and especially our children, about the truths of our history that have been hidden beneath the misinformation that passes for Native American History in our schools. We can simultaneously educate the general public (those who do not refuse to listen, at least) about our true history, demonstrating that we were living in civilized, organized societies while their ancestors were still crouching in caves in Europe. The *truth* must be known and it must be accessible for this simple reason: those who do not know and understand history, and the truth of *our history*, are doomed to relive it.

The American Indian Movement has accomplished much for Native Americans in the last 35 years. It has much yet to accomplish. And it will do so using the devastatingly effective tools of education and peaceful leadership. In a world that is less tolerant of acts of physical activism, and which is, seemingly, more ready and able to be attentive to the needs of those outside the dominant culture, these current methods of affecting change will accomplish much more than those less peaceful methods of former times.

It is difficult to speak of the protection and preservation of Native People and Native culture without talking about the protection and preservation of Mother Earth, with whom our lives and our spirits are so intimately entwined. Since the earliest days of the "explorers," foreigners have been attempting to buy Her, plunder Her, rape Her, and destroy Her, all in the name of profit. They, who do not seem to understand that all life springs from Her and that all things of Her's are sacred—even the very rocks—have pillaged the Earth and scarred Her, so that they could trade Her *true* wealth for *their* form of *meaningless* wealth.

And so it is today, and the "Land" part of "Sovereignty, Land and Culture" has very real meaning in contemporary society. The importance and sacredness of our Mother Earth has just as much relevance today as it did 500 years ago or 5,000 years ago. We, as a People, still feel that we have been put here to protect and defend Her and all that walk upon Her, fly above Her and swim in Her waters. The dominant culture insists that the papers they hold granting them a piece of Her gives them the right to treat Her as they will. The users still despoil the land in order to get the raw materials that they need to run their machines—machines that are made to create one primary product: profit. In the process, much of what the Creator made as a part of our Mother, the Earth, is being destroyed. As the hills and rivers and forests are being turned into housing developments and mines and factories and cesspools, the homes of our People, and of the creatures who are our brothers, are quickly fading into oblivion.

As AIM fights for the rights and freedoms of Native American Peoples, so it fights for the rights of those People to preserve what is left of the natural world. No longer do we fight with lances and bows, but with writs and lobbyists and injunctions. We fight by trying to appeal to the humanity and decency and commonsense of those in power, both in government and in business, and to make them see the wisdom of preserving the Earth so that future generations—of all species—may thrive. So we strive to save the Earth, our Mother, so that we and all our relations can continue to live in the way we were meant to live: taking care of our Mother and serving the Creator.

Random Thoughts on Eco-Racism and Resistance

Kazi Toure

As vast and deep as this subject is, I will attempt to point out some of the obvious, leaving you to conclude what is to be done. One has to be careful of how things are worded these days, as conspiracy charges can be brought from random thoughts.

We have known for years of the dangers of humankind's ability to create inventions that would enhance and promote "better" lives for everyone…or at least that is how the rhetoric is couched. As it turns out, a large number of those inventions have proven to be extremely detrimental to our health and the health of this planet.

From the pesticides/herbicides that are sprayed on plants and vegetables, to injections of hormones in cows and chickens, from the erosion of our forests to the pollution of our waters, and the greenhouse gas emissions that cause global warming, greed spread by imperialism lies at the root of our social and environmental problems. My contention is that everything is connected—everything. What goes on in one part of the world affects people in another part. When Dow Chemical or Waste Management dumps toxic solutions in poor neighborhoods or any community, people drinking the water will be affected. It is a well established fact that some of the most polluted areas in this country are either on Native reservations or in neighborhoods of the poor and people of color. The most appalling and abandoned factories sit on Native reservations or economically depressed communities. Some of the most devastating and environmentally burdened areas are located in Mississippi and New Orleans, locations doubly hit by the recent hurricanes—and we saw the racist and apathetic response by the US government.

Want to know how this country exports the American way to other countries? Often times when US landfills are full, the government places the garbage on barges and floats them down to third world countries that they pay to take the waste. Why? The US consumes anywhere from 25–40% of the world's natural resources while only making up only 4% of the world's total population. As a result, almost 80% of the trash produced in the whole hemisphere comes from the US. The poor nations are forced to choose between contaminating their population or not taking much-needed money. Would you honestly call this anything but racist?

Another random thought: every time we turn on the TV to watch the news, sports events, movies, or any program, we are bombarded with commercials that detail a list of causes and symptoms of depression, while promoting drugs as the solution to the problem. The list is so long that 90% of the American population can identify with many of the symptoms. Missing in the ad and in the social debate, is the fact that depression is also caused by poverty, oppression, and the daily grind of a dog-eat-dog society that does not eat dog.

In the past, as in the present, when people start to organize themselves against the big multinational companies that are engaged in the practice of destroying natural resources—land, water, air, trees—and Mother Earth herself, they are criminalized and either locked up or killed, depending on how well they have organized. Those jailed are known as political prisoners, mainly because they are in organizations that decided to take a conscious, organized action against exploitation and US imperialism.

In the last several decades, young, mostly white anti-imperialists formed under a couple of organizations—the Animal Liberation Front (ALF) and the Earth Liberation Front (ELF)—that have been targeted by the FBI and labeled "eco-terrorist." The radical social movement welcomes these comrades who have joined ranks and share the suffering of other political prisoners, some of whom have been locked up for over thirty years. Since September 11, 2001, the FBI, along with every other law enforcement agency or affiliation, has labeled nearly every organization in opposition to the government's domestic or foreign policies a terrorist group or a supporter of terrorism. According to the FBI, "terrorism" is the "unlawful use of force or violence, committed by a group of two or more individuals, against persons or property to intimidate or coerce government, the civilian population, or any segment thereof, in furtherance of political or social objectives."

By this broad and vague definition, Martin Luther King, Jr. would have been labeled a terrorist. Cesar Chavez of the United Farm Workers, John Afrika of MOVE, and those folks that threw the tea in the Boston harbor would all be labeled terrorists. The latter group maybe should have been labeled terrorist back then, not for throwing the tea overboard, but for dressing up in Native regal and attempting to shift the blame to Native Americans. It was okay for colonists to break away from the oppression of the British government, but it is not okay for people today to break away from the tyranny of the US government. Depending on who is doing the labeling, attempts "to intimidate or coerce...the government, the civilian population, or any segment" could easily be applied to the US government itself. And I repeat, depending on who is doing the labeling.

Those young people who are now carrying on the struggles of John Afrika's MOVE, Cesar Chavez, and all the people who came before them, should be commended, and ultimately joined. All of *our* struggles have a common enemy. It only makes sense that people unite the many struggles that our enemy tries its best to keep divided; that we deal collectively with the giant of US imperialism.

So what happens to be random thoughts for me, hopefully have made some things clearer for you—namely that racism in the United Snakes is alive and well. And for a buck, they will destroy the earth, the very source of life.

What to do about it? You'll have to come to that on your own. But rest assured if you do nothing, your life will not get any better.

That is the way things are, folks. One man's freedom fighter is another man's terrorist.

Grumpywarriorcool
What makes our movements white?

amory starr

Beginning in the Global South with IMF-riots in the 1980s, the anti- or alterglobalization movement is the most recent phase of resistance to 513+ years of colonialism. The movement has taken aim at the institutions, legal frameworks, and justificatory popular ideologies which implement and enforce the privatization and marketization of the ecological and social commons. Around the world, indigenous people, farmers, fisherfolk, youth, workers, and unemployeds are collectively asserting "one no" to this "neoliberalism"/multinational capitalism/imperialism and generating "many yeses,"[1] based in ecological and community-oriented livelihoods and political processes.

The US alterglobalization movement is built on the foundations of Latin American solidarity, internationalist unions, progressive populism, Green Party and other sustainability work, anti-fascist, and do-it-yourself organizations centered in punk rock communities, connections with European autonomism,[2] new agrarian/sustainable cuisine movements including anti-biotech, political pagans, anti-nuclear movements, environmental justice, forest wars, and other forms of radical ecodefense.

The most intense and visible manifestations of the movement use the term "direct action."

Repopularized between 1999 and 2001, direct action has become hegemonic in the US alterglobalization movement. The conjunction of activist punk, political paganism, and radical ecodefense have produced a political framework and culture which emphasizes anti-hierarchy, consensus-based decision-making, open organizing, mutual support among all groups, invitations to cultural diversity, low-budget operations which creatively maximize use of marginal and discarded resources, physical spaces that prioritize low-throughput/sustainability, free services for all participants, vegan food, affirmation of marginal youth cultures including travelers, direct action tactics, carnivalesque imagery, and heroic personal risk.

As Francesca Polletta shows in her important book *Democracy is an Endless Meeting*, these methods of organizing and action have roots in earlier movements such as the Student Nonviolent Coordinating Committee (SNCC), Students for a Democratic Society (SDS), and the feminist movement.[3] At the same time, Direct Action organizing is a jarring departure from much of what has become familiar in labor and community organizing since the 1960s, particularly in its embrace of what many would call "undignified" low- or no-budget physical spaces, unwillingness to impose fees or dues, hostile rejection of any leadership, and the moral priority given to direct confrontation with law enforcement.

> *i'd been in the streets for a couple of years and i finally had to say something about the masculinity of that experience, about how i felt "weak, fearful, trivial" next to other activists who showed "courage, humility, sacrifice." it felt like the gendered story in every war movie i'd ever hated for just that reason. suspended by the agonizing disappointment that i would have to be a street warrior to really contribute to my beloved movement, i hid the halting poem under my bed.* **we have come to recognize ourselves by the glint of riot helmets.**

I didn't know that for radical women in the New Left, the romanticized pressure to "become street fighters" during defense of People's Park in 1969 was "the final straw" that drove them away from the male Left and into the women's liberation movement. I didn't know that their earlier straws were straining our own organizing—"forceful public speaking as the mark of leadership" and the prioritization of "intellectual theory" and "verbal debate" over organizing. I didn't know that that women involved with SDS (which "revered the mind, but ignored feelings"), looked back heartbroken for "doubting their intellectual talents, for accepting men's definition of the world."[4]

While I was suffering from repeated history, I was also struggling mightily with the horrifying news that people of color were describing the alterglobalization movement as racist. (I first heard at the Los Angeles Democratic National Convention protests in 2000, which was actually a bit late as the issues blew up immediately after Seattle.)

I was shocked. This is the movement that **does** get beyond capitalism in its analysis. It's anti-corporate, targeting the enemies of the environmental justice movement. It's challenging the economic policies that are forcing people into brutal migrations. It's discrediting the development theories that tell urban communities they should be grateful for "enterprise zones" and toxic jobs. It's making the connections between redlining and horrific dam projects and high interest loans at trade schools. And we're doing the Black Power thing, taking leadership from people of color (the Zapatistas)! This was the movement I'd been dreaming of because it was about the assaults on communities of color here, indigenous communities everywhere, ordinary people in the Global South, and farmers. This is the movement challenging the devastation of diasporas, taking on economic policies in a context of racist colonialism and ethnocentric "development." This is the movement that understands environmental destruction as livelihood destruction. This is the movement that does it right! How could anti-racist activists not be as thrilled as I was that this movement was actually happening?

I embarked on an admittedly defensive exploration of how this could be. I started reading everything posted on the *Colours of Resistance* web-site,[5] interviewing activists, asking questions, consulting with anti-racist coaches, painstakingly cataloging the charges of racism, and publishing a few articles refuting all but a few seemingly isolated incidents. Finally, just before the next Conventions (a good four years later), I started to get it. And that would just be embarrassing if it weren't that I think I'm not alone.

Of course, globalization is affecting communities of color both here and abroad. Of course, globalization is more than an economic project—it's part of racist imperialism. Lots of white people are working on the grow-ing anti-imperialist movement in the US. But (aha!) it's not *what* we work on that makes our politics anti-racist, it's *how* we do it that matters. And in fact, a lot of the alterglobalization *how* is even pretty good. Consistent with principles of anti-racist organizing, we *do* carefully design campaigns to make connections between distant global institutions and our neighbor-hoods, we *do* emphasize building community as part of our activism, and we *do* work to empower marginalized people. What I have finally begun to understand is that the *how* is deep and subtle.

This essay does explores what it is about the way that we do seemingly anti-racist work that alienates activists and communities of color—groups we'd like to be working with. Before I go any further though, it's important to note that white activists have better and worse moments in struggle with whiteness, so this paper does not generalize about white activists. It seeks to describe the problems with what I call "white organizing." Also I need to note that this essay weaves together the scholarship and the lyrical insights that work here and there to help folks see what is invisible. And several colleagues must be credited for the ideas presented in this multivo-cal text.[6]

This essay does assume that activists see themselves as organizers, by which I mean that they want to expand participation in the movement, rather than operating only as small cells or vanguards. It also assumes that activists are already aware of and working to address the destructive, ex-clusionary and alienating effects of security culture. This essay addresses activists who are interested in examining, self-critically, the impacts of the whiteness of our organizing out of concern for building a participatory and multicultural revolution.

Smuggling My friend Jane is a feminist scholar, active in multiracial queer communities, and she's white.[7] She's radical but not an alterglobal-ization activist. One day she cleared her throat and said, "You activists spend so much time dealing with your fear of the cops and jostling each other to be more brave. Why is pushing yourself around those issues really important but it's not important to push yourself around dancing—as long as you're wearing a tutu and all?" And Aimee, droopy in her tutu, stirred and exclaimed, "Oh! Dancing is wimpy and girly. Cops are macho."

we don't recognize warriors as macho when they're women

Foucault reminded us to be very careful about what parts of the old regime we are smuggling into our revolutions.[8] What I was calling "courage, humility, sacrifice" is the internalized piece of masculinity. Recognizing how feminists might (still) be smuggling masculinity, helped me see how revolutionary anti-racists might be smuggling whiteness.

Where is the smuggler's hold? In feminism, these warriors hide out under the protection of "diverse feminisms." Anybody's version of feminism is legitimate. Among radical countercultures, the same commensurability applies in the discourse of (sub)cultural diversity.

So what? What's at stake in this smuggled masculinity? Invoking "culture" claims a socio-moral status beyond reprove and a horizontality which obviates critique. **It is this framework of cultural diversity which makes it difficult to identify and address internalized oppression within radical and revolutionary countercultures.** The freedom from critique prevents us from discovering what we are missing.

What is missing in a fearless feminism? In fearless activism? Just as Audre Lorde pointed out that anger is loaded with information and energy,[9] artist Dan Cohen describes the value of fear.[9]

> The culture of the barricade, of opposition, needs to celebrate its own lucid rage...but what about that internal world behind the barricades? What happens to the doubts, fears, questions whispered in the silences between confrontations? Those voices of intimate reflection are an enormous archive of knowledge, but remain hidden behind profound doubt and fear.[10]

Feminist warriors smuggling the masculine self-image of "courage, humility, strength" are cut off from this "archive."

Not so Counter-Cultural... Activist cultures are heavily invested, deeply meaningful frameworks designed to create time and space that affirm and manifest our hopes, dreams, and visions. But, like any culture, these precious, hard-won expressions and rituals can be deeply alienating to those who do not share them. While no culture can be a universally welcoming landing pad, that doesn't mean that organizers are absolved of any responsibility for culture. Culture is an unavoidable part of how we do politics, and it must be viewed critically, as any other part of organizing.

White organizing in alterglobalization, radical ecodefense, anti-imperialism, and other movements often draws on "alternative" subcultures which experience themselves as countercultural. These subcultures do, in many ways, explicitly counteract and displace oppressive hierarchies, including racism. But the subcultures smuggle whiteness. It is the unacknowledged whiteness that undermines a subculture's language of outreach, inclusion, and revolutionary change.

For example, the Direct Action framework of "diversity of tactics" establishes unstructured space and participatory democratic processes, which are presumed to provide space for any radical political possibility, including anti-racism. Within this framework, people have the right to participate as they wish, and stylistic differences are enclosed by a framework of cultural diversity. But after Miami and Cancún,[11] I wrote:

> i'm going to stink, i'm going in there even though i'm contagious, i'm going to bring my barking dog, i have the right to do whatever the fuck i want and people just have to deal with it and i'm going to call this "cultural diversity" or "class issues" or "activist dogs." meanwhile other folks around are feeling like another white guy is doing whatever the fuck he wants, which is [again] downright unpleasant for [us folks] who seem to be always subject to some white guy [cop, schoolteacher, boss, landlord...] doing whatever the fuck he wants at our expense even though it's obviously no way to treat other human beings and we don't know anyone in [our group] who would treat people that way nor would [people in our group] let people be treated that way if we had any influence over the situation, which must mean that all these other people in here think that what he's doing is a perfectly fine way to (mis)treat/inconvenience/offend other people...

excessive individualism isn't cultural diversity, it's internalized white privilege

Massimo De Angelis explains that the struggle against globalization requires both local struggles, where "our desires and aspirations take shape" and the increasingly global context of struggle, which is fundamentally the "discovery of the other." As we become a global community of activists, we develop solidarity through a "creative process of discovery, not a presumption."[12] Most poignantly, he writes:

> And if you are irresponsible towards the "other" in your community, then think twice, because the world we are fighting against is based precisely on this persistent indifference to the other...[13]

Assuming that spaces, behaviors, and actions are culturally neutral and therefore inclusive, is an act of indifference or disregard for other people. To create inclusive space, we need not neutrality, but discovery. During my research, Lorance Romero schooled me on how offensive it is to Latino people to have a meeting without having food first, or to eat your own lunch that you brought without offering some to others near you.

> so i'm sitting on the floor, i'm eating my food, i don't even notice any more how many cops are parked across the street, i'm tired, someone just came in the room i don't know i'm not paying attention...all that to me feels like **nothing is going on.** to a person of color (or any person new to this activist culture) entering that space, a lot of things that are going on: there are no chairs and the floor looks too dirty to sit on, people are rude, and there is a frightening army of police across the street.

The discovery Massimo urges means not only getting to know each other, but also interrogating the structural contents of political concepts and space we take for granted which, as it turns out, have a huge impact on the shape of our political work. Take, for example, dignity. For privileged activists, dignity is about washing the blood off their hands by dis-identifying with professionalism, managerialism, and status symbols. For people who wear uniforms to work and don't get to be clean there, dignity, particularly in political space, involves having the aspects of self that capitalism and racism withhold.

> *if i'm willing to be super uncomfortable and not shower for a week so that i can fight for change, maybe i need to understand that spending our precious organizing money on some chairs will enable a whole bunch of really cool people to feel like our meeting is a place they can be comfortable—people who just can't sit on the floor because their legs or back ache, or have come straight from work, or can't afford to get their clothes dirty, or just find sitting on the floor really fucking weird and there isn't a way to explain it to them before they are going to feel like this space isn't a space for them.*

Individualism and its Communities A hallmark of white countercultures is the vision of individualistic self-creation in which oppressive childhood values and institutions are cast off, and political compassion embraces what might best be theorized as "imagined community."[14] This process involves finding community and "chosen family" with those who share political perspectives. Since white activists often face ridicule, threats, or abuse from parents for participating in activism, many find it hard to imagine parents participating in radical political action. People with parents who are supportive, or who might even participate in marches, are considered "lucky" in white activist communities. Experiences of critical mass (such as large protests) are powerful for white activists, in part because of the isolation that accompanies politicization.

Meanwhile, activists of color envision social movements in intimate terms; fighting racism is protecting their mothers, fathers, brothers, sisters, children. Survival and struggle are principles learned at home, from family and elders, at church... Activists' evolving political principles and work need to make sense in the context of their histories, their families, and the spiritual/religious traditions of their communities.

While white activists are also under pressure to conform, revolt is encouraged by white traditions which valorize defiant and expressive individualism.[15] Individualism enables white radicals to reject home and family, and to define themselves anew. Radicals of color are sometimes taken aback by white activists' distance from family, history, and community. People without families and communities may seem like unaccountable, untrustworthy free-agents. It is also hard to assess the extent to which activists who have separated from their birth families for political reasons, are indeed totally cut off from their family's resources; a confusion that leads to seething tensions about class privilege.

This individualistic mode of politics also says that the intellectual content of political actions is more important than their social content. When activists focus energy on clever communications and/or disruptions which even the mainstream media will cover, they imagine that the cleverness and surprising courage of these actions will excite people to participate in various capacities, or if they missed out, hearing about these actions or seeing them on TV will inspire people to participate in the next one. White organizing sees a "good action" (a clever and visible one) *as organizing* because **joining a movement is understood as an individual intellectual act, not a social one.** Individualism pre-dates politics, community follows.

For whites who have left home, subcultures are precious. By necessity, these subcultures celebrate individualism at the same time as they awkwardly endeavor to create the community that many have never previously experienced. These communities' foundation and basis of connection is a commitment to carefully-chosen principles, moreso than the social relationships themselves.

Strange Commitments Activist countercultures often emphasize "prefigurative" practices which embody revolutionary vision as if it were already achieved, thereby calling it into being. Some aspects of prefiguration are rarely contested, such as the need to address multiple oppressions even while organizing urgent campaigns. But other aspects of prefiguration have become controversial flashpoints. Two controversial prefigurative practices are radical democracy and responsible consumption.

In radical participatory democracy, everyone has an equal voice and is welcome to participate without having to establish a reputation or credentials. Leadership, when it exists (most often in the form of "facilitation") is supposed to be temporary, rotating, and random, affirming that all participants have equal (and equally limited) authority.[16] Far from a theoretical ideal, participatory democracy has been refined by Quakers, civil rights organizations, the New Left, feminists, as well as community organizing and direct action movements. Polletta argues that deliberative strategies are developing steadily, as activists try to formalize equality, build the relationships on which collective deliberation depends, and communicate democratic rituals.[17]

Popular in radical environmental and alterglobalization movements, responsible consumption is a personal and collective practice which builds awareness of dependency on third world resources (including labor), and then works to reduce that dependency. Independence involves re-learning subsistence production[18] and creating alternative forms of identity and celebration. ("Look what we found in the dumpster!") Even activists who feel that consumption politics are inadequate in themselves, often practice responsible consumption as a "practice of commitment"[19] to global justice.

These activities are similar to anti-racist practices in that they are *local* (unlike mass actions and international campaigns), *build community,* and *empower* marginalized people. Despite these similarities, other aspects of the culture are off-putting. Participatory democracy's legacy from the civil rights movement was as an idealistic and youthful drama disconnected from more serious struggles. (Polletta re-tells this history.) The hegemonic civil rights/anti-racist organizational style rests on the presence of well-known, established activists. Meetings and actions are dignified and tidy, prefiguring a very different future than responsible consumption—one without the material scarcity imposed by racial inequality.

White organizing assumes that activists arrive at meetings having decided already to be committed and to do inconvenient, uncomfortable things in service of their convictions. It's not necessary to make meetings themselves comfortable or empowering. Participants who are committed will not be daunted by discomfort. If people aren't willing to be uncomfortable, they're not ready for activism. In contrast, anti-racist organizing endeavors to establish legitimacy, comfort, and confidence by affirming values, traditions, culture, ideas, and leadership of people of color, and ensuring that the space is non-dominated by white culture, procedures, and ideas (although white people and ideas may be present.)

Imagining Empowerment White organizing has specific assessments of what is "empowering" for strangers. Conceptualizing new activists as isolated individuals, an "empowering space" is one that will provide "something for everyone" (individuals) through "diversity of tactics." In contrast, anti-racist organizing sees new activists as people embedded in oppressed communities. An "empowering space" is dignified and welcoming for people more accustomed to exclusion and invisibility. It must acknowledge and show commitment to transforming the experience of the marginalized group. And it must be *safe* from daily experiences of racism and violence.[20] These crucial aspects of anti-racist organizing are ill-protected by diversity of tactics.

> *negotiating the order of the line at the taco stand...i was committed to fairness and accuracy to the order of arrivals...then i realized that the uniformed Latino men i was negotiating with were negotiating something else—something more and other than fairness. **perhaps when life is abjectly, incessantly, unfair**, getting some fairness isn't very powerful. it's going to take more than vigilant neutrality (formal equality) to heal these wounds. generosity, kindness, yielding, compassion, and joy are the comfort, the balm, the sanctuary, **and the alternative**.*

My orientation to fairness reflected an arbitrary, individualistic orientation to the mechanics of social justice. This orientation drives white organizing. For example, we create highly formalized methods of equalizing conversation space, methods which take for granted that we all arrive equal, that we all have the same sorts of needs from that space, and comparable capacity to articulate and negotiate them. And that we don't need any generosity, yielding, or compassion.

Smart Radicalism, the Political *sine qua non* In white organizing, radicalism is a fundamental axis around which politics revolve. Invoking the term "radicalism" almost always implies two things. First, it implies a commitment to radical principles and theories of social relations and alternatives, such as anti-capitalism, anti-imperialism, racial and gender liberation, and so on. Second, radicalism entails "correct" interpretation, reasoning, and application of principles in a given situation. Correct theory and application are understood to be the most likely to be *effective* in eliminating oppression. For a position or an action to be correctly radical (as opposed to fetishized, compromised, or misapplied radicalism) is the highest value accorded within radical circles. This hierarchy echoes exclusionary social class structures and could be the unwitting internalization of class elitism within activist countercultures.

In radical white organizing, once people have gathered to participate in social action, a major activity is securing the radicalism of the group, which consists of identifying and vilifying any "reformists" or reformist proposals. It also may involve some kind of subtle litmus test of the martyrial militancy of members—their willingness to engage in high-risk direct action. Those who do not pass are unofficially disregarded. These tests and the resulting rigid (although unacknowledged or even denied) hierarchy is not missed by those demoted, who feel unwanted or excluded. They may not return to future group events, but their loss is considered unimportant by those who prioritize radicalism and/or militance. The performative requirements of sufficiently impressing the radicals may become a preoccupation of remaining members.

While ideological and tactical radicalism exist in antiracist organizing, they are not the standard by which organizations and organizers relate with participants. Instead, friendliness, comfort, safety, generosity, and reliable personal connection are the necessary elements of "good" political work.

> Some antiracists, such as Bernice Johnson Reagon, seek to recenter debates about radicalism by reorienting the terms, showing that Black survival and anything that prioritizes it, is in and of itself already radical. The sociology of race reveals that the radical/reformist distinction is too dualistic and does not take into account the wily ways of both racism and antiracist resistance which require, for example, both state intervention and autonomy from the state, militant action and slow, creeping transformation, etc. Some antiracists have pointed out that the very word "radical" is symptomatic of what they call white culture, an abstract, exclusive, either/or standard that is more distracting or divisive than it is galvanizing, empowering, or productive.[21]

Grumpywarriorcool Then Jane says "And another thing..." Oh boy. "You know I've met about ten of these brave new warrior activists from the anti-globalization movement and there's really a pattern of how they hold their faces. They really have a mean, judgmental look on their faces. it's expressionless, but smirky. And it surprises me, because I would think as activists they'd be wanting to be more friendly to people."

I hit the roof. "I'm having a hard enough time trying to convince people that there might be more going on in radical counterculture than just cultural diversity. Now you want me to try to talk to them about the looks on their faces? Isn't that the very sort of invasion of the person and oppressive, hegemonic pseudo-values that we're *fighting*? What you're asking for is what folks would call 'fake.' They would reject that as not the world they want to live in."

Jane responded "If it's fake to be interested in new people then what are you all about?...If you are fundamentally disinterested in other people, you've got bigger problems than a possible risk of fakeness." Then she paused a bit and observed, "The radical people of color I know are so full of life. But your folks seem like they've rejected love of life, rejected too much expression."

"Well I think part of what grumpywarriorcool is about is like this democratic ethic of not wanting to take up very much space." She said, "Get over it. You better figure out how to be democratic and still be full of life."

Countercultures, alienated from the vapidity, repression, and denial which permeates white public culture and family life, promote some version of "cool"—a refusal to participate in the lie that everything is ok. But cool is a smuggler too. Its cultural roots glorify emotional detachment as the basis of dignity. *Cool Rules: Anatomy of an Attitude* tells the history of cool, complete with a section entitled "a whiter shade of cool."

> *many times over the years in my own home, people have come in the door and they don't introduce themselves and i don't introduce myself and my housemates who know this person don't introduce them. it's obviously the right thing to do in that situation and yet none of us do it. there's something all gushy and vulnerable and uncool about it...*

There's a video called *The Merchants of Cool*.[22] Cool is the internalized piece of commodity culture, consumerism. We don't even realize cool isn't ours! We think we made it up. They've sold it to us and we think it's who we are! Cool is the reification of self-indulgent insecurity. Which is fine if you really are just an angry kid, but it's not okay if you're actually a revolutionary anarchist warrior.

Cool is a problem for activists because it gets us into a place where we then feel undignified and vulnerable smiling, approaching someone, talking to strangers, being unilaterally *friendly*. All of that is very un-cool. Whether cool is a habit or a fragile bulwark for someone who feels they can barely keep it together,[23] the result is very little friendliness, and, ultimately not even what most people would call civility, like greeting people when they come into a common space.

Joyful Warriors Jane wasn't done yet. She asked, "What do you think the face of a powerful activist looks like?...What is the face of a joyful warrior?" As participatory democratic radicals start to think through unintentionally smuggled hierarchies, the possible necessity of temporary leadership, and other complexities of power, it would be useful to discuss together the kinds of power we believe in, how power manifests, and then what is the face, the gesture, the relationship with strangers, and the greeting?

In order to get past our emphasis on smartness, we might want to collectively remember precisely how people became involved in (and left) our groups, and compare the importance of cleverness and friendliness in our organizing experiences.

In critically reflecting on our relations with people and groups outside our own, we may want to analyze to what extent we are driven by "discovering the other" in a responsible way, and to what extent are we driven by indifference and contempt masked as politics.

In taking responsibility for our decisions about resources, we might review honestly and systematically, what resources we have access to, and how best to utilize those to make movements welcoming to more and more diverse participants. In discussing race, class, and gender in activist communities, I have noticed that while we have ready access to language and techniques to recognize, confront, and discuss sexism and racism, we are at a loss when we try to discuss class. Frameworks for addressing classism are underdeveloped and, to the extent they exist, have yet to permeate progressive culture.

These suggestions are tentative and preliminary. I hope it provides a map for bravely discussing these issues, sifting through cultural cargo, and creating new countercultures which are more multicultural. In a powerful invitation—the Black Power exhortation to white allies, so eloquently updated for our movements by De Angelis. **Let us see as central to our politics the replacement of indifference with discovery.**

Notes

1. "One No, Many Yeses" is a Zapatista Principle. See Zapatistas in Cyberspace: <http://www.eco.utexas.edu/Homepages/Faculty/Cleaver/zapsincyber.html>.

2. See George Katsiaficas. *The Subversion of Politics: European Autonomous Social Movements and the Decolonization of Everyday Life*. (Oakland, CA: AK Press, 2006), 235.

3. Polletta, Francesca. *Democracy is an Endless Meeting: Democracy in American Social Movements*. Chicago: University of Chicago Press, 2002.

4. Ruth Rosen, "Leaving the Left." In *The World Split Open: How the Modern Women's Movement Changed America* (New York: Viking, 2000), 136, 119.

5. <http://colours.mahost.org/>

6. Much of the analysis that follows was performed jointly by amory starr and Rachel Luft. The method of analysis used was an intense distillation of perspectives. The version of anti-racism which was used to perform this distillation was not the anti-racism articulated from within the anti-globalization movement, but instead one from outside it, best represented by the influential People's Institute (<http://www.thepeoplesinstitute.org/>), whose analyses were often present in (but not at all completely encompassing of) the anti-racist-anti-globalization discourse. Readers should be aware that references to "anti-racist perspective" below *are not* descriptive of anti-racist-anti-globalization practice. For a comprehensive view of anti-racist pedagogy, see Luft, Rachel. *Race Training: Antiracist Workshops in a Post-Civil Rights Era*. Diss. University of California, Santa Barbara, September 2004. Also see my overview of these issues "how can anti-imperialism not be anti-racist?: a critical impasse in the anti-globalization movement," in *Journal of World Systems Research* 10.1. (Winter 2004).

7. Jane Ward.

8. *Birth of the Clinic.* New York: Pantheon, 1963. *Discipline and Punish.* New York: Pantheon, 1977.

9. Lorde, Audre. *Sister Outsider: Essays & Speeches.* Crossing Press, 1984.

275. also see Lappé, Frances Moore and Jeffrey Perkins. *You Have the Power: Choosing Courage in a Culture of Fear.* Penguin, 2004.

10. Cohen, Dan Baron, "Beyond the barricade," *New Internationalist* 338 (September 2001). <http://www.newint.org/issue338/beyond.htm>

11. WTO 5th ministerial, Cancún México, 10–14 September 2003. FTAA negotiations, Miami FL, 19–21 November 2003.

12. De Angelis, Massimo. "from movement to society." In *On Fire: The Battle of Genoa and the Anti-Capitalist Movement.* Tucson, Arizona: One-off Press, 2001, 118–19,124.

13. Ibid.

14. Anderson, Benedict. *Imagined Communities: Reflections on the Origin and Spread of Nationalism.* London: Verso, 1991.

15. Bellah, Robert. et. al. *Habits of the Heart: Individualism and Commitment in American Life.* Chicago: University of Chicago Press, 1985.

16. See *Anarchism in Action: Methods, Tactics, Skills, and Ideas.* <http://www.radio4all. org/aia/>; *Collective Book on Collective Process* <http://www.geocities.com/collectivebook>; Steward Community Woodland consensus process step-by-step <http://www.stewardwood. org/resources/DIYconsensus.htm>.

17. Polletta, 2002, 178, chapters 7 & 8.

18. Bennholdt-Thomsen, Veronika and Maria Mies. *The Subsistence Perspective: Beyond the Globalised Economy.* London: Zed Books, 1999.

19. Bellah, et. al., *Habits of the Heart: Individualism and Commitment in American Life.*

20. This fundamental difference leads anti-racist organizers to say, "If we're going to keep escalating the tactics, we're going to keep turning people off to them." (Brian Dominick, "Anti-Capitalist Globalization Organizing," *Arise! Journal* (June 2001).) But this interpretation of anti-racism is not without its critics. Ward Churchill argues that pacifism sometimes indicates a pathological commitment to pacifism rather than justice (similar to activists more committed to radicalism, than organizing.) (*Pacifism as Pathology.* Winnipeg: Arbeiter Ring Publishing, 1998.) As noted by a recent collective commentary, tactical moderacy may actually normalize white middle class perspectives. "But to realize our potential for building a mass movement requires, first and foremost, clarity as to who actually constitutes the 'mainstream' and why. The right, the corporate media, and elite policy makers persist in painting 'mainstream America' as white and middle class. Even many white liberals cling to the notion that building a mass movement against war necessitates the use of techniques and rhetoric that 'don't scare away' middle class whites." (Numerous Authors. "Open Letter On Movement Building." 21 Feb. 2003. <http://www.Znet.org>).

21. Rachel Luft, 2003. Reagon, Bernice Johnson, "My Black Mothers and Sisters Or On Beginning a Cultural Autobiography," *Feminist Studies* 8.1 (Spring 1982): 81–96.

22. Pountain, Dick and David Robins. *Cool Rules: Anatomy of an Attitude.* Reaktion Books, 2000. Dretzin, Rachel, "The Merchants of Cool," PBS Frontline <http://www.pbs.org/wgbh/ pages/frontline/shows/cool/>

23. Seems to me that insecurity is now, like eating disorders, a collective phenomenon—it's not a personal pathology or a disorder. See Bordo, Susan. *Unbearable Weight: Feminism, Western Culture, and the Body.* University of California Press, 1995.

Identity Politics and Poetic Solidarity
Roots of Alliance between Feminism and Animal/Earth Liberation

homefries

W hat do women have in common with other species, and the earth as a whole? This is one of the first questions that come to mind when we feminists think about how our liberation struggles might be tied to revolutionary environmentalism. Ecofeminism's most basic precept is that the movements for feminism, earth liberation, and animal liberation must go hand-in-hand. Some argue for this alliance out of a belief that there is something in the essence of *being* a "woman" that connects women to the earth and other animals. Others argue for an alliance that's rooted in shared experiences of specific types of domination and forms of resistance, instead of essential similarities.

Crafting a poetic tension between these identities—one that draws from our common experiences of oppression and liberation—is a third way of grounding an ecofeminist alliance. Analogizing experiences of sexism, anthropocentrism, and ecological destruction through metaphorical language both resonates and leaves us hanging. This offers a kind of shifting ground that's sometimes solid, but often obscured by dim light or darkness. It gets scary not knowing exactly where you're standing—even thinking that the floor has dropped into oblivion—but then sometimes it can feel like dancing on air.

I'm a white female who grew up in Atlanta in the 80s, and now I live in Boston. I have always been financially stable. I'm regarded as "able-bodied" in most ways, and I've benefited from a strong springboard and network of support in obtaining academic degrees. In so many ways these experiences (among others) give rise to the specific perspective on ecofeminism I'll talk about here.

Rooting Alliance in Identity

Some ecofeminists have suggested that the correlation between women and the non-human world is inborn—intrinsic to femininity. By virtue of certain biological traits, such as the capacity to give birth and the monthly cycle of menses, they argue that women are actually "closer" to the earth than men. For example, Constantina Salamone, an early animal liberation ecofeminist, writes, "She [i.e. 'woman'] has the genetic mechanics and suppressed knowledge of simple animal ecology...impressed within the ingrams of her brain, just as she has the surging of the moon-drawn tides circulating within her blood."[1] Linda Vance, another early ecofeminist, explains that she's compelled to be vegetarian "by freeing an intuitive kinship" between herself as a woman and other animals.[2] According to this perspective, women's relationship with the non-human is a form of kinship, much like a mother-daughter union.

In order for these ecofeminists to identify femininity with the non-human world, they have to be able to specify a universal and basically intransigent set of characteristics that inhere to women and signify femininity. But the kaleidoscopic and sociohistorically constructed plurality of "feminine" forms casts doubt about the possibility of universally inherent female traits. Some feminists point out, for instance, that there is male-to-female transgender femininity, corporate executive femininity, Latina femininity, North American white housewife femininity, and "femme" or "butch" lesbian femininities, among many, many others that exist currently or have existed historically throughout many cultures. Taking this line of thought deeper, other feminists question the coherence of abstract or unified gender categories altogether, arguing that what constitutes a person's girl- or womanhood almost always draws from an overlapping multitude of these various feminine identities. Also, what we feel and imagine when we talk about "femininity" may be defined by even more local contexts—our nations, our communities, our families, our schools, our particular constellation of friends, for instance. What does the word mean to you?

Perhaps in talking about "women" these ecofeminists intend to speak only about people with female reproductive capacities. But why are people with female reproductive capacities any more akin to other animals and the earth than those without these capacities? Only a small fraction of the other living beings on this planet experience menses and give birth in the way that human females do.

If "femininity" isn't so easy to define, neither is "nature" or "non-human." The environmental movement often uses "nature" and "humanity" as opposing concepts without offering a clear definition of either. According to standard Western dualistic thinking that frames the vision of many environmental defense activists, Humanity is defined as "not-nature," as Nature is defined as "not-humanity."[3] Kate Soper points out that "Ecological writing...very frequently works implicitly with an idea of nature as a kind of pristine otherness to human culture, whose value is depreciated proportionately to its human admixture."[4] Chaia Heller, an ecofeminist activist, explains how, since the resurgence of the environmental movement in the 1970s, romantic images of "nature" as other-than-human have proliferated. "During Earth Week 1990," she writes, "an epidemic of tee-shirts hit the stores depicting sentimental images of a soft blue and green ball of earth being held and protected by two white man's hands."[5] This image distinguishes "nature" from "humanity," positioning "humanity" as the potential saving grace that is now obligated to defend and rescue "nature." "Our relationship to the natural world is largely mediated by industries of production and consumption that shape our appetites, tastes, and desires," writes Heller. "More and more, the nature we know is some market researcher's romantic idea of a 'nature' he thinks we would be likely to buy."[6] To the extent that thinking about "humanity" as separate from "nature" helps in recognizing and ending domination, it can be liberating. But the suggestion that humanity is fundamentally different from "nature" begs a downpour of questions. What's completely unique to humans? What don't we share with any non-humans? If our non-human ancestors are part of "nature," at what point in our evolution did we make such a clean break?

Because of conceptual problems like these, some ecofeminists have resisted the identification of femininity with the non-human, drawing from "poststructuralist" or "social constructionist" feminism.[7] One straightforward example is voiced by Carol Adams: "I value nurturing and caring because it is good," she writes, "not because it constitutes women's 'difference.' Similarly, I do not value animals because women are somehow [essentially] 'closer' to them."[8]

The force of Adams' work lies in illustrating that patterns of domination such as sexual objectification, reproductive control, and domestic violence have oppressed both those who identify as human and those we identify as non-human alike. Our focus shouldn't be on the issue of whether or not we "women" share an identity with the "non-human." Instead, we should direct our attention toward our shared troubles and the struggles we instigate for our survival.

Rooting Alliance in Poetic Solidarity

One of the crises shared by many of us who are identified as "feminine" by the dominant society is our object status. In a myriad of contexts (imagery, sexual contact or even daily conversation with many males, to name a few) we are treated as mere objects devoid of human subjective powers. Women and others who are viewed as objects are not only seen as unable to observe and assess others, but also fundamentally unable to observe and assess themselves. Life under this stereotype creates a cogent empathic link between women and the non-human (who, like us, are stereotyped as unable to have experiences and form judgments—to live "internally").[9]

The dominant representations of women in popular imagery parallel the way non-human beings—especially other animals—are depicted. They create an ongoing persistence-of-vision in which animals and women are just images flashing before our eyes, triggering some kind of desire. This seems particularly true of imagery used in advertising. For instance, the fragmentation of the body into curvy thighs, delicate ankles, round breasts, and emaciated midriffs (among other parts) is common in advertising. Any grocery store's newspaper advertising insert, for example, will depict various fragments of animals' bodies—a wing, a breast, a rump. This form of visual reduction prevents us from imagining the woman or animal that is (or once was) whole and animated by her own life.

Beyond the basic stereotype that women and non-humans are not self-perceiving, there are other common experiences that run between us. For instance: reproductive control is essential to most efforts of mass-producing living beings. Farming (and particularly factory farming) is probably the most abusive of female animals' reproductive systems. Egg-laying hens, for example, are "forced-molted," meaning they are denied water and light for up to two weeks in order to synchronize their egg-laying cycles. The dairy industry is completely predicated on reproductive control: all cows must be pregnant in order to produce milk, so they are constantly impregnated in order to maintain lactation. Similarly, laboratory animals and companion animals are manipulated or directly forced into mating for human profit. The movement against biotechnology has further challenged the platitude that reproductive autonomy is only a "women's rights"—or only a "human rights"—issue. In agribusiness, genetically modified organisms (which we suddenly learn are in our Corn Flakes and Cokes) are a toxic symptom of reproductive control over crops.

Strip mining is another abuse to the non-human world that has long resonated with some people who identify with "femininity." Ecofeminist, Delores Williams, says, "Strip mining exhausts the earth's body..." She compares "the violation of the land's production capacities in strip-mining" to "the violation of black women's bodies and reproduction during slavery."[10] Slave-owners' routine stripping, beating, and raping of slaves is echoed in the way that coal companies strip forests and wildlife from mountains to dig for the coal underneath.

In all of these ways and many more, the political condition of women connects to the political condition of the non-human world. We can assemble our own metaphors based on the comparison of our own experiences with others: "I abhor some of my culture's ways, how it cripples its women, *como burras*, our strengths used against us, lowly *burras* bearing humility with dignity,"[11] or "[as a slave, I] brought in chillum ev'y twelve mont's jes lak a cow bringing in a calf."[12]

As coal mining eats through Appalachian mountain ranges near my home state of Georgia, I can't help but think about how this decimation echoes the repeated creation and exposure of "feminine" bodies in the public symbolism of mainstream pornography. These images trigger an impotent desire to uncover and penetrate the mystery that they create.

she
had stars blinking
above her body:
a blinding five-fingered flash

above each breast and one
between her legs

underneath, they cast a black
deeper than coal;
everyone drilled down
to see it

they sunk heavy steel hands
into the dark,
grasped at powder and
hauled it up

their carbon covered palms were
drained and grey
once they hit the edge of vision,
robbed by starlight

auger animal, metal monster, digger divine: you've mined
through her shadows
leaving bottomless holes
hook and eye—

but "your love
is impotent
and a mis
fortune;"

goodnight[13]

Poetic association is both real and flexible. It holds power over us at the same time as we hold power over it. The reality of the sexual objectification, reproductive control, and other kinds of oppressions we face (and often resist) with other animals, and the earth, is powerful. When we witness another's suffering with an awareness of our own, it can command our attention, hit our senses vividly, trigger body-memories, sneak into our dreams. At the same time, our poetic identification is elastic; as we fight and change our political contexts, we associate in new and different ways, assembling new metaphors.

Defining ourselves enables us to construct our own metaphors. A metaphor is a comparison of two things through an implicit analogy. Metaphors suggest, instead of describe—they're often vivid and intense as well as loose, obscure, and bewildering. These poetic analogies, I argue, should be the basis for women's identification with non-human life. Sometimes I really can imaginatively identify with a mountain being strip-mined, an egg-laying hen immobilized in a crowded cage, a cat in a laboratory cage, a "lowly *burra*." Although we are not the same, and I'll never know exactly what hens and lab animals and mountain ranges go through, in these moments I'm most inspired to respond with direct aid. These flashes of metaphorical insight are at the root of what motivates many women to resist control over our bodies, as well as the lives of other species and the earth.

"Cross-movement alliances"—such as the blending of feminist and ecological struggles—look increasingly important to understanding and undermining oppression. In Seattle in 1999, people around the world saw "the teamsters and the turtles"—unionists, animal advocates, and environmentalists—marching and chanting side-by-side to stop a meeting of the World Trade Organization. In Québèc City in 2001, I turned around during a large march against the Free Trade Area of the Americas treaty to see a herd of "cattle" (activists dressed in cow costumes to represent animal concerns) walking alongside a cluster of radical feminist affinity groups. It was a colorful scene of mutual action as we chanted *"sol-, sol-, sol-...solidarité."*

Ecofeminism is one example of an active cross-movement alliance, challenging the degradation of billions of lives. As feminists, we can picture our connections to other animals and the earth as a whole, through the lens of metaphors about our shared oppressions. Sometimes these metaphors become electric-shock intersections that grow into vital networks of mutual aid. And, like any net, this system of poetic associations can bend, stretch, break, or change shape through new seasons of rhyme and reason, new ways of describing ourselves and our conditions, instead of trapping us in typecast identities like fish trawled from the ocean.

Notes

1. Salamone, Constantina, "The Prevalence of the Natural Law Within Women: Women & Animal Rights." In *Reweaving the Web of Life: Feminism and Nonviolence*, edited by Pam McAllister. (Philadelphia: New Society Publishers, 1982), 365.

2. Vance, Linda, "Ecofeminism and the Politics of Reality." In *Ecofeminism: Women, Animals, Nature*, edited by Greta Gaard. (Philadelphia: Temple University Press, 1993), 136.

3. Catherine Roach, Chaia Heller, Donna Haraway, Marti Kheel, Greta Gaard and Kate Soper are feminists who have written about various political—often sexist—constructions of "nature."

4. Soper, Kate, *What is Nature?* (Malden, MA: Blackwell Publishers, 1995), 16.

5. Heller, Chaia "For the Love of Nature: Ecology and the Cult of the Romantic." In *Ecofeminism: Women, Animals, Nature*, edited by Greta Gaard. (Philadelphia: Temple University Press, 1993), 224.

6. Ibid., 229.

7. Janet Beihl of the Institute for Social Ecology attempted to argue for a version of ecofeminism that doesn't essentialize "women" or "nature" in her essay, "What is Social Ecofeminism?," *Green Perspectives* 11 (October 1988): 1–8. Chaia Heller and Greta Gaard have also written along these lines. For a general explanation of "post-structuralist" feminism, see Linda Alcoff's well-known essay "Cultural Feminism Versus Post-Structuralism: The Identity Crisis in Feminist Theory," *Signs* v.13 no 3 (Spring 1988).

8. Adams, Carol. "Caring about Suffering: A Feminist Exploration." In *Beyond Animal Rights: A Feminist Caring Ethic for the Treatment of Animals*, edited by Josephine Donovan and Carol J. Adams. (New York: Continuum, 1996), 173.

9. Some anthropologists trace the origins of patrilineage to the commodification of other animals. For example, Clare Janaki Holden and Ruth Mace's recent study of people who speak various Bantu languages in Africa, concluded that as people began herding cows, men began passing "ownership" of the cows to other men as they married into their families, and this was an historical seed for an expanding system of male objectification of both women and non-human life. See Bhattacharya, Shaoni, "Cattle Ownership Makes it a Man's World," *NewScientist* v 14 no 1 (October, 2003).

10. Williams, Delores. "Sin, Nature and Black Women's Bodies." In *Ecofeminism and the Sacred*, edited by Carol J. Adams. (New York: Continuum, 1995), 25.

11. Anzaldua, Gloria. *Borderlands/La Frontera: The New Mestiza.* (San Francisco: Aunt Lute Books, 1987), 21. A *burra* is a female donkey.

12. A woman quoted anonymously in Delores, 25.

13. Poem written by homefries, quotation from Karl Marx's *Economic and Philosophic Manuscripts*, as part of his analysis of worker alienation under capitalism.

Radical Ecology, Repressive Tolerance, and Zoöcide

Richard Kahn

> "In defense of life: the phrase has explosive meaning in the affluent society." *Herbert Marcuse,* Eros and Civilization

The official beginning of the modern environmental movement in the United States is generally considered to be the first Earth Day, which took place on April 22, 1970. Yet, a good case can be made that Earth Day itself, along with the sort of radical ecological politics now associated with groups like the Earth Liberation Front, erupted out of an event that took place the prior year. While drilling for oil six miles off the coast of Santa Barbara on the afternoon of January 28, 1969, Union Oil Company's[1] equipment failures resulted in a natural gas blowout from the new deepsea hole they were excavating. Though the gas leak was quickly capped, the resulting pressure build up produced five additional breaks along a nearby underwater fault line, sending oil and gas billowing into the surrounding ocean.

Ultimately, it took the better part of twelve days to stop the main leaks, and some three million gallons of crude oil were released into an 800-square-mile slick that contaminated the coastal waters, ruined 35 miles of shoreline, and damaged island ecologies. Amounting to a sort of Union Carbide disaster for non-human animals, over 10,000 birds, seals, dolphins, and other species were soon covered with tar, poisoned, or killed by chemical detergents used to break up the slick.[2] Many more animals that did not die were adversely affected through destruction of their habitat, as the region became seriously polluted and took on the smell of the worst regulated oil refinery plant. Fred L. Hartley, then President of Union Oil Company, responded with all the concern of a profit-hungry corporate executive. "I don't like to call it a disaster...I am amazed at the publicity for the loss of a few birds," he confessed.

Despite Hartley's disinterest, Santa Barbara's ecological catastrophe became a national media spectacle beamed into every American's television on the nightly news. Drawing on the nascent environmental consciousness sparked during the 1950s by Aldo Leopold's *Sand Country Almanac* and the 1960s by Rachel Carson's bestseller *Silent Spring*, public outrage erupted at the sort of governmental decision-making that allowed Big Oil to cavalierly despoil the country for profit. It was revealed that oil companies had corrupted the US Geological Survey, whose job it was to oversee the granting of offshore land leases, and that such leases were routinely granted with little investigation, save for that conducted by petroleum corporations themselves (whose data was kept from the public record). Further, corruption also flowed from President Johnson's administration on down. As the Vietnam war was proving overly costly for Johnson, he enacted a policy of producing additional federal revenues from the sale of natural resources (even at pennies on the dollar), in order to manufacture the illusion of budgetary economic soundness. As a result, the Santa Barbara channel had been auctioned off at the tidy sum of $602 million, providing the green light for oil companies to do with it as they willed, while a former proposal to turn the area into a wildlife sanctuary was quietly dropped from the agenda.

Clearly, no one in power had ever stopped to question what the political effects of a giant slick in the Santa Barbara channel would be. Since the 19th century, the community of Santa Barbara had been fighting against the battleship-sized drill platforms stationed obtrusively on the horizon, and so was already mobilized on the issue. In the days following the spill, GOO (Get Oil Out!) was created and it served as an organization to lead activist campaigns for reducing driving time, staging gas station boycotts, and burning oil company credit cards. Santa Barbara was a city of wealth and intelligence, a home to many people with insider connections to alter the usual workings of the status-quo. Citizen pressure led to two major national policy changes: the enacting of a federal moratorium on leases for new offshore drilling (except in huge swathes of the Gulf of Mexico) and the passage of the National Environmental Policy Act of 1970 (NEPA), the Magna Carta of environmental legislation in the United States. Finally, Santa Barbara was also a university town that was a hotbed of 1960s youth activism and counterculture.

The community of Isla Vista, in particular, was known for its radicalism—opposing police repression, staging war resistance, and defending leftist UCSB professors who were being denied tenure and removed from their posts. In 1970, Isla Vista militants responded to the corporate energy-cum-military State by breaking into and burning the local branch of the Bank of America to the ground. The bank made a perfect target for many reasons. On the one hand, the bank was *the* community representative of capitalist business. Whether in its opposition to Cesar Chavez's grape boycott or its support for American imperialism (and hence the Vietnam war) through the opening of branches in Saigon and Bangkok, Bank of America was seen as corrosive to the community's social justice values. But there is a less well-known, though truly vital, reason that the bank was targeted:

Bank of America directors sat on the board of Union Oil and so were themselves seen as responsible for the terrible oil spill of 1969.

In this context, though the Earth Liberation Front's first arson campaigns are dated only to 1997, the torching of Isla Vista's Bank of America stands as one of the very first acts of uncompromising direct action to be found in United States' environmentalism, and thereby shows that radical ecological approaches to politics co-originated with the mainstream movement. However, unlike the mainstream, Isla Vista New Left radicals tethered their ecological sensibility to an anti-capitalist and anti-imperialist stance that demanded a qualitative and revolutionary change in social relations.

Returning to the Question of Social Intolerance

"Civil disobedience has many permutations.
You can block the streets in front of the United Nations.
You can lay down on the tracks, keep the nuke trains out of town,
Or you can pour gas on the condo and you can burn it down."
David Rovics, "Song for the Earth Liberation Front"

While there are dramatic differences between the political and cultural scene of the 1960s and the present, in many ways it seems like old times. Oil is again the center of political discussions as the Bush administration is hunkered down in a costly, and apparently unwinnable, Vietnam of its own making in Iraq. While Bush has promised to honor his father's extension of the federal moratorium on offshore drilling until 2012, Big Oil has been working vigorously to gain access to the continental shelf, amongst other potential exploration sites such as the Arctic National Wildlife Refuge (ANWR) in Alaska. In 2005, utilizing high domestic gas prices and the threat of blocked oil supplies due to war or natural disaster, oil lobbyists grafted an inclusion onto Bush's 2006 Energy Plan that will end the 25-year bipartisan congressional moratorium on Outer Continental Shelf leasing. Further, NEPA itself—the law created to make sure federal agencies properly account for potential environmental impacts before developing federal lands—has come under an all-out assault as the Bush administration seeks to free industries from what it deems to be a time-consuming and expensive legislative regulatory procedure. This, as a January 2005 "mystery spill," unclaimed by any oil company (go figure), once again painted Santa Barbara beaches black, killing some 5,000 birds and other animals. Less than a year later Hurricane Katrina's destruction of offshore refineries produced 50 large slicks along the Gulf Coast, rivaling the giant Exxon Valdez disaster in terms of oil spilled, and became perhaps the greatest environmental catastrophe in the history of the US.[3]

Three and a half decades since the oil disaster in Santa Barbara have brought startling changes. Whereas 1969's spill radicalized students into taking direct action against anti-ecological capitalism and galvanized a national environmental movement in the mainstream, 2005's oil slicks have passed relatively unnoticed. One might argue that, in the present age of mega-spectacle, nothing short of global warming as fictitiously pictured in the absurd movie, *The Day After Tomorrow* (2004), has enough emotional punch to break through the exhausted sensibilities of the oblivious masses. In this sense, the relatively rare devastation wrought by a killer tsunami rouses widespread attention today, while the public passes by news about the toxic burdens brought to bear upon life by corporate and state malfeasance with little more than a bored shrug and occasional blog post. For sure, since the Battle for Seattle, the United States has seen a reinvention of public protest, and while people continue to link images of the 60s with notions of social discontent, recent mass mobilizations such as the unprecedented worldwide anti-war/alter-globalization protest on February 15, 2003 and the demonstration against the 2004 Republican convention that shut down New York City represented dissent on a scale far beyond that ever mustered by the flower-power youth of yesteryear. Why then did the counterculture of the 1960s accomplish so much, while the contemporary Left has largely suffered being overrun, consolidated, and ignored despite its large numbers?

The answer requires reconsidering the past. As Steven Best has noted, the post-9/11 US government has been engaged in a McCarthyesque crackdown on activists, by brandishing them as terrorists, while corporations and the government intone treasured words like "freedom" and "democracy."[4] The State portrays itself as a security apparatus in charge of preserving the liberal ideal of tolerance, while it uses the extremism of groups like the Taliban to smear all of its enemies with charges of tyrannical fundamentalism or terrorism. Thus, animal activists like the SHAC7 are reviled as anti-democratic enemies of the State because of their willingness to directly challenge and attempt to shut down the self-imposed rights of corporations to cavalierly murder animals in the name of science and business.[5] SHAC's corporate and political opponents, conversely, disingenuously promote themselves as "good citizens" who recognize the right to voice even the most unpopular opinions as long as those opinions do not step beyond the bounds of free speech into, as they see it, "intimidation."

Herbert Marcuse, the so-called "father of the New Left," during the 1960s, wrote an important essay called, "Repressive Tolerance." In it, he examines this process by which the liberal State and its corporate members claim that they are fit models of democratic tolerance, while radical activists are subversive of the very ideals on which our society is based.[6] In fact, Marcuse notes that the claim that democratic tolerance means activists need to restrict their protests to legal street demonstrations and intra-governmental attempts to change policy, is highly spurious. Tolerance, he says, arose as a political concept to protect the oppressed and minority viewpoints from being met with repressive violence from the ruling classes.

When the call for tolerance is accordingly used by the ruling classes to protect themselves from interventions that seek to limit global violence and suppression, fear, and misery, it amounts to a perversion of tolerance that works to repress instead of liberate. Thus, Marcuse thought such tolerance should be met without compromise by acts of revolutionary intolerance, because capitalistic societies such as the United States manage to distort the very meanings of peace and truth by claiming that tolerance must be extended throughout the society by the weak to the violence and falsity produced by the strong.

Many have criticized Marcuse for advocating violence against the system in order to quash the system's inherent violence. However, his critique of repressive tolerance is key to understanding why revolutionary violence remains—if not necessarily ethical in principle[7]—a legitimate and essential mode of political challenge. For a tolerance that defends life must be committed to opposing the overwhelming violence wrought by the military, corporations, and the State as the manifestation of their power. Conversely, passive tolerance, by failing to take adequate action to stop violence, is itself a pro-violence stand. Therefore, Marcuse felt that revolutionary violence may in fact be necessary to move beyond political acts that either consciously or unconsciously side with, and thereby strengthen, the social agenda of the ruling classes. Further, he noted that the tremendous amount of concern (even amongst the Left) over whether revolutionary violence is a just tactic fails to correlate to how often violence is actually applied and practiced by radical leftists or social progressives. Meanwhile, systemic violence constantly goes on everywhere either unnoticed and unchecked, or is sometimes even celebrated. This goes to show, Marcuse felt, how hard it is to even think beyond the parameters set by repressive tolerance in a society such as our own, and serves as yet another reason why such tolerance must, by any means necessary, be met with social intolerance.

Marcuse also recognized a wide-range of tactics such as marching long-term through the institutions, and grabbing positions of power wherever possible, if such tactics were undertaken with a revolutionary thrust towards a more ecologically-sound, peaceful, and free planet. Largely forgotten in this respect, is his concept of the "Great Refusal" that means the complete cultural rejection of the mainstream in favor of a life-affirming and ecological world. This idea gripped the counterculture of the 1960s, who created a plethora of new cultural forms and institutions (such as the environmental movement) across the whole spectrum of society.

Certainly, there are also bold new cultural forays in today's radical ecological politics. Increasingly, individuals and countercultural collectives are attempting to reject the mega-war-machine of the mainstream, as they take up veganism, permaculture, and other alternative lifestyles—such as the Straight-Edge movement that mixes urban punk stylings with a commitment to self-control, clean living, and political expressions like animal rights. Relatedly, anarchistic events such as the Total Liberation tour travel the country, and a variety of infoshops are actively investigating green political philosophies like social ecology and primitivism. The last few years have seen a broad array of oppositional technopolitics.[8] Blogs and websites are mushrooming everywhere, and helping to organize affinity groups, cover crucial issues dropped from the mainstream media, and practice hactivism that jams corporate and State networks, gathers otherwise secret information, and attempts to generate anti-capitalist culture. Indeed, as for the latter, hardly an urban setting can be found that is free of some form of regular culture jam.

But as today's popular culture is dominated by media spectacle and all manner of mass-commodified technological gadgetry, eco-radicals must work harder still to distinguish the ways in which their culture represents a positive realization of anti-oppressive norms based on ideals of sustainability, and not just a nihilistic disapproval of a society rightly deemed unredeemable. That is: a politics of burning-down that lacks a correlative social and cultural reconstructive focus should not itself be tolerated. This is not to say that ecotage is a poor tactic—far from it. Though ecological radicals have thus far demonstrated an impressive capacity to fight fire with fire, sometimes quite literally, they need to more strongly develop and promote the sorts of political and cultural alternatives to mainstream American life that are inherently ecological and rooted in a new ethic and sensibility toward nature. Rear-guard, piecemeal, scattershot monkeywrenching actions must ultimately swarm into a revolutionary movement that shakes the foundations of the militaristic and capitalistic system itself.

Reinventing a "Pro-Life" Politics

"Be just and deal kindly with my people, for the dead are not powerless.
Dead, did I say? There is no death, only a change of worlds."
Chief Seattle

George W. Bush has been characterized as a pro-life leader for his desire to overturn *Roe v. Wade*, ban stem cell research, and stop funding for international aid organizations that offer counsel on abortions and provide contraceptives. Of course, in his role as outright war maker in Afghanistan and Iraq, indirect war maker through his global neoliberal structural adjustment policies, and ecological war maker as the worst environmental president in United States history, Bush is anything but pro-life. As the sort of über-representative of the affluent society, its forces, and its values, Bush is a fitting figurehead for a politics of mass-extinction, global poverty, and ecological catastrophe. Let us make no mistake about it, death-dealing politics such as Bush's, extend far beyond the ideological confines of his neo-conservative administration and so, from a perspective of radical ecology, strategies such as the "Anybody But Bush" that progressives attempted to use during the 2004 election cycle could not be more misguided.

Since the first Earth Day, we have witnessed the advanced form of an "endless growth" economy of hyper-production and consumption that is literally devouring the planet. Wholly without precedent, the human population has nearly doubled during this time period, increasing by nearly three billion people. Similarly, markets have continued to worship the gods of speed and quantity, and refused to conserve. The use and extraction of non-renewable energy resources like oil, coal, and natural gas has followed and exceeded the trends set by the population curve despite many years of warnings about the consequences inherent in their over-use and extraction. This has led to a corresponding increase in the carbon emissions known to be responsible for global warming.

Likewise, living beings and organic habitats are being culled and destroyed at staggering rates, all in the name of human consumption. Tree consumption for paper products has doubled over the last thirty years, resulting in about half of the planet's forests disappearing. Global fishing also has doubled, prompting a recent report which found that approximately 90% of the major fish species in the world's oceans have disappeared. Mile-long nets used to trawl the ocean bottoms for commercial fishing enterprises are drowning and killing about 1000 whales, dolphins, and porpoises daily—some of the species near extinction from centuries of commercial hunting. Since the end of the 1960s, half of the planet's wetlands have either been filled or drained for development, and nearly half of the Earth's soils have been so agriculturally degraded that they cannot support life. As giant corporate agribusinesses have consumed the family farm, and as fast food has exploded from a dietary novelty to a cultural staple across the world, vast, unimaginable slaughterhouses—brutal production-lines in which thousands of animals are murdered for meat harvesting every hour—have also become the business standard.

Marcuse himself referred to the sort of systemic disregard for life evinced by such statistics as "ecocide"—the attempt to annihilate natural places by turning them into capitalist cultural spaces, a process that works hand-in-hand with the genocide and dehumanization of people as an expression of the market economy's perpetual expansion. More recently, others speak of ecocide as the destruction of the higher-order relations that govern ecosystems generally, as when corporations seize areas characterized by complexity and diversity, like the Amazonian rainforest, and reduce them to a deforested and unstable monoculture of soybeans for cattle-feed. While it is no doubt possible to disable an ecosystem from sustaining much life, it is not clear that one can actually "destroy" it. Instead, we are witnessing a process by which bioregions are being transmogrified from natural ecologies that support life, to blighted capitalist landscapes unable to sustain biodiversity and complex life. In this way, the current globalization of capitalism that institutes classist, racist, sexist, and speciesist oppression is a biocidal agent.

It is also biocidal in a more philosophical sense. The term *"bios"* is an ancient Greek word that has come to designate natural life as studied by the science of "biology." Originally, though, *bios* meant a sort of characterized life—as in a "biography"—that is demonstrated by the active subjectivity of sentient beings. In this manner, organizations like People for the Ethical Treatment of Animals (PETA) have, as their ultimate goal, the social recognition of animals' *bios*, and accordingly, want them to be afforded the status of being considered subjects of a life, and are therefore deserving of rights.[9] When compared with the larger socio-political context against which PETA struggles, however, the McDonaldization of the planet is obviously moving in the opposite direction. Most beings today, including the great Earth and the sustaining cosmos beyond, are instead increasingly reduced to one-dimensional objects for exploitation.

In stark contrast to the objectification of life that typifies mainstream culture in the United States, as well as to the sense of life as "characterized"—that is represented by the idea of *bios*—the ancient Greeks (in a manner similar to many indigenous cultures) held that life was fundamentally *zoë*—a multidimensional and multiplicitous realm of indestructible being that pervaded both organic and inorganic matter. Thus, in ancient Greek culture primeval and natural places were consecrated to the pagan deity Pan (whose name means "all"), and these were held to be sacred groves where *zoë* was especially concentrated in its power. The final point then, is that today's ruling elite politics is also zoöcidal, though not in the sense that it destroys *zoë* (which cannot be destroyed by definition). Rather, in instituting a transnational network of murderous profanity over the sacred—in paving paradise in order to put up a parking lot—capitalist life is zoöcidal in that it seeks to colonize any and all spaces in which cultures based on understandings and reverence for *zoë* can thrive.

The call to future radicals is clear. They must, if they are not doing so already, integrate the ecological critique into their politics and culture and begin to forge deep alliances with uncompromising non-anthropocentric social movements, such as those in favor of earth and animal liberation. If these dialogues are to achieve real and lasting solidarity, human rights-based groups will need to demonstrate their readiness to move beyond limited non-ecological identity positions and experiment more frequently with modes of living that are without clear precedent in their cultural histories. In kind, animal liberationists and ecological radicals must increasingly move to develop cultural relationships to nature and non-human animals that exhibit the sort of non-classist, anti-racist, non-patriarchal, and anti-hierarchical values that have emerged out of a long history of social struggle. This will mean, at a minimum, beginning to realize a more rigorously radical ecological politic such that they aim to fully abolish *the social logic and institutions* whereby nature is separated from culture and reduced to a "resource" for human uses. Radicals of all persuasions will also have to learn, grow, and ultimately teach the values and practices that unfold a *new sensibility towards life*—the ability to find awe, reverence, and beauty in *all* of life's many manifestations—in order to liberate *the entire planet* from its chains. In this respect, perhaps, the reinvention of a pro-life politics where human and non-human beings are understood as both *bios* and *zoë* represents the great social challenge at the present historical moment.

To reiterate, it is too soon in most cases to describe in detail the ecological values, practices, and attendant ethics that will pervade a post-revolutionary future in which life flourishes. The present moment has come to be fully complicated and polluted by those who traffic in destruction and death, and it is in this global socio-political context—not on the pastoral fields of a wind swept paradise—that the call to eco-radicalism now emerges. Therefore, any sort of desire for the future to be more responsive to the ecological and the ethical requires a clarification of the system as it now exists, as well as the promotion of wider struggle against structures of zoöcide.

Certainly, there is no guarantee that this process will result in either justice or wholeness or peace. But as these concepts and values are virtually nonsensical today while we climb headlong towards Hubbert's Peak,[10] the negation of current behavior patterns—combined with the re-imagination of social alternatives that have been brushed aside in the myopic quest to define life by standard of living indices—provides at least the possibility for real hope to grow and bloom into a powerful resistance movement. Let us tolerate nothing short of establishing a new planetary community and earth democracy.

Notes

1. Union Oil Company exists today as Unocal Corporation.

2. The Union Carbide disaster took place during the early hours of December 3, 1984 in Bhopal, India, when an industrial accident in one of Union Carbide's pesticide plants resulted in the accidental release of some forty tons of toxic gas into the city, murdering thousands, and injuring hundreds of thousands of others. It is generally considered the worst industrial disaster to have occurred, with ongoing contamination, death, and injury to this day.

3. The Exxon Valdez oil spill occurred on March 24, 1989, when an Exxon owned oil tanker struck a reef in Prince William Sound, spilling tens of millions of gallons of crude oil. It is estimated that the deaths of birds, seals, whales, otters, and fish ran to the hundreds of thousands—at a minimum—as a result of this accident.

4. See Best, Steven. "It's War! The Escalating Battle Between Activists and the Corporate-State Complex." In *Terrorists or Freedom Fighters? Reflections of the Liberation of Animals*, edited by Steven Best and Anthony J. Nocella, II. New York: Lantern Books, 2004.

5. On the significance of the SHAC7 trial, see Best, Steven and Richard Kahn, "Trial By Fire: The Shac7, Globalization, and the Future of Democracy," *Animal Liberation Philosophy and Policy Journal* Vol II Issue 2. <http://www.cala-online.org/Journal/Issue3/Trial%20by%20Fire.htm>

6. See Marcuse, Herbert. "Repressive Tolerance." In *A Critique of Pure Tolerance*, edited by Robert Paul Wolff, Barrington Moore, and Herbert Marcuse. Boston: Beacon Press, 1969.

7. By this I mean that both systemic and anti-systemic violence are probably non-ethical, in that neither represents the sort of behavior which would constitute a post-revolutionary society based on an ecological ethic that incorporates peace, beauty, and justice. However, current ecological struggles hardly unfold in ideal conditions, and valid arguments can be made in favor of revolutionary violence that seeks to defend life from being overrun by forces of death.

8. See Kahn, Richard and Douglas Kellner, "Oppositional politics and the Internet: A critical/reconstructive approach," *Cultural Politics* 1:1 (2005): 75–100. <http://richardkahn. org/writings/tep/oppositionalpolitics.pdf>

9. See Guillermo, Kathy (2004), "Response to Nathan Snaza's '(Im)possible Witness: Viewing PETA's Holocaust on Your Plate,'" *Animal Liberation Philosophy and Policy Journal* Vol II No 2. <http://www.cala-online.org/Journal/Issue3/Response_Letter_Snaza.htm>

10. "Hubbert's Peak" is the name given to the world's impending oil shortage, based on the fact that fossil fuels are limited and non-renewable, while societal cravings for them are apparently unlimited and ever-renewable.

Afterword
Katrina!!!

Jalil A. Muntaqim

Katrina, Katrina what made you so mean?
Katrina, Katrina you're worse than a crack fiend!

Bush promises, As Halliburton moves in fulfilling
mandates with no bid contracts as New Orleans and
Biloxi resembles that bomb-out shell that once was
Mesopotamia. As the once contained oil seeps back
from where it came, contaminating the land of the
displaced, considered refugees in the Astro-dome.
The promises of Bush are as revealing as Judge
Roberts confirmation hearing—and we asked to
trust he will be fair. But we know the Bush
political agenda is the neo-cons revelation,
Chapter 6–Verse 5.

Katrina, Katrina what made you so mean?
Katrina, Katrina you're worse than a crack fiend

The levees broke open the heart of America like
the piercing screams of an Afrikan baby thrown
overboard during the middle passage—as
slavery's face grimaced with the knowing the
Federal government cares nothing about black
people. As CNN broadcast their affliction
around the world, embarrassing democracy,
exposing America's history of eco-racism in
living color; but mostly in black and white.
With the 9th Ward in disrepair, white flight
and black despair, proceeding mass gentrification
to ensure the poor are dispersed to new enclaves
of poverty, hidden away from the disaster
of media exposure.

Katrina, Katrina what made you so mean?
Katrina, Katrina you're worse than a crack fiend!

Where are the 2500 Black babies? A reminder of
the retreat from Vietnam and the kidnapping of
Vietnamese babies; as in New Orleans the taking
of babies, leaving the parents behind, to watch
water lines climb, as tears and fears stretched
into the dark unknown; while CNN reports floating
bodies, and the national guard wait on standby for the
next commercial break of red tape, so no one could
escape their watery fate, sponsored by Dick Cheney
and Halliburton.

Katrina, Katrina what made you so mean?
Katrina, Katrina you're worse than a crack fiend!

Hurricane Carter did 25 years for a crime he did
not commit, a prime example of American justice
personified. Hurricanes in America always screw
poor folks. The next hurricane should hit the
White House and leave the Bushes in Shock and Awe,
perhaps, then they will be better off; and we'll
name that hurricane Mumia

2005

Appendix
Earth Liberation Front Communiqués

We include in this anthology the following Earth Liberation Front communiqués, along with the official ELF introduction to its philosophy, ELF guidelines, and an interview with an anonymous ELF member. We include these communiqués not because we favor or support the ELF more than other revolutionary groups, but because as yet this is the most complete collection of communiqués available, one that has not been published together and is not presently available on the Internet. As these communiqués are important for scholarly research and activist reflection, this text has historical and political significance. We gratefully acknowledge the ELF Press Office, which gave us these communiqués to publish here.

About the E.L.F.

The Earth Liberation Front is an international underground movement consisting of autonomous groups of people who carry out direct action according to the E.L.F. guidelines. Since 1997, E.L.F. cells have carried out dozens of actions resulting in close to $100 million in damages.

Modeled after the Animal Liberation Front, the E.L.F. is structured in such a way as to maximize effectiveness. By operating in cells (small groups that consist of one to several people), the security of group members is maintained. Each cell is anonymous not only to the public but also to one another. This decentralized structure helps keep activists out of jail and free to continue conducting actions.

As the E.L.F. structure is non-hierarchical, individuals involved control their own activities. There is no centralized organization or leadership tying the anonymous cells together. Likewise, there is no official "membership." Individuals who choose to do actions under the banner of the E.L.F. are driven only by their personal conscience or decisions taken by their cell while adhering to the stated guidelines.

Who are the people carrying out these activities? Because involved individuals are anonymous, they could be anyone from any community. Parents, teachers, church volunteers, your neighbor, or even your partner could be involved. The exploitation and destruction of the environment affects all of us—some people enough to take direct action in defense of the earth.

Any direct action to halt the destruction of the environment and adhering to the strict nonviolence guidelines, listed below, can be considered an E.L.F. action. Economic sabotage and property destruction fall within these guidelines.

Earth Liberation Front Guidelines:

To inflict economic damage on those profiting from the destruction and exploitation of the natural environment.

To reveal and educate the public on the atrocities committed against the earth and all species that populate it.

To take all necessary precautions against harming any animal, human and non-human.

There is no way to contact the E.L.F. in your area. It is up to each committed person to take responsibility for stopping the exploitation of the natural world. No longer can it be assumed that someone else is going to do it. If not you who, if not now when?

Earth Liberation Front FAQ:

Q: Aren't there environmental groups to take care of these problems?

A: Yes, but obviously they're not getting the job done otherwise there wouldn't be houses for us to burn down! All successful movements in history have had a variety of methods, from education all the way to direct action.

Q: Are you terrorists?

A: No, we condemn all forms of terrorism. A common definition of terrorism is "to reduce to a state of fear or terror." We are costing them money. If change falls out of your pocket, you are not in a state of fear or terror. If you give money to the homeless, you are losing money, but you are not being terrorized. Even if your house is robbed, you are not being terrorized. We are non-violent. Houses were checked for all forms of life, and we even moved a propane tank out of the house all the way across the street just because—in worst case scenario—the firefighters could get hurt. We show solidarity with our firefighters, and we are sorry to wake you up in the middle of the night. Don't be mad at us, be mad at urban sprawl. We encourage all citizens to donate generous contributions this year to your local volunteer firefighters.

Q: Don't companies have the right to property?

A: We are just trying to cause the rich sprawl corporations enough money so they stop destroying the planet, and thus the health, well-being, and existence of humankind. Corporations do not have rights. Humans do. Corporations lost their "right" to property the second the earth's inhabitants lost their freedom to life and happiness. Cancer is not happiness. Dead animals are not life. Polluted air and mudslides affect people's lives. Property is theft.

Q: Why don't you use legal methods?

A: They don't work as well. Mahatma Gandhi disobeyed the law to free his people. Harriet Tubman used illegal methods to free slaves on the Underground Railroad. Nelson Mandela even used violent methods to end the Apartheid. John Brown killed slaveowners and raided a federal arsenal to try to start a slave revolt. How many successful movements in history can you think of off the top of your head that came about only by education? How do you "protest" against slavery? Holding signs and handing out flyers on southern plantations? Today, these "unlawful" people are all seen as martyrs, and someday we will too. Try to realize this NOW. Not all laws are just. Malcolm X says "By Any Means Necessary" in order to obtain freedom. But, we do not hurt people, we never have in our long history, and we never will. We respect all life, even our worst enemies that give us cancerous drinking water. (If someone is going to shoot you in the back six times, do you nicely, kindly ask him to shoot you only three or four times? No, you freakin' turn around and punch them in the face, grab the gun from them, and shove it up their ass!)

The earth isn't dying, it's being killed, and those who are killing it have names and addresses.

What are YOU doing for the earth tonight?

No Compromise In Defense of Our Earth!

Stop Urban Sprawl Or We Will.

March 14, 1997 Mackenzie River watershed, OR

Tree spiking at Robinson-Scott timber harvest site in the Mackenzie River watershed, Willamette National Forest. Joint ALF / ELF claim.

Beltane, 1997

Welcome to the struggle of all species to be free.

We are the burning rage of this dying planet. The war of greed ravages the earth and species die out every day. E.L.F. works to speed up the collapse of industry, to scare the rich, and to undermine the foundations of the state. We embrace social and deep ecology as a practical resistance movement. We have to show the enemy that we are serious about defending what is sacred. Together we have teeth and claws to match our dreams.

Our greatest weapons are imagination and the ability to strike when least expected.

Since 1992 a series of earth nights and Halloween smashes has mushroomed around the world. 1000s of bulldozers, powerlines, computer systems, buildings and valuable equipment have been composted. Many E.L.F. actions have been censored to prevent our bravery from inciting others to take action.

We take inspiration from Luddites, Levellers, Diggers, the Autonome squatter movement, the A.L.F., the Zapatistas, and the little people—those mischievous elves of lore. Authorities can't see us because they don't believe in elves. We are practically invisible. We have no command structure, no spokespersons, no office, just many small groups working separately, seeking vulnerable targets and practicing our craft.

Many elves are moving to the Pacific Northwest and other sacred areas. Some elves will leave surprises as they go. Find your family! And lets dance as we make ruins of the corporate money system.

Form "stormy night" action groups, encourage friends you trust. A tight community of love is a powerful force.

Recon:
check out targets that fit your plan and go over what you will do

Attack:
powerlines: cut supporting cables, unbolt towers, and base supports, saw wooden poles.
transformers: shoot out, bonfires, throw metal chains on top, or blow them up.
computers: smash, burn or flood buildings.
Please copy and improve for local use.

October 21, 1998 Vail, CO

On Wednesday, October 21st 1998 the Earth Liberation Front released a communiqué to the Sheriff's Department, the Owners of Vail Inc. and various media, allegedly from an anonymous Massachusetts Institution of Technology internet address claiming responsibility for what became known as the "largest act of eco-terrorism in US history."

"ATTN: News Director, On behalf of the lynx, five buildings and four ski lifts at Vail were reduced to ashes on the night of Sunday, October 18th. The 12 miles of roads and 885 acres of clearcuts will ruin the last, best lynx habitat in the state. Putting profits ahead of Colorado's wildlife will not be tolerated. This action is just a warning. We will be back if this greedy corporation continues to trespass into wild and unroaded areas. For your safety and convenience, we strongly advise skiers to choose other destinations until Vail cancels its inexcusable plans for expansions. Earth Liberation Front."

December 19, 2000

Greetings from the front.

The Earth Liberation Front claims responsibility for the torching of a luxury home under construction in Miller Place, Long Island on December 19th. Anti-urban sprawl messages were spraypainted on the walls, then accelerants were poured over the house and lighted. Let there be no mistake that this was a non-violent action and the house was searched for any living thing before being set alight. This is the latest in a string of actions in the war against urban sprawl. Urban sprawl not only destroys the forest and green spaces of our planet, but also leads directly to added runoff of pollutants into our waterways, increased traffic that causes congestion and air pollution, and a less pleasing landscape. Our earth is being murdered by greedy corporate and personal interests. The rape of Earth puts everyone's life at risk due to global warming, ozone depletion, toxic chemicals, etc. Unregulated population growth is also a direct product of urban sprawl. There are over six billion people on this planet of which almost a third are either starving or living in poverty. Building homes for the wealthy should not even be a priority.

Forests, farms, and wetlands are being replaced with a sea of houses, green chemical lawns, blacktop, and roadkill. Farmland is being bought out by land developers because of their inability to compete with cheap corporate, genetically-engineered, pesticide saturated food. The time has come to decide what is more important: the planet and the health of its population or the profits of those who destroy it. The purpose of sloganeering is not self righteous posturing as has been reported, but a direct warning to the Earth's oppressors. Apparently, Long Island's growing smog and cancerous water is not a good enough warning to those directly responsible for it. The site of this recent action was warned twice of impending actions with the monkeywrenching of several vehicles and spraypainted messages. It's time for the people of Long Island to put their foot down and no longer passively tolerate our island's rape. It is time for Nassua and Suffolk County Police to realize we are but the symptoms of a corrupt society on the brink of ecological collapse. Law enforcement should be directing their time and resources towards the real terrorists. Those who commit murder and theft upon our populace daily. Big business is the enemy of the people, yet most people remain blind of it due to the massive propaganda and the power they wield. Every major media outlet on Long Island is in their pockets. The time for action is upon us. We are watching.

Earth Liberation Front

December 31, 2000

Greetings Friends,

As an early New Years gift to Long Island's environment destroyers, the Earth Liberation Front (E.L.F.) visited a construction site on December 29 and set fire to four unsold Luxury houses nearly completed at Island Estates in Mount Sinai, Long Island. Hopefully, this caused nearly $2 million in damage. This hopefully provided a firm message that we will not tolerate the destruction of our Island. Recently, hundreds of houses have been built over much of Mount Sinai's picturesque landscape and developers now plan to build a further 189 luxury houses over the farms and forests adjacent to Island Estates. This action was done in solidarity with Josh Harper, Craig Rosebraugh, Jeffrey "Free" Luers and Craig "Critter" Marshall, Andrew Stepanian, Jeremy Parkin, and the countless other known and unknown activists who suffer persecution, interrogation, police brutality, crappy jail conditions, yet stand strong.

Whether it's denying a prisoner vegetarian or vegan food/phone calls (which is a right), or even the terrorism of the Grand Jury, they stand strong. Oppression of our brothers and sisters will only make us up our tactics, by means, frequency, and cost. The more brutality you give our brothers and sisters, the more money we cause the oppressors. Our hearts go out to all of them.

Keep up the fight.

"Never Give In"

April 4, 2001

Take Actions Against Globalization Now!!!

The Earth Liberation Front has very recently paid a visit to a Nike outlet in the town of Albertville, MN. This visit was in solidarity with all people of all nations to fight globalization, and to support the growing anti global sentiment. This is also a call for direct action against globalization in solidarity with all of the anti FTAA actions scheduled in Canada later this month.

After witnessing first hand the treacherous conditions that Nike workers experience daily in sweatshops around the world, it was decided that no NGO organization, could have the immediate impact necessary to end conditions that exist currently at any sweatshop.

Instead, direct action is a more efficient tactic to stop Nike in their footsteps. Unfortunately, due to weather conditions, the visit was short, and although the plan was to destroy the roof, only minor damages were sustained.

Although the roof of this Nike outlet did not go up in flames as planned, this action is still a message to Nike they cannot ignore. In fact, there are only two options for Nike at this point. Option 1—you can shut down all of your sweatshops immediately, and immediately place all assets into the communities that you have stolen from. Along with this, you must close down all Nike outlets, starting with the Albertville, MN location (you are especially not welcome in this town!!!)... Or, Option 2—people across the globe will individually attack Nike outlets, as well as retailers that sell Nike (including college campus shops) until Nike closes down, or adheres to demand #1.

It is important to point out to Nike that the violence they use against the poor, and especially those that do all the work for them, will only be met with violence towards what they hold dearest... their pocket books. All E.L.F. actions are non violent towards humans and animals. But if a building exists which perpetuates and sponsors violence towards people or animals (such as a Nike outlet, or a Gap outlet, etc.), then by god, it's got to be burned to the ground!!! The E.L.F. whole heartedly condones the use of violence towards inanimate objects to prevent oppression, violence, and most of all to protect freedom. Direct action is a wonderful tool to embrace on the road to liberation.
Sincerely,
Philip H. Knight, Chairman and CEO NIKE, Inc.
One Bowerman Drive
Beaverton, OR 97003-6433
Fax: (503) 671-6300

May 21, 2001 Seattle, WA

ELF burns an office and a fleet of 13 trucks at Jefferson Poplar Farms in Clatskanie, Oregon. The ELF simultaneously burned down the office of Toby Bradshaw at the University of Washington. Total damages for both sites exceeded $5 million. This marks the first time in North American history that the ELF has targeted two separate locations in differing states at the same time.

Part 1

At 3:15am on Monday, May 21, the research of Toby Bradshaw was reduced to smoke and ashes. We attacked his office at the University of Washington while at the same time another group set fire to a related target in Clatskanie, Oregon, 150 miles away.

Bradshaw, the driving force in G.E. tree research, continues to unleash mutant genes into the environment that are certain to cause irreversible harm to forest ecosystems.

After breaking into Bradshaw's office at the Center for Urban Horticulture, we inspected the building for occupants and set up incendiary devices with a modest amount of accelerant. Although we placed these devices specifically to target his office, a large portion of the building was damaged. This extensive damage was due to a surprisingly slow and poorly coordinated response from the fire department, which was evident by their radio transmissions.

As long as universities continue to pursue this reckless "science," they run the risk of suffering severe losses. Our message remains clear: we are determined to stop genetic engineering.

From the torching of Catherine Ive's office at Michigan State University to the total incineration of GE seeds at the D & PL warehouse in Visalia, CA, the Earth Liberation Front is growing and spreading. As the culture of domination forces itself into our very genes, wild fires of outrage will continue to blaze.

Part 2

Early Monday morning, May 21, we dealt a blow to one of the many institutions responsible for massive hybrid tree farming in the Northwest. Incendiary devices at Jefferson Poplar in Clatskanie, Oregon, burned an office and a fleet of 13 trucks. Unfortunately, due to a design flaw, one targeted structure was left standing. We torched Jefferson Poplar because hybrid poplars are an ecological nightmare threatening native biodiversity in the ecosystem. Our forests are being liquidated and replaced with monocultured tree farms, so greedy, earth raping corporations can make more money.

Pending legislation in Oregon and Washington further criminalizing direct action in defense of the wild will not stop us and only highlights the fragility of the ecocidal empire.

As we wrote in Clatskanie "You cannot control what is wild."

ELF Earth Liberation Front

August 11, 2002 Irvine, PA

The ELF claims attack on the United States Forest Service Northeast Research Station in Irvine, Pennsylvania causing over $700,000 in damages and destroying 70 years worth of research.

The Earth Liberation Front is claiming responsibility for the 8/11/02 arson attack on the United States Forest Service Northeast Research Station in Irvine, Pennsylvania.

The laboratory was set ablaze during the early morning hours, causing over $700,000 damage, and destroying part of 70 years worth of research. This lesson in "prescribed fire" was a natural, necessary response to the threats posed to life in the Allegheny Forest by proposed timber sales, oil drilling, and greed-driven manipulation of Nature.

This facility was strategically targeted, and if rebuilt, will be targeted again for complete destruction. Furthermore, all other US Forest Service administration and research facilities, as well as all DCNR buildings nationwide should now be considered likely targets.

These agencies continue to ignore and mislead the public, at the bidding of their corporate masters, leaving us with no alternative to underground direct action. Their blatant disregard for the sanctity of life and its perfect Natural balance, indifference to strong public opposition, and the irrevocable acts of extreme violence they perpetrate against the Earth daily are all inexcusable, and will not be tolerated. If they persist in their crimes against life, they will be met with maximum retaliation.

In pursuance of justice, freedom, and equal consideration for all innocent life across the board, segments of this global revolutionary movement are no longer limiting their revolutionary potential by adhering to a flawed, inconsistent "non-violent" ideology. While innocent life will never be harmed in any action we undertake, where it is necessary, we will no longer hesitate to pick up the gun to implement justice, and provide the needed protection for our planet that decades of legal battles, pleading, protest, and economic sabotage have failed so drastically to achieve.

The diverse efforts of this revolutionary force cannot be contained, and will only continue to intensify as we are brought face to face with the oppressor in inevitable, violent confrontation. We will stand up and fight for our lives against this iniquitous civilization until its reign of TERROR is forced to an end—by any means necessary.

In defense of all life,
—Pacific E.L.F.

December 2, 2002 Harborcreek, PA

ELF & ALF joint claim fire at the Mindek Brothers Fur Farm.

At 2:00 AM on November 26, 2002, anonymous cells of the A.L.F. and the E.L.F. visited the Mindek Brothers Fur Farm (4200 Shannon Road) in Harborcreek, Pennsylvania. Before disappearing into the night, a large fire was set which completely destroyed the farm's feed barn and its contents, causing extensive financial loss.

The A.L.F. is also claiming responsibility for releasing 200 breeding mink in May and 50+ in September from the same farm.

Working together, cells from A.L.F. & E.L.F. demolished this feed facility due to its role in the systematic torture and killing of thousands of innocent creatures yearly—animals which possess the same complex emotional/physiological traits as loved household pets, yet are denied all reasonable consideration and confined to a miserable "existence" in tiny wire cages hardly large enough to turn around in.

Imprisoned in fur factories, these solitary creatures are forced to endure intensive confinement for the entirety of their lives, next to, or not uncommonly, packed into the same excrement and disease-laden cages as their doomed relatives. In their natural state, these animals maintain a vast territory encompassing several miles. However, on fur farms such as this one, most of these semi-aquatic animals "enjoy" less than 24 inches of space, living on chicken wire, exposed to incredible levels of disease, cannibalism, and weather extremes. With what is essentially still a wild animal, these squalid conditions produce a perpetual state of chronic distress, unimaginable to human beings. This stress leads to severe psychosomatic illness, causing disturbing behaviors like self-mutilation, cannibalism, and incessant pacing and scratching in attempts to escape from their prison.

After experiencing the blistering heat, filth, intensive confinement, and other amenities of the mink shed for half of a year, they are either gassed, electrocuted, or have their necks snapped. If they are genetically superior, they often stay on the ranch indefinitely in such conditions, only to be killed in the same manner when they lose their usefulness.

These cells have witnessed all of these things and more just as disturbing, first hand at this farm, and feel that they must pose this question to the public.

Would this deplorable situation be allowed to continue if the animals happened to be cats, or puppies perhaps, rather than their canine relative the North American Mink? Clearly, it would not. Brutality is brutality—these animals are no less deserving of basic "rights" than the animals we call our friends, and the law protects as such. Thus it is, in the face of this glaring hypocrisy, with their very real suffering in mind, that we take the justice and mercy that the law fails to provide into our own hands, and provide it for those who cannot act in their own defense.

The economic value of a dead body or a frivolous luxury item can not be compared to the inherent value of a life—thus unnecessary killing is absolutely unjust. This has been recognized by much of the rest of the world, and in multiple cases, fur farming has been completely banned by other "first-world" governments. It is time for the worlds most accomplished and proven terrorist, the United States, to respond and follow suit. If it does not, this inexorable struggle on behalf of innocent life will continue.

December 28, 2002 Philadelphia, PA

ELF claims vandalism against new housing development in Philadelphia suburb.

Letter to Editor / Media Release

Greetings. Recently, we visited a housing construction site in Northeast Philadelphia, along Rhawn St., to give a Christmas present to the developers. There, what was natural land—and a home for birds, squirrels, deer, etcetera—is now a sprawling pit of mud. Others' attempts at stopping this devastation failed; we felt the only thing we could do, and the thing that felt right, was to fight back for those who can't. So we went to the site and attacked construction vehicles however we were able to—glued locks, sugared gas tanks, disconnected hoses, spray painted vehicles, broke windows. Also we attacked the "sample house" on Rhawn St.—the first house built to attract buyers. We covered the walls in spray paint, glued locks, and broke many windows.

We are not "terrorists." We are not teenage vandals. We are middle-aged, long-time residents of Philadelphia/the suburbs who are tired of seeing the earth destroyed for money. New housing units (and these are "luxury houses," starting at $200,000) are not needed; tens of thousands of housing units in Philadelphia are vacant, or for sale. There is no excuse for the terrorism of developers, destroying the little bit of natural land left for money.

We will not sign our names, but we want to. If construction is stopped and the woods allowed to grow back, we will turn ourselves in gladly. We pray the destruction of developers in Philadelphia/the suburbs is stopped—and that our kids don't grow up in a concrete world, built over ashes of the destroyed earth.

"Sally and Peter" Philadelphia/suburbs

January 1, 2003 Erie, PA

ELF torches Bob Ferrando Ford Lincoln Mercury Dealership causing $90,000 in damages. Specifically targeted were SUVs in the lot.

Communiqué follows:

At 5:30 AM on January 1, 2003, the Earth Liberation Front attacked several SUVs at Bob Ferrando Ford Lincoln Mercury in Erie, Pennsylvania. At least four vehicles were entirely destroyed and several others sustained heavy damage, costing an estimated $90,000.

Despite decades of popular environmental activism, the mainstream environmental movement, which began arguably in the early 1960s, has failed in its attempts to bring about the protection needed to stop the destruction of life on this planet. In many ways, it has served only to accelerate this destruction. Its occasional "victories," reforms, or small concessions, have fostered hope in a means of social change that has proven unable to produce tangible protection of life, time after time.

By focusing its energy on temporary "solutions," they have altogether ignored the roots of the problem at hand. Western civilization, with its throw away conveniences, its status symbols, and its unfathomable hoards of financial wealth, is unsustainable, and comes at a price. Its pathological decadence, fueled by brutality and oceans of bloodshed, is quickly devouring all life and undermining the very life support systems we all need to survive. The quality of our air, water, and soil continues to decrease as more and more life forms on the planet suffer and die as a result. We are in the midst of a global environmental crisis that adversely effects and directly threatens every human, every animal, every plant, and every other life form on the face of the Earth.

There is absolutely no excuse for any one of us, out of greed, to knowingly allow this to continue. There is a direct relationship between our irresponsible over-consumption and lust for luxury products, and the poverty and destruction of other people and the Natural world. By refusing to acknowledge this simple fact, supporting this paradigm with our excessive lifestyles, and failing to offer direct resistance, we make ourselves accomplices in the greatest crime ever committed.

Time is running out—change must come, or eventually all will be lost. A belief in state sanctioned legal means of social change is a sign of faith in the legal system of that same state. We have absolutely no faith in the legal system of the state when it comes to protecting life, as it has repeatedly shown itself to care far more for the protection of commerce and profits than for its people and the natural environment. Clearly, the state itself causes and profits from many of the various atrocities against life that we must struggle against. To place faith in that same state as though it will act in the interests of justice and life is utter foolishness and a grave mistake.

Therefore, the E.L.F. will continue to fight to remove the profit motive from the killing of the natural environment, and to draw public attention to that which is deliberately concealed from them by the forces that control our lives and destroy our home.

We urge our sisters and brothers—let us strive to become the revolutionary force we've always spoken of being, and begin to take the control of our lives out of the hands of those who would destroy us. NO COMPROMISE.

Happy New Year Bob Ferrando!

Contributors' Biographies

Ashanti Alston

Ashanti, 49, former member of the Black Panther Party, and a Black Liberation Army, political prisoner for over 12 years, is a New York City based activist, organizer, writer, and storyteller. He is the North-east regional coordinator of Critical Resistance, an abolition movement in opposition to the prison industrial complex. He is a member of Estacion Libre, a people-of-color US-based organization that organizes solidarity visits to Zapatista-controlled Chiapas for other people-of-color. He is also a member of Blacks Against the War. Ashanti has been an anarchist for over a decade, and self-publishes an occasional zine called *Anarchist Panther*.

Michael Becker

According to the files, Michael Becker was born in Alton, Illinois in 1964. He spent the best part of his time growing up in the woods on the bluffs of the Mississippi river and on his maternal grandfather's farm in Missouri. He graduated from Aurora College with a B.A. in Political Science. He completed his M.A. and Ph.D. in Political Science at Purdue University. His dissertation addressed critical interpretations of technology and freedom in the later works of Michel Foucault and Martin Heidegger. He has been a full time lecturer in Political Science at California State University, Fresno since 1992. In addition to articles related to his dissertation research, he has written on Nietzsche's "last man" as it relates to the nihilism of self-narcotizing/necrotizing television culture. His current research concerns philosophical and tactical parallels between the Zapatistas and the Earth Liberation Front, drawing on Deleuze's conception of the rhizome. Becker is active in ecstatic, liberatory direct action from Critical Mass to Earth First! to guerilla gardening. He, Liza, Ayanna, and Jack the dog live with several other families on three shared acres near the geographic center of one of America's most polluted and otherwise gnarly cities, Fresno, California.

Steven Best

Best earned his B.A. in philosophy at the University of Illinois, Champaign-Urbana; his M.A. at the University of Chicago; and his Ph.D. at the University of Texas, Austin. Currently, he is Associate Professor of Humanities and Philosophy at the University of Texas, El Paso, where he teaches courses such as modern humanities, critical thinking, ethics, social philosophy, nineteenth and twentieth century philosophy, animal rights, environmental theory, postmodern theory, and philosophy of science and technology. Best has written and edited seven books and published over 100 articles and reviews. Two of his books, *The Postmodern Turn* and *The Postmodern Adventure* (co-authored with Douglas Kellner), won numerous awards for best Philosophy/Social Theory books of the year. With Anthony J. Nocella, II, Best is co-editor of *Terrorists or Freedom Fighters? Reflections on the Liberation of Animals* (Lantern Books, 2004). Best and Nocella co-founded the Center on Animal Liberation Affairs <http://www.cala-online.org/>, and Best is Chief Editor of the (peer-reviewed) *Animal Liberation Philosophy and Policy Journal* <http://www.cala-online.org/Journal/Journal.html>. Best is also President of Stop Animal Neglect and Exploitation (SANE), Vice President of the Vegetarian Society of El Paso, and runs his own radio show, Animal Concerns Of Texas (ACT). He regularly give talks to groups throughout the country and abroad on various topics such as state repression, direct action, and animal rights. Many of Best's writings are posted on his website <http://www.drstevebest.org/>.

Marilyn Buck

Marilyn Buck is a long-time anti-imperialist political prisoner. She has been imprisoned since 1985 for her support and solidarity with the struggle for the right to self-determination of Black people in the US.

In Texas, where Marilyn was raised, her family took part in civil rights work. As a young woman, she connected her own oppression as a woman through the Black Power movement of the mid–1960s. Politicized greatly by the struggle of the Vietnamese people to rid themselves of US imperialism, Marilyn officially became a political activist when she joined Students for a Democratic Society (SDS). Later, she worked for San Francisco Newsreel to educate politically through the visual media.

Marilyn was imprisoned in 1985 based on her support for the New African Independence struggle. She was convicted of being part of a conspiracy to free US political prisoners, and also for raising funds through bank robbery. Marilyn Buck and her comrades were convicted of participating in Assata Shakur's liberation from prison in New Jersey. Assata remains free in Cuba under political asylum. Marilyn was also convicted of conspiracy for actions opposing US international and domestic policies of war and aggression, including the attack on the US Capitol building in the early 1980s.

The life and death of environmentalist, Judi Bari opened her eyes to the colonization of Nature by the US government, including environmental racism, as the capitalist ruling class destroys and degrades the earth particularly in communities of the poor and people of color.

Since entering prison, Marilyn has become an oft-published poet and writer, seeing it as an avenue to participate in the struggles to change the conditions in the Empire, to educate and inspire. She has a small chapbook, *Rescue the Word*, as well as a CD, *Wild Poppies*.

Drew Dellinger

Drew Dellinger is a spoken-word poet, teacher, and activist. He is founder of "Poets for Global Justice," a collective of artists using poetry and spoken word to build and support movements for justice, tell truths, empower youth, and inspire radical imagination. Poetry can help ignite revolutions by stirring collective action and invoking a world of possibilities beyond the current regime of war, racism, sexism, poverty, greed, and ecological destruction. Poets for Global Justice has rocked mics and inspired minds at events across the country, from mass demonstrations, street protests, and direct actions, to conferences, churches, and classrooms.

Dellinger is also author of the collection of poems, *love letter to the milky way*, with forewords by Thomas Berry and Matthew Fox. He has presented and performed throughout the United States, speaking on justice, ecology, activism, art, anti-racism, and democracy. Dellinger's poetry has been widely published and his work is featured in the film, *Voices of Dissent* and the books, *Children of the Movement* and *Global Uprising*. In 1997 he received *Common Boundary* magazine's national Green Dove Award. He has studied cosmology and ecological thought with Thomas Berry since 1990. Dellinger has been called "an important voice of the global justice movement" by *YES!* magazine and "a national treasure" by Joanna Macy. In September of 2005, Dellinger was arrested at the White House with a delegation of religious leaders, veterans and others demanding an end to the imperialist war in Iraq.

Lauren Eastwood

Eastwood is a visiting Assistant Professor in the Department of Sociology at Syracuse University. Her area of expertise is in Sociology of the Environment, with an emphasis on environmental justice, international environmental policy, and NGO and Indigenous Peoples Organization movements. Dr. Eastwood's past research and publishing involves Eastern European environmental movements before and after the 1991 political transitions. More recently, she has conducted participant observational research on international forest policy making through the United Nations, with a focus on NGO and IPO participation in the various international forest policy making processes. She is currently engaged in continuing this research, as well as beginning projects on (1) the debates surrounding Genetically Modified Organisms; (2) shifting politics of resource extraction in Montana which allow for alliances between indigenous peoples, ranchers, and environmentalists; and (3) Latin and North American revolutionary movements which critique neo-liberal economic and political policies in the current phase of globalization based on platforms of indigenous autonomy and environmental/land tenure concerns. Eastwood brings an activist perspective to her research. Theoretically, her research is informed by a post-structuralist analysis of discourse and power combined with a historical materialist analysis of the manner in which everyday activities are circumscribed and organized by larger social relations, such as the imperatives of trade liberalization and the global military industrial complex.

Davey Garland

Davey Garland is a long time environmental, labor, animal rights, and media activist, having been involved in direct action groups in europe and the UK since 1980. He established a number of projects such as Hunt Saboteurs international, *Blagh Magazine* (Northern Ireland) and stood for the Greens in Northern Ireland before immersing himself in the establishment of Earth First! (Mid-Somerset EF!) in the UK(1991). He founded the radical magazine *Do or Die*, co-founded the Earth Liberation Prisoners support network (ELP) was a regular contributor for *Green Anarchist*, *Green Revolution*, the EF! Journal, *Alarm*, as well as participating as an EF!/IWW activist during this period. An open supporter and advocate of the ELF, he was arrested in 1994 for selling the magazine *Terra-ist*. In his spare time, he authored two books of poems, *Ecowars* (1992) and *Burn the Cages* (1996) (both fundraisers for Mclibel Two and Gandalf 6 respectively). In 1994, due to illness (M.E.), Davey began his studies at Ruskin College Oxford, and then continued to read "Revolutionary Ecology" (Independent Studies) at Lancaster University in 1995. He got his M.A. in Peace Studies in 1998, and is presently doing post-graduate study, focusing on the anti-depleted uranium weapons movement (for which he is a founder and coordinator of the Pandora DU Research Project). He now teaches radical media in Independent Studies at Lancaster University, and is still involved with the IWW.

Terra Greenbrier

Greenbrier is currently involved in a land-based community in North Carolina focused on the experiential practice, learning and sharing of "earthskills." Wild foods, hide tanning, nature crafts, natural and primitive building, and "radical homesteading" form the physical basis for living close to nature. "Truthspeaking," "radical honesty," and emotional healing and growth provide deeper sustenance for coping with the psychic and spiritual disconnection resulting from the process of domestication. Greenbrier is co-presenter of a slideshow presentation called "Feral Visions against Civilization," which has been taken on two separate tours around the US. She has co-presented and facilitated workshops and discussions on Green Anarchy, Civilization, and rewilding.

Greenbrier's involvement in radical culture started with the "Riot Grrrl" radical feminist movement and Food Not Bombs (an anarchist free food sharing movement) in the early 1990s. From there, an intellectual interest in Native American and ecological politics propelled her to get involved in the Earth First! movement in the Pacific Northwest, where she participated in civil disobedience/direct action organizing in defense of native forests, Indian Sovereignty struggles, and related issues. In the late 1990s, Greenbrier participated in, and organized actions against, genetic engineering and biotechnology, and eventually became involved in the anti-capitalist globalization movement.

Through lived experience as well as theoretical exploration, Greenbrier's focus has expanded to encompass a critique of Civilization, rather than confronting the symptoms through symbolic, and ultimately reformist approaches. By developing and sharing lived, visual examples of "decivilizing" ourselves in our daily lives, she hopes to inspire others to explore the possibilities of community-based rewilding.

Fred Hampton Jr.

Fred Hampton Jr. is an unleashed (September 14, 2001) Political Prisoner who has served a little under nine years in various state prisons. In the eyes of the state, Fred Hampton Jr. is a three-strike offender:

Strike One: For simply being African.

Strike Two: For being the offspring of freedom fighters: assassinated Deputy Chairman Fred Hampton Sr., Illinois Chapter Black Panther Party and his mother/comrade Akua Njeri, Illinois Chapter BPP, and...

Strike Three: For continuing the fight for the liberation of African people.

Now that he is unleashed but not free, Fred Hampton Jr. continues to expose the brutal prison conditions and the fight to release still-held political prisoners, prisoners of war, and prisoners of conscience. He continues to push for pardon—based on his innocence—in order to clear his name of the dubious charges.

Chairman Fred of the Prisoners Of Conscience Committee states:

> We are clear that the US Prisons don't operate as a separate entity from the war launched on our people, but as an apparatus of it. Just as we identify the "illegal" capitalist drug economy, the genocidal foster care system, the "we don't care" health care system, chemical and biological warfare (various strands of hepatitis, AIDS, etc.), US enacted legislation under the guise of a "War on Gangs, Guns, and/or Drugs;" there are many additional instruments that are utilized in the war against African and other colonized people.

In addition to organizing with the people to fight against those instruments of war utilized against us, the P.O.C.C. serves to heighten the level of consciousness of those held captive behind enemy lines, implement the Harriet Tubman Code, and make One Prisoner, One Contact a reality. The P.O.C.C. serves to unite the struggle for freedom for those behind and outside the walls of US concentration camps.

Free Imam Jamil Al-Amin, Mumia Abu Jamal, Marshall Eddie Conway, Sundiata Acoli, Jerry "Odinga" Dunnigan, Ruchel Cinque Magee, Aaron Patterson! Hands Off Assata! Long Live Shaka Sankofa, Stanley Tookie Williams, and all other *"Strange Fruit"* this country has created.

Ann Hansen

Hansen served seven years of a life sentence in the Prison for Women in Kingston, Ontario for actions committed with Direct Action. This was a small guerilla group in the early 80s that bombed the Litton plant (that built cruise missile guidance systems), burned down Red Hot Video stores (that distributed violent porn), and bombed two transformers at a Hydro substation on Vancouver Island (to stop the expansion of the pulp and paper industry). In 2001 she published a memoir, *Direct Action: Memoirs of an Urban Guerilla*, which tries to give an honest account of our politics and how and why she decided to start a guerilla group in Canada. Presently she is working with Womyn4justice, a support group for women both inside and outside prison. The group is involved in direct action, public awareness, and working on a long-term project to start a transition house for women being released from prison with a self-run cafe/bookstore.

Josh Harper

Harper is currently under indictment on terrorism charges for his role in advocating direct action through his speaking engagements, video productions, and writings. Since 1997, the US Government has attempted to silence him with grand jury subpoenas, wiretaps, raids on his home, round-the-clock physical surveillance, police beatings, and an array of trumped up charges and bogus evidence. Harper has kept his resolve throughout the continual harassment, and is planning on completing his first full length documentary after the conclusion of his current round of legal proceedings.

homefries

homefries has been focusing on connecting social justice and animal liberation issues for the past several years. She has worked with a grassroots organization called Boston Ecofeminist Action. She facilitates workshops on feminism and animal liberation at conferences, community centers, and universities around the country. She holds a B.A. in Philosophy from New College of Florida and an M.A. in Feminist Theory/Social Movements Studies from Goddard College. Most recently, she has become interested in story-telling as a way of illustrating the intersections between feminism and the liberation of other animals. homefries and two other people started offering a workshop called "How I Became a Teenage Vegan Anarchafeminist." She is also collecting the stories of people around the country for a radio series about how their struggles for social equality are related to non-human animal liberation. homefries' slide show, "Resisting the Symbolic Order: An Ecofeminist Look at Patriarchal Imagery" is available online <www.smartelectronix.com/~marc/rtso>.

Derrick Jensen

Derrick Jensen is the author of many popular books, notably including *A Language Older Than Words* and *The Culture of Make Believe*. The latter was a finalist for the Lukas Prize Project Award for Exceptional Works of Nonfiction, sponsored by the Columbia University Graduate School of Journalism and the Nieman Foundation at Harvard, which cited it as a passionate and provocative meditation on the nexus of racism, genocide, environmental destruction, and corporate malfeasance, where civilization meets its discontents. His most recent book, from which his chapter in this book is excerpted, is titled, *Endgame: The Collapse of Civilization and the Rebirth of Community*.

Robert Jensen

Jensen joined the University of Texas at Austin faculty in 1992 after completing his Ph.D. on media law and ethics in the School of Journalism and Mass Communication at the University of Minnesota. He teaches graduate and undergraduate courses in media law, ethics, and politics. Prior to his academic career, he worked as a professional journalist for a decade. In his research, Jensen draws on a variety of critical theories. Much of his work has focused on pornography and the radical feminist critique of sexuality. In more recent work, he has addressed questions of race through a critique of white privilege and institutionalized racism. Jensen is the author of *Citizens of the Empire: The Struggle to Claim Our Humanity* (City Lights, 2004), and *Writing Dissent: Taking Radical Ideas from the Margins to the Mainstream* (Peter Lang, 2002). He is the author (with Gail Dines and Ann Russo) of *Pornography: The Production and Consumption of Inequality* (Routledge, 1998), and editor (with David S. Allen) of *Freeing the First Amendment: Critical Perspectives on Freedom of Expression* (New York University Press, 1995). In addition to teaching and research, Jensen writes for popular media, both alternative and mainstream. His opinion and analytic pieces on such subjects as foreign policy, politics, and race have appeared in papers around the country. He also is involved in a number of activist groups working against US military and economic domination of the rest of the world.

pattrice jones

As cofounder of the Eastern Shore Sanctuary and Education Center, pattrice jones cares for chickens while promoting agriculture reform in a rural region dominated by the poultry industry. Jones also coordinates the Global Hunger Alliance, which unites animal, environmental, and social justice organizations to promote plant-based solutions to the worldwide hunger and water crises. She has spoken up for animals in venues as diverse as the World Food Summit in Rome, the World Social Forum in Porto Alegre, and the Sustainable Development Conference in Islamabad. An activist since age 15, when she gave up meat and joined the gay liberation movement, jones has organized rent strikes, kiss-ins, street theater, and extremely unlikely coalitions. At the Baker-Mandela Center for Anti-Racist Education, she designed programs concerning racism, sexism, and economic exploitation. She taught a University of Michigan course on social change activism until the course was canceled in retaliation for her own activism. A founding member of Global Boycott for Peace, jones agitates for economic direct action against war in the same spirit in which she advocates veganism. Her articles linking animal and social justice issues have appeared in Bangladesh, Italy, Pakistan, and South Africa, as well as in the US and Canada.

Richard Kahn

Kahn is a Ph.D. student in the Social Sciences and Comparative Education division of the Graduate School of Education at UCLA, where he works with Douglas Kellner in thinking about how the revolutionary developments occurring between humanity, the culture of technocapital, and nature affect the future course of progressive left radicalism. He also holds an M.A. in Education from Pepperdine University and an M.A. in Liberal Arts from St. John's College. He was awarded the Sutherland Prize in Philosophy, for being the most promising student of his tenure, while an undergraduate at Hobart College. He is currently the Chair of Ecopedagogy for the UCLA Paulo Freire Institute. Additionally, his weblog—*Vegan Blog: The (Eco) Logical Weblog*—is the top ranked blog devoted to veganism, animal rights, and ecological consciousness on the Internet. He publishes regularly on topics surrounding ecopedagogy, cyberculture, and radical uses of the Internet. He is also a published poet, folk musician, and web designer.

Lisa Kemmerer

Kemmerer earned a Masters Degree in Theology from Harvard Divinity School and her Ph.D. in Philosophy from University of Glasgow, Scotland. She has taught courses such as ethics, moral theory, and philosophy of religion at numerous colleges and universities. Currently, she teaches philosophy and religious studies at Montana State University, Billings. Kemmerer has published numerous reviews and articles, and has a book in consideration for publication entitled, *Ethics and Animals: In Search of Consistency*. Lisa also has written, directed, and produced two documentaries on Buddhism in North America and Alaska. Besides philosophy and animal rights activism, Lisa is a classical vocalist, guitarist, and flautist, and enjoys painting and writing poetry. A nature lover, Lisa has hiked, biked, and traveled widely around the world.

Marti Kheel

Marti Kheel is a writer and activist in the areas of animal liberation, environmental ethics and ecofeminism. Her articles have been translated into several languages and have appeared in numerous journals such as *Environmental Ethics*, *Between the Species*, and *The Journal of the Philosophy of Sport*. She has also contributed essays to numerous anthologies, including *Healing the Wounds: The Promise of Ecofeminism*; *Reweaving the World: The Emergence of Ecofeminism*; *Ecofeminism: Women, Animals, and Nature*; *Animal Rights and Human Obligation*; and *Covenant for a New Creation*. Kheel developed an early feminist critique of the philosophical dualisms between environmental ethics and animal liberation in a 1984 article, entitled "The Liberation of Nature: A Circular Affair." Originally published in *Environmental Ethics*, the article has since been widely cited and republished in several anthologies. Over the years, her primary goal has been to develop an ecofeminist philosophy that is capable of bridging the seemingly disparate movements and philosophies of feminism, animal liberation, environmental ethics, and holistic health. In 1982, Kheel co-founded Feminists for Animal Rights in the hopes of bridging the divisions between the feminist and animal advocacy movements. She has Masters Degrees in Women's Studies and Sociology, and received her doctorate in religious studies from the Graduate Theological Union in Berkeley.

Charlotte Laws

In Spring 2004, Charlotte Laws was elected to her first political office as a councilperson for Valley Glen, California. She holds a Ph.D. in Social Ethics from the University of Southern California (USC) and has completed doctoral level coursework at UCLA. She also earned two B.A. Degrees, in Philosophy and Theater Arts, from California State University (Northridge) and two Masters Degrees, in Social Ethics and Professional Writing, from USC. She has lectured and written articles in the following areas: the philosophies of Spinoza, Nietzsche, Russell and Mill, postmodernism, ethics, animal liberation/rights, environmentalism, philosophy of science, social philosophy, political theory, and First Amendment law. Some of her more mainstream articles have appeared in *Newsweek*, *Publisher's Weekly*, and the *LA Times*. For three years, she was also a regular contributor to *California* magazine, focusing on philosophy, politics, law, and social issues. Her first book was published in 1988, and her second book, entitled *Armed for Ideological Warfare*, which explores Spinoza's philosophy and the animal rights movement, will be released in Spring 2005. She has been interviewed on a number of television shows, including *Larry King Live*, *Fox News*, *The Late Show*, and *Oprah Winfrey*. Charlotte has been a vegetarian since 1981 and is the Founder and President of the League for Earth and Animal Protection (LEAP), which advocates and educates on behalf of nonhumans and the environment. The website is <http://www.LEAPnonprofit.org>.

Tony LoGrande

Despite being a native Clevelander and an elder of the Wabigoon Lake Ojibway Nation of Northwestern Ontario, LoGrande is relatively new to the realms of social and political activism. He did, in fact, spend the first 33 years of his working life as a factory employee, and was little involved with his Native Heritage (which is Metís, his father being Canadian Cree and his mother European). Tony first started to become interested in his heritage in the middle 1990s, and he began spending time as a volunteer at the American Indian Education Center in Cleveland, assisting the Center primarily with activities related to its annual Fathers' Day Powwow. Tony retired from his factory position in 1999 and, having continued his education starting in the mid-90s, took a position in social service as a counselor for a welfare-to-work organization. When that business closed its doors in 2001, he found himself without specific direction. On the advice of a friend, he moved to the Wabigoon Lake Ojibway Nation to assist an elderly medicine man there. He was subsequently recruited by the Chief and Tribal Council to organize and run adult education programs on the reserve, which he did for about two years. In recognition of his service to the Wabigoon Lake Aanashinabe, he was adopted and named by the Council and elders of the reserve. He has since been designated as a Tribal Elder. Upon returning home to Cleveland, he began volunteering once again at the American Indian Education Center. He was hired by the Center in October of 2004, and is the Assistant Director and Educator, editing the Center's quarterly newspaper, *Smoke Signals*, in his spare time. He has recently become involved in the work of the American Indian Movement, and is dedicated to securing the rights, political and social, of Native Peoples. Tony is completing work on his Ph.D. in Educational Leadership and Adult Education at Cleveland State University.

Jeffrey "Free" Luers

My name is Jeffrey Luers. Most of my friends call me "Free." I have been active since 1996 fighting for a range of issues such as animal rights, gender equality, anti fascism, eco-defense, and others. These issues are not separate—they are one struggle, one fight. My story is only a small part of a greater whole.

In my lifetime I have witnessed an onslaught against the inhabitants of this world lead by the greed of industrialized nations. It is my belief that the oppression of people is rooted in the oppression and exploitation of nature, a fundamental disrespect for life that began with the conquest of Mother Nature and has lead to the conquest of humankind. I struck back in an act of resistance designed to raise awareness and draw attention to a problem that affects every human being, every animal, every plant, and every form of life on this planet. I am speaking of global warming, air, soil, and water pollution. We are in the midst of a global environmental crisis.

On June 16, 2000, I ignited a fire that would forever change my life. I torched three SUVs. I took extra care and used specific fuels to ensure no one would be injured. Approximately 30 minutes after the fire was lit and extinguished, I was taken into custody by three undercover agents who had been following me, one of whom I would later learn to be a member of an anti-domestic terrorist unit. I was arrested on Criminal Mischief One, a charge that carries about one year. In the course of one week that charge would multiply into ten felony counts, including three counts of Arson One. Getting to trial took the course of a year. By trial, I had accumulated 13 felony counts, now including conspiracy with persons unknown. I was looking at a little over 100 years. I refused to take a deal.

My trial was a joke. We proved that evidence had been tampered with, that officers had lied, and that the prosecutor had manipulated evidence to get a legal search. On top of that, the judge refused to allow me to separate the trial, such that I was charged with two different fires. Law requires that upon request separate offences must be tried separately. The final blow came when the judge threw out the testimony of my expert witness. In the end, I was convicted of 11 felony charges. I was sentenced to 22 years and 8 months. I have no possibility of parole.

Craig "Critter" Marshall

Craig Marshall, better known by his friends and enemies as Critter, does not consider himself an activist. He feels he is just doing his part to stop the techno-industrial state from destroying the only planet he has ever known and loved. Critter was recently released after serving a 5 ½ year sentence at the Snake River Correctional Institution for torching some SUVs in June of 2000 in Eugene, Oregon with the hopes of raising attention to the environmentally destructive nature of these vehicles. For a couple of months before being taken hostage by the State, he participated in numerous community projects including cooking breakfast every morning for Café Anarquista, serving free food and coffee to those in need, and helping with Food not Bombs. Prior to that, he spent most of his time defending the Fall Creek timber sales by doing tree-sits and road blockades. His experience in that forest, and others before it, made him realize what we are losing when we don't fight to protect the Natural world from civilization's greedy encroachment.

Jim Mason

Mason is an author, speaker, journalist, environmentalist, and attorney who focuses on human/animal concerns. His latest book, *An Unnatural Order: The Roots of Our Destruction of Nature*, from which his essay is edited (Lantern Books, 2005), looks at the historical and cultural roots of the Western belief in God-given dominion over the living world. Mason is best known for his 1980 book, *Animal Factories*, written with philosopher Peter Singer. Mason's writings have appeared in a wide variety of publications. He is a contributor to *In Defense of Animals* (Blackwells, 2005), edited by Peter Singer. His magazine article, "A Plague of Gypsy Moths" was chosen for the book, *Cases for Composition* (2nd edition; Little, Brown, 1984). His articles have appeared in *The New York Times, New Scientist, Newsday, Country Journal, Orion Nature Quarterly*, and other publications. His 1993 story in *Audubon* about the growing trade in exotic pets was nominated for the National Magazine Award for excellence in reporting. The article sparked national interest and was chosen for the anthology, *Preserving Wildlife: An International Perspective* (Prometheus Books, 2000). Mason and Peter Singer's new book, *Food Matters: The Ethics of What We Eat*, will be released by Rodale in August, 2006. In addition to writing, Jim Mason speaks about animals, nature and the environment at conferences, churches, and universities. He has appeared on NBC's *Today*, CBS *This Morning*, NPR's *All Things Considered, CNN, Midday Live*, and other radio and television programs in major cities. His books have been reviewed in *The Washington Post, The Christian Science Monitor, In These Times, The Chicago Sun Times*, and *The Atlanta Constitution*. Mason's home page is <http://www.jimmason.info/index.html>.

Noel Molland

Molland has been involved with many animal liberation and eco-defense campaigns over the years. He was sentenced to three years' imprisonment for allegedly conspiring to incite animal liberation and earth liberation direct action through the dissemination of Animal Liberation Front and Earth Liberation Front information. Noel is currently volunteering with Earth Liberation Prisoners Support Network (ELP), which he helped to found in 1993.

Jalil A. Muntaqim

Jalil was 19 years old when he was arrested. He is a former member of the Black Panther Party and the Black Liberation Army. For the past 32 years, Jalil has been a political prisoner, and is one of the New York Three (NY-3) in retaliation for his activism in the 1960s and early 1970s.

Two months shy of his 20th birthday, Jalil was captured along with Albert "Nuh" Washington in a midnight shoot-out with San Francisco police. When Jalil was arrested, he was a high school graduate and employed as a social worker. In 1976, while in San Quentin prison in California, and before he was moved to New York, Jalil launched the National Prisoners Campaign to petition the United Nations to recognize the existence of political prisoners in the United States. Progressives nationwide joined this effort, and the petition was submitted in Geneva, Switzerland. This led to Lennox Hinds and the National Conference of Black Lawyers having the UN International Commission of Jurists tour US prisons and speak with specific political prisoners. The International Commission of Jurists then reported that political prisoners did in fact exist in the United States.

Jalil has received awards of appreciation from Jaycee's, NAACP and project Build for his active participation and leadership. After many years of being denied the opportunity to attend college, Jalil graduated from SUNY-New Paltz with a B.S. in Psychology and a B.A. in Sociology in 1994. He would like to pursue his Masters degree, but has not been allowed by DOCS. Jalil has had many essays and articles published, including a compilation of prison writings, titled *We Are Our Own Liberators* and is featured in a video, *Jalil Muntaqim—Voice of Liberation.*

During his imprisonment, Jalil has become a father and grandfather. He states, "I came to prison an expectant father and will leave prison a grandfather." Jalil is presently working to develop a National Prisoners Afrikan Studies Project (NPASP), a non-profit organization dedicated to educating prisoners. Also, he is the founder of the Jericho Amnesty Movement, a national determination to win the release of political prisoners, and the co-founder of the New Afrikan Liberation Front.

Anthony J. Nocella, II

Nocella, a Quaker, is a Social Science doctoral student at the Maxwell School at Syracuse University, where his focus is political repression, terrorism, guerilla warfare, and conflict studies. He holds a M.A. in Peacemaking and Conflict Studies and a graduate certificate in mediation from Fresno Pacific University. He was involved with peacemaking in Colombia with Mennonite Central Committee and the Christian Peacemaker Teams. He has taught workshops in mediation and tactical analysis, and has assisted in a number of legal committees in the Americas. He is a co-founder with Richard Kahn of the Institute for Revolutionary Peacemaking and Education and with Steve Best of the Center On Animal Liberation Affairs. Currently, he is involved with Jericho Amnesty Movement in Syracuse, NY, Syracuse Animal Rights Organization, Central New York Earth First!, is a facilitator of Alternatives to Violence Program at Auburn prison, and is a member of the Syracuse Quaker Meeting. Nocella has written in more than two dozen publications and is author of *Introducing Restorative Justice to Activists: A Peacemaker's Guide for Building Peace with a Revolutionary Group* (PARC 2004), and co-editor, with Dr. Steve Best, of *Terrorists or Freedom Fighters? Reflections on the Liberation of Animals* (Lantern Books 2004). Nocella's web page is: <http://student.maxwell.syr.edu/ajnocell/index.html>.

Sara Jane Olson

Born in 1947, in a rural farming community in North Dakota, to a former fighter pilot All-American jock and a woman from California her childhood was spent with her brothers and sisters on the Great Plains. Her family moved to California, first to Lompoc, then Palmdale, which employed her Dad as a high school coach and English teacher. She studied English and theater at UC Santa Barbara, then moved to Berkeley, where she studied anti-war and anti-racist politics during the Vietnam War. After moving back to the Midwest, she married, bore three daughters, taught English to Shona kids in Zimbabwe, trained as a chef, performed in community theater, ran road races, and worked in a variety of political organizations supporting democracy and equality. Arrested in June 1999, she pled guilty to conspiracy and association with the remnants of the Symbionese Liberation Army in 1975. She is currently serving a term, still yet to be determined by the Court, at Central California Women's Facility in Chowchilla, CA.

Paula Ostrovsky

Paula Ostrovsky has a PhD in Microbiology, and many years of basic laboratory research where she published and presented her work in national and international venues. She abandoned academia to use her analytical skills and writing talents for indigenous causes. She has produced and hosted radio shows serving these causes on WEFT (Champaign, Illinois), KPOO (San Francisco, California), and Berkeley Liberation Radio (Berkeley, California). She has done media and public relations work for the Tashunka Witko Brigade, the American Indian Arbitration Institute, the National Coalition on Racism in Sports and the Media, Chicago Rock Against Racism, and presently, the Leonard Peltier Defense Committee.

Kanahus Pellkey

Kanahus Pellkey is a Secwepemc & Ktnuxa from the interior of British Columbia, Canada. Kanahus Pellkey is Warrior and Spokesperson for the Native Youth Movement. She is a community organizer, and has worked with many Indigenous Nations throughout Turtle Island. In 2001, Kanahus Pelkey and other Secwpmec Youth, formed the Secwepmec Native Youth Movement (NYM). Their mission to Defend their Territory and Protect the clean water, food, and Land her People still depend on for Survival. Kanahus and her People have been battling the governments of BC and Canada for their illegal occupation and theft of Secwepemc Lands, and been fighting against illegal development of Sun Peaks ski-resort, a massive resort destroying Secwepmec hunting, food, and medicine-gathering Mountains. This Stance resulted in over 70 arrests of NYM Warriors and Traditional Secwepmec People including elders nearly 80 years old. As an Organizer and Spokesperson, she has been targeted and assulted by the RCMP. She fled and remained on the "run" until her capture in 2003. When her nephew passed away in a rural BC hospital, the doctors attempted to take the baby away and mutilate the body by performing an autopsy. Kanahus, her sister and husband, and an NYM Comrade fled the hospital with the baby to perform the proper burial ceremony in the mountains. The reaction of the enemy was a massive manhunt in which RCMPigs from across BC, six different divisions, helicopters, and K-9 units were deployed to capture the NYMers. On a cold February night, they were all arrested and denied bail. She was refused bail even though she was breast feeding her four month old son. The Canadian Government held her for Ransom away from her child because of her beliefs and defense of their land and ways of life. Upon her release, she maintained her stance and continues to stand strong against oppressive Canadian control forced upon her Peoples. All charges have since been dropped, and she remains to Stand for her People and her Land, and continues her Uncompromising Stance, This Is Indian Land! Take Back Our Land! Her Warrior Spirit is an Inspiration to all! Fuck the Police! Free Peltier! For more information about Native Youth Movement, please contact nymcommunications@hotmail.com.

Leslie James Pickering

Leslie James Pickering served twice as spokesperson for the North American Earth Liberation Front Press Office, from its birth in early 2000 until the summer of 2002. During this period the Press Office sustained two raids by the Federal Bureau of Investigation, the Bureau of Alcohol Tobacco and Firearms, and local law enforcement agencies. It responded to half a dozen grand jury subpoenas; conducted public presentations; produced booklets, newspapers, magazines, and a video on the ELF; and handled the release of dozens of ELF communiqués. Pickering was the editor of *Resistance, the Journal of the North American Earth Liberation Front Press Office*, and many other independently produced materials regarding the Earth Liberation Front, and has since edited the book *Earth Liberation Front 1997–2002*. He has handled countless local, national, international media inquires, resulting in articles in *The New York Times*, *The Washington Times*, *The Los Angeles Times*, *USA Today*, *Christian Science Monitor*, *Rolling Stone*, *Village Voice*, and many other newspapers and magazines. He has conducted interviews with ABC, NBC, CNN, FOX, CBC, BBC, National Geographic TV, and various other outlets. Pickering has also given lectures at colleges and universities such as Lewis & Clark College, Saint Michael's University, Furman University, Bard College, New York University, Fresno State College, Macalester College, University of West Los Angeles, Princeton University, Mercyhurst College, and Syracuse University. He has a California High School Equivalency Diploma and a BA in Revolutionary Community Organizing from Goddard College. He is now involved in Arissa, and is based in his hometown of Buffalo, NY.

Anthony Rayson

Rayson is an anarchist writer and organizer, who makes meaningful and effective prisoner support activism a priority. He co-founded grassroots groups STAND (Shut This Airport Nightmare Down), Southside Citizen's Coalition, and Chicago Anarchist Black Cross. He runs South Chicago ABC Distribution, crafts and distributes dozens of powerful publications and pamphlets (free to prisoners). These are often written by prisoners to help educate, connect, and empower people, inside and out, and to raise issues and up the struggle.

Robert Roche

To say that the list of Robert Roche's accomplishments and achievements is lengthy is an understatement. Roche's dedication to the Native American Community of Northeastern Ohio began in earnest in 1969 when Russell Means founded the Cleveland American Indian Center (CAIA). He began as a volunteer and was subsequently hired by the Center in 1970. In those early years, Robert served the Cleveland Center as the Youth Director, a paralegal, the Bureau of Indian Affairs Representative for the Child Welfare Act of 1978, and, as the Assistant Director. In this time frame he also worked as the Executive Director under the Comprehensive Education Training Act in conjunction with the Department of Labor in Eleven Northern Ohio counties, including Cuyahoga. During this time he was also self-employed, operating five stores with thirty-five employees, and was the City of Cleveland Minority Businessman of the Year in 1971. In addition, Roche has been active in the American Indian Movement (AIM) since 1972, and was a party to the original Chief Wahoo lawsuit with Cleveland AIM, the Cleveland American Indian Center, and Russell Means which was filed in that year. Another lawsuit was subsequently filed by the Cleveland American Indian Movement against Gateway/Cleveland Indians in response to their policy of prohibiting protesters and demonstrations at Jocobs Field in1995. Roche and others filed a civil rights action in 1998.

Roche left the Center in the mid-80s to pursue other interests. When he returned in 1992, with the help of Candy Cruz, he revived the then defunct CAIC under its current name, the American Indian Education Center. In the ensuing years Roche has been incredibly busy in his efforts to bring clarity to Native American education, culture, and history to the people of the Cleveland community, both Native and non-Native. In his capacity as the Executive Director of the American Indian Education Center, as well as the Executive Director of the Cleveland office of the American Indian Movement, he has been involved in countless projects and undertakings designed to further the goals of those two groups and, more importantly, the welfare of the Northern Ohio Native American community. These endeavors included: the many cultural workshops he has conducted, his ram-rodding of the annual AIEC Edgewater Powwow, his hosting of his own radio and television talk shows, his involvement as Project Director of the Red Spirit Circle, an alcohol abuse treatment program, his speaking at over 80 colleges and universities throughout the United States and Ireland, his administration of a Federally funded Tobacco Grant for smoking cessation, and, his most recent venture, the founding of a Native-focused newspaper, *Smoke Signals*.

Roche has participated, and continues to participate in, diverse community service efforts, from the Earth Day Coalition to the Lorain County Children Services. When asked what he feels has been his most significant achievement, however, he will tell you that it has been his work in the areas of promoting the education of our children to the point where they have professional, marketable skills, and assisting them in their efforts to find and maintain meaningful employment. In addition to his other activities, he is currently teaching a course on the American Indian Movement at Oberlin College.

Kalamu ya Salaam

New Orleans editor, writer, filmmaker, and teacher, Kalamu ya Salaam is founder of the Neo-Griot Workshop, a Black writers' workshop focusing on text, recordings, and videos. He is co-founder of Runagate Multimedia publishing company, leader of the WordBand, a poetry performance ensemble, and moderator of e-Drum, a listserv for Black writers and diverse supporters of their literature. Salaam is also the digital video instructor and the co-director of Students at the Center, and executive director of Listen to the People, a New Orleans oral history project. His latest book is the anthology, *360-degrees A Revolution of Black Poets* (Black Words Press). Salaam's latest spoken word CD is *My Story, My Song*, and his most recent movie is *Baby Love* (75-minute drama). Salaam can be reached at kalamu@aol.com.

Levana Saxon

Saxon began voicing her disgust of the way humans treat each other and other species at age five when she became a vegetarian. At age 9, she began doing invisible theatre in McDonald's, demanding to know where the beef came from. Now she is mostly an educator who uses theater, puppets, and ecopedagogy, a radical approach to education for the earth. She has worked with various groups including Youth for Environmental Sanity, Jatun Sacha, the Praxis Peace Institute, the Institute for Deep Ecology, the Paulo Freire Institute, and the São Paulo World Education Forum. In each setting Saxon has organized and facilitated workshops and conferences, using the arts for children, youth, and adults. In addition. she served for two years as the US Advisor to the United Nations Environment Program Youth Advisory Council and co-founded INIYA, the Indigenous and Non-Indigenous Youth Alliance. She now organizes outside of the NGO realm with PEACE (Popular Education and Action Collective) and other groups, focusing on ending the war and occupation of Iraq, leading people power strategy trainings, and bringing theater and Brazilian percussion into the streets. She also recently worked on the design team to create a new small autonomous public elementary school in Oakland (SEED—the School for Expeditionary Learning, Equity and Diversity), where she teaches giant puppet making and drama. She graduated from the Friends World Program of Long Island University that brought her to work and study in Latin America, East Africa and Europe. She is currently working on a Masters in Education, with a concentration in Participatory Theatre and a credential in Adult Education at San Francisco State University.

Rik Scarce

Scarce is a sociology professor at Skidmore College, where he teaches Sociological Perspectives, Development of Sociological Thought, Contemporary Social Theory, Environmental Sociology, Social Movements & Collective Behavior, and other courses. Scarce's books include *Eco-Warriors: Understanding the Radical Environmental Movement,* Updated Edition (Left Coast Press, 2006), *Contempt of Court: A Scholar's Battle for Free Speech from Behind Bars* (Alta Mira Press, 2005), and *Fishy Business: Salmon, Biology, and the Social Construction of Nature* (Temple University Press, 2000). He is also the editor of *Syllabi and Instructional Materials for Environmental Sociology,* 4th and 5th editions, for the American Sociological Association (1999 and 2003). His scholarly journal articles have been published in *Symbolic Interaction, Society and Natural Resources, Teaching Sociology, Journal of Contemporary Ethnography, Law and Social Inquiry, The American Sociologist, Animals and Society,* and elsewhere. Among the more unusual events in his life, Rik was jailed for five months in 1993 for refusing to cooperate fully with a federal grand jury. His "contempt of court" citation resulted from his assertion of a researcher's right to safeguard confidential communications and his steadfast stance in defense of the American Sociological Association's Code of Ethics. Never accused of wrongdoing, arrested, or tried, he was released when a judge recognized that he would not cooperate further with the grand jury. Rik's current research is a socio-ecological history of the Hudson River.

Maxwell Schnurer

Schnurer received his Ph.D. in rhetoric from the University of Pittsburgh. He is currently an Assistant Professor of Communication at Humboldt State University in Arcata, California. A long time animal rights activist, Schnurer's work focuses on social movements, cultural change, and activist strategies. He is the co-author of *Many Sides: Debate Across the Curriculum* (Idea Press, 2000) and a contributor to *Terrorists or Freedom Fighters: Reflections on the Liberation of Animals* (Lantern Books, 2004).

Jesús Sepúlveda

Sepúlveda is one of the most multifaceted poets from Latin America. He was born in Santiago, Chile in 1967. His notable poem, "Place of Origin," written at the age of 17, portrays the years of violence and rebelliousness during the Pinochet military regime. His recent poem, "Pax Americana," published in various alternative zines, is a mantra of protest against Bush and Imperialist aggression. In 2002, his eco-anarchist essay, "The Garden of Peculiarities," was published in Buenos Aires, two months after the Argentine revolt. Sepúlveda's poetry has been extensively published in Chile, Argentina, Uruguay, Brazil, Bolivia, Costa Rica, Mexico, the USA, and Spain, and partially translated into English and Portuguese. While in Chile, he directed the magazine *Piel de Leopardo* (currently on-line, edited by Lagos Nilsson <http://www.pieldeleopardo.com>), and in Eugene, Oregon he co-directed the bilingual magazine *Helicóptero* in collaboration with Paul Dresman. In 2001, his book of poetry *Correo Negro* was published in Argentina, and in 2003 his collection of poems, *Escrivania*, was published in Mexico. The English translation of "The Garden of Peculiarities" is soon to be released by Feral House, and the second edition of "Hotel Marconi" (published in Chile in 1998) will be published by *Cuarto Propio* in a bilingual edition to be distributed in the USA. Sepúlveda holds a Ph.D. in Romance Languages and teaches at the University of Oregon in Eugene, where he lives with his *compañera*, Janine, and his two-year son, Indigo.

Mark Somma

Somma is a professor of Political Science at California State University, Fresno. He has worked on environmental and related issues for many years. Dr. Somma has published work on political ecology, water politics, environmental public policy and public opinion, and revolutionary environmentalism. He believes that environmental conflict and environmental issues will soon overshadow other issues and dominate social, economic, and political decisions. He strongly advocates decentralized technology and the rapid development of alternative energy so that each house, workplace, and transportation system creates its own energy. He argues for expansion of wilderness lands, a cessation of old-growth logging, strong population control measures, encouragement of organic farming via a radical change in agricultural subsidy policy, and strong controls on bioengineering. In 2005, with Mike Becker and numerous others, Somma recently started the online journal, *Journal of Green Theory and Praxis* <http://greentheoryandpraxis.csufresno.edu/main.asp>.

Somma believes that human society needs a spiritual evolution to sanctify nature and life as a moral and ethical guide. He argues that deep ecology is the pathway to this spiritual evolution, albeit with many key steps remaining in its development. Recently, he organized a conference at Fresno State entitled "Revolutionary Environmentalism: A Dialogue between Activists and Academics." Conference panels and discussion drew a packed house of students and faculty. It also drew the attention of angry right-wing ideologues, agribusiness, and law enforcement, including the FBI. Somma welcomes comments, questions, or suggestions about revolutionary environmentalism addressed to him at markso@csufresno.edu.

Amory Starr

Starr is an activist in and scholar of the anti-globalization movement. Her book, *Naming the Enemy: Anti-Corporate Movements Confront Globalization*, written well before the Seattle protests, was the first systematic and international documentation of the emergence of what is often called the "anti-globalization movement." She participates in a rank-and-file affinity group in all the major North American manifestations, and has worked on many local projects such as community currency, permaculture, union organizing, activist legal work, infoshop, Transform Columbus Day, and many campus campaigns. Her second book, *Don't Be a Tourist: Guidebook to a Global Uprising*, is an accessible introduction to points of consensus, debates in the movement, and tactics.

Bron Taylor

Taylor is Samuel S. Hill Professor of Religion and Social Ethics at the University of Florida, where he is developing the first graduate program in religion focusing on the intersections among peoples' religious beliefs and practices, and their natural habitats. He is the author of many books and dozens of articles on nature religions, grassroots environmental movements (especially radical ones), environmental ethics, and affirmative action policies. His books include a two volume international, *Encyclopedia of Religion and Nature* (Continuum, 2005) and *Ecological Resistance Movements: The Global Emergence of Radical and Popular Environmentalism* (SUNY, 1995). A gateway to the encyclopedia and other published work and initiatives can be found at <http://www.religionandnatutre.com>.

Robert Thaxton, aka Rob los Ricos

Robert Thaxton, aka Rob los Ricos, was born in the Texas Panhandle on the eve of the 1960s. By the righteous (r)age of twelve, Rob began to work with various revolutionary organizations. He eventually left Pampa for the streets of Dallas, Texas, where he joined CISPES (the Committee in solidarity with the People of El Salvador), worked with ACT UP, and KNON-FM, a peoples (Pirate) radio station where he served as program director. In the early 90s, as Rob Thaxton began to fade into a memory, Rob los Ricos relocated to Austin, Texas, to engage in anarcho-specific activity such as Food not Bombs and Earth First! In the late 90s, he lived in Portland, Oregon where he worked with the Anarchist Info Shop. On June 16, 1999, Rob Los Ricos traveled to Eugene, Oregon to attend an anarchist conference and a Reclaim the Streets festival. Arrested by police during the June 18 Reclaim the Streets demonstration-turned-police riot,

Rob was accused of throwing a rock at a cop, and was subsequently beaten by police. He was ultimately charged with rioting, first degree assault, and second degree assault. Used as a Latino-out-of-towner-anarchist-scapegoat example of what can happen to those who dare to rebel, Rob was given a nearly eight year prison sentence.

Rosalie Little Thunder

Rosalie was born on the Rosebud Reservation in South Dakota. She is Sicangu Lakota, a descendant of Chief Little Thunder and matriarch of one of the Little Thunder Tiospayes (extended families). Lakota is her first language, which she has been teaching for more than 30 years. She is currently an adjunct professor at Black Hills State University.

Although Rosalie's livelihood has been as an artist, she is most known for her wildlife activism. Her most recent effort was to appeal to the United Nations Permanent Forum on Indigenous Issues for a global campaign to protect Sacred Species. She chairs the Seventh Generation Fund and South Dakota Peace and Justice Center, and is a board member of Predator Conservation Alliance and the Alston-Bannerman Fellowship program for activists of color.

Rosalie has developed "Cultural Mapping," which is a description of the Lakota Worldview and the refined disciplines that helped Lakota people to survive in a very responsible manner (pre-Columbus). "Cultural Mapping" is being used as a means of cultural healing for people affected by oppression and poverty.

Kazi Toure

A former political prisoner, Toure is the first person of Afrikan descent in the u.s. to be convicted of seditious conspiracy charges, of "conspiring to overthrow the u.s. government." He was captured in February, 1982 and released October, 1991. A longstanding member of the Afrikan Liberation Movement, he is an outspoken critic of the injustice, oppression, and exploitation of u.s. government. Toure was an employee and representative for the American Friends Service Committee in Geneva, as well as in South Afrika, at the World Conference on Racism, Xenophobia, and Other Related "isms." In 2001, he was a recipient of the 2004 National Lawyers Guild Award. He has published poetry and articles in many newsletters and other publications, including in the book *Hauling Up the Morning: Izando la Manana: writing and art by political prisoners and prisoners of war in the US* (edited by Tim Blunk and R.L. Trenton, NJ: Redd Sea Press, 1990). Currently, Toure is working with the Jericho Amnesty Movement in Boston, Massachusetts and speaks around the country on prison abolition and political prisoner support.

John Wade

Wade was born March 15, 1985 in Alexandria, Virginia, and moved to Richmond, Virginia in 1990. He is the third oldest son in a mixed family of six children. His mother died when he was young, and he was raised by his stepmother. His primary political interests concern the abolishment of the death penalty, ending institutional racism, securing civil liberties, providing opportunities for the poor, and of course, saving the environment. Political consciousness came to him in early high school and radical environmental action came in late high school. He is currently serving three years in federal prison for a series of actions against suburban sprawl, the fast food industry, and Ford Motor Company. Wade recently turned twenty and celebrated his one-year anniversary in prison. While "on the street," he worked for a variety of different mainstream environmental organizations such as the Sierra Club, the Nature Conservancy, and the Chesapeake Bay Foundation, along with liberal nonprofits such as American Civil Liberties Union, the Human Rights Campaign, and numerous groups working to end the death penalty. He also worked for the Democratic Party. It might sound like he doesn't value the contribution of mainstream groups, but he does.

Matt Walton

Walton is in the final semester of earning his M.A. in Political Science at Syracuse University. He holds a B.Mus with Honors in Music Composition, also from Syracuse. Walton is involved in labor rights activism and voter mobilization as a project leader with NYPIRG, and is on the editorial board of the *Journal of Green Theory and Praxis*. His current research projects include a study of the effects of Buddhist teachings on leadership and democratic governance in Southeast Asian nations, and a collaboration with Eastside Neighbors in Partnership (Syracuse, NY) to design and implement evaluation tools for their Youth ACTION program. Walton remains an active composer, and his music has been performed in London, New York, and Boston. His newest opera, which is based on the trial and incarceration of Leonard Peltier, premiered with the Syracuse Society for New Music in the summer of 2005.

Wanbli Watakpe

Wanbli Watakpe (Attacking Eagle) is first and foremost an *Akicita* (traditional Lakota warrior), and as such has vowed to stand before the people in times of war and behind the people in times of peace.

He founded the Northern California Chapter of the American Indian Movement in 1969 and was the squad leader for the Little California bunker in the Wounded Knee siege in 1973. He then joined the fishing rights struggle in Washington State. He formed Northwest AIM with Leonard Peltier, Jim and Steve Robideau, and Joe Stuntz. He was arrested with Kenny Loud Hawk, Anna Mae Aquash, and Kamook Banks in 1975, and together with Peltier and Banks he faced the longest pre-trial case in US history. He is a founder of the Leonard Peltier Defense Committee and has served as its Executive Director several times, including the present.

Wanbli Watakpe has also worked to preserve indigenous ceremonies, sacred sites, and Mother Earth. He served the people as educator and social worker, focusing on the preservation of the indigenous family and the development of an indigenous framework to address historical trauma.

He has lectured at San Francisco State University, University of California Berkeley, and San Francisco City College.

Jessica Widay

Widay is a joint M.A./Ph.D. student at the Maxwell School of Syracuse University. She is pursuing a Masters Degree in International Relations and a Doctorate in Political Science. At Syracuse University, Widay has served as a graduate assistant in the Moynihan Institute for Global Affairs, where she worked on the Transboundary Crisis Management project, helping to develop a coding scheme and database for over two hundred transboundary crisis case studies. She currently serves as a research assistant in the Center for Environmental Policy and Administration, examining techno-environmental conflicts. Her interests focus on transnational environmental activism, environmental attitudes & behavior, and environmental education. Widay is currently researching transnational networking among environmental advocacy groups in the United States and Canada involved with the acid rain issue. Prior to her graduate studies, she completed her undergraduate degree at Middlebury College (Environmental Studies and Spanish), and was employed with the consulting firm Booz Allen Hamilton, working on contracts with the Department of Energy, Internal Revenue Service, and Office of Housing and Urban Development. She has lived and worked in Upstate NY, Vermont, Washington, DC, and Madrid. In her free time, she escapes to a family cabin in the Adirondack Mountains.

Adam Weissman

Weissman is working to create a world where human beings reaffirm a sense of reverence for the earth and a kinship with and compassion for sentient living beings, including each other. An anarcho-primitivist, Weissman is part of a rapidly growing movement that looks to abolish government and private property and to develop a post-industrial, post-capitalist, post-agricultural society, looking to pre-civilized peoples as a model for an egalitarian, fulfilling existence in harmony with the earth. He has worked on a wide variety of activist issues like animal rights, sweatshop labor, anti-militarism, environmental justice for indigenous peoples, corporate globalization, wilderness defense, the campaign to free Burma, youth liberation, global warming, genetic engineering, expanding the voices of women and people of color in social change movements, and overconsumption. With the Activism Center at Wetlands Preserve (<http://www.wetlands-pre-

serve.org>), a human, animal, and earth liberation activist group based in New York City, Weissman works to convert the comic book industry to use of recycled paper; to promote the freegan lifestyle and ethic through "dumpster tours" (<http://www.freegan.info>), and to stop the passage of pro-corporate, anti-environment global free trade agreements, as part of the New York City People's Referendum on Free Trade (<http://www.taareferendum.org>).

John Zerzan

Zerzan, known as a founder of green anarchy, has written about technology, social dislocation, and the fate of the natural world for the past 30 years. He is author of *Elements of Refusal, Questioning Technology, Future Primitive, Running on Emptiness*, and is editor of *Against Civilization*. Zerzan is editor of *Green Anarchy* magazine, and translations of his work have been published in France, Germany, Italy, the Netherlands, Turkey, Greece, Serbia, Ukraine, China, and elsewhere. Zerzan's parents came to Oregon from Nebraska in 1940. He was born in Salem in 1943, and grew up in the Willamette Valley. His father was a mechanic, small business owner, and janitor, his mother chiefly attended to raising his two siblings and himself. Zerzan was an organizer and officer of the independent Social Services Employees Union in San Francisco (1967–1970), where he came to see Organized Labor as a bureaucratic and alienated structure. Afterwards, other major institutions, with their external authority modes, struck him as very problematic and not healthy to individual freedom. Thus, he slowly became an anarchist, more from his experiences than from theory. Zerzan has traveled and spoken widely in recent years. Since 1981, Zerzan has made his home in Eugene. He was a member of the East Blair Housing Co-op from 1987 through 2003, has been a volunteer at the YMCA since 1990, and frequently provides childcare on a part-time basis. Zerzan is married, with two daughters and a granddaughter.

FRIENDS OF AK PRESS

AK Press is a worker-run co-operative that publishes and distributes radical books, visual and audio media, and other mind-altering material. We're a dozen people who work long hours for short money, because we believe in what we do. We're anarchists, which is reflected both in the books we publish and in the way we organize our business. All decisions at AK Press are made collectively—from what we publish to what we carry for distribution. All the work, from sweeping the floors to answering the phones, is shared equally.

Currently, AK Press publishes about 20 titles per year. If we had the money, we would publish 40 titles in the coming year. New works from new voices, as well a growing mountain of classic titles that unfortunately are being left out of print.

All these projects can come out sooner with your help. With the Friends of AK Press program, you pay a minimum of $20 per month (of course, we welcome larger contributions), for a minimum three month period. All the money received goes directly into our publishing funds. In return, Friends automatically receive (for the duration of their membership), one FREE copy of EVERY new AK Press title (books, dvds, and cds), as they appear. As well, Friends are entitled to a 10% discount on everything featured in the AK Press Distribution Catalog—thousands of titles from the hundreds of publishers we work with. We also have a program where groups or individuals can sponsor a whole book. Please contact us for details. To become a Friend, go to: <http://www.akpress.org>.

CDs
JUDI BARI—Who Bombed Judi Bari?
NOAM CHOMSKY—The Imperial Presidency
WARD CHURCHILL—Life in Occupied America
ANGELA DAVIS—The Prison Industrial Complex
NORMAN FINKELSTEIN—An Issue of Justice: Origins of the Israel/Palestine Conflict
FREEDOM ARCHIVES—Prisons on Fire: George Jackson, Attica & Black Liberation
CHRISTIAN PARENTI—Taking Liberties: Policing, Prisons and Surveillance in an Age of Crisis
UTAH PHILLIPS—Starlight on the Rails box set
DAVID ROVICS—Behind the Barricades: Best of David Rovics
ARUNDHATI ROY—Come September
HOWARD ZINN—People's History Project Box Set

DVDs
NOAM CHOMSKY—Imperial Grand Strategy: The Conquest of Iraq and the Assault on Democracy
STEVEN FISCHLER & JOEL SUCHER—Anarchism in America
ARUNDHATI ROY—Instant-Mix Imperial Democracy
HOWARD ZINN & ANTHONY ARNOVE (ed.)—Readings from Voices of a People's History of the United States

ORDERING AND CONTACT INFORMATION

AK Press
674-A 23rd Street
Oakland, CA 94612-1163
USA

AK Press
PO Box 12766
Edinburgh EH8 9YE
Scotland

akpress@akpress.org
www.akpress.org

ak@akedin.demon.co.uk
www.akuk.com

For a dollar, a pound or a few IRCs, the same addresses would be delighted to provide you with the latest complete AK catalog, featuring several thousand books, pamphlets, zines, audio products and stylish apparel published & distributed by AK Press. Alternatively, check out our websites for the complete catalog, latest news and updates, events, and secure ordering.